20th CENTURY JOURNEY

THE START: 1904–1930

20TH CENTURY JOURNEY

*A Memoir
of a Life and the Times*

THE START: 1904–1930

BY

William L. Shirer

LITTLE, BROWN AND COMPANY · BOSTON · TORONTO

Grateful acknowledgment is made to the following for permission to
reprint material from their publications:

Norma Millay Ellis, for material from "A Few Figs from
Thistles," Harper & Row, New York, copyright © 1922, 1950,
by Edna St. Vincent Millay.

Harcourt Brace Jovanovich, Inc., New York, for material from
The Complete Poems of Carl Sandburg.

LIBRARY OF CONGRESS CATALOGING IN PUBLICATION DATA

SHIRER, WILLIAM L. (WILLIAM LAWRENCE), 1904–
20TH CENTURY JOURNEY.

INCLUDES INDEX.
CONTENTS: 1. THE START, 1904–1930.
1. SHIRER, WILLIAM L. (WILLIAM LAWRENCE), 1904–
—BIOGRAPHY. 2. NOVELISTS, AMERICAN—20TH CENTURY—
BIOGRAPHY. 3. JOURNALISTS—UNITED STATES—BIOGRAPHY.
I. TITLE. II. TITLE: TWENTIETH CENTURY JOURNEY.
PS3537.H913Z4617 1984 070'.924 [B] 84-21279
ISBN 0-316-78712-4 (V. 1)

*Published simultaneously in Canada
by Little, Brown & Company (Canada) Limited*

PRINTED IN THE UNITED STATES OF AMERICA

CONTENTS

Books by William L. Shirer

There may be many shapes of mystery;
And many things God brings to be,
Past hope or fear.
And the end man looketh for cometh not,
And a path is there where no man thought.
— EURIPIDES

Thing of a day! Such is man; a shadow in a dream.
— PINDAR

Qu'est-ce qu'un homme dans l'infini?
— PASCAL

We are all born wholly uncivilized . . . On a geological
time scale we are still close to savagery.
— JAMES HARVEY ROBINSON

Every son of man travels an unbeaten path — a road beset
with dangers and temptations that no other wanderer met.
His footsteps can be judged only in the full knowledge
of the strength and light he had, the burden he carried,
the obstacles he met and a thorough knowledge of every
open and secret motive that impelled him.
— CLARENCE DARROW

What a wee little part of a person's life are his acts
and his words! His real life is led in his head, and is
known to none but himself.
— MARK TWAIN

Quel homme suis-je? . . . En vérité je n'en sais rien.
— STENDHAL

INTRODUCTION

The writing of memoirs, I find, is a strange and tricky business.

Can you tell the truth? Does memory, blurred and disjointed by the passage of time and fed by the imagination, lead you to recount more fiction than fact? William Allen White was afraid it did. "This Autobiography," he warned in the preface to his memoirs, "in spite of all the pains I have taken and the research I have put into it, is necessarily fiction." The reader, he said, should not "confuse this story with reality. For God only knows the truth." White was merely trying, he concluded, "to set down some facts which seem real and true to me."

That is all I have attempted to do in this memoir of a life and the times. I, too, have done years of research in a considerable pile of personal papers, though some were lost in the war and in travel, for a foreign correspondent led a nomadic life, living out of a suitcase. And I have been haunted and humbled by the warnings of poets, philosophers and memorialists whose abilities and attainments were far above mine. Montaigne thought man was simply incapable of attaining truth because he "was the servant of customs, prejudices, self-interest and fanaticism . . . The bane of man is the illusion that he has the certainty of his knowledge."

Isadora Duncan, who lived such a full and tragic life, used to talk to me about her memoirs while she was writing them in Paris. "How can we write the truth about ourselves?" she would ask. "Do we even know it?" Emily Dickinson thought that "truth is so rare, it's delightful to tell it." Delightful maybe, but difficult.

What is truth? To Santayana "truth is a dream unless my

dream is true." And André Malraux, in writing his memoirs—or "anti-memoirs," as he called them—speculated that "the truth about a man is first of all what he hides," but he differentiated between what a man hides and what he ignores in himself. The two are not the same. Stendhal wrote one book after another about himself in an effort to understand who and what he was, but the search for the truth eluded him. "What manner of man am I?" he finally asked, and admitted: "In truth, I haven't the faintest idea."

There are other problems in writing memoirs. They have to do with the past and with time. "The past is never dead," wrote Faulkner. "It's not even past." You cannot ruminate about the past and write about it without transforming it. Immediately the imagination enters into play until it is impossible to separate memory from imagination. Or to sort out time. Einstein, for whom the conception of time was so important in his theory of relativity, and in mathematics and physics generally, thought it was impossible to sort it out. "The separation between past, present and future," he said, "has only the meaning of an illusion, albeit a tenacious one."

Rousseau, whose *Confessions* is probably the greatest and the most self-searing of all the autobiographies, thought first of writing simply a portrait of himself. He spent twelve years preparing to write it, assembling notes and mulling over notebooks, letters and other material. In the end he rejected the idea of doing a portrait, not only because he thought it would be static but because it would present a final judgment of himself made late in life. Time would play its tricks. Instead he decided to relate "all that has happened to me, all that I've done, all that I've thought, all that I've felt. . . . I cannot be wrong about what I've felt."

But he deceives himself. Like every other who writes of his life, he transforms it by the writing. "That is why," wrote Marcel Raymond, the editor of the Pléiade French edition of *Confessions*, "the history of his soul, which he promised us, becomes, without his knowing it, the legend or the myth of his soul."

An observation or two about my own view of life, as a background to these memoirs:

Only rarely have I paused amid the trivia of living, which make up so much of our existence, and out of which come the setbacks, the triumphs, the sorrows and the rare moments of happiness, to consider how puny and unimportant we all are, how puny, in fact, is our planet. Even the solar system, of which the Earth is a negligible part, is but a dot in the infinite space of the universe. The limited space and time that we can comprehend are nothing in the incalculable extent and age of inorganic nature. Who can say, then, that the purpose of the universe, if it has a purpose, has been to create man? Who can even say that there are not billions of other planets on which there is some kind of human life, perhaps much further advanced than ours, or at least more sane, meaningful and peaceful?

Every person's life is of importance to himself, of course; it is the only one he has and knows. But in the universe of infinite space and time, it is insignificant. *"Qu'est-ce qu'un homme dans l'infini?"* asked Pascal. Nothing. Perhaps Carl Becker, the historian, and one of the most civilized men I ever knew, grasped best our piddling place in the infinite.

> Man [he wrote] is but a foundling in the cosmos, abandoned by the forces that created him. Unparented, unassisted and undirected by omniscient or benevolent authority, he must fend for himself, and with the aid of his own limited intelligence find his way about in an indifferent universe.

And in a rather savage world! The longer I lived and the more I observed, the clearer it became to me that man had progressed very little beyond his earlier savage state. After twenty million years or so of human life on this earth the lot of most men and women is, as Hobbes said, "nasty, brutish and short." Civilization is a thin veneer. It is so easily and continually eroded or cracked, leaving human beings exposed for what they are: savages.

What good three thousand years of so-called civilization, of religion, philosophy and education, when right up to the 1970's, as this was being written, men go on torturing, killing and repressing their fellow-men? In fact, was there not a retrogression here? In my own brief time we vastly multiplied our capacity to kill and destroy. With the advent of the bomber and then the guided missile we not only slaughtered soldiers but also innocent women and children far behind the lines of battle.

We could see in our own country as late as the 1960's and 1970's how good Christian and Jewish men, the pillars of our society, when they acceded to political and military power, could sit calmly and coolly in their air-conditioned offices in Washington and cold-bloodedly, without a qualm or a moral quiver, plan and order the massacre of hundreds of thousands of men, women and children and the destruction of their homes, farms, churches, schools and hospitals in a faraway Asian land of poor peasants who had never threatened us in the slightest, who were incapable of it. Almost as savage was the acceptance by most of us citizens of such barbarism, until, toward the end, our slumbering—or should one say, cowardly?—consciences were aroused.

Sometimes it has seemed to me that man's main accomplishment has been to tear down, rob, pollute, kill. First, his earth. Then his fellow-men. In recent years has come our final, triumphal achievement: a nuclear contraption and a guided missile to carry it, works of such incredible complexity that only our handful of geniuses could create them, works that can blow up our planet in a jiffy, snuffing out life for good. Can, and probably will, given the folly of those who rule us and who have the power to decide.

In such a world what meaning can there be in life, what purpose? All my years I have searched, like so many others, for some meaning. Seldom have I got beyond asking the questions. What is life? For what purpose? How did it originate? Where did we come from? Where are we going? Does death end it all? And what is death? The door to eternity? To nothingness? Malraux came to believe that a man "finds an image of himself in the questions he poses," that he "shows himself more truthfully by the profoundness of his questions than by his answers." As Gertrude Stein lay dying in the July heat of 1946 in Paris she mumbled to someone by her bedside: "What is the answer?" And when there was no answer she said: "Then what is the question?"

I never was able to find many answers myself. There have been some, thought up by others, though none very satisfying to me. The gloomy Schopenhauer found that life was merely the passage from being to nothingness. Sophocles, surprisingly, at the end of a long, full life in the golden age of Greece, concluded that it would have been better for man not to have been born. Sophocles had won all of life's prizes. He had captured the drama awards, been acclaimed Greece's greatest playwright and poet, was handsome, rich and successful, and had lived in good health and vigorous mind to ninety. Yet he could write:

> *Never to have lived is best, ancient writers say;*
> *Never to have drawn the breath of life, never to*
> *have looked into the eye of day.*

Solon agreed. "Call no man happy," he said, "until he is dead."

Did Solon think happiness began thereafter? That is a question we all have asked. The religion of the Greeks, like all other religions, answered that it did. Plato thought that heaven, the Elysian Fields, was the reward for all the injustices and un-happiness on earth. But there were skeptics. Epicurus, for one. "There is no immortality," he was sure, "and therefore death for us is not an evil; it simply does not concern us: while we exist there is no death, and when death comes we are gone."

Without subscribing fully to his view, even after I lost my faith in the Christian certainties of the hereafter, I have always liked the way Epicurus put it.

> Faith in immortality was born of the greed of unsatisfied people who make unwise use of the time that nature has allotted us. But the wise man finds his life span sufficient to complete the full circle of attainable pleasures, and when the time of death comes, he will leave the table, satisfied, freeing a place for other guests. For the wise man one human life is sufficient, and a stupid man will not know what to do with eternity.

George Eliot was equally skeptical. For her, God was un-knowable and immortality unthinkable.

Such, in part, have been the meanderings of my own thoughts as they mixed with those of others and were influenced by them. They will creep in and color, no doubt, this narrative of one life and of the times as the world moved through the first three-quarters of our momentous twentieth century. That brief whiff of time, as time goes, that has comprised my own span, encompassed more changes, I believe, than the previous thousand years. It has been an interesting experience to have been born in the horse-and-buggy age and to have survived into the nuclear era.

Luck and the nature of my job put me in certain places at certain times where some of the main currents of our century were raging. This gave me an opportunity to see at first hand, and to get the feel of, what was happening, and why. To say that "there is no substitute for experience" may be indulging in a stale cliché, but it has much truth in it. Rilke thought that to be a poet *"Mann muss viele Erlebnisse ertragen"*—one has to have a lot of experience, or go through a lot. It is true for all writers and for all those who wish to have a full life.

I love books. They connect you with the past and the present, with original minds and noble spirits, with what living has been and meant to others. They instruct, inspire, shake you up, make you laugh and weep, think and dream. But while they do enhance experience, they are not a substitute for it.

I've always felt it was helpful in my understanding of our country to have been born in Chicago and to have begun to grow up there shortly after the turn of the century. Not that there were not plenty of other equally interesting and certainly more pleasant places to be born in: New York, say, or Cambridge or San Francisco. They were more civilized, probably. And I've always loathed the prospect of having to live in Chicago, a prospect I escaped at an early age. Still, it was in Chicago, I think, around the turn of the century, that one could grasp best what had become of America and where it was going. All the boisterousness and the raucousness, the enormous drive to build, to accumulate riches and power, all the ugliness, the meanness, the greed, the corruption of the raw, growing country was exemplified in windy Chicago. Yet some of the poetry of the land and the city were there too, in the beauty of the lake site, of slender buildings soaring to the blue sky along the water, and the quest for art and learning. You can feel it all in the poetry of Chicago's Carl Sandburg. There, and later in Iowa, I grew up with the Midwest in my blood. The Midwest, too, was not the only good place to begin life in. But it gave us something, for better or worse, that no other region had. It was the heartland. It fed the nation, mined many of its minerals, manufactured most of its goods. More than any other section, I think, it shaped the American nation and whatever civilization we have. My roots were there.

Later when I yanked them up—but not all of them, that would have been beyond me—and went abroad at twenty-one to live and work in Europe and Asia, the fortunes of my job set me down in places where some of the principal events that were shaping our world were transpiring: in India in the early thirties during the revolution for independence that Gandhi was leading; in Paris and London during the twenties and thirties when Europe's two greatest democracies were inexplicably sliding downhill; in Rome when that sawdust Caesar Benito Mussolini, after a shaky start, was fastening Fascism on a civilized people and when the Vatican was beginning to stir, to accommodate itself to the twentieth century, and the Pope was giving up the role of the "prisoner" of Rome; in Berlin during the rise and fall of Adolf Hitler and of the barbarian Third Reich; and finally in the Second World War, which Hitler inflicted on a suffering world.

Without these direct, immediate experiences I never could have gained at least some understanding of, much less have got the feel of, what happened and perhaps why in that troubled time. They helped later in the writing of some history.

Throughout the mature years of my life, and through the writing of these memoirs, something that Leon Trotsky wrote of our times and something else that Henry James wrote about being an American have flickered through my mind. "Anyone desiring a quiet life," Trotsky wrote shortly before he was hacked to death in Mexico by agents of Stalin, "has done badly to be born in the Twentieth Century." As for crotchety old James: "It's a complex fate," said he, "being an American." Complex or not, it was an interesting fate to be an American in the twentieth century. I am glad it was mine.

BOOK ONE

FROM MAIN STREET
TO THE LEFT BANK, 1925

One bright June morning in 1925, a few days after graduation from college, I drove with my uncle out the Lincoln Highway from our town in Iowa headed for Chicago and for points farther east that I had never seen. I planned to make it that summer to Washington and New York and finally, after London—I could not quite believe it—to Paris.

From Main Street to the Left Bank! A lot of college graduates, scornful of the inanities of the Coolidge era, "The Era of Wonderful Nonsense," as Scott Fitzgerald called it, were doing it, if only, as in my case, for a couple of summer months. Paris loomed as paradise, the City of Light and Enlightenment, the Center of Civilization, after our growing up in the American wasteland. We wanted to get away from Prohibition, fundamentalism, puritanism, Coolidgeism, Babbittry, ballyhoo, the booster antics of Rotary and the Chamber of Commerce—all the cant of the bourgeois who dominated our land and made it, we thought, such a mindless, shoddy place to live in.

We had grown up in our college years, despite the efforts of our teachers to keep our minds off current literature, on the novels of Sinclair Lewis, *Main Street* and *Babbitt,* and the thundering of H. L. Mencken in *The American Mercury* against the *homo boobiens* of the American hinterland. They had rubbed in what we knew all too well from our young lives: the cultural poverty of the Midwest small town; the tyrannical pressures to conform to a narrow, conservative, puritan norm; the hollowness of the small-town booster Babbitt businessmen; the worship of business and profits and financial success by our sanctimonious and churchy Christians.[1]

A few months before—fabulous day!—I had received from the great Mencken a letter he had obviously typed himself thanking me for an item I had sent him for his "Americana" column.

DEAR MR. SHIRER:

Thanks very much for the clipping. I believe that Dr. Pinto has started a movement that will sweep the country. Christian people everywhere will be hot for it, once they hear of it. I am trying to set it going in the south.

Sincerely yours,
H. L. MENCKEN

I no longer remember who Dr. Pinto was or the nature of his movement, though it must have been idiotic. Perhaps it was he I had seen quoted in the local *Gazette* as telling the Rotary in nearby Waterloo[2] that "Rotary is a manifestation of the divine."

Such hocus-pocus was not confined, of course, to our Corn Belt. One read in the *Mercury,* in the radical weeklies, and even in the daily press of "manifestations" from coast to coast of the divinity in business and businessmen. There were the indefatigable divine Dr. S. Parkes Cadman, addressing conventions of businessmen on "Religion in Business," and the promotion pamphlet put out by the Metropolitan Casualty Insurance Company, with an introduction by Dr. Cadman, entitled "Moses, Persuader of Men," which declared that "Moses was one of the greatest salesmen and real-estate promoters that ever lived . . . a Dominant, Fearless and Successful Personality in one of the most mag-

---

[1] Dr. Russell H. Conwell, pastor of the Temple Baptist Church in Philadelphia and founder of Temple University, died that year after preaching for forty years on six thousand occasions from coast to coast his famous sermon, "Acres of Diamonds," in which he admonished: "Get rich, young man, for money is power. . . . I say you have no right to be poor. . . . Love is the grandest thing on God's earth, but fortunate is the lover who has plenty of money. . . ." It was probably the most popular sermon—I believe he called it a "lecture"—ever delivered in America and certainly the one most often repeated by the same divine. Six thousand times!

[2] Where Sinclair Lewis had worked as telegraph editor and editorial writer on the *Daily Courier* in 1908, the year after he graduated from Yale. He was fired after ten weeks, the editor informing him, Lewis told me once, "Young man, you'll never make it as a newspaperman. You can't write."

nificent selling campaigns that history has ever placed on its pages."

Jesus Christ, in this respect, was celebrated as even a greater salesman. That summer Bruce Barton's *The Man Nobody Knows* was climbing to the top of the best-seller list. Even in our town, where reading books was not very much indulged in (there was no time for it, our busy businessmen said), the book was selling well and being read, and hailed even in some of the Protestant pulpits. The man nobody knew turned out to be Jesus, "the founder of modern business . . . a great executive . . . whose parables were the most powerful advertisements of all time . . . He would be a national advertiser today . . ."

> He picked up twelve men from the bottom ranks of business and forged them into an organization that conquered the world . . . Nowhere is there such a startling example of executive success as the way in which that organization was brought together.

These idiotic ramblings were hailed by the country as gospel. After all, at the very moment of my leaving that summer the great "Monkey Trial" was getting under way in Dayton, Tennessee. It seemed too absurd to be real, but there it was, spread all over the front pages as I made my way east. John Thomas Scopes, a twenty-four-year-old highschool biology teacher, was being tried for violation of the Tennessee anti-evolution law that made it unlawful "to teach any theory that denies the story of the Divine creation of man as taught in the Bible, and to teach instead that man has descended from a lower order of animals." Scopes, following a state-approved textbook, Hunter's *Civic Biology*, had taught the latter, giving his highschool students a brief outline of the Darwinian theory of the origin of species. For this he was arrested and put on trial. Later it would be learned that Scopes, half in jest, had agreed with some of the bright young townsmen over soda pop at Robinson's drugstore to allow himself to be the subject of a test case.

Overnight it became a celebrated trial, a battle of Christian fundamentalism against modern science, with William Jennings Bryan, thrice the Democratic candidate for President and once Secretary of State, as chief prosecutor, and Clarence Darrow, the knotty, agnostic criminal lawyer from Chicago, who had defended anarchists, trade-union leaders, and more recently Leopold and Loeb in the famous murder case, heading the defense. Hundreds of reporters from the metropolitan papers descended on the hillbilly town, steaming under the summer sun, to recount every word of the two great antagonists. Their dispatches were splashed over the front pages, not only in America but abroad, where the trial was regarded as the latest aberration of the primitive Yankees. By the time I got to England and France, just after the case was finished, people asked in amazement how such a spectacle was possible in the enlightened Republic of Benjamin Franklin and Thomas Jefferson.

The climax of the trial came when Darrow put Bryan on the stand as an authority on the Bible, provoking a scene that the staid *New York Times* called the most amazing courtroom drama in Anglo-Saxon history. Under Darrow's sharp, sarcastic questioning Bryan declared his belief in the literal truth of the Biblical story of Creation. The world, he said, had been created in 4004 B.C. and the Flood had occurred around 2348 B.C.

"Don't you know," asked Darrow, "that there are any number of civilizations—China, Egypt—that are traced back to more than five thousand years?"

"I'm not satisfied by any evidence I have seen," Bryan replied.

"You have never in all your life made any attempt to find out about the other peoples of the earth—how old their civilizations are, how long they have existed on the earth—have you?" Darrow persisted.

"No, sir. I have been so well satisfied with the Christian religion that I have spent no time trying to find arguments against it. I have all the information I want to live by and to die by."

Asked about the religions of Confucius and Buddha, Bryan retorted, "I think they are very inferior . . . The Christian religion has satisfied me, and I have never felt it necessary to look up some competing religion."

Darrow was relentless.

"Mr. Bryan, do you believe that the first woman was Eve?"

"Yes."

"Do you believe she was literally made out of Adam's rib?"

"I do."

"Did you ever discover where Cain got his wife?"

"No, sir; I leave the agnostics to hunt for her."

"Do you believe Joshua made the sun stand still?"

"I believe what the Bible says."

It was a trying day for the perspiring Bryan in the Tennessee heat on the courthouse lawn to which the trial had been moved that day to accommodate the multitude, and he was the object of much derision in most of the big-city press the next day, though the fundamentalists in the state and elsewhere in the South—and no doubt in the North—were reported pleased by the stout defense of their beliefs by the Champion. Scopes was found guilty and fined a hundred dollars, and less than a week later Bryan was dead from exhaustion. Darrow had hoped to appeal right up to the United States Supreme Court, but the Tennessee Supreme Court reversed the decision of the Dayton court on a technicality, thus preventing appeal. At the same time it upheld the anti-evolution law, which remained on the statute books for decades.[1]

It was in such an atmosphere of bigotry and banality that I took leave of my country that bright summer. I was fed up with it. I yearned for some place, if only for a few weeks, that was more civilized, where a man could drink a glass of wine or a stein of beer without breaking the law, where you could believe and

---

[1] Bryan's blatant fundamentalism and his appalling lack of taste that led him to promote the frenzied real-estate boom in Florida had destroyed the image I had had earlier of the great "Commoner." For many of us growing up in the Midwest, Bryan had been somewhat of an idol, the great champion of Populism, the eloquent politician who espoused the cause of the farmer, the worker, the poor, and who in the three times he had run for President on the Democratic ticket had been beaten, we were sure, by the moneybags of the Republicans.

Even in grade school I could recite most of the famous "Cross of Gold" speech, which had won for the unknown thirty-six-year-old Nebraskan the Democratic nomination for President in 1896 and which, in the emotions it aroused and in the effect it produced—in the convention and in the country—was one of the great orations in American history. Who can forget its peroration?

Having behind us the producing masses of this nation . . . the toilers everywhere, we will answer their demand for a gold standard by saying to them: You shall not press down upon the brow of labor this crown of thorns, you shall not crucify mankind upon a cross of gold!

Later I heard him speak, once in our Presbyterian Church in Iowa filled to the rafters, and several times on the chautauqua circuit, where I worked on a tent crew. He had a deep, resonant voice that carried to the far corners of the largest auditorium or tent without benefit of microphone, and he had the magnetism and the art of the great orator, though the content of his speeches was usually disappointingly banal. He repeated one called "The Prince of Peace" thousands of times without tiring of it.

say what you wanted to about religion or anything else without being put upon, where inanity had not become a way of life, and where a writer or an artist or a philosopher, or merely a dreamer, was considered just as good as, if not better than, the bustling businessman. Where, too, you could lead your own life, do as you pleased, get drunk or make love, without Mrs. Grundy or the police or the preacher or the teacher breathing down your neck.

It would be rather far from the truth, though, to give the impression that at twenty-one, just out of a small Midwest college, having grown up the last twelve years in an Iowa town of forty-five thousand in the center of the Corn Belt, I had become so alienated that I thought of myself as permanently fleeing the tawdry land for the civilized haunts of Europe. Probably I was, in many ways, a pretty typical small-town Iowa boy. Though America seemed to have become a rather foolish place in the time of Harding and Coolidge, both Presidents so dreadfully mediocre and so popular and esteemed, I intended, nevertheless, to return and take my chances in it. I had rebelled against much, disliked more, yet on the whole my growing up in an Iowa town in a fatherless family that was financially rather strapped had been a happy one. I had had to work hard to augment our meager income and get on in school, but there was a lot of play and fun, too. Never had I felt a moment of boredom, which was supposed to be chronic in the Midwest Main Street towns. There were moments of outrage, to be sure, of discouragement and sadness and even, occasionally, melancholy. But also of joy, exhilaration, hope, love—and always a zest for life, such as it was. I had learned long before twenty-one that it was never easy, usually baffling, often incredible but sometimes wondrous, not only in America but elsewhere, not only now but always, since the beginning.

For all their blasts against its idiocies, Lewis and Mencken and Dreiser and Sherwood Anderson and Carl Sandburg, my literary idols, loved the country, thrived on it, and seemed to be having a pretty good time. You could feel that, beneath the barbs. Though a lot of writers, artists and students were rushing off to Paris, these giants, all but Mencken from the Midwest, were staying put, mining the rich material that lay at hand. For better or worse, they reminded you, it was the only country you had.

• •

To be sure, in the back of my mind that last year in college was a vague idea that I might be able to prolong my stay in Paris. But it was very nebulous and I did not take it seriously. I had the choice of two jobs already offered, one at the college, the other at the nearby University of Iowa, and I intended to return to one of them—and also to the college girl I was engaged to and hoped shortly to marry. Anyway, I didn't have the money to stay on in Paris. I had borrowed a hundred dollars from the president of the college and, the day before, wheedled the loan of another hundred from my rather reluctant uncle. But two hundred dollars couldn't keep me in Europe more than the couple of months I had• planned.

Still, there was a crazy thought in the dim recesses of my consciousness that would not quite die. A classmate had told me of a friend of his by the name of Bill Bridges, who, after finishing at Franklin College in Indiana, had got a job on one of the American newspapers in Paris. That would be a way of staying on, and I couldn't quite get it out of my mind. One spring evening I mentioned it to my mother, who did not much like it. A few evenings later she called in a distant "uncle" named Franchere, from some French branch of the family, who ran a declining department store in town, The Fair, in which we had a little almost worthless stock. He had served in some capacity, perhaps in the Y.M.C.A., in France during the war and, I believe, had grown up in Paris. He still spoke with a trace of a French accent. He took a dim view of my dream. The climate in Paris, he said, was terrible. It rained all the time; the houses were dank and cold, being largely unheated in the winter, when the sun seldom shone. An Iowa boy could scarcely hope to survive in the place. You were bound to come down with tuberculosis, as he had before he came to the promised land. Besides, he added, there were the temptations of the gay city. When my mother, who was rather innocent, asked what they might be, he replied, very embarrassedly and apologizing for his "frankness," that the women were "loose" and that, as a matter of plain fact, the city licensed legal "houses"—"*maisons*," he said (that was as far as he would describe them)—which abounded in every street. I found this information rather intriguing, but my mother, tolerant though she was, recoiled from it in horror.

Probably she considered the matter closed, and I thought it

wise not to bring it up again. It was only a dream, after all. Bill Bridges had written my friend that there were thousands of students and hundreds of genuine newspapermen applying for jobs in Paris and that not more than two or three made it each summer. So the chances were really nil, though it would do no harm to apply when I got to Paris. I also intended to sound out the city editors of the *World* and the *Times* for a job when I passed through New York, just in case. But I had no illusions that a youngster with my limited experience of a couple of summers during college on a small-town daily could break in at once on those two great metropolitan newspapers—or on the ones in Paris either. So I accepted as settled my return to a job in Iowa and to the girl I had promised to marry. My mother seemed confident that the young coed, if not the job, would fetch me back. She had become extremely fond of her. She was a lovely girl, dark blond, with dancing green eyes, a straight nose, a full and rather sensuous mouth, a trim figure, and a saucy manner and mind. For over a year I had been in love with her. A few months before, I had given her my fraternity pin, after the custom of the campus, as a token of our engagement. I hated to leave her and to be so far away, even for two months. But as June came, and four years of college were wound up in the sentimental exercises of commencement and the farewells to campus and friends, I grew more and more excited at the anticipation of the summer's journey to places that for so long had seemed out of reach. I had the money in hand for the expenses in Europe. I had a contract with a marine agent in Montreal to work my way on a cattle boat from that port to Manchester, England, with a free trip back on a returning boat, without cattle to tend, at the end of the summer. On the way I would stop over in Washington and New York, attend a conference of college newspaper editors at Woodstock, New York, to which I had been invited (all expenses paid), and while away a few days with some distant relatives at Canton, New York, up the St. Lawrence River from Montreal.

I said goodbye to my mother and to my sister, who had been teaching school in a nearby town since graduating from our college three years before. My mother had continued to be uneasy about the venture but she had not opposed it. She had a remarkable tolerance for us children and what she considered our wild schemes and our unruly ways. Though her life had been terribly circumscribed—widowed twelve years before by the sudden death of my father at the age of forty-two in Chicago, with three young children to bring up—she had attained a wisdom which I did not fully appreciate until years later. Left with little more than a small life-insurance payment and the house in Chicago, she had never complained about her problems. By some miracle, for she said she never understood "finances," she had seen us through school, leaving us with complete freedom to grow as we might. My younger brother still had two years to go, and already was not sure he wanted to finish at our college. As rebellious as I, he found it intellectually rather arid. I had bid him goodbye a week before when he went off to Stone City to spend the summer working in a stone quarry nearby, where Grant Wood, who had not yet burst upon the country with his paintings, was talking about setting up an artists' colony.

The parting over, my uncle and I drove past the campus, where I picked up some old pipes and a bottle of bootleg "hootch" I had left in the office of the *Cosmos,* the weekly college paper I had edited that last year. Smoking on the campus was strictly forbidden and secreting bootleg whiskey on the premises in those Prohibition days was not only breaking the law of the land but would have brought instant dismissal had one been caught.

I took a last look at the little campus where I had spent the past four years. The buildings, sidewalks and lawns were deserted and the loneliness of the place which for so long had been the bustling center of my life brought a tinge of sadness at the leaving. They had been pretty exciting years, I thought, as I looked back. For the first time I had loved passionately, been rejected, suffered agony over it, and loved again. I had learned a little, or at least had learned the most important thing of all: that college was but a step in an education that I was determined to pursue all the rest of my life. I had had three or four teachers who had made a dent in my mind. In the town I had got my first daily newspaper experience and this had determined what eventually I wanted to do. I had also had a great deal of fun, and a passion for reading, music, and sports had sprouted and grown.

The morning had cleared after three days of rain, but the downpour, which had helped the corn, the basis of life in our region, had left the highway a quagmire of oozing mud in parts. We managed to make the first sixteen miles to Mount Vernon without mishap, my uncle putting on the gas whenever we saw a mudhole and urging the Model T Ford through it as if he were driving a team of horses. The road ran up to the high ridge where Cornell College in Mount Vernon stood. We got out and sauntered through the deserted campus. Giant elms and maples studded the spacious lawns, and ivy grew on the nondescript buildings and the Gothic chapel. My father had spent four years here (as had my uncle and their two sisters) before going on to law school in Chicago. It was on this campus, I knew, that my father had met my mother, who was majoring in music. It had been little more than a Methodist seminary at the time, full of Protestant uplift, Christian teaching and Bible reading, where, my mother used to tell us with some amusement, drinking, smoking, dancing and the playing of cards were strictly forbidden and a boy and a girl were expelled if they were caught kissing under the shadow of a tree on a moonlit spring evening.[1]

The ridge of the campus ran into Main Street, from which my uncle suddenly detoured. He wanted to have a look, he said, at the "ol' farmhouse" where he had grown up. His father, my grandfather, he explained, had moved there from a larger farm farther west, in Blackhawk County, in the 1880's in order to put his four children through the college in the town. It was only a couple of blocks off Main Street.

"I don't know how he did it," my uncle said. "The place only had eighty acres. But, by gad, somehow he did. Put us all through this little college, your father, your Aunt Lillian, your Aunt Mabel and me. I guess folks were like that in those days. Those pioneer farmers, who never had a chance to go to college[2] —there was too much backbreaking labor from dawn to dark —were determined to give their kids a college education. It became Dad's single purpose in life. When the farm didn't pay quite enough, he opened a butcher shop. Slaughtered his own cattle,

[1] It did teach more than the Bible, of course. It gave my father an excellent foundation in Latin and Greek, which I was not given at college. Several books in his library in Latin, and especially in Greek, are lovingly annotated by him in the margins.
[2] Recently I learned that my grandfather had attended Northwestern College at Plainfield, now North Central College at Naperville, Illinois, where he fell in love with a vivacious lady named Caroline von Triem, and shortly married her.

pigs and chickens. Sold them and his milk and his eggs. We never had much cash, but we sure had plenty to eat. Between the farm and the butcher shop, he managed."

It was an old American story, and generally true of that time. I had not realized that my father's family had lived it. My father had died too early to talk to me about such things.

Soon after we left Mount Vernon we began to run into trouble. Thrice that day in the eighty miles between Mount Vernon and the Mississippi at Clinton the Tin Lizzie got stuck and my uncle had to pay the farmers five dollars each to haul us out with their teams of sturdy horses. He regarded it as a form of highway robbery. The government was also to blame. "The government, what with all the taxes we pay," he muttered, "ought to pave the roads—at least a big highway like this." The Lincoln Highway was the main route across the country but it was largely unpaved, at least in Iowa. Slowed by the mud, even when we did not get stuck in it, we did not reach the Mississippi until dusk. My uncle decided reluctantly that we would have to put up for the night at a hotel in Clinton—despite the expense.

This change of plans was a happy break for me. It gave me the opportunity to have a longer farewell with my college sweetheart, who lived in the town. We had planned to meet for a few minutes over coffee at the local hotel as we drove through, my uncle having been impatient to push on that day to his home in Glen Ellyn, a suburb of Chicago. Instead, after I had telephoned her and explained the delay, she joined us at the hotel for dinner. It was not a very merry meal. Beautiful and lively as she was— my uncle took a great liking to her at once—her mood was far from warm. Weeks before at college she had scarcely disguised a feeling of resentment that I was going away so far for so long. We had had a bit of a quarrel, one of several lovers' quarrels that evaporate the next day and which are the salt of courtship, and she had ended by saying that she wanted very much for me to have this particular experience.

After dinner my uncle excused himself, saying he was an early-to-bed and early-to-rise man. The girl and I drove in her car to a drugstore, there being no cafés or "speakeasy" bars in the town. Over coffee in the little cubicle we began to talk about the future, but she did not seem as optimistic about it as I had expected. She was tense, a little distant and, I began to see, still a trifle resentful. Somehow, she said, she had a feeling that once I saw Paris I would never come back to the small-town Midwest life we had had and which we intended to continue, neither of us, really, knowing any other. My first nine years in Chicago hardly counted since I could scarcely remember them.

I did my best to disabuse her of such thoughts and swore my eternal love but I could not quite put her at ease. We began to slide into a quarrel. It seemed to me an ugly way to part for the summer and I suggested we take a drive. Perhaps the night air would help to clear things up. Toward midnight, with the town asleep, the streets deserted, the storefronts and houses dark, we drove out to the approach to the bridge over the great, wide river, watching the ribbons of light it made across to the far shore in Illinois. We saw the lights of an old paddle-wheeler wheezing slowly upstream, the kind, we recalled, that Mark Twain had piloted and loved in the great days of steamboating on the Mississippi but which now, in 1925, already were a rarity on the river.

I thought the long silence as we gazed across the river and into the night might change her mood but when she spoke again it was clear that it had not.

"I'm sorry," she said, "but somehow I feel that you will never come back . . . that perhaps you won't want to, once you are in Paris . . . and that you're afraid to tell me."

"Listen, darling, I'll be back in a couple of months," I protested. "My two hundred dollars won't last longer than that. I've got a couple of job offers. We can get married and you can finish school. I love you and I want to marry you."

I could not quite convince her and when we parted in front of the hotel I had for the first time in the two years of courtship a dim feeling that maybe we would not make it together after all. I felt even more depressed than she seemed to be. It was a lousy way to start off on what had seemed to be an adventure, the first of its kind I'd ever had. After a last kiss that she made very perfunctory, I got out of the car and stood for a moment at the curb watching her drive off into the darkness. I sat down in a plush chair in the half-darkened hotel lobby to think it over. I had a sudden urge to telephone her and say I would cancel the trip and we could get married then and there. The urge was fleeting. If she thwarted me in this at the very beginning, how could I ever feel free again to strike out beyond the narrow horizon of an Iowa town?

She was, of course, I see now a half century later, wiser than I and more foresighted. She knew me better than I knew myself.

I never saw her again.

Nearly every day for a week I took the train from Glen Ellyn into Chicago with my uncle, who was a vice-president of a publishing house, Henry Holt & Company, in charge of the Chicago office. His main job was selecting, editing and especially selling textbooks, the financial backbone of the publishing business, and, I gathered, he was very good at it. He could talk for hours about textbooks and how many hundreds of thousands he sold every year, but when I tried to turn the conversation to books that interested me more, contemporary novels, he did not seem much interested.

"I leave those to the New York office," he said. "I earn the bread and butter out here with the textbooks." He did mention once that Holt had turned down Sinclair Lewis' *Main Street* but he was more impressed by the opportunity lost than by the book itself.

During that week, I usually parted with him in the Loop, near his office, and wandered over to the Public Library to read up on England and France, grabbed a hasty lunch nearby, and walked up Michigan Avenue to the Art Institute to look at the paintings, especially those of the French Impressionists—the first originals I had ever seen. One day I took the elevated out to 63rd Street to look up the house and neighborhood in which I had spent my first nine years. The house, at 6612 University Avenue, seemed smaller than I had remembered and rather dark and dismal inside, nudged as it was in a row of houses that lined the street. The neighborhood, where I had played as a child, seemed rather run-down. I called at three or four homes I remembered, but the families, whose youngsters I had dug caves with in the nearby vacant lots, had moved away. There were no more vacant lots.

Somehow I could not connect with the teeming city of my birth and early childhood, nor have I been able to since. It had seemed an exciting place in my father's time, bubbling over with energy not only to build and make money out of its advantageous situation at the crossroads of the fast-growing nation, but to create a rich and civilized life for its people. It had been a heady, yeasty place for writers, artists, musicians, architects, lawyers, journalists and cartoonists. Symphony music, the opera, even the theater, flourished. Some of my father's enthusiasms had rubbed off on us youngsters. There were the Chicago Symphony Orchestra of Frederick Stock, the opera of Galli-Curci and Mary Garden, the Art Institute, the Field Museum, the theater, which originated much of its own drama, and the rebellious writers of the "Chicago Group," who, breaking away from Howells and the rest of the effete literary establishment of New York, at last were giving the country a vigorous literature of its own and exposing the cant, the greed, the corruption, the shabbiness of the rich and the mighty.

All the ferment which had made Chicago such a dynamic city at the turn of the century and immediately afterward, all that ferocious energy which Burton Rascoe felt as coming out of some "huge hydroelectric plant," now seemed stilled. Rascoe himself, Dreiser, Floyd Dell, Sherwood Anderson, Francis Hackett, Carl and Mark Van Doren, Harry Hansen, and even the academic literary critic Professor Stuart Sherman had left, or were leaving, for New York. Carl Sandburg had given up his movie reviews in the *Daily News* and his concentration on poetry to move to Michigan to work on his biography of Lincoln. Harriet Monroe stayed on with her *Poetry* magazine. She still carried on the cover Whitman's line: "To have great poets there must be great audiences too." But most of her readers, as well as her contributors, now came from points far away from Chicago: from New York and Europe. *The Dial* had long since moved on to New York, as had Margaret Anderson's *Little Review*, the best of all such publications.

The good people of the beautiful city by the lake seemed content enough. Money was plentiful along with bootleg booze—and fantastic graft. Almost everyone seemed hellbent on having a good time, well seasoned with raw alcohol, and if it all struck a passing cornfed youth as a little frenetic and infantile, they probably were unaware of it, or didn't mind. "Everybody's doing it," the lines of a song hit said. Everybody wanted to be "happy." Wasn't it such "happiness," I mused smugly, that people seek in a country which has no history? We had, of course, a history, brief but interesting and full of violence, and who cared? Henry Ford, one of America's idols, had declared during the trial of his libel suit against the *Chicago Tribune* that "history is bunk"—an opinion probably shared by a good many readers out of the same ignorance that afflicted the automobile wizard, who on the stand had told the jury he thought Benedict Arnold was "a writer."

The newspapers were bursting with trivia: the latest divorce, murder and gang war, the latest "gala" costume party of some North Shore millionaire, the latest pronouncement of some idiotic statesman, politician, businessman, Prohibitionist or divine, the latest romance—or its bust-up—of a Hollywood movie star, the latest surge of the soaring stock market on Wall Street, the frenzied new real-estate boom in Florida, where William Jennings Bryan, no less, before his departure to defend fundamentalism at the Dayton "Monkey Trial," was earning a fat fee sitting under an umbrella on a raft in a lagoon at Coral Gables lecturing the crowds of suckers ashore on the wondrous sunny climate of the former swamp. There were headlines, too, concerning the latest crazes: the progress of a marathon dance—"bunion derby," the newspapers called it—or of some nut perched for days on the top of a flagpole in the middle of the city. Records were being set. Couples danced and grown men sat on flagpoles for weeks, making headlines and winning prizes.

On such fare the newspapers were thriving. It wasn't all their fault. That's the way the country and this city were. That's what the citizens wanted to read. The *Daily News* and the *Tribune*, both of which maintained news bureaus not only in Washington but in the principal European capitals, struggled to leaven the daily fare with dispatches telling what was going on in the seats of government here and in less frantic lands. Thus on one June day in 1925 the *Tribune*, though devoting its banner headline to the acquittal of a local society figure accused of murdering his wife's millionaire ward in order to gain a million-dollar inheritance, found top space on its front page for such headlines as these: "FRENCH VOTE 6 BILLION MORE PAPER FRANCS" and "COOLIDGE KILLS PLAN TO LET U.S. FOOT WAR BILLS."

If the French were foolish in thinking they could save their economy by resort to the printing press, they were no more foolish than President Coolidge, who thought he could continue to collect war debts from our wartime allies after Germany began to default on reparation payments to them. "They hired the money, didn't they?" he reminded the American people. He wanted every cent of it paid back—with interest. To lower the tariffs so that the foreigners could sell enough to get the money to pay their debts to us would be, the President maintained, a betrayal of the American taxpayer.

The Chicago taxpayers did not seem unduly concerned with such matters. Like most people in the country, they had great faith that whatever Coolidge was doing, or not doing, was all right, so long as he kept taxes down, restrained the government from poking its nose into business, and left them free to grub for money and to raise cain. In Chicago they were more interested that summer in the doings of a local character of insalubrious background who was said to be the real ruler of the town and who indeed, any way you looked at it, was an interesting figure. This was "Scarface" Al Capone.

I had read a little about him in the hometown newspapers, but in the city room of the *Daily News*, where I had been sent by an old friend of my father's, Jim Gilruth, a former city editor, to talk about an eventual job, I heard a great deal more. Prohibition had become a gold mine for the underworld. Millions could be made from outlawed beer and booze. Johnny Torrio, a formidable figure in Chicago's gangland, had been the first in the city to appreciate this and within a short time, by 1920, was doing so well selling bootleg liquor that he imported an assistant to help manage the business and, when necessary, to take care of the "competition"—the O'Banions, the Gennas, the Aiellos—with guns. Himself a former leader of the notorious Five Points Gang in New York, Torrio picked a promising young hoodlum from that organization, installing him at his gambling club, the Four Deuces, in a small office on one table of which stood a family Bible. He had printed up for him a business card: *"Alphonse Capone, Second Hand Furniture Dealer. 2220 South Wabash Avenue."*

To the reporters on the *News*, and no doubt to their avid readers, Capone was a fabulous figure. Thug though he was, he had turned out to be, the reporters said, a brilliant businessman, a masterful organizer, ruthless and bold. Indeed his interlocking directorates of beer, booze and brothels were not unlike those of the more legitimate kind which, under the Insulls and Van Sweringens and others, controlled vast enterprises in transportation, public utilities and industry. Ensconced in Cicero, a Chicago suburb, which he ran like his own fief, choosing the mayor, the police and civic officials and even the judges, Capone drove about in an armored automobile, preceded and followed by cars full of trigger-happy gunmen who, to protect their lord, often found it necessary to mow down a good many rivals who got in the way. Most of the killings, some three hundred in all, though, were done by Capone's private army of seven hundred thugs whom he armed with sawed-off shotguns and submachine guns—"typewriters," he called them—stolen from state armories.

By the time I passed through Chicago that summer of 1925, "Scarface" had become the undisputed boss of the Chicago underworld, his annual income estimated by federal agents and reporters to be $50 million from beer and liquor, with another $25 million from gambling and dog tracks, $10 million from prostitution and a further $10 million from various other rackets. Johnny Torrio, once so feared by the lawless and the lawful alike, was fading away before the brilliance and boldness of his erstwhile young assistant. In 1923, after a shoot-out with a rival gang at the Four Deuces during which he was hit by six bullets and Capone saved himself by lying flat on the floor and protecting his head with a brass spittoon, Torrio had begun to be somewhat discouraged with life in Chicago. Two years later, shortly before my arrival in Chicago, he had been gunned down in front of his apartment, spent sixteen days in a hospital, and then gone on to serve a nine-month term in jail. While behind the bars he turned over his underworld empire to young Capone and made plans to return to his native Italy on his release.

By this time, as *The New Republic* noted, "Scarface" Al didn't merely buy the government, he *was* that government. Still, he purchased "protection" from interference by the law, and that meant buying officials. Reporters and frightened timid civic reformers estimated that this cost Capone some $2 million a year but obviously it was a bearable expense. It was said for Capone that he was at least nonpartisan in his political payments. He supported whoever was in office, at one time the "reform" Mayor Dever, at another one of Chicago's favorite politicians, Mayor "Big Bill" Thompson, whose reign at City Hall set a record even for this tolerant city for municipal graft, which was estimated to amount to $125 million annually. No matter. The light-hearted Chicagoans went for "Big Bill." When a few bluenoses accused him of crookedness, he snapped back, "I am for America first!"

When during his second term the city went bankrupt, couldn't pay its teachers, police and firemen, and the mayor was charged with wasting the taxpayers' money, he thundered: "If King George doesn't keep his nose out of America's affairs, I'll bust him in the snoot." In response to such statesmanlike words of wisdom, Chicagoans in 1927 would elect "Big Bill" to a third term.

Behind the scenes, though, it was "Scarface" and not "Big Bill" who ran the city. This was not merely the view of the hard-drinking, cynical newsmen. Frank J. Loesch, president of the Chicago Crime Commission, agreed. "It did not take me long," he would testify, "to discover that Al Capone ran the city. His hand reached into every department of the city and county government."

After a week in the city of my birth I had had enough. I was glad to leave it to "Scarface" Al and get on. Thanking my uncle for his hospitality and his loan of a hundred dollars, I set out for Washington and New York.

A dispatch in the *Tribune* the morning I left attracted my attention: "FRENCH DRIVE REPULSES RIFFIAN TRIBES WITH MANY DEAD. TRIBUNE MAN ALMOST SHOT AS SPY." The cable was by-lined: Vincent Sheean. He had obtained a world scoop by getting through the French and Spanish lines in Morocco and interviewing the Riffian rebel leader, Abd-el-Krim. On the way he had been arrested by some trigger-happy Riffian ruffians on suspicion of being a spy and had barely escaped a firing squad. Well, I thought as I finished reading the piece and gazed out at the endless cornfields of Indiana as the B&O train gathered speed, the life of a foreign correspondent was certainly interesting. A year or two before I had read an anthology of dispatches of some of the great correspondents filed during the World War and immediately afterward, with notes on the careers of the authors. They had struck me as a romantic tribe, dashing from one battle to another, from one revolution to another, from one international conference to another, hobnobbing with the great who made the headlines. But their exciting world had seemed to be far beyond my chances of entering. It was so terribly distant from the placid Iowa cornfields in which I had grown up.

Still. I went back to the smoking car, lit my pipe, and reread Sheean's story. He apparently worked out of the Paris office of the *Chicago Tribune*. I recalled his occasional by-line from there in

the past couple of years. Perhaps . . . when I got to Paris . . .
As the train rolled on I puffed at the pipe, gazed out at the rows
of corn that stretched to the horizon and at the monotonous Midwest villages and towns, replicas of the one I had come of age in,
and thought: Why not? Then I put it aside as a recurrence of the
old pipedream, and began to wonder what Washington and New
York would be like.

In Washington on a sweltering day I saw Calvin Coolidge. I
actually shook hands with the President of the United States,
along with several hundred others, mostly country hicks like
myself, who filed by the great man in awe. It was then a White
House custom, happily for the President soon abandoned, to have
the Chief Executive pump the hands of the visiting yokels once or
twice a week. Apparently such a barbarous ordeal for him was
considered a part of our democracy and kept him in touch with
the ordinary citizens, whose votes, however manipulated, controlled the elections.

A college friend, now a newspaperman in Washington, had
procured a ticket and I had gone to the White House out of
curiosity to see the place at first hand and to get a view of the
President face to face. The spacious rooms of the mansion, reminding one of so much of our history, were impressive—but not
the occupant. Still, one could not help being struck by the awe for
the President in the faces of the good, simple people from the
hinterland as they grasped his hand and heard him say "How do
you do" in his Yankee nasal drawl. It is a phenomenon common
among us to this day, I believe, and no different probably from
the awe the peasants once had for the kings and emperors of
Europe and Asia. It must have been a feeling for the exalted
office, not for the man. Who could possibly be awed by Calvin
Coolidge, the man?

It spoke much for the state of civilization in our country in
1925, I thought, that this prematurely wizened, tight-lipped, New
England mediocrity, a man, as Frederick Lewis Allen would say,
of "uncompromising unoriginality,"[1] with a positive genius for
inactivity, enjoyed a tremendous popularity in the land. Moving
up from Vice-President to President when Harding suddenly died

[1] Frederick Lewis Allen: *Only Yesterday*, p. 163 (paperback edition).

on August 2, 1923, he had been elected overwhelmingly on his own the following year. No doubt, he fitted the times. He still believed, as most of his successors would, in the country's outworn myths, just as most Americans seemed to. Among these was that you got ahead in this world, or at least in America, by hard work, frugal living, impeccable morals and devotion to religion. Coolidge preached that gospel. "The success which is made in any walk of life," he would state in his autobiography, "is measured almost exactly by the amount of hard work that is put in it." This seemed strange from a man who was reported to nap at least two hours after lunch and to spend much time in his rocking chair, apparently not even in meditation.

It seemed to me that afternoon in Washington, as I pondered the reason for the unquestioned popularity of this anemic little man, that it was due mainly to his policy of keeping the government's hand off business and encouraging the businessman to do his damnedest to make more money. Perhaps more so than today, in the 1970's, when we may be a little wiser, business, as we have seen, was enthroned in the land and businessmen had become the arbiters of public opinion and taste, far above the statesman, the philosopher, the poet, the pastor, the priest. Calvin Coolidge believed in them. "Business is the business of America," he told the country on becoming President. At various times thereafter he underlined his beliefs: "The driving force of American progress has been her industries. . . . The man who builds a factory builds a temple, the man who works there worships there. . . . Large profits mean large payrolls. . . ." And about the time I passed through the capital he was preparing a speech for delivery to the Chamber of Commerce of New York in which he would say: "Business rests squarely on the law of service. It has for its main reliance truth and faith and justice. In its larger sense it is one of the greatest contributing forces to the moral and spiritual advancement of the race."

This seemed to me to be utter rubbish, since business "rested squarely" on making profits, but no doubt the country liked it, especially the businessmen. Theodore Roosevelt and Woodrow Wilson had had no such faith in the "moral and spiritual" force of our money-grubbing entrepreneurs, and had tried somewhat to curb their appetites and pare their predatory claws, but Coolidge was content to sit back in his rocking chair and cheer them on to feed unimpeded at the public trough, not even dimly aware that this would lead in four years to national disaster. For the farmers and the workers and the poor, Coolidge seemed to have little awareness.[1] Twice he vetoed farm relief legislation, which was badly needed in my part of the country, where the price of corn and wheat and hogs was going down and the price of farm machinery and fertilizer was going up. Such legislation was "uneconomic," he told the farmers, adding this advice:

> No complicated scheme of relief, no plan for government fixing of prices, no resort to the Public Treasury will be of any value. Simple and direct methods put into operation by the farmer himself are the only real source of restoration.

The farmers of Iowa, who knew better, had voted for him nevertheless. They knew that no "simple and direct methods" could extricate them from the squeeze between the prices they got for their produce and the prices they had to pay for the things they needed to keep their farms running. The former were set by a blind market over which they had no control; the latter were fixed by quasi monopolies, protected by a high tariff. Yet there was no stirring of revolt among the farmers of my part of the country nor of the working people and the poor anywhere. They still believed, as did Coolidge and the rest of the populace, in the shibboleths of America. Anyway, they asked, "What could the little man do?"

The little man had been offered a political alternative in the elections the year before when Senator Robert La Follette, bolt-

---

[1] Or for the poets either. Mark Sullivan, who admired Coolidge and was close to him, tells of being asked by the President, soon after he took office, for advice "'about this job of mine.'" Sullivan suggested that he pay some attention to eminent men in the arts and sciences.

". . . Theodore Roosevelt used to do it" [Sullivan said], "he was always having authors and artists and scientists . . . stay at the White House. If I were President, especially . . . from New England as you are, . . . I'd have some of those New England poets come and visit the White House."

Coolidge, with laconic directness, asked, "Just what poets do you have in mind?"

"Oh," I said, "any of the New England ones—Robert Frost, Edwin Arlington Robinson, Edna St. Vincent Millay—she was born in Maine."

"Frost? Robinson?" asked Coolidge meditatively, searching his memory —"I never heard of them."

—Mark Sullivan: *Our Times*, VI, p. 439, footnote.

ing the Republicans, had run on a Progressive ticket that promised a better break for the farmer, the laborer, the small businessman, for whom the dour Senator from Wisconsin had fought all his life in battling the greed, the corruption, the monopolies of Big Business. Despite my awareness of La Follette's narrowness on certain issues, especially in foreign affairs, I had worked in my small way in Iowa for his election, believing that he had the truer vision of what the country ought to be. The majority, including many farmers, workers, and poor, obviously did not see it. The well-financed election propaganda of the Republicans may have blinded them. La Follette got just under five million votes, Coolidge nearly sixteen million, and Davis, a Wall Street lawyer who was the Democratic candidate, some eight million.

La Follette had just died when I arrived in Washington, worn out from overwork in his losing battles against "the interests." He had been despised by many for his opposition to the war, for his seeming pro-Germanism and for his "radicalism"—a word that frightened the bulk of the American people and apparently still does. There was not much mourning for him except in Wisconsin, which he had dominated with his progressive ideas for a generation.

Woodrow Wilson, too, had died in Washington the year before, in almost total obscurity. He had been the idol of my youth, when I was too young—I was still too young in 1925—to see his Presbyterian shortcomings.[1] Great as these were, Wilson had had vision, and now, it seemed to me, a year after his death and after five years of Harding and Coolidge, there was little vision left—in the White House, in the Congress, in the whole broad land. At least Wilson had stood for "the revival of the power of the people," as he once had put it, for the "New Freedom," the professed goal of his first Administration, and he had flayed at the "interests" and the "privileged." Although he had taken us into the war five months after his re-election in 1916 on the slogan "He

---

[1] ". . . a kind of frozen flame of righteous intelligence," William Allen White thought, after a visit to Wilson at the White House during the war. But White's admiration was expressed in the epitaph he wrote on the President's death:

> God gave him a great vision.
> The Devil gave him an imperious heart.
> The proud heart is still.
> The vision lives.

—*The Autobiography of William Allen White*, pp. 615, 629.

Kept Us Out of War,"[1] he had fought to the point of exhaustion and a paralytic stroke that left him permanently crippled to take us into the League of Nations, which he believed fervently, though mistakenly as it turned out, would keep the world's peace, abolishing war. Compared to Wilson, with all his faults, Coolidge seemed to me a pigmy, but vastly more popular, as pigmies often are in our fickle democracy.

Washington in 1925 had forgotten the ideals of Wilson, and La Follette's dire warnings of the danger of plutocracy. The country was wallowing in the "Coolidge Prosperity," unshared by many though it was. And it was not much disturbed by the taint of the scandals of the recent Harding Administration, whose reverberations were dying down, though they had shown, as Frederick Lewis Allen was later to conclude, "more concentrated robbery and rascality than any other in the whole history of the Federal Government."[2]

The skulduggery during the sainted Harding's reign had begun to come to light soon after Harding's death—the newspapers were still headlining it—and most of my few days and nights in Washington were spent listening to the tales of it in a newspaper city room, where two college friends, John Kennedy and Newall Rogers, had come to work as reporters two or three years before. Kennedy had himself exposed one of them, the story of how the head of the Veterans' Bureau, Colonel Charles R. Forbes, a favorite friend of Harding, had amassed a small fortune by taking a cut from the contractors who built the new veterans' hospitals for the gallant, crippled casualties of the war. This would ultimately cost Forbes a year in Leavenworth.

The oil scandals were still being investigated by a Senate Committee under the indefatigable Thomas J. Walsh of Montana. But enough evidence had already turned up to show that another friend of the President, former Senator Albert B. Fall of New Mexico, who had become Secretary of the Interior, had leased two vast government-owned oil-bearing tracts to two oil tycoons, Harry F. Sinclair and Edward L. Doheny, after Doheny had "lent" him $100,000 in cash and Sinclair had *given* him $260,000

---

[1] Just as President Lyndon B. Johnson had sent a half million American troops to Vietnam shortly after his campaign promise in 1964 that he was not going to send "American boys" there to fight a war that "Asian boys" should fight.
[2] Frederick Lewis Allen, *Only Yesterday*, p. 138.

in Liberty bonds. Eventually the leases would be voided by the Supreme Court, and Secretary Fall sentenced to a year in jail for accepting a bribe.

This was the most sensational of the oil scandals, but there were others, one of them involving the most illustrious graduate of my college, Chairman of the Board of the Standard Oil Company of Indiana, no less, who was finally driven out of the business by the biggest Standard Oil man of them all, John D. Rockefeller, Jr., who was said to have been shocked by the lack of Christian morals among the leaders in the very field in which his father (with an appalling lack of Christian scruples) had built up the immense family fortune.

The newspapermen in Washington, along with investigating committees of the Congress, were still digging up malodorous facts about the pilfering of the "Ohio Gang," which Harding had brought with him to Washington from his native state. Its chief collector of graft had been a small-town businessman from Washington Court House, Ohio, named Jess Smith, an old crony of the President and a protégé of Attorney General Harry M. Daugherty, who had masterminded Harding's rise to the White House. Smith, who shared a Washington apartment with the Attorney General and had a desk near his at the Justice Department, though he had no government post, was an ignorant, unread, crude but friendly man whose familiar greeting to all he met was "Well, whaddayaknow?" and whose favorite song, which he sang often and lustily, was "God, How the Money Rolls In." Soon after arriving in the capital, the money started rolling in for Smith and his Ohio pals from the sale to the highest bidder of liquor-withdrawal permits, pardons, federal judgeships, immunities from prosecution and the considerable assets of the Alien Property Custodian.

The Custodian, Colonel T. W. Miller, for instance, with the approval of the Attorney General, had turned over to a Swiss group some $6 million seized from a German commercial holding during the war. The lawyer who arranged it for the Swiss had found it necessary to spend almost half a million dollars greasing itchy palms in Washington. Jess Smith, the chief fixer, got at least $200,000, and the Alien Property Custodian, Colonel Miller, $50,000. A sum of some $40,000 found its way into the bank account of the Attorney General in Washington Court House,

Ohio, where Smith also deposited his loot. By the time the Attorney General was brought to trial it was disclosed that he had burned the ledger sheets covering his account and Smith's.

Smith had long since disappeared from the scene. Feeling himself cornered, he confided to his divorced wife, whom he still loved, that "they are going to get me," returned one night to the apartment he shared with the Attorney General, and was found the next morning dead on the floor, a bullet in his head, which was resting in an iron wastebasket, and a revolver in his right hand. The Justice Department of Harry Daugherty took over the case, permitting neither an autopsy nor an investigation. Smith's financial records of his graft, meticulously kept, were burned. By Daugherty? It was impossible to prove. But some of the newspapermen believed Smith had been murdered to prevent exposure of corruption in high places. President Harding, to whom Smith had been a boon companion since the early Ohio days, was reported "almost prostrated" by his death. Many believed it hastened his own death a few months later.

Harding's funeral train had paused briefly for a memorial service in our Iowa town on the way from San Francisco to Washington, and our local clergymen had extolled the dead President as an upright and God-fearing man. I was somewhat surprised now to hear the newspapermen in Washington talk quite openly of Harding's drinking bouts in the "Little Green House on K Street," the headquarters of the Ohio Gang, where the President, they said, often dropped in to play poker with his old Ohio friends and imbibe the best liquor his Prohibition officials could provide. Even more interesting was the talk in the city room of the "loves" of the President—a matter which seemed to my innocent mind too fantastic to believe. But according to my newspaper friends, the President of the United States had been "girl crazy" and the year before his election, when he was a U.S. Senator, had fathered an illegitimate child with a young lady from his hometown named Nan Britton, who had been his mistress on and off for years.[1]

[1] Later, in 1927, Nan Britton published a book, *The President's Daughter*, dedicated "with understanding and love to all unwedded mothers, and to their innocent children whose fathers are usually not known to the world." In it she alleged that her intimate relations with Harding had begun in New York in 1916 when Harding was a U.S. Senator and had continued in Washington at various

The week in Washington had opened my innocent eyes a little to what went on in the big world. The picture from Iowa, I could see, had not been very complete. Young hayseed that I was, I was both fascinated and shocked. Nothing in my experience growing up in the Midwest had prepared me to believe that such doings in high places could prevail in the national capital. Some of them, to be sure, already had been reported in the newspapers, but our good citizens had shrugged them off, just as, at the time of this writing nearly half a century later, they have shrugged off the disclosures of American atrocities in Vietnam and remained unconcerned about the savage American aggression in Indochina and the terrible toll it has taken in Asian lives and property.

What did Americans care about the "concentrated robbery and rascality" in their national capital? The answer, it occurred to me, had been given in the national election the year before, in 1924, when John W. Davis, the Democratic candidate, and La Follette, the Progressive candidate, had tried to make an issue of the scandals of the Harding-Coolidge Administration. The American electorate was not interested. It had clobbered both candidates at the polls.

After all, I reflected as I prepared to push on to New York, not even the leading members of Harding's Cabinet, the most

---

places, including the White House, up to shortly before his death. Her child, she believed, had been conceived during a rendezvous in the Senate Office Building, and had been born on October 22, 1919, at Asbury Park, New Jersey, when she was twenty-three and Harding fifty-four. She listed numerous hotels where she had registered with Harding, who introduced her, she said, as his "niece." The manager of a hotel in Plattsburgh, New York, on Lake Champlain, once showed me a register in which Nan Britton had signed in with Harding's Presidential party.

Still later, in 1963, Francis Russell, the biographer and historian, doing research on Harding in Marion, Ohio, dug up another affair with a hometown woman. This was Mrs. Carrie Phillips, the wife of a local department store owner, described as "a willowy redhead" and known "as the best-looking and most elegant woman in town." From 1905 to the time of his candidacy for President in 1920, Harding, according to Russell, maintained a passionate and intimate relationship with Mrs. Phillips, replete with his customary mushy love letters, one of which began: "I love you garb'd but naked, more!" Heirs of the former President resorted to the courts to prevent Russell from publishing his material in a biography of Harding. Finally, at the end of a long and bitter struggle in the courts, an agreement was made in which the correspondence between Harding and Mrs. Phillips was to be turned over to the Library of Congress and sealed until 2014.

honorable of men, had ever protested publicly: Charles Evans Hughes, the eminent Secretary of State and later Chief Justice of the Supreme Court; Andrew W. Mellon, "the greatest Secretary of the Treasury," the Republicans said, "since Alexander Hamilton"; Herbert Hoover, the Secretary of Commerce, who already was being spoken of as the next Republican candidate for President. Nor Harding's Vice-President, Calvin Coolidge, now the President. Was it possible, I wondered, that they knew nothing?

Exciting and bewildering as Washington was to a country bumpkin, I had to move on. I took the night B&O train to New York, full of anticipation of the first sight of the skyline of the great city.

For a small-town boy from the plains the first view of the towers of Manhattan could never be forgotten. It was early morning on a bright June day when the ferry pushed off from the B&O terminus on the New Jersey side of the Hudson and I saw the gleaming skyscrapers across the river. They were clustered in the lower part of the island, the soaring buildings of midtown capped by the Empire State Building being then only in the planning stage. Perched a little higher than the rest stood the white tower of the Woolworth Building, shining in the early-morning sun. I stood at the rail of the ferry, breathless at the sight. It seemed like a magic fairyland along the water's edge.

It was Sunday, and I had to hurry on to Woodstock, where the college editors' conference was due to begin the next day. As I sat in an uptown streetcar, straddling my shiny new suitcase, watching the bustling passengers and glancing at my copy of the Sunday *World,* I felt a warm glow of happiness. I had reached one goal of a cornfed boy, if only for an hour or two. I had set foot on Manhattan. And I would be returning briefly in a week. Then . . . perhaps . . . with luck . . . well, I would brave the city rooms of the *World* and the *Times* just to see. I put the idea aside—London and Paris still lay ahead—recrossed the Hudson on an uptown ferry and caught a train up to Woodstock.

Above the village in a sprawling lodge nestling on a wooded hill beneath the Catskill peaks I spent a delightful week with a dozen other college newspaper editors. They were mostly from the Ivy League colleges, male and female, editors of the *Harvard*

Crimson, the *Yale Daily News,* the *Daily Princetonian,* and whatever the papers were called at Smith and Vassar, with three or four from the great state universities in the Middle and Far West. I was the only editor from a small college (apparently the makeup and content of the *Coe College Cosmos* had impressed the organizers and this had brought me an invitation to the gathering) and on my way to Woodstock I had wondered whether this would make any difference. It did not. The prestigious Ivy League colleges and the great state universities did not seem to have imparted any more wisdom or learning to their charges than had my little college in Iowa. We were all, I felt, starting out in life about equal, so far as an academic education was concerned.

There was much good talk all day long and far into the night: shoptalk about the fun of getting out a college paper that was saucy enough to annoy the administration, half the faculty and most of the alumni; talk of our chances of breaking into big-time journalism; but most of all, talk about the writers who were shaking up the country—Dreiser, Lewis, Fitzgerald, Sherwood Anderson, Willa Cather, Floyd Dell, James Branch Cabell (with his temporarily banned *Jurgen*), James Joyce (whose *Ulysses* was still banned; I would have to pick it up in Paris, where it had been published three years before by Sylvia Beach)—and talk about the poets—Amy Lowell, Sandburg, Frost, Robinson, T. S. Eliot, Edna St. Vincent Millay and others.[1]

Most of us were still a little gone on Fitzgerald and Millay, though they came from the college generation before us. *This Side of Paradise,* which romanticized the high-flying collegians, had appeared in 1920, while I was still struggling to finish high school, and "Renascence," the most loved poem of our time, even before that—in 1917, I believe. But this novelist and this fine poet seemed to be speaking for us, especially about sexual freedom. We never tired of reciting the lines from *A Few Figs from Thistles:*

[1] None of us had yet heard of Hemingway, though, as we would learn later, two slim volumes of his had been published obscurely in Paris a couple of years before and had attracted the attention of Edmund Wilson. But *In Our Time,* a collection of short stories, would not appear in New York until October, 1925, and his first novel, *The Sun Also Rises,* a year later. Dos Passos had begun to publish, *Manhattan Transfer* coming out in 1925, following two war novels, but the *U.S.A.* trilogy still lay in the future. Fitzgerald's best novel, *The Great Gatsby,* and perhaps Dreiser's greatest work, *An American Tragedy,* came out, I believe, later that year of 1925; at any rate I do not recall our discussing them.

My candle burns at both ends;
It will not last the night;
But ah, my foes, and oh, my friends—
It gives a lovely light!

Fitzgerald and Millay had liberated us, we thought, from the heavy hand of puritanism and stodginess not only by their imaginative writings but by the example of their lives. They were gay, uninhibited, saucy, and if they burned the candle at both ends, why not?

Editors from New York came up for a day or two to talk to us of the world we had just been graduated into. One of them, Don Seitz of the *World*, was not too encouraging when we asked how we could get a job on his newspaper, the goal of so many aspiring reporters, for we thought the *World* was the most interesting and best-written daily in the country.

"Go out and get a couple of years' experience on a small-town daily first," Seitz advised us. "Then come and talk to us." Good advice, no doubt, but I had already worked a couple of *summers* on a "small-town daily" and complacently felt that I had learned almost all there was to learn from that experience.

A more interesting visitor was a pale, rather intense young man named Briton Hadden, not long out of Yale, who a year or two before had, with a college mate named Henry Luce, founded a new weekly magazine called *Time*. They were struggling to get a foothold against the established *Literary Digest*, a dull and stodgy publication with an immense circulation, whose articles were made up mostly of quotations from the daily press. *Time*, Hadden said, was writing its own pieces in a fresh, brisk language and with a point of view, though, it was obvious, it, too, mined its material from the daily press. It seemed like a promising idea, though the promise faded later when the money started rolling in, and Hadden was dead of exhaustion within four years of our meeting. Hadden suggested to two or three of us that we drop in on him in New York if we were interested in a job. He also suggested that if any of us had a "thousand or two" to invest, he would be interested in that as well. It struck me as a very long shot even if I could raise such a sum, which was beyond the realm of possibility. But I remember that one of the student editors, impressed by the charms of Hadden, told me he was going to ask his father to advance him a "thousand or two." If he did, and got it, and bought *Time* stock and held on to it, he would be a millionaire today, for recently I read somewhere that $30 worth of that stock in those days is worth $22,000 today.

Suddenly the exhilarating week was over, and I found myself going down the Hudson in an old "Day Liner" to New York. One of the organizers of the Woodstock conference had offered me the use of his apartment near Columbia University. With this costly item of living taken care of, I roamed the dazzling city for a week, up and down Broadway and Fifth Avenue, gazing into the windows of the huge department stores and smart shops, breaking my neck to peer up at the soaring skyscrapers, viewing the paintings and sculpture at the Metropolitan Museum, wandering through the Public Library at 42nd Street and Fifth Avenue, hiking through the Fulton Fish Market, Chinatown, Greenwich Village and the Bowery, marveling at the sights and sounds and the sheer electricity in the air of this bustling metropolis. I took my first subway ride and took in my first Broadway play, the satirical, comic *What Price Glory* by Maxwell Anderson and Laurence Stallings, which had been the leading hit in New York since its opening the year before. It suddenly brought the war home to me in a way I had not felt out in Iowa, where we had taken a rather romantic view of it and its soldier heroes, several of whom I had watched with awe in our town as they sauntered jauntily down our streets in their smart overseas caps when they came back from France. A few of our townsmen who had seen the play had been shocked by its profanity, of which it was full, but it was full, too, of wonderful Rabelaisian exchanges between the rough combat soldiers and between them and a pert, fast-talking young Frenchwoman. The play, I believe, broke through once and for all the stilted, ladylike dialogue of American drama, though today, in the 1970's, our youth undoubtedly would find its profanity rather tame. In this, at least, we've grown up.

One afternoon I summoned up my courage and, armed with the letter of introduction Jim Gilruth had given me in Chicago, made my way to the newsroom of the *World*. I was a little nervous as to what I would do if I were offered a job immediately and the city editor declined to hold it until my return from Europe. I needn't have worried. I never got by the receptionist guarding the newsroom. At the *World*, at the *Times*, and the

Evening Post. This was my first comedown of the trip and it deflated me. It would not be easy to get a newspaper job in New York after all. For a day or so I felt defeated and lonely.

But then one evening my host, who had returned that afternoon to the apartment to fetch some papers, took me to a party in Greenwich Village. It bucked me up considerably; in truth, it dazzled me. The large living room looking out on a back garden was jammed with Village lights—"bohemians" we called them at home—the women gaily togged out in all sorts of colors and mostly with short-bobbed hair and bangs, the men dressed very informally in nondescript jackets (in contrast to my store suit). The conversation and the booze flowed. My friend pointed here and there to some famous journalist whose column I had just read, to writers, poets, painters, editors, whose names I scarcely grasped. A young man who looked like a poet, and perhaps was, whispered to me that Edna St. Vincent Millay was expected any moment. I had worshiped her for years for her poetry, and especially since the year before when she had read her verse one winter evening at our college and chatted with some of us at a reception afterward. She was, I decided, the most fascinating and beautiful woman I had ever met, with flaunting red hair, a highly expressive face, rather sad eyes and a golden voice.[1]

To my immense disappointment she never appeared. No doubt I would have been tongue-tied in her presence, as I had been the year before on the campus, but what did that matter if one could just gaze on this goddess again? I recall being rather tongue-tied on being introduced to one of the most beautiful young women in the gathering, Freda Kirchwey, already, I believe, managing editor of the *Nation.* Her looks, her manner, her talk, her lively mind, stunned me in the most pleasant way. In fact I was soon wonderfully dizzy from listening to all the talk—I had little to say myself, try as I might—and from imbibing all the drinks.

[1] She was so vivacious and charming in her reading and in her conversation it never occurred to me that actually she might be bored to death by these one-night stands in the hinterland. Many years later I noticed among her published letters one to her husband of a year, Eugen Boissevain, written on the stationery of the local hotel in my Iowa town and dated February 5, 1924. "I give my reading still with charm & spirit," she wrote, "[but] I am sunk in a lethargy of boredom. . . . Did you ever go from Chicago to Cedar Rapids [my town] on one of these Middle-Western so-called Parlor-cars?—Well, don't."

My little town in Iowa, I reflected the next day while trying to recover from a hangover, would be a tame place to return to. And I had not yet seen London and Paris. I had not forgotten that either. Despite a free place to sleep in, I was spending money that I ought to save for Europe. Rather reluctantly I decided to move on, to stop for a few days with some distant relatives at Canton, New York, where there would be no way to spend much. From there it was a short distance down the St. Lawrence from Ogdensburg to Montreal, where I was due in a week to embark on the cattle boat for England. I was still eager to get abroad, but the days in Washington, Woodstock and New York, fleeting as they were, had sobered my mind a little about "fleeing the waste-land." If one could get a start in New York or even in Washington, life might turn out to be more interesting and free than I had imagined possible in our Babbitty land.

Upstate New York, lovely as the land was, made one a little sad. The headlong progress of the nation had passed it by, leaving it a rather stagnant backwater. My cousin took me around in his car to see the abandoned cheese factories which once had supplied the country with most of its native cheese. Now Wisconsin was doing that. The upstate farmers no longer had a market for their milk.

My uncle was cheery enough. He had spent his youth and early adult life in the coal mines of Scotland, and after such toil he found farming relatively easy and rewarding, even if it didn't yield much cash. He was now doing little more than raising enough food to feed the family, spending most of his time in the study and contemplation of Herbert Spencer, for whose thoughts he had developed a lifelong passion. He tried his patient best to impart to me the main thrust of Spencer's philosophy, the application of the natural sciences, especially biology and more especially Darwin's theories, to philosophy, psychology, sociology and ethics, but I found it difficult to follow. In college Spencer had scarcely been mentioned.[1]

---

[1] I did not realize until much later what an enormous influence Spencer had in America during the last third of the nineteenth century. John Fiske built his philosophy and his conception of history on Spencer, who flashed across his world when he was eighteen, preparing for Harvard. Oliver Wendell Holmes thought that no other writer except Darwin had such an impact on the American mind.

The old Scot had also been attracted to Henry George, but more for George's biting criticism of capitalism's inequalities, its spread of misery among the masses, he said, than by George's solution for such ills by a single tax on land, which would give back to society the unearned increment in rising land values. The single tax, he argued, would stop the unconscionable profits of those who speculated in land, but it would not touch the real power of capitalism, which lay in the possession of industry, transportation and the banks.

I noticed that my uncle's copy of George's *Progress and Poverty* as well as his several volumes of Spencer and Darwin and other authors were well thumbed. He was obviously an omnivorous reader and I asked him how he had come to that, since he had told me he had little formal schooling, having gone to work in the mines in Scotland when he was scarcely in his teens. "The miners' libraries!" he exclaimed. "You do not know about our libraries?" Whereupon he explained that every union local had an excellent collection of books and that there was little else to do but read through the long, damp, chilly evenings in Scotland. I recalled that conversation much later when Jennie Lee and Aneurin Bevan, climbing toward the top in the British Labor Party, the one having grown up in a Scottish, the other in a Welsh, mining family, told me how, at an early age, they had devoured the books in the miners' libraries.

My uncle in Canton opened a further crack in my mind. Listening to him expound on his reading, it dawned on me that it was not necessary to go to college to become educated. Self-education had made him a well-read, well-informed man, had opened his mind and kept it fresh and receptive, which was more than I had seen in the complacent businessmen in our Iowa town. He had shed the narrowness of his Scotch Presbyterian faith, in which I myself had grown up without ever really taking to it, and his good-natured skepticism about the values and aims of our Christian capitalist world struck a responsive chord in me. De-

---

Hamlin Garland, Jack London and Theodore Dreiser were among his ardent followers. Spencer, Dreiser said, blew him "intellectually to bits." William Allen White once told me that Spencer (along with Whitman, Emerson and Dickens) had been one of the great spiritual inspirations of his life around the turn of the century. When the philosopher died in 1903 at eighty-three, White wrote an account of his life and work for *The Saturday Evening Post*.

spite this skepticism, despite the hardships of a life in the mines and on a farm, he struck me as being one of the happiest men I had ever talked with. He had a wonderfully craggy face behind his drooping mustache and his eyes sparkled with good humor, and the lilt and the brogue of his Scottish tongue sang out to you.

In Montreal all through the first fortnight of July my venture seemed stranded. I was joined there by a college friend, George Latta, who had been working his way through school by operating a Linotype machine at one of the local newspapers. He intended in the fall, if he could work it out with his girl, who wanted him to finish college with her, to enroll at the Art Institute in Chicago to study painting, at which he already showed a marked talent. He had brought with him a collapsible easel and a heavy bag of paints and brushes, determined to do a lot of painting while we were abroad.

But for several days it looked as though we would not get abroad after all. We had arrived in Montreal on July 4, a hot, muggy day, and the marine agent, who had already pocketed our ten-dollar fee, told us to report at the dock early the next morning. But there were no places on the cattle boat that was leaving. There seemed to be dozens of men, mostly college youngsters, ahead of us. Morning after morning, soon after the crack of dawn, we lugged our bags on a streetcar down to the wharves only to find either that no ship was sailing or if one was we were not to be on it. "Tomorrow morning, for sure," the burly agent would assure us, and wearily we would take up our suitcases, board a streetcar and return to the drab rooming house. To husband our meager resources we lived off bread, sausage and cheese, bought at a corner grocery store and eaten on a park bench or on the lawn of McGill University. But this, we reflected glumly, cost money we had planned to spend in England and France. On the thirteenth, after nine days of waiting, we decided we had been duped. There was nothing else to do but go home. We rode down to the docks without our bags and asked the agent for our money back. "Tomorrow morning, for sure," he said, but his eyes seemed shifty to me. "And be sure you're here at six o'clock sharp," he added as a parting shot. "Boat sails at seven."

We decided to take one more chance, and I am thankful we

did. Before noon on July 14 we were gliding down the graceful St. Lawrence, past the high bluffs of Quebec the next morning, and soon settling into the routine of feeding and watering a hundred head of cattle herded on the top deck of the dirty 2,500-ton "limey" freighter. In what seemed no time at all—ten days—we were heading up the Mersey past Liverpool and into the ship canal for Manchester. The work had been easy, the food almost uneatable, the tough British seamen crowded with us in the cramped quarters of the fo'c'sle a very likable lot. Though Manchester was gray and drab, the streets full of unemployed textile workers, this at last was Europe! The next day we caught a train south to Stratford-on-Avon to see where Shakespeare had lived and to take in some of his plays.

This first glimpse of the old world—the grimy slums of Liverpool and Manchester; the pastoral landscape around Stratford, where the meadows were so much greener than those of our Midwest; the spectacle of Shakespeare's plays performed in his birthplace; the winding streets of Oxford lined with steep-roofed buildings of stucco crossed with wooden beams; the hour of punting on the Upper Thames; the accidental bumping into my sister and her college friends at a bus stop after we had roamed around the lawns of the university—all this enlivened our days and prepared us a little, if only superficially, for London. We could understand and make ourselves understood, to a certain extent, in English English. The people were reserved but courteous. The pace of living seemed slower, life more tranquil. It was quite a different world and we were beginning to like it.

London may have been, as the *Encyclopaedia Britannica* (1911 edition) said, "the greatest city in the world," but I did not fall in love with it at first sight.[1] It was gray, sprawling, grimy and ugly. The people in the streets—the British race, as Winston Churchill liked to put it—were, if one could make an initial whopping generalization, not very attractive to look at, the facial features slapped together haphazardly, the complexions as pale as

[1] As did my later friend John Gunther, who opened his book *Twelve Cities:* "I fell in love with London at first sight when I arrived there about 4 P.M. on a gray silken day in the late spring of 1922, and have been in love with it ever since." Gunther was also twenty-one when he first saw London, and like me he had worked his way over on a cattle boat.

paste, the teeth irregular, uncared for, and sometimes missing, the dress so-so, the men in black suits and black derby hats pulled down to their ears, a black umbrella dangling from an arm, the women in ungainly floppy hats, baggy suits and broad-toed, flat-heeled shoes.

London was awesome, just the same. We had found quarters in a pleasant rooming house in Bloomsbury, a stone's throw from the British Museum, and after a preliminary glance at the museum's famed Greek, Roman and Egyptian collections, we set out each morning on the top of a bus to see the sights: St. Paul's, Westminster Abbey, Parliament, Buckingham Palace and the changing of the guard, the Tower, Whitehall, Piccadilly, Trafalgar Square, alighting to see the paintings at the National Gallery and the Tate. We walked and walked: down Fleet Street with its smell of newsprint, past the Inner and Middle Temples, to the Strand, with the Law Courts on the north and in the middle of the street the lovely church of St. Clement Danes, built by Sir Christopher Wren, with its tall white steeple and its bells tolling the quarter hour. Thence to Charing Cross and Trafalgar Square, pausing to browse through the bookshops on Charing Cross Road, where I discovered Foyle's, the biggest and most fascinating bookstore I had ever seen. Evenings I slipped off to the theater, a new and magic world for me. I can still recall the tingle of seeing my first musical comedy, *Rose Marie*, at the Drury Lane.

That week in London, no doubt, was one of the most exciting ones I had yet lived, each day unfolding something new, each stone, it seemed, evoking some history of our forebears. But after a week of rubbernecking I had taken in more than I could digest. It would take more time than we had to sort things out. And there was something missing. We had scarcely talked to the English. In Manchester, on our first day in Europe, I had telephoned one of the editors of the *Guardian*, who had spoken at our college and with whom, after I had procured him a bottle of bootleg whiskey, I had sat up most of the night in his hotel room drinking and talking of newspapering and writing and books. But when I telephoned, he did not remember me. In London I knew no one. One got a flavor of the Englishman, perhaps, in reading the editorials and the letters in *The Times*. But this was only one breed, albeit the ruling one, upper-class, or upper-middle-class, titled families of ancient origin, Lords of the Press and of Big Business who

recently had acquired titles, Tory politicians and their syco-
phants, retired Indian Army colonels, colonial civil servants and
the like. One rubbed shoulders in the crowded buses or subways
with more humble folk, black-coated clerks out of Dickens,
stoutish housewives, rouged stenographers, many of them color-
fully expressive in their Cockney speech, which I scarcely understood. I imagined they led drab and rather empty lives. And the
English workers? I went out to Hyde Park to hear them preach
Karl Marx from their soapboxes and stepladders. But most of the
speakers turned out to be not workers but crackpots, invariably
wearing derby hats, and preaching not Marx but vegetarianism
and other fads, secular and religious.

The workers' spokesmen obviously had to be found elsewhere. I knew, of course, that there was a strong labor movement
here, that the workers were more fully and tightly organized in
unions than at home, and that, unlike at home, they were beginning to make themselves felt politically through the burgeoning
Labor Party. I would have liked to talk to some of them but
could not think of a way to do it. England had had briefly the
year before its first Labor government, and I had met Malcolm
MacDonald, the son of its first Prime Minister, Ramsay Mac-
Donald, when he debated at our college with a group from Oxford, but I was too shy to call him in London, especially after my
little rebuff in Manchester. Probably he would not remember me
either.

We had heard a great deal in America of the class system in
England—our public school textbooks were full of it. From reading the morning newspapers, *The Times*, the *Daily Telegraph*,
the *Morning Post*, the *Daily Mail*, one got the impression that
class distinctions were still very strong, that almost everyone,
high and low, was aware of them and accepted them, and that
there was a vast gulf between the few at the top, titled or rich or
politically successful, and the great mass of people below them.
Of the latter, a growing number were out of work. Unemployment had passed a million, and in the streets you saw groups of
jobless miners and textile workers gathered in groups to sing or to
toot horns and pass the hat. It was a depressing sight in the midst
of so much splendor in this capital of Empire.

Bloomsbury, where we stayed, was becoming well known as
the center of a group of writers and aesthetes, Virginia Woolf,

John Maynard Keynes, Lytton Strachey, Roger Fry, Clive Bell and the already established E. M. Forster, but they were said to be terribly snobbish, looking down their long noses not only at the young writers outside their circle but at the renowned ones, such as H. G. Wells, Arnold Bennett and George Bernard Shaw. I looked for them as we roamed the streets in Bloomsbury—I had seen their photographs in the newspapers and magazines—but I never caught sight of a single one. So though we saw much of this great city and were charmed and fascinated, I missed talking to the English. What were they really like? What concerned them? Probably I would never know—at first hand.

I began to itch to get to our final destination. Paris was the light that had beckoned us all along. One morning we rode down to Dover, stopping off between trains at Canterbury, and took a cross-channel boat to Ostend. After a wondrous first evening on the Continent sipping wine on the square in Bruges, listening to the playing of the bells of the Cloth Hall, and hearing French spoken for the first time, we pushed on to Paris.

How can one recapture the sheer excitement, the intoxication, the unalloyed joy of the first day, the first week, the first fortnight of a raw Iowa youth in this lovely city by the Seine—as it was that late summer of 1925, before another war, the automobile and Americanization changed it? All through that sun-drenched month of August I felt I was treading on air.

There was so much history within every cathedral, church, palace, museum and gallery, and in every park, cemetery, square and street. And so much beauty. Spaciousness. Harmony. Over a thousand years this was what the imagination of kings, archbishops, presidents, premiers, architects, artists, artisans, common laborers, and something in the soul and spirit of the citizens had achieved. It was incomparable. One gloried in it, took in as much as one could, and looked forward feverishly to what the morrow would reveal. Life in such surroundings seemed so unlike what I had known in our modest Midwest town that it seemed we were living, for a fleeting moment, on another planet—or in paradise.

We had booked a room in a *pension* in a courtyard back of 85 Boulevard Port-Royal, just beyond Montparnasse, presided over by an elderly white-haired lady invariably in black who treated us from the beginning as though we were members of the family—a pair of stray nephews, say, from the provinces, come up for the first time to see the great city. This was probably because since the war, which had widowed her, she had been taking in visitors from our hometown, mostly teachers from the college and the high school, who had spent a summer or a sabbatical in the capital. She inquired after several of them as though they were old friends and then, since it was early evening, suggested for our first night in Paris that we stroll down the Boulevard Montparnasse to the Dôme or the Rotonde, have an *apéritif* and then dinner at a small place on a side street which she recommended, where a good meal could be had for five francs (twenty-five cents) and the wine was "not bad."

We dashed off. Except for the evening in Bruges I had never sat on the terrace of a sidewalk café before—there had been none in London and none, of course, in Iowa. Soon we were seated on the crowded terrace of the Dôme, ordering our first *apéritif*, and watching, with the awe and excitement of a peasant, the crowds stroll by, the customers come and go, and tuning our ears to catch the flavor of the animated talk at the adjacent tables. Somewhat to my surprise much of it was in English, American English, some of it flavored with the familiar twang of my Midwest. We sat there for an hour and listened and gawked. Couples passed, the young men with their arms around the women, holding them tight. At a nearby table a heavily bearded fellow pulled a young girl to him, slowly kissed the nape of her neck and then turned his lips to her face. No one seemed to notice but us. I had never seen it in public before. Once there was a stir when a rather buxom auburn-haired lady in a sort of flowing white Greek tunic stopped for a moment to chat with someone at a front table. She was very beautiful and her eyes flashed as she talked. I heard someone whisper that it was the great American dancer Isadora Duncan, and that she lived in a studio around the corner. From talk around us I gathered the terrace was sprinkled with young American writers, but I did not catch their names and wouldn't have recognized many of them if I had. But this, apparently, was where they gathered.

We had another drink and then a third. It was difficult for us to pull ourselves away from the place but finally our hunger overcame our reluctance to leave. The dinner on the terrace of the little bistro nearby turned out to be excellent though, after a bottle of red Bordeaux, I realized it would take some time before I could really savor genuine wine after all the years of the bootleg stuff. But it would not take any more time to be able to savor the delight of eating and drinking in the open air while watching the passers-by in the street. Why hadn't we thought of it back home? I wondered. We returned to the Dôme for a coffee and cognac— we were pushing our education as fast as we could—watched again the throng, which did not seem to diminish as the evening wore on, and finally around midnight we tore ourselves away and wove down the boulevard, happily, home.

Bright and early the next morning, armed with a small guidebook I had bought at a kiosk, we set out to have our first look at the great city. We strolled down the Boulevard St. Michel, through the Latin Quarter, past the Sorbonne to the Seine, where suddenly we caught our first view of Notre Dame up the river. The first one was never to be forgotten. The distant Gothic façade looked pink in the early-morning sun. Slowly we made our way up the quai, past the bookstalls, never letting our eyes off the cathedral. Like everyone else in America we had seen pictures of Notre Dame, but the reality, as we gazed at it from the broad Place du Parvis, overwhelmed us. We were still in a daze after two hours of gazing up at the three magnificent portals of the façade, with their statues and bas-reliefs telling the story of Christianity, and then roaming through the vast interior, half lost in the shadows, which high above were pierced by the refracted sunlight streaming through the thirteenth-century stained-glass rose window of the facade and a second one in the south transept.

On the way to see another Gothic masterpiece, Sainte Chapelle, at the other end of the Île de la Cité, we walked through the narrow, winding Rue de la Huchette. In the space of a hundred yards I noticed three premises with large glazed windows on the ground floor. These could only be *maisons*, the ones my French uncle had warned my mother and me about when I first contemplated the trip to Paris. My uncle had claimed there was one in every block, but here there were three.

From the Place St. Michel we crossed over the river to Sainte Chapelle. Grant Wood, who had studied in Europe the ancient art of painting glass windows, an art apparently "lost" over the last few centuries, had told me it had the most beautiful stained-glass windows in the world. The nave consisted almost entirely of them, the like of which I had never seen, with the refracted colors, all shades of blue, red, yellow and green, shining through.

Satiated by this morning's first glimpse of Gothic glories, we retreated to a café across the street from the Palais, had a sandwich and a beer, and watched the French lawyers in their black gowns filing out from the law courts. Most of the afternoon we spent prowling through the Louvre, pausing, like all the other tourists, before the obvious things, the *Winged Victory,* the *Venus de Milo,* the *Mona Lisa,* the paintings of Rembrandt, Titian, Giorgione, Caravaggio, Van Dyck, Rubens. The first-floor collections of antiquities from ancient Egypt, Assyria, Persia, Chaldea, Greece and Rome were simply too vast and rich to be faintly comprehended in an afternoon, but we paused to marvel just the same at such wonders as the frieze and metope from the Parthenon, the figures of Phidias, Polycletus, Praxiteles and Lysippus, some of the Egyptian sarcophagi, the tablet with the Code of Hammurabi.

Weary from so much trudging we took the Métro up to the Arc de Triomphe, rested on a bench nearby, and then strolled down the Champs Élysées to the Place de la Concorde and retraced our steps up the spacious tree-lined avenue to a café for refreshment. There was not much traffic on the Champs Élysées in those days, a few taxis and buses mostly, and the broad sidewalks were alive with pedestrians. We sat and watched them stroll by as the light of the afternoon waned. We blew ourselves to an expensive dinner that evening on the terrace of Chez Francis, on the Place de l'Alma, by the side of the Seine. Across the river, ribbons of light ran up the Eiffel Tower. Crowded with half-digested impressions we stopped off at Montparnasse for a nightcap, our fatigue lightened by the elation of this first fantastic day in Paris.

And so it went each blessed day that followed until after a fortnight we had achieved a certain acquaintance with much that made this city so memorable: Sacré Coeur and Montmartre, the Opéra and the Grand Boulevards, St. Germain-des-Prés, the Luxembourg Gardens, the Panthéon, the Invalides, the Place des Vosges, the two old islands in the Seine, the Latin Quarter, Les Halles, and St. Sulpice, where Marcel Dupré, who had once given a concert in our college chapel, played the magnificent organ.

Evenings we passed mostly on café terraces in Montparnasse, St. Germain-des-Prés, the Boulevard St. Michel, the Champs Élysées, the Grand Boulevards, or drinking beer at the two fine brasseries on the Left Bank: the Balzar in the Rue des Écoles or Lipp's on the Boulevard St. Germain. It was a magic life, each day and night filled to overflowing, opening up new worlds, ancient and current, to two awe-struck Midwest youths.

As in London, we met no citizens of the country except occasionally when we asked directions. My college French, I saw at once, was quite inadequate. I could scarcely converse in it, though I had better luck making out what was in the Paris newspapers. The headlines in the Parisian press were almost exclusively given over to domestic news. Joseph Caillaux had staged a political comeback by being elected to the Senate. I remembered vaguely about this former Premier and Finance Minister whose political career had been set back in 1914, on the eve of the war, when his wife had murdered the editor of *Le Figaro*, and then seemingly destroyed when, toward the end of the war, he was accused of communicating with the Germans and was imprisoned. But now, said the newspapers, he was back in politics. There were stories about French troops evacuating the Ruhr that summer, which the editorialists said improved the chances for lessening tensions in a Europe striving to recover from the awful devastation of the war. A conference had been called by the European powers for the fall in Locarno to try to set up a lasting peace on the Continent. The newspapers were making much of the trial of the royalist poet and leader Charles Maurras, who had threatened in the columns of *L'Action Française* to have the Minister of the Interior murdered. I noted some glee among staunch republican editors when Maurras received a sentence of two years in prison. I had not known that a royalist movement still existed in the Third Republic. Political life in France certainly seemed to be lively and amusing. Another government, the papers said, was about to fall. But I did not pay much attention. I was just a passing tourist, my neck sore from rubbernecking, my eyes glazed.

As the time to depart approached, I hated the thought of leaving this beautiful and civilized place and going back to the drab Midwest prairies and our narrow way of life. I had had no luck in getting a job. At the end of the first week I had gone to the two American newspapers in Paris, the New York *Herald* and the

Chicago Tribune, to see what the prospects were. They were nil. Eric Hawkins of the *Herald* showed me a thick file of applications. There were at least a thousand names in it, he calculated, though he said he had given up counting them. Mostly college "kids" like myself, he said. He added my name to his file but warned me: "I'm sorry. But I don't see the slightest chance for you." Over at the *Tribune* the application file of David Darrah, the editor, was almost as bulging. He, too, took down my name but offered not the slightest hope. "There are just too many ahead of you," he said. Even if there were not, I reflected, my credentials were not very inspiring. Editor of a small college paper. Two summers or so on a small-town daily. French inadequate. Age twenty-one.

I was disappointed, but less so than I had expected. I was having too good a time, and several more weeks in Paris lay ahead. It had been easy to forget for the moment what I thought I had fled from at home. There had never been a ghost of a chance to stay anyway. I had realized that from the beginning. I began to think of the girl in Iowa. Perhaps when I got home we could get married. That would make life more bearable. My college companion spoke of doing the same thing. George often went out during the day to paint or sketch a scene—Notre Dame, St. Germain-des-Prés, the Arc de Triomphe, St. Sulpice, the Luxembourg Gardens—and I prowled the city alone. A good many evenings he stayed home to write his fiancée, as he had in London, and he frowned a little when I took off to walk the boulevards or see a musical, or drop in at a cabaret or pass the time at a sidewalk café watching the world go by.

In particular, I guess, I was watching the French women, who appeared to me on the whole to be very attractive—vivacious, chic and, some of them, quite beautiful. One night I dropped in at a small cabaret called Noctambules, off the Boulevard St. Michel, danced with two or three girls and invited them to my table for a drink. But they were whores, I concluded, painted, rather coarse and too willing. One night on the terrace of Deux Magots I struck up a conversation with a French girl who was sitting alone at the next table. She certainly looked "respectable"—she said she worked in a publishing house—and she was rather attractive, with very black hair and dark eyes and a cultivated manner. She let me buy her a drink, finally moved over to my table for another and seemed in no hurry to break up our talk.

But in the end, toward midnight, I got cold feet. Feeling rather sheepish at my lack of guts, I asked her for her address and departed.

We began to count the days left. I thought of dropping by the *Herald* and the *Tribune* for a final check on a job, but it seemed too hopeless an errand to bother with. Our last night in Paris came, and having more francs left than we had figured on, George and I went out to do the town. We had a fine dinner near the Place Pigalle and bought tickets to the Folies Bergère, where the great Mistinguette was appearing with her former protégé, Maurice Chevalier. Between acts we started drinking champagne at the bar and continued at several night spots in Montmartre until our francs ran out. The effect was stronger than I had anticipated. But it was our last night in Paris and we were having a wonderful time, bobbing from one cabaret to another. Toward dawn we pulled ourselves together, took a taxi for almost the first time, and arrived at our *pension* just as the sun was coming up. A couple of hours' sleep would fix us up, I was sure, and then we could pack and catch the noon train for England. As we stumbled happily into our room I kicked an envelope that had been slipped halfway under the door. I just kicked it into the room and left it there. I doubted that I could read anyone's letter even if I could bend over to pick it up.

Washing up later that morning, splashing cold water over my face to try to bring myself to—my head felt like a rock—I noticed the envelope lying on the floor by the door. I picked it up and suddenly my head cleared. On the left-hand corner was the imprint of the *Chicago Tribune*, 5 Rue Lamartine, Paris IXe, and over it was scrawled a name: Darrah. It had been sent by *pneumatique*. I tore it open. The letter was in handwriting and I tried to take it in all at once.

DEAR MR. SHIRER:
    If you still want a job would you be kind enough to come in to see me some evening about nine?

DAVID DARRAH

I read it over and over, reciting it to George, not quite believing that it was real.

"You're not going to take it, are you, this last second when we're all set to go home?" George said, resuming his packing.

"You think I'm going to give up a chance like this?" I said.

"It doesn't sound like a very definite offer to me," my friend said.

"I'm going to take a chance on it," I said. There had not been a split second of doubt in my mind about that.

"It'll be a shock to Eleanor," George said, "if you stay."

"If I get the job," I said, "I'll send for her."

He was depressed at having to leave alone and I was beside myself with excitement at the prospect of remaining. He finished packing in silence, and I paced the room, brandishing the letter, rereading it and savoring the miracle of its coming at this very last moment.

I saw my friend off on his train at the Gare du Nord, he trying to convince me to the last moment of farewell that I was making the most foolish mistake of my life. Back in the *pension* I went to bed to sleep off my hangover. But I could not fall asleep. Restless, I dressed and set off through the Luxembourg Gardens and down the Boulevard St. Michel, stopping for one coffee after another along the way, trying to read the papers, the *Tribune*, the *Herald* and a half dozen Parisian dailies. It was becoming a long day. It seemed that 9 P.M. would never come.

At eight, after trying vainly to down some dinner and a half bottle of wine, I walked over to the Boulevard Raspail and caught a Métro to the north side of the city, alighting at a station, Cadet, right in front of *Le Petit Journal*, where the *Tribune* was published. I found the entrance in the back at 5 Rue Lamartine, walked around the block several times until it was nine, and then climbed the steps to the newsroom on the third floor.

Darrah, who sat at a desk in one corner of the little newsroom where the copy-desk men had already gone to work, was rather taciturn. He asked me bluntly how much experience I had had on a copy desk.

"Two years," I said, exaggerating a little.

"How's your French?" he asked.

I told him I had studied it for a couple of years in high school and another two years in college but that obviously I'd have to work on it.

"The pay isn't much," he said, as though he were trying to

discourage me. "Twelve hundred francs a month. That's only sixty dollars."

It came to fifteen dollars a week, I quickly calculated. I had made fifty dollars a week on the hometown newspaper.

"I guess I can get by on that," I said. This was no time to quibble over salary. All I wanted was enough to live on so I could stay on in this city. Living was cheaper here than at home. I had already learned that.

The editor thought a moment, which seemed an age. He was a rather silent man, I could see. Finally he said curtly:

"When can you start?"

"Right away," I said.

On such a slender thread does the course of one's whole adult life hang. From the age of twenty-one mine would now follow a path quite different from the one it had been on. All that became of me, almost all that will be set down in these recollections, stems from that sudden turning point that came when I scooped up from the carpet of the room in the *pension* on the Boulevard Port-Royal as we were about to leave for home in Iowa the *pneumatique* that had arrived out of the blue and that I had responded to in the only way I could.

I had come over to Europe for two months. As it turned out, I would remain there to live and work for two decades, experiencing and chronicling the remaining years of an uneasy peace, the decline of the democracies, the rise of the dictatorships, turmoil, upheaval, violence, savage repression, and finally war.

BOOK TWO

CHICAGO, 1904–1913

In Chicago on the morning of February 23, 1904, my father jotted down in his diary:

> 5 minutes to 3—Baby Boy born. Weighed 7¾ lbs.
> WILLIAM LAWRENCE SHIRER
> Born
> 6500 Greenwood Ave

Three days before, on February 20, my father had noted: "5th Anniversary of Wedding. Dinner with . . ." He and my mother had invited in several friends to celebrate. She must have been highly, visibly pregnant with her second child. Her first, a girl, had been born three and a half years before. Had I arrived three hours earlier, in time for Washington's birthday, my mother told me later, I would have been named George.

Lost, and almost beyond recognition, that time in America, shortly after the turn of the century. Yet it was from that horse-and-buggy era, before there were airplanes, radios, television sets, movies, electric refrigerators, washing machines and dishwashers, oil burners, air conditioners, tractors, paved roads, garages, filling stations, parking lots, traffic lights, shopping centers, income taxes, social welfare, women's suffrage, computers, moon landings, napalm, nuclear bombs, world wars and much else that is commonplace today, like the family automobile, that my roots and those of my generation sprang.

America was a big, raw, undeveloped country then. From the Alleghenies to the Pacific it seemed largely frontier, with the majority of the people living on farms or in villages and small towns, and possessing the virtues—and the shortcomings—of rural life. They were self-reliant, hard-working, thrifty, neighborly, deeply religious; but in their isolation they were also narrow-minded, a little self-righteous and complacent, suspicious of the city and its sophistication, and often hostile to the new ideas and developments that were beginning to sweep the country and, as the twentieth century began, to transform it from an agrarian society to an urban and industrial one, making it a world power with a self-proclaimed Manifest Destiny.

Not one American in two had ever seen an automobile. There were only thirteen thousand cars in the country in 1900, and no paved roads to run them on outside of the big cities. My father considered the newfangled horseless carriage a menace to the streets, though they were so rare in Chicago that as a boy I used to run out of the house to catch sight of one. He applauded the sentiments of Senator Joseph W. Bailey, who told the U.S. Senate in 1909, when cars had become a little more common and had begun to venture out on the country dirt roads: "If I had my way, I would make it a crime to use automobiles on the public highways, because no man has a right to use a vehicle on the public highway that is dangerous to the safety of other people." The "other people" were getting about in their buggies and wagons and on bikes. Woodrow Wilson, president of Princeton University, saw the motorcar as a plaything of the arrogant rich, exclaiming in 1906, six years before he would be elected President of the United States: "Nothing has spread socialistic feelings in this country more than the automobile. It offers us a picture of the arrogance of wealth."

Horses were everywhere. They pulled the streetcars,[1] though fancy electric cars were beginning to supplant them. Sturdy steeds raced through the streets with fire engines in tow or plodded along with drays from the breweries and vans from the factories and stores. They pulled cabs, surreys and buggies through the residential streets, and on the farms, supplemented with oxen and mules, they pulled the plows, harrows, reapers and binders. There were some eighteen million draft animals on the farms and many more than that in the towns and cities. My first memories of life are of horses, stables, blacksmiths, hitching posts along the curbs in front of the stores and before our house, of fast

[1] In 1900 it was estimated that some 100,000 horses and mules drew 28,000 streetcars over 6,600 miles of track in the towns and cities.

rides in summer with a pair of borrowed or rented horses and even faster rides on crisp, wintry Sundays with the sleigh bells jingling—a sound I loved as a boy in Chicago and later in Iowa and which still provokes a tingle in my blood when I hear it occasionally on a frosty evening in my rural retreat in the Berkshire Hills.

The house on Lexington Avenue (now University Avenue), to which the family moved shortly after my birth, was heated by a coal-burning furnace and was lit by gas. Around 1912, my father took the plunge of adding electricity for light, though he refused to give up the gas jets in the long living room. His father, out in Mount Vernon, Iowa, whom we visited summers and sometimes at Christmas, clung to oil lamps until after the First World War, and heated each room with a cast-iron stove. The streets of Chicago all through my youth were lit by gas. Toward dusk we used to wait for the lamplighter, a friend of all of us youngsters on the block, to make his accustomed rounds. He carried a long pole with which to turn up the gas at the top of the light pole. Sometimes, if he was not in a hurry, he would let one of us do it. For a time I dreamt of becoming a lamplighter when I grew up.

Or an iceman! Every three days or so a big, lumbering fellow would lug in with his tongs a fifty- or seventy-five-pound slab of ice for the icebox, sometimes letting me help him and rewarding me, if it was a summer day, with a small chunk of ice to lick. The icebox in those days kept meat, milk, butter and eggs from spoiling. During the long northern winter months we never saw an orange, grapefruit, fresh lettuce or fresh vegetables. Florida and California had not yet been connected with the rest of the country by fast trains with refrigerator cars. During the winter we lived, as did everyone else, out of cans for our fruits and vegetables, or on preserves that my mother had put up during the summer. By spring, my mother once explained to me, everyone was a little run-down from lack of vitamins.

One of the first things I remember in the early years in Chicago was the day a man arrived to install a telephone. There were fewer than two million of them then in the whole country and they were mostly confined to offices and the great houses of the rich. It must have been shortly after my father was appointed Assistant U.S. Attorney, when he felt the need of keeping in touch with his office, associates and friends. The neighbors and my parents' friends were going in for telephones, too, and there was much buzzing of excitement in the first years over being able to talk with someone a few blocks or miles away through an electric wire. The telephone was a clumsy instrument at the time, clamped to a board attached to the wall. Static and a humming almost drowned out the voice at the other end, especially if it was a long-distance call. The automatic dial would not come in for decades.

On the day I was born, war dominated the headlines on the front pages of the Chicago newspapers. From the very beginning, war would bloody the world through most of the years of my life.

On page one of the *Chicago Tribune* of February 23, 1904, John T. McCutcheon had a cartoon reflecting the concern with war. It was entitled "Portrait of the World Drawn from Telegraphic Description" and showed a globe of the world in the shape of a bomb with a hand labeled "War Fever" applying the torch to the fuse. The Boer War, in South Africa, which had captured the headlines on the day the new century began, had ended two years before with the victory, after many embarrassing setbacks, of King Edward's British troops. A new war had just broken out in China between Russia and Japan. The Japanese fleet, said the headlines, was attacking the Russians at Port Arthur. Russian troops were being rushed to the scene over the Trans-Siberian railroad. Bloody skirmishes had already been fought. The German Emperor, according to a dispatch that day to the *Tribu*ne from St. Petersburg, was threatening to send a fleet and an army corps to the Far East "if China fired a shot." Kaiser Wilhelm, the cable explained, "was obsessed by almost a monomania on the subject of the 'Yellow Peril.'" It was this German war lord, the newspapers reminded their readers, who four years before had directed his soldiers about to be sent to China to help quell the Boxer Rebellion to "give no quarter and to conduct themselves so like Huns that for a thousand years no Chinaman will dare look askance at a German."

The United States was flexing its nationalist, militarist muscles, too, after the easy victories over Spain in Cuba and the Philippines six years before. It also was watching the Russo-Japanese War in China. A dispatch from Washington reported that our Pacific Fleet in China waters would be strengthened by the sending of two more battleships and two cruisers.

On the island of Santo Domingo, the U.S. Navy had shelled an insurgents' camp and landed the marines. The *Tribune* warmly applauded the deed in an editorial headed: "A Lesson to San Domingo."

> The shelling . . . and the landing of the marines to punish an unpardonable outrage were acts which will have the hearty approval of the American government and people.

The "unpardonable outrage" had been the firing on an American merchant vessel by the rebels. Taking note that "prominent citizens" of the city of Santo Domingo had protested against the naval shelling as "an insolent outrage against the liberty of the Republic," the *Tribune* replied indignantly:

> The words are ill-chosen . . . If the forceful warning given that the American flag must not be fired upon is not heeded, further lessons of the same kind will be administered unhesitatingly. . . . There is considerable American capital invested in San Domingo.

Ever since the Spanish-American War of 1898 and the annexation of the Philippines, cries of Manifest Destiny were increasingly heard in the land. As the twentieth century began, they had reached a new pitch of intensity. The newspapers on the morning of January 10, 1900, had heralded the maiden speech in the U.S. Senate of thirty-seven-year-old Albert J. Beveridge of Indiana, who had just returned from watching sixty thousand American troops in the Philippines subjecting the natives, who had believed that the American triumph over Spain would give them freedom and independence.[1] Beveridge, with an eloquence popular at the time and in a language that sounds familiar today, had called

---

[1] Mark Twain, the most popular and loved writer in the country, had risked his popularity by his satire on what he considered our betrayal of the Filipinos. He also denounced our armed forces for the "burned villages, wholesale massacre of civilians and the torture of prisoners," calling them our "Christian Butchers, our uniformed assassins."

A good many authors would write similarly of the behavior of our troops in Vietnam sixty years later. The morals of an army and a people apparently do not improve with age. But their hypocrisy grows.

upon his fellow-countrymen to live up to the great destiny that beckoned:

> We will not renounce our part in the mission of the race, trustee, under God, of the civilization of the world. . . . Self-government and internal development have been the dominant notes of our first century; administration and the development of other lands will be the dominant notes of our second century. . . . He [God] has made us the master organizers of the world to establish system where chaos reigns. . . . He has made us adept in government that we may administer government among savage and senile peoples. . . .
>
> He has marked the American people as His chosen Nation to finally lead in the regeneration of the world. This is the divine mission of America . . . We are trustees of the world's progress, guardians of its righteous peace.

Even the genial, intelligent young William Allen White was bitten by the bug. Writing in his newly acquired newspaper, the Emporia, Kansas, *Gazette*, on March 20, 1899, he fairly bubbled over:

> It is the Anglo-Saxon's manifest destiny to go forth as a world conqueror. He will take possession of the islands of the sea. . . . This is what fate holds for the chosen people. It is so written. . . . It is to be.

And yet, as the new century in which I was to live out my life dawned, there was some uneasiness among many citizens about a country, which hitherto had been mostly concerned with its own business of developing a continent, suddenly aspiring to conquer the world. Doubts were expressed that God had made us, or even intended to make us, "the master organizers of the world."[1] What the Republicans called "natural expansion" and

---

[1] For the turn of the century, the New York *Herald* on December 30, 1899, had published Mark Twain's "New Year's Greetings":

A GREETING FROM THE NINETEENTH CENTURY
TO THE TWENTIETH CENTURY

I bring you the stately nation named Christendom, returning bedraggled, besmirched and dishonored from pirate raids in Kiao-Chou, Manchuria, South Africa and the Philippines, with her soul full of meanness, her pocket full of boodle, her mouth full of hypocrisies. Give her soap and towel, but hide the looking glass.

the Democrats thought was "wicked imperialism" had been one of the principal issues of the 1900 elections. The Republicans had won.

Deeper than the malaise over America becoming an imperialist, colonial power was the feeling among many people that something had gone wrong at home. The gulf between the rich and the poor was widening. Vast fortunes were being quickly amassed by the monopolists and manipulators, sometimes by fraud, chicanery and corruption, and often with the aid and connivance of the democratic government—all three branches of it, the Congress, the Administration, the courts. Especially in the more rural West, Midwest and South, millions felt they were being "had" by the eastern financial and industrial interests, which dominated not only the country's economy, with its grotesque inequalities and, for the poor, its brutalities, but the federal and state governments, and thus the politics of the nation. They believed the courts, even including the Supreme Court, were corrupt and unduly prejudiced in favor of Big Business and Big Money, and against the workingman, the shopkeeper, the farmer—in short, against the Little Man. Property was more sacred to the black-robed justices than man himself.

The year 1894, a decade before I was born, had been the darkest year for millions since the Civil War. Prices and wages hit a new bottom. In the Midwest, corn and wheat sold below the cost of production. In Kansas alone, eleven thousand farms were lost by their hard-working owners through foreclosures of mortgages. Four million out of a population of seventy-six million were unemployed, and among those who had jobs, three-quarters of a million were out on strike against drastic cuts of already low wages, their strikes ultimately suppressed by gangs of armed strikebreakers, by the state militia and federal troops, their union leaders thrown into jail. For countless citizens there were no means of getting enough to eat, and all through that black year ragged, hungry bands roved through the country, the fires from their hobo camps along the railroad tracks striking terror among the good townsfolk. One group, "Coxey's Army," under the leadership of Jacob Coxey of Massillon, Ohio, marched on Washington to demand relief for the unemployed and reached the Capitol and the White House lawn before it was repulsed by the police and the guards, its bedraggled troopers arrested for refusing to keep off the grass.

It wasn't only the farmers and the workers who reached rock bottom that year. The middle class and even the rich were hit. According to one historian,[1] 158 national banks, 172 state banks, 177 private banks, 47 savings banks and 13 trust companies failed; 169 railroads, including some of the biggest, such as the Erie, Union Pacific, Northern Pacific, and Atchison, with trackage of 37,885 miles and a capitalization of $2.5 billion, went into receivership; 15,000 other businesses failed. "Businessmen," noted Henry Adams, "died like flies under the strain."

Even the federal government faced bankruptcy. It was saved only when President Grover Cleveland turned desperately to the great banker J. P. Morgan for a loan to the Treasury of $65 million in gold.

What had happened to the American dream, to American democracy? The good citizen was wondering.[2] The "muckrakers" had begun to tell him through magazine articles and books the inside story of the plunder of the country by the railroads, of the shady practices of John D. Rockefeller's Standard Oil to gain a monopoly of the mushrooming oil business, of the manipulation of stock prices on Wall Street by which millions were made by insiders overnight, of how state legislators and judges were bought by the big companies to give away the wealth of the country. The "land-grab" was one of the most blatant. Millions of acres of public land had been given to the railroads ostensibly to encourage more laying of tracks, but also to enable them to make more money. Millions of acres more had been "leased" or "transferred" at a nominal price to private hands for the exploitation of timber and minerals.

Toward the turn of the century many good citizens, struggling to survive, had seen some hope in the agitation for basic reforms to curb the rapacity of the robber barons, to clean up the corruption in government and to distribute the burdens of taxation more equitably. In 1890, Congress had passed the Sherman Antitrust Act to restrain the great combinations of business, but

[1] James Truslow Adams: The March of Democracy—A History of the United States, IV, p. 42.
[2] He was still wondering three-quarters of a century later. "What is new, though," the astute TRB, veteran Washington columnist of The New Republic, wrote early in 1972, "is the failing of the American dream: the dream that the gap between rich and poor was getting smaller. It isn't." The failing of that dream was really not new.

one President after another had disdained to use it, and in the handful of cases brought to trial, the Supreme Court had usually ruled against the government. Not until 1902, under Theodore Roosevelt, did the government finally sue in a big case—against the Northern Securities Company, a holding concern set up by J. P. Morgan to control important railroads in the West. A year before, Morgan had organized the United States Steel Corporation, the biggest corporation in the world, with control of nearly half the steel production in the country; and the Justice Department had not objected. Now, at the news of the Northern Securities Company suit, Morgan was indignant. He felt personally insulted by the President of the United States, who was treating him, he complained, "an honorable man, like a common crook." He told his friends, his biographer relates, "that he had supposed Roosevelt to be a gentleman, but a gentleman would not have sued."

For some years there had been a growing demand for a federal income tax that would assess the national tax burden according to one's ability to pay. In 1894, under the stress of the Depression, Congress had finally passed a bill imposing a straight 2 percent tax on income over four thousand dollars (equivalent to fifteen thousand dollars in the 1970's). There was a howl from the bankers and the businessmen and the press that the law meant the end of freedom in America. They need not have worried. The Supreme Court, by a vote of 5 to 4, held the tax bill to be unconstitutional, Justice Field for the majority exclaiming that the law was "but the first assault upon capital."

The Republic and its freedoms were saved. The free press rejoiced. "The wave of the socialist revolution had gone too far," wrote the editor of the New York *Sun.* The New York *Tribune* exulted that "this attempt to bring about a communistic revolution" had been defeated. "Thanks to the Court, our government is not to be dragged into a communistic warfare against the rights of property and the rewards of industry."[1]

[1] Eventually, as we all know too well, our government was "dragged into a communistic warfare against the rights of property." In 1909, the Sixteenth Amendment, proposed by the conservative Republican President Taft, calling for a national income tax, was passed by Congress, and by 1913 had been ratified by the states. President Wilson lost no time in applying it. But it was extremely mild at first: 1 percent on incomes from $4,000 ($15,000 today) to $20,000 ($70,000 today), with a small surtax on larger ones. Incomes under $4,000 ($3,000 for

The "communistic" bugbear was by now well established in the country and would remain so to this day. It would make periodic suckers of the majority of citizens and of one Administration after another. Richard M. Nixon would rise from obscurity to the White House on it. At any rate, with the "communistic" assault upon the Republic repulsed by the Supreme Court, Andrew Carnegie, the steel king, for instance, was spared from paying any income tax on his 1900 income of $23 million. His workers didn't have to pay anything either—on the $500 they averaged that year. No wonder the happy steel magnate could exult in his book *Triumphant Democracy* that

> there is not one shred of privilege to be met with anywhere in all the laws. One man's right is every man's right. The flag is the guarantor and symbol of equality. There is no party in the state that suggests or which would not oppose any fundamental change in the general laws. These are held to be perfect . . .

Not every American thought they were perfect. Some of my earliest recollections are of talk in Chicago and in Iowa of the Populist movement, which swore to break, or at least to brake, the power and the greed of the Carnegies, who ever since the end of the Civil War, the Populists thought, had left the common people only the crumbs from their rich feasts. Throughout the rural prairie states could be heard the cry: "Raise less corn and more hell!"

By 1892 the Populists had organized the People's Party and were ready to put their case to the polls under the leadership of General James B. Weaver of Iowa, whom they nominated for President on a ringing platform.

> We meet in the midst of a nation brought to the verge of moral, political, and material ruin. Corruption dominates the ballot-box, the legislature, the Congress and even touches the ermine of the bench. The people are demoralized . . . The newspapers are largely subsidized or muzzled; public opinion

---

single persons) were not taxed at all. On a net income of $10,000 ($35,000 today) a married man paid a tax of $60. If he earned twice as much, his tax came to $160. For four years, until 1917, the Federal Income Tax yielded less than customs duties. By 1920, it brought in ten times as much. As we know, that was only the beginning.

silenced, business prostrated, our homes covered with mortgages, labor impoverished [and] denied the right to organize for self-protection . . . the fruits of the toil of millions are boldly stolen to build up colossal fortunes for a few unprecedented in the history of mankind . . .

Years later in highschool in Iowa when I read in a textbook this damning indictment of the state of affairs in the Republic (how had such subversion crept into our safe and patriotic textbooks?), I wondered why our sturdy citizens had not risen up and swept the Populists into power. But they had not. Though General Weaver carried five Midwest states and polled more than a million votes and the Republican incumbent, Benjamin Harrison, was turned out, the sober electorate chose Grover Cleveland, a conservative Democrat and a "sound money" man. After 1896, the year the Populists supported Bryan, the losing Democratic candidate, their fortunes waned. Good times set in. There were abundant harvests and rising prices for them. Business picked up, wages and salaries rose a little. There is nothing like the return of a bit of prosperity to make most of our citizens forget the basic inequalities in their society.

Since the end of the age of Jackson, on the whole the majority of Americans had been conservative and would remain so through most of the years of my life. No matter how raw a deal they were getting, they shrank back from voting for drastic change, except for the desperate Depression years of the early 1930's under Franklin Roosevelt. Often, of course, in our predominantly two-party system, they were given no choice. Actually some of the principal demands of the Populists, which both Republicans and Democrats had branded as "socialistic," were later adopted by the country as it grew to maturity: the graduated income tax, direct election of U.S. senators and the eight-hour day.

For a time, shortly before and after the turn of the century, some good folk, mostly in the rural areas, thought that Prohibition might help to improve the quality of life. They believed that drink was the root of all evil, or of most of it, and quoted Saint Paul that drunkards, along with murderers, were ineligible for heaven. The issue was much debated in our house, my father holding that the Prohibitionists were fanatics and that he was damned if he would give up his freedom to enjoy a stein of beer or a glass of wine. The fanatics would eventually succeed at the end of the Great War (1919) in clamping Prohibition on the nation. But the "noble experiment," as President Herbert Hoover would call it, was a dismal failure. It made lawbreakers out of millions of otherwise law-abiding citizens until finally the country, under the prodding of President Franklin Roosevelt, came to its senses in 1933 and repealed the Eighteenth Amendment.

Probably a majority of the women, but certainly not of the men, as the new century began believed that the time had come for female suffrage, that once women had the vote they would purify politics, drive out the crooks, provide enlightened legislation, and curb the paranoiac tendency of the male rulers to wage war and embroil the nation in other kinds of violence.

My mother, an ardent suffragist, was sure of it, my father less so, and their arguments sometimes became heated. She was incensed at an inane remark by some congressman, which my father had jokingly read to her from a local newspaper, that "a suffragette is one who has ceased to be a lady and has not yet become a gentleman." Years later she would still remember it and say, "Will, that really wasn't very funny. But it was typical of the men who were supposed to represent us in Washington. Do you realize that for nearly fifty years—ever since 1869, when a bill to give us the vote was introduced in the House—that stupid man's Congress has denied us our rights!" The very thought made this gentle woman boil.

The promise that the political enfranchisement of women would greatly improve American political life turned out to be an illusion. When the valiant, highly organized fight that the women had carried on for half a century finally brought them the vote in time for the 1920 elections, they cast their ballots pretty much as the menfolk did, rejecting American membership in the League of Nations, throwing the Democrats out after eight years of Woodrow Wilson, and electing one of the most mediocre presidents in the history of the Republic, and one whose Administration would become one of the most corrupt since the nation was formed. The majority of women didn't even bother to vote the first time they had the chance.

But sexual equality, at least at the polls, had finally been won, and this was one of the splendid achievements of the early twentieth century. The long struggle left the women's rights movement in America exhausted. It would not be revived for nearly another half a century. One of the most important political reforms in the country, the election of U.S. senators by popular vote instead of by state legislatures, where a seat was often auctioned off to the highest bidder, was achieved in 1913, before the women got the vote.

Such was the world and the country in the first years of the century as I began to grow up. Though I was too young to grasp much of what was going on, some of it was bound to rub off on me. In school, in church, above all at home, where I eavesdropped on the discussions of my parents and their friends, the world, the country, the city, began to take shape in my immature but growing mind.

Chicago at the turn of the century was a rip-roaring, wide-open city of one and three-quarter millions, second largest in the nation and fifth in the world. It had grown by leaps and bounds. A few old residents could remember when it had been a frontier military post against the Indians, called Fort Dearborn, established in 1804, and consisting of fourteen houses protected by a wooden stockade. Most of the emigration from the East to the West had had to stop or at least to pause there since it lay at the southern tip of Lake Michigan, which blocked the westward passage to the north as far as Canada. The early settlers came by land and later by water—over the Great Lakes from Buffalo. Most of the great railroads spanning the continent made Chicago their terminus since they had to pass to the south of the lake. The rail lines from Boston, New York, Philadelphia, Baltimore and Washington ended there; the great lines to the West Coast began there. By the time I arrived on the scene, Chicago had become the greatest railroad center of the nation, its biggest market for grain, lumber, livestock and meat-packing. The stockyards, which lay directly west of where I grew up on the South Side, were the largest in the world. On the days when the wind blew from the west (the prevailing wind came from the lake, just to the east) the smell could be overwhelming.

Burgeoning industry and transportation attracted people to Chicago in droves from all over the world. In one single decade, between 1880 and 1890, the population of the city more than doubled. Many came from Europe. By 1900, 35 percent of the people were foreign-born, and if you counted those born in

America of foreign parentage, the statistic rose to 77 percent of all the people in Chicago. The Germans predominated. One of my first recollections is hearing a strange tongue that my father identified as German, and when I entered first grade in the public school in Woodlawn, the study of German was compulsory. In Chicago in 1903, there were 500,000 German-speaking citizens, 100,000 Swedes (and 50,000 Norwegians and 20,000 Danes), 125,000 Poles and 90,000 Bohemians, as we called the Czechs and Slovaks then. Chicago was a Babel of foreign tongues.

It also seemed to many to be a wild and barbaric place. "Chicago!" wrote Lincoln Steffens about this time in his muckraking *Shame of the Cities* articles:

> First in violence, deepest in dirt; loud, lawless, unlovely, ill-smelling, irreverent, new; an overgrown gawk of a village, the "tough" among cities, a spectacle for the nation.

William T. Steed, a British journalist who came to Chicago in the 1890's to explore its corruption and sin, found more than he could digest. He was sure hell would be merely "a pocket edition of Chicago." Brothels, gambling joints and saloons abounded, as did whores in the busy streets, and the notorious First Ward, in the heart of the city, just south of the river, was the fief of two legendary characters my father, a reformer, used to talk about as Hinky Dink and Bathhouse John. They not only ran the First Ward, which included the business and amusement district, for half a century—from 1890 to 1940—but often had control of the whole city. Paul H. Douglas, a former U.S. senator, a professor at the University of Chicago and a "reform" alderman from the Fifth Ward (a post to which my father was about to be elected when he suddenly died), remembered them rather fondly. It was his "good fortune," he said, to have known them personally toward the end of their colorful careers, by which time their graft had netted them an estimated tens of millions. My father, somewhat of a puritan, took a dimmer view, but he would have agreed with Douglas' description of Hinky Dink and Bathhouse John:

> The Bath was the bumbling and none too bright extrovert, while Hinky Dink was the shrewd and laconic introvert. . . . The Bath, with his gayly colored waistcoats, his inability to

speak a coherent sentence, his penchant for owning race horses which couldn't or wouldn't run, and his sponsorship of absurd songs such as "They Buried Her by the Side of the Drainage Canal" and "Dear Midnight of Love," is, in a sense, as irresistibly funny as the Keystone Cops.

But not so was his partner, Hinky Dink. "The Hink" knew the price of everything and, his opponents charged, the value of nothing. It was charged that every saloon, every gambler, every prostitute had to come across at rates which were presumably fixed according to their ability to pay. Mike (as Hinky Dink was rarely called), with his aides, saw to it that this was done and that the vote was delivered on primary and election days.[1]

Nevertheless, despite their graft and its sources of vice, Hinky Dink Kenna and Bathhouse John Coughlin did a lot of good for people in poverty and in trouble. "They fed the hungry," Douglas reports, "and they got jobs for the unemployed. They protected those in trouble with the law." In return they demanded loyalty in the form of votes and money. And if they took their loot—from saloon keepers, breweries, whores in the streets, madames of the houses that lined the city's blocks, and gamblers —did they not also give something in return not only to the poor and wretched but also to the well-to-do, by providing the latter the means of satisfying their Victorian lusts? "The first ward," says Douglas, "gave to the city and to the Midwest the chance to privately enjoy every form of vice that was publicly condemned."

Perhaps my father's views of Bathhouse John and Hinky Dink and the other ward bosses would have mellowed in time, as have those of Douglas. But at his untimely death he was running as Republican candidate for alderman of the Fifth Ward and thus a place on the City Council, with a promise to the voters to drive out the Baths and the Hinks. My father was more attuned to the good works being performed in Chicago by Jane Addams at Hull House.

He came from a family that had emigrated from the German Rhineland early in the 1840's "to seek freedom in this country," as he explained it, and his father was born in Herkimer County,

[1] Paul H. Douglas in his Introduction to *Bosses in Lusty Chicago* by Lloyd Wendt and Herman Kogan.

New York, in 1846. Like most Germans arriving in those days, the family pushed west and settled first in Wisconsin, not far from Milwaukee, and then on a large farm in Blackhawk County, Iowa, near the small town of La Porte City, where my father was born in 1871. The family name originally was Scheurer, a fairly common name in the German Black Forest region. Some time during the trek west it was Anglicized to Shirer. My grandfather attached no importance to the change, explaining to me once, when I asked him, that it was done mainly because the town officials and tradesmen mistakenly kept writing it the way they thought it sounded, and it was simpler to go along with them. Was there also a desire, common among so many families transplanted from the continent of Europe, to fit the name better into the new world of the dominant Anglo-Saxon population? Perhaps not. My grandfather, though he hated the Kaiser and the Hohenzollern autocracy, was proud of his German heritage, often spoke German with his wife, also of German origin, and loved to sing German *lieder*. Still, I gathered he was also proud that he spoke English without an accent, probably the first of his family to do so, and it may have been revealing that he and his wife never taught their four children German. So with my grandfather, the "Scheurers" became "Shirers." It seems a short and simple name, and I have always been surprised to see how few bear it in this vast country. In the Manhattan, New York, telephone directory in the 1970's, there is not a single entry under the name.

Like most boys in Iowa at that time, my father grew up on the family farm, learning at a very early age to help with the chores, milk the cows, feed the chickens and pigs, churn the butter, try his hand at plowing a straight furrow behind a team of horses, and at "plowing" corn and harvesting it. Iowa then was virgin prairie land, its rich black earth just coming under cultivation. Crops matured easily and in profusion, especially corn, which in large part was fed to hogs and cattle. It was not long before my grandfather became chiefly interested in stock-breeding. The farms were isolated and self-contained, furnishing the family most of its food and making it a closely knit unit, independent, self-reliant and yet, of necessity, a sort of cooperative. A small town or a village might not be far away but over the dirt roads in a wagon behind a team of horses it took at least a full day for a farmer to reach it for marketing and shopping and still get back in time for milking.

Life, though primitive, must have been a new and even exciting experience for a family that moved from eastern Wisconsin
westward across the Mississippi and into Iowa at the beginning of
the 1860's. It was new, unsettled Indian country. The first white
settlers had arrived scarcely thirty years before, in what was then
known as Iowa territory, crowding out the Indians, who had lived
there since time immemorial. (One tribe called Ioway had given
the region its name.) By 1846, when Iowa was admitted into the
Union as a state, all the Indians except the Sioux had been driven
out, their vast lands "purchased" for a song. In 1851, that valiant
tribe was "purchased" out of the state and shoved across the Missouri River into the Dakotas.[1] The virgin land was now open for
full settlement and the white men, with their women, began arriving in droves, ferrying across the Mississippi with their covered
wagons and cattle and striking westward for a choice piece of
land, on which they quickly erected sod huts or log cabins and
began scratching up the grassland and started planting.

From 1850 to 1860, about the time my forebears arrived, the
population of Iowa more than tripled—from 192,000 to 675,000.
During the next two decades it more than doubled—to 1,625,000,
and by 1890, a year after my father graduated from the La Porte
City highschool and his father sold the farm to move to Mount
Vernon to give his four children a college education at Cornell,
the population of the state had reached 2,000,000. Iowa had become the leading agricultural state in the Union, its people overwhelmingly rural, fairly prosperous except when prices for grain

[1] The fear of Indians by the acquisitive white settlers persisted for some time,
and not without reason. As late as the winter of 1857 a marauding band of Sioux,
under a drunken chief named Inkpaduta, descended upon a settlement near
Spirit Lake, Iowa, and killed and scalped all of the forty inhabitants except three
young married women and a fourteen-year-old girl, whom they carried away as
captives. Two of the women were murdered in the course of the Indians' flight to
the Dakotas, and the third woman and the girl were later ransomed, the girl,
Abigail Gardner, writing a moving account of how her parents, her grown sister
and three young children were done to death in their little cabin before her eyes.
The killings became known as the "Spirit Lake Massacre" and we youngsters
growing up later in Iowa were excited and not a little frightened at reading
Abigail Gardner's lurid account of it. Sometimes a stray and hungry Indian from
the nearby Tama Reservation would come to the back door of our house to beg
food and my worried mother would lock the doors and windows and, if the man
persisted in knocking, call the police. We were brought up to believe that "the
only good Indian was a dead Indian" and nothing was said to us in those days of
the cruel and savage slaughter and the robbery of the Indians by the white
Americans, one of the darkest sides of our history.

and stock sagged, as they had in the great Depression of 1894, leading the simple life of the countryside, fiercely democratic and egalitarian, yet withal rather conservative in their politics and in their way of life and intensely religious to an extent that seems almost incomprehensible today.

Apparently, too, hungry for more culture, or at least for more education. That was why my grandfather had sold his farm the year my father graduated from highschool and moved on to a college town. His two daughters had revealed a talent for music and wanted to continue their studies in piano and voice. Neither of his two sons obviously were going to take over the farm. They had early become more interested in books than in farming and seemed determined to follow more intellectual pursuits. It must have been a wrenching decision for my grandfather to give up a prosperous farm and strike out on another path at the age of forty-three. He seemed to me later, when I got to know him somewhat, the most mild-mannered and modest of men, though he had a strong, well-chiseled, intelligent face behind his close-cropped beard. But as my uncle had told me the day I set out from Iowa to Paris, underneath the gentle man was a burning passion to give his children the education he had lacked. No doubt it was not an uncommon feeling at the time out in our prairie states.

Obviously there was considerable pride in one's children and ambition for their future. I can imagine my grandfather and his wife beaming with pleasure when they sat in the Opera House at La Porte City on the evening of June 21, 1889, to watch the Seventh Annual Commencement of the highschool and to see their son, Seward S. Shirer, salutatorian of the class, deliver the opening greetings and then launch into his "oration"—"Free Opinion a Preserver of the State." His was the first of eleven orations (in a class of twelve!) interspersed with music, one number of which being a male quartet, in which my father also participated, rendering "Roll On Majestic Ocean." In the rustic high-schools and colleges of those days, orating was the most popular of all extracurricular activities—like football and basketball to-day—and the boy and girl orators were much looked up to in their class. My father, from his early highschool days, was passionately devoted to becoming a public speaker, a passion that continued through college and his practice of law. On this June evening, according to the local weekly newspaper, he "presented his discourse with much ease of manner and without an excess of gestures. He has a good voice." The whole town, swollen by numbers of nearby farmers, must have turned out for the graduation ceremonies. "The audience," reported the newspaper, which devoted five full columns on the front page to the exercises, "was the largest, we believe, that ever assembled in the Opera House."

The graduation over, the Shirer family bid farewell to the farm and packed off for Mount Vernon and Cornell College one hundred miles away.

Iowa was dotted by that time with a dozen institutions of learning which had been founded around the mid-century as "seminaries," affiliated with one Protestant church or another, and gradually had grown into colleges. Cornell College, connected with the Methodists, was typical of them. An advertisement in the college newspaper, *The Breeze*, on January 6, 1892, when my father was a junior and my mother a sophomore, describes the institution.

> Cornell College affords excellent facilities for securing a liberal education at moderate expense. The *Classical, Philosophical, Scientific and Civil Engineering* Courses compare favorably with the leading colleges of the country . . . The *Conservatory of Music* . . . is justly celebrated . . . for its superior Professors from the best Conservatories of Europe and America. . . .
>
> Location beautiful and healthful; twenty-eight experienced professors and teachers; 675 students annually. . . .
>
> *Tuition,* including incidental fees, $11.00 to $12.00 per term. Board, including furnished rooms, $2.75 to $3.50 per week.

Judging from his scrapbooks my father concentrated on history, Latin and Greek, and oratory, and my mother on music; she became a fairly accomplished pianist. And the young ladies, as well as the men, seem to have gone in for oratory. I find a marked copy of the college paper which my mother mailed to my father the fall after he graduated telling of *her* performance at the tribune. Since she was inordinately shy, it must have required some effort. The write-up of the annual "public" of the women's "Philomanthean Society" reminds one of how simple and innocent, by our later standards, that college generation was.

> The stage was tastefully decorated with rugs and roses. The participants marched to the platform to the music of Myers'

Opera House Orchestra of Cedar Rapids. Miss Conklin, Pre-
ceptress, offered a touching prayer. . . . Miss Bess J. Tanner of
Cedar Rapids [my mother] refuted the theory of "Chance" in the
universe. . . . Miss Louana Reeder of Tipton showed the "Secret
Power" of God so manifest in His Works. . . .

The orations were carefully prepared, thoughtful and clearly
and forcibly delivered. . . . Myers' Opera House Orchestra kept
the large audience in good cheer with their first-class music.

My mother, so timid and reticent, refuting the theory of
Chance in the universe! There was a certainty about life on that
rustic campus and almost a literal feeling of God's presence, at
least as revealed in Protestantism. There were daily prayers in
chapel, attendance at which was compulsory. All meetings of
whatever kind were opened by prayer. God must have seemed
very close, the students and faculty conversed with Him so frequently. The Bible was the rock of their life—a fanatical faith in
Protestantism, too, and this caused them to look on the Catholics
with suspicion and even hostility. The same issue of the college
paper contains an initialed essay which begins:

Romanism is the coming foe . . . It condemns free speech,
a fress press, the free public schools . . . teaches idolatry, un-
dermines governments and keeps the masses in ignorance and
superstition . . . A consistent Romanist who unquestioningly
accepts all the Papal decrees . . . cannot be a true and patriotic
American citizen . . .

Despite their Protestant zeal, the students in the early 1890's
appear to have broken away from it at intervals long enough to
have a good time. Horses got the youngsters around. An item in
the *Cornellian* reports that "a carry-all filled with young ladies
went to Anamosa last Saturday to see the penitentiary." An ad for
the Mount Vernon House, the leading hostelry, says: "Free Hack
to and from all Trains." The town was on the main line of the
Chicago and North Western railroad, and several local trains
stopped there daily. It was but a half-hour trip into the big
metropolis of the region, Cedar Rapids, then a town of twenty
thousand, where I later would grow up. There the students could
take in the "Opera" or theater or vaudeville (there were no
movies yet) and do their shopping or even, if they were brave

and adventurous, go to a public dance and have an alcoholic drink, both dancing and drinking, as well as card-playing, being forbidden on the campus and in the college town.

Such was the life and atmosphere in this small-town Midwest Methodist college where my parents grew to maturity, met and later married. It would seem terribly circumscribed to students today. The diversions they take for granted, movies, radio, TV, even the Gramophone, not to mention highly organized and practically professional sports, were unknown. The students in the 1890's made their own diversions and they were very simple but natural. No doubt at most colleges and universities today the instruction is better and certainly more varied and the science laboratories infinitely superior. But perhaps the fundamentals of a liberal arts education were just as good then if not better. At any rate, the little college put a stamp on my parents for the rest of their lives—which in my father's case was to be tragically short.

Though he played on the college baseball team and loved the game—he would later become an ardent fan of the White Sox in Chicago—his chief extracurricular interest was in public speaking. The college orator in those days, unbelievable as it seems to us today, was a more important figure on the campus than a star fullback or a winning pitcher. An item in the Cedar Rapids *Daily Republican* reports my father's return from the annual Collegiate State Oratorical Contest at Iowa College (later Grinnell) in 1893 at which he won second place—and fifty dollars. He was greeted at the depot in Mount Vernon "by the college band and a large number of students who almost mobbed him." No winning football team ever received a warmer reception. No athlete was the subject of more praise.

I recently came across a copy of his oration, which he also delivered at the Interstate Oratorical Contest at Ohio State University that year. It was entitled "The World Citizen" and it contained thoughts which seem rather advanced for a college youth in 1893 and which he championed in later life and which, indeed, are meaningful today. It was a plea for the end of war and for "a world citizen" in a world government. "Throughout the world," he said, "there is a cry on human lips against war." He foresaw that the "bristling armaments of Europe" and the national rivalries there "may be the precursors of a final sanguinary struggle that will forever sicken men of this dread expedient"—a prediction of World War I, which came twenty-one years later, though in foreseeing that it would be the "final" great war because men would sicken of it, he was too optimistic about mankind. Too optimistic also about man's capacity for world government, though he argued that it was already a practical proposition. "The world state is not a dream," he concluded. "It is the natural sequence of political evolution. The interests of mankind plead for it." In this he was a little ahead of his time, a little ahead of our time eighty years later.

His success as a public speaker and the personal encouragement he got from some of the state's leading lawyers, who acted as judges at the various oratorical contests he took part in during his last two years in college, led my father to determine to seek a career at the bar. His family, with three other children to see through college, could not afford to send him immediately to law school but this was not much of a setback. In those days many young men passed the state's bar examination after reading law for a year or two in some attorney's office. This my father did. The year after graduation found him principal of the Blairstown (Iowa) Preparatory School, where he doubled as teacher of Latin and Greek. After school hours he read law in a local attorney's office and in the spring of 1894, he took the state bar examination at Des Moines and was admitted to the Iowa bar. The next year he went to work in a law firm in Estherville, but the prospect of life as a small-town Iowa lawyer apparently did not appeal to him, and in 1895 he moved on to Chicago, enrolled in the Law School of Lake Forest University, graduated in June, 1896, and was admitted to the Illinois bar. He had worked his way through law school by teaching in the public schools of Chicago, a second profession he continued to practice during the first lean years around the turn of the century, after he hung out his shingle and waited for clients.

Chicago was still under the spell of the Haymarket riot and the legal murder of innocent labor leaders that followed, and of the Pullman strike, two bloody events that provoked a paroxysm of hysteria in the press and among the upper and middle classes against organized labor and that embittered the American workingmen—and helped set back their drive to organize in unions—

for a generation. The workers, ill-paid, ill-housed, ill-used and just beginning to organize, were put upon by the police, the militia, U.S. troops and armed strikebreakers, beaten, shot down, killed and wounded, their leaders jailed and some of them executed.

One of my first inklings of the darker side of life came from eavesdropping on the conversations of my parents and their friends about these happenings. Gradually they became imprinted on my budding consciousness, causing me to wonder about the inhumanity of the human race. More than half a century later I was still wondering. The murder of innocent men by order of a court of justice after the Haymarket riot, and the obscene rejoicing it brought in the press and even in the Protestant pulpit, seemed inexplicable in a civilized society even to a small boy, and still does to that former child, now nearing the end of a long life that has witnessed at first hand so much injustice and killing all over the world.

On May 3, 1886, striking workers of the McCormick Harvester plant had clashed with strikebreakers. The police had fired on the former, killing one, wounding several others, and had beaten up many of the survivors. Anarchist and labor leaders called for a protest meeting the next evening in Haymarket Square. Only some twelve hundred of an expected twenty thousand showed up on a cold and drizzling night. The meeting proceeded peacefully enough. Mayor Carter Harrison appeared on the scene to make sure of that and remained until the last of the speakers was winding up and the crowd was beginning to disperse. Relieved that the meeting had brought no threat of violence, he left. A moment or two later, a band of 180 police, which the mayor had forbidden to come to the square, arrived and started to charge the dispersing crowd. Suddenly a bomb thrown from an upper story of a building nearby exploded in the ranks of the police, killing seven of them.

The newspapers, not only in Chicago but throughout the country, cried for vengeance. Protestant preachers joined them. Eight men, including the editors of two Chicago labor journals, who had been on the speakers' platform, were arrested and quickly tried for conspiracy to murder. Though the prosecution did not charge the men with throwing the bomb or with even knowing who threw it—he was never apprehended—all the accused were found guilty. Judge Joseph E. Gary, who presided, summed up the theory of American justice at the trial:

> The conviction has not gone on the ground that they did actually have any personal participation in the particular act which caused the death of Degan; but the conviction proceeds upon the ground that they had generally by speech and print advised large classes to commit murder and had left the commission, the time, place and when to the individual will, whim or caprice or whatever it may be of each individual man who listened to their advice.

Though there was no evidence whatsoever that the bomb thrower had in fact been influenced by the speeches or writings of any of the accused, or had ever heard of them, Judge Gary, whipped by a hysterical press, persisted: "In consequence of their advice, in pursuance of that advice, and influenced by that advice, somebody, not known, did throw that bomb that caused Degan's death."

In pursuance of this theory, and in defiance of the law of Illinois which stated that an accessory to a crime could only be tried when the guilt of the principal had been proved, Judge Gary sentenced seven of the accused to death and one to the penitentiary. One escaped the gallows by committing suicide, two by having their sentences commuted to life imprisonment by the governor, and four were hanged.

This, my lawyer father said, was "judicial murder," a view shared by many in the country though they were in a minority. To William Dean Howells, the gentle dean of American letters, it was "civic murder" and it filled him, he said, "with heartache and horror." He called the executions "forever damnable before God and abominable to civilized men. This free Republic has killed five men for their opinions."

It was not the last time in our "free Republic." Forty years later, when I at last had come of age, Sacco and Vanzetti would be done to death for the same reason. They were "anarchists," too.

One was faced, then, in America from an early age with the intolerance and violence of our people, with the frenzy with which they could be whipped up by an irresponsible press, shoddy political leaders, hypocritical captains of industry and bigots in the pulpit. The hysteria would die down for a time and then suddenly flare up again. Seven years after the Haymarket executions, Governor John Peter Altgeld pardoned the three remaining men then in prison, not only on the grounds of mercy, but because he found that the trial itself and the judgment of the court had been a travesty of justice. This caused a new wave of hysteria in Chicago and throughout the land, and the governor, a man of noble stature, was crucified. The Reverend Dr. Lyman Abbott, one of the country's leading divines, stormed from his New York pulpit against Altgeld as "the crowned hero and worshiped deity of the anarchists of the Northwest." Theodore Roosevelt, the "progressive" Republican, who had acclaimed the Haymarket sentences, attacked Altgeld as a man "who condones and encourages the most infamous of murders." The pardons cost Altgeld his political life.

The frenzy over his "crime" had hardly died down in Chicago before it burst out again in the Pullman strike the summer of 1894. This year, as we have noted, had seen one of the worst depressions in the country's existence. The railroads in general and the Pullman company in particular had slashed wages and had organized to smash the weak unions, which had dared to strike. For years there had been bitter strife in the railroads. A succession of strikes had shut down temporarily many of the largest lines. The strikes had been broken by state militia and federal troops, who had not hesitated to fire on the workers, killing a number of them and wounding more.

George M. Pullman, head of the Pullman Palace Car Company, housed his workers in what he called a "model" company town named Pullman, a suburb of Chicago. He ran it like a feudal manor, fleecing the workers by charging 25 percent higher rents than were prevalent in the area and gouging them at the company-owned stores. But the biggest gouging came in wage reductions. Between late 1893 and May, 1894, according to the findings of a Federal Investigating Commission, Pullman slashed wages 25 percent, though the company continued to pay its 8 percent annual dividend and by the end of its fiscal year in July had an undivided surplus of $2,320,000. When the employees, who were members of Eugene V. Debs's budding American Railway Union, sent a delegation of forty-three representatives to management to protest, they were fired and their families were dispossessed of their homes. Two days later, on May 11, 1894, the workers struck but offered to arbitrate their case. Mayor Hopkins of Chicago and fifty other mayors throughout the country urged Pullman to agree to arbitration. He refused. "The workers," he replied, "have nothing to do with the amount of wages they receive. That is solely the business of the company."

On June 26, the union ordered a nationwide boycott of Pullman cars, offering to keep the trains running if they did not carry sleeping cars. The General Managers' Association, which represented twenty-four railroads terminating in Chicago, countered by declining to run any trains unless the Pullman cars attached to them were allowed to go through. There was an immediate outcry throughout the land that the carrying of the sacred mails was being hampered. In Washington, President Cleveland declared: "If it takes every dollar in the Treasury and every soldier in the United States Army to deliver a postal card to Chicago, that postal card will be delivered." But this was a red herring. No mail trains carried Pullmans and the union had ordered all its members to see that the mail got through.

By the end of June, by lockout or by strike, 125,000 railway workers were out. Twenty railroads could not, or would not, move their trains. Despite the strict orders of Debs that there be no violence, Pullman cars were forcibly detached from two or three trains, delaying them. But Chicago was quiet, the mayor declining to ask Governor Altgeld to call out the militia. The city was quiet, but not its press. On June 30, the *Tribune* headlines were ominous—"MOB IS IN CONTROL . . . LAW IS TRAMPLED ON" —and the readers were told that "through the lawless acts of Dictator Debs' strikers the lives of thousands of Chicago citizens were endangered yesterday." The *Herald* called on the railroads "to defeat the strike . . . and the labor agitators and conspirators." On July 2, the *Tribune* headline roared: "STRIKE IS NOW WAR!"

If it could be made to look like "war," then troops would have to be called out. But first the federal government struck through the courts. I remember years later my father, by then a federal attorney himself, trying to explain to me what happened. The railroads persuaded the U.S. Attorney General in Washington to appoint their own lawyer as a special prosecutor in Chicago to break the strike. At his instigation, and with the help of a notoriously antiunion judge, the federal government got an injunction. It forbade Debs and other union leaders to support the boycott by word, writing or wire—or by any other conceivable means. It was to be the model for forty years of the injunction used by the government to prevent or break strikes.

Having accomplished this, the railroad attorney, now disguised as a special prosecutor, induced the President of the United States to call out federal troops to break the strike. This, thought Governor Altgeld, was plainly unconstitutional. The President had no power to send troops into a state unless they were called for by the legislature, or, if it was not sitting, by the governor. He had not asked for any, and he thought none were needed. He asked President Grover Cleveland to rescind the order, but Cleveland was adamant. Federal troops from Fort Sheridan marched into Chicago and pitched camp as the city was peacefully celebrating the Fourth of July. This was a provocation to the workers. When the troops started moving Pullman-car trains, they reacted.

They overturned freight cars or set them afire to block the tracks. In vain, Debs, defying the injunction by speaking out, urged his men to refrain from violence and "to obey the law." He knew that much of the violence, the setting fire to cars, the first shooting, was done by a force of thirty-five hundred men recruited by the government from the dregs of the city's underworld and deputized as "federal marshals." This was later confirmed by the chief of police and by Mayor Hopkins. The workers, infuriated by being shot at by the marshals and the troops, fought against them, wrecking cars and throwing stones. July 6 and 7 were the worst days. The forces of order, firing on the rioters, killed thirty persons and wounded hundreds more. Flaming boxcars dotted the railroad yards. On July 8, the nation's press exploded in flaming headlines:

FIRED BY THE MOB
Chicago at the Mercy of the Incendiary's Torch
(Washington *Post*)

WILD RIOT IN CHICAGO
Hundreds of Freight Cars Burned by the Strikers
(New York *Sun*)

In Chicago itself the headlines in the *Inter-Ocean* were typical:

FLAMES MAKE HAVOC—UNPARALLELED SCENES OF RIOT
Terror and Pillage
Anarchy Is Rampant—Mobs at Pullman and Burnside Apply the Torch

Joseph Pulitzer's liberal St. Louis *Post-Dispatch* kept its head. Its headlines accurately described the rioting:

SHOOT TO KILL
Volley after Volley Poured into a Desperate Mob

Some of the pulpits were not so objective. One New York minister charged that Debs was "the son of a saloon keeper, a man reared and educated upon the proceeds of human ruin." (*The New York Times* had just run an interview with a doctor who declared falsely that Debs was an incurable drunkard.) A minister in Brooklyn called from the pulpit for rebellion to be put down by gunfire.

> There must be some shooting, men must be killed, and then there will be an end of this defiance of law and destruction of property . . . The soldiers must use their guns. They must shoot to kill.

Out on his western ranch, Theodore Roosevelt agreed.

> The sentiment now animating a large proportion of our people can only be suppressed . . . by taking ten or a dozen of their leaders out, standing them against a wall and shooting them dead. I believe it will come to that.

After the Haymarket riot, Roosevelt had offered to bring his cowboys to Chicago to do just that, but Judge Gary had made it unnecessary.

In Washington the House of Representatives came down on the side of "law and order" and in support of the President's use of federal troops. In a joint resolution it endorsed "prompt and vigorous action of the military force in suppressing interference with the mails and with interstate commerce."

The boycott, or strike, was broken, and the American Railway Union was destroyed, neither the Railroad Brotherhoods nor the recently formed American Federation of Labor having offered it the least support. Debs was indicted for criminal conspiracy and was arrested for that and for violating the court injunction. The conspiracy trial fizzled out before the relentless defense of a young Chicago lawyer named Clarence Darrow, who had left his lucrative job as attorney for the Chicago and North Western railroad to defend Debs. But Debs was sentenced to six months in prison for violating the injunction. The Supreme Court, true to its long record of defending property rights above all others, sustained the conviction. It would take more than a generation of maturing before the country—and the courts and the Congress—would take another view of the injunction and drop it, more or less, as a tool with which the federal government could break strikes. The pros and cons of the Pullman strike echoed for many years in my ears and mind as I began to grow up in Chicago, and this helped to condition my thinking and feeling about the rights and wrongs of management and labor all the mature years of my life.

Out of the Pullman turmoil emerged two men for whom I would have a lifelong admiration, though they were reviled through most of their lives by the possessing classes. These were Eugene V. Debs and Clarence Darrow, who defended Debs, and who would spend most of his long life as one of the country's greatest lawyers defending the workers and the poor in the courts of the land.

Darrow, a homespun, craggy-faced Midwesterner in a crumpled suit, dropped by occasionally to have a drink and chew the fat with my father. Though in the courtroom they were antagonists, my father the federal prosecutor, Darrow the relentless defender, they became good friends. Darrow was certainly the more philosophical of the two, more passionate and compassionate, the more eloquent in moving juries. He was fascinated, I'm told, by my father's classical learning, his knowledge of Greek drama and philosophy and Roman law, and he admired him not only for his fairness and decency in the courtroom, which Darrow felt he did not often meet in a government prosecutor, but for his shrewdness before judge and jury. The admiration must have been mutual. My father, a believing Christian and sturdy churchgoer, must have wondered sometimes about Darrow's agnosticism though he probably shared the older man's skepticism of the Holy Bible as history. At any rate, my father, his friends have told me, learned much from Darrow not only about his profession but about philosophy, history and literature. And as the younger and less experienced of the two, he looked up to him and felt his genius, as eventually I would. I have often regretted that I was not old enough to absorb some of their talk. It was only years afterward, when I had read some of Darrow's great courtroom speeches and read his books, that I was able to grasp the greatness, the goodness, the courage, of this rough-looking, humane, civilized man.

The putting down of the Pullman boycott by the guns of the troops turned Debs, a kindly, moderate, decent man, into a life-long socialist.

> I was to be baptized in Socialism [Debs said of the Pullman struggle] in the roar of conflict . . . In the gleam of every bayonet and the flash of every rifle the class struggle was revealed . . . This was my first practical struggle in Socialism.

He believed that socialism would soon triumph in America as it promised to triumph in Europe, but this was not to be. Yet despite the early rejection of socialism by the American worker and by the electorate—Debs was a perennial candidate for President on the Socialist ticket—he continued to believe in it and to fight for it throughout a long period when to many Americans a socialist was a red menace to the Republic. Vilified, as he was, in the press and pulpit, he remained a kindly man. Darrow once said of him: "There may have lived sometime, somewhere, a kindlier, gentler, more generous man than Debs, but I have never known him." To Dos Passos, in the days he was writing *The 42nd Parallel,* before he turned to the Right, Debs was "a lover of mankind."

Without the right to strike and consequently powerless to bargain collectively, the sullen workers went back to work—where they could find it, for the railroads would not rehire a member of the Railway Union. And many of them became convinced that the power of government would always be on the side of the rich, granting large favors to Big Business while determined to help the employers keep down the majority of workers, depress their wages and prevent them from organizing to improve their condition. Wages averaged out to $500 a year—$10 a week—with the unskilled earning under $450 in the North and less than $300 in the South. In the sweatshops of New York, Boston and Chicago, women were lucky to make $5 a week. The hours were long. The garment workers in Chicago had a seventy-hour work week. In the steel industry there was a uniform twelve-hour day, with a stretch of twenty-four hours every two weeks at a wage of thirty cents an hour.

Strong unions might have alleviated such slave-labor conditions but they were suppressed. Our comfortable middle class regarded them as a threat to the American Way of Life. As the Citizens Industrial Association put it in a ringing declaration published on page one of the *Chicago Tribune* on February 24, 1904, the day after I was born: "Labor Unions are revolutionary and anarchistic and a menace to the entire social and industrial system of the United States." It would take a generation, and much bloody strife, before our free society, of which well-heeled Americans boasted so much, would come to its senses about the freedom of workers to organize.

Every Christmas in Chicago my parents used to get up a large clothesbasket full of food—a turkey, a slab of ham, canned vegetables and fruit, candy—and clothing, and the whole family would pile into a taxi on Christmas Eve and deliver the basket to some hovel near the stockyards to the west of us. It was my first glimpse of the other side of the tracks and I was horrified by the sight of human beings living in such appalling squalor, like pigs in a pigsty. My father and mother, too. While we children stood silent, too abashed to speak, they would chat earnestly with the parents, ascertain their needs and add them to the list of stockyard families to whom they would send food, clothes and a little money over the years.

"Why do they have to live like that?" I would ask my father on our return. Perhaps he was embarrassed by the question. He was already becoming moderately affluent as a federal attorney and staunchly believed in the system, though he was always talking about how it had to be improved. I seem to remember that he talked that way to the poor families we visited each Christmas, sympathetically deploring their plight, but assuring them that it was bound to improve in our free country, which offered so much more opportunity than the old ones from which they had come.

That must have been of little comfort to them. Even then, despite our annual Christmas visits, it was only years later when I read Upton Sinclair's novel *The Jungle* that I really grasped the horror of the life of the stockyard families, almost all foreign-born, mostly Slovaks, Poles and Lithuanians. The book had a searing preface by Sinclair's fellow-socialist Jack London, then at the height of his popularity as novelist and short-story writer:

> It [the book] depicts what our country really is, the home of oppression and injustice, a nightmare of misery, an inferno of suffering and human hell, a jungle of wild beasts.

And Van Wyck Brooks, reviewing Sinclair's exposure of life in the stockyards, summed up the horror for the immigrants working there:

> Ignorant and stunted by European tyranny only to be utterly destroyed by American indifference, they were swindled by house-agents, political bosses . . . and judges who refused to recognize their rights. No one either knew or cared when their babies were drowned in the stinking green water that lay about their wretched shacks, when their daughters were forced into prostitution, when their sons fell into boiling vats because the employers had provided no safety devices.

No one in America either knew or cared? It was a refrain that would haunt an American all through the twentieth century. My own family cared a little—the stockyards were so near to us—but I cannot say that the degradation there cast much of a shadow on our lives. I know that after each Christmas visit to that forlorn place we quickly shed our depression and began to enjoy the holiday, with all its rich food and presents and its professed Christian spirit of Good Will Toward Men—like most good, churchy, hypocritical Americans.

There was another spell, and a happier one, that still hung over the Chicago of my birth. It was cast by the great World's Fair, the World's Columbian Exposition, which, opening a year late, in 1893, had celebrated the four hundredth anniversary of the discovery of America. People still talked about it in the years that I was growing up in Chicago. Some of its buildings still stood not far from us in Jackson Park and we youngsters never tired of visiting the exact replicas of Columbus' three ships, *Pinta, Niña* and *Santa Maria,* which the Queen of Spain had sent over for the exposition, and which remained moored in a lagoon of the park.

The Republic had never seen anything quite like the Chicago fair. It suddenly revealed to twenty-seven millions of Americans who visited it—more than one-third of the country's population—that there was another world beyond their own drab and circumscribed one, the world of art and architecture, of color and beauty. The fair did what our literature and art had not been able to do: it stimulated the imagination of the whole nation, not only for color and beauty but for the promise of a new age of electricity.

Even Henry Adams, who had about given up on America and gone back in his studies and meditations to the medieval France of Mont-Saint-Michel and Chartres to find what meaning he could in human existence, was deeply impressed, devoting a whole chapter in his autobiographical *Education* to his experience of a fortnight at the Chicago exposition. "He found matter of study," he wrote (the book is written in the third person), "to fill a hundred years . . . The Exposition itself defied philosophy . . . As a scenic display Paris had never approached it . . . The first astonishment became greater every day." Full of wonder, the usually skeptical Adams sat down on the steps "to ponder and to brood . . ." as he had never done "on the benches of Harvard College." "Education," especially his own, he says, "ran riot in Chicago."

What impressed him more than the architecture of his friends Richard Hunt, Henry Richardson, Charles McKim and Stanford White, which was mostly derivative from the Paris Beaux-Arts, was the Electrical Building, where humming dynamos furnished electric power to the whole fairgrounds and brightly illuminated millions of light bulbs in the gleaming White City. He "lingered long," he recounts, "among the dynamos, for they were new, and they gave to history a new phase . . . For the historian alone the Exposition made a serious effort . . . The historical mind can think only in historical processes, and probably this was the first time since historians existed that any of them had sat down helpless before a mechanical sequence." In a land whose homes, offices and factories were still lit by gas or the kerosene lamp and coal-fired steam engines were the main source of power, this old-fashioned but keen-minded Yankee philosopher was awed by the sight in Chicago of the dawn of the age of electricity.

It is difficult to comprehend today the imprint the Chicago World's Fair made on America and Americans. My father and mother, their relatives and friends, talked of it even after it was long gone, and so did almost everyone else in the country. Years later, in his autobiography, Theodore Dreiser exulted about the fair, "this vast and harmonious collection of perfectly constructed and snowy buildings . . . as though some brooding spirit of beauty, inherent possibly in some directing over-soul, had waved a magic wand . . . and lo, this fairyland." Maud Howe Elliott, daughter of Julia Ward Howe, and like her mother, an ardent feminist leader, remarked that though she had seen the Sphinx and the Acropolis,

> neither of these superlative legacies of the past impressed me more than . . . this miraculous city . . . arisen as if by magic. For the first time in the history of our nation . . . art has asserted itself and triumphs over its handmaidens, commerce and manufacturing.

One great Chicago architect, Louis Sullivan, in whose office Frank Lloyd Wright was then serving his architectural apprenticeship, disagreed. Sullivan had designed the ornate Transportation Building and he took a dim view of most of the other edifices, straight out of the Beaux-Arts as they were, and designed by the New York architects, who for a long time had dominated the American scene. "The virus of the World's Fair," he wrote later, brought "a violent outbreak of the Classic and the Renaissance in the East, which slowly spread westward, contaminating all it touched."

> Architecture died in the land of the free and the home of the brave. . . . Thus did the virus of a culture, snobbish and alien to the land, perform its work of disintegration . . . The damage wrought by the World's Fair will last for half a century.

All in all, though, Henry Adams, who thought his native land was pretty much of a cultural desert, believed that the World's Fair was a landmark in our history.

Chicago asked in 1893 [he wrote] for the first time the question whether the American people knew where they were driving . . . Chicago was the first expression of American thought as a unity. One must start there.

One had to start there, too, with the first expression of a new and dynamic American literature. No one who began to grow up in Chicago just after the turn of the century could escape the excitement of the literary revolt that was making the city, addicted to commerce and industry though it was, the center of a new, vigorous American writing, far different from what for nearly a century had been coming out of what Chicagoans called the "effete" East. There was a literary ferment in the air that stirred my father and his friends and rubbed off on me at a tender age. All the forces that had been arousing the Midwest since the rise of Populism and labor unionism in the eighties now burst out in literature. The raw new writers were in revolt: against the old, against the Establishment in business and government and letters, against the vulgarities of the Gilded Age, against the "prissy," conformist literature of the Atlantic seaboard, against the betrayal of the American promise. They set out stubbornly to paint life in the Republic as it was and to expose the corruption, chicanery, hypocrisy, ugliness, greed and brutality of a society dominated by the few who were powerful and rich.

Hamlin Garland, out of Wisconsin and Iowa, was the first, perhaps, to explode the myth of idyllic rural life in the Midwest. His early tales of the grim, backbreaking, spiritually empty life on the Midwest farms (*Main-Travelled Roads* in 1891 and *Crumbling Idols* in 1894) upset a good many comfortable Americans, including my father and mother, who tended to look back on life in rural Iowa with fond nostalgia. Stark as these tales were, recalling the early Knut Hamsun, as a picture of the drab life on the Middle Border, they were also an expression of the passionate protest of agrarian America against the inroads of industrialism and the blind marketplace. Garland was one of the first germinal forces in the new Midwest realism, though he seems to be forgotten today. In fact, with the triumph of industrialized America, he had little more to say, ending up in California, where he went in for spiritualism—an early example of the promising American writer who failed to grow up.

A few blocks from us lay the campus of the new Rockefeller-endowed University of Chicago, where my father had many friends, and to which President William Harper had attracted a group of brilliant teachers: John Dewey, Robert Herrick, Thorstein Veblen, and the scientists Jacques Loeb and Albert Michelson. My father greatly admired Herrick, now largely forgotten, a gentle, erudite, refined professor of English out of Harvard, who seemed a little out of place in the raw, rapacious city. He hated it for its vulgarity and its crude materialism, and yet in his novels he showed, like Dreiser, a deep understanding of it. Understanding, but not acceptance. In all his novels there was the one theme: the greed and corruption and tawdriness of the businessman, the inanity of his drive for profits and success, the emptiness of his life, the foolishness of his fashionably dressed, idle wife, and the tragedy of America worshiping—and being dominated by—such idols of clay.

Though he detested the prevailing culture of the money-grubbing entrepreneur, as he lived under it in Chicago, he had little hope that it would change. For the poor and downtrodden, he had little hope either, for they seemed to him to have accepted their miserable lot without protest, lacking any will to revolt. He could only pity them, as he did in *The Web of Life*, a novel about the Pullman strike. They faced "decay, defeat, falling and groaning, disease"—but who in the great Cliff City by the lake cared?

> Hunger and sorrow and sordid misery; the grime of living here in Chicago in the sharp discords of this nineteenth century; the brutal rich, the brutalized poor; the stupid good, the pedantic, the foolish—all, all that made the waking world!

Of all the lights at the University of Chicago, there were two who attracted me later and stirred up my mind: John Dewey and, especially, Thorstein Veblen, whose *The Theory of the Leisure Class*, published in 1899, started the demolition of the Manchester school of classical economics (which dominated economic thought in the universities and in business) and exposed more powerfully than Herrick or Dreiser or Frank Norris the vulgarity of the trader's world. I do not recall that my father ever mentioned reading the book, which came out just as he was embarking on his career at the bar, and which, though little noticed at the time, was destined to become an American classic. I don't believe Veblen's revolutionary ideas ever touched him; after all, most of the academics either rejected them or passed them over in silence. I suspect that what little thought my father gave to Veblen was in discussions with some of the faculty about Veblen's difficulties at the university, first over President Harper's refusal to promote him because "he did not advertise the university," and at the end his forced resignation because of "woman trouble"— his wife had left him and another woman had moved in.[1] My father, who was terribly strait-laced about such matters, undoubtedly took a dim view of Veblen's involvement with "other women."

As happens so often in America to men of originality and the guts to express it, Veblen was almost destroyed by a hostile culture. Drifting from one lowly university job to another, he came to New York late in life as a contributor to the *Dial* and a lecturer at the New School for Social Research, never quite losing the accent of his Norwegian-immigrant parents (who had raised him on farms in Wisconsin and Minnesota), always finding it difficult to write in English, though his prose ultimately achieved great distinction, forever the loner, the intellectual wayfarer, the disturber of the status quo, but refusing to compromise or adapt, and publishing more books, *The Theory of Business Enterprise, The Instinct of Workmanship,* among others, which eventually would further enlighten Americans about their business society; a tormented genius, a tragic yet basic figure in American writing and thought, passing the last days of his lonely life in a shack in the brown hills above Palo Alto, where he died on August 3, 1929. By that time I had been working in Europe for four years but had continued to read him, and his going seemed like a personal loss. He had been one of my mentors since college days and had helped to influence my own revolt against the smug status quo. I remember reading that Veblen had directed that "no tombstone, slab, epitaph, effigy, inscription or monument be set up to my memory." He didn't need one. His works were memorial enough.

John Dewey, a colleague of Veblen at the University of Chicago, was quite a different man and saw America in quite another light. He had come to the university on condition that he be given

---

[1] The same difficulty later beset Veblen at Stanford, after his wife finally left him for good. "The president doesn't approve of my domestic arrangements," he wrote to a friend, "nor do I. What is one to do if the woman moves in on you?"—John Dos Passos: *The Big Money,* pp. 118–119 (paperback edition).

The longest and, to me, the best of the moving, poetic thumbnail portraits in Dos Passos' *U.S.A.* trilogy is of Veblen.

facilities for an experimental school for children to test his new theories of progressive education. My parents had thought of enrolling me in it but in the end decided on the neighborhood public school. It was a decision I had nothing to do with, but I never regretted it. Though later I came to see some good in progressive education, with its emphasis on letting the child develop freely and creatively rather than making him learn by rote, and even sent my own children to a progressive school, I believe I came out none the worse from the twelve-year incubation in the public schools of Chicago and Cedar Rapids, Iowa.

So Dewey's name came early to me, through my father, who admired him, and then I forgot it until I began to read him in college and thereafter. Somehow I never quite got through to him. Given the conditions of American life, he seemed too optimistic about it, too certain that if only we could straighten out our educational institutions and learn wisely from experience, the future for our society, despite all its present antagonisms and inequalities, would be bright. A man of great good will, sensible and generous, Dewey became for a time the prophet of a new and better society for Americans. But for me, as I grew older, and insofar as I could penetrate his monotonous and abstract prose, which kept throwing me off, Dewey built his hopes on sand. I think he lacked a sense of history and, more important, a sense of the tragedy of life. He seemed incapable of grasping the tragic view, and I myself felt that he turned his mind away from the forces that were making our society what it was. One was moved by his idealism, inspired by his belief that a new and civilized spirit was not only possible but probable in America, but one felt—or at least I felt—that the structure of his philosophy was shaky. One hoped that he was right, but the hope gradually faded.[1]

Like a magnet, Chicago, the bustling, aggressive frontier capital of booming industry, trade and transportation, drew the

[1] Late in his long life, though, Dewey became prey to doubts until he was forced to come to some somber conclusions: that the mass of Americans had needlessly surrendered their liberties to a few; that rugged individualism had become ragged individualism; that to talk of free individuals, equality of opportunity, the automatic blessings of democracy, was to overlook certain facts (as he had done); and that genuine liberty had been greatly diminished in America as the result of the concentration of economic power in the hands of the few.

new young writers of the Midwest prairies to its teeming streets. Theodore Dreiser had come there from his native Indiana in the last years of the fading nineteenth century, working at odd jobs, searching for an identity and a calling. He would soon be on his road as a newspaper reporter in St. Louis, Cleveland and Pittsburgh, and then as a magazine editor in New York, and would finally stumble into his true calling when he turned to the novel and came back to the sprawling lake city for the raw material for his first books.

Sister Carrie, published in 1900 by Doubleday and all but suppressed by the publisher, is the story of a country girl who goes to Chicago and makes her way by liaisons with a bouncy salesman and later with the sleek Hurstwood, the flashy owner of a "fashionable saloon." The few who got to read it before it was withdrawn from distribution—it was not republished until 1912 —were shocked by Dreiser's seeming lack of morals in depicting Carrie so sympathetically. But it was Hurstwood, the hustling man of business, who most interested the author, and in two following novels, *The Financier* and *The Titan,* he would base his principal character, Frank Cowperwood, on a real-life buccaneer of finance who lorded it over Chicago in those days. This was Charles T. Yerkes, the traction magnate, a typical, hard-driving, crooked practitioner of acquisition, who, after a dazzling financial career in Philadelphia which had ended when he was sentenced to prison for embezzlement, had come to the Windy City in 1882. His past was no great handicap for a man beginning again in Chicago.

Yerkes had fascinated Dreiser in his early days in Chicago. Unlike my father, who thought Yerkes was a criminal and ought to be put back behind bars, Dreiser saw in the gaudy financier, the builder of the municipal streetcar and elevated railways who bribed city officials right and left to get and hold his questionable franchises, the type of man who represented success and power in America. Dreiser, the novelist, would not judge him. He would portray him as he was: a symbol of the money-grubbing civilization in which such robber barons flourished. That was the way America was at the time. That was the way its successful men were and behaved. In fact, Dreiser, the more he looked into the model of his chief character, came to have a sneaking admiration for him.

Yes, Cowperwood [Yerkes] was a crook—but how strong, how able, how he got things done! . . . what a heroic Renaissance man, what an artist![1]

And Chicago was a perfect setting for him. Dreiser had scant sympathy for the reformers, such as my father, who were always threatening to clean up the city. Let it be as it is, he admonished a reporter who came to interview him about his books.

A big city is not a teacup to be seasoned by old maids . . . Chicago is a big city where men must fight and think for themselves . . . Leave things be; the wilder the better for those who are strong enough to survive, and the future of Chicago will then be known by the genius of the great men it bred.[2]

As it turned out, Chicago would become better known, at least in the country, not for the genius of its buccaneer businessmen but for that of the writers it bred.[3] Besides Veblen, Dewey, Herrick and Dreiser there were others, and after them—a generation hence—would come still others whose writing would constitute a sort of literary renaissance in America between the two world wars.

No one made a greater splash among the brash, young new writers at the turn of the century than Frank Norris, who was fated to die in 1902, at thirty-two, before he could complete his trilogy of novels on Wheat, an ambitious, sweeping undertaking concerned with man's struggle with nature and human greed that would tell the story of the lost promise of America.

Born in Chicago in 1870 of affluent parents, moving with his family to San Francisco, a city as wild as Chicago, he went to Paris, where he studied painting and discovered Zola, spent a year at Harvard absorbing the lectures of Lewis E. Gates, the American apostle of Impressionism, and quickly, with a great

1 William A. Swanberg: *Dreiser*, p. 172.
2 Chicago *Journal*, March 18, 1914.
3 Most of the pioneer Chicago tycoons had passed along by the turn of the century or shortly thereafter. Cyrus McCormick, the biggest of all, had died in 1884 and his business had ultimately been taken over by J. P. Morgan as the International Harvester Company. George Pullman had passed along in 1897, three years after the Pullman strike; Philip Armour in 1901; Potter Palmer in 1902; Gustavus Swift in 1903; Charles Yerkes in 1905; and Marshall Field in 1906.

burst of energy and an appetite for the bigness and violence of life, turned to writing. In *McTeague*, his first novel, begun in college and published in 1899, he told the story of a crude, violent dentist and his life and loves in the wasteland of an American city. But Norris' ferocious energy, his gusto for American life, found their true outlet in the trilogy on Wheat, in which he proposed to narrate in broad strokes an epic of America and Europe, using Wheat as the symbol of man's life force. He would tell its story from the planting and harvesting in the great fields of California's San Joaquin Valley, where the farmers battled with the monopolistic Southern Pacific Railroad over outrageous freight rates, through the manipulation of its price in the speculative jungle of the Chicago grain market, to its ultimate destination in Europe, which bought it to sustain life for its hungry millions. "It's an idea as big as all outdoors," said the exuberant young Norris. For behind the story of Wheat, Norris saw in his project the telling of American and European history, the conquest of the western frontier, the rise of acquisitive, soulless business enterprise, the anarchy of the market exchange, the primitive struggle of the fertile earth against the blind force of the machine.

The first book of the trilogy, *The Octopus*, the tale of wheat-growing in California and the farmers' battles with the railroad, came out in 1901. The second, *The Pit*, published a year after his death, was a biting satire on the Chicago grain market, where both the grower and the ultimate consumer were fleeced. Norris did not live to write the third. He succumbed to appendicitis—something my father remembered in his own last days eleven years later when he lay dying of the same ailment. My father, much more conservative in temperament and outlook, could not believe that Norris had painted America quite truthfully. I heard much lively talk of his books about the house. My father thought Norris' picture of the anarchy and corruption of the Chicago pit was exaggerated. He believed, as did most Americans at that time, that the law of supply and demand, as it worked in the "free" market, was holy, even God-given, and that it should not be tampered with. For a farm boy this was puzzling. The farmers of the Midwest, where he had grown up, knew better.

There were new poets, too, unlike anything the country had seen since Whitman, walking the humming streets of Chicago in that time, poking into its filthy slums, its stinking stockyards, its bluestocking North Side, its First Ward brothels, saloons and gambling joints, its swarming life along the lake and the river, which gave the city one of the busiest ports in the nation or indeed in the world.[1]

The best of them was Carl Sandburg. Born in Galesburg, Illinois, in 1878, spending his youth riding the rails, living from odd jobs up and down the land, soldiering in the Spanish-American War, entering West Point (where he was a classmate of Douglas MacArthur's), which he endured for two weeks, attending Lombard College in Galesburg, he had come to Chicago shortly after the turn of the century, where he worked as a reporter, and later movie critic, on the *Daily News*. Journalism gave him a living and the opportunity to get to know the city, but his great passion was poetry. Sandburg loved Chicago. He saw its ugliness, its brutalities, its tragedies and wrote of them in tough, lean lines that brought a fresh breath and a robust new language to American poetry. Yet he saw its beauty, too: the fog and mist over the lake, the whistle of a boat, the gulls gliding in over Michigan Avenue, the sand dunes "of the white moon" along the shore, the winter blizzard howling in to blanket the streets, the fish crier on Maxwell Street "evincing a joy identical with that of Pavlova dancing"—and always the great city "with lifted head singing so proud to be alive and coarse and strong and cunning, flinging magnetic curses amid the toil of piling job on job . . . shoveling, wrecking, planning, building, wrecking, rebuilding" under the smoke and dust.

No other poet—or writer—quite got the feel for Chicago that Sandburg conveyed in his first book, *Chicago Poems*, published in 1916, when he was thirty-eight. The oft-quoted title piece, "Chicago," had appeared two years before in one of the early issues of Harriet Monroe's *Poetry* magazine and launched him in his career as poet.

CHICAGO

Hog Butcher for the World,
Tool Maker, Stacker of Wheat,

[1] The annual tonnage of shipping on the Chicago River far exceeded that of the Suez Canal.

Player with Railroads and the Nation's Freight Handler;
Stormy, husky, brawling,
City of the Big Shoulders:

They tell him the city is wicked, crooked and brutal, "and I believe them."

> *Of my city the worst that men will ever say is this:*
> *You took little children away from the sun and the dew,*
> *And the glimmers that played in the grass under the*
>   *great sky,*
> *And the reckless rain; you put them between walls*
> *To work, broken and smothered, for bread and wages,*
> *To eat dust in their throats and die empty-hearted . . .*

More truly, more lyrically and eloquently than any other, Sandburg, the poet, captured the agony and the achievements of my native city.

From the Illinois prairies had come also another remarkable poet, Vachel Lindsay, the wandering troubadour, who hoped by his poetry, with its sweeping rhythms and buoyant melodies, not only to recapture what he thought was the true spirit of the nation but to arouse in its citizens an appreciation of the beauty that lay all around them and which somehow, in their drab and complacent towns and villages, they had missed. Lindsay was an American minstrel, traveling up and down the land, reciting and singing his poems to the accompaniment of his guitar, carrying in his pack copies of a sixteen-page booklet, *Rhymes to be Traded for Bread,* which he literally did. (One of the brightest evenings of my college life was spent listening to him.) I believe he burned himself out in the readings he made on a thousand campuses and elsewhere; and perhaps the adulation that the poet received from the young on such numerous occasions, year after year, was ruinous to his creative springs—though it was not to Carl Sandburg, who also brought his guitar and his readings to countless campus audiences, or to Edna St. Vincent Millay. Perhaps he realized this. Apparently out of despair at thinking he had failed, he killed himself in 1931, at fifty-two, by swallowing a bottle of Lysol.

Another Chicago poet, gloomier and grimmer than Sandburg, but more conscious of the tragedies, the mean and frustrated lives in the small towns of the Midwest, was Edgar Lee

Masters, who practiced law in the city and who for nine years was a law partner of Clarence Darrow. He wrote many volumes of poetry and prose. One was truly great, *Spoon River Anthology*, a group of imagined epitaphs, some self-composed, of mostly thwarted souls who lived and died in Spoon River, which was much like Lewistown, Illinois, where Masters had grown up. These were the doomed, anonymous citizens of the flat American prairies, resurrected by the poet and allowed one last defiant word about the joys and sorrows of life in rural America. Later I would see some of their likes in Iowa.

Masters wrote himself out in *Spoon River*. Some critics thought he might have been spoiled by its success. It seemed almost as if the book had been a miracle, for the poet's subsequent work—novels and biographies as well as poetry—never approached its excellence. Some critics, such as Louis Untermeyer, who had hailed *Spoon River* as a landmark in American literature, found most of his later work tiresome. This was one of the mysteries of the writer's experience, especially in America— the drying up or the wasting of the creative spring. Yet it could be said for Masters, I think, that in some of the many volumes he continued to turn out until his death in 1950, flawed as they were, he never gave up his search for the meaning of existence and an understanding of its tragedy.

Masters and Sandburg had been encouraged by the publication of their early work in a remarkable periodical, *Poetry: A Magazine of Verse*, founded in Chicago in 1912 by Harriet Monroe. It was to give more impetus to, and have more influence on, modern American poetry than any other publication in the country. It more than liberated poetry and the poets; it exploded them. Just as influential to new writing in general was another literary review that sprang up in Chicago two years later, in 1914, under the auspices of Margaret Anderson, who had come to the city in 1912 from Indianapolis with a dream of shaking up literature and art. This is exactly what she did, opening the columns of *The Little Review* to an array of writers, then unknown, but soon to become famous: Sherwood Anderson, Hart Crane, T. S. Eliot, Ford Madox Ford, Hemingway, Joyce, Marianne Moore, Ezra Pound, Gertrude Stein, Wallace Stevens, William Carlos Williams, Yeats and many others. *The Little Review* found few readers but many authors. Like *Poetry*, it helped to launch from Chicago the brightest period in American writing.

There were lesser literary lights in Chicago, some of whom my parents much admired. My father's favorite among these was Finley Peter Dunne, a second-generation Irish-American, who skipped college to become a reporter and who at twenty-one was city editor of the *Times*. Five years later, in 1893, when he was twenty-six (the year the World's Fair opened and Henry Ford built his first car), Dunne launched on the American scene a character named "Mr. Dooley," who once a week polished the bar of his saloon and casually remarked to a customer: "I see be th' pa-apers, Hinnissy . . ." Mr. Dooley saw a lot "be th' pa-apers," and for a quarter of a century his humorous deflation of the country's politicians and its fat cats and their pretensions was eagerly read by millions of Americans either in the Chicago *Evening Post* or in syndicated columns in other journals from coast to coast.[1]

It was funny stuff and fun to read and like all great humor it was full of satire and wit and skepticism, as perhaps was natural in an Irish-American writer whose literary idol was Montaigne. It

[1] His influence lives on. As late as the summer of 1972, seventy-nine years after Mr. Dooley first sprang from the fertile mind of Dunne, Arthur Schlesinger, Jr., was using one of his sayings to begin an article in *The New York Times Magazine* on the plight of the Democratic Party after Senator George McGovern's nomination for President. Mr. Dooley had made a point a half century before that the historian wanted to stress.

". . . I've seen the Dimmycratic party hangin' to the ropes a score iv times. I've seen it dead an' buried an' th' Raypublicans kindly buildin' a monymint f'r it . . . I've gone to sleep nights wonderin' where I'd throw away me vote afther this an' whin I woke up there was that crazy-headed, ol' loon iv a party with its hair sthreamin' in its eyes, an' an axe in its hand, chasin' Raypublicans into th' tall grass. 'Tis niver so good as whin 'tis broke."

As the Presidential election campaign warmed up in the fall of 1972, Mr. Dooley's wisdom was again being quoted in the newspapers. On Sunday, September 17, 1972, the Op Ed page of the *Times* carried a four-column article at the top of the page giving some of the gentleman's best quips on "Speakin' iv Polly-ticks." On Congress:

"Well, I see Congress has got to wurruk again," said Mr. Dooley.
"The Lord save us fr'm harm," said Mr. Hennessy.

On the Vice-Presidency:

"Th' prisidincy is th' highest office in th' gift iv th' people. Th' vice-prisidincy is the next highest an' th' lowest. It isn't a crime exactly. Ye can't be sint to jail f'r it, but it's a kind iv a disgrace."

was Mr. Dooley who uttered the words that were to be echoed ever since: "The Supreme Court follows the election returns." Every week my father used to sit at the breakfast table and read to us the latest sayin' of Mr. Dooley, chuckling and cackling as he read.

Was there something in the windblown air of the sprawling prairies of our mid-continent—arctic cold in winter, scorching hot and humid in summer—that bred the kind of writers who were ushering in a new era in American writing that would last through the first half of the century? Or was it just a coincidence, an accident of geography? At that time, too, in Chicago and in the Midwest most of the authors who would make the literary renaissance of the 1920's and 1930's were being born:[1] Dos Passos (in Chicago), Hemingway (in suburban Oak Park), Archibald MacLeish (in nearby Glencoe), T. S. Eliot (St. Louis), Sinclair Lewis (Sauk Centre, Minnesota), Scott Fitzgerald (St. Paul, Minnesota), Kay Boyle (St. Paul, Minnesota) and Carl and Mark Van Doren in rural Illinois. Some were growing up farther west, Ezra Pound in Idaho, John Steinbeck in California. Two were somewhat older, Willa Cather and Sherwood Anderson, both born in 1876; she spending her youth on the frontier in Nebraska, the scene of her early novels, and he coming from Ohio to Chicago, where for a time he was one of the leading lights of the Chicago Group. Many of these younger ones, not much older than I, I would get to know in the golden twenties and early thirties in Paris.

Something of this literary ferment in Chicago, a constant subject of talk in our household as I grew up, must have brushed off on me so that a little later, out in Iowa, I felt it in my bones. At the time, I must confess, I was beginning to feed on quite another literature, the stuff American boys began with, the Rover Boy series of juvenile novels and, above all, the works of Horatio Alger, Jr. Is that name forgotten today? Almost. But when I was a boy, before the First World War, Alger's books were a constant delight. We youngsters read them avidly. They became our gospel. It was in them that we first learned the wonders of the American success story, of the inevitable rise from rags to riches

[1] Some of the painters, too, who would give us a vigorous Midwest native art between the two world wars: Thomas Hart Benton, born in the Ozarks of Missouri; John Steuart Curry, born on a Kansas farm; Grant Wood, prevailing over poverty in the Iowa town we would shortly move to.

if a boy was only earnest, diligent, thrifty, hard-working and believed in the glittering promise of American life. The heroes of all the books—there were more than a hundred of them, with such titles as *Bound to Rise, Luck and Pluck, Sink or Swim, Tom the Bootblack,* and they sold a total of twenty million copies—were identical: a boy born poor, early becoming fatherless, forced to earn his own living when he was fifteen, cheated on his way up by innumerable villains and beset by evil temptations, but in the end, by force of character and ambition and unending toil, rising to wealth and power.

Could it all be true? I used to ask my father. Sometimes he would hesitate and then say that if I didn't believe the Alger heroes—the rise of Tom the Bootblack, say—one had only to look around to see parallels in real life. It had actually happened, he said, to Andrew Carnegie, John D. Rockefeller and Edward Harriman, to cite but three examples of penniless boys who by hard work and vision had ended up as multimillionaires, building vast fortunes on steel, oil and the railroads. Alger's tall tales were, of course, trash, trashily written. But it would take some years to get the illusions he created out of my youthful system. I suspect some of my contemporaries never succeeded in that. The American success story, which they first learned from Horatio Alger, Jr., became a part of them, however much in the end they may have failed. They fervently continued to believe in it to the bitter end.

There was something else that lent excitement to growing up in the first years of the century. Life not only in Chicago, the Midwest and America but in the whole Western world was experiencing swift and sweeping changes that overnight, so to speak, utterly transformed it, ushering in an era that was scarcely recognizable to the old, which materially, except for steam power and the railroads, had remained pretty much the same for centuries. The inventiveness of man in mechanics suddenly burst forth. The imagination of even a child was kindled. The new inventions of grown-up men were more exciting than the most sophisticated of our toys.

In 1903, the year before I was born, the Wright brothers had flown the first airplane above the sands of Kitty Hawk, North Carolina, and in Detroit a tinkerer named Henry Ford had built his first automobile for what seemed then an unpromising market. That year, too, brought the first movie with a connected story,

The Great Train Robbery, which few saw because there were no motion-picture houses in existence. It was shown in a handful of vaudeville houses and shabby vacant stores soon to be transformed into "nickelodeons." The advent of the flying machine was overlooked by the big-city press, as was for a time the possibilities of wireless, which had been invented in 1895 by an Italian physicist, Guglielmo Marconi. Hard-nosed American newspaper editors believed that airplanes and the wireless were too fantastic to be real and that motion pictures were merely a passing fad.

Not until 1908, five years after the first flight at Kitty Hawk, did they send reporters out to see what those cranks, the Wright brothers, were up to, though by that time they had built several machines and flown them successfully over Ohio. We boys playing in the streets of Chicago were certainly aware of them. We were flying little planes powered by rubber bands. On September 27, 1910, according to my father's diary—a day I have never forgotten—he took us to Grant Park, by the lake, to see our first "aerial show." A half-dozen sputtering little biplanes flew back and forth. I thought it was the most wonderful thing I had ever seen. Not so my father. As the little planes buzzed about overhead he muttered: "If God had wanted us to fly he would have given us wings."

His view of the motorcar, as I have mentioned, was equally dim. He thought it ought to be banned from the streets of Chicago[1] so that they would be safe for kids to play in and for horses and buggies to proceed unmolested. Sometimes on weekends

---

[1] It had made its first appearance on those streets long before he arrived—in 1892 —when William Morrison of Des Moines, Iowa, apparently the first in the country to build an electric motorcar, brought it to the big city. At first the Chicagoans could not believe their eyes. A local newspaper described the startling appearance:

> Ever since its arrival the sight of a well-loaded carriage moving along the streets at a spanking pace with no horses in front, and apparently with nothing on board to give it motion, was a sight that has been too much, even for the wide-awake Chicagoan. . . .
> So great has been the curiosity that the owner when passing through the business section has had to appeal to the police to aid him in clearing the way.

The sight of the new contraption moving along on its own "with no horses in front" was what astounded people. The U.S. Army took no chances. In 1899 it announced: "Three automobiles have been purchased by the War Department for the use of officers. Each is equipped so that a mule may be hitched to it, should it refuse to run."

when he was working with us on the front lawn, we would pause to watch a car noisily chug by. "They ought to be outlawed!" he would mutter, and resume his gardening. But of course, as time would shortly show, that was like King Canute wanting to stem the tides of the sea. The automobile would soon swamp America and alter it beyond my father's imagination.

The Ford was the first car I remember by name, though there were others whose names I've forgotten, some propelled by steam or electricity. In 1909 Henry Ford started to turn out the first of his fifteen million low-priced Model T's that were to push the country into the automobile age and make it possible for the first time for most Americans to own a car. Our family eventually bought one. It was an ugly contraption. It shook and rattled. To many it was a joke and indeed the canny Ford got his greatest promotion out of publishing an annual book of jokes about the Tin Lizzie, as it came to be called. From the beginning he believed that the key to success in the motorcar industry was to produce a low-priced vehicle that most Americans could afford. And as the Model T came off the assembly line in increasing numbers, the price went down: from $950 at first to $550 in 1913 to $365 in 1916. And profits went up: to $25 million in 1913, to $30 million in 1914, to $59 million in 1916. By 1926 the Ford Motor Company had a *cash* balance of more than $300 million.

Henry Ford became a legendary figure in my youth, but not always because of his genius at producing low-priced cars. He had his odd quirks. I remember reading about some of them on the front pages. For a time he ran an avowedly anti-Semitic magazine called the *Dearborn Independent,* in which the Jews were held responsible for most of the ills of this world. During the Great War, Ford sent off a "Peace Ship" filled with an odd assortment of pacifists to Europe to try to stop the slaughter, a well-meant but preposterous mission. At the beginning of 1914 he provoked apoplexy among the leaders of the eastern financial and industrial establishment by doubling wages at the Ford plants: $5 for an eight-hour day against the prevailing wage of $2.34 for nine hours.

The New York Times bemoaned the step. "The theory of the management of the Ford Motor Company is distinctly Utopian," it said, "and runs against all experience." It predicted "strikes and unrest in the shops of other companies" and "certain failure for the experiment so manifestly based upon a vision of universal uplift through a single venture in the field of beneficence." *The Wall Street Journal* was horrified. It thought Ford's doubling of wages was un-Christian. "To double the minimum wage, without regard to length of service, is to apply Biblical or spiritual principles where they do not belong."

So those of my age grew up in America with the motorcar and with the airplane, though the latter was slower to develop. We saw them revolutionizing transportation and, indeed, a part of our lives. The horse-and-buggy age faded away. My father wasn't happy about it but he kept abreast of what was going on, and often when he came home from work, he would read to us from the newspapers and try to explain the latest events in what often must have seemed to him a cockeyed world. I have a dim memory of him trying to explain to us one Sunday morning after church a phenomenon called "wireless." This must have been on an October day in 1907 when the first press wireless message was flashed across the ocean to *The New York Times* and the story was front-paged in the Chicago newspapers. Marconi's discovery, which had been greeted with general skepticism when first announced eleven years before, had at last proved practical. It, too, would radically change our world.

Later my father would take me to a friend of his who had built a wireless set in his attic and who, miraculously, it seemed to me, could receive dots and dashes over the air from distant places and translate them for us into words. It was to me as exciting as the airplane.

Beyond these mechanical inventions that were beginning to change our way of life drastically, there occurred five breakthroughs in pure science around the turn of the century, of which little was known at the time except among a handful of scientists in Europe and America. These were even more important than the mechanical discoveries, for eventually—within fifty years—they changed our world more than in all the previous time of man on earth. As Albert Szent-Györgyi would later put it, they marked the beginning of a new period in man's history: the discovery in 1895 of X rays, in 1896 of radioactivity, in 1897 of electrons, in 1900 the quantum theory by Max Planck and in 1905 the theory of relativity by Albert Einstein.

So in this, too, the turn of the century was a great dividing line. In the brief space of ten years was revealed a world that could not be experienced by our senses or measured by simple rulers or thermometers or perceived by the mathematics and physics of Newton. For the first time man became aware of a cosmos whose existence he had not suspected and to which his senses gave him no clue. He slipped into it not only as a stranger but without the faculty of understanding it. All he knew, and still knows, is that a few men of genius have found it exists and have penetrated some of its secrets.

Even had I been older, and heard of them, I could not have grasped the significance or meaning of these breakthroughs in theoretical science that were occurring around the time I was born. I am sure that neither my father nor his friends at the University of Chicago grasped them either, if they heard of them—with two exceptions. Professor Albert A. Michelson won a Nobel Prize in 1907 and Professor Robert Millikan another one in 1923 for their discoveries in the field first cultivated by Planck, Einstein and others. I believe my father knew both of these scientists over at the university, but probably their work was beyond his understanding. It would have been incomprehensible to him, as to most others, that as the twentieth century, so full of bright promises, began, we were being thrown into a cosmic world that man was not prepared by millenniums of experience for and in which perhaps he could not for long survive. Father could not possibly have imagined what we in the final third of the century have had to take for granted: that a mad American President or a mad Russian Chairman could press a nuclear button and in an hour or two exterminate man from the earth.

Certain happenings in the world, which Father read to us before we were old enough to follow the newspapers ourselves, were as exciting to us as the coming of the motorcar, the airplane and the wireless. One was the news on September 6, 1909, that Commander Peary had reached the North Pole on April 6. He had telegraphed the word to New York as soon as his ship made port in Labrador five months after the discovery. Though still a very young child, I can remember how the news electrified the city and no doubt the country. Around our house and among the boys I played with on the street, we talked of nothing else. For more than twenty years, explorers had been trying to get to the Pole; Peary himself had made eight attempts, and only the year before, in 1908, Dr. F. A. Cook had claimed that he had reached the Pole. For the next couple of years even we youngsters at school and at play in vacant lots argued and fought over who had reached the Pole first, Dr. Cook or Commander Peary. In the end the good doctor, we were told, was proved a fraud. Apparently he had never got near the Pole.[1]

The next year, 1910, when I was six and had enrolled in first grade in the neighborhood public school, the talk turned to Halley's Comet, then flashing across the sky. Newspapers speculated whether this time it might hit the earth and perhaps destroy it. This provoked the first great fright of my life. Was the world to come to an end just when I was getting started in it? One boy who sat at a desk near mine said his father predicted that the comet would collide with the earth and finish it—finish us all— off. I remember coming home from school frightened to death and waiting for my father to come home from work so I could ask him if my companion's father was right and that we were doomed. Father brushed off the threat. Halley's Comet, he said, had been making passes at the earth for centuries but had never come very near. There was nothing to fear. But for months I had nightmares in which I saw the comet hitting the earth in one blinding flash. And as soon as I was old enough—my fears apparently still lingering—I looked up the comet in a boy's book of astronomy. It had been observed as early as 1066, the book said, had passed very near to earth in 1456, when its great tail stretched out over 60 degrees of the sky and looked like a gigantic saber, and had been identified in 1682 by the British astronomer

---

[1] Nearly three-quarters of a century later, in the 1970's, one was not so sure. Evidence was unearthed that Dr. Cook may well have got to the Pole, or near to it, as he claimed. But against the endorsement of Peary by the U.S. Navy, the President of the United States, and the National Geographic Society, which had sponsored Peary's expedition, the lonely Dr. Cook could scarcely get a fair hearing and the press denounced him as a fraud. His stock plummeted when he was convicted of using the mails to defraud the public in an oil exploration in Texas and was sentenced to twelve years in Leavenworth prison, which he served. Two reputable authors who investigated the life story of Cook, Andrew A. Freeman in *The Case for Doctor Cook* (1961) and Hugh Eames in *Winner Lose All: Dr. Cook and the Theft of the North Pole* (1973), believe that he was innocent in the Texas case, that he was indeed the first to reach the North Pole and that he was probably one of the "most unjustly put-upon figures in American history."

Edmund Halley, after whom it is now named. Halley predicted that it would appear every seventy-six years, and it has. It will be back in 1986 but perhaps it will not frighten the youngsters as it did us in 1910. The world, even of boys, is less innocent today.

There was another happening that brought us a sinking feeling of the danger lurking in our world. On the night of April 14–15, 1912, the *Titanic*, the world's largest and most luxurious ocean liner, en route from England to New York on its maiden voyage, struck an iceberg in the North Atlantic and sank with the loss of 1,500 of its 2,200 passengers and crew. It was the worst disaster at sea in history. For days the story dominated the front pages of the Chicago newspapers—by this time I read them avidly—and people talked of nothing else. How could it happen, they asked, to a giant liner that had been advertised as unsinkable. Hundreds had drowned because there were not enough lifeboats for everyone. They had not been thought necessary on an "unsinkable" ship. From that disaster the Atlantic iceberg patrol was created and stringent new regulations requiring lifeboats on all ships for all passengers and crew.

There was one other event, and one in which my father directly participated, that he talked to us a good deal about. This was the U.S. government's lawsuit against Standard Oil of Indiana, one of the first cases he worked on as an Assistant Federal Attorney in Chicago. We could always tell when Father was involved in an important lawsuit. His efforts to hide his feelings and the strain he was under were of no avail. He would be slightly irritable and somewhat sharp with us. Apparently he had been that way during the Standard Oil trial. But, as my mother later told it, he had come home in a happy mood the day (April 3, 1907) Judge Kenesaw Mountain Landis found Standard Oil of Indiana guilty (on 1,462 counts of accepting rebates) and fined it the whopping sum of $29,240,000, the largest fine in the history of American law. Father often talked to me a little later about the case and once took me to visit the celebrated judge, whom he much admired but who struck a little terror in him, as in other lawyers, when he faced him at the bar. Notwithstanding, the two men became good friends outside the courtroom. Landis, then nearing fifty, was a stern, gaunt man who resembled the portraits of Andrew Jackson, but in his chambers the morning my father took me in to see him, he seemed to melt, putting aside the work at his desk to talk to me about school and play and whether I was following the White Sox. Like my father, he loved baseball in general and the White Sox in particular (their stadium was not far from us on the South Side), and later, when that team accepted bribes and became the "Black Sox" after the 1919 World Series scandal, Landis left the federal bench to become the first commissioner of baseball, to clean up the game and restore public confidence in it.

Judge Landis' unprecedented fine of Standard Oil of Indiana was set aside as excessive by a Court of Appeals in 1908, much to my father's disappointment. But I remember his satisfaction in 1911—by this time he had begun to discuss a good many things with me—when the U.S. Supreme Court dissolved the parent Standard Oil Company. He apparently thought that at last the power of monopolies was broken. He didn't live long enough to see how mistaken he was. He would have been surprised, I'm sure, to see that, dissolved though it was supposed to be by order of the Highest Court, Standard Oil of New Jersey, the parent company, continued to thrive.

This would become a familiar pattern. Part of the story of America, I would begin to learn, and continue to learn to the end, was the power of the giant corporations to defy the supposedly more powerful federal government and, when that occasionally failed, to side-step the application of its laws. The tricks of highly paid corporation lawyers—honorable men mostly, no doubt, but, like their employers, carried away by their greed for monopolistic profits in this land of milk and honey—usually won out.

Always in my youth there were fires in Chicago. Buildings were always burning down. One of my first memories is of the excitement we had watching fire engines drawn by four huge horses racing down Drexel Boulevard, their bells clanging, their hoofs clanking on the brick pavement. In 1871, the city had been all but destroyed by a great fire, which became part of the lore of all boys growing up in the city. Often my father recounted the story of the burning, of how it had started when Mrs. O'Leary's cow kicked over the lantern while she was milking in the barn, igniting the straw and setting a fire in De Koven Street, in the Irish section, from which, fanned by high winds, it spread over the city, laying waste the business section, leaping the river to the North Side, until a vast area of more than three square miles with seventeen thousand buildings lay smoldering in ashes and a hundred thousand people—a third of the population—were homeless.

Another Chicago fire, with a greater loss of life, affected my father personally. On Christmas Day, 1903, he noted in his diary: "Call from Bessie and Nina Chapman." They were, I believe, his second cousins and, as he later told me, they had come to Chicago for the holidays and wanted to see as much of the theater as possible. He had promised to take them to a matinee at the Iroquois Theatre to see Eddie Foy, one of his favorite comedians, who was playing in *Mr. Bluebeard*. Then his daughter, aged three and a half, had come down with whooping cough, and Mother, pregnant with me, was having dizzy spells, and he had begged off, telling his cousins he would send over two of the tickets he had bought. On December 30, he noted in his diary: "Iroquois Theatre Burned. 600 Lives Lost. Bessie and Nina Chapman Perished."

It was the most disastrous theater fire in the nation's history.

I grew up in Chicago under a father who was a strict disciplinarian and who seemed to a boy sometimes to be thwarting his freedom and his imagination. Corporal punishment was still the fashion in the best of families in those days and I received my share, usually a whack on the hands with the back of a hairbrush from my gentle mother when she was provoked into extreme action, and perhaps two or three "lickings" from my father which hurt more and were more humiliating since he wielded his razor strap with some vigor. After these I would be put to bed with no supper, feeling miserable and full of burning resentment against the perpetrators of such outrageous punishment. I recall these episodes, but I remember far better all the good times: playing cowboy and Indian in the nearby vacant lots, where we also dug caves, shooting marbles in the autoless streets or racing up and down them in scooters we made from roller skates, and in the winter, ice-skating on the Midway. Above all, there were the vacations that my parents shared with me, the glorious, long summer ones at Onekama, Michigan, far north on the opposite shore of Lake Michigan or, sometimes, before or after that, a month at my grandfather's farm at Mount Vernon, Iowa, where we helped to feed the cattle, pigs and chickens, climbed trees and nearly every day raced down the mile-long hill that descended steeply from Main Street in our "roller-coaster" wagons. Then we would hurry off to a swimming hole—one was in an abandoned stone quarry, another in the bend of a creek—take off our clothes and jump in. It was the highlight of the day. In those days in summer the old swimming hole became the center of our life. Two or three times we spent Christmas vacation on the farm, then deep in snow, and there was the new thrill of coasting down the hill on sleds or taking a ride in Grandfather's sleigh behind two horses, their bells tinkling, their noses and mouths belching white clouds of vapor in the icy, crisp air.

At Onekama, on a beautiful lake connected by a narrow channel with Lake Michigan, my father taught us how to swim, row, sail a boat and fish. It was there, when he was relaxed, that I got to know him best. In the boat, sailing or fishing, or on a picnic hike through the sandy countryside picking berries, he would tell tall tales or, sometimes, fascinate us with stories of his youth on an Iowa farm or at school and college, or of some of his recent cases in the court. He was a passionate fisherman, and occasionally when he returned, proud and beaming, with a big catch of muskellunge, bass or perch, my mother would tease him about "acting like a schoolboy." For me, and probably for him, the vacations ended all too soon.

Yet, as his diaries remind me, he was happy to get back to work. He loved the courtroom, its rough-and-tumble battles, its strategies, its often unexpected denouements. He was never happier than when crossing swords with a defense lawyer, trying to sway a jury or fencing with an unpredictable judge. Apparently he had no great concern for money and was never tempted to quit the federal attorney's office for the more lucrative jobs in the city's prestigious law firms, where corporation law was beginning to attract young lawyers who wanted to make money fast. He felt more at home fighting the corporations, with which the bulk of his cases were concerned. His salary as Assistant United States Attorney was extremely modest. I find in his papers a letter from the U.S. Attorney General in Washington, Charles J. Bonaparte, dated 1908: "Sir, Your compensation is hereby increased from $2,500 to $3,000 per annum, commencing April 1, 1908." At the time of his death, five years later, he was making $4,000. Multiply that by four or five times, it would still be a modest salary today, and a fraction of what he would have earned in private practice.

Slowly but steadily, Father got involved in politics, and I think toward the end his ambition grew in this field. In 1904 he was a sergeant at arms at the Republican convention in Chicago, which renominated Theodore Roosevelt for President,[1] and between the nomination and the election that year, he worked part-time for the Republican National Committee at a salary of twenty dollars a week. When, two years later, he got his federal appointment from the Roosevelt Administration, he continued to work, insofar as a government official was permitted, for the party. He joined the Hamilton Club, the Chicago citadel of Republicanism. He worked for the re-election of his district congressman, James R. Mann, author of the famous Mann Act against white slavery, who apparently was grooming him as his eventual successor. I imagine Father considered himself a "progressive" Republican, after the manner of his nominal boss in the White House, Teddy Roosevelt. Perhaps he had also taken note that the Republican Party offered him the most advantages. There had been only one Democrat in the White House—Grover Cleveland—since before the Civil War. "The Republican Party of Lincoln," I remember him saying once, "is the party of the future." (It would never, after I had grown up, be that for me.)

It was the debacle of the Republican Party in 1912, when Teddy Roosevelt broke away from President Taft to run on a Progressive ticket and thus, by splitting the Republican vote, assured the election of Woodrow Wilson, the Democratic candidate, that led my father to try for elective office. He could expect no advancement to the federal attorneyship with a Democrat in the White House, nor even perhaps hold his post for long as Assistant Attorney. The Democrats, out of office for so long, were hungry for jobs. Shortly after Woodrow Wilson's election in November, 1912, Father announced that he would be a candidate for the Republican nomination for alderman from the Seventh Ward. If he won, he said, he would use his position on the City Council to help clean up the city and curb the power of the likes

[1] As Vice-President, Roosevelt had succeeded McKinley in 1901 when the President was assassinated at the Buffalo Pan-American Exposition by an anarchist, Leon Czolgosz. When Mark Hanna, the Ohio millionaire and political boss who had masterminded McKinley's elections in 1896 and 1900, heard the news he exclaimed: "And now look, that damned cowboy is President of the United States!"

of Bathhouse John and Hinky Dink of the notorious First Ward. I believe Father saw the post as a stepping-stone to eventually going to Congress as successor to his friend Congressman Mann, who spoke of retiring. All that fall and early winter he campaigned informally, addressing meetings, stopping by at shops to chat with the proprietors and customers. Often he took me with him. Away from the shelter of home, it gave me one of my first glimpses of the world of grownups. I felt six feet tall.

Getting about a little made me gradually aware of how people dressed, what the women wore and the men and the children, and of the habits of our elders in their smoking and drinking, though it is difficult to remember clearly, and I have had to refresh my memory by going back to old catalogues and advertisements of the time. The dress is scarcely recognizable today, though it has changed less for men than for women. The ladies in those days imprisoned themselves in tightly laced whalebone corsets (these were supposed to give the female form the shape of an hourglass and a waist that could be "easily clasped with two hands"), long skirts that brushed the pavement, full-sleeved shirtwaists with a high, choking collar, layer upon layer of underclothing, black cotton or wool stockings, and large hats adorned with feathers or flower-and-ribbon arrangements and attached to the hair with "hatpins." Gradually women's skirts rose inch by inch above the ground, partly because the advent in the 1890's of the "safety" bicycle, which had replaced the high-wheel one, induced women to risk riding and they found that long skirts got tangled in the wire spokes. Even when women went bathing, they respected the proprieties. I still remember them on the beach at Onekama, wading into the water fully clothed in "bathing" costumes whose skirts fell below the knees, their legs stockinged, their feet in slippers.

Bobbed hair for women was unthinkable. Trousers for women were equally taboo. Most states had laws forbidding women to wear men's clothing. When a stout middle-class Iowa lady of Council Bluffs, Amelia Jenks Bloomer, wife of a prominent lawyer, began a crusade in the 1850's for more sensible women's clothing, and designed a form of female trousers later named after her, the bloomer, she was denounced by the preachers, jeered at in the press, and finally driven to transfer her battle to England, where she fared no better. Another American woman, Dr. Mary Walker, who had served as a nurse in the Civil War and found that in the field a woman had to wear men's clothing, was arrested several times for not abandoning it when peace came. It took a special Act of Congress to keep her out of jail.

Men's clothing in those days was almost as uncomfortable and forbidding as women's. A man wore a heavy three-piece woolen suit, usually black or dark-blue serge, the year around. Despite the heat of summer and the total absence of air conditioning, it had not yet dawned on a tailor or a clothes manufacturer to design a lightweight suit, though a few made flannel jackets and trousers, which afforded some relief. A man's shirt had a high, starched, detachable collar and detachable cuffs, hard as a board. If a man was a big shot in business or in politics he often drove to the office or to a meeting in a frock coat and high silk hat. The average man was less formal and sported a derby hat, changing it when summer came to a hard straw hat or a Panama. He never went out in the street hatless or without a necktie. More often than not, he wore buttoned shoes. A buttonhook lay on every man's dresser.

What did we children wear in those days? Judging from photographs, we boys wore blue-and-white sailor suits until we were four or five (the girls wore middy blouses until they were much older) and for children's parties we were dressed in ridiculous "Lord Fauntleroy" suits. At six, boys graduated into "knickers" and jacket, to which we were condemned until we entered high school at fourteen, when we received, proudly, our first pair of "long pants," which stamped us as men.

Few men and no women (except those regarded as "fallen") smoked cigarettes then. My father, I think, was typical. He was fond of cigars after dinner or at social affairs with men. At the office or while relaxing at home or on vacation he smoked a pipe, a habit I must have inherited for I have been an inveterate pipe-smoker since I was sixteen. A surprising number of American men chewed tobacco, and every office, hotel lobby, public building and even many a parlor in the home had a cuspidor, at which a man took careful aim and spit his tobacco juice. Visiting Europeans were horrified at the sight.

Though very different in temperament, my father and mother got along very well. There must have been much love and devotion between them and they were immensely loyal not only to each other but, I think, to marriage itself, which they regarded as sacred. Like all couples they quarreled occasionally. Two or three times I was the unhappy witness to, or eavesdropper on, an exchange of angry words, which only showed that they were human but which to me was a shattering experience, providing one of the first moments of fear in my life. It was a fear, I suppose, that a child gets that his parents might separate or divorce, though I'm sure they never faintly contemplated it. Divorces were much looked down on then in an American community and amongst one's friends, though there were not nearly so many of them as today—one in every twelve marriages in 1905 against one in three in 1970. I'm sure both Father and Mother looked forward to a long and happy life together. And to raising their three children, whom they adored but were too wise to spoil.

It is only now, as I look over what I have written in this chapter (and much that I've cut out), that I realize how big a figure in my early life my father was. He has crept into many of these pages on his own and dominated them, as I see now he did our family life. He was gone so early, when I was nine, that for the rest of my own long life he seemed a shadowy figure whom I had scarcely known. I remember some things. He was tall for those days, six feet, and slender, with black hair which he parted in the middle, bright, kindly eyes that sometimes grew contemplative and sad, a finely chiseled straight nose, a strong and sensuous mouth, and a strong chin.

After his death, his friends tried to sum up his character, and I recall something of it myself. The main attributes, some contradictory as in all human beings, were gentleness, patience, courage, firmness, industriousness, perseverance, and absolute honesty and integrity. His friends and associates spoke of his high ideals, his firm principles, to which he adhered rocklike without mistaking narrowness of view for principle. They said he was unostentatious, even in the midst of a courtroom battle, that even there, as a prosecutor, he had an innate sense of fairness that sometimes surprised the defense. They praised his dependability, his absolute loyalty to associates, friends and family. They marveled at the way he threw himself into whatever he was doing, civic work, church work, his work as prosecutor, without sparing himself. The *Chicago Tribune* thought it was the strain of the last case he prosecuted in the courts that brought his end.

Judging by the library he left, and his notebooks, he read a good deal of history and biography and some poetry, but few novels. He loved to read in classical Greek and Latin. His books in those now almost dead languages are heavily marked with under-linings and filled with marginal comments. They must have ab-sorbed a good deal of his reading time. How he found time for general reading, after the long hours he must have spent reading the law in preparation for his court cases, and considering the time he spent with his children, I don't know. We saw a lot of him week-ends and during vacations when he played with us, taught us carpentry in his tool shop in the cellar, went ice-skating with us in the winter, rowing on the lagoons of Jackson Park in the summer, and, as I have mentioned, shared his love of fishing and boating with us.

In these days since Freud, when it is customary to blame one's complexes, faults and failures on the hostility between a child and his father or mother, or both, I cannot offer that excuse for my own shortcomings. I admired and loved both my parents, not excessively or obsessively, but genuinely. There was no re-sentment, no feeling of hostility or neglect. Ours was a closely knit family. Perhaps this was partly because the pace of life was slower in those days and without the jarring distractions of auto-mobiles, movies, radio and TV, and the other gadgets which people take for granted today and which consume so much of their lives. Parents had more time for their youngsters. We liked one another's company and all the good talk in the household. We were spared that phenomenon of family life around the TV with everyone, young and old, gawking for hours at the inanities of the idiot box. If my father had lived, I probably would have rebelled against him, at least against his conservatism and his strait-laced principles, but that, too, I was spared.

What were my father's influences on me, assuming that noth-ing is inherited? It is hard to say. Perhaps the greatest were the sense of honesty, integrity, modesty, tolerance, and the love of music, learning, literature and life.

Then on a gray, wintry day in the middle of February, 1913, with the snow piled up along the streets and sidewalks, an abrupt change came, and the wondrous world I had known in Chicago for nine years came to a sudden end. Toward the end of January, Father had become ill and taken to bed, the first time this had ever happened in our house. He was exhausted by the strain of a big case in which he had been the chief government prosecutor, a trial which the newspapers had been front-paging for weeks and on which he had worked night and day for months. He complained of an excruciating pain on the right side of the abdomen. The doctors diagnosed it as an intestinal and stomach ailment brought about by nervous exhaustion. They duly prescribed medicine to take care of it, but as events turned out it did more harm than good. For days we listened with growing apprehension to my father in the upstairs bedroom groaning from pain. This, too, was a new experience for us, for he was a stoic man. Finally my mother, in desperation, called in one of Chicago's leading physicians, Dr. Billings. He took one look at my father, felt his abdomen and sides, quickly diagnosed appendicitis and called an ambulance to take him to the hospital for an emergency operation to remove the appendix. Before the ambulance reached the hospital the appendix burst and peritonitis set in. Surgeons removed the organ and put Father on the "critical" list.

It is amazing how little was known about appendicitis in medical circles in those days. Today it is scarcely more serious than infected tonsils that have to be removed. It is easily diagnosed, the operation is routine and a patient is out of the hospital within four or five days. But in 1913 not much was known about it, it was not easily diagnosed, and the operation was considered a serious one, from which many died.

For the first time in our lives we were faced with the prospect of Father's death—something a nine-year-old boy can scarcely conceive, and I couldn't. Two or three times we children were led into Father's room in the hospital and his stricken face and unrecognizable, feeble voice struck terror in us. Still, the doctors said he was making a game fight for his life. His stamina and will to live might carry him through. Ten days after the operation it seemed that they had. When we saw him again he looked a little better, there was more strength in his voice, a little color in his cheeks. He smiled at us and assured us he would be home in a few days. We felt an immense relief. Mother, stoic from the outset, relaxed for the first time, taking us to an ice-cream parlor on the way home. On February 12 the *Evening Post* published a heartening news item.

Seward S. Shirer, Assistant United States District Attorney, is pronounced out of danger by physicians in attendance at the Washington Park Hospital. Mr. Shirer was operated on for appendicitis about two weeks ago. His condition had been critical and for a time his life was despaired of.

At home we rejoiced at the good news. We began to make preparations for his homecoming. Mother talked of taking Father to Southern California to recuperate and said she would take us along to see the "Wild West" for the first time. At school, where I had sat brooding in the fourth-grade class, unable to follow the lessons, my spirits revived. But not for long. Scarcely had we taken in the good news when the bad news followed. The poison of peritonitis, which had seemed checked, began to spread. Specialists were called in, a second operation was performed, but to no avail. At 12:40 on the morning of February 18, six months short of his forty-second birthday, two days before his fourteenth wedding anniversary, Father died. My mother, his father and brother, and the United States Attorney, James H. Wilkerson, were at his side. We children were awakened during the night and told. I simply could not comprehend that my father was gone for good.

"He died in the prime of life," I heard our Presbyterian minister intone at the private funeral service held in the living and dining room of our home, which followed a Masonic memorial service at the Woodlawn Park Lodge, where all the eulogies that accompany a man to his grave had been spoken. But I could not quite believe that he had died. Somehow I felt that by some miracle, like one in the Bible, he would come back to us. Not until a few days later, when we went to the Woodlawn Cemetery for a brief ceremony of cremation and I saw in the ashes all that was left of his physical being, did I accept his death as final.

It seemed to me such a senseless thing—then and forever after. The more I thought about it as I grew older, the more it confirmed for me the meaninglessness of life, its pointlessness. My father thought as he lay dying, I was told, that it was God's will and accepted it. I did not. If in his case it was God's will, how could you believe in the justice of God? What justice was there in snatching away a man at forty-one who had prepared so long and so well for life and who was just at the point of fulfilling himself? Should not a man be born to fulfill himself? Otherwise, why be born and struggle so to no end?

A world itself died with my father in 1913, or shortly thereafter, for the next year there came the Great War, which left the world my father had known in shambles. For two generations man in the Western world had lived in peace. Human beings had faith in themselves, in God, in the future; they had a sense of security. They believed that progress was the eternal law of life and that despite a few flaws in society the human race was moving inexorably along a splendid road that led toward a promised land where everyone would be free, happy and even well-off. Science, technology, invention, promised a millennium. Machines would liberate human beings from drudgery and give them a life of abundance, freeing them for the pursuits of leisure. The advances of medicine would ensure longer life and a healthier one. The rapid development of long-distance transportation and communication by the railroads, fast transatlantic liners, the telegraph, telephone and wireless, and the promise of automobiles and even airplanes, would bring men together from the far corners of the country and indeed of the globe and make them good neighbors. Never since the Renaissance had man's creative genius flowed so richly. Doubts were few, and later, in our own age of doubt, Osbert Sitwell, the poet, could look back on what he remembered as the golden age before 1914 and marvel at its high spirits, the grace and beauty of life, the absence of disillusionment.

My father had lived in that kind of a time. It had not known world wars, cold wars, revolutions, genocide, Fascism, Communism, totalitarian dictators and nuclear bombs. So far as the world was concerned, Father died, I am sure, in complete peace of mind. He could not have faintly imagined that a year later the assassination of Archduke Ferdinand, of whom he probably had never heard, at Sarajevo, a faraway Balkan town of whose existence he undoubtedly was totally unaware, would cause the earth he thought so reasonable and good to be littered with the shattered corpses of millions of men who had been as decent, as innocent, as full of faith and hope as he. Nor could he have had the slightest foreboding that this senseless mass slaughter would be repeated on an even greater scale a quarter of a century later in a second world war, that thereafter the children of the planet would live in fear of the world being reduced to ashes in an hour or two by the nuclear bomb, and that as the century approached its three-quarter mark, his own country, the richest and most militarily powerful nation in the world by that time, could, while professing its love of peace, devastate with its bombs and shells a faraway little peasant country in Asia that had never even threatened to harm us. Nor could he, an honest, forthright man, foresee a President of the United States brainwashing his people into believing that "war is peace."

A few American writers and philosophers, as we have seen, were beginning to warn in the first decade of the century that in America, despite its blessings and achievements, things were far from right. But I do not believe my father heard them. I doubt if he noted, for instance, that William Dean Howells, the dean of American letters, whom he certainly admired, was arriving at the bitter conclusion that civilization was coming out all wrong in the end and that he abhorred it. Nor would he have agreed, if he had known, with what Mark Twain, one of his favorite authors, was writing in private, that "the damned human race is a race of cowards," that civilization had been corrupted by the grab for wealth, that the American dream had collapsed. On the contrary, Father died, I am certain, in the belief that the American dream was coming true.

A few weeks later my mother rented the house in Chicago and we packed off in time for the second semester of school to her parents' home in Cedar Rapids. There among the rolling cornfields of Iowa I was to grow up and come of age.

BOOK THREE

GROWING UP IN IOWA, 1913–1925

Cedar Rapids in the spring of 1913, when we arrived, was a sprawling Iowa town of thirty-five thousand lying on the banks of the Cedar River in the heart of the Corn Belt amidst one of the richest farmlands on earth. Dominating the skyline against the surrounding hills were the towering grain elevators, twelve stories high, of Quaker Oats, the largest cereal mill in the world. A bustling business district four blocks wide, dotted here and there with an office building six to ten stories high, ran up from the river an equal distance to the railroad tracks, where all day long and through the night rumbled the passenger and freight trains of four major railroads, one of them the trunk line of the Chicago and North Western, which carried the transcontinental trains from Chicago to Omaha and thence by the Union Pacific to the West Coast. To get to or out of the business section one had to cross the tracks at the peril of one's life and often wait for a quarter of an hour or more for a long freight train to pass. The flagman—there were no traffic lights then—at each of the half-dozen street crossings was a familiar figure, waving his red flag at the approach of a train during daylight and a red lantern at night. When it rained or snowed, especially at night, it was difficult to see his dim warning signal, and you took your chances. Many a limb was lost and not a few lives on the gamble.

The town, clean, conservative, complacent, churchy and mostly Protestant, prosperous and growing, was dominated by the merchants and the bankers, the manufacturers and the realtors, many of whose pioneer families had made their first pile from soaring real-estate values when the site grew steadily from a

128

river village to a busy "metropolis," the marketing center of east-central Iowa. These early settlers had bought considerable stretches of land for next to nothing, often at the government price of $1.25 an acre, and later sold it for five, ten, a hundred, a thousand times more when their farms were broken up into small but costly lots for businesses, factories and homes.

Now, at the time of our arrival, their children and grandchildren lived in great white-frame or red-brick Victorian houses along the wide elm-shaded streets which sloped up beyond the tracks and they were beginning to move to even greater homes on the hilly, wooded outskirts. They were beginning, too, to abandon their handsome carriages and prancing horses for the automobile: electric coupes, Stanley steamers and noisy, chugging gasoline-driven rigs.

Though I had occasionally visited the town on vacation when we lived in Chicago, I felt a complete stranger as we, my mother, brother, sister, and I, alighted from the train at the Union Station into the welcoming arms of my gray-haired grandparents, who helped gather our baggage and drove us away in a horse-drawn cab. My mother looked as depressed as I felt. She had not yet recovered from the trauma of her husband's sudden death and the collapse of all her dreams. She was returning by force of circumstances to her parents and to her hometown, which she must have felt she had outgrown after the exciting married years in Chicago. She had discussed the prospects with us, young as we were, during those bleak February days after Father died. He had left her with $10,000 of life insurance and the house in Chicago, valued at $6,500, which she could rent for $50 a month. There seemed to be only one way out: to go back to her birthplace and her parents and with their help try as best she could to raise her three young children there.

From the Union Station you could see a large sign, erected by the Chamber of Commerce to catch the eye of the tens of thousands who passed by on the passenger trains of the four railroads: "CEDAR RAPIDS SUITS ME! IT WILL YOU!" So far as I was concerned, suddenly jerked away from the great city to this rural place, that remained to be seen.

Gradually, as I grew up, I learned a little about the town. Though its Chamber of Commerce and its other boosters, who were legion, did not like to be reminded of it, Cedar Rapids had been founded by a notorious horse thief. The town's first citizen turned out to have been an unsavory character by the name of Osgood Shepherd, who arrived in 1837, the year before Iowa was designated by Congress as a territory and, the Indians having been driven out, opened for settlement by white Americans. Shepherd built a log cabin by the side of the rapids after which the town would be named, fetched his wife and two children the following year, and enlarged his crude hut into a "tavern." Though business was good, with hundreds of pioneers stopping to rest their horses and oxen and to refresh themselves before fording the river's rapids and pushing farther west, Shepherd's most lucrative business appears to have been stealing horses. According to a history of the town compiled by a pious Presbyterian minister who, as a boy, knew Shepherd, the tavern became a hangout for a number of hard-drinking, shady characters who had formed a gang of extremely successful horse thieves. Shepherd protected his interests with a trusty rifle, driving off settlers who tried to claim land nearby and intimidating all who tried to look too closely into his "horse-trading" business. Finally in 1841 he sold out his squatter's rights to a group of newcomers who had their eyes on the rapids as a source of water power for mills.

These new arrivals were of a different breed. Coming from the East after a stop or two in Ohio and Michigan, they were sober, upright Christians of some education who had a keen eye for the opportunities of business in the raw, undeveloped region. They saw that the rapids of the river, where it fell fourteen feet, was an ideal spot for building a dam and harnessing power that would turn the wheels of mills to saw lumber, grind wheat, oats and corn, and drive the looms for weaving wool. The raw material lay all around in the rich farming land that was just beginning to be tilled and grazed. The finished products could be sent down the river in flatboats to the Mississippi and from there to the great markets of the land. A thriving, growing town could rise by the river's banks. Later, railroads, which already were being built in the East, might come in and open new possibilities. The town site lay directly west of Chicago, from which thousands of pioneers were moving westward across the Mississippi and into the newly proclaimed Territory of Iowa and beyond.

Seven settlers had bought out Shepherd and his land along

the rapids. From them, and a dozen or so others whom they persuaded to come out from the East in the 1840's and 1850's to contribute capital and skills in building the dam and the mills, set up shops, develop transportation, organize the town, and stimulate the growing of crops and livestock on the fertile land all around, came most of what in my time were known as "the first families." My mother had often described them to my father, but he was not much interested, having got away from the small-town Iowa life, with its narrow little elites, as soon as he could.

These first families formed a closely knit group. They intermarried. They formed partnerships for one new enterprise after another. Their wealth increased. They owned most of the land and most of the important businesses. They built railroads and a steamboat line. They set up newspapers. They established Protestant churches. They founded a college. They built hotels and one of them built the Opera House, which for half a century was the pride of the state and in which I as a youngster would hear most of the great singers, musicians and stage notables of the world. Like the aristocracy in Europe, they strengthened their hold by bringing in fresh blood occasionally: suitable husbands for their daughters and energetic young entrepreneurs with the capital and the drive to start new industries. The mill of one of the latter became and remained the home of Quaker Oats. The plant of another became for fifty years the largest meat-packing house west of Chicago.

And if in the beginning these hardy pioneers had little education and less culture and no time or means to acquire much, by my time their children or grandchildren were packing their youngsters off to the Ivy League colleges in the East, subsidizing the local appearance of symphony orchestras, of musicians like Paderewski and Kreisler, of stage luminaries such as Sarah Bernhardt, and the beginnings of a poverty-stricken young painter who eventually would become known throughout the land. They knew how to hold on to their money and multiply it, and yet many of them were generous in their contributions to the welfare of the town, seeing to it, among other things, that the community had public schools as good as any in the country, and that the hospital was first-rate. They gave liberally to the Public Library, after Carnegie had provided the funds for the spacious building, and to churches, the Y.M.C.A. and the Y.W.C.A., the Boy and

Girl Scouts, and other good works which help make life bearable in the small communities, especially for the restless young, and keep the common people more or less content with their lot.

And yet as I grew to manhood in the town, I would find them, full of Christian zeal though they were, unduly conservative, rigid and complacent, somewhat smug, a little snobbish and determined to clamp down on the rest of us a deadly conformity to their narrow mores, which is one mark of all our small towns and which in the end I declined to accept. I came to feel that our local aristocracy, if you could call it that, was, for all its assumption of superiority, based merely on money, as it was elsewhere in the land. At any rate, it had built the town from raw beginnings and now lorded over it.

In 1841, the year the seven settlers had bought out the squatter horse thief, one of them purchased four thousand bushels of wheat, put it on three flatboats and ventured down the river to the Mississippi and thence to St. Louis and finally to New Orleans, where he sold it. It was the hamlet's first business venture, accomplished even before the first gristmill was set up by the dam. Two years later the first paddle-wheel steamboat, the *Maid of Iowa,* arrived below the rapids with fifty passengers and one hundred tons of cargo. Most of the passengers, including a Methodist minister, remained, were given free lots to build on, and doubled the population. An outlet for the town's goods and cheap transportation for what it imported had been found. For several years the traffic on the river thrived. To get in on a good thing, the local businessmen, most of them the original settlers, had their own paddle-wheel steamer built at Pittsburgh at a cost of twenty thousand dollars, a shallow-draft 155-footer, piloted it down the Ohio River and up the Mississippi and the Cedar to the town, where it arrived the summer of 1858 with eighty-four passengers and three hundred tons of goods and was welcomed with a salute of cannon and fireworks and a general celebration. Before the river froze, the steamer made twelve round trips to St. Louis and greatly added to the growing prosperity of the town and to the bank accounts of the owners.

But, burning with enterprise as they were, they had already turned to a still better mode of transportation, which would quickly transform the village into a good-sized town. They had their eyes on the railroads, which were beginning to stretch out from Chicago toward the Mississippi. When the Chicago and North Western reached the river in 1856, the local leaders joined it in organizing the Chicago, Iowa and Nebraska railroad to extend the line westward through Cedar Rapids and eventually to Council Bluffs and Omaha, on the Missouri River.

On a typically hot summer day, June 15, 1859, the first railroad train chugged into Cedar Rapids from Chicago, its five crude passenger cars filled with dignitaries from as far away as New York. Almost all of the village's sixteen hundred inhabitants, swelled by two thousand more from the surrounding counties, including a band of Indians from the nearby Tama Reservation, turned out to greet it and join in the celebration of rejoicing. After inspecting the snorting, wood-burning "iron horse" and filing through the passenger cars, they assembled at the "grove" which rose a few blocks beyond the tracks and sat down at long tables under the elms to feast on barbecued oxen and imbibe the local apple cider. When the celebrants had recovered from their dinner, they gathered at Daniels Hall for a grand ball, which continued until dawn. It must have been the greatest binge the citizens of Cedar Rapids ever went on. In my youth old inhabitants were still talking of it. The town, as they said, had been made.

In the next ten years it more than tripled its population to seven thousand as the railroad brought in new inhabitants and sparked new business enterprises. In the following decade, when the same local promoters built four hundred miles of a new railroad, the Burlington, Cedar Rapids and Minnesota, eventually connecting the town with Minneapolis-St. Paul in the north and St. Louis and Kansas City in the south, the town doubled in numbers. It was becoming a bustling little hub, with access by rail to the north, east, south and west. Manufacturing enterprises, powered by new steam plants, sprang up like mushrooms. The surrounding farmers, of whom my grandfather Shirer was one, began to ship their corn and hogs by rail to Chicago, where they fetched good prices. In return they received shipments of farm machinery at much less cost than previously. Major railroads eventually took over the local lines. By the time of my arrival the town was served by four of them: the North Western, the Rock Island, the Milwaukee and the Illinois Central.

· ·

An energetic, imaginative, driving, acquisitive, God-fearing man by the name of George Greene had by my time in Cedar Rapids been established in the minds of the populace as the town's first citizen. Its true founder, the squatter Shepherd, whom Greene and his six fellow-settlers had bought out and sent on his horse-thieving way, had been pushed into limbo. By all accounts Greene was a remarkable person, the epitome of the early settlers, who in a few decades in the nineteenth century transformed the Midwest prairies of the Indians into one of the richest agricultural, commercial and industrial regions on earth.

Born in England in 1817, brought to Buffalo, New York, at the age of two, orphaned at ten, schooled for only four years in New York State "academies" but finding time to read law, he set out with his bride in 1838 for the Iowa Territory, settled near Cedar Rapids, acquired land, taught school, studied law, was admitted to the bar in 1840 and the same year was elected to the territorial legislature. He was twenty-three. The next year he induced six other settlers to join him in getting possession of the water-power site at the Cedar River rapids. From then until his death in 1880 he built up the town from nothing, owned or participated in most of its enterprises, built mills, bridges, railroads, steamboats, office buildings, industrial plants, hotels; started banks, a printing house, a newspaper, a church, even a college; directed real-estate businesses throughout the Mississippi Valley and one in New York City; practiced law not only in the town but for four years in Chicago; served as a justice of the Iowa Supreme Court for seven years; developed his thousand-acre farm on the outskirts of town into an experimental agricultural station and made a small fortune from its 150,000 fruit and ornamental trees; and fathered twelve children from two wives.

Though I was no hero-worshiper, I came to wonder, as I learned about the man, how on this crude frontier he could crowd so much into a life that ended at sixty-three. I could not help but admire his sheer creativity if not his acquisitiveness, and admire also his generosity, for he gave away much of his fortune in land and money to the community. The old man had died long before my time, but the Greene family, I believe, was still considered first, though it was no longer the richest, among the local gentry.

My mother's parents were not part of it. Though they were of solid English-Scottish-Welsh stock, they had arrived in Cedar

Rapids relatively late, three years after the Civil War. And they were—and remained—of modest means. Still, as I gradually learned, there was a good deal of American history wrapped up in their families that few among the town's elite could match. But they were very modest about it, especially my grandfather, Frank Tanner, to whom I took a liking at once.

The Tanners, from whom he was descended, had emigrated from Wales and the west of England in the middle of the seventeenth century and settled in Rhode Island soon after the establishment of that colony, being, according to a family genealogy book, "dissenters from the strictness of the Puritans and sympathizing with the liberal principles of Roger Williams." Grandfather, I soon saw, was far from being a puritan, and perhaps this quality struck me from the beginning of our friendship.

His great-grandfather had moved "upcountry" from Rhode Island to Connecticut in 1740, settling in an area called Cornwall, in the wooded, hilly northwest corner of the colony. By one of those coincidences with which life is so full, I bought a small farm near Cornwall after the Second World War and found to my surprise that not only the Tanners but my grandmother's forebears, the Lawrences, had been among the first settlers in the region in the 1740's. Until then I had paid scant interest to family history and genealogy—the subject did not interest me—but perhaps because of advancing age and my surprise at finding so much early family history in the neighborhood, when I had no idea it existed, I began to delve into my background among old county records and family papers. Frank Tanner's great-grandfather and father turned out to be characters who reminded one of much of the early American story.

The great-grandfather, a certain Thomas Tanner, had been born in 1741 in Cornwall, a few miles up the road from my farm. At eighteen he enlisted in a Connecticut regiment and served two years during the French and Indian War. By 1773, with war with the mother country threatening, he helped form in Cornwall a company of militia and when war broke out two years later he was appointed second lieutenant of the company and went off to fight under General Washington. He took part in the first battles of the war, at Long Island, the retreat to New York, Harlem, Washington Heights and Fort Washington, where, with more than two thousand Connecticut and Maryland troops, he was taken prisoner. Released after the war, he moved over the line to New York State and settled in New Lebanon, which by another coincidence is but a few miles from my present residence in the Berkshire Hills. There he resumed farming and building—he was a master carpenter—and became acquainted with the Shakers, several hundred of whom arrived in the settlement in 1787 and set up seven communities. Apparently he was puzzled by them but he admired them, for a family record comments: "A plain, honest and industrious people they have followed their principal occupation of agriculture, horticulture and broom manufacture. Though a singular order of society, they have been very peaceful and prosperous."

Perhaps the Shakers were a little too solemn for him, for in 1793 he removed to Cooperstown, New York. There my grand-father's father was born. The family genealogy book tells his story tersely: "He received an elementary education, married, followed farming and had four children. In 1852, affected by the prevalent 'gold fever of California' he started thither, 'via the cape,' but died at sea August 11, aged 47. He was an active and excellent christian man and his untimely death much lamented."

I don't believe much in heredity but I have been rather inter-ested to find that these two direct forebears were men of imagina-tion and even of adventure, one a combat soldier in our first two wars, the other seeking his fortune in the California gold rush and daring to set out in an old square-rigger on the dangerous voyage around the Horn. And in these days of soft living it was instruc-tive to learn in the family papers of a harder sort of life for one's forebears not so long ago. One family member recalled the "older times" in Cornwall and New Lebanon "where for a few years resided our ancestors in their log cabins, subsisting on coarse and scant fare, dressing in home-made linen and woolen, having few privileges of education and culture, enduring many deprivations and hardships, but living in joyful hope of better times and richer blessings."

And what wonderfuliy queer names they gave their children! William Tanner, brother of Thomas, who also grew up in Corn-wall, named some of his children Tryal, Ephraim, Ebenezer and Consider. His sister, Mehetabel, had a child she named Submit.

Frank Tanner was eight when his father died at sea. Thus my grandfather was left fatherless a year younger than I was to be.

He was pretty much on his own, as I was, from a tender age. In 1861, at seventeen, he enlisted in the Union Army, first as a drummer boy, and served in an infantry regiment throughout the war, participating in a number of major battles of which Gettysburg, with its great slaughter on both sides, remained implanted more than all the others in his mind.

More than half the books in his small library were devoted to the Civil War and many of these to the Battle of Gettysburg, which he often fought over again with some of his war-veteran cronies at the local chapter of the Grand Army of the Republic. Two or three times before he died that very year we arrived I persuaded him to fight it over with me. At first he was reluctant— probably he thought I was too young to understand—but finally he would get down his books, unroll his maps, and go over the battle from beginning to end, climaxing his recital with Pickett's bloody Confederate charge and telling how it was at last thrown back in the worst carnage he had ever seen. A modest man, not very articulate, on these occasions alone he became inspired and I would sit there spellbound, poring over the illustrations in the books and studying the maps, fighting the battle with him over every foot of ground.

According to the family lore he had been seriously wounded three times during the war, but he would never speak of this when I asked him, turning me away with Sherman's quip that war was hell and adding: "It wasn't fun, son, fighting in that war— don't let anyone tell you it was." But it was not long before I became aware that his four years in the field with the Union Army had been the one great adventure of his life. It was over for him at twenty-one, when adult life normally is just beginning. Mustered out in 1865, he returned to his hometown in upstate New York, two years later married the girl he had left behind, and, restless after so many years of excitement, set out for the West and settled in Cedar Rapids, where he earned a living as the Midwest representative of a glove manufacturing firm at Gloversville, New York.

Of Grandma Tanner's family I learned little, perhaps because she was the one woman in my life I grew to hate. But by another coincidence while I was living on my Connecticut farm after the war, I discovered that one of her forebears had been the first settler to move into northwest Connecticut above Cornwall and found the town of Canaan, where eventually he built a large frame house that still stands and which I pass frequently. He was a certain "Colonel" Lawrence, my grandmother's maiden name. Grandma talked occasionally about the "Lawrences of Massachusetts" and that sometimes aroused my grandfather to add: "Damned Anglican and Methodist bishops, those Lawrences!" And indeed some of them were, right down to my own day, but I remember the Lawrences from family and newspaper pictures, mostly from their rather bulbous noses with flaring nostrils. Grandmother was no exception. What we called the "Lawrence nose" gave them—and especially her—a somewhat mean countenance that I found unpleasant to look at.

And she was mean. She scolded and nagged not only her husband but me. She went further with me. We had scarcely settled in the household at 811 Second Avenue, across the street from the Sinclair mansion and a few doors below the Van Vechtens, when she took to cuffing me on the slightest pretext. I took the blows for several months, accepting the fact that this was the way of life when you were forced to live with an ugly old grandma. But then I began to brood at the outrageousness of it all, and one day it dawned on me that I was bigger and stronger than she. The next time she hit and shoved me, I decided, I would hit and shove back in self-defense. One morning she gave me a good punch and sent me sprawling to the floor of the living room. This was what I had been waiting for, and I felt good. I got up and faced her. "Grandma," I said, "this is the last time. You're never going to do that again."

"And why not, son?" she said, taken a little aback.

"Because . . ." and I whacked her in the cheek and pushed her across the room until she stumbled over a chair leg and fell flat on the floor, where she lay moaning and groaning until my mother came from the kitchen in answer to her cries. There was a terrible scene. I felt guilt swelling up my insides. I hadn't meant to knock her out. My mother and I knelt down beside her, and after my sister, frightened to death, had fetched some smelling salts, we revived her and carried her to bed, where she lay complaining the rest of the day. She never hit me again, and her scolding dropped way off. And though my mother gave me a good bawling out, I felt that secretly she sympathized.

One thing always puzzled me about this grandmother. Mean

and bitchy though she was, she had a passion for flowers and for raising them. From early spring to late fall she worked away at her flower borders: lilacs, peonies, roses and plantings for cut flowers. Her flower beds were neat and tidy and she weeded them daily. One of our differences was over my lack of enthusiasm in helping her. I hated weeding. But I had to admit that it paid off. Her flowers were admired up and down the neighborhood. Grandma not only kept the house filled with a dozen varieties of blossoms but gave large bouquets of them to the neighbors. She was justifiably proud of them. But how, I wondered, could a woman with such a passion for flowers be so nasty to human beings? If you loved the promise and the beauty of plants, why not show the same love and understanding toward your husband and grandchildren?

I hated her, but I loved my grandfather. He was a very gentle old man—incidentally, five years younger than she—with a sense of humor and a tolerance of others that included even his nagging wife. He never flared back at her scoldings, but with a wan smile on his lips below a spreading walrus mustache he would saunter off after one of her outbursts to his little den on the second floor at the top of the stairs, where he would sit at his desk smoking his pipe and read the newspapers or a book from his small bookcase, usually a volume on the Civil War. It seemed to me that he spent a lot of time there and I didn't blame him.

He was not at all an intellectual, as was my father. I believe he never went back to school when he returned from the war. Most of his subsequent life he spent on the road selling gloves for the Gloversville firm. By the time we arrived, in 1913, he had pretty much retired, apparently with just enough money in the bank to live comfortably in the large frame house with its four big bedrooms and a bath on the second floor, a bedroom for him and his wife on the first floor, which also had a bath, a large dining room, a larger sitting room and a spacious parlor, and outside of which ran a porch along the front and one side.

Porches were an integral part of one's house, of one's family life, in those days in those parts. On warm summer afternoons the ladies sat out on them in rocking chairs, fanning themselves, sipping lemonade or ice tea, and greeting, chatting with, or noting carefully those who passed by on the sidewalk and in their buggies or new automobile contraptions in the street. Everyone in town lived their summer afternoons in this way except the few notables whose large mansions were set well back from the street behind ivy-covered brick walls. On the unbearably hot Iowa summer evenings (when nearby farmers swore they could *hear* the corn growing) the old folks would gather again, the men now joining the women, in their rockers, fanning themselves with one hand and brandishing sticks of punk with the other to help keep off the mosquitoes. Some families screened in their porches but my grandmother was against it. "You can't see a soul through those screens," she would say.

I suspect my grandfather missed the old life on the road, with its good fellowship among the salesmen and traveling lawyers and judges in the smoking cars on the trains and in the lobbies and bars of the sprawling small-town hotels where he would put up for a day or two to display his wares. For if not exactly a backslapper, he was a warm and friendly man.

He still liked to saunter down to a saloon on a late afternoon before dinner to have a friendly drink or two, usually with G.A.R. veterans—a practice which drove my grandmother into paroxysms, for she was not only a teetotaler but wanted everyone else to be one, especially her husband. We could see him through the sitting-room bay windows returning from his haunts, striding up the wooden sidewalk happily and perhaps whistling an old army tune, and my grandmother would swear that he was tottering from drink, though his gait seemed steady enough to me. He would hardly get inside his own house and lay his derby hat on the rack when Grandmother would rush up to him, not for a kiss, but to sniff his breath and then to rage about what she called the evils of "demon rum," though he never drank anything but whiskey. He would maneuver his way around the old lady, greet the rest of us, and ask in a quiet voice, "Is dinner ready? I don't mind saying I'm hungry, my dear ones."

"For the sake of these innocent young children, if not for me," Grandmother would howl, when she had caught up with him, "you ought to desist, Frank! You ought to be ashamed!" As if she gave a damn about us! His only answer would be to pick up one of us and carry us into the dining room, where, as my mother spread out the dishes and platters, he repeated, "I declare, I'm hungry as a wolf." Finally, having restored peace by his refusal to stoop to answering his shrewish wife, he would sit down with us to one of those huge, heavy, Midwest dinners fit for threshers.

He died quietly in his sleep at the end of that first year, and for me it was the second blow within twelve months. My father gone, and then my grandfather—the two men I loved and looked up to. Grandmother lived on for another four torturous years. She, too, passed away in her sleep the year the country entered the war, in 1917, and I must confess, though I kept it to myself, that I was glad to see the last of her—the first and last time I have ever had that feeling about anyone.

All through that first year in the Iowa town, the world continued to unfold to me and I developed the habit of poring over newspapers from the first to the last page. Though Grandmother thought it was wasteful, Mother subscribed to the *Chicago Tribune,* an early edition of which arrived before breakfast, perhaps partly out of nostalgia for the city where she had known her greatest happiness and fulfillment, brief as it was, and partly because she wanted us to grow up with a metropolitan newspaper, however bad the *Tribune* was, despite its claim to being the "World's Greatest Newspaper." In the afternoon we had two local journals, the *Gazette* and the *Republican and Times,* whose feuds —something which, alas, has disappeared from the American scene with the consolidation of rival newspapers—afforded much amusement and occasional excitement in the town.

Checking recently in old files of the town's newspapers recalls the events which bestirred us that spring and summer of 1913. Locally, there were many death notices of Civil War veterans. The *Gazette* noted that in Iowa alone they were dying at the rate of four hundred a year. Soon there would not be enough of them to parade on Memorial Day. But on the holiday that first year, Grandfather put on his faded, old blue uniform and joined the parade for what proved his last time. We stood proudly along the curb watching him as he marched by, keeping more or less in step with his gray-haired comrades to the music of a fife-and-drum corps. Gradually, as the ranks of the Grand Army of the Republic thinned to a handful, the Memorial Day parades faded away, as did the memory of the Civil War. I did not yet know, though I would find out soon enough—the next year, in fact— that bigger and bloodier wars would follow, and that for the rest of my life there would be millions of veterans of one war after another to keep the parades going.

One front-page headline that must have shocked my grandmother, though not her tolerant husband, proclaimed: "DIS-ORDERLY HOUSE RAIDED!" So they had them in this town, so de-voted to Christian uplift! Later, when I had become more aware of the world, I would learn that there was indeed a "red-light district" along the river, where whores prowled First Street and "houses" flourished. Some of the old bloods talked of a "Madame Taylor and her girls," who prospered around the turn of the century despite constant "raids" by the police and who were patron-ized in secret by certain citizens of the most impeccable public reputations. So the town was human after all. Another front-page headline declared: "CONVENTION OF STATE LIQUOR DEALERS PRO-CLAIMS ANTI-SALOON LEAGUE A MENACE." It would shortly prove more of a menace than they realized.

Still another headline read: "CHERRY SISTERS END ENGAGE-MENT IN FRUIT SHOWER." The dispatch was datelined Boston. The Cherry Sisters, if not the greatest pride of Cedar Rapids, were at least at this time its chief claim to fame. Their stage show was so terrible that millions paid to see it out of perverse curiosity. Their acting was so ludicrous that they had to be protected by a wire netting in front of the stage to fend off the showers of cabbages, rotten eggs, tomatoes and old shoes hurled at them by apparently hilarious customers. From my mother and others I gradually learned the grotesque story of these famous ladies. Born on a farm a few miles out of town, they apparently concocted the idea of "going on the stage" to pay off the mortgage. After a "tryout" at the nearby town of Marion, they made their "debut" in Cedar Rapids at Greene's Opera House on the night of February 17, 1893. Next day the *Gazette* commented:

> Such unlimited gall as was exhibited last night at Greene's Opera House by the Cherry Sisters is past the understanding of ordinary mortals. . . . Their knowledge of the theatre is worse than none at all, and they surely could not realize last night that they were making such fools of themselves.
>
> If modesty could not have warned them that they were act-ing the part of monkeys, it does seem that the overshoes thrown at them would have conveyed the idea in a more substantial manner. . . . But nothing could drive them away and no com-bination of yells, whistles, barks and howls could subdue them.
>
> Let it be understood that the audience was not a gang of hoodlums. Quite the contrary. The parquet and dress circle were filled by the best people of the city.

A clipping in my father's files from the Chicago *Record*, hailing the arrival of the Cherry Sisters in that city, tells what happened subsequent to the *Gazette* review:

The sisters were deeply hurt and they sued the editor for libel. When the case came to trial the judge decided that the jury would have to witness a performance in order to decide whether or not the article was libelous. It is claimed that the foreman arose and said: "Judge, there's seven of us here that saw the show, and we'd rather go to jail for contempt than sit through it again."

Despite, or probably because of, the notices, the fame of the Cherry Sisters spread and before long they were playing at Hammerstein's Olympia in New York before packed houses at one thousand dollars a week. It was the great impresario Hammerstein, I believe, who after the first night's volley of overripe fruit and vegetables benevolently devised a great wire screen to protect them from the paying customers. It became one of their most important props as they toured the land. Their acts, if they could be called such, consisted of patriotic recitations, with the three girls, Addie, Jessie and Effie, wrapped in American flags; of various idiotic songs such as the "Ta-ra-ra" which they composed; and of the two skits which they wrote, "The Wanderer's Return" and "The Gypsy's Warning," about the perils which beset innocent young ladies in the wicked cities of the land.

Shortly after the end of the First War, the Cherry Sisters returned to Cedar Rapids, apparently broke despite all the money they reportedly had made, and opened a bakery. My mother used to send me out to it to buy homemade bread, pies and cakes, which were excellent. The three sisters struck a youngster like me as strange relics from the past, dressed in long garments, with the choke collars of the nineties, under their aprons, their wizened faces heavily powdered and painted.

"Tell me about the big time," I asked Effie, the oldest of the sisters, one day while buying a loaf of bread and some cakes. I was already an aspiring journalist. But she was reticent and her sisters said absolutely nothing. "We're putting it in a book," Effie said. "You'll see." According to rumor, the manuscript "got lost." At any rate it was never published, and probably was unpublishable, if it was ever written.

In 1924, the year before I left the town for good, Effie ran for mayor on a "reform" ticket and actually polled a few hundred votes. The last of the sisters to survive, she died in 1944 in a shabby rooming house for the aged. *The New York Times* had not forgotten her. It devoted a whole column to her obituary.

There were other items in the newspapers as 1913 slipped by in our town. Buffalo Bill, one of my heroes, whom my father had taken me to see in Chicago, was reported "at death's door," and in Rome J. P. Morgan, no hero at all, had died. In Washington the new Democratic President, Woodrow Wilson, who had promised the country "a new freedom," had proclaimed the "doom," as the headlines put it, of the trusts and the lobbyists, and we could not know then that this was never to be. My mother read avidly the news of the agitation for votes for women. Most of this news came from far-off London. Mrs. Pankhurst, the headlines said, had "PLEADED NOT GUILTY TO ARSON CHARGES." Another dispatch from Britain was headed: "SUFFRAGETTES IN ENGLAND DISRUPT DERBY—TRY TO STOP KING'S HORSE." Mother lamented the lack of interest for women's suffrage in the town, but Grandmother said she couldn't see what all the fuss was about.

Mother was also surprised, after her long absence, to find so much "entertainment" available in such a small town. She clipped an ad from Greene's Opera House:

Henry W. Savage Offers Tremendous Spectacle
EVERYWOMAN
150 People
Special Symphony Orchestra
Entire Trainload of Scenery and Effects

Did she complain about the prices?—two dollars for seats in the parquet and dress circle, one dollar in the first balcony, seventy-five cents in the second, only fifty cents in the "gallery," which was called "nigger heaven," and where we youngsters ended up.

At the Majestic, the "top in vaudeville from the Orpheum Circuit" was offered—"any seat, any time, ten cents." The price of a ticket to the two movie houses, the Columbia and the Crystal, was five cents, though they advertised an orchestra and featured the great stars from Hollywood who soon would become my great heroes or secret loves: Charlie Chaplin, Douglas Fairbanks, Theda Bara, Pearl White, Norma Talmadge, Marguerite Clark and Mary Pickford. The People's Theater—Hy-Tone Repertoire, with "a change of bill Sunday and Thursday," offered one thousand seats at ten cents, reserved seats at fifteen cents.

So we would not be without "entertainment" in this rustic place.

What I remember most distinctly in the newspapers from that first year in Cedar Rapids was the talk of a threat of war in Europe. The Balkan wars were ending, the headlines said, but the peace was precarious. The scrapping little Balkan states were involving the Big Powers, especially Russia and Austria-Hungary, in their troubles. In Berlin Kaiser Wilhelm II was continuing his bombastic threats—against Russia, France and even England, which was alarmed by the rapid growth of the German Navy. The continental powers were arming feverishly. I followed it all avidly, if with little understanding.

"Why do you read all that war stuff?" Grandma would say. "T'ain't none of our business. Europe's a long ways away, son." It was in truth, especially from our Iowa cornfields. But still . . .

The next summer, 1914, when the big war came, we were in Montana, visiting our uncle, my mother's only brother. For us children it was our first glimpse of the "Wild West"—cowboys, Indians, roundups, bucking broncos, the clear air of the mountains, the carefree, outdoor summer life of the Rockies. We loved it. Uncle Dode, a fat, jovial, rough fellow, who had railroaded all his life, was foreman of the Milwaukee Railroad shops at Miles City, a wide-open frontier town of some ten thousand inhabitants. Like most fat men, he was jolly, shaking the room when he laughed, but he also had a hot temper, especially when provoked by his wife, who turned out to be as shrewish as Grandmother.

They had been separated or divorced and had recently re-united, and were childless. She took a dim view of three young brats taking over her household and tried all summer to curb us. "Little children should be seen and not heard!" she would admonish us. Uncle would growl at her and sometimes, unable to bear either her or us, he would stamp out and go down to the Elks for a fresh start at a meal with his cronies. Despite his occasional irritation at the table, Uncle Dode came to like us. He would sweep us off to lunch at the Elks or to one of their rowdy Saturday-night "entertainments," proudly showing us off to his friends. He steered my brother and me around the Milwaukee shops, let us ride in the cabin of a switch engine and once, for a moment, sit in the engineer's seat in the cab of one of the huge steam locomotives on a passing train to the coast, strengthening my secret ambition to become a locomotive engineer when I grew up.

Miles City was a stop on two transcontinental lines, the Milwaukee and the Northern Pacific, which carried passengers and freight between Minneapolis-St. Paul and the northwest coast at Portland and Seattle. My brother and I, at eight and ten, never tired of gawking at the long cross-country passenger trains, pulled by giant, snorting steam locomotives. Nearly every day we would go down to one of the two depots to watch a train come in.[1]

There was much else, of course, in the life of a boy in Montana that summer. My uncle owned one of the first automobiles in the town, a contraption called the "Krit," into which he piled us evenings for a drive in the country to "cool off," and on Saturdays and Sundays for a visit to a ranch. There we could ride horses and talk with my new heroes, the cowpunchers, or picnic on the banks of the Yellowstone River or up in the mountains. Never had I had such a wonderful summer—despite my aunt.

And then, in August, the war in Europe broke out, and I spent less time outdoors and more time indoors reading the news-

[1] The last of such trains stopped there more than half a century later—on the evening of May 1, 1971, as I was preparing notes for this chapter. A long dispatch from Miles City to *The New York Times*, replete with a photograph and a map, noted it and the passing of an era. It passed, too, in Cedar Rapids the same day when the last of the through trains made its brief, mournful appearance. Hundreds of towns and cities like Miles City and Cedar Rapids had the same experience that weekend as the great railroads from coast to coast ceased their passenger service and Amtrak took over to try to maintain a skeleton service over a few once great lines. What especially angered the good citizens of Miles City, according to the *Times* dispatch, was that the railroads in Montana were allowed to retain 1,439,137 acres of land which the federal government *gave* them during the nineteenth century to encourage them to extend their lines west to the coast. In Montana most of this land is extremely valuable for ranching, coal and oil.

"Damn it," said one customer to the *Times* man in the bar of the Golden Spur in Miles City as he stamped his cowboy boots, "if the railroad is not going to run passenger trains then I say let's make them give back the land and oil and coal we gave them."

papers, the Minneapolis and St. Paul papers, that came in a day late, and the local gazette, all their front pages black with huge headlines. First there were the declarations of war at the end of July and the beginning of August—Austria-Hungary against Serbia, Germany against Russia and then against France, England against Germany when the Kaiser's armies invaded little Belgium. By the first week of August all the major European powers except Italy were at war and each day I pored through the newspapers, studied the maps which my grandfather had taught me to read, thrilled at the first news of the Russian advance into East Prussia, of the French into Alsace-Lorraine, of the gallant defense by the Belgians of their great forts of Liège and Namur, for I had already decided in my infinite wisdom who I was for and against. The German invasion of Belgium had made it easy. The bellicose Kaiser had to be stopped. The Prussian militarists, the violators of brave, neutral little Belgium, had to be defeated. The French, the British, the Russians, must see to that. I had played with a boy of my age whose parents had come over from Germany. *His* hero was the Kaiser and he boasted that the Germans would soon be in Paris and St. Petersburg. We argued and then fought with our fists over who was right and wrong and who would win, and in the end, little pure-in-heart that I was, I told him I didn't want to see him any more.

"Why not?" he asked.

"Because you're the enemy, that's why," I said. "You and your Germans." I hated them both.

We spent a few days on our way home toward the end of August in St. Paul, my mother and sister shopping, my brother and I standing all day in front of a newspaper office around the corner from the hotel. Huge bulletin boards gave the latest news from the battlefronts. The great Belgian fortress of Liège had held out against a powerful German army for two weeks. And I remember the cheers of the crowd in the streets, after Liège had fallen, when a bulletin announced that the second great Belgian fortress of Namur was still holding out.

By the time we returned to Cedar Rapids at the beginning of September, however, the news had turned ominous. The Russians, after their initial successes, had suffered a disastrous defeat at Tannenberg at the hands of a couple of German generals named Hindenburg and Ludendorff. On the Western front Belgium had all but fallen, northern France was overrun and the Germans were marching on Paris. It was difficult to take any interest in school that fall.

And then at the end of the first week in September what seemed like a miracle happened. When all seemed lost and the French government had fled Paris for Bordeaux, the French, supported by a small force of British, had halted their retreat in front of the capital, turned on the Germans and driven them across the Marne in headlong retreat, destroying the legend of their invincibility. For weeks on end I read the local and Chicago newspapers to piece together the "miracle" of the Battle of the Marne.

So Paris, miraculously, was saved, and France. The war, people said, might be over by Christmas. The pundits wrote in the newspapers that none of the warring powers had the resources to continue the struggle on such a colossal scale much beyond the holidays. No one knew then, especially in America and more especially in our small Iowa town, where the war seemed far away but terribly fascinating to follow just the same, that four murderous years of war lay ahead, that our country would be drawn into it in the end, that young soldiers from our community would be killed, that ten million men would be slaughtered, and that most of the wealth of Europe would go up in smoke.

One day at the end of September, as I sprawled on the floor poring over the war maps, my mother admonished me. "When are you going to get back to your studies? They tell me you're not doing very well in school. It's a shame."

Jackson School—all the grade schools in the town were named after Presidents—was a solid, square, red-brick, two-story building with the eight grades occupying four large corner rooms on each floor. The office of the principal was tucked at the top of the second-floor stairs. It did not take me long to realize that its occupant, Frances Prescott, was a remarkable woman. Irish, tall, straw-haired, vivacious and possessed of enormous energy, she dominated the school and made it for me, at least, an interesting and challenging place. She was the first of three or four educators who took me in hand and stimulated an urge to learn and a curiosity about life.

Though it was a small public school in a small Midwest

town, it could boast of two former pupils who already were world-famous. These were the Wright brothers, and we soon learned that it was here in our school and across the street on Fourth Avenue where they lived, that the two youngsters had first got the inspiration to build flying machines. Their father, Bishop Milton Wright, of the United Brethren Church, had moved with his family from Dayton, Ohio, to Cedar Rapids in 1879 and enrolled Wilbur, eleven, and Orville, seven, in Jackson School, where my mother was in the third grade.

One day, according to the story I grew up on (and which is confirmed in Orville Wright's autobiography), the bishop brought home a toy, a helicopter built by a Frenchman, Alphonse Penaud. Powered by a rubber band, it would lift off for the ceiling and then fall. The young Wright brothers were so fascinated that when it finally broke down, they themselves built another and then several more. But when they constructed a much larger one in the backyard it would not rise. They did not understand, Orville wrote, that the bigger the flying machine the more power it had to have. So they abandoned the project and took up flying kites, and I remember one of the older ladies of the town, a great beauty, Mrs. Walter Douglas, who had seen her husband go down on the *Titanic*, telling of how as a girl she made tails for their kites out of old rags. The Wright boys, she remembered, were even then obsessed with anything they could make fly.

One other pupil at Jackson, who preceded me by eight years, was destined to become well known in the nation. This was a sprightly young lady by the name of Mamie Doud, whose father was an executive of the Sinclair Packing Plant, where later I would toil one summer on an assembly line of butchered hogs. The Douds lived directly across from the school. At nineteen, after the family had moved away, Mamie married a young Army lieutenant by the name of Dwight Eisenhower.

Early at this school I developed a passion for writing, showering the teachers with my compositions, whether they asked for them or not. The title of one of these childish pieces I still remember: "How Vodka Saved the City," though I cannot recall how vodka had this remarkable effect or how I knew anything about this strong Russian drink, which I had never tasted. Probably it evolved from something I had read in a magazine about the stirrings of the Russian Revolution in St. Petersburg, and I was no doubt influenced by Dostoevsky, whom I had just discovered on my own at the Public Library and was reading avidly. Outside of reading and writing, geography and American history—the last taught abominably from atrocious but patriotic textbooks, though I did not realize it—I had little interest in other studies. Arithmetic I detested and barely passed in it.

And in memory, at least, what happened outside of school was much more interesting. Winters in Iowa were arctic, with the thermometer often falling below zero and the snow piling up in the streets. My main job at home was keeping the coal-burning furnace in the cellar going. We had a large bin that held ten tons of soft coal and a smaller one for a ton or two of anthracite and all winter long I kept shoveling. Early each morning I would hurry to the cellar to stoke up the fire, shaking down the ashes, removing the clinkers and heaping on coal. The last chore of the evening would be to bed down the fire with as much coal as the burner would take, topped by ashes to make for a slow burn, and hope that it would last until morning.

Cold and icy though they were, with the prairie winds biting your face and freezing your fingers, the winters I loved. Shoveling the sidewalks was fun and you could always pick up a quarter or fifty cents clearing them for a neighbor or two. Then there would be sleigh rides with friends whose folks kept horses and sleighs, ice-skating on nearby ponds or on the river, and best of all, sliding down the long, steep hill on B Avenue on your own sled. At the top of the hill in a mansion set back from the street lived a beautiful girl I knew, Mary Safely. We had met, I think, in Sunday School, and when we were tired and cold from sledding, she would invite me in for a hot chocolate and cookies, making a wonderful end to an almost perfect day.

Not so pleasant through those icy, snowbound winters was carrying papers. When I reached twelve, and the seventh grade, I acquired a paper route. Each weekday afternoon after school and before dawn on Sunday mornings I would lug a sack of fifty or sixty copies of the *Republican* from the newspaper office to my "territory" on the outskirts of the town, fold each one, and toss it onto the front porches of the subscribers. In the spring, summer and fall it was easy. I did it on my bike, and the job was over in an hour. But winters, with the snow piled high and the thermometer often below zero, I had to trudge through the drifts, pulling a sled on which I had tied the bulging bag of papers. Sunday mornings in the darkness, before the daylight had mitigated the temperature a little, could be especially grim, and I would often arrive home with my toes, fingers and ears frostbitten.

The pay was five dollars a month (with a ten-cent fine for each complaint that you had failed to deliver a paper—if the wind blew any away, that was no excuse, the fine was levied), but we needed even that kind of money in our household and I felt rather proud to be earning at least a part of my own living, something that became ingrained in me early, and stuck. Even before that I had earned a little selling eggs from the flock of hens we kept in a coop in the backyard and vegetables from our garden, and from mowing lawns, digging dandelions, tending furnaces and doing odd jobs for neighbors. It wasn't, I think, that I subscribed to the American work ethic so praised by President Nixon in the 1970's—I preferred playing to working—but that I felt I had to contribute to holding together a family I loved.

And so when America entered the war in 1917 and labor became scarce, I lied about my age, which was thirteen, and took on other jobs, weekends, vacations, summers, working for a time trucking freight in the North Western freight depot and one summer at the National Oats factory, where the pay was three dollars for a ten-hour day and we were told we were helping "win the war" because our product went to feed the gallant soldiers overseas. Certainly going to work at a man's job when I was still a boy never stunted me in the least. Just the opposite: it gave me an education I was not receiving in school or at the family's First Presbyterian Church or at home. It gave me my first contacts with manual workers and the toughness and drabness of their lives. Also with their rough language, which may have lacked the grace of our middle-class talk (and some of its hypocrisy) but was wonderfully expressive. At first it shocked me, but soon I got to appreciate it, especially during the summer working on an assembly line at National Oats, where most of the workers were young women who swore like troopers and used four-letter words which I had never heard before and who after a hard ten hours trying to keep up with the machinery of an assembly line would invite you to go over to nearby Daniels Park "for a drink and a roll"—an invitation I appreciated but was too exhausted and especially too afraid, in my Boy Scout purity, to accept. I found these workers more interesting and more earthy than the people I associated with in school and church. I liked them.

When we got into the war in the spring of 1917 I tried to get into it, too. I was already a foolish little warrior. I wanted to fight for freedom. All during the previous spring I had often played hooky from school in order to hang around the National Guard armory, where our two local companies were mobilizing to go off to the Mexican border to protect our sacred soil from the depredations of Pancho Villa and his Mexican "bandits." Big for my age and looking considerably older than twelve, I had tried to enlist. The next spring, when the Great War came, and not only our two National Guard companies were called up but a new unit, an artillery battery, in which almost the entire male student body of Coe College enlisted, I was again struck by war fever and tried to join up. No luck. So I enlisted in the R.O.T.C. unit in the high-school, which I had by then entered, proudly donned a uniform, toted a gun in the daily drills, and hoped fervently that Uncle Sam somehow would overlook our tender age and send us off to fight the Huns.

When the Armistice came on November 11, 1918, and the town went wild in celebration, I was bitterly disappointed. I was old enough to thank the Lord, as my mother did, that so many lives would now be spared, especially those of the many I knew among the thousand or so young men who had gone off to the war from our town.[1] Already a number had been killed. Gold stars hung in the windows of several homes, and some of the wounded were back, hobbling the streets, a leg gone, an arm missing, a patch over one eye. A young doctor who had married a cousin of ours and then gone off to France had just returned, his lungs burned out by German poison gas, slowly dying.

Nevertheless, I found it hard to swallow the fact that I would never fight in the war to make, as President Wilson said, and I believed, the world safe for democracy. Well, I would get ready for the next one. The following summer, in 1919, as the troops were being demobilized, I again lied about my age—this time by only a year—and went off to an R.O.T.C. camp at Camp

[1] But I was too young to realize that if not among the Americans (53,000 killed in action) then certainly among the British (900,000 killed in action), the French (1,357,800 killed in action) and the Germans (1,800,000 killed in action), the flower of youth had been wiped out in the bloody carnage of the war.

Funston, Kansas, to learn how to soldier. It was the most exciting summer I had ever had, drilling all day, playing soldier all day, writing home to a beautiful highschool girl on Y.M.C.A. stationery that was headed "With the Colors," which greatly impressed her. I was so full of the martial spirit that after the camp was ended I stayed on as a highly paid (one hundred dollars a month) civilian Army field clerk, but in uniform, and lived and messed with regular Army soldiers who had just returned from the battlefields of France and who, I thought, made me one of them, even sewing a red discharge stripe on my sleeve, which I had no right to have. When school time came that fall of 1919, my mother wired that it was time to come home and go back to school. Reluctantly I abandoned my post. But there were a few days of glory when I returned to school in uniform, phoney discharge stripe and all, and strutted from class to class as if I were a returning war hero. Finally the patient principal, Miss Abbie S. Abbott, one of the most remarkable women in my young life, suggested that the war was over, had in fact long been over, and that I put my uniform aside and get back to studying, like the others.

I was never very happy in highschool, before my foolish military posturing or afterward. But Miss Abbott pulled me through some difficult years and pounded some sense into me—some sense for education and for life and for riding its ups and downs. She always looked to me part Indian, with her high cheekbones, aquiline nose, dark skin and hair, and I supposed she had come east perhaps from Oklahoma. Actually she had come west from Massachusetts, one of New England's gifts to the Midwest, taking over Washington High School in 1886 when it was a small building of four rooms with sixty pupils and three teachers on the edge of Greene's Square across from the Union Station, building it up to an imposing stone edifice with a thousand students and fifty teachers and making it one of the finest public highschools in the country. She was stern, but warm and friendly, with sad, reflective eyes that occasionally sparkled with humor, and she seemed to me to be a little skeptical, even slightly sardonic, in her view of life and in her attitude toward the school and the town—not quite in line with the boisterous boosters. I felt her uniqueness from the beginning and often went to her to discuss my problems, sometimes at considerable length. She alone seemed to understand my difficulties, my frustrations, my unhappiness, and she taught me how to live with them.

There were two major disappointments, and in retrospect they seem childish enough. The first was that I did not "make" one of the two Greek-letter "literary societies," which were actually fraternities, for there was nothing literary about them; I did not even make the one for sophomores, from which one graduated into the two older ones in the junior year. For the first time in my life I felt left out, scorned, rejected. It was my first confrontation with that snobbishness of American bumpkins that starts in highschool and continues in college with the fraternities. Out of five hundred boys in the highschool, some eighty were taken into the two Greek-letter societies, but to be cast with the great majority did not console me. I soon found that it was almost impossible to get a date with an attractive girl if you were not a member. The two fraternities automatically provided the school with debaters for the debating teams, and I found I was excluded from something at which I thought I was pretty good. The two groups filled almost all the places in other school activities.

Among these was the school paper, *The Pulse*, whose staff was chosen from juniors and seniors. By my junior year I was already the highschool correspondent for one of the local dailies and was seeing my by-line in it over various feature stories about the town, and once about the "Dutch Colonies" in nearby Amana. But I was ambitious to make the school paper. I never did, and this, too, rankled. I couldn't understand why. Miss Abbott consoled me, urging me to start a new fraternity of "rebels," since I was the most promising rebel she had ever seen. "I'm challenging you!" she would say with a sparkle in her eyes, but I was too full of false pride to accept. "And since you're already writing for a daily paper, why do you want to be on a little school paper?" she would ask, but I did not appreciate her logic.

What I appreciated, at least later, was that this gifted woman gave me some of my first insights on how to deal with what then seemed adversity and how not to be thrown by it. Above all, she gave me a friendship that must have been rather unusual between a school principal and a raw, ignorant young pupil, and as a friend she counseled me on what education—and life—were all about. I was lucky to have gone to school to her, as I had been lucky in Jackson School before, where Frances Prescott had befriended me as a mere tot and had helped to show me the way. (Miss Prescott had an even greater influence on a young genius, a youthful painter who had barely survived poverty, named Grant Wood, whom she befriended, providing him with a job teaching art in her school, and kindling him with her own steadfast faith in him as an important artist.) These two remarkable women, Miss Prescott and Miss Abbott, in these public schools in this rural town, had, by their friendship, by their encouragement, by their faith in me, done more for me than they probably ever realized.

My own realization of this would come only later. At the end of my junior year at Washington High I was so restless to get away from the school and the town that I left immediately after the last examination for a job I had got—after again lying about my age by a couple of years (I was sixteen)—on a chautauqua tent crew. A year later, much to my mother's disappointment, I skipped the graduation ceremonies, asked Miss Abbott, who was retiring that year after thirty-five years at the school, to mail me my diploma, and again went off to work on chautauqua, see the country and get a closer view of the people in the smaller towns[1] of mid-America, whom Sinclair Lewis had just written about in his novel *Main Street,* and of the sophisticates from the big outside world who lectured to them and entertained them in the summer's heat under the brown chautauqua tents.

Chautauqua is gone now, and probably forgotten. Most young people I talk to nowadays have never even heard of it. But chautauqua was one of the most unique and enduring of American institutions. Theodore Roosevelt, who once had been a part of it, called chautauqua "the most important American thing in America." For half a century it brought a little culture and much uplift into the drab and circumscribed lives of millions of Americans in twenty thousand Main Streets from one end of the country to the other.

It developed in what was to be its final and most successful form—chautauqua under a tent—in the fertile mind of a young man in Cedar Rapids. I worked for him one summer vacation in the mail room, getting out mountains of promotion literature, and spent the last two summers of my highschool life on a tent crew,

[1] Cedar Rapids by now had passed the forty-five-thousand mark and had become, as we thought, practically a city.

riding the smoky, cinder-spattered trains day and night on the bumpy branch lines, putting up the canvas and tearing it down in twenty Midwest towns, erecting seats, stages and lighting, collecting tickets, filling in in a chorus or a play when someone got sick or lost, listening to the perspiring orations of William Jennings Bryan and other luminaries, flirting with actresses from the "Broadway" stage and musical companies, and, like a sailor in all the ports of the world, falling momentarily in love with a local girl in a new town each week.[1] It was a wondrous, romantic interlude in my young life, and largely made up for all the emptiness of the highschool years. And during it I learned a great deal about a part of our country, our people—the terrible limitations to life in all our Main Streets and yet the yearning of so many, especially the young, to reach out for something beyond the small town, for "culture," for good music, for the drama of the stage, and for contact with minds that soared above the gray and narrow confines of rural civilization. In part, for a week, chautauqua responded to those yearnings.

One day in Cedar Rapids early in 1903 a thirty-one-year-old businessman named Keith Vawter, who ran the Redpath-Vawter Lyceum Bureau, wrote J. Roy Ellison, who managed a lyceum bureau in Nebraska: "Come and join me. I've got an idea. Bring any money you have." He had, indeed, a new idea for chautauqua, which by then had become a rather venerable institution in the country. It had been founded a quarter of a century before at Lake Chautauqua, New York (from which it got its name), by a young New Jersey Protestant minister, John H. Vincent, and an Akron, Ohio, businessman named Lewis Miller. Their idea was to form a sort of summer school for Sunday School teachers in pleasant surroundings on the shore of a lake. It was an instant success. Forty earnest youths showed up the first summer, then hundreds, then thousands, to drink in the wisdom of the eminent men of the day. Several U.S. Presidents, past, present or future, came to talk: Grant, Garfield, Hayes, McKinley and Theodore Roosevelt. They

---

[1] Despite our contract with the management, which stipulated, among other things, that " 'girling' is forbidden. This is not a social event but a summer's work." The contract also stated that "use of profane language will be just grounds for immediate dismissal." It also forbade smoking, "except in the crew tent." The crews, mostly college boys, obviously were supposed to set a wholesome example.

were joined by William Jennings Bryan, Booker T. Washington, Mark Hanna, Eugene Debs and many others.

Actually, chautauqua derived from the old lyceums, which had been started in 1826 by Josiah Holbrook of Millbury, Massachusetts, to widen the horizons of a provincial people by bringing to them well-known speakers and artists. By 1835 they were doing this in three thousand localities, to which came such luminaries as Ralph Waldo Emerson, Horace Greeley, Daniel Webster, Oliver Wendell Holmes and, biggest catch of all, Charles Dickens, first in 1842, sponsored by James Redpath, who, on the success of this enterprise, founded the Redpath Lyceum Bureau, the most successful of them all. The lyceums were urban, confined to the cities and the larger towns. Chautauqua was designed for the smaller places.

From Lake Chautauqua, the movement spread. By 1900 there were two hundred chautauquas in thirty-one states, almost all of them set up in permanent pavilions by the shore of a lake. Essentially they offered a program of education and self-improvement, with a chance to hear good music as well as notable speakers, in pleasant summer surroundings. But there were not enough pavilions, or nearby lakes, to reach a mass audience. Young Vawter, who ran half a dozen "lake chautauquas" in Iowa, pondered this limitation and came up with an idea to overcome it. To Ellison, who arrived in Cedar Rapids from Omaha with his life savings and a receptive mind, Vawter proposed that they buy circus tents and take chautauqua to those towns that had no regular pavilions. They managed that first summer of 1903 to set up chautauqua under a tent in six towns. By the end of the season they both had lost all their savings and had gone into debt. Pondering their failure, they came up with two new ideas that were to revolutionize the business, spread chautauqua from coast to coast and bring them fortunes.

The first notion was to build a circuit. They would buy a dozen tents, keep seven of them in operation each week and book talent into each of them day after day, repeating the process every week. Thus a speaker, or a road company, would perform under a new tent in a new town on seven successive days, week after week, throughout the summer. This assured them of work seven days a week, with short hops between engagements keeping down their travel expenses. It also promised to yield handsome profits. With seven tents daily attracting a paid attendance of a thousand or so each, that meant a total of seven thousand paying customers a day for the circuit and the money was bound to roll in.

But the two young impresarios had an even brighter idea, one that would guarantee, so to speak, a fortune at no risk to them. They would appeal to the pride of a community and induce the civic-minded businessmen to put up a financial guarantee for a week of chautauqua. This guarantee varied from $2,000 to $2,500 a week and usually meant that if the local committee could sell enough season tickets to fill the tent, it broke even. If not, it made up the deficit. This was foolproof. If Vawter and his partner could put this across on Main Street they were bound to make a lot of money.

They put it across. They knew their small towns. I used to listen to our "superintendent," a young preacher with a gift of gab (Vawter hired only ministers of the Gospel for this job), make his pitch at the end of our sojourn for a new contract for the next summer. No mention of any profits the Redpath-Vawter chautauqua might be interested in. Not a word about the local committee taking all the risks and Vawter taking all the profits. With a zealousness he had learned in the pulpit he would convince these local Babbitts that as the "leaders of the community" they owed it to their town to bring again next summer this marvelous institution of uplift, culture and inspiration. "This splendid community cannot afford to do without it. You know that better than I," he would intone. And in case there was any hesitation—as there was when the good burghers faced coughing up a hundred dollars apiece to make up a deficit—he would threaten dire consequences.

"I will be frank with you," he would say. "We have a long waiting list. There are dozens of towns in this part of the state, some of them not far, which are awfully envious of you. If I offered them this contract I'm now presenting you, they would sign it in a minute. They're dying to have chautauqua in their community."

It worked. Year after year for a quarter of a century, the local communities signed up—and sometimes had to cough up when there were deficits. The brown chautauqua tents spread all over the land when summer came. More circuits were added. One summer that I worked, chautauqua played five hundred towns in

Iowa alone. Cedar Rapids prided itself on "Chautauqua Week," with a big tent spread on the athletic field of Coe College.

For an Iowa highschool boy of sixteen or seventeen, his ego swollen by the realization that his mates on the tent crew were all in college—and three or four years older—those two summers on chautauqua, while filled with hard work, were a joy, and a further education. I loved the traveling, the variety of the land as we jolted along in a day coach through the rolling cornfields of Iowa, the lake-studded countryside of Minnesota, the flat wheat-lands of the Dakotas, the hills of Missouri with its faint flavor of the South. And there was something in the life on the trains and in the red-painted depots, where we changed trains or arrived at our destination and departed, that was appealing to a raw youth. I sort of envied the life of the trainmen, who lived in a world of their own and had a camaraderie, a distinct life-style, that seemed to give them more satisfaction in their work than I had seen in offices and factories. They were, among other things, gargantuan eaters, and I remember the boardinghouses across the square from the depot where we would find sustenance during the week we were in town, and where we were joined, especially on early mornings, by the railroad men starting or finishing a shift and gobbling down immense breakfasts of oatmeal, bacon and eggs, pancakes, hot biscuits and coffee.

After the last evening performance of the week, we would take down the big tent and stuff the canvas into large bags, pile our props into trunks and by midnight or shortly after catch a train (passenger trains swarmed even the branch lines in those days) for our next location, arriving there often by early morning or before noon and, after a hearty breakfast or lunch, pitching the tent on the lawn or the football field of a local high school or college. Soon the tent was up, the stage built, the lighting strung out, the bench seats arranged, our own little tent behind the stage, where the crew slept, erected, and we were ready for business. Strolling down Main Street to get an ice-cream soda, we could see that the advance man had done his job. Streamers stretched across the avenue proclaiming "Chautauqua Is Coming!" The message was repeated on banners fluttering from automobiles, trucks, drays and carriages, and all the businessmen on the sidewalks or in their offices and shops were wearing large buttons that said "I'll Be There!"

By the time chautauqua opened for the first matinee we were

back on the grounds for the last chores: rolling an upright piano onto one corner of the stage, planting Old Glory behind it so that our speakers could point to it with customary patriotic pride, and fetching a pitcher of ice water and a glass to tide them over their long-distance runs in the suffocating heat. The tent would fill up, our preacher-superintendent would come beaming on stage and, when the applause was over, open the week's festivities: "Well, here we are, my friends, bringing you and this great town [mentioning it by name, if he could remember it] another great week of chautauqua. And if you thought it was good last year, wait till you see what we have in store for you *this* year—the greatest program, I can say in all modesty, that chautauqua has ever presented anywhere. It's all here for you, afternoons and evenings, for the next seven days." And he would spin through it with great aplomb. "That peerless American statesman William Jennings Bryan" would be back, but he could hardly finish his sentence because of the applause. For Bryan was the great spellbinder of the chautauqua circuit, the biggest drawing card it ever had. There would be other speakers, of course, and a new "Broadway hit," and the Ben Greet Players with a new presentation of *Hamlet,* and two orchestras, and, of course, Sousa's great band, a famous musical sextet "straight from New York," an opera company "from Chicago" presenting *Pinafore,* a great "diva" from the "Metropolitan Opera of New York"—and on and on he would go, the audience breathless with anticipation, though it had known for weeks from advance flyers just what the program would be.

Finally the superintendent would present a beautiful young lady (invariably a pert college girl trying to earn next year's tuition, and a welcome member of our crew) who would be in charge of "junior chautauqua." She would not only keep the youngsters occupied while their parents were absorbing culture, but would labor doggedly all week to whip them into giving a pageant or a play on the last afternoon, which, however terrible, would delight the fond mothers and fathers and help to deepen their impression of all the wholesome good that chautauqua had brought to the community.

Wholesomeness. Inspiration. Uplift. Enlightenment. A high and pious moral tone. That was what chautauqua deliberately sold to the good people of these barren towns. Its programs catered to their puritan morals, the fierceness of their conformities and the fundamentalism of their religious beliefs. Yet they did a little more. If the lectures (of Bryan, of the Reverend Russell H. Conwell, with his sure-fire "Acres of Diamonds" speech, of Billy Sunday, the fire-and-brimstone evangelist, and of countless others like them) were full of moral uplift and "inspiration" (proclaiming "Mother, Home, and Heaven"), the good music, the good plays (which sometimes had to be toned down a bit) and occasionally a lecture by a nonpreacher (Stefansson, the Arctic explorer, Opie Read, the humorist, and such politicians as Debs, William Howard Taft, Herbert Hoover, Al Smith, and Senators George Norris and Robert La Follette) made a dent on the starved minds and the pinched souls of these rural people and perhaps even stirred their crushed ideals.

The epitome of high moral uplift though we on chautauqua were, we sometimes ran into the earthy problems of the flesh. More than once a "Broadway" actor or a "foreign" member of one of the bands or orchestras (French? Italian?) seduced a young lady who, stage-struck, had come back stage to pour out her heart. And one summer our handsome young superintendent, a Baptist preacher and a whiz at enticing a new contract out of the local businessmen, got into trouble. I had rather envied his success with the local girls in one town after another, though his promiscuous amorousness had surprised me since he often showed me snapshots of his wife and three children, for whom he professed great devotion. In one of our last towns that summer, a pretty young coed home on summer vacation from college showed me an engagement ring our minister had given her, and indeed before the summer was out they were married—the first case of bigamy I had ever seen at first hand. Keith Vawter, a deeply religious and moral man, was livid when he learned of it from the aggrieved first wife, and later from the authorities, and put me through the coals when I returned to Cedar Rapids for not having reported it.

Those summers on chautauqua were educational for me in many ways. For the first time I became aware of girls, of how attractive some were and what pleasure you could have in their company. The "New York" sophistication of the young women in our "Broadway" companies fascinated me, but some of the local girls, home from college, were interesting, too. And, on quite another plane, I saw more clearly that Sinclair Lewis was essentially truthful and accurate in his searing portrait of Main Street. His novel of that title had been published in October of 1920, had swiftly climbed to the top of the best-seller list, and by my second summer on chautauqua, in 1921, had swept the country. Everyone in Cedar Rapids had been reading it and I now found it had penetrated even the smaller towns. One week we pitched our tent in a Minnesota town not far from Sauk Centre, the Gopher Prairie of the book, where Lewis had grown up and which he had so devastatingly satirized. The country around was highly indignant. Sinclair Lewis, people said, had libeled them. Their Main Streets, they said, were not as dull, their people not such clods, as the now famous author—the success of the book had skyrocketed him into national fame—had depicted. By the end of my second summer on chautauqua, after working twenty Main Streets, I concluded that Lewis had not greatly exaggerated. These people in the crossroads towns did live drab lives, they exacted from one another a withering conformity on a dreadfully low level, their towns were unlovely. Piety and boosterism were not enough for a decent, meaningful life. Yet, one had to admit, they were not aware of what they were missing. They seemed happy enough. Or, at least, content. Chautauqua had really not helped much.

And by then, I began to see, it was destroying William Jennings Bryan. He had been, after all, one of America's foremost political figures—three times the Democratic candidate for President, and Secretary of State, for a time, under President Wilson. He had leaped to fame in 1896 as the great Populist leader from the Midwest who swore to tame the great robber barons, the "malefactors" of wealth, and to restore the government to the common people. He had been the idol of millions, including me. Now, by 1920 and 1921, all this lay behind him, forgotten. He had become, it seemed to me, an empty shell, a vain and foolish old man, blabbering banalities about the wonders of fundamentalist Protestantism and the sinfulness of sin, especially drinking, though, to his credit it must be added that he never tired of extolling the virtues of Peace.

If he had faded as my own idol, I could see that he remained the idol of the millions who came to hear him under the stifling chautauqua tents. He packed them in, day after day, week after week, summer after summer—for a quarter of a century. But if, more than any other person, he had made chautauqua, it was obvious by 1920 and 1921 that chautauqua had destroyed him. It stultified his mind, deadening it against the reception of new ideas as the world continued to change. He repeated the same speech, day after day, year after year, to the same roaring applause, which fed his vanity but left his mind emptied and dry. There was no one against whom he could sharpen it. His eloquence remained unimpaired, as did his magnetism at the tribune. But even as he continued to sway the masses with his repetitious oratory, he retreated more and more from reality, perhaps unaware of the banality, the triviality, of the haven he had found under the chautauqua tents.

He no doubt was unaware, too, that his last appearance on chautauqua in 1924 marked the approach of his own end and that of chautauqua. It had been chautauqua's golden jubilee year, celebrating the fiftieth anniversary of the first meeting on Lake Chautauqua, and an audience of thirty million Americans in twelve thousand towns across the country had made it the biggest year in its history. I was finishing my junior year in college and working on a daily newspaper and had no idea that chautauqua was doomed, though if I had been a better journalist I might have. The changes in American life made this inevitable.

The demise of chautauqua was swift. In 1925, the year after the jubilee, the summer I set out for Europe, hundreds of towns balked at renewing their guarantees for chautauqua. Dozens of tents remained in the big warehouse in Cedar Rapids. What killed chautauqua? Panicky management at first blamed the local businessmen, who had finally become tired of guaranteeing the costs of a week of chautauqua. But this was a superficial explanation. What brought chautauqua to a sudden end were the automobile, the movies and above all the advent of radio. By the mid-twenties almost every rural American family had a car and could drive to the larger towns and cities to see a good movie or take in a concert or a play. But it was radio that dealt the death blow. Radio stations were popping up in hundreds of towns; they were being formed into networks. The country folk could now sit in their living rooms and, without paying a nickel, hear far better music and a much richer variety of talks and drama piped in from the great cities every week throughout the year than chautauqua had afforded them once a week in summer. Chautauqua had served its purpose. It had played a role in American life for half a century. Because of radio it went the way the great national magazines, *Look, Life, The Saturday Evening Post* and others, would go a generation later when television came. The medium of communication had changed. By 1932 the last of the chautauqua tents was put into storage—or to other uses— forever.

During my second tour on chautauqua, in 1921, there had been on our crew an attractive girl just out of college named Peggy O'Neal. She had shown much imagination in handling the youngsters and nursing them through their "pageant" on the last day in town. She was black-haired, blue-eyed, very Irish and quite lovely. We had traveled all summer together and had become extremely fond of each other. As the season approached its end she suggested that we get married, settle in some college town and run a book and art shop there. But I had not yet got to college and I wanted to try it first on my own, and I was not really in love.

All summer long I pondered where I would go to college. I thought first of the University of Chicago, whose campus I had known as a youngster; of the nearby University of Iowa; of Drake University in Des Moines. But we didn't have the money. So I enrolled that fall in the local college, Coe, where my sister was a senior, and where I, like her, could save the main expense of board and room by living at home. Most of the men among my fellow-graduates from Washington High who came from the old or better-heeled families were going off to college in the East, to Yale, Dartmouth, Princeton, Williams and Amherst. I do not recall that I was envious. My horizons were still limited. My father had found it no handicap, apparently, in afterlife to have gone to nearby Cornell College, which was very much like Coe except that it was situated in a village and was Methodist while Coe was Presbyterian[1] and its campus lay in the heart of an expanding town. It would be easier to find jobs in a place of fifty thousand than in Mount Vernon, which had remained a village of under

[1] Coe had already dropped direct affiliation with the church in order to get some Carnegie Foundation money for a teachers' pension fund and for a new science building, an act of divorcement which showed that a Christian institution of learning was worldly enough to realize where the sources of important money lay. It lay in the big foundations, no longer in the churches.

two thousand. For one thing, Cedar Rapids had two daily news-papers, and I had my eye on a job on one of them, which would not only help put me through college but would provide an ap-prenticeship to a profession that I had about made up my mind to follow.

With no high hopes, after the disappointments of highschool, but determined to get some kind of college education, I returned from chautauqua at the beginning of September, bid a senti-mental farewell to Peggy O'Neal, and registered as a freshman at Coe.

Its origins, like those of most Midwest denominational col-leges, were pious and primitive, narrow-minded and zealously Christian; and in my time, three-quarters of a century later, Coe had not entirely outgrown them nor did it desire to. What later became Coe College had begun in 1851 as a crude seminary to train young men for the ministry, presided over by the pastor of the Presbyterian church, one Williston Jones, and his wife, who between them taught writing, grammar, geography, algebra, arithmetic, Bible, Latin and Greek, and held classes in their home and church, whose grounds only sixteen years before had be-longed to the Indians.

Under various names, Cedar Rapids Collegiate Institute, Parsons Seminary and Coe Collegiate Institute, it prospered and fell apart until in 1881 it was incorporated as Coe College on a campus of eighty acres on the edge of town purchased from a fund of fifteen hundred dollars donated in 1853 by a Catskill, New York, Presbyterian farmer named Daniel Coe.[1] During the next forty years the student body grew from fifty to nine hundred and the faculty and buildings increased accordingly. Most of the students were like me: they came from solid families of modest means, many fresh off the farm and from the small towns. Most had to earn at least part of their way. The teachers were as poor

---

[1] The rules for student conduct laid down that year stipulated:

    1. All are expected to be present at morning and evening worship, and to attend church and Sabbath school on the Sabbath.
    2. No games of chance are permitted. The use of fire-arms or gun-powder is strictly prohibited.
    3. All profanity, the playing of cards, the use of intoxicating liquors, the use of tobacco on the college grounds, attendance upon balls or theaters, visiting drinking or billiard saloons . . . are strictly prohibited.

in purse as their pupils, for salaries were meager, and it always seemed a wonder to me that they were so dedicated to their work and, especially, that a few at least were so outstanding. In my four years there were two or three who aroused my sluggish mind. I doubt if any student in any college anywhere has better luck than that.

There were limitations, of course. There was an isolation from the great centers of learning that was more than geographical. The library was woefully lacking in books and space. The science laboratory facilities were inadequate. The intellectual level of the place was low,[1] not only among the students but among the run of the faculty, its ranks littered with a good many mossbacks. Both pupils and teachers and of course the administration and the trustees were proud of the Christian atmosphere of the campus, as if that made up for the intellectual and cultural deficiencies.[2]

Two years of Bible study were required, but not an hour of philosophy; in fact, there were no courses in philosophy.[3] I stumbled on Santayana, Bertrand Russell, William James, Dewey and Bergson wholly by chance, and on the more ancient philosophers not until well out of college. And with a few exceptions, history, economics, sociology and psychology were taught in a humdrum fashion, though the exceptions were notable. The English Department had scarcely heard of anything written since the Victorians, and foreign-language literature was entirely ignored, as if Sopho-

---

[1] "The intellectual quickening of the Twenties was not pronounced," the *Coe College Courier,* the official alumni publication, recalled in its centennial number in 1951. "Only the Shirer brothers raised their voices . . . Most of the women who went to Coe were looking for husbands."

[2] Professor George W. Bryant, my Latin teacher and track coach, a graduate of Coe and Princeton, never tired of injecting God into athletics, which he had built up over a quarter of a century from scratch. "Intensely religious men," he said, "make the very best kind of football players, and atheists a rather indifferent lot. Let football then be made a religious game, and let our college men make their religion a football game." This last exhortation revealed that he was not so religious as he thought.

But the sincerity of a young coed addressing the Y.W.C.A. on a somewhat similar subject could not be doubted: "Health is not a luxury or a private convenience," she said, "but a religious requisite . . . Do we, as college women, play every game in such a way as to give Christ, the umpire, the preeminence?"

[3] The president, who had done his postgraduate studies in philosophy at Columbia, in defending compulsory Bible study assured the trustees that "study of the Bible by a devout Christian student will prepare him for life. The Bible is the world's best treatise on 'Pushing to the Front' or on 'Getting On in the World.' "

cles, Euripides, Sappho, Dante, Montaigne, Cervantes, Goethe, Balzac, Stendhal, Tolstoy, Dostoevsky and their like had never lived. These shortcomings, however, rarely disturbed the complacency of the campus. What you did not know—or learn—wouldn't hurt you, as long as you remained a good Christian. Still, I suppose, the college reflected the educational and cultural standards of a Midwest rural state, though a new president, the first professional educator the college had had as its head after a long series of Presbyterian preachers, was striving to improve them.

All this I would eventually learn. In the beginning I was a practicing Presbyterian, green and ignorant, a country bumpkin, except that my mind may have matured a little from a good deal of extracurricular reading of novels and history in books profusely borrowed from the Public Library during my highschool years. By the time I entered Coe I had read a good bit of Shakespeare, Milton, Dickens, George Eliot, Irving, Cooper, Hawthorne, Emerson, Thoreau, Mark Twain, Balzac, Dumas, Defoe, Tolstoy, Dostoevsky, Shelley, Keats, Byron, Whitman (and Longfellow and Whittier, of course), Gibbon, Prescott and Mott. Obviously there were many gaps.

For all the complacency of the college and the town, there was a ferment in the world in 1921 that stirred even us. The Great War had turned a lot of things upside down. The age I had been born into had come to an end in 1918, its staid certainties, its simple faiths and beliefs, swept away in the carnage. Americans, though their country had come into the war late and had not suffered or sacrificed much, were tired of wartime restrictions, mild as they had been. They were weary of President Wilson's ideals and his preachments about making the world permanently peaceful and safe for democracy. The year before, in November, 1920, they had rejected Wilsonianism and elected as President a Republican, Warren G. Harding, an amiable but mediocre small-town Ohio newspaper publisher and U.S. Senator, by a majority of nearly two to one. Iowa had backed him three to one. Harding had promised a period of "normalcy." Now our good people had their wish: to be left alone by their government, and by history, free to make money and whoopee, freed from concerns about the wicked, war-torn world beyond the seas.

We were going on a spree, leaping into the jazz age, the era of wonderful nonsense, of flappers and sheiks, of automobiles, racy Hollywood movies, the newfangled radio, booze and bootleggers, and uninhibited sex. The year before, too, Scott Fitzgerald, just three years out of Princeton, had published his novel *This Side of Paradise*, celebrating the new freedoms of college youth, especially in drinking and sex. It had shocked our town and our college, but it had made an impression, nevertheless. It was still being bootlegged around the campus when I arrived—along with liquor, which had been outlawed in the country the year before by the ratification of the Eighteenth Amendment, and which we students were forbidden to touch on the pain of expulsion.

This, like sex, raised certain problems on our pious campus. Just about the entire student body of men at Coe had gone off to the war in 1917, and now most of them had returned, hardened by combat in France, cynical about puritan morals and resentful that Prohibition had been put over on the country while they were away. In France they had learned something not only about the hell of combat, about life and death, but about women and drink. They were not to be tamed by the stern moral precepts of a Christian campus, whose elders and innocent younger students had not gone through that searing experience. The fraternity I joined was full of these men—hardened beyond their years, we youngsters thought, with admiration—and they raised so much hell and drank so hard that our local chapter was suspended for a year by the national organization and was disciplined by the college.

So it was in this Presbyterian place of learning among such fine men that I first learned, among other things, to drink and to survive the poisonous alcoholic concoctions that Prohibition, in its folly, had foisted upon the country. And to look at girls with a less inhibited approach.

The young college women, coming as they did from stable, God-fearing, rural homes, were also affected by the freer new time. Despite the edicts of the stern dean of women, they began to shorten their skirts from the ankles to the knees; they bobbed their hair, though this, too, was frowned on; and they began, in secret, to smoke and—horrors!—to kiss and pet.

All this is obviously tame to the college generation of the 1970's, which, apart from the drug culture of some, goes much further toward a civilized relation of the sexes. In my time in my college the relaxations in morals of the jazz age seemed a scandal to parents and faculty and to many zealous students. Girls who went with their boys to a public dance hall were severely disciplined and threatened with expulsion. A young man caught embracing his girl in a dark corner of the lobby of the women's dormitory was liable to be thrown not only out of the dormitory but the college, along with her.

From the first, college began to be more interesting and rewarding than highschool. My studies and some of the teachers were more challenging, but aside from that, I felt accepted, as I had not been in highschool. I was invited to join a fraternity. I made the staff of the school paper, one of the best-edited college weeklies in the country. I quickly won a place on the debating team. All three were achievements denied me in highschool.

I also threw myself into the juvenile rah-rah spirit of this provincial campus. In after years I almost convinced myself that this had never happened to me, that from the start I had been too sophisticated for such nonsense. But the truth is that I was just like the rest—at least for the first couple of years. I cheered the football team, especially when it upset Iowa State and tied mighty Wisconsin; yelled myself hoarse at pep meetings and games; and joined exuberantly in Homecoming Week, with its silly parade of idiotic floats, its parties and dances, its welcome to delirious old grads returning to the one place in which they had found much happiness in life, and the climactic big football game with either Cornell or Grinnell. I blush today, half a century later, to read the childish rubbish I wrote in a "humor" column in the *Cosmos*. It is full of the most dreadful trivialities and smart-aleckness of college life.

Gradually, though, I began to grow up. Perhaps it was the off-campus experience of the long summer vacations that helped most. The first summer, 1922, I worked the harvest fields of western Nebraska. The following two summers were spent on the Cedar Rapids *Republican* as sports editor and feature writer. These jobs gave me a somewhat wider view of the adult world, just as the summers "soldiering" at Camp Funston and working on chautauqua during the highschool years had.

In the wheat fields that first summer I got a glimpse of the wonderful world of the Wobblies, of the I.W.W., before that remarkable group of migratory American workers, who left an imprint of tough radicalism on our West, passed into history. For nearly a quarter of a century the I.W.W. (Industrial Workers of the World), organized by "Big Bill" Haywood, had been raising hell up and down the country, launching strikes and battling with employers, strikebreakers, state militia and federal troops. By the time I hit the harvest fields in the summer of 1922 the catchall union was about finished. Still, most of my fellow-workers were card-carrying Wobblies, the last of a colorful breed, and at night around the barns, after work, they used to sing the old songs[1] of Joe Hill, the troubadour of the I.W.W., and tell of his untimely end when he was framed, they said, in Utah on a murder charge and was executed in the prison yard at Salt Lake City.[2]

I must say I liked these rough men, riding the rails of the western country from one job to another, working the wheat fields in the summer, picking lettuce, grapes and oranges in California in the winter, with months of loafing in between. They were contemptuous of authority, of "settling down," and happy to be on the road. They seemed wonderfully free. Some of them were surprisingly well read. There was one old "hobo," as he liked to call himself, with a craggy, weather-beaten, but kindly, intelligent face, whose spare luggage included a bag of books. He quoted Jack London, Upton Sinclair, Henry George, Spencer and Marx all day and upbraided me for not knowing enough of them to argue with him.

"What the hell do you guys read in college?" he would tease me. "How the hell can we have some intelligent discussions when you haven't read anything?"

Saturday nights the Wobblies from all around would gather at a barn dance, sing, square-dance, get drunk. Though most ranchers were suspicious of the I.W.W. bums, as they called them ("Didn't I.W.W. stand for 'I Won't Work'?" they would say), and some feared them as Bosheviks intent on overthrowing the Republic, those in our area that summer were tolerant enough—

---

[1] Their favorite was "Hallelujah, I'm a Bum!"

[2] "Don't mourn for me, organize" were the last words he sent out to the working stiffs of the I.W.W. Joe Hill stood up against the wall of the jail yard, looked into the muzzles of the guns, and gave the word to fire.

"They put him in a black suit, put a stiff collar around his neck and a bow tie, shipped him to Chicago for a bangup funeral, and photographed his handsome stony mask staring into the future."—John Dos Passos: *Nineteen Nineteen*, p. 421 (paperback edition).

after all, you couldn't get your wheat harvested without them—
and set up the barn dances, hired a fiddler and brought in their
wives and daughters to provide partners. Perhaps the farmers
thought this was a good way for the tough harvesters to let off
steam. There were a few fights and one brawl between some local
hands and the Wobblies over a girl, but on the whole the barn
dances were peaceful enough—the I.W.W. stiffs had a sense of
brotherhood—and I myself had a wonderful time.

So even in the harvest fields that summer, my real education,
as opposed to that of academe, continued. These Wobblies,
knights of the road, as they jocularly called themselves, set me to
thinking as no professor had that first year in college. I had been
raised to believe that you got a crack at the good life by hard
work, sober habits, Christian behavior and a college education.
But here were these "tramps," with whom I worked from sunup
to sundown that summer, drifting up and down the land, working
just enough to enable them to eat well, happy as larks and attuned to life and nature more than I was, showing me that you
didn't have to live conventionally, settle down, get a steady job,
get married and have children, join a church, a lodge, Rotary or
Kiwanis, and all that, to fulfill yourself.

With such thoughts, bound to sound subversive if expressed
in the churchy, Republican, wholesome-family atmosphere of
Cedar Rapids and Coe College, I returned in the fall to school.
Not much happened there that second year. But off campus I got
the break I had been waiting for. I got a job that fall as sports
editor of the daily *Republican*. Every morning from seven to ten I
got out two pages of sports, then dashed off in a streetcar to
classes. The pay, twenty-five dollars a week, struck me as tremendous. I could help pay the family grocery bills, buy a couple of
rather badly needed new suits, replace my shabby shoes, and still
have enough left over to splurge weekends with the girls.

When the next two summer vacations came, I worked full-
time (the ten- to twelve-hour day which was customary on small-
town dailies in those pre-Guild days), editing the sports pages,
covering the local baseball team of the Three-I League and turning out a steady flow of general feature stories for the local news
pages. My full-time pay was increased to thirty-five dollars and
finally to fifty dollars a week, which was considerably more than
the "World's Greatest Newspaper" would pay me the first years in

Paris. The stuff I turned out undoubtedly was mostly junk. But it probably chronicled—and mirrored—faithfully enough the life of an Iowa town in the Prohibition days of the early 1920's.

One day a speaker in chapel, Sidney F. Wicks, editor of the *Manchester Guardian,* which *was* one of the world's greatest newspapers, had given me some advice about going into journalism. "You can learn all the technique of newspapering," he said, "in three months in a newspaper office." I found this to be true, and this early experience of reporting, editing and rewriting copy, and knocking out headlines against a deadline would save my life, or at least my job, when I went to work for the Paris edition of the *Tribune.*

Wicks had given me a further piece of advice, which was more important. "Acquire a background," he admonished. "Read Plato, Socrates, Shakespeare, Carlyle, Anatole France and a lot more like them. It takes longer than learning the mere trade of journalism. But without it, you won't be very good." On this piece of advice, I have worked all my life.

The Cedar Rapids *Republican,* the older of the two dailies, had been launched in 1872, but by the time I began to labor on it in the early 1920's it was second in circulation and prestige to the *Gazette* and it was gradually running down. It had had from 1898 until recently a remarkable editor, Cyrenus Cole, who had given it a certain distinction. He was a sort of Iowa William Allen White, learned in literature, Biblical, classical and modern, who tossed off quotations from the Bible, the Greeks, the Romans, Shakespeare, Milton, Balzac and others with alacrity and wrote in a simple, graceful and somehow haunting style. Shortly before I arrived he had got himself elected to Congress and had gone off to Washington. He had been to me one of the more interesting personalities in the town—there were half a dozen others—and I had read him avidly as a youngster and got to know him when I was the highschool correspondent of the paper.

Later I would sometimes reflect on him and his career. Here was an editor and a writer of unusual talent—the New York *Tribune* had once tried to lure him away as an editorial writer—who fell victim to the fatal flaws of so many men who rise from humble origins to prominence. He went with the upper crust, with the moneybags. Born of Dutch parents on an Iowa farm, penniless at first and later poorly paid on Iowa newspapers, despite his brilliance, he rejected the Populism and the radicalism of the Midwest, which were protests of our hard-working common people against the domination of the country by the wealthy of the East, and became a standpat Republican and an ultraconservative. (Herbert Hoover, born in West Branch, twenty miles from Cedar Rapids, and early orphaned, would follow the same path.) In 1900, enamored of Mark Hanna, the Ohio boss who was putting over President McKinley for a second term, Cole, at Hanna's insistence, wrote one of the chief Republican campaign books, designed to combat Bryan's Populism in the Midwest and the bimetalism of Adlai E. Stevenson, Bryan's running mate. In my own time, Cole sneered at Iowa's Populist phenomenon Smith Wildman Brookhart as "Wild Man" Brookhart when Brookhart ran against the standpatters and won a seat as a Republican in the U.S. Senate in 1922.

Cole's heart, he later revealed, had been broken in 1912 when his beloved Republican Party split between President Taft and former President Theodore Roosevelt, and Woodrow Wilson, the Democratic candidate, was elected.

> Amid the wreckage of the Standpatters [he later wrote in his memoirs], I sat in gloom . . . To me the Republican Party had been synonymous with my country, and the Standpatters had been the bearers of my political ark.

He never quite recovered. When finally in 1921 he resigned as editor and won our district's seat in Congress, his talents as a civilized and graceful writer seemed spent. His weekly letters from the capital became exercises in banality. He touted his standpat Republicanism. He seemed unable to see an inch beyond his party. He found the mediocre, floundering Harding "a great President" and on the Coolidges he was ecstatic. "When I think of Calvin and Grace Goodhue Coolidge in the White House," he wrote, "I cannot but wish that their lives be repeated in all the homes of America." Cole's kind of success, it seemed to me, destroyed not only his writing but his judgment. In retrospect, his career as a newspaperman, congressman and something of a philosopher reminds me of the remark of Brooks Adams, brother of Henry, to Justice Holmes that "philosophers are men hired by the well-to-do to prove that everything is all right."

All newsrooms have bizarre characters and ours was no exception. There was Belle Bever, the society editor, unmarried, in her late sixties, her neat white hair tucked under a large hat that she never removed, a member of one of the oldest families and never forgetting it, sitting like a ramrod in her little cubicle of an office, scribbling her copy with a pencil. She had been with the newspaper since the 1880's and had become a sort of social arbiter in the town, knowing each family's place in the social hierarchy, writing up their marriages, their soirees, the births of their children. She knew all the secrets, too, the skeletons in their closets, and kept them out of the paper. She avoided the raucousness of the newsroom and kept to her cubicle the day long in splendid, imperious isolation. I held her in some awe. She seemed to me an eerie survival from the past and the gulf between us was too vast for communication across it. Her lengthy chronicles of the doings of the socially prominent struck me as drivel but she believed they were one of the most important parts of the newspaper, and most of our readers probably agreed with her. If only, I used to think, she had a sense of irony, of proportion, a little skepticism—but then she would not have been the willowy relic she was. Every newsroom ought to have at least one relic—a link to the past, a reminder of a world buried by time and changes.

Frederick J. Lazell, who succeeded Cole as editor, had been with the *Republican* since 1896, and it was he who quickly taught me the ropes of reporting and editing. He was a prodigious worker, pounding out on his typewriter editorials and articles from dawn to dusk. Newspapering was in his blood and getting out the daily *Republican* was his life—with one exception. He was a passionate gardener, a sort of local John Burroughs, who not only found time somehow on weekends to cultivate one of the finest gardens in town but to write five books about it. I liked and admired him and learned much from this modest, kindly man. His love of newspapering, of the smell of ink and paper, of the excitement in the newsroom when a big story broke, rubbed off on me and became a part of me for ever after.

Like Cole and so many other editors I would eventually work with, and like all of us, he had his flaws. For all his mastery of the technique of newspapering he was not a man to take a lonely stand against the current. In his office he submitted to the powers that be. At home he cultivated his garden.

Since the *Republican* was slipping, a pair of new young publishers decided my first year on the paper to hire a "big-time" city editor to jazz up its columns. A craggy-faced man of forty, he was one of the last of the breed of old-time newspapermen who drifted from town to town across the country, hard-boiled, cynical, able, fast-talking, and given to heavy drinking and running after women. Within a week he was giving our staid journal flaming headlines more suitable for a Hearst paper. The town was bewildered by such a display in such a conservative old publication. We reporters too. But we liked the man. After putting the paper to bed, he would regale us provincials with tales of the big time, of his work on so many great papers—the New York *World,* the San Francisco *Chronicle* and many others, and perhaps he actually had worked on some of them.

One Monday morning he failed to appear. For several days he had been complaining that some girl was trying to get him, and he had been drinking more heavily than usual. He had also taken to borrowing a little, five, ten, fifteen dollars at a time from each of us, "to meet some lousy debt in New York," and had duly given us I.O.U.'s. By afternoon, when we had somehow got the paper out without him, the office began to fill with the family and the lawyer of a young lady of the town who claimed our dashing editor had mulcted several hundred dollars from her in connection with a marriage proposal. They were followed by several merchants who maintained the man had run up large bills with them. But they arrived too late. The weekend had given our man a good start. Probably, I mused, he was already sitting at a city desk in another town safely distant—under a new name.

My two years, part-time and full-time, on the esteemed *Republican* passed quickly and pleasantly. The first summer, 1923, was climaxed by covering, for a change, two stories of more than local interest. President Harding's funeral train stopped briefly in Cedar Rapids on the morning of August 6. It is difficult to recall today the outflowing of grief in the country for this undistinguished President who suddenly departed this earth in San Francisco on August 2, just before his Administration would be revealed as one of the most corrupt in the Republic's history. I must admit I shared in it. It would take years of growing up before I realized how maudlin we Americans become on such occasions. By then, of course, one knew more of Harding than on that hot August day when his remains were riding through our town and the church bells tolled and people wept.

There was an A.P. dispatch that day that carried the headline: "HARDING BELIEVED FIRMLY IN CHRIST. GAVE HIS LIFE TO BRING GOVERNMENT CLOSER TO THE PEOPLE." (We did not know then that he brought government closer to the crooks.) Over at the *Gazette* a front-page editorial mourned: "Never has misfortune struck a more untimely blow. . . . There is something infinitely pathetic in the quiet death of this great man. . . . His spirit lives on." The scene in Cedar Rapids, where fifteen thousand citizens, a third of our population, turned out to express their grief as the funeral train passed through, was repeated in scores of towns along the way from coast to coast. A *New York Times* reporter aboard the train wrote that it was "the most remarkable demonstration in American history of affection, respect and reverence for the dead." Nearly a decade later Frederick Lewis Allen in his classic book *Only Yesterday* pondered over this.

> . . . everywhere people felt that a great-hearted man, bowed down with his labors in their behalf, had died a martyr to the service of his country. The dead President was called "a majestic figure who stood out like a rock of consistency"; it was said that "his vision was always on the spiritual"; and Bishop Manning of New York, speaking at a memorial service in the Cathedral of St. John the Divine, seemed to be giving the fallen hero no more than his due when he cried, "If I could write one sentence upon his monument it would be this, 'He taught us the power of brotherliness.' . . . May God ever give to our country leaders as faithful, as wise, as noble in spirit, as the one whom we now mourn."
>
> But as it happens [Allen thought], there are some problems —at least for a President of the United States—that the spirit of brotherliness and kindness will not alone solve. The problem, for example, of what to do when those to whom you have been all too brotherly have enmeshed your administration in graft, and you know that the scandal cannot long be concealed, and you feel your whole life-work toppling into disgrace. That was the problem which had killed Warren Harding.

Allen, the sober editor of *Harper's*, recounts the rumor that Harding committed suicide by taking poison, which was the theme of Samuel Hopkins Adams' novel *Revelry;* and he weighs the implications of Gaston B. Means, a Department of Justice detective and a member of the gang which was deeply involved in the corruption in Washington, that "the President was poisoned by his wife, with the connivance of Doctor Sawyer," his personal physician.

The motive, according to Means, was a double one: Mrs. Harding had found out about Nan Britton and the illegitimate daughter and was consumed with a bitter and almost insane jealousy; and she had learned enough about the machinations of Harding's friends and the power that they had over him to feel that only death could save him from obloquy.

"Both the suicide theory and the Means story," writes Allen, who was the most responsible editor I would ever know, "are very plausible." But, of course, both could not be right. The published accounts of the President suffering ptomaine poisoning from eating crab meat on the Presidential boat on the return from Alaska, Allen treats with skepticism. There was no crab meat in the steward's pantry, he found, and no one else in the Presidential party was taken ill. Furthermore, he points out, the fatal "stroke of apoplexy" in San Francisco occurred when the President was recovering from pneumonia.

Mrs. Harding was apparently alone with him at the time, and the verdict of the physicians, not being based upon an autopsy, was hardly more than an expression of opinion.

Whether all this was true or not we shall probably never know for certain. What we eventually learned, as Allen says, is that Harding knew too much of the skulduggery in his Administration to be able to face the future. All during the Alaskan trip, according to William Allen White, he kept complaining to Secretary Herbert Hoover and other confidants that he had been "betrayed" by his friends. "Whatever killed him," Allen concludes, "—poison or heart failure—did so the more easily because he had lost the will to live."[1]

[1] All quotations from Allen from his *Only Yesterday,* pp. 120–121 (paperback edition).

Of all this we knew nothing that August morning when Harding's funeral train passed through. My own dreadfully sentimental story, a faded copy of which lies before me to haunt me, is best passed over in silence. The last two paragraphs are typical.

> Mrs. Harding was seated at a table peering distantly out of the screened window, and as the car . . . went by, the heart of the throng went out to her who but a short time ago was the first lady of the land.
> "What a brave, brave woman," remarked one, and her comment was silently accepted by the rest.

"Scoops"—getting an exclusive story—are part of the fleeting glory of the newspaper game, and I suppose I got my share in the ensuing twenty-five years in Europe and Asia, though I have come to think that they are not nearly as important as most editors, and reporters, think.

No doubt I felt a little puffed up when, a few days after the Harding funeral train story that August, I scored a scoop for my sport pages with an exclusive interview with Jack Dempsey as he was passing through on his way to fight Luis Firpo in New York.[1] It wasn't much of a story, but then no one else on the two local dailies had ever talked with the great heavyweight champion before.

The stationmaster at the Union Station had tipped me off that Dempsey would be on the train from the West Coast and he had given me the number of his Pullman car. In the best fashion of the intrepid cub reporter I burst into the champion's stateroom, elbowing away a couple of hangers-on who were on guard. The trouble was that Dempsey was fast asleep, snoring. I woke him up.

"Excuse me, Jack," I howled, "but how do you think you'll do against Firpo?" He rubbed his eyes, gave me a scowling look, and muttered, "How's that?" I repeated the question. "I'll knock him out," he said. The scowl became more menacing—many an un-

---

[1] He would knock out Firpo a few weeks later to remain the heavyweight champion of the world, probably the greatest we ever had. It was one of the briefest and most exciting heavyweight champion bouts ever fought. In the first round Firpo knocked Dempsey down twice, once through the ropes; Dempsey dropped Firpo five times. He finished him off in the second round in less than a minute.

easy opponent had faced it in the ring, I knew. "And who the hell let you in? Who the hell are you?" I identified myself. "Well, what do you want? You woke me up." I told him. He sat up in bed, glowered at me and finally smiled. "O.K. What do you want to know? Where are we anyway? Iowa? Ohio?"

I told him he was in Cedar Rapids, Iowa, and by his glance I realized he had never heard of our fair town. "Go ahead." He grunted. "How you going to fight him?" I asked. And so on. And he gave the answers any reporter could have made up.

"Thanks very much, Jack. And good luck with Firpo," I said, and put out my hand to the great man. "O.K., son," he said, shook my hand, and turned his face to the wall to resume his slumber.

The next day I ran into the editor of the rival *Gazette*, Verne Marshall, on the street. "Damned good scoop on Dempsey," he said. "Our sports editor hasn't recovered yet."

Verne Marshall was another of the half-dozen personalities in the town who interested me and who might have made it in the "big time" and who, in fact, briefly did. He had been one of my idols in the highschool years ever since the day he came to an assembly and vividly described his experiences as an ambulance driver at Verdun. A crusading editor, who ran a front-page editorial column after the manner of Arthur Brisbane for Hearst, he often stirred up our placid town. Later, in 1936, he won for the *Gazette* a Pulitzer Prize "for the most meritorious public service of the year" by exposing corruption among state officials and a slot-machine ring.

The strain of battling against America's entry into World War II unhinged him. He became one of the fiercest and most effective of the speakers (after Lindbergh) for America First and the No Foreign War Committee, devoting all of his time and his considerable energies to their cause, speaking day and night to one rally after another from coast to coast, taking on all comers in radio debates, and achieving what perhaps pleased him most— national recognition—sharing the platform and the radio studio with our leading isolationists, Herbert Hoover, General Robert E. Wood, Senator Burton K. Wheeler and Lindbergh. But the strain began to tell. Marshall's fanaticism and his ceaseless activities proved too much for his nerves. He neglected the *Gazette* and finally gave it up altogether in December, 1940.

I remember a summer Sunday evening in 1941 that I was

spending at the Long Island home of William Paley, who owned the Columbia Broadcasting System, for which I was then working. I had recently returned from Berlin and from covering the first part of World War II. Verne Marshall was in our New York studio waiting to make a speech in answer to President Roosevelt, whom he accused of trying to drag us into the war. Elmer Davis, the bright star of the C.B.S. news team, had been appointed to introduce him. Suddenly, Davis was on the telephone to Paley saying that Marshall refused to be introduced by him. "He calls me a damn warmonger, and he looks as if he were about to tear up the place," Davis said in his dry Hoosier drawl. "He says he will go on only if he is introduced by his old Cedar Rapids friend Bill Shirer. What do we do?"

I had talked to Marshall since returning home and we had agreed to disagree—violently. I suggested to Paley that since C.B.S. had offered "equal time" to Marshall to reply to the President, it was his fault if he refused to use it. Paley handed me the phone and asked me to talk to him. I told Marshall that Davis, despite his personal opinions, which I shared, was the fairest and decentest guy in the world, and could introduce him more gracefully than I could. Finally he calmed down and agreed to go on. He made an extremely effective speech; he was a magnetic personality on the air. I remember that he frightened several of Paley's guests, who included a fair sprinkling of notables—Herbert Bayard Swope and a number of editors, among them—who feared the America Firsters might still prevail in the country.

The next day, I took Verne out to lunch in New York. It was a painful experience to one who had known him in his prime in our town. He was on the edge of a breakdown. It soon came and it finished him.

Among others in Cedar Rapids who left a certain mark on me were two learned and eloquent preachers—one who might have made it in the big world if he had wanted to, and one who did. Dr. Edward Read Burkhalter was entering on his seventieth year in 1913, when we arrived, after thirty-seven years as pastor of the First Presbyterian Church. Born and raised in New York City, graduated from Princeton and the Union Theological Seminary and with a German university doctorate, he had become at twenty-six the pastor of the Presbyterian Church at New Rochelle, a suburb of New York, and an instructor in Hebrew at the Union Theological Seminary, where he had been promised an eventual professorship. Why he left such a fertile and civilized field for the raw prairies was somewhat of a mystery in our town, though he often told me why. He had fallen in love with a young graduate of Mount Holyoke Seminary (as it then was) who lived in Burlington, Iowa, whom he married, and he had simultaneously fallen in love with the land beyond the Mississippi. After six years and three children in New Rochelle, they could not resist the call of the West, and when in 1876 a call came from Cedar Rapids, then a frontier town of seven thousand, they accepted it, and never regretted it.

Dr. Burkhalter was my neighbor and early mentor. His learning, especially in Hebrew, Greek and Latin, was prodigious, and if most of it was lost on me, his passion for it was not. Over the back fence which separated his garden from ours, we talked for hours through the years. For one thing, he was the most vivid link to the past, to history, that I had. As a boy of six he had watched from the windows of Barnum's Museum in New York the funeral procession of President Zachary Taylor pass up Broadway. As a student at Princeton in 1861 he had gazed at Lincoln as the President-elect passed through Trenton on his way to Washington to be inaugurated. He had graduated from Princeton the next year and, rejected for military service because of poor health, had spent the last two years of the Civil War studying in Germany: at Bonn, Heidelberg, Berlin.

He would talk for hours about his life in the Prussian capital, of the flavor of the university, where the great Fichte and Hegel had taught in the first years of the nineteenth century and where Treitschke was still lecturing—those three towering philosophers who would have such a formidable, and disastrous, influence on the German people and nation. But the university was not the exclusive center of young Burkhalter's life. He loved, he said, to watch the old King of Prussia review his troops on the Unter den Linden. His one great disappointment was that he had never been able to catch sight of Bismarck, who six years later would make the Prussian King the Emperor of Germany and arrange for him to be crowned as Wilhelm I in the Hall of Mirrors at Versailles, after the defeat of France by Prussia.

The young student kept in touch with home through his

friendship with the American Minister in Berlin, N. B. Judd, a close personal friend of Lincoln, who regaled him with stories of the President, eagerly told him of the latest Northern victory and continually assured him that the Union would soon triumph. It was an exciting life for the young American, the days filled with lectures at the university, with watching Bismarck building up aggressive Prussia into a German Empire, and with following, through Lincoln's Minister, the culminating years of the American Civil War.

Berlin obviously had left an indelible mark on Burkhalter—it had implanted in him a devotion to scholarship, a sense of history, a feeling for the Germans—but fascinated as I was by his stories, it seemed a faraway place that would never concern me as it had him. My grandfather Shirer, who loathed the Hohenzollerns and the Prussians, had told me that Berlin was an ugly place filled with ugly people. As I listened to Dr. Burkhalter talk of it across the garden fence, I could not have had the faintest inkling, as a youth with horizons that scarcely stretched beyond the town limits, that it would be my fate to live and work in Berlin through most of the barbarous Nazi time and that the great city would leave an even deeper imprint on my life than on his.

Nor could I appreciate Dr. Burkhalter's learning, though it filled me with some awe. Later in my highschool and early college days, when he was trying unsuccessfully to interest me in taking up Greek and Latin, and more successfully to widen my reading, he did succeed at least in making me take note of some of the subjects of his scholarly pursuits. To my untutored mind they were formidable. Like all great scholars, he carried his learning easily, and he was tolerant of my intellectual limitations.

"You must read Augustine," he would say to me. He had acquired, he said, eight volumes in Latin of the saint and six volumes of Chrysostom, to boot. "At least read the *Confessions*. They're much better than his *City of God*. Of course, Augustine didn't know much Hebrew, and less Greek—only Latin, and this sometimes led him into error. But read him! A genius. A philosopher. And what a poet!"

It was the first time, I think, that I had heard anyone in Cedar Rapids excited about a poet. Or about Augustine. Or about dozens of other old authors. Or about history. And the ancient philosophies and controversies. For years he steeped himself in the study of the Council of Nicaea and the Arian quarrel, quoting Sozomen, Theodoret, Athanasius, Hilary of Poitiers, Basil and the Gregorys. He would tell of his joy in coming across Bernard of Clairvaux's *Sermons* in the library of the University of Chicago, and of how disappointed he was with the *Summa* of Thomas Aquinas, whose six volumes he had purchased, and which, he admitted, he found dull reading, full of the vices of Scholasticism.

Steeped as he was in the old literature, Burkhalter took a lively interest in the goings on of the town. He was an early advocate of the ecumenical movement when it was little known or understood in our place. He insisted on bringing the ministers of all our churches, including the two Catholic churches, together in the Ministerial Union, over which he presided and to which he lectured on tolerance of one another's faiths. He was much criticized at first for bringing in the Catholics, who were looked on with some suspicion and even hostility in our Protestant-dominated community, but he brushed it aside, and one colorful Irish priest, Father Toomey, who defied his bishop in Dubuque by joining with his Protestant brethren, became one of his closest friends and admirers. "What that saintly man has taught me! About life. Religion. Even about our early church! And what a fine friend!" he once told me.

Burkhalter died as he was nearing eighty, at the end of my sophomore year at Coe, which he had done more than any other to build up from a miserable seminary into some semblance of a place of learning. He never achieved national fame, though his scholarship was recognized in the General Assembly of the Presbyterian Church, where he fought for years for the revision of the Westminster Confession and for otherwise bringing that church into the twentieth century. To me he was a great man. There must be two or three of them in many of our towns, unknown and unrecognized in the nation, but of importance nevertheless in the light they shed on the smaller communities, even on the likes of me.

Joseph Fort Newton did achieve a national reputation after he left our town. When Dr. Burkhalter was not preaching, I used to play hooky from the family pew at the First Presbyterian Church and steal up Third Avenue to the People's Church to hear an even more eloquent minister—another of the local personalities who early helped to put me on a new tack. This was Dr.

Newton, who, before he became a preacher, had learned news-paper writing under Henry Watterson on the Louisville *Courier-Journal*. He was not only an inspiring speaker but a graceful writer, who also wore his great learning easily. His little brick church, Unitarian and Universalist, with no written creed, would be packed to the doors and I would have to edge my way in and stand at the back.

Newton had an inquiring mind (one of the first I would meet) and posed cogent questions about religion, philosophy and life that were not often heard in our parts. Some called him a "radical" and were disturbed by his growing influence in the town, especially on the young, but he was so eloquent, so persua-sive, so imposing in his personality and looks—both rather Lin-colnesque—that the criticism and suspicion of his unorthodoxy never got off the ground. He did two things for me personally: he helped to open my immature mind to questions and to doubts about religion and the status quo of American society; and having a passion for literature, he provoked me into a more serious read-ing of it. Though he said in later life (in his autobiography, *River of Years*) that he "had found himself in Cedar Rapids," I often wondered whether it was true. He seemed a little too enlightened for our town, and after eight years there, he departed not only our community but our country, to become the pastor of The City Temple in London. Later he returned to large pastorates in New York and Philadelphia, wrote many books, conducted a nationally syndicated newspaper column and became a popular speaker on the radio.

Billy Sunday, the most famous evangelist of his day, was born near Cedar Rapids and often returned to us to hold a fort-night's revival orgy in a tabernacle which the local citizens erected especially for him. I used to go occasionally to see his show, for he was a great rabble-rouser and showman, who got hundreds at each session to "come to Christ." Apparently for all his showmanship he was a warm and decent man, a former pro-fessional baseball player and heavy drinker "who had found God" and wanted to share his discovery. But I found the emotions he aroused in getting the brethren to hit the sawdust trail—and thousands did in our community, and hundreds of thousands in other places all over the country—a bit tawdry. He left me cold, as does the Reverend Billy Graham today.

Though he was no longer living in Cedar Rapids in my time,

Carl Van Vechten, who was born and raised there, remained a sort of invisible force, especially for the young and rebellious in our town. Though he scandalized the proper people with his novels, which they thought dirty if not downright wicked, the town followed his rise to fame as a novelist, New York drama and music critic, "arty" photographer, champion of jazz and of Harlem, and husband of the beautiful Russian actress Fania Marinoff, whom he married after divorcing a local woman. The Van Vechten house was a few doors up from ours on Second Avenue and I used to earn a little pocket money there, mowing the lawn and picking dandelions, after which the old Mr. Van Vechten, Carl's father, a genial man with a hearty laugh, would take me for a ride in his surrey behind a pair of fast-stepping steeds. But I could never get him to talk of his famous son—he seemed a bit bewildered by his celebrity.

In 1924, when I was in my last year at college, the publication of Van Vechten's novel *The Tattooed Countess* caused a great hullabaloo in our town. Maple Valley, the locale of the book, was in reality Cedar Rapids as it was in 1897, two years before our author graduated from Washington High School, and some thought they recognized not only the chief character, the Countess Nattatorrini, née Ella Poore, in Maple Valley, but most of the other characters in the book. And they did not like the comments of the Countess on her birthplace, to which, in the novel, she returns after a glittering life for a quarter of a century in Europe as the wife of an Italian aristocrat: ". . . this God-forsaken hole full of stupid fools . . . a dull, sordid village . . . this narrow, provincial town . . . where life is inverted [and] everybody is busy trying to conceal his vices . . ."—and so on. "Get ready for a shock!" an editorial in the *Gazette* warned when the book came out.

> In his new book Carl Van Vechten presents his old home town as Maple Valley, and pictures Cedar Rapids as it was back in the nineties. . . . A former generation of Cedar Rapids folk moves through its pages with a realism that makes possible fairly accurate identification. Some of the readers will hardly forgive the author for the things he wrote.

Van Vechten was a brave man, and that fall he returned to his hometown, full of amiability, praising our fair city for the way it had grown, and professing astonishment that anyone could identify his characters from real life since, he said, he had "invented" them. I first met him then, and "off the record" he advised me to get the hell out of Cedar Rapids as quickly as possible. He was a genial, civilized man with that overblown air of sophistication that comes to Iowans who have settled on Manhattan Island. He was the spokesman of the Speakeasy Intelligentsia, obsessed with the social manners of New York's bohemians, who, as Alfred Kazin said, "did nothing, nothing at all," though it seemed to me they did plenty of drinking and sleeping around. Van Vechten's novels fascinated me when I read them in the flapper twenties, but on rereading them in the 1970's I find them rather slapstick and thin. They have not aged well. Later I would occasionally see Van Vechten in New York. He never spoke of our hometown in Iowa. Perhaps in the last decades of his active life—he lived to 1964, when he was eighty-four—he could not bear to think of it. New York had become for him (as it never did for me) the one and only center of the civilized life in America.

I got to know in the years growing up in Cedar Rapids a struggling, impoverished young painter who would become one of America's finest artists and our town's most famous citizen. The life of Grant Wood is the story of a Midwest farm boy of indomitable character and enormous but slow-to-mature talent that finally flowered into genius, who fought through the first half of his life not only against grinding poverty but against the multitude of disappointments, false starts and setbacks that come to artists at all times in all countries.

His family was of old Quaker stock, and like so many others in our community, had come west after the Civil War, in their case from Virginia, and gone into farming. His grandfather and father tilled a couple hundred acres near Anamosa, a pleasant, sleepy town not far from Cedar Rapids, for a quarter of a century, and when the father died in 1901, when Grant was ten, the mother moved to Cedar Rapids with her four children and, with part of the five thousand dollars left from the sale of the farm, bought a modest house not far from us, on 14th Street. She was the inspiration of Grant's life—and in a way, of mine. It was in her that I first grasped the wonder and the beauty of human fortitude, of how a human being could survive degrading poverty, and the numbing heartbreaks and hardships that went with it, with grace and dignity. Like her son, she refused to be defeated by what life at its worst had brought her. All this Wood has preserved for posterity in his painting of her—*Woman with Plants*—a copy of which hangs before me now in my study. It is one of the great portraits painted in our time. Wood thought it was his most enduring work.

I remember when Grant returned to Cedar Rapids in 1916, halfway through the first war. Sometime after graduating from Washington High School in 1910, he had gone off to try to make his way as a painter, studying first under Ernest Batchelder at the Minneapolis School of Design and then moving on to the Art Institute in Chicago, which he attended evenings after a day's work in a silversmith's shop learning a trade he thought might be helpful in his painting. Soon he and three friends set up a silversmith's shop on their own, but the business failed to provide a living for them, and after two years of it, Grant gave up and returned to Cedar Rapids, broke.

He found his mother about to be evicted from their home. Her income from sewing and baking could not meet the mortgage, and one of our finest banks foreclosed without mercy— when did a banker, even in our town ("Cedar Rapids, the City with a Soul" proclaimed a Chamber of Commerce billboard at this time), show any compassion or even understanding? The Grant family moved to a tar-paper shack, which Grant hastily built on a piece of land owned by a generous friend out by Indian Creek beyond the fringes of town. Later Grant replaced it with a solid one-story frame house, where the family could live in some dignity and where he could paint.

In the meantime America had entered the war and Grant enlisted, serving for two years in an Army camouflage unit. Returning home, he finally found a job that would provide him and his family a living. My old principal at Jackson grade school, the lovely Irish ball of fire, Frances Prescott, took him in as an art instructor, on a modest but steady salary—twelve hundred dollars a year, I seem to recall—and saw to it that he had plenty of time for his painting. With such unaccustomed prosperity, Grant saved some money and was able on the strength of his job to borrow enough more to spend the summer of 1920 in Europe and in 1923 another fourteen months to study at the Julian Academy in Paris, where he fell completely under the spell of the French Impressionists and began turning out competent canvases derived from their fine works.

Oddly enough, at home, Wood's greatest encouragement came from our leading undertaker, John B. Turner, a canny, warm-hearted old Scot, and his son, David Turner. These strange morticians, busy as they were with embalming and burying the dead, saw in Grant Wood's life a great promise. If he could escape from the drudgery of teaching, get himself a decent studio in which to work and devote all his time to painting, they were confident that he would not only become a great artist but would make enough of a living from his work to decently support himself and his mother. They had just moved their mortuary to the Sinclair mansion across the street from us, and having converted from horses to motor vehicles, they offered Grant the spacious old barn and coach house, where I had played as a boy with the Sinclair children, to fix up as a home and studio, rent-free. Moreover, they offered him a fat fee to redecorate their new premises and promised to buy his paintings to hang on their walls. It was in this studio, which Grant himself fixed up—he was a fine carpenter as well as a decorator—that he would paint almost all the pictures that would bring him national recognition. The Turners purchased seventy of them. At last Grant could achieve that goal of painters and writers: to live from his art, with no more time wasted laboring at something else.

But that was no final triumph. It was just a beginning. Wood was still uncertain of what he wanted to do with his talent. He was turning out a few portraits of local worthies and they were remarkably good. During summers in Europe he was painting pleasant, unoriginal landscapes of Paris' Luxembourg Gardens and the French countryside. But I could see that last year in college, when we occasionally met, that he was terribly unsatisfied, that though he was thirty-four and had been painting since his youth and now was giving his full time to it, he was still struggling to find himself, seeking some light about himself that would set him on the road to true accomplishment.

That light broke through to him the next summer in Paris during an exhibition of his French landscapes, the first show he had ever had outside of Cedar Rapids. One balmy August evening we sat on the terrace of the Deux Magots, opposite the lovely old tower of the Église de St. Germain-des-Prés, and for hour after hour Grant, usually so hesitant and sparing of speech, talked about it with the exultation of Saul on the road to Damascus. It was the turning point of his life as an artist.

These few unusual and spirited men, three editors, two preachers, a novelist, a painter, helped to shake me out of the rut of growing up in a Midwest town. There was not a single businessman among them, but there were two labor leaders who should be mentioned.

Cedar Rapids in those days was pretty much a nonunion town—even anti-union. None of the larger plants were organized, and the labor leaders, like the workmen, were sort of second-class citizens so far as the community was concerned. You never saw them on the boards of the myriad civic groups or among the deacons of the churches—perhaps most of them were Catholics. Those places were reserved for the business and professional men of our sterling middle class. However, to me two of the labor leaders were interesting and important figures. I met them both while carrying papers; their offices were on the last paper route I had. Later, personally or as a reporter, I occasionally dropped in on them for a talk.

The national headquarters of the Order of Railway Conductors was located in Cedar Rapids. It was a big union in the days of passenger trains and the president at this time was a taciturn and formally dressed man named Shepherd, who, like the presidents of our banks and big businesses, rode to work every morning in a chauffeured limousine. He was not a very communicative man but I sometimes got through his reserve and once I asked him why a labor leader wanted to maintain a Pierce Arrow and a chauffeur to drive him to and from work.

"Well, maybe for the same reason that the bankers do." He smiled. "This is an important office, even if the town doesn't know it. I have a lot of problems dealing with a quarter of a million men and the relentless efforts of the railway magnates to keep them down. I can't waste my time in trying to drive these new-fangled gasoline contraptions."

For all his zeal for the union, he struck me as a conservative man, and this somewhat surprised me. "Well, it took half a century to build up the Railway Brotherhoods," he would explain. "You youngsters from comfortable families have no idea how we had to fight against the owners for decent wages and hours. We've won a lot and we want to conserve it. So call me conservative, if you want."

"You dress like a banker," I taunted him once, as he was leaving his office, wearing his usual neatly pressed dark suit, his invariable stiff wing collar, an expensive derby in his hand.

"Why not?" He laughed. "Maybe I'm just as important." I doubt if our town thought so. Shepherd seemed a lonely figure in our business-oriented middle-class surroundings. But from him I got my first impression of the new breed of big-union presidents rising in our country, men as intelligent, as prudent, as conservative—and as highly paid—as their businessmen counterparts, and just as concerned with the trappings of office, such as a chauffeured limousine. Like Samuel Gompers, the president of the American Federation of Labor, they were determined to keep the union movement confined to a narrow craft basis, were as opposed to socialism and "radicalism" as the Chamber of Commerce, and, in contrast to Europe, where powerful labor parties were rising, they kept the American labor movement out of politics and were very lukewarm about pushing for economic and social reform. As Shepherd, echoing Gompers, often reminded me: "We stay out of politics. We're concerned with wages and hours and conditions of work for our men." That apparently was all, and to me it did not seem enough.

R. G. Stewart, the editor of the weekly labor paper, *The Tribune,* was a warmer and more outgoing man. And if his readership was small, confined mostly to the few thousand unionized skilled workers in the community—printers, linotypers, pressmen, carpenters, painters, bricklayers and the like—he considered himself, his newspaper, the unions and the workingmen as important as anyone or anything else in Cedar Rapids. And he said so in his bludgeoning editorials. He was a forceful writer and he took a lively interest not only in local matters but in national and world affairs, about which he read avidly and pondered more than most in our town. I used to leave him to the last when delivering my papers so that I could linger in his office and chew the fat with him. I was a fairly frequent caller on him during the rest of my time in the town. We argued hotly about many things and this sharpened my mind. Above all, though, he was interested in journalistic writing and he would challenge or praise my pieces in the local newspaper and especially my editorials in the college weekly, which he followed more closely and critically, I fear, than any of the students or faculty. When I graduated he paid me editorially a tribute that I blush to quote from but which at the time, exaggerated though it was, gave me more encouragement to get on in journalism than I received from anyone else.

A Tribute to a Worthy Kid

In a week or so Coe will list among its graduates a lad who will some day make his mark in the newspaper world. His name is William Shirer . . . He has served with distinction as editor of the Cosmos, the weekly publication of the college. Under his guidance the editorial page has become something different and distinct in college journalism . . . Editor Shirer has written in a vein that marks him as a student of human nature and affairs and world events far beyond the average writer of his opportunity and years.

Given a larger field in the daily press and his writings would have been accepted as sound, fearless logic in good English carrying weight and conviction to the average citizen. Many there are in the newspaper field who do not have the abilities of this young college lad. A bit pessimistic at times, due perhaps to hardships endured while he worked his way through college, . . . he realizes the injustice of many things that today are classified as proper under the rules and customs of organized society. "Bill" is already a big man in a newspaper sense although he may not know it. He will become bigger as life unfolds before him.

That, of course, remained to be seen. But Stewart's words did much to encourage this "worthy kid" to press on. It stirred his ambition and gave him confidence. No one else downtown had taken any notice of him.

Besides the influences of these men, there were three others of a different kind that broadened the life of a country bumpkin in our town: the large and compact group of Czechs—we called them Bohemians, from their native land of Bohemia—who made up one-quarter of the inhabitants of Cedar Rapids and who, sticking largely to themselves and their own language to a point where some old families thought they were almost un-American, brought something of the values and color of Europe to our midst; the "Dutch Colonies" in nearby Amana, which, at a time when red-blooded Americans began to foam at the mouth at Communism, not only in Russia but at home, were carrying out a successful experiment in Christian communism; and visitors from outer space who brought to the town and the campus some music, poetry and provocative thought, providing a breath of excitement from a distant and larger world of art and the mind.

Every spring Walter Damrosch came with his New York Symphony Orchestra for three days of concerts during the May Festival. Later the Minneapolis Symphony Orchestra took over. Though I had got my first taste of symphony music in Chicago as a mere tot, it was in Cedar Rapids, listening to these spring concerts, that I developed a passion for it that has grown with the years.

The college, rather than the town, which did not go in much for "culture," of which it was a little suspicious, was responsible for most of the music we got to hear. It was through its auspices that I first heard many of the great musicians: Paderewski, Kreisler, Heifetz, Casals, Schumann-Heink, Geraldine Farrar and Amelita Galli-Curci. Like many youths, I fell in love with Farrar and Galli-Curci—the latter had a sort of Mona Lisa Italian face— and kept colored photographs of both of them on my desk. I remember the first time I thrilled to Galli-Curci's pure, high soprano voice and also, on this occasion, to her poise. In the midst of an operatic aria the artificial ceiling of cheap muslin bunting in the old auditorium fell down and engulfed most of the rapt audience. Her voice broke off and she stood there, poised and statuesque, watching the drapery flutter down until most of the listeners were smothered in it, while those who could were making for the exits for fear the decrepit old building was caving in. After the debris had been cleared and the frightened had returned to their seats, Galli-Curci resumed her program, her poise untouched, her beautifully lyric voice unaffected by the interruption.

If poetry was not widely regarded in Cedar Rapids—though we had our Shakespeare and Browning clubs—it was not the college's fault. It booked one poet after another: Millay, Sandburg, Vachel Lindsay, John Cowper Powys and others, and part of the joy of their visits to me was to talk with some of them after their readings—far into the night.

My mother

My father

The author at two or three or so

The Shirer home in Cedar Rapids

Right, Grant Wood in his studio in Cedar Rapids, across from our home. Wood rebuilt it from an old horse-barn I played in as a youngster.

Downtown Cedar Rapids

RALPH CLEMENTS

Above, Washington High School in Cedar Rapids in 1921, the year I graduated

Above right, my high school graduation picture

Below left, the author after putting up a Chautauqua tent

Below right, reading from left to right, my brother, John, my sister, Josephine, and myself, 1923

Williston Hall, at the left, the oldest building on the campus, later torn down. The office of the *Cosmos*, the Coe College weekly, was in the basement.

Right, The *Cosmos* gave me my first by-line.

The staff of the *Cosmos*, 1925. The author, its editor, is on the far right.

As a freshman, the author, third from the left in the center row, made the college track squad as a hurdler, but not a very fast one.

The 1926 *Acorn*, the college yearbook. Beside one's photograph, one's "activities" were noted.

LIAM L. SHIRER
          Cedar Rapids
        History

Kappa Epsilon; Pi Del-
psilon; Pi Kappa Delta;
pa Phi Sigma; Sachem;
lent Council; Treasurer
hman Class; Track (1,
Vesper Choir (1); De-
(1); Dows Debate (1);
nos (1, Sport Editor 2.
aging Editor 3, Editor-
hief 4).

The *Chicago Tribune* building, Chicago

The John T. McCutcheon cartoon on the front page of the *Tribune*, February 23, 1904, the day the author was born in Chicago

The lordly Colonel Robert Rutherford McCormick, publisher and editor of the *Chicago Tribune*

MATERIAL BOTH PAGES: CHICAGO TRIBUNE

Below, left, "Bathhouse John" Coughlin and, *right,* Michael "Hinky Dink" Kenna ran the notorious First Ward, the center of Chicago, and kept it wide open for sin and its profits.

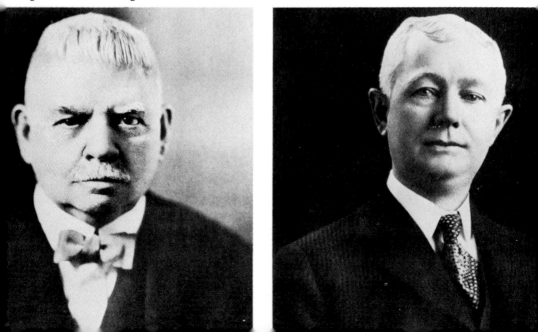

William Jennings Bryan. Three times Democratic candidate for President and Wilson's first Secretary of State. He was a populist hero to the author as a youth, but less so after summers listening to him on Chautauqua and, at the end, reading about his defense of fundamentalism at the Dayton, Tennessee, "Monkey Trial."

Clarence Darrow, Chicago's greatest lawyer and defender of the workers and the poor, was another hero. He was a friend of my lawyer—father, and came by occasionally at our home for long talks.

Edna St. Vincent Millay, as the author remembers her at their first meeting in 1924 following her lecture at Coe

Below left, Carl Sandburg, reporter and movie critic of the *Chicago Daily News,* who became the city's finest poet and later the distinguished biographer of Abraham Lincoln

Below right, Theodore Dreiser at his desk. Chicago gave him the material for some of his best novels. "The wilder the better," he said of it.

The author at work in the Paris office of the *Chicago Tribune,* 1927

Below left, interviewing Gene Tunney, Paris, 1928. Just retired as the world's heavyweight champion, he was on his way to Rome to get married.

Below right, Charles Lindbergh, waving to the crowds after his transatlantic solo flight from New York to Paris

Sylvia Beach, publisher of *Ulysses,* with James Joyce in Paris

Ezra Pound in the garden of his Paris studio, 1923. He had already begun to champion Hemingway.

Georges Clemenceau. A bitter rival of Poincaré, the "Old Tiger," as premier, led France to victory in the First World War and dominated the Peace Conference at Versailles in 1919. Defeated for the Presidency, he lived his last embittered years in the 1920's in self-imposed isolation, writing books and predicting that France would go down in twenty years—an accurate prophecy.

Raymond Poincaré, war-time President of France and later Premier, as he returned to his home in Lorraine after his retirement in 1929. Dying, five years later, he looked across the nearby border toward Germany and said, "They will come again." They did.

Ernest Hemingway. His journalistic friends were confident
in 1925, while he was at work
on his first novel, that Hemingway, a former newspaper
correspondent himself, would
make it big.

Gertrude Stein (left) and her
companion, Alice B. Toklas.
Miss Stein did not approve of
the author's admiration for
Joyce nor, at the end, of Hemingway.

BOTH PHOTOS: PHOTOWORLD

F. Scott Fitzgerald at his desk in Paris. Some nights the novelist would take over the editor's desk at the *Paris Tribune,* harangue Thurber and me and our fellow copyeditors, and try his best to keep the paper from going to press.

James Thurber. Nights around the *Paris Tribune* copy desk in 1925, he talked to me about his determination, despite all the setbacks, to become a writer.

John Gunther. Also Chicago-born, Gunther was a correspondent in Europe for the *Chicago Daily News*. In Vienna, though working for rival newspapers, we became fast friends and remained such until Gunther's death in New York in 1970. In Vienna in the early 1930's, Gunther's chief ambition was to become a novelist. The success of his "Inside" books tempered that ambition.

Sinclair Lewis and Dorothy Thompson. In Vienna in 1931–32 they tried to save their marriage. It was there, too, that Lewis confided to the author that he was at work on the great American novel, which would be nothing less than a history of America. Nothing ever came of it.

Isadora Duncan. In our brief friendship, she became one of the inspirations of this young newspaperman's life.

Greene's Opera House did not provide us with much opera except for Gilbert and Sullivan, which I never liked; my education in opera would have to wait for Vienna, Berlin and New York. But it did bring us many plays and some of the actors famous in those days, Cedar Rapids being a convenient stopping place on the railroads between bookings in Chicago and Omaha, Minneapolis and St. Louis. I cannot remember many of the plays except for Shakespeare. Most were Broadway hits now mercifully forgotten, such as *East Lynne* and *Way Down East*. But the names of some of the great stage celebrities linger in the mind: Otis Skinner, John Drew, Richard Mansfield, Lillian Russell, Marie Dressler, Eva Tanguay, Modjeska, Mrs. Scott Siddons, Minnie Maddern Fiske. Names unknown to the present generation, but where are their likes today?

The most memorable to me was Sarah Bernhardt. She arrived toward the end of the first war when she was in her seventies. One of her legs had been amputated in 1915 and she could scarcely move on her wooden leg, but the curtain would be lowered briefly to enable her to take a new stance. Besides her "divine" presence one remembers the golden voice, the rolling cadences of her French, and though I did not understand a word of it at the time, it seemed so wonderfully rich in sound, like a kind of music, that I swore I would learn it some day, which, in the years in Paris, I did.[1]

Visitors from afar but of a different sort were three young members of the Oxford debating team who arrived on campus in my senior year to argue against the merits of Prohibition with our debaters. How they happened to stop off at our little Midwest

[1] We stage-struck youngsters (sometimes I would work as an extra stagehand, moving scenery and props between acts, when a great star I wanted to see at close hand came to town) grew up in Cedar Rapids on a strange legend about Sarah Bernhardt. It was that she had been born Sarah King in the village of Rochester, twenty-five miles down the Cedar River from us, that her mother had died when she was five, that she had run away soon afterward, entered a French convent at St. Paul, and, having learned the new language, set off to Paris, where she began her fabulous career in the theater. The legend grew when in 1905 it was reported that a veiled but elegantly dressed woman had stopped off briefly at Rochester to lay a bouquet of roses on the grave of the elder Mrs. King. When reporters noted that Sarah Bernhardt had played an engagement at nearby Iowa City the previous evening, they put two and two together, as reporters sometimes are tempted to do, and concluded that it was the great Parisian actress who had made the mysterious visit to the grave of one who must have been her mother. Ergo! The great Sarah Bernhardt, the most famous French actress of our time, was an Iowa girl!

college—they were on a world tour and had debated at some of our leading universities from coast to coast—I do not remember, but I do recall the considerable impression they made on me. It was obvious from the sharply contrasting styles of the debate that they had received quite a different education than we were getting. They spoke extemporaneously, with wit and humor, calling lightly on history to buttress their arguments and cracking jokes to enliven their arguments. Our debaters, in contrast, uttered formal memorized speeches—they had memorized even their rebuttal points—and were dreadfully serious in recounting statistics to prove that Prohibition was necessary in order to achieve "industrial efficiency, social progress and a high standard of living" and was therefore "economically sound." Such claptrap, so solemnly presented, made me wince.

"Alcohol is a poison. It lessens the span of life," one of our debaters proclaimed earnestly.

"That may be," rejoined one of the visitors, "but alcohol has been used for some seven thousand years, and if it's a poison you must admit it is a mighty slow one. Anyway, it's better to live only half as long and see twice as much. Would you trade your birthright for a mess of dotage?"

Malcolm MacDonald, son of the then British Prime Minister in the first Labor government in English history, twice brought gasps from the staid audience—once when he quoted a letter of Lincoln's castigating those who objected to beer drinking and once, during an argument over the harmful effects of alcohol on health, when he revealed that the King's physician prescribed liquor for the King.

After the standing vote of 437 to 95 to uphold our team's staunch defense of Prohibition—there were few in our conformist audience who dared stand up in public against it—I invited the three gentlemen over to the *Cosmos* office to have a drink of some bootleg whiskey I kept in the lower drawer of my desk and to chew the fat. We talked about the coming elections in Britain and America. They could not understand how a dimwit like Coolidge was overwhelmingly favored to win re-election as President.[1] MacDonald's father was facing defeat, though young

[1] The day before, our students and faculty had shown their Republican standpatism in a straw vote that gave Coolidge 631 votes; Davis, the Democratic candidate, 94; and La Follette, the Progressive candidate and my favorite, 69.

Malcolm MacDonald, running for office for the first time, hoped to win a seat in the Commons. He seemed to me a very stimulating young man, though later when I occasionally saw him in England and other parts of the world—he became eventually a distinguished colonial official—he struck me as being, unlike his flamboyant, handsome father, Ramsay MacDonald, rather colorless and, though competent, of no great stature. Another of the men, Christopher Hollis, would later become a well-known journalist and writer, and the author of *A Study of George Orwell,* whom he had known since their days together at Eton.

All these visitors from beyond our narrow little Iowa world helped to keep us from stagnating in the small-town life. They did not so much assuage my own thirst and hunger as to stimulate it. They stirred up in me, at least, a resolve to one day break out of the Midwest provincial life, though in all truth I did not entertain very high hopes that I could, or would. My self-confidence would mature slowly.

The Bohemians in our town interested me, if only because they seemed so different from most of the rest of us and were proud to remain apart, devoted to their own Slavic European way of life, which we thought strange and certainly inferior to ours, but which obviously seemed the best to them. Later all this would change as they, like the other nationalities in the country, became absorbed in the dominant Anglo-Saxon culture.

But in my time our ten thousand or so Czechs lived pretty much to themselves in the south part of town, beyond the river and the railway tracks, those dividing lines which in so many American towns separate the poor from the rich. In our case they separated not only the poor but the Czechs, though the latter did not seem to mind it, not even when some among them who already were making it financially began to move into the more affluent neighborhoods and to intermarry with our Wasps.

Most, however, remained where they were, making the south part of town a sort of Bohemian settlement, preserving their identity through their schools and their religious, social and fraternal organizations, the largest of which was the Sokols, primarily devoted, as it was in the old country, not only to physical culture but to maintaining Czech nationalism and culture. These "foreigners" in our midst were democratic, thrifty and hard-working, plying their trades as tailors, blacksmiths, harness makers, bakers, grocers, carpenters, cigar makers, butchers, shoemakers, and proprietors of cafés, which our good Anglo-Saxons called "saloons," rather frowning on the lusty beer drinking and singing that took place in them, though when Prohibition came they were pleased to buy the beer the Czechs made, which if not genuine Pilsen was the best you could buy in the entire dry state of Iowa.

From the Bohemians came most of our local music. They furnished the bands we had and most of our music teachers. My sister studied piano and I the violin with two of them, and two or three of their pianists made it to the big world. They were justly proud of their great composer Anton Dvorak, who in the latter years of the nineteenth century had spent two or three summers in our midst. Whenever a symphony orchestra came to town they would persuade the conductor to include in the program Dvorak's E Minor Symphony, "From the New World," which the composer had written in Iowa.

Into the drabness of rural Midwest life, the Bohemians also brought a lot of color. Saturdays and Sundays, especially before Lent, they staged their native dances, the women in their bright-colored peasant dress, the musicians striking up lively tunes from the old folk music of Central Europe, the gaiety and good-natured banter accelerating.

Gradually they introduced me to a new world—the old world, from which they had come—and to a segment of European history not taught in our public schools. I remember a Czech doctor saying once: "You remember 1620 for the landing of the Pilgrim Fathers on Plymouth Rock. But it's a historic date for us, too. At the Battle of White Mountain near Prague in 1620, during the Thirty Years' War, we lost our independence. The Austrians, our conquerors, have suppressed us ever since."

But the Austrians could not suppress the Czechs as a nationality, and their centuries-old struggle to maintain it and to regain their freedom was much on the minds of the Bohemians in Cedar Rapids. I remember during the first war how they worked for Thomas Masaryk and the Czechoslovak government-in-exile in the United States, raising incredible sums of money to help finance them. And I recall the rejoicing in "Bohemian town" in 1918 at the war's end when Masaryk returned to Prague to proclaim the Czechoslovak republic. As a lad of fourteen, I joined in the celebration, not knowing that my own life and work would be intermingled for a while with these people in Europe, that I would get to know their two heroes, Masaryk and Beneš, and become a good friend of Jan Masaryk, the old President's son, follow the ups and downs of the Czechoslovak republic between the wars, see it at Munich sold down the river to Hitler by the Prime Ministers of France and Britain and that, finally, one day in New York after the second war I would sit up through the night arguing with Jan, the Foreign Minister, against his returning to Prague, where shortly afterward, the Communists having taken over, he would meet an untimely and mysterious death. Fate is strange.

In those early days in Iowa I saw Christian communism work—right in the midst of our hustling, rugged capitalism. Although most of our good people hated communism, or thought they did, or were told to, they loved to visit the "Dutch Colonies" at nearby Amana, where a sturdy people of German stock were living under communism, liking it and thriving on it.

The pious, prosperous communists at Amana did not, of course, receive their inspiration from Marx, of whom probably they had never heard, but from Christ, whose message they believed ordained communal living as the best way of life. This was considered almost sacrilegious by our sanctimonious people, who inclined to agree with the gospel of the advertising hustler Bruce Barton, who preached that "Jesus was the founder of modern business" and that "free-enterprise capitalism" was the true Christian way of life.

The Amana Society, occupying twenty-six thousand acres along the Iowa River twenty miles southwest of Cedar Rapids, was known as the Community of True Inspiration and traced its origin back to 1714, when a small group of German Pietists broke away from the Lutheran Church to found their own sect. Its members believed that God continued to reveal Himself through chosen prophets, or "Divine Instruments," hence the title of "True Inspiration" that they gave themselves. In Germany they refused both military service and the taking of loyalty oaths to the state and were much persecuted by the Lutheran Church and the civil authorities. To escape persecution some eight hundred of these Pietists, under the leadership of Christian Metz, their chief prophet, emigrated to America in 1842 and founded a settlement on five thousand acres near Buffalo. It was there that Metz claimed to have received a revelation from God that the flock should live under "absolute communism," sharing all work and its rewards, living in communal homes, eating from communal kitchens in communal dining rooms, eschewing any form of private property. When the region around Buffalo became crowded and the soaring price of real estate made it difficult for the settlers to acquire more land, they moved on to Iowa in 1855, purchased eighteen thousand acres of fertile soil and woodland along the Iowa River and soon added eight thousand more. Metz wanted to call the new community Bleibtreu (Remain True) and wrote a song to commemorate it:

> *Bleibtreu soll der Name sein*
> *Dort in Iowa der Gemein.*

But the Elders, on reflection, decided to adopt a more English-sounding name, Amana, from the mountain mentioned in the Song of Solomon, which in Hebrew meant the same thing, and the choice, according to the records of the Society, was approved by the Lord on September 23, 1855. Christian Metz, the chief Divine Instrument, died twelve years later at seventy-two, having seen his Iowa settlement put down its roots and prosper under its God-inspired communism. He was succeeded by Barbara Heinemann, who died at ninety in 1883. After that, up through my time, no Divine Instrument was found to reveal God's continuing word, but the Society got along well enough under the rule of the Elders.

Like hundreds of others in Cedar Rapids we used to take the train down to Amana to have Sunday "dinner" in one of the communal eating houses and wander around and see communism lived. It was quite a different world. Six villages were scattered around Old Amana, and with their winding main streets along which were rows of gabled houses, they resembled an old German village except that the houses and indeed the churches and all other buildings were unpainted—the Amanaites believing that paint was a worldly luxury. There were great barns and sheds at one end of the villages and neat factories and workshops at the other. Back of each home was a tidy vegetable garden beyond which stretched communal gardens, orchards, pastures and fields of grain.

The homes themselves contained no kitchen or dining room because the families ate in the communal dining halls where all the cooking was done. Though most of the members were married and had children, the sexes, I noted with some surprise, were always separated at meals as well as in church or meetings, the men sitting on one side, the women on the other. Both men and women were dressed simply and rather drably in clothes made by themselves or by the community tailor, in keeping with a determination to live as unworldly as possible.

Over the years I began to see how this unique experiment in communism worked. It was, to begin with, completely democratic—as opposed to Marxism—the ruling Board of Trustees being elected annually to preside over both the spiritual and temporal affairs of the Society. Each year it had to give an accounting of the community's business affairs to all members. It also acted as a court of justice, its decisions being final.

The rules governing the commune called for each member to receive "free board, dwelling, support and care in his old age, sickness and infirmity" and to be "entitled further out of the common fund to an annual sum of maintenance for him or herself, children and relatives." The idea of society being responsible for providing every citizen with work, food, clothing, housing and decent care in old age had not yet dawned on the rest of us in America in those days, nor has it been fully accepted, at least in practice, to this day.

A lot of people in Cedar Rapids thought it queer. They admired the Amanaites for their thriftiness, piousness and hard work. The products from the Amana farms and factories (especially the high-grade woolens) were among the best in the state. But we could not accept a community where our sacred "free enterprise" was not permitted, where there were no profits for the farmer and the businessman, where all that was produced and all the profits gained from selling to the outside world went to the community for the common good. Besides, these strange people spoke a foreign language—for German remained the exclusive tongue in Amana. They stubbornly refused to speak English, like the rest of us.

Still, we could not overlook the fact that the people in

Amana, despite their communism and drab dress and buildings, seemed extremely happy. Businessmen could not understand how the men in the Amana workshops and factories could be satisfied with no wages. Yet they could not dispute the findings of Iowa's leading historian of the colony, Bertha M. H. Shambaugh, when she wrote: "Each worker labors with the air of a man in physical comfort and peace of mind, and with the energy of a man who is working for himself and expects to enjoy all the fruits of his labor."

Strange! It bothered the esteemed and learned editor of the *Republican*. "To have and to hold," he wrote, "is human instinct that cannot be stamped out even in the name of religion." And he quoted Châteaubriand: "Make no mistake. Without individual property none are free."

But the success of Amana belied the words. Still, it was an isolated island in the world of rugged American individualism, and it was obvious that it could not forever remain unaffected by it. Long after I left Iowa, the pull of American "free enterprise" civilization began to be felt, especially among the young. A number of the youths in Amana had to be sent off to the state universities to study the new techniques in farming, to learn engineering, medicine, pharmacy, even marketing, for the Amana products, its fine woolens above all, were being sold throughout the country. The more colorful, materialistic, complicated, joyful worldly life outside had its attractions for the young. Some did not return; many who did questioned the values of the strict communal life.

In 1932, in the midst of the Depression, which had put the commune in the same financial difficulties that all capitalist enterprises in America were in, though the Amanaites had plenty to eat, the pure communism of the Amana Society was dropped after the issue was put to the voters, and a new cooperative corporation was formed in its place. The twenty-six thousand acres and all the dairies, shops and factories were held intact in a cooperative enterprise. Members were given stock, they shared in the profits, and wages were introduced. The former editor of the *Republican*, now a staunch conservative Republican member of Congress from our district, was jubilant. He hailed the end of pure communism in our midst, though it really had never corrupted us. He was happy, he said, to see it replaced at last by what he called "a modified form of capitalism." It was not pure capitalism, to be sure, but it was no longer pure communism. Our greedy, profit-based way of life had, to a certain extent, triumphed!

My college days finally came to an end in the late spring of 1925, a spring more lovely than I had ever remembered on our Midwest prairies, though perhaps it merely seemed so because I was in love with a young coed I hoped to marry soon. The days and nights since early April had been soft and warm, the air full of the perfume of lilacs and other spring flowers. And I felt good that this last chapter of one's youth was coming to an end in such a splendid season. Relief, too. Twenty-one years of growing up is a long time.

What had I got out of the four years of college? All through the final months I had wondered about that. I had taken note of what Henry Adams thought of his four years at Harvard.

The Class of 1858, to which Henry Adams belonged, . . . was aggressively commonplace.

Could that not be said of my class of 1925, though our standards were different?

The four years passed at college were, for his purposes, wasted.

I did not believe that my own four years at this lesser college had been wasted.

Henry Adams never professed the smallest faith in universities of any kind . . . nor had he the faintest admiration for the university graduate, either in Europe or in America . . .

That remained to be seen so far as I was concerned, though in time, over the next fifty years, I would largely, though not completely, come to share a similar lack of faith.

The chief wonder of education is that it does not ruin everybody concerned in it, teachers and taught . . . Harvard College taught little, and that little ill, but it left the mind open, free from

bias, ignorant of facts, but docile . . . The graduate knew little,
but his mind remained supple, ready to receive knowledge.

Was that not the main thing I had got out of college? I had
learned little—in history, literature, foreign languages, economics, science—but this prairie college at least had left my mind
open, in fact, had opened it, making it "ready to receive knowledge." Whatever knowledge ultimately came would be through
nonacademic sources, with the exception of two years attending
lectures at the Collège de France while I was working on a newspaper in Paris.

The saintly, unprofessorial genius Mahatma Gandhi, in the
years in India and the time with him in London, would become
the most influential of my personal teachers, though like everyone
else I would eventually learn most from life. Not all, though.
Much more than in college, books, when one began to range far
and wide in them, would add some depth and breadth to one's
knowledge, providing an increasingly solid link with provocative
minds and spirits of the past and present; and to books must be
added works of art and music. Foreign languages would come
through the luck of working and living in France, Germany,
Austria, Italy and Spain, though even with this advantage the
learning of them was for me a slow and painful process, and of
the four acquired in twenty years in Europe, two (Italian and
Spanish) would be forgotten for the lack of opportunity to use
them when I returned home for good, leaving German and especially French, with which one could roam in two rich literatures
and continue to converse with citizens of two old cultures.

"The mind, like the heart," André Maurois wrote in his memoirs, "is formed early and many of us remain all our lives what our
childhood made us." If so, it is a pity. For though our childhood
shapes us, to remain what it made us would condemn many
adults to a state of arrested development. They could never grow
up.

Sometime, probably in my junior year, I began to awaken a
little and to question. I was troubled by doubts, and too immature to realize that this was all to the good. Doubts about the
religion I had been born into and largely accepted without question. Some of these doubts and this questioning were reflected in

the editorials I wrote for the college paper my last year when I was editor and which probably few students read and which the teachers, if they read them, did not much like. (My younger brother would be driven from the editorship of the paper two years later for raising similar questions, which moved him to finish college in another place.)

A quarter of a century later the official alumni publication in celebrating the college's centennial would remember me as "the crusading editor of the *Cosmos*" and recall that, among other things, I had "condemned" the English Department as a "Victorian swamp" and "called for more Lewis, Dreiser, Wharton and Mencken" and that my "agitation" eventually (long after I left) leavened Shakespeare and Milton "with liberal doses of modern writing." My editorial was headed: "Give Us Light!"—a tall order for any college.

A glance at my youthful editorial outbursts that last year reveals that I flailed about a good deal trying to shake up our staid campus. Chapel, daily attendance at which was compulsory, had become so dull and boring that one week I let loose with an editorial: "Chapel: A Good Place to Snooze." I kept hammering away at other shortcomings, and with all the zest of an aroused bumpkin, I exhorted the administration, the faculty and the students to make the college a true place of learning, which it was not yet. I added a plank to the *Cosmos* "Platform": "Make Coe Preeminent Scholastically"—another tall order. "The college at its best is but a rude educational affair," I lamented in one piece, and asked: "Are we Coe students intellectually defunct?"

Not only the state of the campus bothered me, but the state of the town, country, world, and I roved far and wide in my questioning, causing many students and teachers to ask whether I was editing a *college* paper or a journal of world affairs. "This is an age of blundering ignoramuses," I concluded toward the end of my editorship. I swung at a local pastor for preaching a sermon during the 1924 Presidential campaign on "Why Christians Cannot Vote for La Follette." I castigated the town's leading citizens, including the president of our college, for opposing the Child Labor Amendment, which was then up for ratification by the states. When it was rejected by thirteen states, I wrote bitterly that it had been defeated by the lies of employers, who now could continue to fatten their pocketbooks at the expense of overworked children. Even the Communist bugbear had been raised—not, as it turned out, for the last time.

> There were all sorts of stories about the amendment spring-
> ing from Russian influence . . . from the Bolsheviks. That is a
> gag that Americans still go into convulsions over.
> . . . The Child Labor Amendment has been laid away until
> some more enlightened period in American history dawns. . . .
> We can only take cognizance of the state of intellectual decay of
> our leaders . . . But maybe things will change in time. Even the
> reactionary regime of Metternich came to an end—in time.

I was not always angry. I find I wrote a number of editorials lauding the lives of some of the great men who died in 1924 and 1925. There was a tribute to Conrad: "A Great Writer Passes"; and another, in the midst of the antics of Homecoming Week, to Anatole France, in which I marveled that Paris had given the great writer an homage at his funeral usually accorded only to France's military heroes. I wrote of the loss in 1924 of Puccini, of Woodrow Wilson, of Lenin.

> Lenin also cut a deep notch in history, the U.S. Chamber of
> Commerce, Secretary of State Hughes and the Cedar Rapids
> *Republican* to the contrary notwithstanding. . . . He earned a
> place near the front rank of world characters.

That Bolshevik! The trustees and the town's worthies fumed. My terrible subversion was called to the attention of the president of the college. And the clamor did not subside when I paid a tribute to Samuel Gompers, the president of the American Federation of Labor, on his death. "A distinguished American," I maintained. "Sam Gompers will be recorded among the nation's greatest when the future history of America is written."

Horrors! That man! That labor agitator! Why, at the very moment of his death he was under sentence to serve a year in prison for contempt of court! The piece stirred up our good non-union, anti-union town more than it did the campus. Most students probably had never heard of Gompers—or of Puccini, Conrad, Anatole France and Lenin, for that matter.

If I was not always angry, I was always skeptical—at least that last year in college when I could publish my thoughts. Mark Twain was a constant inspiration. I used to publish at the head of the editorial columns a quotation each week, and many were from Twain, or from Bertrand Russell, another subversive in the eyes of many staunch Americans. Thus in one issue, from Mark Twain:

> My idea of our civilization is that it is a shabby, poor thing and full of cruelties, vanities, arrogances, meannesses and hypocrisies.

I had been fascinated and somewhat shocked by the publication of Mark Twain's posthumous autobiography in 1924. The most popular writer we ever had, the great humorist, the toast of bank presidents and business tycoons, the supposed optimist about life in America, had turned out to have held, secretly, a devastating opinion about the shabbiness and crookedness and, above all, the shams of our touted American civilization. He had not dared publish the book during his lifetime, and its publication had been held up for fourteen years—he had died in 1910. One week I shared a little of it with our readers, most of whom would probably not get it first hand. It was pretty strong stuff for youngsters brought up to believe in, and conform to, all the myths about American life and character.

> We are discreet sheep; we wait to see how the drove is going, and then go with the drove. We have two opinions: one private, which we are afraid to express; and another one—the one we use—to please Mrs. Grundy.

I remarked that Mark Twain sounded almost as if he were commenting on the Presidential election that year when he wrote of the idiocy of

> party loyalty, party allegiance—a snare invented by designing men for selfish purposes—and which turns voters into chattels, slaves, rabbits, and all the while their masters and they themselves are shouting rubbish about liberty, independence, freedom of opinion, freedom of speech . . . and forgetting that their fathers and the churches shouted the same blasphemies a generation earlier . . .

But weren't the American people noted for their tolerance? Not to Mark Twain.

All the talk about tolerance, in anything or anywhere, is plainly a gentle lie. It does not exist. It is in no man's heart; but it . . . drivels and slobbers from all men's lips.

Having released this bit of Twainean subversion to our subscribers, who outside of their textbooks read little or nothing, I waited for a mighty response. This would surely stir them up. Not a single student or faculty member responded. Perhaps those who had grown up on Huckleberry Finn and Tom Sawyer thought I had perpetrated a literary hoax. It is a charitable view, at least.

A couple of professors and the president opened up my mind a little in the four years in college, and I concluded that this was as good a piece of luck as any student, in any college or university, ever had. Two or three such teachers is about the limit. Perhaps in a few institutions for a brief time a student was luckier —at Harvard, say, around the turn of the century when such men as William James, Royce, Santayana, Palmer, Charles Copeland and Eliot Norton were stirring up a generation of students. My own two daughters, who went through Harvard as Radcliffe students in the 1950's and 1960's, seem to remember only two or three teachers who left an impression on them. Perhaps those were lean years, scholastically, at that famous college.

Harry Morehouse Gage, who came to Coe in 1920, the year before I entered, was the first genuine educator to become president—his predecessors had been ministers whose hearts belonged to the Presbyterian Church—and in his twenty-one years at the helm he succeeded in making the college one of the best of its kind in the Midwest. His graduate studies at Columbia had been in philosophy (while in New York he had also picked up a divinity doctorate at Union Theological Seminary) and to our backwater Iowa college in 1920 he had brought a determination to make it, if he could, a place of learning. He never lost sight of that goal, though like all college presidents, he had to devote a great deal of time and energy to raising funds for the endowment and to placating the conservative Board of Trustees and the equally conservative worthies who dominated the town. This necessitated making compromises which often disturbed me.

We used to argue about them, for by my senior year we had become rather close friends, almost at times confederates. I liked his passion for learning, especially in philosophy and literature, but I detested his capacity for compromising—on anything. He was not only a staunch Republican, as were most of the people in Cedar Rapids and Iowa, but at one time while I was in college he was also president of the local Rotary. This puzzled me, and once I burst out: "How in God's name can you, a philosopher, a civilized man, preside over a bunch of illiterate boobs?"

In time, for he was a patient man, he made me see, I guess, that the many compromises he made with those who tried to run the college according to their narrow standards stemmed from a conviction that they were necessary in order to advance his main objective, which was to try to make the college—and indeed the town—a more civilized place. Life, he argued, was a series of compromises but they were bearable if they enabled you to achieve what you set out to get. He might, for the record, he would say with a twinkle in his eye, call me to account for some of my editorial outbursts, which he did. Privately, he encouraged me to continue. "You're one of the few around here, among the students or faculty," he said once, "who has an inquiring turn of mind. That's what education is all about. You're critical, but you base your criticism on facts and on intelligence. Keep it up. But don't quote me."

He did his best, though not always with success, to convince the trustees, faculty and students that whatever the prevailing prejudices, a college had to be the sanctuary of truth and freedom, and he meant, as he put it once in the guise of a prayer (it sounded less radical that way), "truth coming from any source whatsoever, and freedom which knows no bounds save those which have been set by the truth."

He was one of the first to try to teach me tolerance of the opinions and actions of others, a lesson that was hard for me to learn. He encouraged me to read more in philosophy so that I might comprehend that no great mind had a monopoly of the truth and that the greatest philosophers often were in fundamental disagreement with one another. And, though he was a little disappointed at my growing skepticism of Christianity, he urged me to drive hard down the road I seemed to be going. We had become good friends and when I graduated that June of 1925 he lent me one hundred dollars to help me get to Europe.

Lynn Garwood, head of the Sociology Department and the

most controversial figure on the faculty, was one of the two teachers who somehow made a dent on my sluggish mind. Though he was supposed to teach sociology, he ranted far and wide in his lectures, into economics, history and politics, probing and questioning all the sacred cows and all the accepted myths of American life. He helped to deepen my own skepticism while trying to increase my knowledge. He had grown up on a small farm in Ohio, worked his way through college and university, and absorbed a sort of Midwest Populist distrust of all the forces of reaction which, with McKinley, had come to dominate America. And he was so fearless in expressing his ideas that he frightened not only the trustees but many of his colleagues on the faculty, who thought him a "radical" and believed he was poisoning the minds of the young Christian students. I loved him, not only because he continually shook me up with his probing mind but because he was such an eloquent, learned, civilized and fearless man. We became fast friends, and many years later, after he had retired and I was lecturing in a city near his Ohio farm, he joined me after the lecture and we sat up in a bar and later in my hotel room most of the night resuming the dialogue we had had in college. In any place he would have been one of the great teachers of my generation.

Perhaps, too, Ethel R. Outland, professor of English and journalism, the second member of the faculty to arouse me from my provincial torpor. A graduate of Coe, she had done graduate work at Radcliffe and obtained an M.A. at the University of Wisconsin. She was not much liked by most of her students, who chafed at her rigorous adherence to high standards both in the study of literature and in their writing. She could not stand sloppy thinking and especially sloppy writing and it was from her that I first got a feeling of what a struggle it would always be to write the American language and of how fine the awards were if you realized this and persisted. As time went on she turned her attention more and more from literature to journalism, perhaps feeling that few of us would make it as authors (one of her pupils, Paul Engle, became one of our finest poets) but that we might make it in the newspaper world. In this field, too, she insisted on clear, concise writing and also on getting as wide an education as possible in the liberal arts, especially in literature, history and economics. Under her influence the college weekly became one of the best-edited and -written college newspapers in the country. Unlike some members of the faculty and administration, she abhorred censorship and in my time there was no interference of any kind with the student editors in running the publication. (Obviously there was a lapse two years later when my brother was forcibly retired from the editorship.)

A number of editors of the *Cosmos* went on to distinguished careers in journalism and this pleased Miss Outland more than anything else in her life. She kept in touch with them, read their dispatches and articles, and often criticized them when she thought them slipshod. In my own case, long after she retired in 1949, after forty years of teaching, she continued to keep a scrap-book of my dispatches, articles and the brickbats I received along the way. They are helping to guide me in these memoirs.

Thanks to these remarkable teachers, to a good deal of extra-curricular reading, and to the development that goes on in a youth of which he is largely unconscious and which he cannot explain—perhaps it is often a matter of chance—I think I got out of my four years in college what was most essential in any college education: a hunger to learn and a realization that college was only a beginning and that one's education could go on, if you wanted it to, to the end of your life.

The foundation you got in college was shaky, to be sure. But at least it was something to build on. Without it, unless you were a genius, you might be handicapped.

College was never for me, as it was for so many, the greatest and the happiest experience of one's life, something you looked back to with nostalgia as the best time you ever had. The problem was to grow up after college, when one's life really started to unfold, but I came to see that for some, life was all downhill after they left the campus, their dreams dashed, their ambitions frustrated, their inner life not solid and deep enough to sustain all the defeats. There is something pathetic in watching alumni returning for homecoming or commencement, determined to put the clock back and to revert to happy college days. It is part of the American story—of men and women who after college never grew up.

There were two alumni of Coe, both graduates of the class of 1886, who did grow up, who indeed became nationally known—

for quite different achievements—and I have often reflected on their lives and their reputations. Occasionally they returned to the campus to speak. The college regarded one, a Standard Oil tycoon, as its most distinguished graduate and the other as the most eminent scholar it had turned out, though somewhat of a "radical" whose thoughts and writings went a little to the left of what was thought safe in our parts.

Edward Alsworth Ross by my time had become one of the country's leading sociologists, holding the chair in that department at the University of Wisconsin. Orphaned at eight, shunted about to a succession of aunts and finally to a nearby farmer whose pious Presbyterianism led him to send the boy to Coe, Ross, after his graduation, pursued his doctoral studies in Germany, where he quickly discarded most of what he had learned at our college, abandoning his faith in orthodox economics and the prevailing social views and exchanging, so to speak, his Presbyterianism for philosophy. After a stormy academic debut—he was kicked out of Stanford in 1900 for opposing the gold standard and the importation of cheap Chinese labor—he found a haven at Wisconsin, where he was free to develop and express his progressive ideas and where he became a member of La Follette's brain trust.

For more than a quarter of a century Ross stirred up the country with his provocative books and lectures, and one of his works, *Social Control* (1901), had a profound influence in pointing the way not only to social planning that the nation eventually would be forced to adopt but to the growing role of the intellectual in positions of power in an increasingly complex society. He foresaw the brain trusts of Franklin Roosevelt and John Kennedy and the participation in the high echelons of government of a swarm of professors from the universities. Mercifully, he did not live long enough to see how disappointing most of the academics, in which he placed such high hopes, would turn out to be once they had gained admittance to the seats of the mighty and been corrupted by unaccustomed power.

To all colleges in the mid-twenties, a poor boy who made good, who became rich, who became a corporation magnate, was a hero. And to even a Christian college like Coe it mattered little that its "most distinguished graduate," Colonel Robert W. Stewart, class of 1886, and presently Chairman of the Board of

Standard Oil of Indiana, turned out, as a Senate Investigating Committee and the special prosecutors appointed by President Coolidge to look into the Harding scandals concluded, to have participated in one of the shady oil deals of the time and that as a result John D. Rockefeller, Jr., himself would drive him from his job at the top.

Like Ross, Stewart came from a poor family. His father was a blacksmith in Cedar Rapids, who later bought a farm nearby, where his son grew up helping with the chores and the hard labor of tilling the soil. A bright and ambitious youth, Stewart, after his graduation from Coe, went on to Yale, where in two years he earned a law degree, and then returned to the West, this time to South Dakota, to begin the practice of law. He was so successful prosecuting big corporations, the biggest of which was Standard Oil, that the company—this was a common experience in our parts in those days—hired him as its western attorney. From that beginning he rose rapidly to the top of the biggest oil company in the country.

Then in the early 1920's he got into trouble. In 1924, my junior year, the revelations of the Teapot Dome oil scandal began to rock the country. Two years before, Albert B. Fall, a former senator from New Mexico and Secretary of the Interior under President Harding, secretly had leased the government-owned Teapot Dome oil reserve in Wyoming to Harry F. Sinclair's Mammoth Oil Company after Sinclair had given him $260,000. The investigation of Sinclair's "gift" led to other questionable oil deals. And that is where our Colonel Stewart came in.

In 1921 he and three other oil executives, including Sinclair, had set up a dummy Canadian corporation, the Continental Trading Company, to conceal a transaction with the owner of the rich Mexia oil field by which the four individuals were able to pocket a quick profit of three-quarters of a million dollars each. When the Senate Investigating Committee and the special prosecutors got on its trail, Continental was swiftly dissolved and its records were destroyed.

As for Colonel Stewart, he turned over his three-quarters of a million dollars to an employee to be held in trust for his company—the trust agreement was written in pencil—but he neglected to inform his Board of Directors of this little windfall until 1928, seven years later, when the government investigators forced disclosure. Like most of the other oil men who had set up Continental, the colonel took up temporary residence in foreign parts, in his case Cuba, from which he was persuaded to return in 1928 by Mr. Rockefeller to face the Senate Committee. To this inquisitive body he first swore: "I did not personally receive any of these bonds. I did not make one dollar out of the transaction." Two months later, after the acquittal of Sinclair,[1] Stewart became more frank. He admitted that the bonds had been delivered to him personally and that he had failed to tell the directors of his company of them until years later.

All this was too much for Mr. Rockefeller. He forced Stewart out of the chairmanship of the board of Standard Oil of Indiana. But as the thoughtful editor of *Harper's* commented: "The business world as a whole seemed to find nothing wrong in Colonel Stewart's performance."

My little Presbyterian college apparently found nothing wrong either. It gladly and gratefully received $200,000 from him to build a splendid new library, which it called the Stewart Memorial Library. It already had elected him to the Board of Trustees and named him as its commencement speaker in 1923.

I was halfway through college then and went to hear him, curious to have a look at this man who had always been held up to us as an example of how a graduate from our rather obscure institution could make good in the big world. As he arrived for commencement, the college weekly hailed this graduate of 1886 as "one of our most famous alumni." The only allusion he made to the current headlines was in the title of his talk: "Present-Day Tendencies in the Witness Box." He had already made an appearance before the Senate Committee but had spilled nothing. Of his commencement speech, the college paper wrote:

> Colonel Stewart's speech was a scathing denunciation of bloc politics, radicalism, syndicalism and the other "isms," and a brilliant defense of capitalism, which he declared the forces of syndicalism were seeking to undermine.

[1] Though the federal courts voided the Teapot Dome lease on the grounds that it had been obtained fraudulently, Sinclair was eventually acquitted of conspiracy to defraud the government. He did serve two brief sentences in jail, one for contempt of the Senate after he had refused to answer questions, and the second for contempt of court when it was revealed that he had hired Burns detectives to shadow the jury at his trial, one of whose members told of being offered "an automobile as long as this block" if he voted right.

"Capitalism," he said, "was essentially based on freedom . . . The world has no place for shirkers, and the advocate of syndicalism is at heart a shirker . . ."

Stewart warned against the feeling prevalent in America that there is no need for worry over communist propaganda. . . .

"A big country," he declared, "needs big business." Stewart admitted there was inequality in America, but cautioned: "Nature is the cause of inequality among men, and Nature cannot be reformed."

So it was "Nature," not "capitalism," that was the cause of inequality in our land. It was "syndicalism," by which I took it he meant the trade-union movement, which by encouraging the "shirkers" was undermining our capitalism "based on freedom." At the time, I cannot recall that I found the bluff colonel's "scathing denunciation" full of hokum and red herrings, though my suspicions were sprouting. I was only nineteen, still crammed full of provincial ignorance.

A year later, as a diary entry shows, I must have begun to wake up—about a lot of things. It is dated June 29, 1924. I had just finished my junior year in college. I was going back in the fall for the last year. In February I would reach my majority. The entry is headed: "On Nearing Twenty-One." It runs to fifteen hundred words. I cite a few of them because the diary shows not what I now—half a century later—believe were my thoughts then (fifty years could color them far beyond the truth) but what they actually were at the time, in all their naïveté.

I wonder what there is about the age of twenty-one that makes one so unsure of himself . . . Curiously enough . . . I find myself without conviction toward everything making for life. In the matter of morals and religion and politics and education . . . I find myself expressing grave doubts. I am at sea . . . Where instinct tells me I ought to be sure of at least a few cardinal principles, I find myself sure of not a thing.

In the field of morals I find myself questioning the foundations on which the regularly accepted standards have been erected. . . . I wonder what "right" really means after all? . . .

Prohibition is a case in point. If I take a drink I am breaking the law. But I cannot comprehend why I am breaking any moral law . . .

As to religion I am no more in the clear. It took but haphazard study of the Bible to relieve me of any orthodox conceptions I entertained during early years. If I read the New Testament free from the fanatic prejudice that makes divine every word of it, I am left wondering why so many people have seen in the life of Jesus wonderful enough precepts to make him their God and associate him as being the son of the supreme being. . . . It has seemed to me that Jesus was a human being, a revolutionary leader with a revolutionary idea and possessed of a new philosophy of life the most of which I concur in. As a man of history he seems to me a great person . . . But as to his being the only true God . . . there is much room to doubt . . .

If the Christian religion is the one true religion I wonder what the powers-that-be in its heaven will do with those millions of other human beings who have believed that Mohammed or Confucius or Buddha were true gods. Certainly these people cannot be condemned for worshiping in the only way which their environment permitted . . . In the rewards of after-life how are those millions who were not Christians to be disposed of?

I wondered if our organized religion as expressed in the churches was "not hypocritical in its stand on practical problems" because it feared to lose financial support. The attitude of the Christian churches on war, for instance: "How can the church worship Christ and shrink from taking a stand on the outlawing of war?" And I expressed fear that I was losing my sense of partriotism, I who at thirteen had tried to enlist in the Great War and then, at fifteen, had gone off for my foolish soldiering at Camp Funston.

The diary breaks off in the midst of this soul-searching. Perhaps it overwhelmed me. Perhaps I went off to a baseball game to get my mind off such subversive thoughts. But they continued to haunt me all the last year on the campus.

In June, 1925, commencement suddenly was on us, and the windup of the college years and of my youth in this Iowa town. In his baccalaureate sermon President Gage called on the graduates to "build in America the great temples of Christian democracy. Paganism," he said, "is reactionism . . . a resolute refusal to take the new way."

This was in itself—the irrelevant crack about paganism aside —not bad advice. A Christian democracy could be a good thing; it should lead logically to a Christian social democracy, too. The trouble was, it seemed to me, that we didn't have it and I did not believe we ever would. There was nothing very Christian, or even democratic, about our profit-greedy, money-dominated, elite-ruled democracy.

With these thoughts—full of doubts and uncertainties—and with this scattering of learning picked up in four years on this bucolic campus, I took my diploma and slipped out of the town in which I had spent the last twelve years growing up.

I had no idea it would be forever. It was not, as I sometimes later fooled myself into thinking, a flight. The long years here through grade school, highschool and college had had their moments of excitement and on the whole I would remember them as fairly interesting, pleasant, even somewhat meaningful. Admittedly, in the last two or three years the state of the country and of the town had more and more depressed me. The bigotry and banality, the inanities of a society dominated by quacks, by fundamentalism, puritanism and the puerility of President Coolidge, were not what a youngster looked forward to returning to and trying to live with, to live the only life given to you. Still, this was the place on earth you had been born into and you had to make the best of it. Perhaps there were ways. I would take my chances.

In the meantime there lay ahead nearly three months of escape from this Midwest town, months of freedom and abandon in the great faraway cities I had heretofore only dreamt of seeing: Washington and New York, London and Paris—especially Paris! The prospect was immensely exciting. And in the back of my mind, though not very strong, was the thought that with luck, in which I had always believed, though the odds were a thousand, or maybe a million, to one against me, I might prolong my stay abroad. Perhaps long enough to sort out myself and get a beach-head on another way of life.

With a last glance at the now deserted campus I set off with my uncle in his flivver for Chicago. Though I did not know it, it was the first step on a new road I have followed ever since and which would take me, before I returned home twenty years later, to distant places in Europe, the Near East and Asia through times of great upheaval and inhumanity.

BOOK FOUR

GROWING UP IN PARIS, 1925-1927

To be twenty-one, fresh out of Iowa, alone, utterly free, and with a job in Paris in the mid-twenties! In the ensuing weeks, months and years I felt I was getting as near to paradise on this earth as any man could ever get. They were the happiest and the most wondrous, if not the most important and eventful, years of my life. Few setbacks, disappointments or sorrows marred those radiant days. These, as they were bound to, would come—but later, and mostly in other places.

In this golden time one could be wonderfully carefree in the beautiful, civilized city, released from all the puritan, bourgeois restraints that had stifled a young American at home. Each day was filled to the brim—with genial work, and people and play, and unfamiliar places to see. There was time and just the right atmosphere for a little contemplation, much reading, much talking, good eating, and a great deal of meandering through the teeming, narrow, winding streets, across the parks, up and down the boulevards, to the museums, the old churches, the splendid cathedral, the busy markets, and, to wind up, to the terrace of one of a hundred cafés where one could sit in the bracing air, watch the crowd go by, read newspapers or books, chew the fat with new friends, flirt, and drink as much, or as little, as one chose.

On days off each week there were trips to the countryside, the environs of Paris: St. Germain, the Valley of the Chevreuse, Versailles, Fontainebleau, Barbizon; and on some weeks to the cathedral towns: Rheims, Rouen, Beauvais, Chartres—Chartres above all and often, its cathedral, the crowning glory of the Gothic. Occasionally in the spring or fall we would cycle through the battlefields of the Great War, the war I had missed by a couple of years or so, concentrating on the ruined forts around Verdun, where a million French and Germans had been slain, ending up sometimes at Compiègne, where the Armistice had been signed on November 11, 1918, in the old *wagon-lit* car, now sheltered in a museum. I would see that old railroad car much later on a sad occasion, after history had taken one of its most calamitous turns.

There was all that and much more in those first exciting years in Paris, and soon there would begin a deepening and passionate love for a woman, a black-haired, dark-eyed, vivacious Parisian. We will call her Yvonne.

Shortly after 9 P.M. on the pleasant summer evening of August 20, 1925, a few hours after the train I had expected to board for the beginning of the trip home had departed the Gare du Nord, I went to work on the night copy desk of the Paris edition of the *Chicago Tribune*. A few minutes before, David Darrah, the taciturn young editor, had taken me on, generously overlooking my meager credentials as a newspaperman and my even more meager knowledge of French, which one had to know to translate the Havas (the French news agency) dispatches and the clips from the Paris newspapers that came across the desk for rewrite. Perhaps he wanted at least one copywriter who "came" from Chicago, the home base of the newspaper, and who presumably knew something about it, and perhaps I had failed to mention that I had left the city when I was nine, scarcely knew it, and didn't much like what little I knew. At any rate, he had taken the gamble and hired me—at a salary of twelve hundred francs a month, or sixty dollars. And he had put me immediately to work. Nervously, fearing my ignorance and inexperience might be put to such a test at once that this first night would be my last, I sat down at the large copy desk and looked at the men around it.

A lanky, owl-eyed man with thick glasses sitting next to me introduced himself. He said his name was Jim Thurber. He seemed warm and friendly and introduced me quickly to the others, tossing in a crack or two: "Elliot Paul, he's the only one of us writers who's got himself published—three novels, I believe." Paul laughed softly. He was rotund, bearded, partly bald and there was a hint of mischief in his eyes behind a look of utter innocence. "Eugene Jolas." Thurber pointed to the next one, a heavyset, broad-shouldered man with the fine classical lines of an old Roman in his jovial face. "He's our poet—in three languages. German. French. American. Sometimes he gets them mixed up. Our other poet over there," he went on, pointing to a gentle-looking man who resembled Shakespeare a little and who was sitting at a separate desk, "is Virgil Geddes, finance editor, I believe." Quickly Thurber went around the rest of the desk, but it was difficult to catch the names. There was an Englishman who spoke in a thick Oxford accent and seemed rather learned; an Irishman with an equally thick brogue and a jaunty lilt of speech who told me during the evening that he and his novels were banned in Ireland—"that curs-ed coontry." In the slot sat a cheerful, roly-poly man, Bernhard Ragner, who was night editor and who helped me through the first evening by tossing me copy that was easy to edit and headline, and sparing me all but two or three small items to rewrite from French.

Later a number of these men around the copy desk that first night would become widely known as writers: Elliot Paul, Jolas (who with Paul would also found *transition* a couple of years later), Virgil Geddes and, above all, Thurber, who, after he joined *The New Yorker*, would develop into the finest humorist of our time and remain my lifelong friend. But all that lay in the future. None of us, except Paul, had any inkling of what would happen. We were young, anonymous, happy and perhaps hopeful. Before the first evening's work was done, it felt good to have fallen in with a group of such congenial, civilized, very individualistic men.

Early in the evening a rather down-and-out-looking fellow around thirty-five, with sad eyes and a couple of days' growth of beard, shuffled in and went over to talk to the sports editor, a bubbly, talkative Texan who had introduced himself to me as Herol Egan. You could hear them talking slyly about likely winners in the horse races.

"Harold Stearns," Thurber whispered to me.

"Not *the* Harold Stearns," I said incredulously.

"*The*," Jim said.

He wore a soiled, beat-up felt hat, which seemed to be glued on his head, for he never removed it, though it was a rather warm evening. His melancholy face was unwashed, unshaved, and his hands and fingers were dirty. I was taken aback by his shabbiness. This was not at all the Harold Stearns I had imagined from my college days, when he was one of my heroes, one of the brightest of all the young intellectuals who in Greenwich Village were stirring up the country, shaming it for its lack of culture and taste and goading it to take notice of the new young writers and the new young literature. After working his way through Harvard he had become a leading contributor to the newly founded *New Republic* and later the youthful editor of *The Dial,* and in 1921, when he was thirty, he had sent to the publishers a book he had conceived and edited, *Civilization in the United States,* which had burst upon the country and shaken it up—and shaken me up—when it came out a year later. I had got the news of it in the college library one day. Thumbing through *The Nation* I had come across the book section, then edited by Carl Van Doren, which was devoted in its entirety to *six* reviews of the book. Next morning I had bludgeoned the librarian into ordering a copy. It and a book of his own essays, which Stearns published at the same time, *America and the Young Intellectual,* aroused me from my provincial slumbers. Civilization in America, they proclaimed, had gone all wrong. Life had become tawdry, vulgar, uncreative, a mad grab for the dollar. Artists and writers—all the creative individuals—could not grow on such barren soil. They must flee abroad, to Paris if possible. Only there could they fulfill themselves.

Having sent his two books to the printer, Harold Stearns had taken his own advice and in the summer of 1921 boarded ship for Europe. A dozen reporters had come to the gangplank in New York to chronicle the departure of the young literary lion and to note his last words.

"How long you going to stay away?" one asked.

"Perhaps forever," Stearns said. There was no future in the American wasteland for a writer, he added. You had to go to Europe, for God's sake, not only to write, but to live. He had gone, to Paris, and I had not heard anything of him since.

And now to my amazement—and disillusionment—there he was, a woebegone figure, chatting to the sports editor about the horses. I did not know then—he would tell of it ten years later in his memoirs[1]—that he had gone back to America for a couple of

[1] *The Street I Know.*

months at the end of 1924 to see his son, whose mother had died in childbirth, and been even more disillusioned with the country than when he had first left it, and that only a few months before this first evening of mine on the *Trib* he had returned to Paris, as he said, "almost completely broke and without a job or a friend or a woman to keep me. That summer and autumn of 1925 were the summer and autumn of my discontent." A woman named "Belinda," he says, had left him "with enough money for a few weeks." But soon it was gone and he had wandered the streets of Paris "literally wondering where the next meal was coming from."[1]

His next meal on this August evening of 1925 was coming, it developed, from the sports editor. At the 10:30 P.M. coffee break, when we adjourned to the terrace of the Trois Portes, Egan mentioned that Stearns had come not so much to discuss the horses as to tap him for a "loan" of a hundred francs.

"He said he hadn't eaten all week," Egan told us. "Next time I'm going to turn him over to you guys. We've got to share the burden."

We all shared the burden in the next years, at least a hundred of us who could not help liking Stearns or feel sad as we watched the slow degeneration of one once so splendidly endowed and so promising. He already had gone, as Hemingway would say, "into the period of his unreliability," balancing, as Evan Shipman, Stearns's friend, added, "his disreputable life like a comic juggler." Hemingway was putting him in as Harvey Stone in the novel he was writing that year, *The Sun Also Rises*, which came out in 1926. And Kay Boyle, the finest American woman writer in Paris in those days, would make Stearns the principal character in a novel of hers[2]—"the most satisfying book," she would say, "I ever wrote."[3]

I often saw Stearns in the next years, sometimes after midnight when you would find him perched at the bar of the Select in Montparnasse, sipping champagne and already drunk from it, looking a little like a silent Buddha, and people would say cruelly: "There lies civilization in the United States." The next year he came to the *Tribune* to write a horse-racing column under

[1] *Ibid.*, pp. 255–259.
[2] *Monday Night.*
[3] Kay Boyle and Robert McAlmon: *Being Geniuses Together*, p. 328.

the not-very-subtle name of Peter Pickem. By that time he was working on a "foolproof" system to pick the winners. He had given it, he said, much thought. I lost many a hundred-franc note, each one constituting a twelfth of my monthly salary, following his thinking. The nags Stearns bet on for me at the races almost always failed to place, and he would explain that he hadn't yet got the "kinks" out of his system. Something had gone wrong. But even when it didn't, when the horses he had coaxed you into betting on won, Harold would tell you when he got back from the races, his sad face full of greater sadness, that somehow he had forgotten to place your bet—and perhaps he had.

I got through that first night without difficulty and about 1 A.M. we knocked off, setting out, Paul, Thurber, Jolas and I, on foot for the Latin Quarter, a couple of miles away, where we lived. It was a pleasant walk we made nearly every night, down the Rue Cadet from the Rue La Fayette, across the boulevard and down the Rue Montmartre and through Les Halles, the great marketplace of Paris, which at that hour was just coming alive, full of carts and wagons and trucks disgorging fruit, vegetables, fish and meat, a place of chaos and wild shouts and curses from the drivers and vendors. The cafés in the quarter kept open all night and we would stop at a zinc bar to refresh our spirits on a cognac. Then we would push on through the Place du Châtelet past the Théâtre Sarah Bernhardt and on across the north branch of the Seine to the Île de la Cité, skirting the Palais de Justice, and then across the second bridge to the Place St. Michel and a few blocks on turn into the Rue des Écoles where the Balzar seemed to be waiting for us. This was an Alsatian brasserie, with the best beer in Paris, and fine *choucroute garni*, I soon learned, and it inevitably became our final stop, where we downed a few beers and a plate of sauerkraut and sausage. Around it lay the complex of buildings of the Sorbonne and other branches of the University of Paris, and even at the late hour we arrived, around two in the morning, there would be a cluster of professors having a nightcap. That first night someone pointed out Édouard Herriot, a stout man who obviously enjoyed his food and drink, and who had recently been Premier and undoubtedly would be again.

The Balzar closed at 3 A.M., the waiters hustled us out, and I walked up the Boulevard St. Michel, past the Luxembourg Gardens, whose gates were closed after dark, to the Boulevard Port-

Royal and my darkened *pension,* which a few hours before I had thought I would be leaving, forever, and thinking of George, who by this time would be well on his way to Manchester to catch our cattle boat home. The room seemed empty and lonely without him. I missed him, but was awfully glad I was not now with him. Exhausted but not sleepy I fell into bed and reflected on this momentous day. The first evening on the *Trib* had been wonderful. I felt confident I could stay on, and that meant staying on in Paris. I could hardly wait to get back to work the next evening.

The Paris edition of the *Chicago Tribune* was like no other newspaper on earth. One could be skeptical of the claim that the *Tribune* in Chicago was the "World's Greatest Newspaper," as it proclaimed each day from its masthead. In truth, it was far from being the greatest, and there were some in Chicago—and elsewhere—who thought it one of the world's worst.

But there can be no doubt that its Paris edition was the world's zaniest newspaper, a crazy journal without peer, and not at all what its owner, the lordly Colonel Robert Rutherford McCormick, intended it to be and thought it was.

The first issue had been published on the Fourth of July, 1917, as the first ragged contingent of American troops under General John J. Pershing, in their broad-brimmed campaign hats, marched down the Champs Élysées. It was called the Army Edition of the *Chicago Tribune* and its purpose was to provide the soldiers with a little touch of home: comics, sports, and news of how the home folks were supporting the war. It was, as Aleck Woollcott, then on the *Stars and Stripes,* said, "Colonel McCormick's gift to the American Expeditionary Force." The colonel, then commanding an artillery regiment, was very proud of it. Before the end of the war it was being read by a million doughboys and, moreover, making a modest profit, which was turned over to the A.E.F.

After the Armistice, McCormick decided to keep the paper going. He wanted a rival to the Paris *Herald,* which James Gordon Bennett of the New York *Herald* had established in Paris thirty years before. The colonel, as I was to learn at first hand, took a dim view of New York publishers and New York newspapers, feeling that they were not quite American. What Europe needed, he decided, was a red-blooded American newspaper to interpret America's attitude toward Europe, which he felt our troops had liberated from the terrible threat of German domination. He wanted the Europeans to know what the *Tribune*, and therefore America, thought of what they were up to: the Versailles Treaty, which he opposed; the war debts, which he wanted promptly paid; the League of Nations, which he believed subversive; the Allied occupation of the German Rhineland, which he didn't much like. He wanted to impress on Europe the new power of the United States and what it intended to do with it. All this, he believed, could be done by maintaining a European edition of the *Tribune*. It would be "America's voice in Europe," he said. It would be "American and not European."

But it never turned out that way. For reasons neither the autocratic colonel, nor anyone else, ever understood—and perhaps the mystery is insoluble—the Paris *Tribune* became the organ of the expatriates of the Paris Left Bank, mostly written and almost entirely read by the bohemians of Montparnasse, who scorned all the standards and values of America, and especially the colonel's dear Midwest. The Paris edition was concerned chiefly with the writers and the painters and the drunks of the Latin Quarter, reporting on their books, their little magazines, their paintings, their lives, their loves; more interested in literature, the theater, the art exhibitions, the concerts, the gossip of the Left Bank cafés than in the goings on of the Right Bank American colony, which was full of businessmen and social climbers, or in the politics and the economics of a Europe going downhill in that brief interlude of peace between the wars, or even in the news from home.

Far from being "America's voice in Europe," the fantastic little newspaper turned out to be the voice of the American voluntary exiles who had fled their homeland, who doubted whether it was worth saving, and who believed that Europe was the only place in which they could live and work in freedom and decency. Had McCormick read its columns, or understood them, he either would have suffered a stroke of apoplexy or killed the paper immediately—perhaps both. It was far more "un-American" than the New York newspapers, which he despised.

Getting out the Paris *Trib* each evening, I soon found, was primarily a work of the imagination. Our news sources were so meager that to fill our eight pages we had to resort to a good deal of embroidering and sometimes to outright fiction. The London office filed by telegraph early each evening a few hundred words of what it could lift from the British newspapers and news agencies, but there were very few American items, and news from home was what an American newspaper in Europe was supposed to feature. For that we depended on a skimp one hundred words a day from the New York correspondent of the home edition, which arrived by cable around 10 P.M. If used as received they would have filled no more than a few inches of one column, but we had from eight to ten columns on the front page and inside to fill. So after our return from the coffee break we would pitch in to enlarge one hundred words of cable from home into several thousand words. That was where one's imagination came in.

Especially Thurber's. He turned out to be a genius. The night editor would toss him eight or ten words of cablese and say, "Give me a column on that, Jim." And Thurber, his owlish face puckering up, would say, "Yes, suh," and he would glance at the cable and go merrily to work. That fall and winter he seemed to specialize on President Coolidge, whose inanities gave him so much pleasure that they seemed to tide him over all the dreary, cold, rainy days that season.

Early in October the President addressed the American Legion convention in Omaha and a cable duly arrived giving us these bare facts: "Coolidge to Legionnaires Omaha opposed militarism urged tolerance American life." That was all Thurber needed, and he set to work composing a column and a half of the finest clichés that had ever resounded from Washington, or Omaha, and most of which, I have little doubt, Coolidge actually used.

Thurber was at it again a few weeks later when the President spoke in Washington to the international convention of the Y.M.C.A. and our cable merely reported: "Coolidge tells international convention Y.M.C.A. American youth needs more home control exparental action." The President's inane homilies, the state of America's wayward, rebellious, jazz-age youth, the worse state of their frenzied thirsty parents in an age of bootleg gin and dizzy paper profits on the bullish market—Jim put them all in as his imagination soared. The result was another classic.

Pretty soon Thurber became impatient if Coolidge was silent for long, and unable to restrain himself, Jim would simply make up a dispatch about our great Yankee President. Once he had Coolidge addressing a convention of Protestant churches and proclaiming that "a man who does not pray is not a praying man."

That fall Christy Mathewson, the great baseball pitcher, died, and I remember the night editor handing Thurber a five-word cable: "Christy Mathewson died tonight Saranac." Jim, like me, loved sports and, at that time, especially baseball, about which he knew a great deal. He took the cable and muttered, "Too bad. A great pitcher. A great man." And he sat down and batted out from the recesses of his memory—we had no morgue of background clippings—one of the finest tributes I have ever read, replete with facts about the player's pitching records, stories of some of the great games he had pitched in World Series, and an assessment of his character on and off the diamond.[1]

All of us around the copy desk became more or less proficient at this sort of "expansion" of the news. I had a chance at it a week after I arrived when the U.S. Navy dirigible *Shenandoah* went down in a thunderstorm over Ohio and I wrote two columns of "vivid" description from the usual ten-word cable. Less than a month later I did it again when the U.S. submarine S-51 was sunk in a collision off Block Island and thirty-four crewmen were lost. The harrowing details of these two tragedies that came out of my imagination perhaps outdid the facts a little, had we known them. Just as Thurber was our ace for fictionalizing President Coolidge, I was in demand for inventing the details of horrendous accidents in the air or on the sea.

We shared our "coverage" of sports. All we got by cable that fall on the big football games was a score by quarters. From that we proceeded to construct a play-by-play account, putting in all the color we could think up, and rising to some heights in our account of the Harvard-Yale and Army-Notre Dame games. The old grads about Paris, we were told by our local reporters, would discuss for days the great end runs, off-tackle smashes, forward passes, blocked punts and spectacular drop kicks (an art now lost) that we conjured up. The scores, of course, were factual.

Since even giving free rein to our imaginations could not fill up the paper with news from home, we had to stuff a number of

---

[1] Charles S. Holmes in his biography of Thurber, *The Clocks of Columbus: The Literary Career of James Thurber,* pp. 75–76, confirms my memory of some of Thurber's splendid rewrites.

columns with local news, mostly about the goings on of the Anglo-American colony in Paris. In this endeavor our reporters often found their assignments so stultifying that they would slip in, as pranks, the most outrageous happenings, all invented, expecting that the copy desk would catch them, be amused, and kill them before they got into print. But occasionally they escaped the notice of the copyreaders, proofreaders, and editor, and ended up on the front page or inside—with shocking results.

There was the story of a lovesick young American whose passion for a movie star was not reciprocated, with the result that he shot himself. The aim was bad and the youth, after having a minor wound dressed at the hospital, was released. "So tonight," the reporter concluded his story, "the lovesick young man is safe in the arms of his mother instead of in the arms of Jesus." The item made the front page and the next day all the good American Christians in Paris were on the phone to the *Trib* protesting such sacrilege. The reporter was fired.

Thurber himself was incorrigible in composing the most outlandish tales and waiting, devilishly, to see if the editor would catch them. Once, on a dull night for news, he wrote a long piece about a dozen international figures, including renowned statesmen and social leaders of Western Europe, being involved in blackmail, burglary, rape, gambling and various other nefarious crimes. The lurid tale got by both the copy desk and the proofreading desk, was set up in type with a sensational headline, and was caught only at the last minute by Darrah, the managing editor, who almost fired the apologetic Thurber on the spot. "That would have cost the *Tribune* a billion dollars in libel suits," Darrah admonished him. It was more than even Colonel McCormick could afford.

The classic example of a terrible prank that did get published was still talked about around the copy desk when I arrived, though it had happened two years before. The then Prince of Wales, later and briefly King of England and thereafter the Duke of Windsor, had visited Paris and gone through the usual boring ceremonies of laying cornerstones, visiting hospitals, receiving war veterans and having tea with the British colony. Reporters got tired of following the Prince around, and the British Embassy, to help them, issued a handout covering royal activities of the day. A *Tribune* reporter named Spencer Bull picked up the handout for the last day, paused at a nearby café for a few drinks, repaired to the office to write the story, and having done so felt the urge to add a few lines of his own invention—for the delectation of the copy desk but not for publication. The Prince, according to the handout, had reviewed a contingent of British Boy Scouts, and this struck the reporter's imagination. So he added to his account the following lines:

> Stopping before one manly youth the Prince inquired: "What is your name, my lad?"
> "None of your goddamned business, sir," the youngster replied. At that, the Prince snatched a riding crop from his equerry and beat the boy's brains out.

No one was more horrified than Spencer Bull to see his story played up on page one the next morning. He had often sneaked in such stuff, he said, and always someone had caught it in time. Everyone on the editorial and business staffs of the *Trib* was called out of bed at dawn, when the editor discovered the story, to snatch all copies of the *Trib* from the newsstands. But several hundred copies had been dispatched to London and there, according to the lore around the copy desk, our newspaper was banned for six months. The Prince of Wales must have been a good sport. He accepted the *Tribune*'s profuse apologies and never sued. Spencer Bull was fired.

Not all of our work on this zany newspaper was horseplay. There was a great ferment in the literary and artistic world of Paris that year. And Europe itself, after the agonies of the long war and the upheavals of the first uneasy years of peace, seemed at last to be settling down, trying to find through the League of Nations and various nonaggression pacts a way to avoid another devastating conflict. The Paris *Trib*, despite its high jinks, covered these developments more thoroughly than its rivals, the Paris *Herald* and the Paris *Times*,[1] helped, in the last instance, by

---

[1] The Paris *Times*, founded a year before, in 1924, by Courtland Bishop, an American millionaire living in Paris, had no connection with *The New York Times* and was strictly a nonnewspaper. It had no news sources except what it could lift from the London and Paris newspapers, and almost no circulation. But it was well written by a staff of talented young men who worked for even less than we did on the *Trib*. These included Vincent Sheean, who always maintained he was fired as a correspondent of the *Chicago Tribune* (after his great scoop of interviewing

the dispatches of the home edition's foreign correspondents from the European capitals and, in the first, by the enterprise of its local reporters, who were more interested in artists and writers than in anything else. These were the things I became chiefly interested in, beyond my personal life, involved, as it was, in the excitement of discovering Paris.

Dada was dead and had been replaced by surrealism. The French literary reviews, which I began to read, took these movements very seriously, recounting their quarrels, manifestos and absurdities. I found them hard to follow. Tristan Tzara, the wild Rumanian poet who wrote in French and who had founded Dada in a Zurich cabaret during the Great War, said that "Dada had no meaning," and from the little I read of it I agreed, though there were some like Malcolm Cowley, who was first taken in by it early in the twenties, who thought it reflected the dizzy times brought about by the war and dominated, as the Dadaists said, by "aggressive madmen." If politics were looney, so could literature be. But I did not find this very interesting.

The young American writers in Paris were not much affected by the shouting of the Dadaists and the surrealists. They seemed to think that struggling with their native language and trying to liberate it from the prewar gentility and sterility absorbed all an American writer's time and energy. They were greatly influenced, however, by an Irish genius, James Joyce, who had settled in Paris after the war and who in 1922 had given the English language a masterpiece, *Ulysses*. Many a night that cold first winter when the news was slow we sat around the copy desk discussing it. But as I had not yet read it—it had been banned at home as immoral and licentious and the first five hundred copies shipped from Paris by Sylvia Beach's bookshop, Shakespeare and Company, its intrepid publisher, had been seized and burned in New York by the U.S. postal authorities—I took no part in the talk. It would be some time before I could afford to buy the book, which cost 125 francs. What little money I had for books I was spending on French volumes purchased for a franc or two at the book stalls

---

Abd-el-Krim in the Riff) for taking too much time out for dinner one night in Paris and who worked on the newspaper sporadically when he was in town and broke; Hillel Bernstein, Larry Blochman and Georges Rehm, all of whom later wrote several books; and Martin Summers, subsequently foreign editor of *The Saturday Evening Post*.

along the Seine, so that I could improve my French and begin to get a feel for French writing.

One soon became aware, however, that something was stirring among the young American writers in Paris. Around the copy desk Paul and Jolas and Thurber talked of the great promise of a man I had never heard of, Ernest Hemingway, who was living in the quarter, had been a part-time foreign correspondent for International News Service and the Toronto *Star*, had already published two slim volumes of poems, sketches and short stories brought out by obscure American avant-garde houses in Paris, and was, they said, working on his first novel. Most of the American writers on the Left Bank, one soon learned, merely talked of writing—they were going to get down to serious work on "the book" next week or next month, but they never did; they never got beyond sitting on café terraces and at bars—but Hemingway, everyone said, worked hard and took his writing with deadly seriousness.

In the company of Paul and Jolas I first ran into him one afternoon at the Closerie des Lilas. He was sitting with Ezra Pound, of whom I was somewhat in awe since he already had a reputation as one of the best of American poets and he was only the second great poet, after Edna Millay, I had ever met. Moreover, he looked like a poet, with his red beard, arty wide-brimmed hat and expressive face. I had heard the crack Gertrude Stein made of Pound, that he was "a village explainer, excellent if you were a village, but if you were not, not," which, as I would learn, was typical of so much nonsense that she wrote, though not all was nonsense. I had heard of Pound's generosity toward new young writers, the help and encouragement and advice he gave them. He was already championing Hemingway and some said that he had saved T. S. Eliot from disaster by suggesting extensive revisions in *The Waste Land,* the poem that still exercised a spell over my generation, and this was confirmed forty years later when the photostats of the original manuscript notes and memos were published.

Immediately, Pound was in an argument with my companions about the merits, if any, of the little literary magazines then flourishing in Paris. Margaret Anderson had moved her *Little Review* here, Ernest Walsh and Ethel Moorhead had launched earlier that year *This Quarter,* Jolas and Paul were planning to start *transition,* "to revolutionize the word," they said, and Pound himself, with Ford Madox Ford, was editing the *Transatlantic Review,* with editorial help from Hemingway, who was one of its chief contributors.

Hemingway did not join in the discussion. Somewhat to my surprise, after all I had heard of him, he did not look or talk much like a writer. He was big and athletic, with a ruddy complexion and bright, lively eyes. Turning to me he began to talk of sports: the six-day bicycle races at the Velodrome d'Hiver, the fights at the Cirque de Paris and a new French middleweight boxer he thought might make it, the tennis and Suzanne Lenglen, the graceful, vivacious French champion. He was playing a lot of tennis, he said, and doing even more boxing—he was even trying to teach Ezra Pound the art—and when he ran out of amateurs he took on the pros at a nearby gymnasium where he could pick up ten francs a round sparring with them before their fights. I wondered how he found time to write. He said not a word about writing, which I was hoping he would, for like most of the young Americans in Paris I was already trying to write poems and short stories and finding it more difficult than I had anticipated. I had thought at first that this was a good opportunity to talk about it but, without saying so, he made it clear he did not want to touch on the subject and I was too timid to bring it up. Still, it was a pleasant encounter. He seemed friendly enough to a stranger who must have seemed to him very young and immature, a bit of a hayseed from his own Midwest, and I was struck by his directness and especially his modesty. This last would dissolve somewhat, as it does for almost every writer when acclaim comes, and it came for Hemingway suddenly the next year when *The Sun Also Rises* came out and he was hailed by many reviewers, as Pound had been saying all along, as the best prose writer of the new generation.

I saw a bit of James Joyce that first year. My first meal of the day, after working the night shift and sleeping until noon, was lunch, which I often took in a pleasant little restaurant at the foot of the Rue de l'Odéon, near the Boulevard St. Germain. Joyce often dropped in there, after stopping at Sylvia Beach's bookshop up the street. At first I just stared at the great man, noticing his appearance, his medium height, his slimness, his hair brushed back from a high forehead, his graceful, narrow hands and a certain air of being high-strung. He usually wore dark glasses, so that you could not see his eyes, which had given him much trouble (glaucoma); the disease was threatening him with blindness—a terrible fate for a writer. We took to nodding to each other when we entered and one day, summoning up my courage, I stopped at his table and introduced myself as a journalist on the Paris *Tribune* and a great admirer. He was extremely courteous but I could feel that he liked his privacy and I did not press upon it, so that for the most part we exchanged little more than pleasantries—a great disappointment to me. As with Hemingway, I was burning to talk about writing. Joyce did invite me to his readings in the back room of Sylvia Beach's Shakespeare and Company, but as I had only one night off a week I managed to make it only once. It was a memorable evening. He was working on a new book which he called "Work in Progress" and I had seen excerpts from it in one of the little reviews. But I could not make much out of it—he seemed to be writing in a dozen languages, which indeed he knew, but which I didn't, and in the process he was creating a new language, which was scarcely English. It was hard to follow in print. But when he read it in his musical tenor voice, with all the lilt of the Irish, it suddenly came alive. *Finnegans Wake*, as it was later entitled, was a joy to hear from Joyce's lips but for me almost impossible to read.

Other writers came through Paris, Sinclair Lewis, Dos Passos, Dreiser, Sherwood Anderson, whom one bumped into at the Dôme or at some party, and it was a thrill to meet them, though I certainly did not get close to them, with the exception of Anderson, an immensely likable man, with whom I had a couple of long, heady talks about writing and writers. I would get to know Lewis and Dos Passos later.

Edith Wharton, whom I much admired—I thought *Ethan Frome* was one of the finest short novels I had ever read—was living in an elegant country house at St. Brice-sous-Fôret, a dozen miles north of Paris, having removed there from her long-time residence in the Rue de Varenne after the war. After I went over to the dayside as a reporter I often tried to think up an excuse for going to interview her, but she was said to be terribly haughty to newsmen and I never got up quite enough nerve to make the call.

Another and greater literary idol was living that fall and winter on the Right Bank, near the Étoile. But it was not necessary to go to him. One night he came to us.

Out of the blue shortly before midnight he staggered into the newsroom, seated himself in the slot of the copy desk, which happened to be empty, looked bleary-eyed at us—he was drunk as a lord—and exclaimed, "Come on, boys. Let's get out the goddamned paper."

"Who the hell is he?" I whispered to Thurber.

"A guy named Scott Fitzgerald," Jim said loudly.

"Never heard of him, eh?" Fitzgerald said, eying me with a surprising belligerence. "You too young, eh . . . ever to have heard of him." He had the clean-cut profile of a young man in an Arrow Collar ad but his angular nostrils and jutting, pointed chin, between which the thin-lipped mouth seemed tucked in, jarred one who had heard of his handsome face. His hair parted in the middle added to his collegiate look, reminding you of the snooty college boy who came to a football game smothered in a long coonskin coat with a pretty, equally snooty girl on his arm.

"I've heard of you all right," I said. "What's more, I've *read* you. I think you're terrific." *Gatsby* had just come out, Thurber had lent me his copy, and I thought it the most beautifully written novel from any of the new writers. But of course since college days and the first novel, *This Side of Paradise,* I had thought he was "terrific" and that more than anyone else he spoke for the new "flapper" generation that had come of age with bootleg gin.

"Well, thanks," Fitzgerald said. "And now, how about getting out some goddamned copy so we can get the goddamned paper out?"

"Yes, suh," Thurber chimed in.

It was very hard getting the paper out that night. Fitzgerald would not move from the slot, and when Ragner, the night editor, returned, he had to find a place around the copy desk and whisper his assignments and stuff the copy we wrote into his coat pocket before Fitzgerald had a chance to tear it up. To add to the turmoil the great writer started to sing and kept insisting that we join him.

Getting Fitzgerald home proved even more difficult than getting the paper to bed. Liquor made him combative. When the night editor had slipped out with the last copy bulging from his pockets and disappeared downstairs to the printers, we finally extracted Fitzgerald from the slot and half carried him downstairs. Spotting a bar across the street, he made for it, pulling a couple of us with him. At the fifth or sixth bar, as we made our way slowly across town, our man gave signs of passing out.

"Let's get him into a taxi and take him home," Jolas proposed, and though Jolas was a big, chunky man, and Elliot Paul, Thurber and I were no midgets, this proved as difficult as everything else during the evening. Scott would not hear of going home. But at the next bar he passed out, and we shoved him into a taxi, half sitting on him when he stirred, and drove to his apartment in the Rue de Tilsitt near the Étoile.

But the job was far from over. The apartment house stood back behind an iron grille fence and from an upper story a woman appeared at a window and shouted, "Scott, you bastard! You're drunk again!"

"Zelda, darling . . . Yuh . . . Yuh . . . re . . . wrong . . . dead wrong . . . I . . . I'm as sober, darling . . . really . . . I am . . . as . . . as . . . a . . . polar bear." He sort of sang out the words as best he could.

So this was the celebrated Zelda, Scott's beautiful wife, queen of the flappers. Zelda, the vivacious, destructive partner in the Fitzgerald saga, a vital part of the Fitzgerald myth that grew and thrived in the good and the bad years between the wars.

With two of us hauling away at his arms and the other two pushing, we tried to lug the famous writer through the gate. No go. He broke away. Now he was furious as only a frustrated drunk can be. Circling around behind us he ran to the curb and picked up a piece of iron grating from around the trunk of a tree. He was about to bash in Thurber's head from behind when Jolas jumped on him and brought him down. Jim, blind in one eye, had not seen him rushing up on his bad side. Finally, we just carried him in, while Zelda, in pajamas, welcomed him with curses, and then, suddenly changing her mood, insisted that we stay and have a drink, which we mercifully declined. She was almost as pretty as her friends said, but somehow, to me at that first glance in the light, there was a flaw in the beauty of her face that I noticed at once but could not define. The features had not been put together quite right. They did not quite blend.

It had been for me a rather disillusioning evening. I was not yet grown up enough to realize, I guess, that it mattered not a damn how much of a nuisance a writer could make of himself, especially when drunk. The only thing that counted was how he wrote, and Fitzgerald wrote as well as anyone and often, as in *Gatsby,* better. I was never a part of the circle that clustered around Fitzgerald in Paris and down on the Riviera in the mid-twenties—the Gerald Murphys, the Archibald MacLeishes, the Hemingways and Dos Passos. I saw Fitzgerald very seldom, and then mostly at the Ritz Bar, which was part of my beat when I became a reporter and which he seemed to prefer to the cafés of Montparnasse—it was full of Ivy Leaguers who had gone into business or banking and apparently it was compatible for a Princeton graduate such as Scott. But I often speculated about his life and writing in those years, wondering if all the alcohol, the foolish self-indulgence, the burning of the candle at both ends, had fatally diminished his wonderful talents and his capacity to grow.

For it was all downhill after *Gatsby*. Downhill to a tragic end at forty-four, an age when in Europe, at least, a writer, a Thomas Mann, for example, was just coming into his full stride, when decades of creativity, if you did not squander what some mysterious power had given you, lay ahead. Zelda, I felt from the first glimpse, had not much helped him—but is that the responsibility of a writer's wife? Hemingway, somewhat hypocritically, thought in this instance it was, and complained that Zelda was ruining Fitzgerald as a writer. Destructive as she may have been, to him and to herself, could she be greatly blamed for his falling away? I doubt it. Blindly, arrogantly, he seems to have willed it himself. Like so many writers of his generation, as it would turn out, he could not stand—or survive—early success, the fame, the acclaim, the fortune it brought. There are no second acts in American lives, he once wrote, and he seemed bent on proving it in his own case.

The Parisians complained that the fall and winter of 1925–1926 were unusually dreary and trying. It rained and rained, then it snowed. The Seine reached the highest flood level in a quarter of a century, overflowing its banks and flooding the cellars of buildings along the quais. The thermometer and the franc tumbled to new lows. It was difficult to keep warm even if you were one of the few who had the newfangled central heating. And the falling franc—caused partly by falling governments—brought rising prices, diminishing the value of my own modest franc salary. A record snowfall almost prostrated the capital, which had no means of digging out. The French you ran into said it was the most miserable winter they could remember. But I had no complaints. I found life that first winter, dark and chilling though it was, wonderful. Paris was unfolding itself to me in all its splendor and enchantment.

I had found a room in a hotel in the Rue de Vaugirard, halfway between the Boulevard St. Michel and a corner of the Luxembourg Gardens that lay across from the Odéon theater. The Hotel de Lisbonne turned out to be as fantastic a place to live in as the Paris *Tribune* was to work on. Despite its staunch buttresses that jutted out on to the sidewalk, it tilted a little toward the street, as did most of the other eighteenth-century edifices nearby. A plaque reminded us that two great French poets had once lived there: Baudelaire and, later, Paul Verlaine— the mad Verlaine, who, as Jules Lemaître said, was a barbarian, a savage, an infant, but one who had music in his soul and heard voices from afar that no other poet had ever heard; the mad Verlaine, who one day in Brussels, in a moment of drunken rage, had tried to kill his closest friend, Rimbaud, also mad, also a great poet, and had served two years in a Belgian prison for the attempt, though Rimbaud had escaped with only a bullet hole through his wrist. The wild spirit of Verlaine hung over the hotel. We all read him avidly and, I'm afraid, tried to emulate him, his writing, his drinking—more successfully in the last than in the first.

The rooms were rather spacious. In each was a large writing table and bookcase well lit by French windows that extended from the floor to the high ceiling, a comfortable double bed, a dresser, a washbasin beneath a large mirror, and the inevitable *bidet*, which had to serve as a bathtub since there was no bathroom in the place (there had been one on the first floor but the proprietor used its tub as a coalbin). The wallpaper was atrocious in its loud, clashing colors and sentimental designs that jarred the daylights out of you until you stopped noticing it. Old and somewhat dilapidated as it was, the hotel had one modern convenience: central heating. The only trouble was that it seldom went on, but when it didn't you could stir up some heat in a fireplace that burned coal.

What more could you ask for in a hotel for 250 francs ($10) a month? Well, one thing: a more comfortable toilet. There was a so-called "stand-up" toilet by the stairwell on each floor. But it took some practice and a good deal of dexterity to use it. The

French called it a "Turkish toilet" and perhaps it was easier for the Turks than for us. They, apparently, had invented it. On the floor of a tiny closet, dimly lit by a 25-watt bulb that went on when you shut the door, was a small cement crater in the midst of which was a four-inch hole. On each side was a raised footrest, similar to one on a bootblack's stand. The trick was to achieve a proper balance without keeling over and then, at the end, keeping your balance, to reach high for the nail on the soggy wall from which cut-up old newspapers hung and, finally, to reach for a knobless, rusty old chain that hung somewhere above in the murky semidarkness. Gradually one became fairly skillful—there was no other recourse—and one's leg and thigh muscles grew strong enough to perform the acrobatics. But one's guests, especially if they were American, found it hard to adjust to, and I almost lost the fine companionship that first winter of a lovely Vassar girl, who was taking the usual course in Civilisation Française at the Sorbonne, because of this Turkish contraption at the end of the hall. A well-bred girl from a well-heeled New York family used to all the modern plumbing that American civilization provided, she said it made her very angry at the French, whose civilization she had come across the Atlantic to study and which, in some ways but not in this, she said, she admired.

I never encountered these Turkish stand-ups elsewhere in Europe, not even in Turkey, but one day years later I ran across one in the corner of a regal chamber in the winter palace of the King of Afghanistan in Jawalabad on my way from Peshawar to Kabul. A French archeologist in our party thought it was very primitive, but I reminded him that I had become well acquainted with the likes of it in the very center of the glittering capital of his country.

By the time I arrived, the Hotel de Lisbonne was full of Americans, mostly from the Paris *Tribune*. Nearly half of our staff had settled down there and this made the place very convivial though it detracted from one's privacy. Each knew pretty much what the others were up to, especially romantically, but at our early age that did not seem to matter greatly. We had long bull sessions in each other's rooms, read and criticized each other's writing, argued over books and most everything else, planned joint adventures for the afternoon or evening, and advised and consoled those who threatened to fall apart from drink, frustration or unrequited love. The friendships formed at the office were cemented in the hotel—in some cases for life.[1]

The Lisbonne quickly became the geographical center of our life away from work. A stone's throw in one direction lay the Boulevard St. Michel, center of the so-called Latin Quarter, lined with sprawling bookstores crowded with teachers and students from the Sorbonne and the other branches of the university, whose buildings were clustered just beyond the avenue. The students jammed the café terraces and the modest little restaurants, which were even more numerous than the bookshops. They animated the boulevard itself, filling its sidewalks with a sea of exuberant youth. Being of their age and just out of school myself, I found them congenial, more mature and less conformist than my college generation back home—perhaps, in part, because they were not confined to a campus or dormitories or silly fraternity and sorority houses but lived unchaperoned in modest *pensions* and hotels, free to live their own lives, like everyone else in Paris, without some awful dean of men or women keeping a beady eye on them.

A stone's throw away in the other direction was the Luxembourg Gardens, which I had come to love even before I went to work. Nearly every afternoon when the weather was good I ambled over there, sometimes stopping at the Odéon theater, whose colonnades sheltered bookstalls where one could pick up inexpensive editions of all the French books. Then across the street and into the gardens, past the Médici Palace, where the august French Senate sat, to the great fountain behind it, where the youngsters, more immaculately dressed than their American counterparts, gathered after school to sail little boats in the large octagonal basin beneath the fountain or to take rides past the statues of the queens of France on decrepit old donkeys shepherded by a weather-beaten old French couple who had the concession.

Usually, until the winter set in, I took a book and after wandering around the park sat down on a bench, paid a withered old woman, whose streetcar conductor's cap denoted her official

[1] Ned Calmer, a resident, a reporter on the *Trib,* and later a war correspondent and commentator for C.B.S., found that the Hotel de Lisbonne had left such an impression on him that more than a quarter century later he wove a novel around it: *All the Summer Days,* published in 1961.

status in the Third Republic, ten centimes for its use, and read, looking up occasionally to watch the throng pass by, struck by the beauty and verve and neat dress of some of the French women, and sometimes, if one of them sat down to share the bench, striking up a conversation (I seized any opportunity to practice my French) and eventually, maybe, going off with her to a café or restaurant for further talk and acquaintanceship. Most of them were students, and more interesting, I thought, than the coeds at home. They were certainly less inhibited. They had absorbed what seemed to me an amazing amount of knowledge, of history, literature and even philosophy, from their education—much more than I had. Perhaps they, too, were looking for husbands, as was said to be the case at my own college, but if so I never caught the message. They certainly were not waiting for marriage in order to enjoy making love. I learned a great deal from them that first year in Paris, and in the process greatly improved my French. Perhaps, as Voltaire advised, it was the only way really to learn a foreign language.

Across the street from the Lisbonne, in a hotel somewhat more elegant than ours, though far from being deluxe, Santayana spent a part of each year. Though he had once taught a year at the Sorbonne as an exchange professor from Harvard, he never felt much at home with the French *esprit*, perhaps because he had remained at heart, though he wrote in English and had had his entire academic career at Harvard, very much a Spaniard. I had begun reading his five-volume *The Life of Reason* in college and had recently discovered, to my delight, that I could borrow the last volumes from the American Library in Paris. Santayana seemed to me to possess the most original philosophical mind in America (or in Spain, the land of his birth), and somehow his philosophy, which was an attempt to assess the progress of humanity through the evolution of its literature, art and science toward some kind of life of reason, struck a sympathetic chord in me, though later I would move away from it, as I think, judging by his later writing, he did. Unlike most philosophers, especially the Germans, he wrote beautiful prose and he had a deep streak of poetry in him that was bound to rub off on you. When I learned that he was living across the street, I sought to meet him, if only to tell him how much his writing had meant to me.

Alex Small, a *cum laude* graduate of Harvard, who had gone

to work on the day staff of the Paris *Trib* about the time I joined
the paper, and Harold Stearns had both taken courses under Santayana during their college years before the war, and some of
their best talk late in the evening after work, when we had had a
few drinks, was about him. They kept promising to take me across
the street to meet him. Unfortunately they would wait until they
were in their cups and it was past 3 A.M. Then they would say,
"Come on, let's go and wake up Santayana. Undoubtedly he will
remember us. We'll have a fine talk." I desisted at that late hour
and in our condition, and tried to persuade them to desist. Once
Small, high as a kite, broke away and said he was on his way to
see the great philosopher, but I doubt if he got very far. Probably
the concierge threw him out. I could never get my friends to call
at a decent hour and I was too timid, or too intimidated by Santayana's greatness, to try alone.

Perhaps it was just as well. I would eventually find it terribly
disillusioning to meet the great in person, with the exception of
Gandhi and a very few others. Perhaps this would not have happened with Santayana. I always felt a certain closeness to him, or
at least to his spirit, by reading his books: after the *Reason,* his
soliloquies, essays, the autobiography, *Persons and Places,* and his
one novel, *The Last Puritan,* both of which to his surprise became
best sellers in America, selections of the Book-of-the-Month Club,
no less. The volumes continued to flow from his ageless mind
until he died at eighty-nine, in 1952, in a convent in Rome.
Though born a Spanish Catholic, he had rejected organized religion while projecting a faith in what he called the unknowable
and an acceptance of the mystery of life.

Down the street from the Place de l'Odéon, in the Rue
de l'Odéon, Number 12, was Sylvia Beach's bookshop, Shakespeare and Company, where you could not only buy but also rent
American and English books. It had become sort of an American
landmark on the Left Bank and there on almost any day you
would bump into American writers. Hemingway, Sylvia said, was
her best customer. He had come in one day, she told me once, in
1921 with a letter from Sherwood Anderson, an old friend of his
from their Chicago days. He was a very shy but attractive young
man, she said, who looked hungrily at her bookshelves and explained sadly that he did not have the money to join the rental
library. A generous woman with writers, especially with Joyce,

whose *Ulysses* she nursed through publication in 1922, and to whom she gave all the financial support she could, and sometimes more, Sylvia had told the bashful Hemingway that he could pay the deposit later when he had the money. He had gone off happily with an armload of books.[1]

Sylvia Beach was the daughter of a Presbyterian minister who had been pastor of a church at Princeton when Woodrow Wilson was president of the college. They had become close friends and later the Reverend Mr. Beach had performed the marriage ceremony for two of Wilson's daughters in the White House. Sylvia had come to Paris with the American Red Cross during the war and, drawn not only by the city itself but by the friendship of Adrienne Monnier, who had a French bookshop, La Maison des Amis des Livres, at Number 7 in the Rue de l'Odéon, had stayed on. Monnier had helped to set her up in business. They became inseparable. Miss Beach, when I first met her, was a sprightly young woman with rather sharp features, gay brown eyes, and brown hair that fell to her shoulders in some disarray. Her manner and clothes, like her friend's, were manly, which put me off a little at first, innocent Midwesterner that I was. But she was friendly and warm, laughed a good deal, made jokes and liked to gossip a little about the writers who frequented her shop. She was not malicious at all except when it came to Gertrude Stein, who with her companion, Alice Toklas, dropped by very occasionally. She liked Toklas. "She has finesse; she's grown up," she would say. "But Gertrude is a child. She's interested only in herself, only in her own writing"—a comment that surprised me at first but to which I would later subscribe. Probably Sylvia's attitude stemmed from Stein's obvious jealousy of Joyce and her sour remarks about his writing. To Sylvia, this was blasphemy.

I was too poor to buy American books and besides I was spending most of my time and what few spare francs I had on acquiring and reading French books—the whole vast literature was opening up for me as my knowledge of the language improved—and though I loved to browse among the shelves and tables of Shakespeare and Company, or be invited to tea in the back room, where in winter a fireplace blazed and there was

[1] Hemingway later described the first meeting at Shakespeare and Company with Sylvia Beach. "No one that I ever knew," he wrote, "was nicer to me."—*A Moveable Feast*, p. 35 (paperback edition).

much good talk, I did not hang out there often, as did Hemingway, Ezra Pound, Robert McAlmon and a number of other young writers.

I spent more time across the street at Adrienne Monnier's, where French books cost a quarter the price of American books. It was a fascinating place. Many French writers I was beginning to read, some of them already famous, gathered there. You would drop in to look at the new books, or search for an old one, and likely as not, off in a corner, a group of French writers would be arguing and gesticulating. At one time or another you saw André Gide, Jules Romains, Paul Claudel, Louis Aragon, André Breton and Valéry Larbaud. Gide and Romains with their novels, and Claudel with his poetry and drama in verse, were already bright lights in the French literary world and I was reading them avidly —more avidly then than later, when my enthusiasm for them cooled. Gide, despite his enormous reputation and his later Nobel Prize (1947), never wrote, I concluded, one great novel. But for years I lived under the spell of his lucid prose.

André Breton in 1925 was the acknowledged leader of surrealism—Monnier's La Maison des Amis des Livres was its headquarters—and he would stick to the movement to the end, long after Aragon, his disciple, had left it for Communism and the pages of the party's daily, *L'Humanité*. Larbaud, a minor poet but an interesting man, was at this time in the period of his enthusiasm for Joyce and particularly *Ulysses*—"the greatest writer and the greatest novel of our time in any language," he said, and he was hard at work translating it into French. At Monnier's one also ran into a group of contemporary French composers: Darius Milhaud, Georges Auric, Francis Poulenc and Arthur Honegger. You could hear some of their music being played more and more frequently around Paris. Though it seemed to me to derive from Debussy, I found it new and refreshing.

In an apartment above Shakespeare and Company lived a boyish, young American composer who that year and the next, 1925–1926, suddenly burst into fame and then just as suddenly, as the decade ended, slipped back into limbo. This was George Antheil, a boy prodigy of two of our chief literary lights, Joyce and Pound, whose enthusiasm for him—at least in the midtwenties—knew no bounds. Born in New Jersey of Polish origin, he had come to Europe to get his compositions played—they were too far-out for America—and Paris had taken him up and made something of a sensation of him. French critics had not liked his first concert at the Salle Pleyel in 1924, finding his piano and violin concertos and his quartet "impotently dissident" and "too much a feast of cacophonies." But by the time I arrived in 1925, the press, both French and American, was building up interest in what was said to be a revolutionary breakthrough in modern music. Antheil, they reported, was putting the finishing touches on his *Ballet Mécanique,* which would do for modern music what Picasso was doing for modern painting: breaking away from all the old forms and creating something absolutely new. Fernand Léger, the French painter, was making a film to be shown during the playing of the piece. Like the music, it would portray the postwar world, dominated by industry, dynamos, machinery and the din of whirling wheels. The orchestra, the critics revealed, would include sixteen electric player pianos hooked up and synchronized, six electrically driven airplane propellers, a dozen smaller fans, numerous xylophones, bells, gongs, drums and other instruments for producing sound.

All through my first summer and winter in Paris there was much talk and a great deal of publicity about the coming revolutionary breakthrough in music. Joyce and especially the talkative Ezra Pound were quoted in praise of Antheil as the coming musician of the twentieth century and the new composition as likely to be a tremendous musical event. That winter, while Antheil was revising his masterpiece, he sometimes came to the *Tribune* with Elliot Paul or Irving Schwerké, the latter our paper's music critic, a sound musician who had studied piano with Moriz Rosenthal and was enthusiastic about new composers, though the previous year he had taken a dim view of Antheil's first concert. I found the precocious composer an extremely likable young man, with an open, almost cherubic face, a sense of humor and modesty, and a simple manner of talking. He seemed to know a great deal about classical music and would explain that he was merely trying to go on from it into new forms.

Finally, on June 19, 1926, the great day came. The *Ballet Mécanique* was given its premiere at the ornate Théâtre des Champs Élysées. Ezra Pound, who had organized and publicized it, was there, and Joyce, T. S. Eliot, Serge Diaghileff, and many others from the Parisian world of music, theater, ballet, art and literature.

The ballet had hardly started, with Antheil sitting at the master player piano working away at the electrical controls, when bedlam broke loose. Above the din of the sixteen mechanical pianos, the whirling airplane propellers and fans, the gongs and all the rest, you could hear a great shouting arising from the throats of the audience—pro and con. Several exchanged punches, something I had never seen among the French, though perhaps Americans were mostly involved. The swirling wind from the propellers blew the wig off a portly old man, picked it up in the air and sailed it to the back of the theater. All around me men and women were putting their coat collars up around their ears, pulling their hats over their ears and raising their umbrellas, but whether it was to deaden the noise or to protect themselves against the violent wind or to express protest I couldn't tell. Probably all three. Several umbrellas were blown inside out.

Suddenly Ezra Pound bounded up on the stage.

"Silence, imbeciles!" he shouted in a mixed American and French accent. "Get the hell out of here if you don't like it! Or at least show some elemental manners!" By now the poet had broken into plain American. He beckoned to his protégé to proceed. There was really no need, for the mechanical contraptions had continued to grind away despite the explosions of the audience. Apparently they could not be stopped, even by Antheil, who sat grimly at the controls to the bitter end. At the conclusion, as Elliot Paul reported the next morning in the Paris *Tribune*, "the combatants filed out peacefully," Antheil was greeted with "uproarious applause" by those who remained, "and there was an atmosphere," Paul continued impishly, "about the theater most wholesome for the art of music. Everyone knew they had been somewhere."

That was true. Where else but in Paris could you participate in such a spectacle? For me it was an exciting evening, though Antheil's noisemaking did not fit in with any conception I had of music. It must have been exciting for young Antheil, too. He must have thought he was on his way, a new Beethoven perhaps. He had already rejected Stravinsky, then living and composing in Paris, as a "false-noter." He could not have had any idea that electrifying evening how his own life and work, in the end, would turn out.

Four years later, in the spring of 1930, when I was stationed in Vienna, there was a great deal in the Austrian and German newspapers about the world premiere of Antheil's opera, *Transatlantic* (whose American title was *The People's Choice*), in Frankfort. The German and Austrian critics praised it highly, and Schwerké, who had been slow to appreciate Antheil, wrote from Frankfort in the Paris *Trib* that "it was one of the most brilliant successes in modern operatic history. . . . It reveals one of the outstanding talents of the time and is an opera of which America should be proud."

What happened to this brilliant young American composer after that? I heard no more in Europe about his progress. Years later when I was home on leave and visiting briefly in California, someone showed me a syndicated column in a San Francisco or Los Angeles newspaper. It was by-lined by George Antheil from Hollywood. It did not concern itself with music. It was, in fact, a junky column of advice for the lovelorn. Could it be the George Antheil of Paris days? I could not believe it.

Schwerké claimed that Paris was the music capital of the world. Maybe so. I heard a good deal of music in those first years there. Often on my night off I climbed to the top balcony at the Opéra, where a seat cost only twenty-five cents, enjoying almost every minute of whatever was being performed and gradually becoming acquainted, at least, with the vast operatic repertory. Sunday afternoons before work I took in a concert of one of the symphony orchestras, usually with Elliot Paul, who had a sound knowledge of music, and who deplored the playing and conducting but loved, as I did, the music. One afternoon he whispered to me, "Look at those bastards in the viola section. They're reading *L'Intran!*" *L'Intransigeant* was the popular, large-circulation afternoon newspaper. Sure enough, whenever there was a break in the music for the viola players, they would snatch up the journal from the floor and scan it. Probably it was the sports page and they were playing the horses. Sloppy though the playing may have been, it gave me an introduction, which had begun very early in Chicago and then in Iowa, to the great symphonic composers: Bach, Beethoven, Mozart, Schubert, Brahms, Tchaikovsky, Saint-Saëns, Berlioz and others. Kreisler, Heifetz and Rubinstein gave annual concerts in Paris and I saved my francs to take them in. And it was at the Salle Pleyel that I first heard the magic of Segovia on the guitar. There were chamber concerts galore all through the winter. This was a new form of music for me and from the beginning I developed a passion for it that would grow in Vienna, Berlin, and, when I came home, in New York and at Tanglewood.

There was some fine church music in Paris and I took to going to the Catholic churches to hear it. After lunch, I would make my way up the Rue de l'Odéon and after stopping at the bookshops head around the corner to the Church of St. Sulpice. There on almost any afternoon Marcel Dupré would be practicing on what he called the finest organ in France. I had heard him play once at home when he came over to preside at the inauguration of a new organ some millionaire had given to the chapel at Coe. Now day after day I could sit in the vast reaches of this old church and listen to the thunderous music of Bach and others as only Dupré, the finest organist of our time, could play it.

That winter, in further pursuit of the French language and a little more knowledge of history and literature, I began attending lectures at the Collège de France. This was a prestigious and unique institution. It had been founded in 1530 by Francis I, at the prodding of the great classicist Guillaume Budé, who wanted advanced studies freed from the pedantry of the Church-dominated Sorbonne, which at that time taught little but theology and stubbornly kept science and Greek and Latin literature off its curriculum. The Collège soon became the center of learning in France not only for the "pagan" classics, as they were called, but for science. In the nineteenth and early twentieth centuries it had become preeminent in mathematics, chemistry, physics, biology, philosophy and the classics. It had remained free from the heavy hand of the government-run university system in France. It had no formal enrollment, no tuition, no examinations, no grading, and granted no degrees. I simply dropped in for the lectures, which were free. These were given by some of the most illustrious scholars in France. Henri Bergson was the leading light of the Collège de France at the time, but that first winter he was ill and, to my disappointment, gave no lectures. But there were others almost as good and I advanced a little further not only in the language but in history and literature.

I felt frustrated at missing Bergson. Though he wrote beautifully and lucidly and could soar like a poet, I found reading his philosophy hard going. His influence on French writers, artists, educators, labor leaders and especially on the military had been immense before the war and scarcely abated after it, and I was trying to grasp why. You could still feel the impact on France of his *Creative Evolution,* which had come out in 1906 and was still widely read—a book, I recalled, that had sent William James into ecstasy and prompted him to write Bergson: "You are a magician and your book is a marvel, a real wonder . . . Your name will surely go down as one of the great creative names in philosophy." So far as I could see, the book overstressed the importance of intuition and the irrational—as against the intellect—as the springs of man's creativity, and of *élan vital* as the driving force in men and societies. This was surely true of poets and painters. But Bergson's teaching led also to Sorel, to Proust and to Freud. Foch and the "young Turks" at the French War College before the war had applied it to their new theories of the *offensive à outrance,* the *attaque brusquée* and an *élan vital* with which they hoped to win the next war. And an obscure young officer, whom I and the rest of the world would hear of only much later, Charles de Gaulle, was making Bergsonism the core of his own philosophy of action. Still, Bergson's anti-intellectualism (he was, after all, a formidable intellectual himself), his denial of the value of rationalism and reason, troubled me. Eventually I did come under the spell of his flowing prose. It was no surprise in Paris that in 1927 Bergson was awarded the Nobel Prize for literature. He was already a member of the French Academy and the most eminent figure at the Collège de France. In France, at least, and in Stockholm, I noted, philosophers were given their due.

Occasionally I went over to the Sorbonne for some special lecture listed on one of the bulletin boards there. One spring evening in 1927, a year that would bring another turning point in my life and a new line of work that necessitated giving up my studies at the Collège de France, I went over to the amphitheater of the Sorbonne to hear a lecture by H. G. Wells. He was then at the height of his world-wide reputation as a novelist, essayist, journalist, prophet and, recently, historian. His *Outline of History* had come out in 1920 and had swept England and America, where it already had sold two million copies. It had done almost as well in France and the rest of Europe. Not only the ordinary reader had grabbed it up but many historians had acclaimed it. Toynbee thought it was magnificent.

In his lecture Wells seemed to me to be summing up one of the main themes of all his work: that the poor human race was doomed unless it established a world state, and that this could come only from a creative elite dedicated to the salvation of mankind. He had harped on it again and again in book after book. We could only be saved by entrusting our fate to a small class of samurai, who would put each one of us in his place and make us toil for the good of humanity, as they—and Wells—saw it.

This, to me, was awful. But Wells kept trying to explain that the choice was that or nothing. He spoke in faltering French, heavily accented not only with English but with Cockney English, and in a highly pitched, squeaky voice that carried little conviction to me.

This obsession with an elite to whom we must turn over our imperfect world was surprising for a lifelong British liberal who now considered himself a socialist, for elitism was the core of Fascism, so far as it had any core at all. Mussolini in Italy blabbered a good deal about it. And in Germany a rightist fanatic by the name of Adolf Hitler had just published the second volume of a book called *Mein Kampf*, which preached, like Wells, according to an article in a French paper I had read, that the earth could be saved only by an elite—a race of supermen made pure in blood by biological selection, who would have the wisdom and the ruthlessness to keep our erring world in order. Dispatches from Munich had said the book was becoming the Bible of a revived Fascist movement called National Socialism, which had flourished in the chaos of postwar Germany and then apparently died away after Hitler had failed in his ridiculous Beer Hall Putsch in Munich in 1923 and been imprisoned. Now here was the socialist H. G. Wells, the most widely read of English writers, preaching in the Sorbonne to the French about the virtues of an aberration that Mussolini and Hitler had seized upon as a justification for dictatorship, though he was himself an anti-Fascist. Disappointing! Another one of my literary idols was crumbling.

Then in Paris, for me in those first years, was the discovery of French food, and wine. Getting acquainted with French cuisine, for a Midwest hayseed who had grown up on rougher fare, mostly pork, potatoes, apple pie and milk, was an adventure, an education, that brought much pleasure and a feeling of well-being then and forever after. Unlike today, in the 1970's, it cost very little. Almost everyone in Paris with a job or a modest income could afford to eat well. Not at every meal—that would have taken away the joy—but often enough to appreciate it.

Most of my regular meals I took in quite ordinary places: at the restaurant, already mentioned, at the foot of the Rue de l'Odéon, where I often lunched; at a little Russian place called Knam, in a narrow little street, Royer-Collard, near the Panthéon, where I dined before going to work; and at Gillotte's bistro, Le Rendezvous du Petit Journal, on the Rue Lamartine, below the plant of the big Parisian daily of that name where our paper was published and where we poorly paid slaves of Colonel McCormick toiled. Gillotte's was not only a handy place to meet and to eat and drink, but Madame Gillotte, who ran it, though there was a Monsieur Gillotte about, gave us generous credit when our francs ran out between paydays. She was a vivacious, talkative, stout, middle-aged lady with a gravelly voice, an infectious laugh which broke out at the slightest pretext, and beneath a rather rude manner lay a heart of gold. She would never, she said, let anyone who worked on the newspapers across the street, French or American, go hungry. The wine at Gillotte's was good and inexpensive and the food not bad, especially when Madame cooked up one of her specialties: a *blanquette de veau*, roast rabbit or a *cassoulet de Toulouse*.

Knam was more than just another little Russian restaurant. There were hundreds of them in Paris then, run by Russian émigrés from the Bolsheviks, most of whom were, or claimed to be, nobles. Knam, though its excellent food was unbelievably cheap (a *prix fixe* of six francs, or thirty cents, for a meal), was something special. The proprietor, a rather frail man in his thirties, had been, I believe, a professor at the University of Moscow, and his stouter, dark-haired, beautiful wife, a teacher in a secondary school. They had made of their modest little restaurant a gathering place for young faculty members of the University of Paris and especially for refugees from Russian Bolshevism and Hungarian Fascism—the two mixed surprisingly well—and for refugees from American puritanism, as we liked to think ourselves. A number of us from the *Trib* who lived in the quarter ate our dinners regularly there, and then took a bus from the nearby Rue Gay Lussac that delivered us practically at the door of our office in time for work. But on nights off we would often drift back to the Knam and order a more expensive à la carte dinner, starting with caviar and vodka. As the evening wore on, and everyone would be getting to their second or third bottle of wine or to more vodka, the Russians—Monsieur and Madame, the waiters and cooks and guests—would produce balalaikas and guitars and there would be much gay music, playing and singing, and, in the end, dancing, until a pair of gendarmes would arrive and after a few free vodkas reluctantly proclaim that the legal closing hour was long past.

At the Knam I got my first experience with Russians, and I have liked them ever since. Somehow they seem to have more in common with us Americans than any other people, sharing a passion for talk, singing and spontaneous drinking. Perhaps it is partly due to the effect the vast horizons in both our countries have on our character and our outlook.

I also met at the Knam for the first time a number of Hungarians and took a liking to these wild, unpredictable people who, however adverse their temporary predicament, seemed endowed with almost an animal capacity to get a good deal out of life. Count Michael Károlyi came often to the little restaurant. There was no Hungarian wildness about him. He was the mildest of men and looked like an absent-minded professor. In 1918 he had led the bloodless revolution in Budapest that had taken over at the collapse of the Hapsburg monarchy and established a mildly socialist democratic government, setting an example by handing over his numerous estates to the peasants. Within a year he was out and his regime was finished, supplanted for five months by a Communist dictatorship under Béla Kun, which in turn gave way to a White government that provided Europe with its first Fascist state. Aside from the fact that the victorious Allies in Paris had betrayed him, it was easy to see why Károlyi had failed. He was too decent, too gullible in his faith in the essential decency of man. He lacked any trace of the ruthlessness of his successors.

It was through him that I first began to grasp the meaning of what was brewing in Europe. Ruthless men, ruthless gangs, who knew what they wanted, were beginning to take over, or were waiting in the wings. Hungary, he used to say, was the first country outside of Russia to have a Communist dictatorship. It was suppressed by Allied troops. And Hungary, he insisted, then became Europe's first Fascist state, set up with the connivance of the so-called democratic Allies under the leadership of Republican France.

"Look," he would admonish me. "We had Fascism three years before Mussolini's march on Rome. Don't overlook its attraction in Germany. Here in Paris, and over there in London, everyone is afraid of Bolshevism. I think Fascism is more dangerous. It has more of a chance of taking over. Keep an eye on that little fellow in Munich—Hitler. He may look as comical as Charlie Chaplin. But he's really not funny at all."

I liked Károlyi, but I didn't take his political warnings very seriously. And though I could see that he was an example of the failure of decent, democratic Europeans to take over after the war and the revolutions, and build a bearable society, I could not see, as he did, that the future belonged to the more ruthless totalitarians. Mussolini was regarded in Paris as somewhat of a joke. He made the trains run on time. No one in Paris or London, or even, from what I heard, in Germany, paid any attention to that little man in Munich with the Charlie Chaplin mustache mentioned by Károlyi.

In October, 1925, shortly after my arrival, the Pact of Locarno had been signed. It had brought a relaxation to Europe. It had drawn a defeated Germany back into the community of Western nations. Freely signed by a German government that appeared to be not only democratic but stable, Locarno guaranteed peace, so everyone in Paris thought, for generations. The frontier between France and Germany and between Belgium and Germany, over which armies had poured for centuries to bring war, was solemnly guaranteed by the four big powers, France, Great Britain, Germany and Italy. And by the terms of Locarno, Germany was welcomed into the League of Nations, which would see to it that the peace was kept. Editorials in the esteemed *Times* of London and *Le Temps* of Paris assured us that Germany at last had been won over to the merits of democracy and peace.

So I did not pay much attention to the forebodings of Count Károlyi. He was often surrounded by young Hungarians, exiled students mostly, who shared my skepticism of the political prognostications of this lovable man. They were lusty youths, noisy in their cups and extremely likable. Like me, they were trying to figure out some personal future in a world that had temporarily made them exiles, and at the moment they were getting as much out of life, such as it was, as they could.

On my nights off, if I had saved some francs, I often splurged in the more expensive restaurants. One made an evening of it, a celebration. There were few "American bars" in those days—Paris had not yet become Americanized—and instead of having cocktails or hard liquor to start the evening off, we would gather for an *apéritif* on the terrace of a café: the Deux Magots, say, opposite the lovely old Church of St. Germain-des-Prés, with its solid eleventh-century Romanesque tower; or the Dôme in Montparnasse, alive with Left Bank Americans but also with Kiki, the voluptuous French model, whom we all loved;[1] or the Café de la Paix, on the Grand Boulevard around the corner from the Opéra, where the French mixed with tourists from a dozen foreign countries, many of them Americans whooping it up in the gay city. On any one of those terraces we would sip a sherry or a vermouth. This was the best of all preparations for a good dinner with good wines. It whetted your appetite. A couple of martinis or whiskeys would have ruined the palate and the mind for both food and wine.

Part of your pleasure was discussing where you would dine. If it was steak you wanted, you might taxi out to the slaughterhouse district in the northeast and go to Dagorno's. It served the best in town. If it was fish, you went to Prunier's near the Madeleine. In those days it was superb, with its oyster bar and its fine dry white wines. If you wanted a fancy decor where the food was quite good, you might go up the Champs Élysées to Fouquet's. You could also have your *apéritif* on the terrace there, and watch the crowd pass up and down the broad sidewalk. There were few cars then on the Champs Élysées to poison the air and puncture your eardrums. Sometimes I liked to go over to Chez Francis, on the Place de l'Alma, overlooking the Seine, with the Eiffel Tower beyond and the golden dome of the Invalides showing across the

[1] And for whose memoirs Hemingway would write a preface, the first he ever wrote. Kiki, as I remember her, had thick black hair, pearly white skin, a sensuous nose and mouth, and large, blazing eyes. Hemingway wrote of her "fine face" and "wonderfully beautiful body" and thought she "dominated" Paris in the 1920's.

river to the left. There was a large terrace where you could eat in good weather and watch the lights go on up and down the Left Bank and shoot up on the tower. The hors d'oeuvres, sole, and salmon were excellent, and there were fine dry white wines to match them. Prices were reasonable.

There was no limit to your choice of restaurants. We might go off to Pharamond's, in the center of Les Halles, for *tripes à la mode de Caen*, for which it was justly famous; to the Petit Riche, in the Rue Le Peletier, which, judging by its old furnishings, had changed little in a century and where you could find a Vouvray Perle wine that if it was right—and you took your chances with this fickle vintage—was one of the glories of France; to Flo's, a sprawling, old-fashioned Alsatian brasserie in the Cour des Petites-Ecuries, where the *choucroute* and *charcuterie* and the beer were excellent, a place buried so deep in an ancient, dilapidated court off the Faubourg St. Denis lined with old stables that no tourist had ever found it. Often we ended up at a favorite place of mine on the Place St. Michel not far from my hotel.

This was Rouzier's Rotisserie Périgourdine, whose menu boasted that it was the *"Temple des Gourmets"* and in those days it literally was. It offered oysters of all sorts, and clams, an immense *hors-d'oeuvre varié* that was trundled to your table on two or three different carts, and a variety of fish and meats so large and so appetizing that you hardly knew which to choose. Among its regional specialties was a lobster, *La Trimbale de Homard à l'Armoricaine*, a roast rabbit billed as *Le Lièvre à la Royale* (*Grande Spécialité*) and truffles *"cuites sous la cendre"*—cooked under the ashes—and, for dessert, a *soufflé St. Michel*, of which the chef, who usually brought it in himself, had a right to be proud. The wine list was the largest I ever saw in a Paris restaurant—more than two hundred vintages, ranging from a Médoc of the current year at ten francs (forty cents a bottle) to three vintages of 1902, a quarter of a century old, a red Bordeaux (Château du Lyonnat), a red Burgundy (Clos de Vougeot) and a white Burgundy (Montrachet), which were priced from fifty francs (two dollars) to seventy-five francs (three dollars). The food was equally inexpensive, the fish and the meat dishes, including lobster, sole, steak *au poivre* and *côte de veau*, priced from fifty to seventy-five cents, a fraction of what they cost in that restaurant today.

So there was always Rouzier's nearby, and if you were dining late, Lipp's across the street from the Deux Magots, where the beer was good and the *choucroute* and the cheeses. By midnight Lipp's would be full of Left Bank Americans. It was there I met, among others, the beautiful Kay Boyle, already one of the freer spirits among the young American women writers, and who has had more staying power—she is still writing poetry, essays, short stories and novels half a century later—than any of the others. Sometimes when Vincent Sheean and Hillel Bernstein were in town (that is, broke and working on the Paris *Times*), they would take me to a favorite little Italian restaurant of theirs on the Boulevard St. Michel opposite the Luxembourg Gardens where the spaghetti and fettucine and Chianti were the best in the quarter and where, after the other customers had left, the *patron*, his plump wife and Jimmy Sheean would gather around the piano and sing arias from a dozen Italian operas (Jimmy seemed to have memorized them all) late into the night. So much of the good life in those youthful years in Paris centered around the cafés and restaurants. There one came not only to drink and eat but to talk and talk, to sing and laugh and argue, to flirt and pay court.

There was one other place which we reserved for very special occasions. Three or four times a year late at night after work we would gather there for a bit of revelry. This was deep down in the cellars of the Hotel du Caveau, where no one would be disturbed by our boisterousness. Elliot Paul in his *The Last Time I Saw Paris* has celebrated that little hotel and its *caves* and the winding little Rue de la Huchette on which it was located and which, for me, turned out in time to be one of the most fantastic streets in the city.

It was only three hundred yards long, winding its way from the Place St. Michel to the Rue du Petit Pont, behind and parallel to the quai and the Seine, about thirty yards away. But it was long enough to house three bordellos, the principal one just across the narrow street from a *Bureau de Police* with a sign over the frosted window proclaiming Le Panier Fleuri—The Basket of Blossoms—and presided over by a redoubtable woman we knew as Madame Mariette. My French uncle in Iowa must have been thinking of the Rue de la Huchette when he warned me in my mother's presence that Paris was full of *maisons de joie*.

Near the end of Huchette toward Notre Dame was the Hotel du Caveau, an ancient, dilapidated edifice that tilted back from the street. Inside it was dark and dank. "There," writes Elliot Paul, "I found Paris—and France." There, in the recesses of the hotel's cellars, we found an ideal spot for our occasional binges. A spiral stone staircase led down to the first *cave* and then below it to another, surrounded by supporting Roman and Byzantine arches and with a gravel floor of pebbles dredged up in times past from the Seine. It had once served as a dungeon. For our feasts the *patron* laid out a fine table in the middle of the vast vault, roasting a whole pig or a lamb or a goat, and fetching some fine old wines from the nearby wine cellar that lay behind an iron grille. Harold Stearns and Alex Small, both out of Harvard no less, would, after they had consumed enough wine, break into bawdy recitations. As the night wore on, Paul would get out his guitar, sing a few old songs, French and American, and then persuade us to join him in a howling chorus that was seldom in key. It was the one place in Paris where we could make as much foolish noise as we were capable of without disturbing neighbors or attracting the attention of the police. No sound escaped the thick walls of the dungeon. Toward 6 or 7 A.M. we would finally have enough, pick ourselves up as best we could, and stagger home.

By that time Madame Mariette's Le Panier Fleuri would be closed. It shut down after a twelve-hour day at 2 A.M. But sometimes on an afternoon or a night off we would stop to pay a visit and have a glass of champagne with Madame and her girls. They were very cordial and the young ladies, though far from beautiful, were attractive enough. Neither they nor their mistress, it was clear, thought of themselves or their lives as immoral. They were invariably gay and seemed to enjoy what they were doing. This at first surprised me. I had often wondered about prostitution. Not only as a Midwest puritan but as an earnest critic of the hypocrisy of society I had deplored its exploitation of young women. But why, I wondered, had prostitution flourished in all societies throughout history and become by now the oldest profession on earth? The theories about it were familiar, and I believed them: that it was a consequence of harsh economics, which had always wasted and cheated the poor, and of society's condonement of male exploitation of women. Now, in this *maison* across from the police station, I thought I would find the answer at first hand and test the theories.

But I never quite succeeded. It was obvious that the girls considered prostitution as a decent means of earning more than an average income while they were young. It paid better than standing on your feet all day in a department store, and then perhaps selling yourself to make ends meet after hours. I had met one young woman, a sprightly brunette, rather cultivated and very intelligent, at the Galeries Lafayette, where the pay of the salesgirls was wretched, who had had to do that in order to pay the bills for rent, groceries, clothing and the care of her child. The girls at Madame Mariette's did not feel that they were being exploited by economics or by men. And what was marriage, they said, especially among the rich, but a form of prostitution? Women sold themselves into marriage for money, didn't they? These matters, I must admit, did not weigh on us or, so far as I could see, on the girls as we sat around in the little salon of Le Panier Fleuri sipping champagne and chatting with the *patronne* and her charges. Each of the girls—Mireille, Mado, Suzie, Daisy, Germaine (I'm indebted to Paul and his book for recalling some of the names)—was a distinct human being. Each had her own personality. All accepted the luck of life. Soon, when they were thirty or so, they would follow a very old custom in France; they would return to their native towns and villages with a sizable *dot* of their own, carefully saved from their earnings of some five dollars a day, find a man, marry, have children and settle down to a most respectable bourgeois rural life.

As for Madame Mariette, we all regarded her as a good friend. Paul in *The Last Time I Saw Paris* paid her tribute. "I think of her as a friend," he wrote, "an interesting and beautiful woman . . . On our street she was second to none . . . in her love and solicitude for France." She considered herself not only a patriot but a useful citizen of *la patrie,* which she loved.

Most of the time we went to the Hotel du Caveau for quiet pursuits, to have a drink, a meal, or twice a week to climb to the top floor where Elliot Paul lived in a two-room apartment with an attractive, dark-haired, middle-aged Frenchwoman, who graciously gave us tea and an hour or two of French conversation to help improve our speaking the language. With her black hair combed severely back and her clothes invariably black, she looked the picture of a respectable middle-class woman. According to Paul she came from Tours, where the purest French was supposed to be spoken, so we were getting the very best practice in the language available in all Paris. Her voice, her enunciation, were very cultivated. She could draw us into a conversation on almost any subject: music, art, history, literature, the theater. Her cultivation and her almost classically sculptured face fascinated me. In her eyes there was something enigmatic and I detected in her a restlessness, as in Flaubert's Madame Bovary, which Elliot did not seem to notice.

One summer day she disappeared. We arrived for tea and our lesson. She was not there, and Paul did not know where she was. He seemed disturbed. We had been surprised that so bohemian a man as he could settle down so comfortably in such a bourgeois manner with such a staid woman. It had not been very much like him. Now she was gone, and he was hurt and unsettled.

One day toward the end of the summer I was walking to work with a *Trib* copyreader, Swede Swenson. Suddenly, while we were passing near the Bibliothèque Nationale in a quite fashionable little street off the Rue de Richelieu, Swenson turned to me and said, "Let's stop off in a 'house' I know near here and have a glass of champagne. There's a woman you'd be interested to see." I could not think of any such woman in this quarter. I did not feel like having champagne and we were already late. But he insisted, and into the place we went. It was much more elegant than Le Panier Fleuri in the Rue de la Huchette. But there was no mistaking what kind of a place it was. And to my astonishment there was no mistaking the stately lady who presided over the establishment. She was sitting behind a raised counter reading a book. Several girls lounged around, reading movie magazines. The woman smiled, stepped down, pointed to the divan and joined us there, insisting on ordering champagne.

"You are surprised to see me here?" she said to me.

"No," I lied.

"You were the innocent one," she said. "But I think you noticed that I did not feel at home there with Elliot."

"I thought sometimes you were restless," I said.

"I was. To get back here."

"You were a fine teacher," I said. "I learned a lot of my French from you."

"Well, it was of some use then." She smiled.

We drank our champagne and got up to leave.

"May I ask you one question?" I said.

She nodded and smiled. She was really a very attractive woman and looked out of place here. She was so solid and cultivated and middle class.

"Where did you meet Elliot?"

"Here," she said. "He took me away."

The first year in Paris passed swiftly. I loved every moment. The summer of 1926, the first full one in France, was fabulous, the best I had ever had. It brought another turning point, as it did in quite a different way for two friends of mine, a struggling painter and a struggling writer, who broke away from Paris and went home to America in order to try to find themselves, soon did, and became justly famous.

So many things began to happen that lovely summer. A new job on the dayside of the *Tribune* as a reporter propelled me, though I did not immediately realize it, toward the career I would follow for the next two decades. It was a job that led to many other things: to meet, for instance, three remarkable American women already known on two continents as creative artists. I fell romantically in love with one of them, though she did not know it, and really in love with a dynamic Parisian, who did. It must have been the season—the days warm and bright, the parks and the countryside abloom, the evenings soft, the skies by day fleeced with snow-white clouds and illuminated at night by a million blinking stars—and my age, twenty-two. The season. One's youth. The job. As Al Laney, the night editor of the rival Paris *Herald* and later a gifted sports writer for the *Herald Tribune* in New York, would write of what it was like to work on either paper in those days: "Never in the history of journalism have so many men had such a wonderful time on so little money."[1]

Part of a reporter's job on the Paris edition of the *Chicago Tribune* was boring enough, and for a time I regretted having left the night copy desk, though the work there had become rather routine after nearly a year of it. It had left my days free. I guess I merely wished a change. And in the back of my mind was a

[1] Al Laney: *The Paris Herald*, p. 12.

feeling that from being a reporter on the local paper I might graduate to the foreign service of the Chicago edition, a goal some of us who realized we were not going to become writers like Fitzgerald and Hemingway—at least, not very soon—had in mind. The seeds of ambition to become a foreign correspondent probably began to sprout in me that second summer in Paris. The job paid better, and in dollars. And there was a certain glamour about it. One got around—all over Europe and even to Asia—and participated in the great events of the day that were making history. But the chances of making the foreign service were not very good. Only once every couple of years did Henry Wales, the Paris bureau chief, pick someone from among the twenty of us on the local paper. A tough, gruff little man, a hard-boiled police reporter in New York before becoming a war correspondent and then chief of the Paris bureau, he had shown no interest in me.

The boring part of the new job was covering the sprawling American colony in Paris. It was made up of some twenty-five thousand Americans and they spawned as many organizations, and exactly the same kind, as their counterparts did at home: a Chamber of Commerce, a Rotary, an American Legion, a million-dollar American Hospital, an American Library, American schools and churches, and dozens of others. At the apex of this transplanted American society stood the American Club, whose weekly luncheons I had to cover much too often. The speeches were long and dull but had to be reported at great length. Occasionally though, a French premier or a finance minister or a general would use the forum for launching a new turn in French politics and then my story would be front-paged and used by Wales for his dispatch to Chicago and, presumably, fetch me a few marks with him. The climax of the American Club's year was its Fourth of July banquet, and there a young reporter could bump into the men who ran France, the President of the Republic, the Premier, several other Cabinet ministers, and—more interesting to me—France's three illustrious marshals who had led the country and, in one case, the Allies to victory in the Great War: Foch, the Allied generalissimo; Pétain, the hero of Verdun; Joffre, the hero of the Battle of the Marne. They did not get on well with one another—the rivalries of the war still cooled their relations—and this, which they were too proud to hide, made them especially interesting to me. I must say they were the very

picture of eminence, with their finely chiseled faces, their imposing manners, not strutting or belligerent like a Prussian's, but very
impressive. Foch's genius was written all over his face, his bearing, the way he talked.

All three, but especially Foch, had a tremendous admiration
for the American Ambassador, Myron T. Herrick—in part, I suppose, because in 1914 he had remained in Paris when the Germans approached and the French government fled to Bordeaux.
Herrick was a handsome, friendly, silver-haired man, grown old
by this time, no intellectual heavyweight but intelligent about
people. In all his years in Paris he had been unable to learn even a
rudimentary French and I often wondered how he conversed
with Foch, as I watched him do at a half-dozen banquets, since
the marshal knew no English. One evening, as the guests were
standing around chatting, I decided to approach them to see
what language they spoke. Herrick introduced me to the marshal
—for the fourth or fifth time—and the two men resumed their
conversation, not minding my eavesdropping. I still remember
how it went, and in what language.

HERRICK: *Ça va, Maréchal? Ça va, eh?*

FOCH: *Oui, ça va. Ça va très bien. Et vous?*

HERRICK: *Oui, ça va, Maréchal. Ça va. Ça va. . . .*

This continued for five minutes, and never got beyond those
words.

Even more boring than covering the American colony was
reporting the shenanigans of the American tourists who poured
into Paris from the transatlantic boats in droves in the mid-
twenties determined to whoop it up in the gay city. Part of my
beat was to meet the boat trains at the Gare St. Lazare and to go
on from there to the plush hotels on the Right Bank to interview
the more notable of the Yankee trippers, especially those who
came from Chicago. It was a curious thing, but an American who
blew into Paris as a tourist, his pockets stuffed with traveler's
checks, his mind emptied of whatever had filled it at home, his
manners—if he ever had any—forgotten, became at once a simpleton and a barbarian: loud, vulgar, inane, and insensitive to the
French, who after all were his hosts. He couldn't have been that
bad back home. While the wife (whom he invariably called
"Mother" or "Mama") made for the Louvre and some "culture"
and then for the fashionable couturier shops for new clothes, he

made for the nearest bar and soon was blotto, a condition in which he remained until the end of his stay and friends poured him onto a departing boat train.

A more interesting assignment was sports. For some reason the legend grew around the office that I had been a crack sports reporter back home, though my experience had been confined to being the esteemed sports editor of the Cedar Rapids *Republican*. So one of my first jobs was covering the French tennis championships that spring. I played the game badly and had never seen an important match. But one learns sports writing quickly and there was much to write about tennis that year. Not only had France produced the famous "four horsemen"—Cochet, Lacoste, Borotra and Brugnon—who had begun to better the Americans and Australians at Forest Hills in New York, Wimbledon in England and here at the French championships, but it had the dazzling Suzanne Lenglen, Europe's greatest woman tennis star, who suddenly that year (1926) was being challenged by a teen-age American in pigtails, Helen Wills. They had fought an epic match on the Riviera in February, the details of which had been emblazoned on the front pages of all the Paris newspapers and which Jim Thurber, then getting out our Riviera edition (a newspaper even more fantastic than our Paris edition, since Thurber wrote almost all its daily contents out of his head), had reported for us in rather epic prose, as if it had been a chapter out of a Henry James novel, a struggle between an innocent young American and a sophisticated European. Lenglen, who darted gracefully around the court like a dancer, had narrowly defeated the "poker-faced" Wills, who slugged the ball like a man, 6–3, 8–6. It was, Allison Danzig, the veteran *New York Times* tennis reporter, recalled thirty-four years later in a column in the newspaper, "the tennis battle of the century in sport's golden age."

Now in Paris in June there was to be a rematch, and the prospect overshadowed the men's singles finals, which the French were confident would go, like the women's finals, to one of their own, either Cochet or Lacoste, two rising young stars who were threatening to end the long domination of international tennis by the Americans and Australians. For days before the tournament began, the Parisian papers built up tension for the expected battle between Lenglen and Wills. And then, a couple of days after the championships began, there was an anticlimax. Helen Wills was rushed to the American Hospital for an emergency appendicitis operation, and was out of the game for the rest of the summer. Suzanne Lenglen danced her way to another championship. She went on to Wimbledon, which she had won six times in the last seven years. But she was not to win there again. Partway through the Wimbledon championships she withdrew and announced she was turning professional. Wills, I am sure, would certainly have blown her off the courts the next year. In women's tennis the day of the graceful, elegant player who won by shrewd placements was over. The future belonged to the slugger with the blazing serve.

Ironically, my covering of sports, especially tennis—though I was much more interested in politics—would help me more than I realized, or suspected at the time, to get a chance to become a foreign correspondent. From that summer on until the end of the decade I would be whisked away from whatever I was doing to cover the French and Wimbledon tennis championships, the British Open and Amateur golf tournaments (though I knew absolutely nothing of golf), and in 1928 the Winter Olympics at St. Moritz and the Summer Olympics at Amsterdam. They would furnish pleasant interludes to more serious work.

I was now getting my baptism in reporting French politics, part-time though it was. Raymond Poincaré, a dried-up little man with a high, shrill voice, dominated them that year, though the figure of his archrival, Georges Clemenceau, an embittered old man, still cast a shadow over the country. Together these two old political warriors, Poincaré as President, Clemenceau as Premier, had with their iron wills and fanatical determination kept France intact in the Great War when toward its end a series of defeats, a tremendous bloodletting and widespread mutinies at the front had brought the country to the brink of collapse. They had prevailed until victory came in November, 1918.

Then after the Peace Conference in 1919 they had faded away—Clemenceau, as it turned out, for good; Poincaré only for a while. Of the two, Clemenceau was much more interesting as a human being. Nicknamed "the Tiger," he had battled his way through the tumult of French politics for nearly half a century, playing a glorious role in his fight for justice for Dreyfus and for many other causes. Considered by most Frenchmen to be the *"Père de la Victoire"* in 1918, he had dominated the Paris Peace

Conference but had been thwarted by the false promises of Britain and the United States of guarantees for France against future German aggression.

He had been thwarted by his own countrymen, too. When the National Assembly met at Versailles in January, 1920, to elect a new President of the Republic it was generally assumed that because of his immense prestige—he was still Premier—he would be chosen by an overwhelming vote. But the Assembly, torn by sordid intrigues, had chosen another man instead, a nonentity named Paul Deschanel, who was on the verge of insanity and soon, passing over the line, had to be removed from his high office. This defeat was a blow that finished Clemenceau's long political career and left him bitter and despondent over the nine remaining years of his life. "Everything I have done," he said two years later, "has been wasted. In twenty years France will be dead." Prophetic words! I tried several times to get an interview with him, but he always turned me down, as he did all other reporters, pleading that he had nothing of interest to say, though the books that he continued to turn out belied that excuse. He was almost the last of the old school of political figures in France, widely read in history, literature and philosophy, passionately devoted to the arts and their practitioners—he was a friend of Victor Hugo, Zola, Alphonse Daudet, Claude Monet, Sarah Bernhardt, among others—and incorruptible in his search for truth, as he saw it, even amidst the corruption of French parliamentary politics.

Poincaré, equally incorruptible, was of a different stripe. President of the Republic during the war, Premier both before and soon after it, he had that summer of 1926 come out of retirement to save the franc, which had tumbled to new lows and threatened to bankrupt the country. As a reporter I saw a good deal of him until his final retirement three years later. At first he struck you as so dried-up, so precise and pedantic, his high-pitched nasal voice so shrill and piercing, his eyes slit like a pig's, his beard so pointed, like a devil's, that he seemed scarcely human. He had no warmth at all, no charm, and even his manners were ice-cold. I used to watch him harangue the Chamber of Deputies, screeching out his bloodless figures, the point of his beard wagging, his forefinger thrust out as if to jab any member who interrupted him, frigid, concise, making no attempt to soften his verbal blows or ingratiate himself with anyone, enemy or even friend.

"We never see you except in times of trouble!" a Communist deputy yelled at him as he presented his new government, put together to save the franc. Poincaré grinned through his slit eyes as if he took it as a compliment. What carried him through in these days of financial chaos in France was a universal respect for his integrity and his amazing capacity for hard, grueling work. There were few in French politics of that sort. When new elections were held two years hence, in 1928, the people gave him a substantial majority. They seemed grateful that he had "saved the franc" and rescued the country from the brink of bankruptcy, though, as invariably happens, the cost fell heaviest on the poor, burdened with higher prices and taxes, and on many of modest means who found that their government bonds purchased before and during the war with gold francs, representing in many cases their life savings, had been reduced in value by four-fifths by the devaluation of the currency.

I saw the old man at a reception in the Finance Ministry shortly before he resigned in the summer of 1929 when I was in Paris on a temporary assignment. He looked exhausted from three years of untiring labor and from a recent illness, and ready at last to retire from politics, which had been his life for forty-one years. He went back to his native Lorraine, on the border of Germany, which he had hated all his life and still mistrusted and feared, settling down to finish the last five volumes of his memoirs, *Au Service de la France,* and to turn out articles for the press. Nearly a half century in politics had not brought him wealth, as it had so many others. He had to write to earn a living.

Years later I tried to reflect on the man and his life. Disliked by Frenchmen on the Left—and by almost all the American correspondents who covered him, none of whom were "radicals"—Poincaré was certainly a man of rather narrow vision, for whom the world outside of France remained almost incomprehensible. He was cold and austere in temperament, often petty in his dealings with others, but nonetheless possessed of considerable intelligence, a clarity of thought, a broad culture and a character that could not be corrupted. He had a devotion to the Republic, a passion for his country, that often carried him into a rage of chauvinism. And yet this had helped him to play a major role in preparing France for the First World War, in enduring and winning it, and in the end leading the country out of financial chaos.

He lived on, writing voluminously, until October 15, 1934—long enough to see his world at home and abroad cracking up. The world-wide depression had again laid France low, and across the Rhine Hitler had resumed the path of Wilhelm II, whom Poincaré, as President of the Republic, had confronted before the war. Dying in his beloved Lorraine, Poincaré is said to have glanced over the nearby frontier toward Germany and whispered with almost his last breath: "They will come again."

There were two other figures in French politics whom we covered with some interest in those days. Aristide Briand was the most durable of all the politicians, the great survivor. Between 1906 and 1932 he participated in twenty-five ministries. No other public figure could match that record. He was Premier eleven times, Foreign Minister seventeen times (doubling as Premier in seven governments) and held various other cabinet posts over a quarter of a century. Whether a government was Right, Left or Center, he was usually in it. Though he began in politics as a left-wing Socialist he soon drifted toward the Center. Lacking any firm belief in the doctrines of the Left or the Right, he was essentially a conciliator, believing that politics was the art of compromise. No other figure of his time in France matched him as an orator. I often went over to the Chamber in Paris to watch Briand work his magic and to try to fathom the mystery of how great speakers communicated. I never solved the mystery (not even later when I listened to most of the great speeches of Hitler, a genius for communicating with an audience—at least of Germans—speeches of Mussolini, Churchill and Franklin Roosevelt) but I was fascinated by Briand's art. He created an emotion in the audience much like that of a great pianist playing one of the soaring Beethoven sonatas. Many in France doubted Briand's sincerity, but it seemed to this young reporter that during the last seven years of his life—from 1925 to 1932—as Foreign Minister in eleven successive governments, he did more than any other French statesman to try to achieve a decent peace and avert another war.

His record in this was impressive, but apparently it did not impress the conniving French politicians. As with Clemenceau in 1920, they denied Briand, despite his world-wide reputation, the

Presidency of the Republic in the balloting in the National Assembly in 1931. They chose instead another mediocre man, Paul Doumer, who would not be remembered even by the French, except for the fact that he was assassinated the following year. Shattered, again like Clemenceau, by the blow, Briand died on March 7, 1932, at seventy. The structure of peace he had so painstakingly built up in Europe would soon be in shambles.

If the durable Briand was the great survivor in French politics, Joseph Caillaux was the master of the art of staging comebacks. No one seemed to like him, even his friends. Vain, conceited, arrogant, he had a talent for antagonizing even those who agreed with him. Nevertheless, he had made his mark on French politics for a quarter of a century, and starting shortly after my arrival in Paris in 1925, he had made another of his surprising comebacks. I found him an interesting and colorful character to watch and sometimes I would stop in the corridors of the Senate to chat with him. Behind the overblown self-confidence and chilly arrogance was, I thought, a lively mind. Talking to him made one forget his monocle, with which he played continually, his shiny bald pate, which turned to crimson when he became excited, his eagle eyes over a beak of a nose. And I was impressed, I suppose, by what I had read and heard of his tempestuous past.

Premier in 1911 when the Agadir crisis in Morocco had threatened to bring France and Germany to war, he had kept his head in the face of German provocation and coolly negotiated a settlement that averted war, but which brought him down as an "appeaser" of Germany. But he was soon back in the Cabinet as Finance Minister and it was while in this exalted political post that in January, 1914, *Le Figaro*, one of the leading conservative dailies in Paris, began to publish a series of articles by its editor, Gaston Calmette, designed to destroy Caillaux once and for all. After charging him with a "pro-Germanism" that bordered on treason, Calmette climaxed his attack by beginning publication of facsimiles of passionate love letters which Caillaux had written to his eventual second wife (signed, in English, "Your Joe") when both had been married to others and which his first wife had stolen. This was too much for the second Madame Caillaux, and on the late afternoon of March 16, 1914, she called at the offices of *Le Figaro* and greeted its editor with six pistol shots in the stomach. Her trial for murder began in July and all but blotted out news of impending war in the Paris daily newspapers. Madame Caillaux's defense was that her revolver went off six times "by itself," and a jury of gallant Frenchmen acquitted her on July 28. The date should be noted. Austria declared war on Serbia that day, France, Germany and Russia began mobilizing, and within a week all of Europe was at war. No wonder it came as such a surprise to so many Frenchmen. All through July they had read little in their newspapers except the juicy daily accounts of the murder trial.

Caillaux had resigned as Minister of Finance at the end of June in order to help defend his wife at the trial. The newspapers believed his political life was over. Indeed his situation became worse as the war continued. Long suspected of being secretly in touch with the Germans, and never hiding his conviction that the war should be stopped and a compromise peace negotiated, he was deprived in 1917 of his parliamentary immunity as a senator at the insistence of Clemenceau, who accused him of treason and wanted him hanged. Caillaux was arrested and jailed on January 14, 1918, on the charge of corresponding with the enemy and plotting against the security of the state in wartime. Finally brought to trial in 1920 before the Senate sitting as the High Court of Justice, he was found guilty by a vote of 150 to 91 of communicating with the enemy, though "without premeditation." He was condemned to three years in prison and the loss of civil rights for ten years. This time he really seemed finished.

But from that blow the resilient Caillaux also recovered. Amnestied along with many others in 1924, he soon got himself re-elected to the Senate, appointed to two Cabinets as Finance Minister in 1925–1926, the period I used to see him, and for a time he was the elected president of the Radical-Socialist Party, the country's largest. I must say that he stuck throughout his life to the championship of rapprochement with Germany, whether it was led by Wilhelm II or by Adolf Hitler. Was it out of a terrible conceit and false pride? It was impossible to argue with him about it, even after it became clear, at least to me, that a rapprochement with Hitler's Germany was impossible. He stubbornly spoke out for it in the Senate to the last, at the time of the infamous Munich Pact in 1938 and thereafter to the final days of peace in 1939. Caillaux died on November 21, 1944, at the age of eighty-one, just as France was being liberated.

I happened to be in Paris then, alternating that fall between the capital and our First Army front just beyond the German border. A few lines in *Combat,* the newspaper that a young writer, Albert Camus, was making the liveliest and most intelligible in liberated Paris, announced Caillaux's death. Camus' reaction was: So what? Over at the Provisional Assembly where General de Gaulle that day was making the principal speech, no one mentioned the news of Caillaux's end. No one was interested. But I regretted that I had not gone to see the old man before he died. It would not have been to exult about how wrong he had been about Germany and how right I had been. But I would have been curious to see that if at the end of a long life, and after four years of brutal German occupation of France and all the slaughter in Europe that Hitler had brought about, he had finally seen the light, at least about Germany. Probably he had not. None of us who have had deep convictions want to be proved wrong. As Hamilton Fish Armstrong, editor of *Foreign Affairs,* who knew Caillaux well and admired him, concluded: "Conceit was his ruin."

All through those first golden years of mine in Paris, despite the tumbling franc and tumbling governments—one political and financial crisis after another until Poincaré temporarily halted them—France experienced what its people would later look back to as one of the happiest times of the Third Republic. The country had made a remarkable recovery from the devastation of the Great War. It was prosperous, the people were relaxed, the old Continent at last was at peace. The successive crises did not greatly concern the citizens—these were provoked, they were sure, by the intrigues of roguish politicians in Parliament. Not since Napoleon, and before him the Sun King, Louis XIV, had the country enjoyed such well-being. In cold figures it was producing 126 percent more than before the war.

Since the defeat of Germany, France had become the greatest power in Europe. Her hegemony was acknowledged by all the nations. Her army, the most powerful in the world, stood watch on the Rhine. France, after two German invasions in less than half a century, seemed secure at last. And Paris, the inimitable city, had become once again the cultural capital of the world. Attracted by its beauty, its charm, its civilities, its balmy air of freedom, its appreciation of the life of the mind and the spirit, foreigners flocked to it from all over the world in search of the civilized life which the Parisians already enjoyed. I was one of these lucky ones.

Beneath the glittering surface though, if one had scratched deep enough, there might have been discerned the seeds of coming trouble. The bloodletting, which had blotted out the best of the youth, and the destruction of the war, its annihilation of the old order, the hatreds it had aroused in Europe, the revengeful spirit of the defeated—all these, though seemingly forgotten, were costs that had not yet been paid in full. Had I been a better reporter I might have at least faintly felt this. But I was too young, too immature, and I was too filled with the excitement and happiness of my personal life to be aware of what was forming under the surface of this country and all the others in Europe. Later, when it began to surface, poisoning the air, and undermining the Western democracies, I was surprised. Disillusioned, like everyone else, I tried to comprehend its scope, hoping that somehow it would go away and leave the people of Europe, who had suffered so much in the Great War, and leave me, who was living and working in their midst, free to pursue some meaning and happiness in our lives.

But all that lay some years ahead. Now, in 1926, after a year in Paris, I was sharing the feeling of well-being in France and Europe. Peace and prosperity seemed assured for the rest of one's life—so forgetful are we of history, the fickleness of fortune, the transientness of existence, the folly of the human race!

Also, after some initial, youthful infatuations, I was truly in love. I had been overwhelmed by the first sight of Yvonne but it took some months, and some ups and downs, before we came together. She was Parisian to the bone, chic, sophisticated, witty, bursting with energy and animation, and yet underneath rather contemplative, full of wonder about life, exhaustively curious about it but always skeptical, and determined to make the best of it that she could. She had black hair and eyes that seemed black and that expressed best her whole personality—eyes that flashed and blazed and danced and laughed, but that also had some inexpressible depth that on occasion would indicate sadness and sorrow. It was her eyes that overpowered me from the first glance and remained forever a wonder and a mystery.

Yvonne was five years older than I—twenty-seven when we

met—and, it was soon evident to each of us, she had much to teach me. Perhaps it was my innocence and ignorance that intrigued her. I remember my shock when she soon told me that she was married—it seemed like the end of the world. And it took some time to get it into my puritan head that, like many other young Parisian women after the war, she had emancipated herself to the point where she was determined that marriage would not prevent her from leading her own life. It would take years, in fact, for me to see that she considered her marriage to be worth maintaining, on her terms. It was this that defeated us. I could not understand it or accept it. I chafed at not being able to be with her all the time. I was slow to learn that devouring, possessive love is almost always bound to be fatal.

Yvonne was something of a free-lance journalist, though she spent most of her time with the Paris *Tribune*. She was a sort of troubleshooter in a city where there were occasional snares for foreign newspapers and newsmen. She would swing an advertising deal with a large European concern or a government tourist agency, smooth out some difficulty with state or local officials, or fix up an interview with someone which we Americans on the staff had been unable to arrange. She wrote little herself, though she was interested in writing and writers, especially American, and later she would work with Hemingway whenever he was in Paris, typing his manuscripts and helping him to answer his mail.

Despite her marriage and the exigencies of our respective jobs, we managed to have a great deal of time together, especially when I was working nights and she would make her day free. We would get away for a couple of days in the country, a couple of weeks in the Alps, and occasionally she would accompany me on a foreign assignment. We talked endlessly about everything under the sun and our passion never abated. I was hopelessly in love. In itself our love seemed permanent, sure to go on for the rest of our lives, but I tried to make it more permanent by marriage and this she did not want. When in the course of time she changed her mind, it was too late. I at last, after much heartbreak, had given up, and moving to another capital had gone my separate way.

Two friends of mine tore themselves away from Paris that summer of 1926 and went home in search of themselves as artists. Both were discouraged and broke. Both were stubbornly determined to find a way. They had come to the conclusion that only at home, however much they disliked it, could they work out their problems. France and Europe had been a good place to live and work—for a time—but now, they felt, had no more to offer them. They needed to come to grips with the material of places and people they knew best—their own. Both were late starters and they had reached an age when they realized that if they did not begin to make it soon they might never make it.

Jim Thurber, who would soon be thirty-two, was struggling to become a writer and make a modest living at it, but he was unsure of what he wanted to say and in what manner and form. Grant Wood, a friend from our days in Cedar Rapids, was in the same situation as Thurber. He was thirty-five, a talented painter of great promise, but he had not yet found what he wanted to express in his canvases. By the summer's end Wood had finally seen the light. It would take Thurber a little more time.

Jim had left our night copy desk shortly before Christmas of 1925 to go down to Nice to help get out the *Trib*'s Riviera edition, which over the winter months catered to a weird assortment of European royalty, aristocracy, politicians, adventurers and gigolos, outnumbered though by American millionaires, divorcées, social climbers, gamblers, fugitives from justice, and just plain but well-heeled tourists in search of the sea, the sun and some fun. These were just the sort of oddballs Jim liked to write about and he made the paper crazier than the Paris *Trib*. It afforded even more play for his powers of invention. Thurber found the winter at Nice highly amusing but when he returned to Paris in the spring he seemed very uneasy. It had all been a waste of time, he now felt. He would be thirty-two before the year was out, and where was he getting?

"Goddamnit, nowhere," he would answer himself. All through the spring he poured out his frustrations to me. I thought he was exaggerating, but that was part of his charm. I knew that he had written a number of humorous pieces for the Sunday supplements and magazines at home. He had shown me some of them, and I thought they were awfully good—very funny, in any case. And shortly before he had gone south he had sold a wonderfully comic piece to *Harper's*, "A Sock on the Jaw—French Style," for which he said he received ninety dollars, an incredible sum to us since it was equivalent to six weeks' salary on the *Trib*.

Still, he was unsatisfied.

"A guy has to face it," he would argue, lapsing into a jargon he saved for such moments. "I'm thirty-one going on thirty-two and I ain't going to be no novelist. Not even a playwright. I tried. But nothin' happened. Yes, sir, Bill, I ain't going to be no Fitzgerald or Hemingway. Look what they've done, and they're not yet thirty."

Fitzgerald would turn thirty that fall, but already at twenty-four, Jim reminded me, he had published his first novel, *This Side of Paradise,* and the wonderful *Gatsby* last year, when he was only twenty-nine. Hemingway was even younger, twenty-six, and though he had published only two slim volumes, *3 Stories and 10 Poems* and *in our time,* he was already being acclaimed on the Left Bank by Ezra Pound and Gertrude Stein and others as the best writer of his generation—"better even than Fitzgerald." Everyone knew that his first serious novel, *The Sun Also Rises,* would be out that fall, and from what Fitzgerald, Dos Passos and MacLeish, who had read it in manuscript or proofs, said, it was better than anything yet written by the younger writers. It was the talk of Paris all that summer. Whether Jim had seen it, I don't know. He had been a little disappointed a few weeks before by Hemingway's *The Torrents of Spring,* a snide parody of a sentimental novel, *Dark Laughter,* by Sherwood Anderson, who had befriended Hemingway in their Chicago days and helped him get his first book published in Paris. But Thurber thought the first two books wonderful and he had heard that the *Sun* was a giant leap forward.

"He's only twenty-six and he writes a great novel!" Jim exclaimed. There was no jealousy in his voice, just admiration.

I was no help to my friend. I admired what he was writing.

"So what the hell!" I said. "You're thirty-one and you haven't yet written the great novel. Most of the great writers were late starters. At least you're on your way."

But he would not agree. He was in a black mood of despair, and I was too young and immature to see that he was sizing himself up better than I realized. In that lovely late spring of 1926 in Paris, he *was* still unsure of himself and did not know what direction to take and in what way, nor did he know that this uncertainty was the best thing that could happen to a man who was serious about his writing, even if he was going on thirty-two.

The most important thing of all was, as the Greeks advised, To Know Yourself. It was also the most difficult.

Broke and despondent, Thurber took ship home at the end of June, leaving his wife, Althea, in Paris until he could make enough in New York to pay her passage home. He told me later that he landed in New York with one last ten-dollar bill in his wallet; no job, no prospects. He took a cheap furnished room near the Village and wrote and wrote, and received rejection slip after rejection slip—twenty of them from the recently founded *New Yorker,* to which he turned as a last hope since it had begun to publish the sort of sophisticated but sometimes wacky humor he liked best to write.

Finally the next spring, after he had been forced to take a job as a reporter on the New York *Evening Post* in order to eat and pay his wife's passage home, he broke through the chilly thick walls of *The New Yorker.* A short piece of his was accepted, a story about a crazy nut who, after a quarrel with his wife, took to going round and round in the revolving door of a department store until he had hung up some kind of a record and made the front pages and received lucrative offers from vaudeville and Hollywood. E. B. White, the genius of the magazine, took Jim to meet the editor, Harold Ross, who offered Thurber a job at the top, as managing editor, on condition that he do no writing. Jim took it, and soon, after proving to Ross that he would never make it as editor, resumed writing—most of it for *The New Yorker.* It was the turning point in his career. He would go on to become in his articles, essays and books the best writer of humor we had.

Many years later when I came back to live and work at home, we became neighbors in Cornwall, Connecticut, and began again to see a good deal of each other. He was almost blind then and soon would be plunged into total darkness. But he continued to write, slowly and with much difficulty (he could no longer draw) as he adjusted himself to dictating and scrawling lines that he could not see. He chafed under the handicap but it did not stop him, and I never heard him utter a word of bitterness about it, or of self-pity. On the contrary. I remember one evening in the 1950's, four or five years before his death, when we gathered at his place for our Saturday-night talkfest—Jim, Mark Van Doren, Lewis Gannett and our wives. He had been brooding about the lousy state of the world—it had added a new depth to his recent writing—but on this occasion he seemed in better spirits than usual.

"I feel pretty good tonight," Jim said. He had just finished another book. "With this one I have now written more books since I couldn't see than before."

It was his final triumph.

Another friend of mine was discouraged with his work that summer and at its end went home. Like Thurber, Grant Wood was utterly dissatisfied with what he was doing. But unlike him, he had by the end of the summer discovered in himself not only what was wrong but what he would do about it. He talked it out with me one August evening on the terrace of the Deux Magots as we sat sipping light wine and gazing at the tower of the old Church of St. Germain-des-Prés across the street.

He had borrowed a thousand dollars from a real-estate dealer in Cedar Rapids and had come back in the spring for one last attempt to try to make it in the art capital of the world. Grant was no stranger to Paris or Europe. He had spent several months over here in 1920, fourteen months in 1923–1924 when he worked at Julien's Academy in the Rue du Dragon, and now he was back for another extended tour. He spent the spring and early summer painting landscapes in Paris, Provence, Normandy and Brittany, returning to the city at the end of June to arrange forty-seven of his paintings for an exhibition at the Galerie Carmine, a small but prestigious art gallery in the center of Paris. I took Elliot Paul to see the paintings the day Grant began sorting them out. Elliot was impressed and at the *Trib* office that night we passed the hat to raise a little money, as Elliot put it, to help bring the young Iowa artist to the attention of some of the leading French art critics. This was an old custom in Paris but knowing Grant, who was the most unworldly of men, I took care that he knew nothing of it. Paul and I wrote up some advance notices of the exhibition and dispatched them, with a few hundred francs in each envelope, to half a dozen critics. Whether this had the desired effect I don't know. In any event, some of the criticisms were quite good and our extra inducements may not have been at all necessary.

Grant was pleased at the notices. He sold a few canvases but not enough to defray the expenses of the trip. When the exhibition closed down in August—the warm midsummer weeks had been a bad time to exhibit, what with the exodus of Parisians to the seaside for vacations—he was depressed and in some kind of a revolt, I felt, against himself. Not because of the notices or because he had sold so few pictures, I soon discovered, but because of something else much more important and profound. He poured it out to me that evening at the Deux Magots, he who in all the years I had known him at home was so reticent and awkward in speech. Now, as we finished one carafe of wine after another, he let loose a torrent of words.

"Everything that I've done up to now was wrong," he said. "And, my God, I'm halfway through my life."

"You're only thirty-five," I said.

"All those landscapes of mine of the French countryside and the familiar places in Paris! There's not a one that the French Impressionists didn't do a hundred times better!"

I could see he was warming up.

"All these years wasted because I thought you couldn't get started as a painter unless you went to Paris and studied, and painted like a Frenchman. I used to go back to Iowa and think how ugly it all was. Nothing to paint. And all I could think of was getting back here so I could find something to paint—these pretty landscapes that I should have known Cézanne and Renoir and Monet and the others had done once and for all."

"Well, Picasso has broken away," I said. "Apparently he finds Paris a good place to work."

"Picasso's a European. Spanish and now French. He feels at home here. Besides, he's a genius."

"Maybe you'll be one," I chipped in.

He laughed. "Listen, Bill. I think . . . at last . . . I've learned something. At least, about myself. Damn it . . . I think you've got to paint . . . like you have to write . . . what you know. And despite the years in Europe, here and in Munich and the other places, all I really know is home. Iowa. The farm at Anamosa. Milking cows. Cedar Rapids. The typical small town, alright. Everything commonplace. Your neighbors, the quiet streets, the clapboard homes, the drab clothes, the dried-up lives, the hypocritical talk, the silly boosters, the poverty of . . . damn it, culture . . . and all the rest. You know it as well as I. You grew up there, too."

"I got away," I said. I was beginning to see what had happened to Grant. He had come to a conclusion about himself and his art.

"I'm going home for good," he said. "And I'm going to paint those damn cows and barns and barnyards and cornfields and little red schoolhouses and all those pinched faces and the women in their aprons and the men in their overalls and store suits and the look of a field or a street in the heat of summer or when it's ten below and the snow piled six feet high." He hesitated a moment. "Damn it, isn't that what Sinclair Lewis has done in his writing—in *Main Street* and *Babbitt?* Damn it, you can do it in painting, too!"

Though I could not know it for sure, when we finally broke up after midnight, Grant had that August evening arrived at the great turning point of his life, as an artist. No doubt his decision had been simmering in him all summer. I'm sure he had talked it out with others, too—undoubtedly with an old friend of his from home, John Reid, a Cedar Rapids businessman, who was in Paris that summer and spent much time at the gallery during the exhibition.

Later Grant told me that on reaching home that year he had gazed at his mother standing to greet him at the door of his studio in the loft of the old coach house of the Turner mortuary. She was wearing a familiar green apron with jagged edges and at her neck an old cameo he had brought home to her once from Italy. Behind the wrinkled, weather-beaten face was a great radiance. He hastily made a sketch. Strange, he thought, that he had never seen in her a subject for a serious portrait. He had seen no such face in Europe, or at least none had struck him. Soon he was at work on the portrait—one of the great ones painted in our time and eventually called simply *Woman with Plants.* I knew, as I have mentioned, the woman with the plants very well in my youth. Grant had captured much more than the face I remember. He had portrayed her indomitable spirit, her triumph over poverty and hardship, the radiance of a woman who would not be defeated by life.

From afar I followed Grant Wood's career in the ensuing years after he found himself and his genius unfolded, and, as John Steuart Curry said, "he jarred America awake to the endless glories of American landscapes. Life. People." Two or three times when I was home briefly on leave we got together and talked in his studio in the old barn I had played in as a youngster. By this time he had become famous, though he remained as modest as he had been in his plodding younger years. He brought me up to date on the reaction, local and national, to some of his controversial paintings. It had taken him three or four years, he said, after he returned home from Paris at the end of that summer of 1926, to get very far down the new road he had determined to take. The portrait of his mother was finished in 1929.

The next year, 1930, he suddenly burst into national fame. His painting *American Gothic* was entered in the annual exhibition of new paintings at the Chicago Art Institute, won the Harris prize and was purchased by the Art Institute for its permanent collection—at a price that Wood had modestly set on entering it: three hundred dollars. The work was the sensation of the Chicago exhibition that year, attracted unusual crowds, and brought critics from New York and elsewhere to write about it. Overnight Grant became known throughout the country. Cedar Rapids suddenly had a hero of its own—and an artist, at that. And it had something to talk about: not only the nationwide acclaim for a local boy and his painting but the fact that it knew the gaunt figures in the foreground of the canvas, the farmer and his wife. Everyone in town knew them. The rigid, severe-looking farmer's wife, with her straight hair parted in the middle and dressed in an apron, was Grant's sister, Nan Wood. The farmer at her side, a gaunt, solemn, long-faced, thin-lipped man with a black store jacket over his overalls and collarless shirt and firmly grasping a hayfork, was Grant's dentist. Nan was not pleased at the way her portrait came out. Dr. B. H. McKeeby, the dentist, was horrified to find himself, a good-humored city man who had never held a hayfork in his life, depicted so starkly. The farmers around protested that no countryman had a house with a Gothic window such as Wood had painted in the background.

American Gothic of course was partly satire—this would underlie many of Grant's canvases from now on. He wanted, I think, to show in the faces of the farmer and his wife some of the starved narrowness as well as the staunchness of the inhabitants of the Corn and Bible Belt. The Gothic window of the run-down farmhouse was itself a sign of the pretentiousness of rural folk. There was satire in the very title of the work. American Gothic! A farmer with a hayfork! Its long, thin prongs in the very foreground of the picture did indicate, though, the long, lean lines of the Gothic. But beneath the satire was Wood's success in portraying artistically and also with deep sympathy and understanding the reality of the drab prairie land, its wretched homes, its weather-beaten, pious, narrow-minded, hard-working people. He had found his material at home, among his neighbors and family.

But he wanted still to say something more boldly, more satirically, not only about Iowa but about America. He found a subject in the Daughters of the American Revolution, which had an active chapter in the town and whose members included my mother, a rather reluctant one since she did not like the D.A.R.'s super-patriotism. Grant didn't either. He had been incensed when the national D.A.R. put Jane Addams, whom he had admired since his Chicago days, on its blacklist. And he had been much put upon by the local D.A.R. and the American Legion (of which he was a member) because he had had to go to Munich and enlist the help of German craftsmen to finish the large stain-glassed window he had been commissioned in 1927 to do for the planned Cedar Rapids Memorial Building. They denounced it for having been made in Germany. Actually it always seemed to me to be one of his most interesting works. Wood was one of the few American painters who had mastered the almost lost art of painting stained-glass windows.

Now, in 1932, he turned his attention to the D.A.R. He painted three dried-up, sexless, smug old ladies sipping tea and obviously puffed up with pride to be standing before a copy of Emanuel Leutze's well-known painting of Washington crossing the Delaware, with the peerless Commander in Chief standing defiantly in the prow of the boat surrounded by his soldiers, from whom the good ladies claimed to be descended. Entitled *Daughters of Revolution*,[1] it was a savage satire and when it was shown at the Carnegie International Exhibition in Pittsburgh that year it caused an explosive controversy across the nation. There were demands that it be withdrawn, and when Wood declined, it was

---

[1] Grant had originally called it *Daughters of the American Revolution* but a local businessman friend of his (the one who had lent him a thousand dollars to go to Paris in 1926) persuaded him to soften the title lest the indomitable ladies of the D.A.R., aroused to fury, put his very life in peril. Perhaps the businessman, Henry S. Ely, saw also that a less identifying title might avoid troublesome lawsuits.

placed in the most inconspicuous place the museum directors could find. Nevertheless, it drew huge crowds and continued cries of outrage from the D.A.R. and other super-patriotic groups. The newspapers and magazines devoted columns to it and to the storm it aroused. Seldom, if ever, had a painter in America received such attention. Grant, I gathered, was highly pleased. He called the three grotesque ladies in his painting "those Tory gals" and added to a reporter: "I don't like Toryism. I don't like people who are trying to set up an aristocracy of birth in a Republic." The painting was exhibited later at Chicago's Century of Progress, along with Wood's *American Gothic* and his *Midnight Ride of Paul Revere,* where it attracted large crowds and further notoriety. It was eventually sold to Edward G. Robinson, the actor.

Other museums and private collectors now competed to buy Grant Wood's paintings and at last he was able to get out of debt. Marshall Field III, King Vidor, Cole Porter, Gardner Cowles, Kenneth Roberts, J. P. Marquand, Cornelius Vanderbilt Whitney, were among the purchasers. But though his canvases began to fetch large sums—ten thousand dollars or more—Grant, who cared nothing for money, never was able to put much aside. In the mid-thirties he married a local woman but the marriage soon went on the rocks. At that time he moved on to Iowa City, where he taught painting at the University of Iowa, became immensely popular with his pupils, rather unpopular with some of his staid colleagues in the art department and brought needed prestige to the university. He died of cancer in Iowa City on February 12, 1942, two hours short of his fifty-first birthday, some two thousand dollars in debt, and was buried beside his mother in the little Anamosa cemetery on the banks of the Wapsipinicon River near where he was born. He was one of the best and most original of our American artists and a fine, warm, modest, civilized human being.

Since his death I have often thought that Grant Wood's discovery of himself amid the cornfields and barnyards of Iowa, after so many years spent groping among the refinements of Paris and Munich, was, in a way, a fulfillment of Emerson's bold prophecy in his famous Phi Beta Kappa address at Harvard on "The American Scholar" nearly a century and a half ago. "Our day of dependence, our long apprenticeship to the learning of other lands, draws to a close," Emerson said, and though he was thinking primarily of scholars and writers, his words applied to

American painters as well. "Events, actions arise, that must be sung," he said, "that will sing themselves."

It was easy to see later that Jim Thurber and Grant Wood had made a wise decision for themselves when they decided to go home and strike off on new paths. I would have to take another road. I could never go back home to those arid surroundings that had helped to shape me, as they had Grant, but that also had made me a rebel against their narrow ways and peculiar values. The kind of life and work I now wanted could only be found, I thought, in a different world—specifically, for a long time to come, in Europe. After a year in Paris I was beginning to know myself well enough to see that, as Jim said of himself, I was not going to be a Fitzgerald or a Hemingway or a Dos Passos or even a lesser creator of fiction and poetry. I had another disposition. Whereas they, as all good novelists and poets must do, had turned inward to find the sources of their creativity, from which they could build in their writing a world of their own, a very personal world, but which if it were good would have universal significance, I was beginning to turn outward—after a year of trying to write poetry and short stories—to what was going on in the world.

History now seemed more interesting to me, especially contemporary history. I was beginning to see, of course, that aside from the aesthetic satisfaction one got from novels, one also absorbed from them a good deal of history, of the feel of certain times in the life of a country or a civilization. My own feeling for life in nineteenth-century England, France and Russia came not so much from the histories I read but from the novels: in the first instance from George Eliot and Dickens; in the second, from Balzac, Stendhal and, eventually, Proust; in the third, from Tolstoy, Gogol, Dostoevsky, Turgenev and Chekhov. Perhaps in the end, when you were mature enough, you could better tell of the times you had lived through in a novel than in a straight history. It was a goal I never lost sight of, until much later I would try for it—and fail.

Vaguely the idea began to take root that there might be a great deal of history to write about from here for a daily newspaper back home. Something was brewing in Europe. Underneath the surface of well-being there were already certain indications. The General Strike in Britain that spring had shown the malaise in British society. Its failure had brought out the determination of the upper classes to keep the lower classes down on depressed wages, which were near the starvation level. Obviously class war in Britain was far from over and the upper classes were winning it. In Italy the murder of Matteotti, a Socialist deputy, by Mussolini's Fascist thugs, was an inkling, I thought, of how brutally far the Fascists would go to stifle opposition to their rule. When, that summer of 1926, the murderers were either acquitted or let off with nominal sentences, it was obvious that law in Italy would henceforth be what Mussolini wanted it to be. From then on Italy would be a totalitarian state.

Germany, it is true, seemed to have settled down. That fall she was admitted to the League of Nations. But some of the American correspondents in Berlin who came to Paris for a vacation (Sigrid Schultz of the *Chicago Tribune*, Edgar Mowrer of the Chicago *Daily News*, H. R. Knickerbocker and Dorothy Thompson of the New York *Evening Post*) spoke of it as being the calm before the storm. Anti-Semitism and right-wing nationalism, they said, were far from dead. A well-known seventy-four-year-old Jewish German scientist and writer, Professor Gregorious Itelsohn, had been attacked and killed in Berlin by an anti-Jewish mob. Royalists and other ultranational groups, who wanted an end to the Weimar Republic, were marching in the streets again. Hitler, the correspondents said, was silent because all the state governments had banned him from speaking in public. But he was quietly reorganizing the Nazi party, and his book, *Mein Kampf*, which thundered against the Jews and the Republic, seemed to be selling moderately well. The correspondents gave the democratic Republic more than an even chance to survive. Still, they said, Germany bore watching.

Russia, too. Though the United States smugly continued to refuse to have diplomatic relations with her, the Soviet Union now had embassies in all the major capitals of Europe and was emerging from the long isolation imposed on her by the West. Since Lenin's death two years before, in 1924, a struggle for the succession had been going on in the Kremlin. Leon Trotsky, who as Lenin's closest collaborator was believed in Europe to be the logical successor, was ousted from the Politbureau that fall of 1926 and seemed finished. A man named Stalin was reported to be coming out on top. Few in Europe, in contrast to many in America, regarded the Soviet Union as a threat, though most professed to be scared to death of Communism. And almost everyone in the West was certain that Russia would never be a great power again. Bolshevism, they said, just couldn't work over the long run. The *Chicago Tribune*'s "Russian correspondent" covered the Soviet Union from the anti-Communist citadel of Riga, in Latvia, where he could give free rein to his Bolshevik-hating imagination. He invented a "people's revolt" in Russia nearly every month. Still, according to some of the correspondents of American newspapers who actually worked in Moscow and who sometimes came out to Paris—Walter Duranty of *The New York Times*, William Henry Chamberlin of the *Christian Science Monitor*, Louis Fischer of *The Nation*—some interesting things were transpiring in Russia. The terrible Bolsheviks, whom American and French cartoonists invariably depicted with knives clutched between their teeth, were in complete control, they said, the country was getting stronger, Germany was helping it, and the West ought to take notice.

And France? Poincaré certainly was restoring some financial equilibrium—but for how long? I had begun to suspect that in France the possessing classes were even more greedy and venal than in Britain and at home. All through the crisis of the franc they had sent their capital abroad and thus further weakened the country's precarious position. Appeals to their patriotism were in vain. The tax system was shocking, soaking the poor and sparing the rich. Yet all attempts to reform it, to make it somewhat equitable, were defeated in a Parliament that had been elected in 1924 on a radical wave. Once when I served for a few weeks as "financial editor" of the *Trib* I had been struck by an article in the *Journal des Finances* by an eminent professor of law, Gaston Jeze. He had served on a Committee of Experts named by the government to draw up a plan to restore the state's finances. Though himself a conservative, he had thrown up his hands.

> Personally [he wrote] I believe that taxes on acquired wealth would be the fairest solution. But such taxes have met an invincible resistance among the possessors, who are the most powerful. That is a fact. The selfishness of possessing classes is not reducible. We have to adapt to it.

One could see that it was a fact all right. But the well-heeled were not satisfied. They feared that democracy in France, however badly it was served by Parliament, might continue to threaten their moneybags. They began to look over the Alps at Italy to see if perhaps the rights of Big Business and Big Finance might not be better protected by a system of government that had destroyed democracy. That very summer of 1926 I started to look into a movement, Redressement Français (French Resurgence), that had just been founded by the electricity magnate Ernest Mercier, with the support of some of his business colleagues. It frankly proclaimed that the democratic Parliament was incapable of solving the affairs of state in the complicated postwar world. It wanted instead a Parliament and government of "technicians" who knew how modern capitalist society ought to function. It was up to business to furnish these new leaders. François Coty, the perfume king, who had bought the conservative daily newspaper *Le Figaro* in 1922, was also beginning to despair of democracy, subsidizing numerous right-wing anti-Parliament movements which would later emerge as a full-fledged Fascist organization, Solidarité Francaise.

Very few in France paid much attention to these things in 1926 and I do not pretend that I did. Only later, with the benefit of hindsight, would I write:

> One can begin to see at this time, in the mid-1920's, the possessing class in France alienating itself from the rest of the nation. Since the bulk of the working class felt *itself* somewhat cut off from the nation—for opposite reasons—the Republic obviously was in more trouble than many realized.[1]

I certainly did not faintly imagine the consequences. But my work on the newspaper in Paris kept me digging away at these matters, and at many others. And the more I dug and wrote, the more I felt I wanted to go on in journalism. It was one way for a young man to be able to chronicle current history, try to understand it and comment on it. But to do it well, you had to graduate from the somewhat frivolous Paris *Tribune* and become a foreign correspondent.

Since the door to that had not yet opened, though it looked as if it might in a year or two—Henry Wales, the *Tribune*'s chief correspondent was beginning at least to notice my existence—I would try to get as much experience as I could as a reporter for

[1] *The Collapse of the Third Republic,* p. 158.

the local edition in Paris. I had heard of the advice of Gertrude Stein to Hemingway—she would even give it to me shortly—that if you wanted to write seriously you had to get out of journalism, but I did not take it much to heart. Hemingway often repeated what Stein had told him on the subject, and which she later included in *The Autobiography of Alice B. Toklas:* "If you keep on doing newspaper work you will never see things, you will only see words and that will not do." This had struck me as a piece of the nonsense she was so full of. Journalism offered probably the best way to "see things," as Hemingway initially had found. He had been a good correspondent. Some of his dispatches from the scene of the Greek debacle in Thrace and Asia Minor, when the Turks had driven the Greeks into the sea, had been brilliant pieces of reporting, and the experience had given him material for some fine sketches and short stories.

Moreover, the "cablese" in which a foreign correspondent had to write his dispatches to save expensive tolls had influenced Hemingway's style, helping him to pare his prose to the bone and keep it lean, as he himself conceded. "It's a great language," he insisted to a group of American correspondents drinking in a café in Lausanne during the peace conference to settle the Greco-Turkish conflict. They had asked him to read some of his dispatches from the scene of that war and were surprised by how much vividness, color and emotion Hemingway had got out of this shorthand language. Most of the correspondents fretted at its restrictiveness, but Hemingway liked it. "I had to quit being a correspondent," he told Lincoln Steffens later. "I was getting too fascinated by the lingo of the cable."[1]

It was a lingo that I began studying that first year on the *Trib*, just in case Wales took me on in the foreign service. Every noon when I came to work on the dayside I would go over the cable file to Chicago of the night before. The lead story, an interview Wales had had with Poincaré, might begin like this:

EXCLUSIVE POINCARE CHICATRIBWARD UNTRUTH UNPAY WARDEBTS AMERICAWARD STOP FRANCE UNINTENDS UP-GIVE REPARATIONS DUE EXTREATIES STOP TWO LINKED QUOTE UNREPARATIONS UNWARDEBTS PAYABLE UN-QUOTE UNBELIEVES GERMANS UNFUNDS PAY FULLEST

[1] *The Autobiography of Lincoln Steffens,* p. 834 (paperback edition).

STOP UNBEFORE POINCARE ADAMANTEST REGERMANS
DELIBERATE STALLING STOP BRISTLING CHICATRIBWARD
UNEXCUSES EXGERMANS . . .

In the *Tribune* in Chicago that morning the cable would
appear as follows:

> In an exclusive interview today Raymond Poincaré, the
> French Premier and Minister of Finance, told the *Chicago
> Tribune* that there was no truth in the report that France would
> not pay its war debts to the United States. But France, he em-
> phasized also, has no intention of giving up the reparations due
> her under treaty agreements from Germany.
> Reparations and war debts, Poincaré maintained, must be
> linked together. "Unless France receives reparations from Ger-
> many," he said, "she cannot pay her war debts." The French
> Premier added that he does not believe that the Germans lack
> the funds to pay reparations in full. Never before has Poincaré
> expressed so adamantly his views regarding what he conceives
> as deliberate stalling by the Germans. He fairly bristled as he
> discussed the problem with a *Tribune* correspondent. He said he
> would accept no excuses from the German government.

One got the hang of cablese quickly. Every word you could
leave out saved one dollar in cable tolls. Affixes saved dollars
more. To write cablese you had to strip narrative of everything
extraneous. Soon it would become the language I wrote in for
many years. And while it apparently was good for Hemingway,[1]
it worked badly for me. It made for a stilted style, a barrenness of
language. Pretty soon it was the only way you could write. It
would take the writing of a long book, mercifully unpublished,
during a year off in Spain to get the jargon out of my system.

My work as a *Tribune* reporter that summer of 1926 led me
to meet three remarkable American women who were already
famous—an opera singer, a writer, a dancer.

---

[1] George Seldes, a *Tribune* colleague, often recalled the meeting in Lausanne
when Hemingway talked of the influence of cablese on his writing. "I remember
his bringing in one of his cableized items and reading it to Steffens with astonishment and satisfaction, saying that it was a new language. I believe this experience in cablese influenced Hemingway considerably." Seldes confirmed this
in a letter to Tom Wood.—Wood's unpublished manuscript, *Influence of the
Paris Herald on the Lost Generation of Writers*, p. 140.

Mary Garden had come back from Chicago to Paris to make her farewell appearance in *Louise* at the Opéra Comique. It was there and in this opera that she had made her dramatic debut a quarter of a century before. I was curious to meet her. My father, as I have recalled, had raved about her. He would come home from the opera in Chicago and tell us that she was the most beautiful and dynamic woman he had ever seen on the stage. Several times he had taken us children to see her in a matineé—in *Louise, Salome* and *Thaïs,* I think—but we had been much too young to appreciate all that Father saw in her. Now that I was grown up I wanted to see for myself. The French newspapers were publishing some fabulous accounts of her debut in Paris and I wanted to talk with her and perhaps separate the truth from the myth. My father, I'm sure, had never got up the nerve to go back stage to see her, but now I had an advantage over him. It would be easy enough to get an interview with her for the *Tribune.* In fact, since Chicago considered Mary Garden as one of its own, the home edition had cabled Wales to cover fully her return to Paris and I was picked to do it.

One day she invited me to tea in her hotel suite. I felt at once that my father had not exaggerated. Though she was by her count forty-nine—and I had no reason to doubt it, though that age seemed much older to me at twenty-two than it would now—she *was* astonishingly beautiful, with strong, fine features, rich dark hair, a full and sensuous mouth, and enormous, lively eyes that quickly expressed half a dozen changing moods. Her magnetic personality overwhelmed me. In the weeks before her appearance at the Opéra Comique we met often in her suite and she told me a good deal about her life.

I knew that she had been born in Scotland—in 1877, she said—but I had assumed she had come from there to Paris to try to break into opera and that after her triumph here she had gone to Chicago, her name already famous. Nothing of the kind, she said. She had gone with her Scottish parents to America when she was six, living in such odd places as Chicopee, Massachusetts, and Hartford, Connecticut, and finally moving on to Chicago when she was eleven. From the very beginning, she said, she wanted to have some kind of a career in music. She had taken up the violin when she was six, played her first concert in Chicago when she was twelve, and then, dissatisfied, had given up the violin for the piano, which she studied for several years. So though it was not generally known, she had really grown up in Chicago, struggling like hundreds of other youngsters there to become a musician. When she was sixteen or so, she gave up the piano and took up singing lessons. Her mother, whose maiden name of Mary Garden she later adopted, thought she had a good voice. After three years of vocal studies in Chicago, she set out for Paris to study under some of the great voice teachers in the French capital—among them, she remembered, Chevalier, Fugère and Trabadello. This was in 1896. She was nineteen, talented and ambitious.

I had heard and read so many accounts of how she suddenly made it in Paris that I questioned her at length about it. The story was really very simple, she said, and not uncommon at all. It had happened to others, and would continue to happen if you were lucky. In the spring of 1900, after four years of training in Paris, she had, through the help of her teachers, caught on as understudy to a well-known French singer named Mlle. Rioton, who had the title role in Charpentier's *Louise*, which, dealing as it did with life in Paris, was one of the most popular operas in the repertoire of the Opéra Comique.

"It happened on the evening of April 13, 1900," Mary Garden said, her luminous eyes lighting up. "How can I forget that date! Thirteen has been my lucky number ever since, but that 'thirteen' was the luckiest of all." Mlle. Rioton, she said, had not been feeling well, but managed to get through the first two acts of *Louise*. At the second curtain she collapsed. A doctor tried to revive her. But it was obvious that she could not go on for the last act. Mary Garden, standing as she had each night for weeks in the wings, was hurriedly summoned by the director, hastily dressed, and, without time to warm up, found herself for the first time in her life before the footlights in a major opera house. She had just turned twenty-three.

"The rest," said Miss Garden, who was no shrinking violet, "is history. But you must have heard it when you were a wee tot in Chicago."

"Not like you've told it," I said. "My father would have given almost anything to be in my steps this moment."

"You say he was an admirer. He should have come back stage." She laughed. "Those were the great days in Chicago," she said, as if her mind for the moment was turning back to them.

What happened that night of April 13, 1900, at the Opéra Comique *was* history—for opera lovers and especially for those in Paris. Though Mary Garden had sung only the last act, she was hailed the next morning in the Parisian press as the new bright star of opera. She took over the part and played it, she said, for one hundred more performances that season. New York took notice but it was not, she said, exactly in a hurry. It was not until seven years later, in the fall of 1907, that Oscar Hammerstein, who had brought over so many singers from Europe, engaged her to sing the title role in *Thaïs* for her American debut in New York. And it took three more years to get to Chicago, where she sang for the first time on November 5, 1910, at the Chicago Grand Opera. She was home again, after a fourteen-year absence, and she remained there to the end of her career, the great star of the Grand Opera Company and eventually its general director.

Her voice had cracked a little by the time she sang in Paris that summer of 1926, but she was as beautiful and as electrifying as ever, and the Parisian critics made much of her. Above all, Mary Garden was a great actress, one of the few of her time in opera. Galli-Curci, her contemporary in the Chicago Opera, might have had a better voice, clearer in the high ranges, more lyrical, but she moved about the stage, as Jane Heap wrote in *The Little Review*, "like a lost cloak-model." In one issue of the *Review* Miss Heap recalled these lines of Euripides to express what she felt about Mary Garden:

> . . . *This Cyprian*
> *She is a million, million changing things.*
> *She brings more joy than any god; she brings*
> *More pain. I cannot judge her. May it be*
> *An Hour of mercy when she looks on me.*

I must confess that in my own small way I felt a little like that about Mary Garden after the weeks of seeing her. My father would have envied me. I felt crushed when I was unable, because of my job, to accept her invitation to visit her on the Riviera. But the radiance of her brushed off on me—to stay forever.

Gertrude Stein was as ugly to look at as Mary Garden was beautiful. One day that summer the city editor hung up the phone and yelled at me: "For God's sake, go over and see Gertrude Stein. She's after some more publicity. Go and see what the hell it is this time."

To me this was an exciting prospect. I stood in some awe of this lady. Though little of what she had written over the last twenty years had been published, and she was said to have written a great deal, her reputation as a writer of great originality, who was transforming the English language as much as Joyce, was already considerable, as was her reputation as a formidable personality. Around the office she was called the Mother Goose of Montparnasse. Elliot Paul and Jolas said she was a genius. A segment of her long novel *The Making of Americans* had appeared, at Hemingway's insistence, in Ford Madox Ford's *Transatlantic,* and now Robert McAlmon was publishing the whole thousand pages of it at his Contact Editions press. I had tried to read the segment but had found it almost unintelligible. But I was intrigued by the chance to meet the author.

Hemingway, who was a close friend and admirer of Miss Stein's at this time—a relationship that was fully reciprocated—had warned, among other things, that if you brought up the name of Joyce in her commanding presence you would not be invited back. I kept that in mind as I hailed a taxi below the office and set out for the address which everyone knew: 27 Rue de Fleurus, just off the Luxembourg Gardens. I had recently started reading *Ulysses* and had already concluded that Joyce was the greatest writer in English of our time, Gertrude Stein to the contrary notwithstanding. But I would keep that to myself.

Miss Stein lived in a pavilion in a courtyard behind 27 Rue de Fleurus. I was ushered by a maid into a large studio salon. Though it was rather dark in the room I could make out the paintings, which already were famous and which occupied every inch of space on the walls. Gertrude Stein and her brother Leo had been among the first in Paris to acquire Picassos—the great Spanish painter was one of her oldest and closest friends—and the first things you saw were two canvases of his, a portrait of Miss Stein done before the Great War and his nude of the girl with the basket of flowers. I thought I also recognized a couple of Matisses and one or two by Juan Gris. Soon a small, dark, middle-aged lady with a strongly aquiline nose came in. She did not introduce herself but I was sure she was Miss Stein's "companion," Alice B. Toklas. She said Miss Stein would be there presently, sat down and resumed some needlepoint she had been working on, and we passed the time of day. Then the author came in.

She was so bulky that, as a note I jotted down reminds me, I thought she looked like a full-blown old Irish washwoman. But this first impression soon changed. Above her heavyset body was a face that reminded you of a Roman emperor, masculine and strong and well chiseled, and her eyes were attractive and intelligent. Her hair was closely cropped, like Caesar's. She greeted me in a low, mannish but pleasant voice. She wanted to talk about, it developed, her recent lectures at Cambridge and Oxford, which, she said, had been a great success and which had not been reported fully in the American newspapers in Paris. In fact, I did not recall that they had been mentioned. This had surprised her, she said, because besides being acclaimed by the students and faculty at the great British universities, she was, after all, the greatest living writer in the English language. It had to be an American, she explained, and it had to be she. Just as England had made our literature from the sixteenth through the nineteenth century, America had made it in the twentieth.

"You know the Big Four in American literature, don't you?" she went on. "Ending with me?" Before I could express my ignorance she answered her question. "There is a natural line of descent. Poe to Whitman to Henry James to myself. I am the last. The only living one."

I kept scribbling notes of these astonishing claims, and this seemed to please her.

"You should have been at Oxford," she went on. "Or Cambridge. Not only the students—the young are always brighter than the old—loved it. But the faculty people. One professor—I think it was at Oxford—came up later and said that listening to my lecture was the greatest experience of his life. He had been as excited, he said, as when he first read Kant's *Critique of Pure Reason.*" And on and on she went.

My God, I suddenly thought, I have landed in the presence of a megalomaniac! It was fascinating but scarcely believable. For she was obviously a most intelligent person, reputedly widely read, a disciplined writer, a student of not only literature but history. Equally obvious after the first few minutes was that the only subject she knew, that she could talk about, that she could

write about, was herself. Her greatness. Her genius. It was difficult to break into the torrent of her words. But finally I managed
it, saying I would do a story on her lectures in England. Did she
possibly have a copy of the text, so that I could quote from it?
She went to her desk and found one and handed it to me.

"It will be published this fall by the Hogarth Press in London," she said. "You know, that wonderful publishing house in
London of Virginia and Leonard Woolf. Miss Woolf, you know, is
one of my admirers."

I had been reading Virginia Woolf's reviews and literary
comments in the London press but I could not recall her ever
mentioning Gertrude Stein. But perhaps I had missed a few
pieces.

My hostess then turned her talk to her long novel, *The
Making of Americans*. She was pleased that at last it was being
published in full—all one thousand pages of it. She had waited a
long time. She had spent two years writing it—between 1906 and
1908. But no one would publish it, though anyone could tell it
was a masterpiece. It was really a monumental work, she said,
really the beginning of modern writing. Hemingway had seen
that at once. He had insisted on Ford Madox Ford publishing an
excerpt in Ford's *Transatlantic*. Hemingway himself had copied it
from the original manuscript and then had read proof on it and in
doing so, she said, he had learned a lot about writing that he
needed to know. Now Robert McAlmon was publishing it in full
in his little press in Paris, though she was having plenty of trouble
with him. This, I knew, was nothing compared to the trouble *he*
was having with her, for McAlmon often dropped by the *Tribune*
to talk of his problems. At this point, one small drop of humility
in the great woman emerged. She was grateful to Hemingway
and now to McAlmon for giving the public this great book. Mc-
Almon, she added, wrote a great deal and she admired him for
it—but unfortunately it was rather dull stuff. Perhaps he should
concentrate on publishing. She had much more to give him that
might make his press famous.

"Well, a thousand-page book is a good start for a small publisher," I said.

"There is much more," she said.

For the first time she paused, looked at me with her keen
lively eyes and I felt she was sizing me up.

"You are very young," she said.

"Twenty-two," I said.

"Well, Hemingway was about that age—maybe twenty-three —when he first came to see me. I like young men, you know." I quickly figured from something I had read that she was fifty-two. I must have seemed like a child.

"Are you writing anything?" she asked.

"Some bad poetry and short stories," I said.

"If you know it's bad, that's good," she said. "All you young men ought to get out of newspaper work," she added. "It's bad for a writer. I told Hemingway that the first time I talked to him. A good thing for him, he took my advice."

I felt for an instant like arguing the point. A great many writers, I was about to say, started in newspaper work. Hemingway himself was a good example. I was beginning to feel flattered at being mentioned in connection with Hemingway. But I desisted. I did not want to get into an argument. I felt I would not be invited back if I did.

"What are you reading these days?" she suddenly asked. And quite deliberately I made the mistake I had told myself I wouldn't make.

"At the moment, *Ulysses*," I said. She was not as put back as I expected.

"Why bother with that?" she said. "It's a waste of time, really. All the young men are reading it. But why? Joyce is a second-rate writer, really. Compared to me, anyway."

I did not argue that point either. Miss Stein seemed to lose interest in continuing the interview. But she was cordial enough in bidding me goodbye. Perhaps she did not want to jeopardize the write-up I would give her. It was the last time I called at 27 Rue de Fleurus for eight years.[1]

---

[1] The beautiful and talented Kay Boyle, whom I met for the first time that year and formed a friendship that has lasted to this day, subsequently told me of her first—and last—meeting with Gertrude Stein a couple of years later. Kay had started to be published in *transition* and other Left Bank quarterlies and Miss Stein, noticing her work aside hers, had asked a friend to bring her for tea. But Kay had been forced to spend most of her time talking with Alice B. Toklas, who told her of the marvelous recipes she had found in Spain, especially one for *gazpacho*. Afterward Kay's friend confessed to her that Miss Stein had asked him not to bring her back again as she had found Miss Boyle "as incurably middle-class as Ernest Hemingway."

Kay Boyle recounts this in one of her books and adds an account of a meeting between Eugene Jolas and Gertrude Stein which I once heard Jolas tell and

Back at the office I studied the text of Miss Stein's lecture. It was entitled "Composition as Explanation" and in it, for the first time, I believe, she tried in public to explain herself and her writing. The text was also a good example of her writing. I found it hard to follow. Despite the title, Miss Stein did not really explain. The first paragraph of the lecture was typical:

There is singularly nothing that makes a difference a difference in beginning and in the middle and in ending except that each generation has something different at which they are all looking. By this I mean so simply that anybody knows it that composition is the difference which makes each and all of them then different from other generations and this is what makes everything different otherwise they are all alike and everybody knows it because everybody says it.

And what is composition? That was the title of her lecture, and she was going to explain it.

Composition is the thing seen by every one living in the living that they are doing, they are the composing of the composition that at the time they are living is the composition of the time in which they are living. It is that that makes living a thing they are doing. Nothing else is different . . .

Everything is the same except composition and as the composition is different and always going to be different everything is not the same. Everything is not the same as the time when of the composition and the time in the composition is different. The composition is different, that is certain.

She talked a great deal about what she called "a continuous present" in her writing. And what was that? "A continuous pres-

---

which eventually was published in *A James Joyce Miscellany*. In *transition* Jolas had championed both Joyce and Stein. One day Miss Stein complained.

MISS STEIN: Jolas, why do you continue to lay such emphasis in *transition* on the work of that fifth-rate politician, James Joyce? Haven't you understood yet that the leading English-language writer today is myself, Gertrude Stein?

JOLAS: Miss Stein, will you excuse me, but I do not agree with you. (*Jolas rises, walks to the door, picks up his hat.*) Miss Stein, I bid you goodmorning. (*Exit Jolas.*)

—Kay Boyle and Robert McAlmon: *Being Geniuses Together*, p. 334.

ent is a continuous present," she says. A little later: "The time of the composition is the time of the composition." It reminded me of Jim Thurber making President Coolidge say that a praying man was a man who prayed.

Gertrude Stein had long made repetition one of the foundations of her writing, and this lecture was full of examples:

> And after that what changes what changes after that, after that what changes and what changes after that and after that and what changes and after that and what changes after that.

By this time I was losing myself in the gibberish. Miss Stein later, in 1934–1935, after fame at last came to her with her *Autobiography of Alice B. Toklas*, gave five lectures in America. I got the texts, which were published the next year, and I tried very hard to make something out of them for I really wanted to understand the phenomenon of Gertrude Stein, but to me they were more of the same. The same meaningless repetition, the same inanities. One American lecture, "What Is English Literature," begins:

> One cannot come back too often to the question what is knowledge and to the answer knowledge is what one knows.
> What is English literature that is to say what do I know about it, that is to say what is it. . . .
> Knowledge is the thing you know and how can you know more than you do know.

In the American lectures there is more of a childish cuteness that convinces you that Gertrude Stein really never grew up. Thus:

> What is the use unless everybody knows what I want to say and what is the use if everybody does want to know everything that I want to say.

She will pause often to be "cute" with her audience. Thus:

> Oh yes you do see. You do see that . . .
> And so I know that it is.
> That is natural enough.

What is it . . .

Do you quite see what I mean. I know quite completely what I mean . . .

All the lectures are wonderfully revealing about the author herself. In one, "The Gradual Making of *The Making of Americans*," she defends her habit of doing all the talking.

I always as I admit seem to be talking but talking can be a way of listening . . . And I began very early in life to talk all the time and to listen all the time. At least that is the way I feel about it. I cannot remember not talking all the time and all the same feeling that while I was talking while I was seeing that I was not only hearing but seeing while I was talking . . .

It was not altogether convincing. If you do all the talking, what is there to listen to? A few sentences later Miss Stein informs us almost unconsciously that the great subject of her life— herself—was cultivated early.

While I was at college and doing philosophy and psychology I became more and more interested in my own mental and physical processes and less in that of others.

In that respect she never changed.

Eight years later, in 1934, I saw Gertrude Stein again. I was back briefly in Paris working on the Paris *Herald* until I could find a better job. As with the first time, she wanted some publicity —why else should she invite over such an unknown as me? I found her in a happy mood. She who had craved general recognition as a writer had at last received it. Her *Autobiography of Alice B. Toklas,* which unlike all her other work was written in a simple, light narrative style, had just become a best seller in America and she was going home for the first time in ages to help promote it and—unbelievably—to go on a lengthy lecture tour from coast to coast. She was as happy as a child.

"I'm a celebrity at last!" She smiled. "And I love it. And the money from royalties is coming in—the first I've ever earned. I'm excited." She had lived her whole life on a comfortable inherited income. The prospect of earning money from writing had never occurred to her. And now that she was earning it she was delighted as a boy or girl who has made his or her first dollar.

I found Miss Stein also happy about the prospects of seeing in America a performance of her opera, *Four Saints in Three Acts,* which her friend Virgil Thomson had put to music. We got to talking about music and I find a note of this conversation expressing surprise at not only her ignorance of music but lack of interest in it, except of course for what Thomson was doing for her libretto. I had not yet read the Toklas book in which she remarks that "music she only cared for during her adolescence. She finds it difficult to listen to it, it does not hold her attention." But then nothing did but herself. Still, she seemed to me this time more mellow and relaxed, as if achieving recognition at last from the general public had eased a great burden of frustration she felt she had borne too long.

By this time she had broken completely with Hemingway. In fact, as I soon found from a copy of the "autobiography," she had said her farewell to him with surprising malice. She had resented, as had almost everyone else in Paris, Hemingway's spiteful parody of Sherwood Anderson in *The Torrents of Spring,* a curious lapse of taste by one who had been befriended and encouraged by Anderson in the apprentice days in Chicago. Anderson had given him letters of introduction to Miss Stein and others in Paris and had continued to praise him. Anderson, whom I saw that second year of mine in Paris, was hurt, but he tried not to show it. Now in the "autobiography" Gertrude Stein brought in Sherwood Anderson and made him share—perhaps unjustifiably, for he was the last man to hold a grudge—a contempt for Hemingway that had long been festering in her.

> Gertrude Stein and Sherwood Anderson are very funny on the subject of Hemingway. The last time that Sherwood was in Paris they often talked about him. Hemingway had been formed by the two of them and they were both a little proud and a little ashamed of the work of their minds. . . .
>
> And then they both agreed that they have a weakness for Hemingway because he is such a good pupil . . . it is so flattering to have a pupil who does it without understanding it, in other words he takes training and anybody who takes training is a favorite pupil. They both admit it to be a weakness. Gertrude Stein added further, you see he is like Derain. You remember Monsieur de Tuille said, when I did not understand why Derain was having the success he was having that it was because he looks like a modern and he smells of the museums. And that is

Hemingway, he looks like a modern and he smells of the museums.

But what hurt Hemingway most, his friends later said, was Miss Stein's crack that he was yellow, he who had written so much about "courage under pressure" and certainly believed he had shown it. But Gertrude Stein recounted that she and Anderson "admitted that Hemingway was yellow, he is, Gertrude Stein insisted, just like the flat-boat men on the Mississippi river as described by Mark Twain."

To be sure, in this book, Miss Stein kept professing her gratitude to Hemingway for having got published an excerpt from *The Making of Americans* and for paying her court when he was very young, green and unknown. "She always says, yes sure I have a weakness for Hemingway. After all he was the first of the young men to knock on my door. . . ."

For some time after an initial cooling they did not meet. Miss Stein had not liked what she saw of the manuscript of *The Sun Also Rises* and told Hemingway so. "There is a great deal of description in this, she said, and not particularly good description. Begin over again and concentrate, she said." Hemingway had not taken her advice—something she could not easily forgive —and perhaps she had not welcomed the acclaim his first novel soon received. Finally they met again, only for Miss Stein to accuse the bohemian young author of being "after all ninety percent Rotarian." According to the "autobiography," in "their last conversation she accused him of having killed a great many of his rivals and put them under the sod."[1]

Hemingway tells the story of the last meeting quite differently. He had been incensed at reading what Miss Stein had written about him. He had thought first of answering her in *Esquire* but then desisted, he told its editor, because he disliked taking pot shots at former friends—to attack her now would be like "socking" a dummy or a ghost. But he was angry enough to insert a piece in his book on an African safari answering Miss Stein's taunt that he was "yellow." All her former talent, he wrote, had now degenerated to "malice and nonsense and self-praise."[2]

[1] The quotations from Miss Stein are from her *The Autobiography of Alice B. Toklas,* pp. 210–220 (paperback edition).
[2] Carlos Baker: *Ernest Hemingway—A Life Story,* p. 267.

Hemingway waited a long time to tell of the final break, and it was not published until after his death. "The way it ended with Gertrude Stein was strange enough," he wrote. On a lovely spring day he had walked down from the Place de l'Observatoire to bid the lady goodbye. She and Alice Toklas were leaving for the south in her rattly old Ford. The maid gave the caller an *eau-de-vie* while he waited, as he had so often, for his hostess to appear. Then something happened.

> The colorless alcohol felt good on my tongue and it was still in my mouth when I heard someone speaking to Miss Stein as I had never heard one person speak to another; never, anywhere, ever.
>
> Then Miss Stein's voice came pleading and begging, saying, "Don't, pussy. Don't. Don't, please don't. I'll do anything, pussy, but please don't do it. Please don't. Please don't, pussy."
>
> I swallowed the drink and put the glass down on the table and started for the door. The maidservant shook her finger at me and whispered, "Don't go. She'll be right down."
>
> "I have to go," I said and tried not to hear any more as I left but it was still going on and the only way I could not hear it was to be gone. It was bad to hear and the answers were worse. . . . That was the way it finished for me, stupidly enough . . .[1]

If the way it ended for Hemingway was "strange enough," his account of it is even more strange for the reader. Everyone, including Hemingway, knew that Gertrude Stein and Alice B. Toklas had lived together as lesbian lovers for a quarter of a century, and that all lovers of whatever relationship quarrel. Even given Hemingway's well-known aversion to homosexuals and their relationships—in the same book he writes "I must admit that I had certain prejudices against homosexuality"—it is more curious that a man who had lived so fully and observed so much would have been shocked at overhearing a quarrel of two homosexual women who had lived together for so long. That the shock was so great that it ended a long and close friendship in the matter of a few seconds is a mystery. It is somewhat out of character for Hemingway.

Was what he overheard a lovers' quarrel about himself? Miss

[1] Ernest Hemingway: *A Moveable Feast,* pp. 116–117 (paperback edition).

298 | 20TH CENTURY JOURNEY

Toklas made no bones of her dislike of Hemingway. Perhaps she was jealous. "Don't you come home with Hemingway on your arm," she told her companion once.[1] She believed that there was a strong sexual attraction between her friend and the young writer and once, in 1924, when she felt it had become unbearable for her, she left 27 Rue de Fleurus for a time. "I had to get rid of him," she later told one of Miss Stein's biographers.[2] Did she choose that day as Hemingway waited in the salon sipping his *eau-de-vie* to do it? It was not the first or last time that Miss Toklas, seemingly so self-effacing as she sat at her needlework while Gertrude Stein regaled the writers and painters who came to the Rue de Fleurus, insisted on her friend getting rid of someone. Virgil Thomson, a close friend of both of the women, cites other cases and says that once in his presence, long after the rupture with Hemingway, Miss Toklas ordered her companion to break with the young French poet Georges Hugnet, with whom Thomson believes Gertrude, from the evidence of her love letters to him, had fallen deeply in love at a time when she was fifty-six and he twenty.[3]

I saw Gertrude Stein for the third and the last time ten years later, in 1944, soon after the American Army, with which I was briefly a war correspondent, entered Paris. It, too, was a strange occasion. Miss Stein and Miss Toklas, though they were Jewish, had refused to leave France, even after the Germans had occupied southern France, where the pair had taken refuge, and the Nazis had begun to root out the Jews and send them to their deaths in the extermination camps. But the two American women had not been molested and as soon as Paris was liberated they returned to the capital and to the new apartment in the Rue Christine into which they had moved the year before the war.

To my astonishment Gertrude Stein had become the darling of the American G.I.'s and she loved it. I doubt if many of these soldiers had ever heard of Gertrude Stein before they entered Paris that late summer and I doubt even more that more than two or three of them had ever read her or could read her. But it made no difference. They loved her as she held open house for them in her new apartment. A famous writer carries some kind of aura

[1] Gertrude Stein: *The Autobiography of Alice B. Toklas*, p. 220.
[2] Virgil Thomson in *The New York Review of Books*, April 8, 1971, p. 4.
[3] *Ibid.*

even for the illiterate. But it seemed to me a rather curious role for the kind of woman Miss Stein was, though there was no doubt that she was enjoying it. In her childish hunger for adoration from the young she was at least consistent. When I had first met her in the mid-twenties she had got this from the young American writers in Paris, and now, in the mid-forties, she was getting it from the young G.I.'s. In her last days she seemed, too, to have become a rousing American patriot, she who by choice had been expatriated for forty years.

"These G.I.'s, aren't they wonderful!" she beamed as she looked over her flock sprawled on the floor munching cookies and drinking wine or, most of them, Coke. "They make me patriotic all over again. Of course I was always patriotic. I was in my way a Civil War veteran, but in between there were other things, but now there are not other things. We are all Americans, aren't we, boys," she said, turning to her admirers on the floor, and they shouted back their agreement. She was forever spouting the obvious. We were not Chinese, obviously, or even French or English or Germans.

Miss Stein had seen something of the American doughboys in France in the first war and she pretended to feel very strongly that there was a great difference between them and the G.I.'s. You could see it in the language, she said. It had changed. The doughboys had not yet possessed it, she explained. But the G.I.'s had.

"The G.I. Joes have this language that is theirs . . . they dominate their language and in dominating their language which is now all theirs they have ceased to become adolescents and have become men. They've become," she went on, "more American, all American, and the G.I. Joes show it and know it, God bless them."

So far as I could remember from the talk of the returning doughboys I had seen at home and at Camp Funston during the summer of my foolish soldiering after the first war, *their* language had been just as expressive as that of the G.I.'s, with whom I spent most of the fall of 1944 up at First Army front. But I did not argue. I guess I never argued with Miss Stein.

Later I read her last book, *Brewsie and Willie,* in which she attempted to get down in print the G.I. language that she had suddenly become so enamored of. But it was not the language I had heard in the camps, along the roads, around the airfields and up at the front just beyond the German border that year, nor was it a literary rendering of it. One had to go to James Jones, Norman Mailer and others for that.

The spectacle of Gertrude Stein at seventy holding this kind of a salon in Paris did not jell, it did not pour, as she had said of other occasions, and I left rather depressed. She would never grow up, and now she was seventy. She died in Paris two years later, on July 27, 1946.

Was Gertrude Stein a great writer, as she so confidently believed? I doubt it. "She realizes that in English literature in her time she is the only one. She has always known it," she boasted once. This was preposterous, but her vanity knew no limits. That she had a certain influence on Sherwood Anderson and Hemingway, there can be no doubt. They got under their skins some of the rhythms, the paring down of description to the bare bones, and especially the patterns of repetition she practiced, though they had artistry enough to keep the repetitions under control, which she, with her "a rose is a rose is a rose,"[1] lacked the discipline and the discernment to do. Her repetitions became tiresome beyond endurance. They often struck me as smart-aleck and reminded me of the rambling of a child.

I realized in the years in Paris and Europe, and I realize even better today in my old age, that there are many things I do not understand and at least a few authors whose writings are beyond my grasp but whom others praise. Gertrude Stein has had her admirers. Edmund Wilson at the time of the Toklas "autobiography" thought she was one of the remarkable women of the time, William Carlos Williams was grateful to her for a certain breakthrough in our language, and other good critics have written well of her. Books about her and her work continue to pour out. She intrigues the literary scholars.

To me she failed in almost everything that makes writers and writing great and memorable. She lacked what all the good writers have had: the power to communicate with her readers. One thinks of Tolstoy, Dostoevsky, Dickens, Balzac, Stendhal, and our own fine novelists between the wars, Faulkner, Heming-

---

[1] No doubt a rose is a rose is a rose, though, as someone added, so, too, a pose is a pose is a pose.

way, Dos Passos, Fitzgerald. Unlike them and unlike two of her contemporaries, Proust and Joyce, to whom she compared herself more than favorably, she never penetrated the heart of things or of human beings. She could be dazzling with words but there was no substance, no meaning, beneath them.

She lacked the tragic sense of life. There is no hint of human suffering in her writings. She wanted to know, as Hemingway noticed, "the gay part of how the world was going; never the real, never the bad."[1] And in their one meeting Edmund Wilson's impression was of "a quick and original intelligence dealing readily from the surface of the mind with the surfaces presented by life."[2] Perhaps the nature of her life had helped to make her oblivious to the harshness and tragedy of living. She had seemed to remain all her life the protected child, living—with the exception of the royalties from the "autobiography"—on an inherited income which while not very large apparently was adequate to sustain a comfortable life isolated from the poor, the wretched, the troubled, the wounded, the defeated.

With her torrent of repetitious words and phrases and sentences which often degenerated into mumbo jumbo, she asked, as someone has said, the American language to bear too heavy a burden. Words were not enough, however cleverly strung together. Great literature demanded more: that words convey substance, meaning, something that matters to the guts, the heart, the mind.

The most beautiful and wondrous of the three noted American women I met that eventful year in Paris, and the greatest artist, was Isadora Duncan.

One day around noon I was sitting in the slot of the *Trib* copy desk, filling in for the city editor on his day off. Except for me, the newsroom was deserted. I was glancing through *Paris-Midi* to see what the early news looked like. Suddenly I felt a tapping on my head and shoulder, and before I could look around, a pair of lovely arms locked about my neck. When they released me I turned to see who my tormentor was. She was one of the most beautiful women I had ever seen. I had seen photo-

[1] Ernest Hemingway: *A Moveable Feast*, p. 25.
[2] Edmund Wilson: *The Shores of Light*, p. 585.

graphs of her, and once, I recalled in a flash, had caught a glimpse of her at the Dôme on my very first evening in Paris. It was certainly Isadora Duncan, the great American dancer. You couldn't help but recognize her instantly. I was thrilled. She was furious.

"I've come to raise hell with your impossible paper," she began. "You've been printing more lies about me."

I pulled out a chair and invited her to sit down.

"No. I will stand up," she said. "I'm too furious with you to sit down. Why do you print all those lies about us?"

Us? I did not understand.

"About me and my poor beloved late husband," she said.

My mind began to clear, though I was torn between gazing into the lovely face of this dynamic woman, whom I had admired from afar for her dancing and for what I had heard of her rich and unconventional life, and listening to her angry complaints. I began to remember a few things I had read in the newspapers.

She had been briefly married to the raging Russian peasant poet Serge Essenin, seventeen years her junior, and there had been accounts in the newspapers and magazines of wild scenes in hotels in Berlin, New York and Paris in which he had broken the furniture, torn down the chandeliers and threatened to toss her out the windows. In glancing through some old files of the *Trib* I had come across a piece—in 1923, I think it was—in the form of a letter she had forced our newspaper through her attorneys to publish denouncing us for what we had written of an alleged scene between her and her violent young husband in the Hotel Crillon. I remembered very clearly now, as she talked on, reading in the newspapers that the body of Essenin had been found a few days after last Christmas hanging from a hook in the very room in the Hotel d'Angleterre in Leningrad where he and Isadora Duncan had first gone after their marriage in Moscow in 1922, when she was forty-four and he twenty-seven. She had received the news in Paris on last New Year's Eve, and though she had left Essenin the year before—the marriage apparently had been an ugly mess from the beginning—she was reported to be deeply stricken. We had duly mentioned this in the *Trib* but she had not liked the way we had done it. Now obviously, though I had not seen it, we had published something that further enraged her. But there was nothing unpleasant about her anger. I sat there, as a matter of fact, listening to her, enthralled. Though she kept scolding me, I was immensely attracted to her. I hoped she would talk on and on.

"You're very young, aren't you," she finally said. "Have you the faintest idea what I'm talking about?"

"I'm trying to understand," I said. In fact I wanted to hear more, just so she would not suddenly go out of my young life—she had come into it so suddenly and unexpectedly. So I made, what for me, was a bold move.

"What about talking it out over lunch?" I suggested.

"Fine," she said, smiling for the first time. "Will you take me out to lunch? Maybe that will calm me down."

"Will you wait half a second?" I said, and went into another room, called the city editor, explained the situation, and said I was taking the great Isadora Duncan out for lunch—it was the only way to appease her—and that it might be a lengthy afternoon and that probably I would not get back until much later. He heartily approved.

"Be sure and get the bill and put it on your expense account," he said. "And for God's sake, calm her down. She threatened to sue us once, you know. Talk her out of it if she tries to bring *that* up."

It did not prove necessary. By the time we got into a taxi to Fouquet's her mood had completely changed. She forgot what it was that had so angered her, or at least she did not bring it up. Over some good food and wine—and I ordered dishes and vintages I could never have afforded myself—she began to talk of herself and above all of her Art. She was self-centered, like all great artists, but not megalomaniac like Gertrude Stein. I sat beside her entranced. She had reddish hair that hung long over her shoulders, large luminous eyes that looked bluish-green to me, a strong, slightly upturned nose and a rather sensuous mouth. It was hard to keep from gazing at her neck and arms as she talked. I had never seen a woman's neck quite so harmoniously proportioned and with such beautiful lines and contours. The arms had the grace of those of a Greek goddess that one remembered from the statues and friezes at the Louvre and the British Museum. She had a resonant voice, rather low in pitch. And though she had lived most of her stormy life in Europe and spoke, I had read, French, Italian and German, she had not lost her American accent, which was as pronounced as mine.

She began to speak of her hopes that her former home in

Neuilly, which she had been forced to sell for a song, would be restored to her so that she could make of it what she called a new Temple to the Dance. A committee was being formed in Paris, she said, to buy it back. Her life, she went on, had been divided— if you left love out—between dancing and teaching the dance. It would have been easier if she had stuck solely to her dancing. It had brought her fame and a fortune. But she had been obsessed by the dream of teaching the young. Did I know, she asked, that she had founded schools in Athens, Berlin, Moscow, Paris and even in New York? Unfortunately all in turn had gone under.

"How?" I asked. "Why did they go under?"

"Lack of money," she laughed in a sort of sigh. "Always the lack of money, though I spent almost all I made on them, and it was a lot. Maybe, like all artists, I had no business sense. But I made up for it in work, in dedication. It was a dream I couldn't let go of. It brought me disaster, time and again, and left me broke."

The idea of being broke seemed to intrigue her. "I've been broke most of my life." She laughed again. "And I'm broke now. Despite all I've made. Millions. And all the help from rich friends. But I go on. I shall devote the last years of my life to this new school in Neuilly. It will be a temple—not only to the dance but to all the arts, music, poetry, drama." Her enthusiasm, her passion, were utterly convincing. I could imagine this new temple rising as the center of art in Paris, the crowning glory of her life. And, child that I was, I began to imagine falling in love with this beautiful and unique genius of a woman. I was already worshiping her. Maybe she noticed.

"Will you take me home?" she suddenly asked. I had not noticed the time racing by. I looked around. The restaurant had nearly emptied. "There's a lot more I want to talk to you about," she said.

"That would be wonderful," I blurted. I should have gone back to the office. But at the moment I couldn't have cared less if I never saw it again. We finished our champagne. I paid the bill, which was on the *Tribune*, and out on the Champs Élysées I hailed a taxi and we drove to her apartment.

She had just moved into the new Studio-Hotel in the Rue Delambre behind the Dôme in Montparnasse. She ushered me into a large two-story studio, rather sparsely but comfortably furnished, with a long plush divan near the big window and a baby-grand piano opposite. Above was a narrow balcony running along one side of the room, off which, I gathered, were bedrooms and a bath. On a small table I noticed a photograph of Eleonora Duse, the great Italian actress and love of the poet D'Annunzio. It was a sad, haunting face.

"I saw her when I was a child," I said. "I have never forgotten."

"Ah, Eleonora! How I miss her," Isadora responded, and I remembered that Duse had died only a year or so ago. "What a tragic life! Full of so much sorrow. But what a spirit! What an artist! No one compared with her on the stage." She hesitated a moment. "She was my close friend. Especially in time of need. Above all, the time right after my children were drowned and I felt I couldn't go on living. I went to her in Italy, somewhere in the countryside. She grieved with me. She saved my life."

We sat down on the divan.

"I wanted to talk with you about my memoirs," Isadora said. "Perhaps you could help me." She turned to me with a wonderfully quizzical look in her eyes. "Would you like to?"

"I would love to," I said. By this time I would have done anything she asked.

She reached for a couple of bundles lying on a table. One seemed to be typed manuscript, the other in her own handwriting. She started leafing over the latter and was obviously bemused. She emitted little bursts of laughter as she perused it.

"My God!" She laughed, putting the bundle down at her side. "I'm halfway through the damn thing and I'm still a virgin!" The idea seemed to her so comical that she laughed and laughed. "I've got to come to grips with love," she finally said. "My first love. It was in Budapest, you know. I finally lost my innocence there. And I was certainly no longer in my teens."

I could not think of anything to contribute to this interesting subject. It must have happened a long time ago. According to the legend at least, she had had many great loves in her life.

"It was in Budapest," she said and for a moment the memory made her face radiant. "I fell madly in love. I'm calling him 'Romeo' in the book. He was playing Romeo in Romeo and Juliet in Budapest when I arrived to give my first performance there. He was the most beautiful young man I had ever seen."

From what she said it was obvious that there had followed a very passionate affair, but it had not lasted long. The young actor apparently proposed marriage but made it plain that he expected Isadora to give up her career and content herself with being his devoted wife, gazing upon him in the evenings from a box in the theater as he played his great roles on the stage. At such a preposterous proposal, Isadora, as she described it in her memoirs, "felt a strange chill and heaviness." She fled from the very idea and from the young man.[1] She would tell the story of this first love and first disillusionment in love fully and dramatically in the memoirs. She must have written it shortly after this first meeting of ours, for it seemed to be bubbling up through the layers of her memory. And recalling the beginning love led her back to her last, Essenin, for a moment, and how shabbily she thought we had treated him.

He was a genius, a great poet, but unfortunately, she said, he had his moments of madness and things happened for which he was not really responsible. Such men, no more than she, should never marry. Though she had had two children, tragically drowned in the Seine just before the war, she had resisted marriage to their fathers. She did not mention their names but I knew from my reading that they were, first, Gordon Craig, the English stage designer and son of one of her friends, the great actress Ellen Terry, and then Paris Singer, millionaire heir to the sewing-machine fortune. She had never intended to marry—it complicated an artist's life beyond enduring—but then in Moscow in 1922, when she was "old enough to know better," she said with a wan smile, she had married Serge Essenin, mainly because it seemed the only way to get him out of Russia so that she could have him with her on her tour of Germany and America.

Beside the difference in ages there had been a second difficulty that had contributed to their problems. Essenin spoke only Russian; she knew scarcely a word of the language.

"How did you communicate?" I asked.

"With love." She smiled. "We were terribly in love."

I did not feel I knew her well enough after only a few hours to pose the next question, but she answered it without my asking.

[1] He was Oscar Beregi, a rising young actor in the National Theater, and this first love affair of Isadora's occurred before I was born, in the spring of 1902.

"It was not enough in the long run. You have to communicate with words, too. Not knowing Russian I could not talk to him, or he to me. I could not really appreciate his poetry. Everyone in Russia said it was magnificent, even Gorki told me, and I believed it. But I could not know for myself. Serge used to read his new poems to me. I could feel the music in the words. But I could not understand them. And this he resented—more and more as time went on, though God knows we had so little time together."

It was getting late, and I did not want to overstay my welcome. I hoped she would invite me back. As I got up to go, a slim, dark young man with intense eyes came in.

"This is my young Russian pianist genius," she said, introducing us, but I did not catch his name. He went over to the piano and began sorting out some scores. Obviously he was at home here. I felt a tinge of jealousy. He seemed even younger than I.[1]

"Come back again," she said to me. "We have open house here almost every evening, and you're invited. But perhaps you could drop by in the afternoon sometimes to help me with these memoirs."

I said that I could and promised that I would. In somewhat of a daze and feeling at the top of the world, I left.

In the ensuing time—there would not be much for though we could not know it she had less than a year to live—Isadora Duncan told me something of her life and loves, her art and her ideals, her sorrows and setbacks, and later in her memoirs, *My Life*, I would find it pretty much as she had related it to me in snatches. I suspect that there was considerable editing of her book, not only by a coterie around her whose eager members were not as helpful to her as she thought, but after her death by her publishers, who found themselves with an unrevised manuscript, which they said, however, was given to the public "essentially as she wrote it." Though she had much advice, much of it

---

[1] He was Victor Seroff, a brilliant young Russian pianist, and Isadora's closest friend, I believe, during the last few years of her life. After her death he went to America, where he became a well-known pianist and author of books on music and musicians. He waited until 1971 to publish his biography of his friend, *The Real Isadora*. It is by far the best and, I believe, the most truthful and accurate of the many biographies of the great dancer. It dispels many myths.

probably bad, she wrote the book herself. It is "essentially" hers. There was no ghost writer. I was of little help myself in the half dozen or so afternoons I spent with her during the following months ostensibly giving advice. Invariably she would put the manuscript down and soar off to talking of herself, her life, her art, which was much more interesting to me.

During the few evening parties I went to at her apartment, there was no opportunity to talk of the work in progress. There were too many people, too much general talk. But these evenings remain in my memory. The studio was jammed with Isadora's friends and admirers from the Paris world of art and politics. There were invariably some luminaries from the French Communist Party, among them her old friend Charles Rappaport, its leader in the Chamber of Deputies, a heavily bearded, bespectacled, rotund man with a puckish sense of humor, who when Isadora insisted on declaiming on Communism would loudly threaten to do a Greek dance. It was their little joke apparently, though Isadora, like Lincoln Steffens and some other Americans who had been to Moscow, still believed, in 1926, that the Soviet Union was the wave of the future—Stalin had not yet completely taken over to clamp on the Russian people his brutish dictatorship and to dispose of art and artists and what freedom and life they had. Sometimes two rising young Communist poets, Louis Aragon and Paul Éluard, would be there, and also Paul Vaillant-Couturier, the amiable, witty editor of the party's daily newspaper, *L'Humanité,* and his attractive American wife. No one at that time, at least in Paris, had conceived the idea, later so popular at home, that to associate with Communists at a gay party was to contaminate oneself. Joseph Paul-Boncour, the handsome, silver-haired, silver-tongued orator and Socialist politician, who, I believe, was Isadora's lawyer, was often there, and Cécile Sorel, the beautiful and stately actress from the Comédie Française, who spoke the purest and the most melodious French I had ever heard.

Some time after midnight the talking and the drinking would subside, the young Russian pianist would sit himself at the piano, and Isadora would dance. I sat on the floor entranced. I had never before seen such natural, graceful, rhythmic movements of a human body. They seemed to flow harmoniously out of some intense inner fire. She was nearing fifty and had taken on a little weight. But her dancing was still a magnificent thing. Invariably her last dance would be the carmagnole, her tribute to the French Revolution, in which she glided across the room trailing a bright-red scarf—the scarf that in the end would kill her.

Did she have a premonition of death? I have since wondered. Usually so ebullient, she did have days when she seemed depressed. Her health was failing, she thought. The plans for buying back her old home in Neuilly and making of it a Temple to the Dance were not getting anywhere. She was practically broke, she said, though I wondered how she could constantly entertain as she did—a party in her studio nearly every evening. Advances on her book were coming piecemeal, a few hundred dollars after she turned in each batch of her manuscript. It was far from enough. But her darker moods were brief. Mostly she talked exuberantly and with pride of her life and read me bits of what she was writing down, scarcely able to suppress a chuckle at some of her follies. Some of the peaks and the valleys of that life remained indelibly in my memory: her growing up in San Francisco, her early triumphs in Europe shortly after the turn of the century as she evolved an art of dancing unlike any other.

She had arrived in St. Petersburg at dawn one winter day in 1905 on her first tour of Russia and driving alone to the hotel had witnessed the mournful funeral procession of the workers slain in cold blood by the Czarist police in front of the Winter Palace the day before, January 22—a scene she never forgot. If the Winter Palace massacre was one of the turning points in Russian history, it was equally so, Isadora said, in her own life. "If I had never seen it," she wrote in her memoirs, "all my life would have been different. There before this seemingly endless procession, this tragedy, I vowed myself and my forces to the service of the people and the down-trodden . . . The despairing rage of that dawn was to bear fruit in my life hereafter."[1] True, but considerably later. For in the weeks in Russia that followed, she consorted only with the high and the mighty, the grand dukes, the aristocrats and the rich, living it up at their gala parties and joining them in the quaffing of much champagne. If her gilded hosts mentioned "Bloody Sunday," it would have been only, I suspect, to approve the slaying of the unarmed workers who had gone to the Winter Palace to present a humble petition to the Czar. The

[1] Isadora Duncan: *My Life*, pp. 174–175.

downtrodden workers, they would have assured her, were getting out of hand.

She had met Gordon Craig in Berlin, fallen madly in love with him and borne him a child, Deirdre. Later, in Paris, she met Paris Singer, with whom she had a second child, Patrick. It was a stormy liaison. Apparently a somewhat cultivated rich gentleman of the old school, but with little appreciation of art and artists, he was not cut out for life with a wild artistic genius. Isadora obviously appreciated the luxury he made possible and the monetary support of her school. But they quarreled frequently and separated often. "All money brings a curse to it," Isadora wrote in her memoirs in recalling her life with Singer (whom she refers to only as "Lohengrin"), "and people who possess it can not be happy for 24 hours. If I had only realized that the man I was with had the psychology of a spoilt child . . ."[1]

They were brought together temporarily again by what Isadora always said was the greatest tragedy of her life. In the spring of 1913 Singer had returned to Paris from Egypt after a four-month separation and there had been a reconciliation as the millionaire renewed his acquaintance with the two young children and spoke of at last going ahead with the building of a large theater for Isadora near the Champs Élysées in the heart of the city. He already had bought the property. There was a gay reunion with the children at lunch in an Italian restaurant. Afterward Isadora had to go to a rehearsal—she was performing with six of her pupils at both the Châtelet and the Trocadéro. The children were dispatched home with their nurse in a limousine. Along the Seine the engine stalled, the chauffeur got out to crank it, forgot that he had left the car in reverse gear, and after starting the motor watched horrified as the limousine backed away from him down the bank of the river and toppled over into fifteen feet of water.

Back in the studio Isadora was resting before her rehearsal, munching a chocolate and rejoicing that her lover had returned and that on this spring day she was, as she later wrote, "perhaps the happiest woman in the world. I have my art, success, fortune, love," she told herself, "but above all, my beautiful children."[2]

Singer suddenly appeared and gave out a loud cry.

"The children," he said. "The children—are dead!"

[1] Ibid., p. 247.
[2] Ibid., p. 289.

I do not believe Isadora Duncan ever recovered from that blow. It ended, she said, "all hopes of any natural, joyous life for me—for ever after." There are some sorrows, she said, that kill.

Ultimately, as she had told me, she found solace in the great tragedienne Eleonora Duse, with whom she went to stay in the Italian countryside near Viareggio. Instead of telling her to stop grieving, Isadora said, Duse grieved with her. "Her heart was so great," Isadora would write in recalling this time in her reminiscences, "it could receive the tragedy of the world, her spirit the most radiant that has ever shone through the dark sorrows of this earth." The actress tried to instill in her American friend her own tragic sense of life. "Isadora, don't, don't seek happiness again," she said one day as they walked along the beach. "You have on your brow the mark of the great unhappy ones of the earth . . . Do not tempt fate again."[1] Later, Isadora said, she wished she had heeded that advice.

But she did not. In fits of depression when she was alone she would swim out to sea and hope that she would not have the strength to get back to shore. One afternoon she was lying exhausted on the beach when a young man came up.

"Is there anything I can do for you?" he asked.

"Yes," she replied. "Save me—save more than my life—my reason. Give me a child!"[2]

That night on the roof of her villa he did. It was the last she ever saw of him. The child would come in August, 1914, in Paris, as millions of young Frenchmen were being mobilized for the war, from which more than a million of them would never return. Death was in the air. Isadora's baby, a boy, died a few hours after birth.

In her days of recuperation at Viareggio, Duse had often sung to her a mournful song from Beethoven, *In Questa Tomba Oscura.* It is a song we shall hear again at the very end.

I saw Isadora Duncan for the last time the night Lindbergh landed at Le Bourget Air Field in the spring of 1927. In the preceding weeks I had dropped in on her half a dozen times to "work" on the memoirs and to check up on how a rather mysterious committee of admirers was progressing on repurchasing her old Neuilly home for the new school. On February 15 I sat in on a

---

[1] *Ibid.*, p. 310.
[2] *Ibid.*, pp. 312–313.

session of the committee at Isadora's studio and wrote a long piece that night for the *Tribune* saying that the Temple of the Dance was about to become "a reality." The house would be picked up at a public auction. Émile Bourdelle, the great sculptor and long a friend of the dancer—she had been the inspiration of his friezes for the beautiful Théâtre des Champs Élysées—had donated a statue worth fifty thousand francs and other gifts of money were coming in. But somehow the project did not go through, and this was another blow to Isadora, the dashing of still another hope, one of her last. She had envisioned spending the rest of her life developing this final memorial to her art.

All spring, too, Isadora had been sick at heart at the impending execution of Sacco and Vanzetti. She had clipped a newspaper photograph of Governor Fuller of Massachusetts and hung it on her mantelpiece with a scrawl of hers in red ink: "Down with Philistines!" It had been widely hoped that Fuller would commute the death sentences but all he had done that spring was to postpone them. Most of Europe was incensed at what seemed to Europeans a judicial murder. There were riots in Paris and mobs had attempted to storm the American Embassy. I had been assigned to the story and had made the front page, even in Chicago. Several times Isadora asked me to attend protest meetings in her studio. There was no thought of dancing on these occasions. She was angry and spoke bitterly of American injustice. Sometimes she would dash off to a larger meeting of protest in some Paris hall. Occasionally she felt so frustrated she would leave her studio at midnight and go down to the Montparnasse cafés around the corner to express her feelings to the throng at the tables along the sidewalk.

One night she got into a violent discussion at the Select with Floyd Gibbons, a legendary war correspondent of the Chicago *Tribune,* who had lost an eye at Château-Thierry and wore a black patch over it. Gibbons, who always supported the status quo, made the mistake of defending the execution of the two Italian anarchists—"They were given a fair trial," he contended. This made Isadora furious and brought Gibbons a tongue-lashing such as, I believe, he had never heard before. Soon sympathizers on both sides joined in and there was a fray with glasses and saucers hurled about until the police intervened to break it up.

Sacco and Vanzetti were scheduled to be executed in Boston that evening, and even after the fracas had been quelled Isadora could not calm down. It was beginning to rain, but undaunted she set off down the Boulevard Raspail, followed by a small crowd, and marched on for two miles to the American Embassy, on the other side of the Seine. There before the locked gates of the Embassy, guarded by a platoon of steel-helmeted gendarmes, she held high a burning taper and kept a silent vigil in the chilling drizzle for the rest of the night. At dawn an American reporter arrived and informed her that the executions had again been put off.

"Thank God!" Isadora sighed and quietly left.

I thought of her in a new way that spring. To me she had become something of a saint.

She despaired of her own country. The execution of Sacco and Vanzetti would be the last straw. "It will put a lasting curse on our poor country," she kept saying.

Her feelings toward her native land were aggravated, I think, by the memory of her last tour in America four years before. It had been a disaster. She had been treated savagely and shabbily, and this had both perplexed and somewhat embittered her. She had not been prepared for the anti-Bolshevik hysteria in America after the war. Arriving in New York, she and her young Russian poet husband were whisked off the boat and taken to Ellis Island, searched, and interrogated for twenty-four hours until at last they satisfied the immigration authorities that they had not come to contaminate America with "godless Communism." Resentful at such a reception in her own country Isadora could not refrain from haranguing her audiences at the end of a performance. At Symphony Hall in prim Boston she let go, blasting her audience for its Philistinism and chauvinism, and finally, flaunting her traditional red scarf, shouting: "This is red! So am I! It is the color of life and vigor." Several elderly ladies and gentlemen stamped out of the hall enraged, muttering that the woman was a Bolshevik and ought to be deported to red Russia. Next day Isadora read the headlines.

RED DANCER SHOCKS BOSTON
ISADORA'S SPEECH DRIVES MANY FROM BOSTON HALL
DUNCAN IN FLAMING SCARF SAYS SHE'S RED

The Honorable James Curley, mayor of Boston, calling the dancer's performance "disgraceful," revoked her license for any further appearances. Isadora had similar experiences in nearly every other city on the tour. In Chicago the fire-and-brimstone evangelist Billy Sunday told his worshipers that the great dancer was nothing but a "Bolshevik hussy" and that she ought to be sent back "to Russia and her Gorki."[1] The mayor of Indianapolis threatened to pack Isadora off "in the wagon if she goes pulling off her clothes. Isadora," he told reporters, "ain't foolin' me any." Essenin, lonely and frustrated in a country whose language he could not speak and which had never heard of him as a poet, was of no help. He drank too much bad Prohibition liquor and smashed up the furniture. He did not endear himself to the staid Bostonians when he showed up for Isadora's performance at Symphony Hall in a Cossack's uniform, complete with a large dagger in his belt. In the hubbub at the end he was accused by a Boston newspaper of having waved a red flag and shouted "Long live Bolshevism!"

Though she refused to call off her tour, as the press urged, or to cease her defiance of the Philistines, Isadora was sick at heart. She had not expected such treatment from her fellow-Americans. Soon after New Year's, 1923, she gave a final performance in New York and booked passage to Europe on the first available boat. It was the last time she saw her native land. She knew it was to be the last. To reporters at the dock she said: "This is the last time you will ever see me in America . . . So goodbye, America! I shall never see you again!"

I was surprised to see Isadora at Le Bourget the night Lindbergh landed. Her young Russian friend was with her. They had been en route for dinner at Chantilly, they said, and, like everyone else in Paris that evening, had been caught up in the traffic that was pouring out to the airfield after news had come that Lindbergh had been sighted off the coast of Ireland that afternoon. Isadora looked wan but she was as excited as all the rest of us at the prospect of witnessing the arrival of the first man and plane to fly across the Atlantic to Paris. There was an unholy jam of people in the little terminal but we managed to edge toward the bar, where Isadora, as usual, ordered a glass of champagne. It was almost impossible to talk above the din and the bustle.

[1] Gorki, the great Russian writer, had scandalized America around the turn of the century by arriving in New York with his common-law wife. Isadora, of course, was legally married to the young man who accompanied her.

"Do you think he will make it?" she kept asking. The French were doubtful, even after the bulletins reporting the spotting of Lindbergh's plane. They had lost two of their great aviators, Nungesser and Coli, a couple of weeks before. I had covered their take-off for New York from this very airfield. Nothing was ever seen of them again and presumably they had gone down in the Atlantic. It had depressed me—death so suddenly for two brave men I had seen fly off so jocularly and hopefully into the dawn. A Frenchman next to us was talking of them, and Isadora mentioned how saddened she had been when no news came from the two flyers. The Frenchman had drawn certain conclusions and insisted on airing them.

"How can a lone American in a ramshackle plane make it," he said, "when two great French pilots of much more experience and in a much better plane—the best France could make—failed?"

"Why not?" Isadora answered. She seemed to light up with pride that an American seemed on the verge of succeeding.

The crowd, which jammed every inch of the small terminal, the restaurant and the observation roof above, grew more and more excited as the minutes passed and darkness began to close over the airfield. Outside, tens of thousands were milling about. Every few minutes, at the sound of a plane overhead, everyone would dash out of the terminal and join these outside in pushing toward the runway along which the lights had now been turned on. In one of the melees, Isadora and her companion disappeared. I had long since lost track of them when the plane we had been waiting for touched down at 10:24 o'clock and pandemonium broke loose and we reporters fought our way through the dense sea of wild, jubilant, shouting, pushing bodies to try to get to the new American hero. Someone later said they saw Isadora join in the delirious cheering. She was so excited she tossed her hat in the air.

I spent most of that summer on an assignment in London, and Isadora, I heard, after a performance at the Mogador in July, went down as usual to the Riviera. Except for a fortnight covering the tennis at Wimbledon, it was a rather miserable interlude for me, torn away from Paris and from Yvonne for the first time, and not taking to the grime and ugliness of London, the bad food, the absence of sidewalk cafés and chic women, the depressing blight of unemployment and poverty and slums, the sight of the conspicuous luxury of the rich in their great town houses and country estates, and the arrogance of the upper classes, who ran the place and indeed, as they still believed, most of the world.

Returning toward the end of August to help cover the national convention of the American Legion, which was to take place in Paris in mid-September to celebrate the tenth anniversary of the arrival of the American Expeditionary Force in France, I was caught up first in the renewed rioting over Sacco and Vanzetti. These two martyred Italo-Americans, the first a shoemaker, the second a poor but poetic fish peddler, whom I believed to be the innocent victims of a vicious frame-up, were executed a few minutes after midnight August 22 at the State Prison at Charlestown, Massachusetts. The next evening Paris exploded with rage and hundreds of riot police had to be called out to protect the American Embassy from being sacked and burned by a huge and angry mob. Covering the riot that evening helped keep my own mind and heart off this frightful legal murder by the complacent Establishment of Boston. It was no consolation to know that it had happened before in America and to recall from my boyhood in Chicago hearing my father tell of the "judicial murder" of the unfortunate martyrs of the Haymarket riot—they, too, had been dubbed anarchists and enemies of American society and so had to die. I kept thinking of what Isadora Duncan would have done had she stood with me as the mob tried to storm the Embassy. She would have stood there at the barricades, I was sure, cheering, cheering the furious throng on, flaunting her reddish hair and waving her red scarf.

I did not know how she was faring on the Riviera, though I heard from someone that she was despondent, destitute and wondering where the next meal was coming from. But one discounted such reports. Isadora herself often exaggerated how badly off she was. But not this time, I would learn later, not this last time.

On September 11 she wrote a letter from Nice to her steadfast friend Victor Seroff, the young Russian pianist,[1] who had returned to Paris after helping to get her resettled on the Riviera: "We are in a H— of a fix here . . . We have nothing to eat—and no way of getting out unless I can sell the furniture here . . .

[1] To whom I am indebted for much of the account that follows. See Victor Seroff, *The Real Isadora*, pp. 428–434.

There are a few inspired moments in life and the rest is *Chipuka.*"[1]

Seroff received the letter in Paris on September 14. That evening on the Promenade des Anglais in Nice Isadora Duncan was dead, her neck broken when her old red scarf became entangled in the spokes of the rear wheel of a red, low-slung Italian racing car, a Bugatti, just as it started. Isadora had long had her eyes on that car, Seroff says, since she had first seen it in a display window of a car dealer in Nice. She loved fast driving. And though she could not possibly afford to buy the car she had prevailed on the proprietor to give her a demonstration. A mechanic had driven the car around to Isadora's studio at 9 P.M. to take her for a ride. Eagerly she had got into the Bugatti, wrapped her scarf around her neck against the cool breeze from the sea, and told the driver she was ready. Probably she had not noticed that there were no fenders on the little racing car and that it was slung so low that the rear wheels came up to her shoulders. Certainly she did not notice that the fringes of her scarf had dropped between the spokes. The driver started the motor, shifted gears, accelerated and the car took off with a roar. The pull of the scarf broke her neck in that instant and killed her.

A little group of friends who had stood by mockingly applauding her getting off in the sleek little car was struck dumb. But later they remembered her last words, spoken in the same kidding manner but which in time would have a deep and prophetic meaning to them and to the world.

"*Adieu, mes amis,*" she had cried out. "*Je vais à la gloire!*"

And so she did.

Isadora Duncan was buried on September 19 at the Père Lachaise cemetery in Paris beside the graves of her two children. I pleaded in vain with my boss, Henry Wales, chief of our foreign service, to which I had recently graduated, and with the Paris *Tribune* editors to allow me to cover the last rites of a great American woman. But none of us reporters, they said, could be spared from covering the big story of the day: the parade of twenty thousand American Legionnaires down the Champs Élysées past the reviewing stand where Marshal Ferdinand Foch himself, the generalissimo of the victorious Allied armies, and

[1] A Russian word for nonsense.

General John J. Pershing, Commander in Chief of the victorious American Expeditionary Force, would salute them.

"What the hell," Wales barked at me in his best hard-boiled police-reporter manner, "she was only a dancer."

For several days we had been covering the antics of the boisterous Legionnaires and their wives whooping it up in gay Paree. I had heard of their annual drunken carnival at home, but this was the first one I had seen, and it depressed me. For weeks our Embassy and Consulate had been working with the French police on how to handle the drunk and the disorderly. Bob Murphy, a consul (and later a prominent diplomat under Roosevelt, Truman and Eisenhower), was in charge of this. Several special stations were set up where the good Legionnaires could sober up without being subjected to the usual treatment of the Paris police: a good kicking and beating up. The chief of police, the amiable, pro-American Jean Chiappe, had instructed his charges to go easy on the American war heroes, who, he reminded his men, had helped save France. He had also called upon the Parisians to be indulgent and understanding of these deserving visitors. They might cut up a bit, but they meant well.

For a week now I and other reporters had watched them cut up, taking over the Montmartre night clubs, invading the café terraces, especially that of the Café de la Paix on the Place de l'Opéra, drunk on the wine and liquor that were forbidden at home by Prohibition, bellowing their barbershop tunes on ancient street corners, slapping incredulous French men—and women— on the back, occasionally breaking up the furniture in the night spots and in the hotel lobbies, loud, noisy, rampageous and occasionally violent from alcohol, but on the whole good-natured. Many had never seen Paris before and probably would never see it again. They wanted to make the most of it. Who among them had ever heard of Isadora Duncan that morning of September 19 as they began to assemble around the Arc de Triomphe for the march down the Champs Élysées behind a score of blaring bands, while in another part of the capital, unknown to them, the funeral procession of a fellow-American began the long trek to Père Lachaise.

The authorities had informed the mourners that they must avoid the Champs Élysées because of the Legion parade. So the cortege, led by Isadora's brother, Raymond, in a Greek tunic and sandals, made its way in the drizzle from Auteuil past the

Champs de Mars and the Pont de l'Alma, skirting south of the Champs Élysées, to the Rue de Rivoli, across the river from the Tuileries, past the scenes of so many triumphs of Isadora—the Trocadéro, on the opposite bank; the Théâtre des Champs Élysées, with the Bourdelle friezes inspired by her, beyond the Place de l'Alma; and farther on the Châtelet and the Gaieté-Lyrique, where her dancing had taken Paris by storm in the distant days before the war—then on to the Place de la Bastille, where the workers gathered each July 14 to celebrate the Revolution, and finally to the cemetery, where so many great French were buried and now a great American would be.

At the Rue de Rivoli, Seroff, who marched with Raymond Duncan behind the hearse, reports, the procession was halted by a regiment of Chasseurs Alpins, which was being sent to guard the southern approaches to the Champs Élysées against possible disturbances by sympathizers of Sacco and Vanzetti, who had threatened to break up the Legion parade. The regimental commander, his breast full of medals, raised his sword in salute to the cortege and the regimental colors and the tricolor were lowered.

Only a few hundred faithful had trudged mile after mile in the procession through the rain but at the cemetery several thousand persons were waiting when the cortege arrived. A French poet and friend of Isadora's, Fernand Divoire, spoke briefly, fighting back the tears.

> She was the renovator of the dance. She delivered it from everything that was not human . . . Today there is a void in the hearts of thousands. They saw for an instant the most beautiful representation of Joy that our century has known.

Then a baritone from the Opéra sang the song that Eleonora Duse had first sung to Isadora at Viareggio when she had come in sorrow over the death of her children, Beethoven's "*In Questa Tomba Oscura.*"

> *In this dark tomb*
> *Let me be at rest.*
> *When I was living,*
> *Then it was you should have*
> *Thought of me,*
> *Oh, ungrateful world!*

It seemed to some as though it were Isadora Duncan speaking these last words from the grave.

All this, this last sad chapter, I missed that day, except for a few incomplete reports I read in the French newspapers. The two American newspapers, the New York *Herald* and the *Chicago Tribune*, all but ignored it. Not one reporter from them was assigned to it. They all were needed, as I was, to cover the Legion parade down the Champs Élysées.

FEW ATTEND ISADORA DUNCAN'S
RITES AS COMPATRIOTS PARADE

The small headline was buried on an inside page in the welter of Legion news carried over from page one. The "few" at the last rites had actually numbered more than five thousand. But no reporter had been there who might have corrected the headline. Later Al Laney, the sensitive night editor of the Paris *Herald*, regretted his news judgment. "We published not a line of the moving ceremony at Père Lachaise," he wrote. "But there were fifteen columns about the Legion parade."[1]

"Yes, we wept when we saw her," Élie Faure, the French critic and art historian, once wrote of Isadora Duncan. "We discovered that primitive purity which every two or three thousand years reappears from the depth of our worn-out conscience." And France's two great sculptors of the time, Auguste Rodin and Émile Bourdelle, both friends of Isadora, called her a supreme artist, the greatest dancer they had ever seen.

Perhaps her genius was too large to be comprehended by her compatriots, especially that drizzling September day of 1927 in Paris when she was buried and the Legion bands blared their way down the Champs Élysées.

I had not fully grasped it myself. There had not been time. But though I was never an intimate or close friend, it had grazed me briefly that last year of her tragic life, and I would always be grateful. Not until the years with Gandhi would I again be touched by such greatness in a human being.

[1] Al Laney, *The Paris Herald*, pp. 244–245.

BOOK FIVE

FOREIGN CORRESPONDENT, 1927–1930

Sooner than expected I achieved the goal I had not lost sight of since coming to Paris. Early that summer of 1927 I graduated from the Paris edition of the *Chicago Tribune* to the foreign staff of the home edition. I became a foreign correspondent. Thus at twenty-three I got a fairly early start in an occupation that would fill my days and nights well into middle age. From the outset the job offered more money—fifty dollars a week, in dollars, against the fifteen dollars a week in francs I had been receiving, which with the continuing fall of the French currency had dwindled to the equivalent of twelve and then ten dollars a week. More important, the job opened up the prospect of travel, perhaps adventure, even a bit of glamour. Most important of all, as I saw it, being a foreign correspondent would enable me to do what I now wanted most to do: report at first hand from day to day the events that were making the history of our time—in Europe and perhaps even in Asia, where the *Tribune* also covered the news with its own correspondents.

True, Europe in 1927 seemed to be settling down to a long period of peace, exhausted from the slaughter and destruction of the war that had ended nine years before. It might be that American foreign correspondents would not find much to write about. But already, as I have mentioned, one felt a stirring underneath the placid surface. The Versailles Treaty had not solved the German problem. Germany was defaulting on its reparations. France as a consequence was stalling on paying its war debts to America. The Germans had signed the peace treaty because they were forced to. For the moment, basking in a certain prosperity made possible by loans from America, they were quiet. But as a brief visit to Berlin showed, they had not really accepted the treaty of peace. You felt they were merely biding their time until they were strong enough to break free from it.

The victorious Allies, under the Wilsonian doctrine of self-determination, had restored the independence of Poland and Czechoslovakia; made a new nation, Yugoslavia, from the union of Serbs, Croats and Slovenes; and vastly increased the size of Rumania. The collapse of the Hapsburg Empire had left Hungary and Austria small countries with scarcely the means of self-support. That collapse had also left the successor states without viable economies and burdened with minorities that ran into the millions, and who clamored for self-determination of their own. Farther east, Russia was coming out of the isolation imposed on her by the Allies. It was obvious—by 1927—that the Communist dictatorship after ten years in control would not be overthrown, either from within or from without, and that the Soviet Union, with its vast area and resources and a population far superior to that of any other European country, was still a Big Power that would have to be taken into consideration by the West. This was a prospect that filled the Western citadels of capitalism with foreboding, which was not lessened by the growing strength of Communist parties, controlled from Moscow, in their midst.

Perhaps, after all, there would be plenty for us to write about. The course of history would always be unpredictable. I cannot say, though, that I had the slightest inkling of how it would unfold or, that pleasant summer of 1927 after I turned twenty-three, that soon and for the ensuing eighteen years my job would throw me into the reporting of the turmoil of revolution in India, the rise of Hitler in Germany, the not-so-funny clowning of Mussolini in Rome, the inexplicable decline of the two great civilized Western democracies, France and Britain, the renewed Balkanization of Eastern Europe, the death of the League of Nations in Geneva and the burial of its Wilsonian hopes for peace, and finally, the greatest war and the most savage oppression the planet had ever gone through.

Curiously enough, it was my work as a sports reporter that helped me land a job on the foreign staff. Ignorant as I was of sports and inexperienced in covering the big-time events, my stories of the French tennis championships and an occasional prize fight attracted the attention of the Chicago office, which published them, and of Henry Wales, the chief Paris correspondent of the home edition. The emergence of France's "big four" in tennis, Lacoste, Cochet, Borotra and Brugnon, to challenge the supremacy of the Americans and the Australians, had made tennis in Europe, at Paris and at Wimbledon, important news on the sports pages at home. And the challenge of young Helen Wills added to the interest.

The *Tribune* for some years had had one member of its Paris bureau double at sports. This had been Don Skene, a brilliant, hard-drinking young man who wrote better copy in whatever field than anyone else on the foreign staff. But he was bored by covering the international political and diplomatic scene, was not particularly enamored of life in Europe, as I was, and recently he had quit the *Chicago Tribune* to return to New York to work on the *Herald Tribune* and devote full time to his greatest love, covering sports. There he would become one of the finest sports writers in America. I replaced him, though remaining on the Paris edition. Still, I hoped I would eventually succeed him on the foreign staff.

Maybe covering sports part-time wouldn't have been enough. Then in May, in the midst of reporting the tennis, fate intervened in the form of a young American aviator I had never heard of until a few weeks before. My coverage of the landing of Charles Lindbergh in Paris on the evening of May 21 after the first nonstop transatlantic flight from New York—an achievement that stirred the imagination of the world and made the young American flyer a world hero—apparently cinched the job. It was the biggest and most exciting event I had ever covered. In fact, it was the biggest news story of the year, in Europe as well as in America. The staid *New York Times* gave it a three-line banner headline on the front page, a treatment usually reserved only for declarations of war or the conclusion of peace, and devoted all of page one to it, and all of the four following pages, though it was a Sunday, when the *Times*, like all morning newspapers, went to press early and the story had broken late—at 4:30 P.M. Saturday, New York time.

All that fine spring of 1927 the public on both sides of the Atlantic had been aroused by the prospect of the first nonstop flight from New York to Paris or from Paris to New York. Eight years before, on June 14–15, 1919, Captain John Alcock, a British pilot, and Lieutenant Arthur W. Brown, his American navigator, had flown nonstop across the Atlantic for the first time in history, covering the 1,960 miles from Newfoundland to Ireland, where they landed in a peat bog, in sixteen hours and twelve minutes. It had been a rough flight through fog and ice, "a terrible journey," Alcock reported. The flight from New York to Paris or vice versa would be even tougher. It was nearly double the distance, some 3,600 miles.

Despite eight years since then of development of both flying machines and motors, there still seemed to be by 1927 no airplane capable of covering nonstop the distance between New York and Paris. Captain René Fonck, the great French war ace (he had shot down seventy-five German planes during the war), had tried it the year before, on September 21, 1926, in a huge trimotored plane designed by Igor Sikorsky. But his heavily laden craft had crashed on take-off from Roosevelt Field, on Long Island, killing two of the four-man crew. Still, this disaster did not deter either Fonck or others, who by the early spring of 1927 were determined to attempt the flight. Early in March we had a dispatch from New York saying that it looked like a four-way race: Commander Richard E. Byrd's trimotored Fokker *America,* Lieutenant Commander Noel Davis' trimotored biplane *American Legion,* René Fonck's new Sikorsky, and a Wright Bellanca owned by Charles Levine, an eccentric businessman who was reported to be feuding with his two pilots, Clarence Chamberlin and Bert Acosta. Brief mention was made of a possible "dark horse," an unknown "St. Louis mail pilot named C. A. Lindbergh," who was having a plane built by a small, obscure company in San Diego called Ryan Airlines, and who, unlike the others, planned to make the flight alone.

Aviation experts and the press did not take this dark horse very seriously. They did not believe that a lone man could fly the Atlantic. It would be physically impossible to keep awake or at least alert enough to give constant attention to a plane's controls and navigation instruments for thirty-six to forty continuous hours. All the other planes had crews of two, three, four men. Most professionals called Lindbergh's proposed solo flight foolhardy and even "crazy." Lloyd's of London, which gave odds on the most risky undertakings, refused to quote odds in his case.

Nor were his prospects deemed any brighter when mishaps came during last-minute trials to his competitors in planes far larger and sturdier and with more powerful motors.

On April 16 Commander Byrd's Fokker, with Tony Fokker himself at the controls, crashed on landing after a short test flight and was badly damaged. Byrd's left wrist was broken; his chief pilot, Floyd Bennett, suffered a broken leg and a dislocated shoulder; and the copilot, George Noville, suffered severe internal injuries. Ten days later Lieutenant Commander Davis' plane, *American Legion,* considered by many to have the best chance to succeed in the flight to Paris, dived into a marsh just beyond the runway at Langley Field, in Virginia, after a trial take-off with full load. Davis and his copilot were killed.

Meanwhile, in Paris, we had a transatlantic take-off to cover ourselves. Two seasoned French pilots, who had been among the most illustrious of war aces, Captain Charles Nungesser and Captain François Coli, were readying their specially built Levasseur biplane, *L'Oiseau Blanc,* for a flight from Paris to New York. It had a 500-horsepower motor, the most powerful ever built. With such a plane and such experienced pilots the French felt certain that they would beat the Americans in the friendly rivalry to be the first to make the crossing between Paris and New York. At the end of April, Wales had sent me out to Le Bourget to check on their progress. I found them superbly confident, brushing aside my question as to the wisdom of making an east-west flight against the strong prevailing winds over the stormy North Atlantic. They had no doubt they could make it against the headwinds. Their only concern, they said, was getting off the ground with their heavy load of eleven thousand pounds, but this did not really worry them. They intended, they confided to me, to drop their landing gear as soon as they reached sea.[1] This would greatly reduce wind resistance and increase their speed, they calculated, by fifteen miles an hour.

"How are you going to land in New York—without landing gear?" I asked incredulously.

"Easy." They laughed. "The 'bird' is watertight. We're going to land her in New York harbor. Maybe right in front of your Statue of Liberty!"

[1] There were no retractable landing gears in those days.

They were both brave, likable men with great confidence in themselves and in their plane. "After all, we survived the war," they said. "This flight is much less risky."

All night long on Saturday, May 7, I stood around the hangar at Le Bourget and watched the mechanics loading gasoline and oil, tuning up the engine and checking every inch of the solid plane. Soon one's ears became deafened by the roar of the powerful engine. Nungesser and Coli were in a jubilant mood, wisecracking to their friends. Shortly before dawn that Sunday the last weather reports came in and Nungesser made the final decision to go. He embraced his wife, waved to the crowd of several hundred well-wishers, and with Coli scrambled into the open cockpit. The engine was started, revved up and in a moment they were off into the early dawn. The heavily weighted plane seemed to gather speed so slowly that for a moment I was in agony. Down the field it gradually gathered momentum—there were no concrete runways in those days—but the way it was going in the soft grass I did not see how it could become airborne in time. Halfway across the field it lifted half a dozen feet and then hit the ground again. We all gasped. But Nungesser kept going at full throttle. Toward the end of the field the plane finally rose and just cleared the trees. In a moment it disappeared toward the northwest.

It was too late for a story in our Paris paper but I phoned a brief account to Wales's assistant for Chicago, which, six hours behind us in time, still could get it into the late Sunday editions. I was too excited to go home to snatch some sleep. Returning to the office I wrote the story for Monday's Paris *Trib* and waited for the bulletins of the plane's progress. It was reported over the Channel west of Cherbourg, off Land's End and finally at noon over Ireland and heading out to sea. That was the last ever seen of it.

But we did not know of this sad fate for a couple of days. On Monday morning an American news agency reported that the plane had been sighted over Newfoundland headed for New York. This report, broadcast over the radio and in special editions of the newspapers, set off a wild celebration in Paris. Everyone started toasting the success of the historic flight in champagne. Parisians snake-danced through the streets. Offices and stores shut down. I joined in the celebration. To have watched those two brave Frenchmen set off so confidently on so hazardous a flight and then to know they had succeeded filled you with pride in men.

The awakening was an agony. By Tuesday morning it became evident that the report from Newfoundland had been false. The plane had not been spotted on the seaboard by anyone. By now its fuel had run out. It was possible that the plane had crash-landed in some lonely spot in Newfoundland. But as the days passed, this hope, too, had to be abandoned. I went around the rest of the week in a daze of depression. All Paris was in mourning for its lost heroes. French aviation authorities urged that further attempts to link Paris and New York by air this year be called off. The development of the airplane, they said, had simply not gone far enough. It was foolhardy to risk more lives in the enterprise.

Already six lives had been taken: four in the American planes and two in the French, and three men in the Byrd plane had been seriously injured. Voices rose on both sides of the Atlantic asking the American flyers to abandon the project. An officer of the French Air Force, General Duval, issued a statement saying that even if one of the Americans succeeded after the failure of Nungesser and Coli, it would prove nothing. "The crossing," he admitted, "can be made once, perhaps twice, but not as a regular service until there is an enormously greater development of aviation. A single successful trip will only encourage illusion."

And suddenly what had seemed to us in Paris to be a friendly rivalry between the French and Americans to be the first to fly between the two cities began to degenerate into an ugly quarrel. When we informed the American Ambassador, Myron T. Herrick, on May 10 of cables saying that the Bellanca might take off any moment from New York to Paris, he warned Washington that such a flight, "when the fate of the French aviators is still in doubt, might be misunderstood and misinterpreted here."

Indeed, as gloom about the fate of Nungesser and Coli spread over the French capital so soon after the untimely celebration, the Paris newspapers began to publish dark rumors, no matter how unfounded. It was reported that the U.S. Weather Bureau had declined to furnish the French aviators with the latest weather reports over the North Atlantic. One newspaper claimed that the reports had been furnished but that they were deliberately falsified. American wire services were blamed for broadcasting the fake report that the French plane had been sighted over Newfoundland. It was branded as a cruel hoax.

Already there had been anti-American outbreaks in Paris that spring. There was deep resentment that the United States was acting like Shylock in demanding that France pay its war debts to America in full even after the Germans had defaulted on reparations. The threatened execution of Sacco and Vanzetti, as I have noted, further exacerbated French feelings. And they were not improved when the franc tumbled to a new low and brought increasing numbers of rubbernecking American tourists to France to take advantage of it. One day recently in the Place de la Concorde I had seen a sightseeing bus full of gaping Yankees stoned by angry Frenchmen. It was no time, the Ambassador thought, for an American plane to drop out of the skies from New York. It might be torn to pieces by an angry mob.

But the Americans, according to the cables from New York, were going ahead anyway. The dark horse in the race, they said, seemed most determined of all. Lindbergh's small monoplane had finally been completed, and after a few preliminary tests at San Diego, he had taken off in it on the afternoon of May 10 for an all-night nonstop flight over the Rocky Mountains to St. Louis. His backers in St. Louis had tried to dissuade him. They thought it too risky. No one had ever made that flight at night before. But he had insisted. He needed, he said, the experience of dead-reckoning navigation, which he intended to use on the Paris flight. Arriving in St. Louis three hours earlier than he had calculated—he had flown the 1,550 miles in fourteen and a half hours, a record—he was told of Ambassador Herrick's warning against any American attempt to fly to Paris so soon after the loss of Nungesser and Coli.

"I am very sorry," he responded, "that Nungesser and Coli seem to have failed in their brave attempt to cross the Atlantic in the wrong direction. I hope they will be picked up. But their experience, whatever it proves to be, will not affect my plans."

And with that he resumed his flight. On May 13 we received a dispatch that the dark horse in the race had suddenly shown up the afternoon before in New York. Lindbergh had flown his tiny plane, *Spirit of St. Louis,* from San Diego to New York, with one stop at St. Louis, in the elapsed time of twenty-one hours, clipping five hours from the transcontinental record. But he had arrived, it seemed, too late. He was told that the Bellanca, the plane he had once vainly tried to buy, was set to take off at 2 A.M. To increase the tension, Byrd's rebuilt Fokker flew in a few minutes after Lindbergh. It looked now like a three-way race, with the Bellanca favored to get away first. But that night the Weather Bureau reported worsening conditions over the Atlantic and they continued to be bad for the next few days. The departure of the Bellanca kept being postponed. By the time the weather began to clear, the plane was grounded by a court injunction brought by one of its pilots, whom Levine had summarily fired on the very eve of an expected take-off. Lindbergh's chance of getting away first, so forlorn a few days before, had improved. His luck was holding. On Thursday, May 19, we got a cable from Chicago advising that Lindbergh, after all, might be the first to take off, though the weather continued bad, with rain in New York, fog over Newfoundland and a new storm brewing in the mid-Atlantic.

The dispatches still did not take Lindbergh very seriously. Aviation writers were calling him "Lucky Lindy" and the "Flying Fool" and saying he would need all the luck in the world to succeed in the flight. A few experts, we noted, however, reported that he was not only a highly skilled pilot but that he had prepared for the Atlantic crossing more carefully than was generally known, working out the navigation problems and calculating the risks, insisting on every possible check of his plane, motor, instruments and weight load at take-off, the most hazardous moment of all, before he would think of attempting the flight. He was really taking "no tremendous chances," he told the reporters. Still they were skeptical, as were the aviation experts, about a man being able to fly for thirty-six hours over the ocean alone and, at that, in what seemed to them to look like a rather rickety little plane. It didn't even have forward vision from the cockpit, they noted. The main fuel tank had been installed directly in front of the pilot's seat. Lindbergh would have to look out of the side windows to get his bearings and to guide his take-off and landing—if, they added, he ever got off the ground with a full load, which he had not yet done, and if he ever landed. After dark it would be very difficult to put the plane down with such restricted vision, they thought, and the flyer had never done it. He responded with a grin, they reported, that he planned to get to Paris before dark.

. .

Shortly after 1 P.M. on Friday, May 20, as I was getting ready to go out to St. Cloud, as usual, to cover the tennis, a bulletin came into the office saying that Lindbergh had taken off from Roosevelt Field for Paris at 7:52 A.M., New York time. We would have some thirty-six hours to make plans to cover him, if he made it. Not many on our side of the Atlantic thought he would. He had barely got his heavily loaded plane off the ground in time, the cables said. In London, where Lloyd's had refused to quote odds, government circles said the flight was suicidal. On my way to the tennis I stopped off at the headquarters of the International League of Aviators in the Bois de Boulogne, where a number of well-known French and other European flyers were discussing the news over lunch. Most of them said that Lindbergh was a brave man, but crazy. A man could never make such a long flight alone even if his plane held out. Colonel Clifford B. Harmon, a wealthy American aviation pioneer, who was president of the league, summed up the prevailing sentiment.

"I do not think," he said, "that a man can stay awake thirty-six hours by himself with nothing but the sea, sky and air as an environment and a motor roaring away monotonously. If he could only get five minutes sleep, two minutes, or any short catnap now and then, it wouldn't be so bad. But Lindbergh can't afford to risk forty winks. The flight is a desperate thing. But brave!"

I noted down his ominous words for a story that evening and proceeded out to St. Cloud to cover the men's semifinals of the French tennis championships. Five thousand people had jammed the stadium in anticipation of a great match between the American and French champions, Big Bill Tilden and little René Lacoste. This was a tennis-mad crowd, aroused by the prospect of a Frenchman dethroning the great American with the cannon-ball service. There was very little talk among the fans of Lindbergh's departure. I had a few words in the President's Box with Ambassador Herrick, a courtly, kindly old man, of whom I had grown quite fond. Yes, he had heard of the flight, he said, just before leaving the Embassy. He didn't know much about the fellow . . . what was his name? . . . ah, yes, Lindbergh. But I could see that he lacked the feeling of excitement building up in me. No, he said in answer to my question, the Embassy had no plans for a reception. They would have to wait and see. What really aroused him at the moment was the prospect of a titanic struggle between Tilden and Lacoste. Perhaps he had been told by his air attaché that the lone flyer would never make it.

The match over—Tilden won in straight sets, 6–4, 7–5, in a hard-fought duel—I grabbed a taxi and returned to the *Trib* to write my story. But I didn't have much heart in it, dramatic as the match had been. I kept stopping to read the cables telling of Lindbergh's progress up the coast from New York. North of Plymouth, Massachusetts, he was spotted heading out to sea for Nova Scotia, flying only a couple of hundred feet above the water, his plane a little wobbly under the crushing load of 450 gallons of fuel. Around midnight, our time, he had been seen approaching Newfoundland, and a little after 1 A.M., when we had to go to press, he was reported to have circled over St. John's and then, as darkness approached, turned his plane out over the desolate North Atlantic, beyond the range of the last observers on the ground. For the next sixteen hours or so there would be no word of him. In Paris we could go home to snatch some sleep—and to hope.

To my surprise, our managing editor, the good-natured, roly-poly Bernhard Ragner, had not shared my excitement about the flight nor seen it as the great story I was sure it was—if the young flyer made it. He had told me that evening not to bother to write a story about the pessimistic reactions out at the League of Aviators to Lindbergh's take-off, but to turn my notes over to another reporter, who might be able to use them in a wrap-up he was doing. When I asked Ragner if I could go out to Le Bourget to help cover the arrival he said, "Sure. But you have to cover the tennis first." To my disappointment, he assigned the main story to our young city editor, Jules Frantz. But he said I could help. He was already tagging me as a sports writer, I realized, who ought to be content to stick to his subject.

Hank Wales and his young assistant, Jay Allen, of the foreign staff, were entirely different. They were gearing up to cover what they suspected might well be the biggest story of their careers. And they suggested I do a little boning up with them myself if I expected to do a really good story for the local edition. All that Friday night we sat up in the office studying maps, poring over aviation manuals and magazines, telephoning French airmen all over town for their views, and checking in the files the stories of the Alcock-Brown flight and others. Wales was no scholar or even student, as Allen was, but he was shrewd. And he had come up with a plan, he told us, that might get his dispatches to America long before any others. All his competitors would be filing by the American-owned co-op Press Wireless Service or by Western Union Cable, and these services would be jammed with copy. He would take a chance on Commercial Cable, which the American correspondents seldom used. And instead of pounding out the story in the office, as the others would be doing, waiting for messengers to take copy through the Paris traffic to Press Wireless and Western Union, he would install himself at the cable head in the Rue des Italiens and feed his stuff in short takes directly to a telegrapher with a direct line to Chicago. It was a strategy that would pay off. It was also my first lesson in coping with one of the problems of a foreign correspondent: getting the story was only part of the job; the other part was seeing that it got through to your newspaper quickly—if possible, ahead of your competition.

"And when you're through with your story for the lousy Paris edition," Wales said in his best police-reporter manner, "get the hell over to Commercial Cable and give me a hand." It was the first time he had given me any encouragement.

I got to the office early on Saturday morning. There was no news of Lindbergh. No ships at sea on the Great Circle Route had reported spotting him. Some of the Frenchmen in the news-room of *Le Petit Journal* below us thought that was a bad sign, but I argued it was not necessarily so. Perusing the morning Parisian newspapers I noticed a change in the French attitude. Banner headlines proclaimed that Lindbergh was out over the North Atlantic, and there were cables saying that the plane, when circling over St. John's, Newfoundland, seemed to be functioning well and flying very fast. The "crazy" young American might make it, after all, the newspapers informed their readers. He might be in Paris before midnight this day. If so, the Parisians would give him a hero's welcome. All the recriminations about the Americans double-crossing Nungesser and Coli seemed to be forgotten.

I ate a hasty lunch and drove out to St. Cloud to continue my coverage of the tennis. It was a lovely, not too warm, sunny day, with the chestnut trees in full bloom and their scent filling the balmy air. Paris in the late spring was always at its loveliest and this was one of the finest days we had yet had. If Lindbergh made it to Ireland and his gas held out, he would have no trouble landing at Le Bourget. The low clouds and fog of the previous week had evaporated.

The stands were again jammed with tennis fans anticipating a great doubles match between the Americans, Tilden and Francis T. Hunter, and the French champions, Borotra and Brugnon. It was a hard-fought, seesaw struggle with the Americans taking the first set and the French the second. Midway through the third set I noticed activity in Ambassador Herrick's box and went up to see what it was about. The benign white-haired Ambassador was leaving in a hurry. He had just got word from the Embassy, he said. Lindbergh had been sighted over Valentia, Ireland. That would put him roughly only some six hundred miles from Paris. I glanced at my watch. It was a few minutes past 4 P.M. At a hundred miles an hour Lindbergh could be here by ten, an hour after dark. Mercifully, Borotra and Brugnon raced through the last set to take the match, and I hurried back to the office to write it up and then get off for Le Bourget Air Field.

Shortly after six o'clock Lindbergh was reported over Plymouth, England, heading across the Channel toward the Cherbourg peninsula in France. There now seemed little doubt that he would make Paris. Hank Wales came barging into the newsroom to read the bulletin.

"Let's get going!" he grunted, and he, Allen and I bolted down the stairs and hailed a taxi. "Make a note of this for the background story," he told Allen. "Plymouth, Massachusetts, was where he left the American shore. I figure he made Plymouth, England, in a little less than thirty hours. How long did those Pilgrims take by sea? Two months, at least, eh? I want a lot of that sort of stuff in our story tonight."

Hardly had we got beyond the Porte de la Villette on the northeast edge of the city before we ran into a traffic jam such as none of us had ever seen before. Ahead of us lay a solid line of cars, bumper to bumper, barely moving up the narrow two-lane road.

"Where the hell did they all come from?" Wales growled. There were few privately owned cars in Paris in those days, and not even enough taxis when you needed one. But now every motor vehicle in town of whatever sort seemed to have converged on the road to Le Bourget. There were all kinds of little makeshift trucks and three-wheeled motor carts full of shouting young men and women. We had plenty of time—more than three hours before Lindbergh could possibly arrive. We stuck it out for an hour or so and made perhaps two of the four miles to the airfield. Then our patience snapped. We paid off the taxi driver and joined a sea of people who were making it on foot. By the time we got to the terminal, the largest crowd I had ever seen surrounded it and spilled off on the field beyond. It must have numbered more than a hundred thousand and before long, according to police estimates, it would reach close to half a million. Everyone seemed in high spirits and excited, and, like all French crowds I had seen, a bit unruly. Gendarmes kept gesticulating and shouting to keep back, but the mass pushed on. Finally a couple of companies of soldiers who did guard duty on the military side of the airfield across from us came rushing in at the double, bayonets fixed, and for a moment restrained the mob from occupying the grass runway.

Flashing our press cards, we fought our way into the terminal, a small building a tenth of the size of the postwar structures at Le Bourget. We were thirsty and hungry from the long walk in the dust and heat and managed to push ourselves to the bar where we got a carafe of wine and a sandwich. It was there and then that we ran into Isadora Duncan and her Russian friend, had a glass of champagne together, and talked briefly as best we could in the din and the shoving. Shortly after nine o'clock it began to grow dark. Two or three times during the next hour, at the sound of a plane over the field, the crowd would dash out of the terminal and join the sea of humanity on the field. The floodlights along the landing strip would flash on. But they turned out to be only military planes landing on the far side of the field. The crowd grew restless and some voiced their skepticism. "All those reports over Ireland, England and Cherbourg were probably false," a Frenchman addressed me. "Like the ones about Nungesser and Coli. I'm sorry, but I don't think your Lindbergh is going to make it, after all."

The police and Major Pierre Weiss, commandant of the Le Bourget military field, who himself had set a long-distance record the year before by flying nonstop from Paris to Persia, had in the meantime worked out a last-minute plan with Ambassador Herrick for a reception. Lindbergh would taxi up to the terminal between two rows of police and troops and the Ambassador and a Franco-American committee would welcome him in a little ceremony, with toasts in champagne, on the observation deck. Wales instructed Allen to remain with the Ambassador while he and I went out to the field and shoved our way through the crowd to a spot along the runway where the flyer was expected to bring his plane to a stop on landing. There we would be able to catch his first words and put to him some questions about the flight.

By ten o'clock it had grown quite dark. Still no sign or sound of Lindbergh. Wales and I were just approaching the landing lights when we heard a plane above the field. A small searchlight picked it up. There was no doubt this time. All the Paris papers had front-paged a picture of the little plane. And this was surely it. It glided down to the far end of the field, where I had last seen Nungesser and Coli finally get off the ground, banked and came in gracefully between the runway floodlights, touching ground about two hundred yards from us. I glanced at my watch. It was 10:24 of May 21. It seemed incredible. He had flown from New York to Paris, I calculated, in thirty-three and one-half hours, but this was no time to do any more figuring than that. We had to get to the plane by the time it stopped. That proved more difficult than we had foreseen.

All the police and all the soldiers that the authorities had managed to mobilize to keep back the crowd were swept away as the tide of people surged forward past them. It looked to me for a moment as if Lindbergh would be unable to bring his plane to a stop and cut his motor before the propeller shredded the first wild spectators rushing toward him. By luck he stopped a few yards away from where Wales and I were standing. Confidently we pushed forward to greet him. But bedlam had broken out. I saw Lindbergh pushing his tousled head out of the tiny cockpit window under the wings, a wide grin on his face. Then he ducked back as thousands surrounded the plane. When he looked out again his grin was frozen in an expression of dismay. The mob was beginning to climb all over the plane, tearing off pieces of fabric from the fuselage and wings as souvenirs. There was utter confusion and the young man who had just flown alone from New York to Paris in a historic flight seemed for the moment helpless. Finally, I saw two French aviators in uniform fighting their way to the cockpit. One of them, Lieutenant Detroyat, jumped on one wing, took Lindbergh's helmet from his hand and tossed it to the frantic crowd. Hundreds of screaming men and women tried to snatch it. This diverted the crowd for a moment and the two French airmen led Lindbergh away to a nearby car. They also directed Air Force trucks to surround the plane and tow it to a military hangar.

So far as I remember none of us reporters got as much as a word from Lindbergh at that hectic moment—it was not possible—though several would concoct fanciful interviews as they pounded out their stories that night. Wales and I, somewhat downcast, made our way back to the terminal where, on the roof, the American Ambassador and his committee were waiting to receive the hero. We arrived just in time to witness a scene which in retrospect provided the only comedy of the evening. A blond young man with an aviator's helmet, a torn shirt and the remnants of a necktie was dragged before the committee. He certainly looked like Lindbergh. The courtly Ambassador, beaming at last, stepped forward to present him a bouquet of red roses.

"But I'm not Lindbergh, Mr. Ambassador," he insisted.

"Of course you are," Herrick replied, holding out the roses.

"I tell you, sir, I'm not Lindbergh," the young man repeated. "My name is Harry Wheeler. Everyone got confused because of this—" and he held up the crumpled helmet. "Someone threw it to the crowd and I happened to catch it."

"If you're not Lindbergh, then where is he?" the Ambassador asked.

"Some French officers took him to a hangar on the other side of the field while that crazy mob was almost killing me."

The Ambassador finally was convinced, and a young American named Harry Wheeler, after a moment of glory, which he had not sought and not liked, passed into the limbo of the history of this epochal flight and of this brave and gifted flyer, after having contributed through no fault of his own a somewhat comical footnote to it.

While Jay Allen left to make his way across the field to the military hangar to see if he could find Lindbergh, Wales and I lit out for Paris, four miles away. It was already past eleven, late for filing dispatches for the Chicago Sunday edition, which went to press early. Wales had to get off the lead story, and there was no time to lose. But when we pushed our way out in front of the terminal we found the traffic jam even more hopeless than before. There were taxis, but they were unable to move. Among Wales's preparations for the evening had been the scouting of side roads back to the city.

"Willy, we've got to hoof it," he said. "I know some short-cuts." We started to jog down the cluttered main road and then hit off on a narrow lane. Wales was nearly twice my age of twenty-three and had never taken any exercise, I believe, since the end of the war. Soon he was huffing and puffing. But on we ran, until I began to get out of breath myself. We must have run for nearly three miles when we spotted a taxi. The driver had set out for Bourget, got caught in the logjam and was now turning back on this side road.

"A thousand francs to you, monsieur," Wales addressed him as we jumped into the back seat, "if you make it back fast." The man did, racing along the bumpy road and careening around the sharp curves. It was a dilapidated old contraption and I thought it would fall apart before we reached the outskirts, where the pavement would be smoother.

"It must be one of those famous taxis of the Marne," I said.

"Yeah, probably is," Wales grunted. I could see he was formulating the story in his head.

I dropped him off at the office of Commercial Cable opposite *Le Temps* and turned back to our office in the Rue Lamartine. "As soon as you're through, Willy, beat it back here. And bring all the cable stuff there is and the early editions of the French papers." He spoke in his customary rasping voice out of the side of his mouth. As I burst into the newsroom I remembered that Ragner had assigned Frantz, the city editor, to write the main story but there was no sign of him. Perhaps he was not as good a sprinter as Wales and I.

"I guess it's your story," Ragner said, turning to me. "But don't make it too long." He still had not grasped the significance of the event. I argued with him, but to no avail. "Better get going on it," he advised me. By this time it was midnight and we went to press an hour later. I batted out the story as best I could in the state of my excitement and with a deadline only an hour away. Forty minutes later, as I was winding up, Frantz rushed in, breathing hard. He had not found a taxi as we had, and had run the entire four miles. He implored the editor to let him write a follow-up, but got the same treatment I had received the night before. "One story is all I want," said Ragner.

By 1 A.M. I was back at Commercial Cable with Wales, having brought the Havas coverage (Havas was the French news agency) and the early edition of the Paris newspapers along with some telegraphed copy from our London office about Lindbergh's flight over Ireland and England.

"Feed me all you can," Wales growled, looking up for a second from his typewriter. "And when you've finished, get on the phone and find out where the hell the guy is. Allen should know by now!" I knocked out a few pages and Wales handed it over to the telegrapher along with his own takes. Our copy was going out instantly on the cable and I was sure we were getting out the story first.

About 2 A.M. Jay Allen phoned. He was at the Ambassador's residence in the Place d'Iéna. Lindbergh had finally shown up there a few minutes before but the Ambassador had insisted on him getting some much-needed sleep and had put him immediately to bed. Jay sounded glum. No story, even after they had finally tracked the flyer down. Wales grabbed the phone.

"Listen, Jay. Tell Herrick you fellows have got to see him."

"What you think we've been telling the old boy?"

"Well, keep telling him. And if that doesn't work, barge up to the bedroom yourself. We got to talk to him."

"Hold on a second," Jay suddenly said. After a moment he came back. "I think we're going to see him."

"Okay," Wales huffed. "Come directly over here when you've got it. Remember, don't stop off at the office."

Half an hour later Jay rushed in and started to bat out the first interview Lindbergh had given since his landing. Later he told us that just as the Ambassador was trying to shoo the correspondents out of his residence, Lindbergh sent down word that he didn't feel like sleeping and would talk to reporters briefly. The whole dozen of them bolted upstairs to the guest bedroom, where they found the aviator sitting on the edge of the bed clad in oversized pajamas lent him by his host. Simply and modestly he answered questions about his flight. It was the first account of it he had given the press, but by this time Wales and, I believe, most of the other correspondents had already dispatched thousands of words quoting Lindbergh about every stage of his crossing. It was surprising, when I checked up later, how near the mark they had come. It was surprising, too, at least to a cub like me, that the foreign correspondents had put so much trust in their imagination.

We wrapped up the story about 4 A.M. and stopped by an all-night café around the corner on the boulevard for coffee and croissants. Wales was in a surprisingly good mood considering his fatigue. Before we had finished, a cable had come in from Chicago saying his copy was arriving even before that of the wire services. He turned to me as we were devouring a plateful of croissants. He had been glancing at the first page of the Paris *Trib* and running through my hastily written account.

"Not bad," he grunted. "In fact, damn good." As a matter of fact he had used quite a bit of it himself.

"Willy," he finally said in his clipped, out-of-the-corner-of-his-mouth manner, "I think maybe you got what it takes. The secret of this business is to turn it out fast under pressure. Maybe"—and he hesitated—"maybe I can find room for you."

The next day he did. I became a foreign correspondent.

My first assignment was to continue on the Lindbergh story. The flyer, who had been utterly unknown a week before, had awakened that May Sunday in Paris after ten hours of sleep to find himself a world hero. By his successful lonely flight against all the odds,[1] he had captured the imagination of millions on both sides of the Atlantic. He was all over the front pages of every newspaper in the Western world. Presidents, kings, prime ministers, cabled congratulations. For a whole week Paris feted him as it had no other foreign visitor in its history. The President and the Premier of France received him and pinned on him the Cross of the Legion of Honor. He addressed the French Assembly. Half a million people jammed the streets when he drove to the Hôtel de Ville for an official reception by the city of Paris, which awarded him a gold medal. Day after day the Parisian press filled its columns with encomiums for the twenty-five-year-old flyer and reports of every move he made. The anti-American feeling in the capital disappeared. "Lindbergh has brought you the real spirit of America," Herrick told the throng at the Hôtel de Ville.

I saw a good deal of Lindbergh that week. Despite the strain

[1] Even when he reached St. John's, Lloyd's of London, which had refused to quote odds on him, relented only to the extent of betting 10 to 3 that he would not reach Paris.

and all the plaudits, he remained simple and modest, full of poise as he was called upon to address one meeting after another, flashing his youthful grin, and using the personal pronoun "we" in talking of his plane and himself. I had never seen a man, let alone one so young, bear such fantastic adulation with such good grace and modesty.

At the urging of the government in Washington he flew on to Brussels, where he was received by the King and Queen and was given another decoration. Then on to London, where the stolid British acclaimed him as wildly as the French had. The King and Queen had him in to Buckingham Palace, the Prime Minister (Stanley Baldwin) to 10 Downing Street, the Prince of Wales to York House. He was presented to the House of Commons and the Lords, a rare honor, and at a gala dinner offered by the Royal Aero Club heard himself praised by the Chancellor of the Exchequer, Winston Churchill.

At the insistence of Washington he abandoned a new plan to continue his flight around the world and reluctantly accepted the proposal of the President of the United States to return home on the U.S. cruiser *Memphis*. No American ever received such a welcome home by his government and fellow-countrymen as did Lindbergh over the weeks that followed his arrival in Washington on the *Memphis* just before noon on Saturday, June 11, three weeks after he had landed in Paris. Our scant cable service from America was greatly expanded so that we could enable our readers in Europe to follow a spectacle unprecedented, I believe, in the American experience.

President Coolidge, who had sent an effusive cable of congratulations to Lindbergh on the completion of his flight in Paris, now praised him even more effusively in a welcoming ceremony at the Washington Monument, where the largest crowd the capital had ever seen gathered after a triumphal parade up Pennsylvania Avenue. The usually laconic Yankee President let loose with torrents of words. Lindbergh was "a boy representing the best traditions of this country . . . this wholesome, earnest, fearless, courageous product of America . . . a valiant character driven by an unconquerable will . . . this genial, modest American youth, with the naturalness, the simplicity and the poise of true greatness . . . this sincere and genuine exemplar of fine and noble virtues . . ." On and on he went, in one of the longest speeches of his career, as the tens of thousands in the crowd applauded and millions more all over the country listened on a fifty-station radio hookup. When he finished, the President smilingly (he who rarely smiled) pinned on the new hero the Distinguished Flying Cross. Lindbergh and his equally modest mother were put up at the temporary White House at 15 Dupont Circle (the Executive Mansion was undergoing extensive repairs), given lunch and later a gala dinner attended by Cabinet officers, leaders of Congress and other notables.

Two days later New York gave the flyer an even more tumultuous reception. Police estimated that more than four million people turned out for the ticker-tape parade, the ceremony at City Hall, where the mayor, James J. (Jimmy) Walker, awarded him a Medal of Valor, and another in Central Park, where Governor Al Smith pinned on him New York State's Medal of Honor. Next day *The New York Times* gave its first sixteen pages over to the story of the stupendous welcome. It continued for three more days. At a dinner given by the city for four thousand guests at the Hotel Commodore, even the venerable, dignified, austere, bearded Charles Evans Hughes, former Secretary of State and eventually to be named Chief Justice of the Supreme Court, shed his usual formality and coldness and almost outdid Coolidge in warmly lauding Lindbergh: "He has kindled anew the fires on the eight ancient altars of the temple of thought . . . This is the happiest of all days for America, and as one mind she is now intent upon the noblest and the best . . . Our boys and girls have before them a stirring, inspiring vision of real manhood . . ." On and on he, too, went. The Republic had never seen such adulation for a private citizen.

Almost everyone was sure, though, that Lindbergh's fame, unprecedented as it was, would be ephemeral, over in a few weeks. Fame, after all, was fleeting, and some who had tasted it briefly urged him to get the most out of it he could. Gertrude Ederle, who the year before had been the first woman to swim the English Channel (and in record time) and had been given a ticker-tape parade down Broadway on her return, and who now, largely forgotten, was playing a small-town vaudeville circuit, publicly advised him that "he had better get the money now; later it may be too late." Gene Tunney, heavyweight boxing champion of the world, had the same advice: "He ought to commercialize his stunt [sic] for every cent that is in it, for in a year from now he will be forgotten."[1]

But he was not forgotten. His fame spread. It went on and on. Toward the end of July he set off in the *Spirit of St. Louis* on a three-month aerial tour of the nation sponsored by the Guggenheim Fund and the U.S. Department of Commerce that took him into eighty-two cities in the forty-eight states, during which he flew twenty-two thousand miles, made 147 speeches and was acclaimed from coast to coast by an estimated thirty million people. Even before he left, he had received 3,500,000 letters, 100,000 telegrams and 14,000 packages from hero-worshipers. And this was only the beginning. For nearly thirteen years Lindbergh remained the idol of the nation, its most publicized citizen, its one authentic hero.

Fame, which so many of us seek, to a certain extent (even if we don't admit it), and which seems so sweet and exhilarating when it comes, can turn into a curse. It did for Lindbergh. It deprived him of the last vestige of what he wanted most: privacy; subjecting him to the worst indignities at the hands of a sensational yellow press and of vulgar, empty-minded hero-worshipers. That was bad enough. But there were other consequences. Sudden fame threw him into the company of the rich and the powerful, whose conservative and sometimes reactionary and even antidemocratic view of the world appeared to gradually rub off on him. Worse, the fantastic adulation of his fellow-countrymen seems to have eventually tempted him to use this immense following for political ends, both foreign and domestic, a course that once embarked upon finally, after thirteen years of being worshiped as a nonpartisan hero, would prove disastrous.

Perhaps my friend Kenneth S. Davis, in his perceptive study of Lindbergh as hero,[2] best described the predicament: "When Lindbergh returned to the United States he sought to bestow upon his countrymen the boon of safe and easy flight, but his countrymen demanded of him other gifts which it was not in his nature, or in the nature of mortal man, to bestow."

[1] Actually Lindbergh, within a week of his flight, received offers of every conceivable kind amounting to a total of five million dollars. Aside from a few testimonials for products used in his flight, he turned them all down.

[2] Kenneth S. Davis: *The Hero: Charles A. Lindbergh and the American Dream*, page 10.

Fame, which brought Lindbergh so many honors and such unprecedented adulation, would in time bring also disillusionment, bitterness, tragedy, deep sorrow (when his first child was kidnapped and murdered), and a confusion about life and politics and war and peace on this bickering earth. I, who had seen him at the first moment of his glory in Paris behave with such modesty and grace and intelligence, would be saddened the next time I saw him. This was in Berlin in the Nazi time. He seemed to me to have been taken in by Nazi propaganda and—worst of all—to have become shockingly admiring of a mindless, bloody, barbarian dictatorship which I was watching from day to day inflict such monstrous suffering on human beings, depriving them of the very freedoms which the famous flyer proclaimed he valued at home. And I was appalled when on October 18, 1938, Lindbergh was awarded by Adolf Hitler—and accepted—the Service Cross of the German Eagle with Star, the second-highest German decoration, conferred on distinguished foreigners who, in the official words of the citation, "deserved well of the Reich."

The timing could scarcely have been worse. For the evening Hermann Goering hung the Service Cross around Lindbergh's neck was just three weeks after Munich, when Czechoslovakia had been sold down the river, and Europe, which Hitler had pushed to the brink of war, trembled to see what aggression the Fuehrer would engineer next. It was a time when the Jews of Germany had just been deprived of their civil rights and put upon, beaten up, arrested and slain by Nazi thugs. It was a time when Germany was on the eve of a new wave of persecutions of the Jews by the giver of the decoration to Lindbergh.

I would not be surprised then when in Berlin during the first year of the second war I would read in the German newspapers of Lindbergh's pronouncements that, after the fall of France, Britain was doomed and that America must abandon the idea of helping her to survive and make its accommodation with the conquering Hitler. They were highly pleasing to the Nazi gangsters such as Joseph Goebbels, the Propaganda Minister, who ordered them played up in the German press. One, I recall, was particularly pleasing: Lindbergh's assertion in a magazine article that appeared just before Hitler invaded neutral Denmark, Norway, Holland and Belgium that it was Germany—Hitler's Germany—that held today "the intangible eastern border of European civilization." Nazi Germany defending European civilization? I saw the barbarous dictatorship destroying it. Nor was I greatly surprised, though I was appalled, when home on a protracted leave from the war in 1941 I read of Lindbergh's speech in Des Moines on September 11 of that year in which, mouthing Hitler and Goebbels, he attacked the Jews for trying to get us into the war against Germany. "Their greatest danger to this country," he proclaimed, "lies in their large ownership and influence in our motion pictures, our press, our radio and our government."

That—and his misjudgment of Britain and Nazi Germany and indeed of the temper of his own country—was the end, I believe, of Lindbergh as hero. It was a far cry, I mused to myself that early autumn day, from the May evening in Paris fourteen years before when I had watched this modest, courageous young man drop out of the sky at Le Bourget to the acclaim of the whole world. It had been such a shining beginning.[1]

---

[1] Charles Lindbergh died on August 26, 1974, of lymphatic cancer at seventy-two, a few weeks after this section about him was written. His sudden end came on the isolated island of Maui, Hawaii, his vacation retreat, to which he had returned the week before after learning from his physicians at Columbia-Presbyterian Medical Center in New York that he had terminal cancer. He was buried there, according to his last wishes, in his khaki work clothes in a rough-hewn wooden coffin built by his Hawaiian neighbors.

During World War II he was denied a renewal of his commission in the Army Air Corps which he had resigned on the eve of Pearl Harbor in resentment at President Roosevelt having branded him a "defeatist." But in 1944 he flew to the Pacific theater of war as a consultant to the manufacturer of a Navy fighter to check its capabilities in actual combat and, though a civilian, flew fifty combat missions against the Japanese, one of which in a dogfight over Biak Island almost cost him his life. Just before and after the war he helped Pan American develop its global routes; encouraged Dr. Robert Goddard, an obscure professor of physics at Clark University in Worcester, Massachusetts, whose pioneering in rocketry and space flight was ridiculed by almost everyone else; and worked with Boeing to perfect the postwar jet commercial planes.

Ten years before his death, as he entered his sixties, Lindbergh, who had spent most of his life furthering the development of aviation and its technology, became interested in conservation and devoted much of his remaining time and energies in promoting the protection of the natural environment. "If I had to choose," he said now, "I would rather have birds than airplanes."

If he had to choose again, he also said, he would not have acted differently than he did in denouncing the Jews and Roosevelt for trying to get the country into the war, nor in hastily proclaiming Britain's doom in 1940 and 1941, nor in declaring his admiration for Nazi Germany as the defender of Western civilization, nor his acceptance of its Service Cross medal at a time when Hitler was trying to stamp out that civilization, nor his fervor for the crackpot philosophical ideas he

· ·

The excitement of becoming a foreign correspondent was soon dampened by my being posted for most of that first summer to grimy London. After Paris the citadel of the British Empire seemed almost desolate. I chafed at being torn away from a job that I was just beginning to get the hang of. The prospect of leaving Paris, even for a couple of months, was depressing. The separation from Yvonne seemed more than I could bear. And I would miss working with Wales and his young assistant, Jay Allen, who had replaced the mercurial Vincent Sheean.

I had been warned by several members of the local staff that Henry (Hank) Wales would be a tough man to work for—mean, harsh, suspicious and a bit of a bully. He could be all of these at times but the more I got to know him the better I liked him. Once he took you on he was loyal to you and understanding, especially when you made mistakes or got into trouble. One overlooked his rasping voice, coming out of one side of his mouth, and his bull-dog face, which I soon realized was a sort of mask hiding a more gentle and insecure character. He had been a police reporter in New York before the war, and a war correspondent in France

got from his friend, the Nobel laureate scientist, Dr. Alexis Carrel, about the desirability of the rule of the elite, which he promulgated on his own and which led him once to write in his book *Of Flight and Life* of the superiority of Americans on this earth and to warn that "for Americans the doctrine of universal equality is a doctrine of death" and that "if we ever become an equal people among other peoples of the world our civilization will fail."

To the end of his life he felt he had been wronged by President Roosevelt, never admitting how viciously he had attacked the President as a warmonger and how wrong he had been in predicting the triumph of Hitler and the defeat of Hitler's enemies, and how ignorant he was of the consequences to civilization if that had happened.

Still, in the world of flying he was a genius, courageous, intelligent, probing, imaginative. He wore the sudden and unprecedented fame thrust upon him with magnificent modesty, and except for the brief period of his floundering in politics and history, the complexities of which escaped him, he remained true to himself. And though he spent much of his life after the Paris flight in the company of the rich and the wellborn, whom he admired, he loved the simple life, feeling most at home in the world of nature, the blue skies, the wilderness and the jungle.

When he learned that the end had come he preferred to have it in a quiet and isolated place, far from the splendid houses he had known here and in England and as far as possible from the chatter and the bustle of the great cities which had so wildly acclaimed him, departing this life dressed in old work clothes amid the simple natives of the unspoiled Pacific island. This, too, was in his character.

from 1915 on. There he had picked up French, which he spoke fairly fluently but with a clipped American accent. As unintellectual as most former police reporters, he frowned on Allen and me when he caught us reading books in the office on dull days, and he never joined in our talks when Jay and I passed the time arguing about Stendhal, Proust, Hemingway, Fitzgerald and other writers in whom we were passionately interested.

"What do you see in all those guys?" he would ask, turning away to bury his head in a newspaper. But out of sheer experience he knew his way about Paris, France and Europe and wrote well of their politics if not of their culture. "Culture?" he would say. "What the hell is that!" His contradictions were odd. He would sternly advise us not to "fool around" too much "with girls," but he had an eye for them himself and lived with an Argentine woman to whom he was not married, keeping her in such seclusion that few even knew of her existence. He never took her out with his friends. A strict Presbyterian, he went to church every Sunday morning, but he spent his evenings in bars and night spots.

Jay Allen, four or five years older than I, was the exact opposite of Wales. Cultivated, sensitive, an omnivorous reader of books, he had gone East from his native Seattle and the University of Oregon to graduate work at Harvard, where he had studied French literature and written his thesis on Stendhal, and then, having married a college sweetheart, joined the exodus to Paris. Rather high-strung and nervous, he transferred his tensions into some of the best writing on the newspaper. Wales had no particular beliefs in anything except being a good reporter. Liberalism and conservatism, democracy and dictatorships, were all the same to him and he never showed any bias one way or the other in reporting from democratic France, Primo de Rivera's dictatorship in Spain, Mussolini's in Rome, Stalin's in Moscow or the rather liberal League of Nations in Geneva. This lack of any ideology whatsoever probably was more of an advantage for an American correspondent than Allen and I realized.

But we could not share it. Allen was passionately against the dictatorships, whether of the Right or the Left, and he made little pretense of being objective when he began to report on the rise of a German rabble-rouser in Munich named Hitler, on the antics of Mussolini, or on the suppression of democracy in Spain first by

Rivera and later by Franco. Rivera jailed him for one of his stories from Madrid and Franco threw him into prison later for his reporting on the civil war. Though a member of our Paris bureau Allen spent a great deal of time in Spain in those years and finally became so personally concerned with the survival of the Spanish Republic when Franco turned on it with his Italian and German Fascist legions that he quit his job with the *Tribune* to devote all his time to try to save it—alas in vain, as it turned out.

I shared most of Jay's views, and this helped to bring us together in a close friendship that lasted until his death forty-five years later. Fundamentally, I think, we both were probably little more than Jeffersonian liberals in our outlook on life, though later the autocratic, erratic seigneur who owned and ran the *Chicago Tribune,* Colonel Robert R. McCormick, accused us both of being "communistic" and actually apologized in the news columns of his paper for ever having hired us. But that came much later, after he had often praised us (and also dressed us down) and, in my case, after he had run many a full-page ad lauding my work as a correspondent.

For the moment, that June of 1927 in Paris, I was engrossed in learning the ropes of my new job. As low man on the totem pole, I had the night shift, working from 3 P.M. to 3 A.M., with a couple of hours off for dinner at eight. Because of a time difference of six hours between Paris and Chicago, we could file until three or four in the morning. But Wales usually knocked off at 6 P.M. (noon in Chicago) after writing a piece gleaned from the afternoon papers or from covering the Chamber of Deputies or some other political event. Inevitably he adjourned to Harry's New York Bar where he sat down to drink with a clique of veteran correspondents, men who had come over first to cover the war and now were heads of bureaus. Among them would be Edwin L. James of *The New York Times* and Floyd Gibbons, a legendary war correspondent for the *Chicago Tribune* and now free-lancing for the magazines. They were old friends from the war days and rather alike, fast-talking, tough-talking, in the manner of old police reporters, which they had been. Gibbons was a familiar figure in the bars of Europe in those days, with the face of an Irish prize fighter and that black patch over one eye. Jimmy James, like Wales, was a stocky little man, but more dapper and flamboyant and garrulous and, I think, with a greater grasp of European politics. He wrote fast and well but with no style. Somehow, perhaps from his work, he had become a great favorite of the staid and dignified Adolph Ochs, owner and publisher of the *Times*, who would soon bring him home as his new managing editor. No greater contrasts between two men could be imagined. Jimmy, a true boulevardier, loved and haunted the bars, the night clubs and the horse races. It was difficult to picture the sedate Ochs even visiting such places, but when he came over to Paris he did, in tow of his exuberant, cigar-chewing Paris bureau chief.

While Wales was ambling over to Harry's New York Bar promptly at 6 P.M., I would be returning from an afternoon spent covering the Chamber of Deputies, the Senate and the Foreign Office, with stopovers to check at the American Embassy and Consulate. Back at the office, I would phone Wales at Harry's and discuss how much to file. My main job began at 10 P.M., when I returned from dinner. There were the file of Havas and the early edition of the Paris morning papers to read. Often they would contain a promising story but it had to be checked on the telephone—itself a formidable task since French telephones and operators (dials had not yet come in) rarely functioned. Later, at 2:30 A.M., came the final editions of the papers, a dozen of them, which had to be read rapidly because of our deadline. By this time my French, thanks mostly to Yvonne, had become adequate for this chore. If a story looked big enough I was supposed to phone Wales. This often meant calling several cabarets before I located him. He would be loath to leave. "Willy," he would say, "you can do it." And I would, and the next morning in Chicago it would be by-lined with Wales's name.

That was the rule in the office. All the dispatches that Jay or I wrote were signed "Wales." We got a by-line only when we went off on a special assignment or when the boss was out of town reporting from another place. To the editors in Chicago, Wales, who put in a rather short working day—an hour before lunch and from 3 to 6 P.M. after lunch—must have seemed from our dispatches to be a tireless correspondent, working around the clock. Allen and I did not complain. We were happy to find such interesting employment and to get this sort of training. And when occasionally we pulled a boner it was Wales who received the flak from Chicago. He never shunted the blame off on us. Still, I began to wonder how I was ever to come to the attention of my employers back home. Sometimes when a cable of mine made the front page it was Wales who received the congratulations. "Good work, Willy," he would say and chuckle. "Chicago likes your stuff." I wondered how Chicago would know. Somehow, I gradually learned, the regal lord of the *Tribune* did. Whatever his faults, and they were legion, he had an uncanny instinct about what his minions on the foreign service were doing.

The aura of Colonel Robert Rutherford McCormick, editor and publisher of the *Chicago Tribune,* pervaded our office. Even the cynical, hard-boiled Wales spoke of him in awe—and usually in whispers. The foreign service was the colonel's pet project. He ran it himself, rarely informing either his managing editor or his foreign editor of the Napoleonic orders he sometimes peppered us with[1] or of his cryptic criticisms scrawled on the margin of our dispatches which came almost daily. Nor apparently did he bother to tell them of certain nonjournalistic assignments he would give us which often kept us away from our reporting for days or weeks.

Since I had begun to work for this imperious and eccentric press lord, I thought it prudent to check up on him and his background. A good deal of the story of the mighty McCormick family I had heard as a youngster in Chicago. I merely had to brush up on it. Everyone in Chicago knew the story of Cyrus McCormick, the colonel's great-uncle, who invented the Virginia reaper and founded what became the giant International Harvester Company. Cyrus, with two brothers, one of whom was William Sanderson McCormick, the colonel's grandfather, had arrived in Chicago from Virginia in 1847 and set up a farm machinery busi-

---

[1] Though his combat experience in France as a major and then a colonel in an artillery regiment had been brief and limited, Colonel McCormick regarded himself as a military genius. Whenever it looked to him, though not necessarily to us, that war might break out in Europe he would bombard us with cabled instructions that Napoleon would have been proud to compose. "Wars always start at dawn," he would cable. "I want each of you correspondents to be at your posts at dawn not later than tomorrow morning." And he would assign each of us to a strategic spot he had picked out from an old map in his office, instructing us how the battle would probably begin and develop, and where to position ourselves and what to look for. We would proceed as rapidly as possible to our posts, but nothing ever happened. Much later during World War II I learned, what reading Tolstoy and Stendhal should have taught me, that a lone observer in a battle hasn't the faintest idea what's going on. All is confusion.

ness based on their new harvester. The brothers, I believe, eventually quarreled and Cyrus, the genius of the family, pushed the other two out of the business. The colonel's grandfather died in an insane asylum in 1865 and the grandson sometimes spoke of the streak of insanity in the family. "All the McCormicks," he would say, "are crazy—except me," though some of us who worked for him wondered about the validity of the exception. Judging by my brief experience with the colonel's mother, who was a Medill, there may have been a thread of insanity in that family, too.

This was a formidable woman. Born Katherine (Katrina) Van Etta Medill, she was the daughter of Joseph Medill, who came to Chicago in 1855, went to work on the *Tribune*, which had been founded in 1847 by persons now obscure, as a printer and in twenty years gained control of the newspaper and made it into the largest and most powerful journal in the Midwest. An early promoter of Abraham Lincoln for the Presidency, he became one of his confidants. And his strong-minded daughter, who could only have known Lincoln when she was a child, came to worship his memory as the greatest man America had ever had, as she once admonished me, though I did not need much convincing.

Katrina Medill married Robert Sanderson McCormick, son of the younger brother of Cyrus, thus uniting the McCormicks and the Medills in the *Chicago Tribune*. But this McCormick had little interest in journalism or apparently in the rough-and-tumble life of Chicago, and through family influence at the White House he got an appointment in 1901 as Minister in Vienna. The following year he was made Ambassador in St. Petersburg and thereafter Ambassador in Paris. Thus our Colonel McCormick, who was born in 1880, spent some of his formative years in three of the most important capitals in Europe, where he picked up foreign languages and a feeling for European politics and life. The Ambassador, in contrast to his wife, appears to have been a rather weak-willed and incompetent man, out of his depth in old-world diplomacy. At any rate President Theodore Roosevelt relieved him of his post in Paris—a blow from which he never recovered. I never heard the colonel mention his father. Perhaps he could not bear to think of his mediocrity and his failure. But he worshiped his mother, whose imperious manner he inherited, and who obviously had a strong influence on him. He apparently even forgave her for dressing him in his early years as a girl; she had done this, it is said, because of her deep sense of loss when her first-born, a daughter, died in infancy and she prayed God for another girl and got a boy instead.

Now in her old age, Mrs. McCormick came every summer to Europe to stay in Paris and Versailles and later take the waters at Carlsbad. A staff member was always assigned to rent a special Pullman for her use, meet her at Cherbourg, get the special car attached to the boat train, accompany her to Paris, and put her up at the Ritz. I escaped that assignment but was then instructed in the line of duty to take "tea" with her for several days at the Ritz. I still remember the first day. Her talk, though disjointed, turned out to be fascinating as she reminisced about the early days in Chicago and then the glittering days at the courts in Vienna and St. Petersburg and, above all, the times in Paris shortly after the turn of the century, which she loved most of all. I gathered that she must have had a drinking problem for the "whiskey" she offered me turned out to be a concoction invented by her doctors which obviously looked and tasted to her like whiskey but which had no alcohol and to me tasted like dishwater. Nevertheless, I manfully gulped it down—it was part of the job. Finally, after a long afternoon, I stood up to go.

"Just a minute, young man," she said. "I want you to send a cable for me."

I took out my pad and pencil.

"This is to Mr. Lincoln," she said.

"To *who?*" I started to say and then caught myself.

"Mr. Lincoln," she began, "White House, Washington, D.C." And she proceeded to dictate a cable to Abraham Lincoln. It went on and on. I do not now recall its contents but I have a faint recollection that it described the situation in Paris, in France and in the rest of Europe, as she saw it a few days after arrival. Perhaps it was based on what she had seen in the Parisian newspapers, for she remembered her French. I knew from subsequent conversations, or rather from listening to her monologues, that she loved France and the French, rather disliked the British, as did her son, and had a distinct antipathy to Japanese, Germans, Jews and Roman Catholics. Perhaps there was something of these opinions in the cable she dictated to me for the martyred President. When I got back to the office I handed the message to Wales.

"Forget it," he grunted. "Mr. Lincoln, I believe, is dead."

The next non-journalistic assignment was for me to go up to the battlefields of northern France, search out the battlefield at Cantigny, report on how it looked today, find a dugout in an old barn from which command post Colonel McCormick said he had directed his artillery in the engagement, and pick up a pair of binoculars and other personal objects which he believed he had left there in the heat of the battle when the Americans advanced that summer of 1918, nine years before. Cantigny, a minor battle in the annals of the American Expeditionary Force, loomed large in the colonel's mind, or at least in his imagination. He had named his great estate west of Chicago after it. McCormick's instructions to me were accompanied by a detailed map which he himself had drawn, showing the farm and exactly where the old barn lay.

I think I actually found the place, after several days of meandering around. The farm looked like any other. The rows of wheat waved in the June sun. There was no sign that it might once have been a battlefield. The peasant farmer greeted me somewhat suspiciously and when I told him what I was up to he glanced at me as if he thought I was crazy.

"If there was a battle here," he said, "it didn't amount to much. I've been plowing these fields for years. Never even turned up a mine or an old shell, as some of my neighbors did."

I noticed that his barn was new.

"I've been asked to visit my American colonel's command post in the basement of the barn," I explained. "He left his binoculars."

"Are you crazy?" he responded. "There ain't nothing there. Only some machinery and what's left over from last year's hay."

Nevertheless, I insisted, and reluctantly he took me over to the barn. No trace of a dugout, though I sounded out the floors and looked in every corner. Nothing but some plows and harrows and a cutter bar and several bales of old hay. I had brought out a local French photographer to take shots of the famous battlefield and of the colonel's command post. Obviously he, too, thought I was looney. But I instructed him to photograph the fields, the barn and the interior of the barn. I needed proof to convince the colonel.

McCormick never answered my "report." But he didn't fire me either. Perhaps he concluded that I was just a dumb reporter who had never been under fire as he had, and wouldn't know a battlefield when I saw one.

I returned to Paris a little despondent over my failure, but Wales quickly cheered me up.

"He never fought in the Battle of Cantigny," Wales said. "He wasn't there."

I couldn't believe it. "Yeah," Wales went on. "Somebody—I think on one of the opposition papers in Chicago—checked up on it in the War Department. The colonel was away on sick leave—it was during the flu epidemic that hit thousands of soldiers. Don't tell anyone," he added slyly, "but some people think the colonel was not even sick—just on leave having a good time in Paris. What the hell! That's nothing to be ashamed of. You took your leave when you could get it. And had some fun in gay Paree."[1]

After that I was usually passed by on such assignments. When I was working in London, for example, one of the tasks of the foreign staff there was to buy new freight boats in Scotland for the *Tribune*'s fleet that transported newsprint from its paper mills in Canada to Chicago. Another assignment was to buy ponies for the colonel's polo team at his country estate. Though he was violently anti-British, McCormick insisted on buying his boats and ponies in Britain. But I was so inept in this business that I was soon relieved of the assignments. I didn't know anything about ships or ponies. I wondered though why the fiercely patriotic McCormick, who was for America First and hated the British, didn't buy his boats and ponies back home and help American business and labor. But to wonder at that was to underestimate his acute business sense.

London, after Paris, that summer of 1927, seemed grim. And nothing experienced or observed during my stints there in the

[1] Frank C. Waldrop, a friendly biographer, confirms McCormick's absence from this battlefield. "The colonel," he writes, "did not fight the Battle of Cantigny at all."—Frank C. Waldrop: *McCormick of Chicago*, p. 170.

This does not mean that the colonel did not have a distinguished war record. After the war he was awarded the Distinguished Service Medal.

following two summers made it any brighter or more attractive. It wasn't the work, but the life. The work was interesting enough. It was something, after all, to see and write about—those last Indian-summer days of the British Empire on which, as the old saw had it, the sun never set. On the eve of the war in 1914 it had covered one-fourth of the land of this earth, with a population of 450 million, of which only 70 million were white. The peace treaties had added another million square miles and seven million more people. Even a green, upstart Yankee observer like myself could see that the sun was starting to set on it now, over all the oceans, though the British themselves seemed blind to this.

The mother country itself, from which the Empire was ruled and milked, one could also see, was in dire trouble, beset by massive unemployment, grave economic, financial and social difficulties, and the gnawing acrimony of growing class strife. The workers, who for so long had known and accepted their place, were getting restive, though God knows there was nothing revolutionary about them. The shadow of the General Strike of the year before still hung over the island. The workers had lost the strike and been forced—the coal miners especially—to return to their jobs at lower wages at near-starvation levels. You could sense their bitterness, and also their despair.

The Tory government and the ruling classes, which had joined to put down the strike, were, after an initial fright, again full of confidence and a sense of privileged well-being. They had taught the striking workers their place. Winston Churchill, Chancellor of the Exchequer, had branded the strikers "the enemy" and demanded their "unconditional surrender" and got it. Legislation was quickly put through the Commons that summer of my arrival outlawing such strikes in the future.

Secure from any more labor trouble over decent wages and seemingly unmindful of the festering sore of unemployment, which remained steadily at more than a million, the wellborn and the well-to-do were enjoying what the newspapers described as the most brilliant social season since the war. While small groups of shabbily dressed out-of-work miners and cotton-mill workers stood around Charing Cross, Trafalgar Square and Piccadilly Circus, tooting horns and passing the hat for pennies to help feed their families, shiny, chauffeur-driven Rolls-Royces delivered their more opulent fellow-countrymen to elegant soirees in the great

houses of Mayfair and Belgravia, to the teas and balls at Buckingham Palace, or conveyed them to the cricket at Lord's, the tennis
at Wimbledon, the yacht races at Cowes and the horse races at
Ascot. Occasionally you would catch a glimpse of them in their
finery: the men in top hats and formal clothes, gray or black
according to the time of day; the women, bejeweled, in their
elegant satins and silks. They seemed not to have a care in the
world—except for their pleasures. When the hot weather came in
August and the London Season ended, they abandoned the uncomfortable city for their spacious houses or castles in the country, where the social whirl continued until fall and armies of well-
drilled, faithful and duly subservient servants catered to their
comfort and pleasure.

The foundations of the Empire might be crumbling (though
this they could not see) and the country going downhill (which,
if so, they thought was only temporary) and millions of citizens
unable to earn enough to provide three meals a day and a decent
roof over their heads (didn't they get a dole, or wages as high as
the economy would allow?), but these wellborn, well-heeled
people had to have the pleasures they had become accustomed to.

I wondered whether they were not a little like the nobility
and aristocracy around the glittering court of Versailles, whose
ladies and gentlemen danced away the last years before the
Glorious Revolution. Not, so far as my ignorant eyes could see,
that there was the slightest danger of revolution in Britain, or
that there ever would be. The rulers had too tight a grip on the
island. The ruled might complain about their plight and even go
out on strike, but they would never do anything more drastic than
that. Class distinctions were so old and so entrenched that everyone, high and low, accepted them. This to me was one of the first
wonders to be observed among these strange people on this tight
little isle.

It did not take long in London for a foreign reporter to grasp,
however, that the class structure was infinitely complex, replete
with myriad hierarchies within hierarchies, each with a different
composition, each seemingly knowing its rung on the social
ladder. Education was one place to look in order to try to understand it. This took one into a world quite unlike anything one had
experienced in America or even in France.

You had to come from Eton or Harrow, from Oxford or Cambridge, to climb to the top in the Tory party, in the Tory government, in the upper reaches of the prestigious Civil Service, especially in the Treasury and at the Foreign Office. In fact, you had to go to either of the great universities in order to get a decent higher education. And since their enrollment, as well as that of Harrow and Eton, was necessarily restricted in numbers and, with few exceptions, limited to the wellborn and rich, this meant that the vast majority of the young men and women in England were excluded not only from a good university education but from its rewards in public office. In no other country in the world was the old school tie so important. The fact was, so far as I began to see, there were two systems of education in England: one for the poor, the other for the privileged and rich.

The first was bad; the second was in most ways excellent. Education, more than any other institution, instead of strengthening democracy and the sense of equality among men, buttressed the distinction between classes. The great dividing line was whether one had been educated at a "public" school (in reality, private schools such as Eton and Harrow) or in what Americans would call a public school. And to a slightly lesser degree, whether one had been to Oxford or Cambridge or to one of the inferior universities. In 1927 the majority of men in the Tory Cabinet, in the Tory party in the Commons, in the higher echelons of the Civil Service and of the Church of England, came from the "public" schools and the two great universities.

Stanley Baldwin presided over the Tory government as Prime Minister during my first two summers in London. From a family of industrialists who four generations before had founded a great ironworks, he seemed to me to be the embodiment of John Bull and British solidity. Ignorant of foreign affairs, suspicious of foreigners, and limited by his experience in business, he would muddle through until 1929. Something of a mystic, despite his early life in the iron business and his later life in politics, and with a certain literary bent, he was also unabashedly an old-school-tie man. His education at Harrow had left an indelible print on him. He left no doubt of this in his volume of nonpolitical addresses, *On England*. "When the call came to me to form a government," he wrote, "one of my first thoughts was that it should be a government of which Harrow should not be ashamed." He was determined, he adds, to "do nothing in the course of my . . . career which shall cause any Harrovian to say of me that I have failed to do my best to live up to the highest ideals of the School."

But were those ideals so high? The highest ideal of that school, so far as I could judge from the few graduates I met, seemed one of insufferable snobbery. No doubt there were other ideals I was unaware of. And whatever his limitations, which were those of the upper class, Baldwin could never be accused of snobbery. But he, like the other products of the "public" schools, took it for granted that they were best fitted to run the country, and perhaps this was a sort of unconscious snobbery.

Even more than in America, the lucky few possessed most of the wealth of this fading land. A bare 1 percent of the population owned two-thirds of the country's wealth. A tiny group, one-tenth of 1 percent, owned a third. The vast majority of citizens, three-quarters of them, had less than five hundred dollars of capital. London itself was an example of the concentration in a few hands of the city's real estate, valued at billions of pounds. One titled gentleman owned nearly three hundred acres in the West End, the income from which in rents was staggering. Some twenty others owned most of the rest. Of the eight million inhabitants of the capital only forty thousand owned any land at all in it, and that in small parcels. An Englishman's home might be his castle but he did not have the wherewithal to own it. Nearly all of the gainfully employed—eighteen million of them—earned on an average only a little more than a thousand dollars a year. They were lucky if they could pay the rent. Yet the majority of them, even the majority of the manual workers, never voted for the Labor Party, which promised them a bigger slice of the pie. They seemed content with the crumbs left them by the Tories. Their loyalty to the ruling classes, their great respect and love for the monarchy, seemed touching but very puzzling to this youthful Yankee observer. But it could not be doubted. It was part of the fabric of the nation.

Also puzzling to one so ignorant as I was not only how the small governing class maintained its supremacy but how from this oligarchy a genuine political democracy had emerged. The more I read English history those summers in London the more I began to comprehend. Democratic freedoms in England came not from a revolt of the masses as in France but from the revolt of the upper classes against the Crown, from whom by the middle of the seventeenth century they had snatched political power and freedom for themselves. It had not been a popular revolt as in France or even in America. The cries of the Parisian mobs for *égalité* had not been heard in London. The masses remained unconcerned by the long struggle of the upper classes against the King. It was the latter class that won political freedom for England.

But political democracy did not bring equality, nor in England was it meant to. Part of the genius of the top crust of society was its success in convincing the lower orders to vote to leave the governing of the country to it. The common people, being in the vast majority, had the votes to install a government of their own—in this case, the Labor Party. But they were too stupid to do the obvious. They joined with the privileged in subscribing to the dictum of Walter Bagehot, the Victorian economist and author of *The English Constitution:* "Sensible men of substantial means are what we wish to be ruled by."

Yet Bagehot, whom I began to read that first summer, had evidently been frightened by the prospect that the common people might wake up and combine to take over the governing of the nation. The very thought horrified him. He solemnly warned

> that a political combination of the lower classes . . . is an evil of the first magnitude . . . ; that their supremacy in the state means the supremacy of ignorance over instruction and of numbers over knowledge. So long as they are not taught to act together, there is a chance of this being averted, and it can only be averted by the greater wisdom and foresight in the higher classes.

Curiously enough, in my reading that first summer, I found one nineteenth-century figure, one of the greatest aristocrats from one of the oldest and most distinguished families, who did not share the forebodings of his class or of Bagehot. This was Lord Randolph Churchill, father of Winston Churchill, and successor to Disraeli, who died in 1881, as leader of the Conservative Party. "The Labor Community," he wrote in 1892, to the consternation of most of his fellow-Conservatives, "is carrying on . . . a very significant and instructive struggle . . . for the practical utilization in its own interest of the great political power it has acquired."

It was merely attempting to do, he saw, what other groups

before it had done in *their* own interests when they ruled the nation.

> Our land laws [he wrote] were framed by the landed interests for the advantage of the landed interest, and foreign policy was directed by that interest to the same end. Political power passed very considerably from the landed interest to the manufacturing capitalist interest, and our whole fiscal system was shaped by this latter power to its own advantage, foreign policy being also made to coincide. We are now come, or are coming fast, to a time when Labor laws will be made by the Labor interest for the advantage of Labor. . . . Personally I can discern no cause for alarm in this prospect.

But a third of a century later, when my acquaintance with London began, there was some alarm among the higher orders, though little reason for it so far as I could see. What Bagehot had feared had come about, at least to some extent. A Labor Party had been formed around the turn of the century and had begun to send a handful of members to the Commons. By the time of the 1914 war it had some forty M.P.'s and in 1922 it had emerged for the first time as the second political party in Britain, surpassing the Liberals, polling more than four million votes and winning 142 parliamentary seats. In elections the following year it increased its strength to 191 seats, against 159 for the Liberals and 258 for the Conservatives. The great Liberal Party of Gladstone and Lloyd George was now expiring, making Labor the real opposition party. The next year, 1924, when the Tories and the Liberals could not agree on a coalition, Ramsay MacDonald had been called upon by the King to form a minority government, the first Labor regime in history. There had been quivers in the City and in Mayfair. It was feared by the upper classes that a "socialist" government might quickly wreck the country. But nothing so untoward happened. It lasted only nine months and accomplished little—certainly nothing to frighten a rabbit. Since that time the Conservatives, with an immense majority in the House of Commons, had been in firm control, putting down the workers, reducing their wages, drifting along and muddling through one blunder after another in both foreign and domestic policy to the general content of the ruling classes. The country was quiet and apparently content.

That did not make for news, which was my principal business. In fact, the only issue which stirred passions in Parliament that summer and the next was over the revision of the Prayer Book, a matter which aroused little interest among our Christian readers in Chicago. I covered some of the debates in the Commons, but they put me to sleep. Admittedly I never understood the issue, if there was one, or why it caused such a fuss in both houses of Parliament (the Lords passed the revision, the House twice rejected it) and among the Anglican clergy. Though the press, especially *The Times*, devoted columns to the debate, I could not discern that there was any concern among the people, high or low, most of whom, as at home, didn't go to church anyway, though professing to be Christians.

More productive of news for us was the breaking off of diplomatic relations with the Soviet Union by the Tory government after another red scare. This was my first actual experience with the Bolshevik bogy, which I would later see exploited to fool the populace in other countries, Germany and France and, above all, my own. For when I finally returned home, it was to live through the McCarthy hysteria. We had had in America, to be sure, the Palmer raids on "reds" immediately after the war. Thousands of alleged Communists had been arbitrarily arrested and jailed by the Attorney General, "the fighting Quaker"; hundreds who were aliens were deported to Russia. Millions of Americans professed to be scared to death of the "red threat." But in due course and distracted by a glittering prosperity and the elevation of trivialities to a way of life, we had recovered our senses.

Somehow one expected our prosaic British cousins to be more immune from the red scare, but they had turned out to be just as vulnerable as we. In 1924 the electorate had been panicked into voting out Labor and giving the Conservatives an overwhelming majority by the publication, just before the polling, of an alleged letter from Zinoviev, head of the Communist International, to the British Communist Party calling on it to carry out a whole array of seditious acts. That the letter was obviously a fake, probably forged by a group of White Russian émigrés in Berlin and conveniently sent for publication to the *Daily Mail*, a rabidly anti-Soviet newspaper, made no difference to the British electorate. The voters held the Labor government to be "too soft" on the Bolsheviks and turned it out.

Now, in 1927, the summer of my arrival, the Tory government again expressed alarm at the threat from Moscow. In May a large detachment of police had raided the offices of the Soviet Trading Agency in London. No incriminating documents had been found. The government had been fooled by a false tip. To hide its embarrassment it broke off diplomatic relations with the Soviet government. This was something the people could understand and approve.

Our readers in the Chicago area, too. Our esteemed newspaper gobbled up such stories and plastered them all over the front page. They assured our readers that there *was* "a threat of Communism" to our free Western world and reassured them that the British government, once more in the safe hands of the Tories, knew when it was time to break with the "atheistic" reds in Moscow. Their own government in Washington, in its infinite wisdom, had never recognized the Bolshevik government, though it had been in power for nearly ten years. So far as Washington was concerned, the U.S.S.R., with its vast territory and population and its great potential power, did not exist.

General Charles G. Dawes, who arrived in June, 1929, as the new American Ambassador just as I was beginning my third summer tour of duty in London, was occasionally a source of sprightly news for us. As one of Chicago's most eminent citizens he had to be covered closely by a Chicago newspaper, though our Colonel McCormick, I gathered, deplored his internationalist views. He was, on his record, the most distinguished American to serve as Ambassador here in a long time, having been, among other things, Comptroller of the Currency under President McKinley, Director of the Budget under President Harding, Vice-President under President Coolidge, author of the Dawes Plan, which eased German reparations and stabilized the German currency, and winner of the Nobel Peace Prize, with Sir Austen Chamberlain, the British Foreign Secretary, in 1925. He also had had a distinguished war record as organizer of supplies for General Pershing's American Expeditionary Force in France. Between public service he had found time to organize the Central Trust Company of Illinois and acquire a sizable fortune. He was eccentric, energetic, unpredictable, with a flair for publicity. And, though a conservative banker, lawyer and public official, he had a wonderful contempt for stuffed shirts.

On his arrival in London he had shocked the English by

publicly announcing that no liquor would be served in the American Embassy. As long as there was Prohibition at home, he said, there would be Prohibition in our Embassy. But a much greater shocker was his announcement that he would wear no fancy Ambassador's uniform (with sword). He showed up at Buckingham Palace to present his credentials to the King attired in formal evening clothes—white tie and tails—though it was only noon. Dawes was also a formidable practical joker. He thought up all sorts of schemes for the Embassy servants to carry out just for the sheer fun of shocking austere British guests. For me he brought a freshness to the drab London scene. One kind deed he did for me brought the severest reprimand I had yet received from the lord of the *Tribune*.

I had dropped in on the Ambassador one Saturday morning for a chat, and he had mentioned that he was putting the finishing touches on a speech he had to give that evening at Oxford. I told him that in that case I would have to traipse along with him to cover it.

"Why spoil your weekend?" he said. As a matter of fact it was one of the very few weekends I had ever been invited to the country. I had planned to get away from London on a noon train and for once had Sunday off.

"Listen," Dawes said. "I'll have this lousy speech typed up in an hour and send it over to you. You can get it off to Chicago and take off for your weekend."

The text arrived shortly before noon. I glanced through it, wrote a brief one-paragraph lead, pasted a thousand words of his copy on the cable, edited them, and dashed for my train. When I returned to the office Monday morning there was an angry cable of five hundred words waiting for me from Colonel McCormick.

SHIRER. YOUR PIECE ON DAWES OUTRAGEOUS. DO YOU THINK BRITISH ARE GOING TO GIVE YOU A TABLET IN WESTMINSTER ABBEY. THESE RESERVED FOR ENGLISHMEN. AMERICANS SHOULD NOT STRIVE FOR THEM THOUGH YOU HAVE.

And it went on and on. If I wanted to "go British," all right. But the *Tribune* wanted only true Americans on its staff. "STOP TOADYING TO BRITISH. BE AMERICAN," it ended.

I forget now even the subject of Dawes's address at Oxford, though I have a vague recollection that in view of the criticism he had received in London he had written a speech about "Some Things We Americans Owe to the English"—something like that. Not a line in my dispatch had expressed my own opinions. All except my hastily written perfunctory lead had been quotes from the Ambassador's talk. I composed a cable to my lord reminding him of that and assuring him I had no desire at all for a tablet to me in Westminster Abbey. Then I tossed it in the wastebasket. I was learning how to get along with the imperious colonel. I was beginning to suspect that he was a little mad.

As a matter of fact, I shared some of his bias toward the English. Over those last three summers of the 1920's I found them often insufferable—insufferably condescending to an American—and with astonishingly bad manners. There was some consolation in the realization that they had been this way for a long time. On his first visit to London in 1787 Thomas Jefferson, then our Minister to France, had been shocked by British behavior, even that of King George III, who had turned his back on the author of the Declaration of Independence after John Adams, the American Minister, had presented him at Court. "The British," Jefferson wrote a friend, "require to be kicked into common good manners." Probably they were even worse during the Victorian heyday of Empire. Denis Brogan, the historian, who was a Scot, used to tell me, and later wrote, that in those days "the English were probably as insufferable a nation as the modern world had seen." He thought they were improving in the 1920's.

If they made me somewhat anti-British, they themselves were anti-American. This was especially true of British officials, many of them at the Foreign Office, the Admiralty and the India Office, with whom a correspondent had to deal. They appeared to assume that an American was rather an uncouth fellow, who spoke the mother tongue badly with a jarring nasal intonation, who lacked culture and cultivation and was woefully ignorant, especially of history and of what really was going on in contemporary England and Western Europe, which they still regarded as the center of the civilized world.

America lay outside that world, crass, money-grubbing, without tradition and history—a veritable upstart among the nations. Yet I discerned a certain uneasiness, a certain jealousy, even a growing resentment, especially among the Conservatives, who ran the country from 1924 to 1929, that America was becoming so quickly a world power to rival their own. What seemed most absurd to me was that the Tories actually suspected that the United States, so isolationist since the rejection of the Versailles Treaty and Wilson's League of Nations after the war, and so little concerned with Britain or Europe, was trying to undermine the Empire and perhaps even grab a part of it for itself. The Admiralty was still a great power in Britain, one of the centers of the Conservative Establishment, and was regarded by most Britishers as the cornerstone of defense and the protector of the Empire. Was it not the British Navy, without a rival in the world for centuries, that had made England great and kept it great? Even so, I was surprised at the resentment still prevalent in naval circles, and among the backers of a big navy, at the Washington Treaty of 1921, which had imposed numerical equality in battleships between Britain and the U.S.A. and thus, they thought, curtailed British naval power. The British had torpedoed the naval limitation conference in Geneva in this very summer of 1927 because they could not accept equality with us in the number of cruisers. They thought the American demand for parity in naval strength was unnecessary; the United States did not have an Empire to defend. Or were the Yankees casting covetous eyes on the Empire?

So a Yankee in London shared in being the butt of the slight distrust and the condescension which the upper-crust English had for foreigners. The attitude seemed to be that you were a little unfortunate and undoubtedly handicapped by not being English. You struck them as a little odd, even funny. Perhaps Gilbert and Sullivan expressed one facet of how they felt. In most of their works everything foreign was funny to an Englishman. Gilbert and Sullivan opera had always bored me. But the well-born in London loved it. It made them laugh at the inferior ways of foreigners. I can't say that I minded what these people thought of me and my fellow-countrymen, or of other foreigners forced to dwell in their midst. But I was puzzled by their attitude and by their manners. H. G. Wells offered at least a partial explanation. He thought that since the members of the ruling classes had all been raised by governesses they had the minds and manners of governesses. No doubt there were other causes. These good folk lived on an island. They were insular. A veteran Dutch news-paper correspondent in London later wrote a book entitled: *The English—Are They Human?* I sometimes wondered.

That they had many fine qualities I was quick to concede. I liked the Englishman's respect for privacy. I appreciated his re-serve when he first met you. There was no backslapping that knocked the breath out of you. He did not get chummy and call you by your first name the instant he met you. He might, and usually did, have an air of superiority, but he was not boastful. He appreciated character in a person and was not taken in by dazzling self-aggrandizement. He might, and did, subscribe to a host of conventions, many of them superficial and some silly, but in his personal life he was an individualist. He did not mind eccentricity in another individual as long as it was not phoney. His word meant something to him, and to those to whom he gave it. He had a sense of fair play. He was a good sport. And though he might appear to be a cold fish, his flair for understatement went down well with me.

And I began to admire some of his conceptions of public service, his devotion to it and, above all, his high standard of honesty in it. Within the limitations of the upper-class mind and character which I have already dwelt on, he had made the Civil Service into an institution unique in the world: disciplined, skilled and absolutely incorruptible. It was the glue which kept the government together. And though more than half of its mem-bers came from "public" schools and 80 percent from Oxford and Cambridge, it was open to others through a series of rigorous examinations which all had to pass. Politicians would come and go through the various ministries and some would fall by the wayside, but behind each of them while they held ministerial office was a permanent undersecretary and a staff of civil servants who provided continuity, stability, brains, and devotion to duty, integrity and honesty. The presence of the Civil Service gave the people considerable confidence in their government, even when they despaired of the politicians.

Fleet Street, where we had our offices, and which was the center of London's newspaper world, was a fascinating place. The shadow of Lord Northcliffe, the first of the great English press lords, still hung over it, and the puckish antics of Lord Beaver-

brook pervaded it. Northcliffe was to England what Joseph Pulitzer and William Randolph Hearst were to America: he founded
the "penny press," the popular newspaper read by millions.
Launching the *Daily Mail* in 1896 he made it an instant success,
driving up the circulation until it reached more than a million
and made him a millionaire. In my time in London in the late
1920's it had begun to slip. The *Daily Express* had pushed ahead
of it, in interest and in circulation. Lord Beaverbrook had replaced Lord Northcliffe and the latter's brother, Lord Rother-
mere, who had taken over on Northcliffe's death in 1922 as
Britain's press lord. A small, pudgy gnome of a man, Beaverbrook
was a ball of fire, directing every facet of the *Express* and the
Evening Standard, editorial and business. He had been born and
raised in Canada, had made a fortune in promoting companies
there before he was thirty, and restless for new worlds to conquer
had come to London before the war, bought the *Express,* raised
its circulation from 400,000 to 4,000,000 and plunged into
politics.

There were racy features and pictures and large, sensational
headlines galore in the *Mail,* and even more in the *Express,* but
practically no news. And even the news columns were colored by
the view of the owners. It almost seemed that the *Express* was
merely a means for the impish, irrepressible, exuberant Beaverbrook to extract as much fun as he could out of life and also to
propagandize his pet political policies, many of which were
crackpot.[1] Unashamedly he would boast that his reporters and
editors wrote what he told them to, and that he paid them well
for doing it. But his puckish spirit enabled him to inject into his
newspapers something no other press lord permitted. His chief
cartoonist, a genius, David Low, of left-wing Labor outlook,
made fun of everything Beaverbrook in his newspapers advocated
or stood for. He punctured the complacency of the Establishment. His "Colonel Blimp," a walrus-mustached old simpleton
who stood foursquare for the ruling classes, for King and Country, for the Army and the Navy, and for all the nonsense about
Empire and flag, became a renowned, if ridiculous, "character," a

---

[1] Beaverbrook once told the startled members of the Royal Press Commission, who
were investigating the state of British journalism: "I ran the paper purely for the
purposes of making propaganda on my own issues . . . I have only an interest in
a paper so long as propaganda is going on."

byword, a relic, a part of English life in those days. Everyone you ran into would greet you with the latest inanity of the mustachioed old colonel and join you in chuckling over it.[1] Low was largely responsible for building up circulation in the *Standard,* Beaverbrook's evening newspaper. Low helped me, and doubtlessly many others, to survive London. He reminded you that the British after all were human, that they had a sense of humor, that the humbugs would be exposed.

Occasionally, just to shock people, Beaverbrook would allow one of his columnists to lampoon him personally. But for the most part his staff wrote what they were told to write, or what they knew the noble lord would expect them to write, and this was true of all the other newspapers, too. No columnist, no "political correspondent"—the man who reported on or interpreted the top political developments—was independent. There were no Walter Lippmanns or Scotty Restons in Fleet Street, and this was a pity. The lack left a tawdry color to British journalism.

In fact, with the exception of *The Times* and possibly the *Daily Telegraph,* the London newspapers, with their great national circulation in the millions, were pretty shabby, making no attempt to provide their readers with more than a modicum of news or even to present objectively what little they published. Almost every news story or column was slanted to fit the prejudices of the owner. British reporters, correspondents and editors were so badly paid that many of them were forced to moonlight at side jobs in order to make ends meet. I got to know a number of them, and liked them, but they were rather an unhappy lot. Since they had to write what their publishers dictated, they were a little ashamed of their jobs. Over their cups in a pub they used to recite a little jingle that was going the rounds in Fleet Street.

> *You cannot buy or bribe or twist*
> *That saint, the British journalist;*
> *But, seeing what the man will do*
> *Unbribed; there's no occasion to.*

[1] "Gad, sir," Colonel Blimp would always begin, and then let loose. "Gad, sir," one cartoon had him saying to Low, who often put himself or Beaverbrook in his drawings. "Lord Bunkum is right. Splendid Isolation, sir! We must insist on fighting everybody ourselves without interference." Or: "Gad, sir, if we want to keep our place in the sun, we must darken the sky with our airplanes." Or, Blimp in a steam bath to Low: "Gad, sir, Lord Beaverbrook is right. The Tory party must save the Empire if it has to strangle it in the attempt."

Even the elegant Harold Nicolson, who abandoned a brilliant career as a diplomat, and who already was a well-known author, quickly became disillusioned when he went to work as a columnist for Beaverbrook at the end of the 1920's. His published diaries later revealed his frustration and sense of shame.

The Times of London was different from all other British newspapers. It had become a British institution. It was the voice of the British Establishment and, indeed, of the British government, whether Tory or Labor, for it formed a close attachment to whatever group was in power, and mirrored its views. But on the whole it expressed the attitude of the traditional upper-class Englishman. And it had immense prestige in the country. Every politician, every businessman, every labor leader, everyone in the top crust, read it to find out what was going on. It covered Downing Street, Parliament, the law courts and events abroad more completely (and more objectively) than all the other London newspapers combined. Though conservative and a little stuffy, it was well written and superbly edited. Geoffrey Dawson, its editor in my time, was accounted one of the dozen most influential men in England. His editorials—"leaders," as they call them in Britain —not only usually revealed what the government was up to but guided it, or pressured it, toward policies and objectives that *The Times* favored.[1]

But aside from its columns of news and editorials and sports pages, which were the best in the country, it provided amusing reading in other fields. Its first page was given over to classified ads in the form of personal notices of every conceivable kind: of births, engagements, disengagements, marriages, illnesses, deaths, bankruptcies, anniversaries, reunions. Noble lords and ladies saved time and money by publishing their thank-you notes in a classified ad on page one instead of sending out letters. It was accepted taste in the highest circles to do so, and an insertion cost only twenty-five dollars. Anonymous persons, who did not trust the royal mail or the government telephone or telegraph, communicated with one another in cryptic messages full of mystery.

Inside, *The Times* published a daily Court Circular, recounting briefly the activities of the royal family, and beneath it a

[1] Later Dawson, for instance, would play a key role in edging Edward VIII off his throne after the young king insisted on marrying Mrs. Wallis Simpson, an American twice divorced; and later in strongly backing Neville Chamberlain's disastrous policy of appeasement of Hitler.

few choice items about what the wellborn were up to in their social life. The "Letters to The Times" section on the editorial page was an institution in itself. Everyone wrote to *The Times,* from prime ministers to George Bernard Shaw and H. G. Wells, from bishops to labor leaders and cricket players. It was almost as much of a forum for British opinion as the debates in Parliament. And, finally, when spring came, there would be the inevitable letter, usually from some country vicar, and anxiously awaited by the multitude of bird-watching readers, claiming that the writer had seen the first tufted titmouse of the season.

There had been a time just before the war when many feared that *The Times,* as an institution, might crumble. This was when Northcliffe bought it. But though he changed editors he did not change the newspaper much, and when he died, insane, in 1922, it was sold by his brother to the son of a former American, Colonel J. J. Astor, and to John Walter, a descendant of the first owner. Astor, with his American fortune to draw from, put up $15 million for *The Times,* taking 90 percent of the shares and offering Walter the remaining 10 percent. To protect *The Times* from the dangers of future changes of ownership a trust was drawn up providing that no shares could be acquired outside the two families without the consent of the trustees, who include the Archbishop of Canterbury, the Chief Justice of England and the Governor of the Bank of England.

Later this notable newspaper would falter at a crucial time for Britain. Abandoning its objectivity and good sense, it would become an apostle of appeasement of Hitler, even stooping to suppress the brilliant dispatches of its Berlin correspondent, Norman Ebbutt, the best informed of us all in the German capital in the mid-thirties, because the editor thought they might displease the brutal Nazi dictator.[1] *The Times*'s loss turned out to be my gain, for Ebbutt, frustrated at seeing his stories killed in London, would turn them over to me, then a greenhorn in the maze of Nazi politics, and his information, so often exclusive and devastating, would see the light in America.

Radio, of whose advent I was little aware at home or even in France, was developing rapidly in London in those last years of

---

[1] "I do my utmost, night after night, to keep out of the paper anything that might hurt their [German] susceptibilities," Dawson wrote in 1937 to one of his correspondents. Ebbutt was expelled from Germany a few months later.

the 1920's, and in quite a different way than in America. In Britain neither the news nor any other kind of program on the radio was for sale. There were no sponsors, no exasperating interruptions for commercials. Broadcasting was supported financially by an annual license fee of five dollars on each radio receiver in use. It was run by a public corporation, established by an act of Parliament, but not, in theory at least, subject to its dictates. It was a monopoly. No private broadcasting was permitted.

This had its good and bad points. The B.B.C. (British Broadcasting Corporation) did not measure the success of its programs by the number of listeners attracted, as at home. It did not have to cater to the tastes of the vast majority for commercial reasons. It did not pitch its broadcasts to the lowest common denominator. There was no pressure on the content of programs from greedy sponsors. In this sense British broadcasting was freer than at home. But it was not free. The heavy hand of monopoly lay over it. If you didn't like the programs on the B.B.C. there were no other networks to turn to, though later a good many Britishers switched to stations on the nearby Continent for release from boredom. And though the B.B.C. was theoretically independent from the government, it hesitated to differ from it. Sometimes its objectivity could be measured better by what it suppressed than what it broadcast. During the General Strike the year before, the B.B.C., then in the process of being transformed from a privately run monopoly, financed by the manufacturers of radio sets, to a public monopoly, broadcast only news that was favorable to the government trying to suppress the strike.

This was the work of Sir John Reith, a dour, driving Scotch Presbyterian puritan, who presided over the first and then the second B.B.C. with an iron hand. He was a tough, ruthless, narrow-minded tyrant who believed fiercely that the power of radio over men's minds should be used exclusively for good, as he saw it. He wanted it to improve their lives, heighten and deepen their appreciation of the good things, such as classical music and serious thinking. He insisted that it give a stamp of Christian morality on all that it did. He would not allow popular entertainment to be broadcast on Sunday. To him, "controllers" (I always thought of them as censors), who watched over program content and shaped it to Reith's narrow views, were more important than producers, writers or performers. When they caught Harold

Nicolson, who became a popular commentator on the B.B.C., trying even to mention Joyce's novel *Ulysses* in one of his broadcasts
on modern literature, they forbade it, on the direct orders of
Reith. When Nicolson insisted, Reith terminated his contract.

Thus it was that controversy on the air was avoided like the
plague, and the news was given by announcers specially trained
to speak in a deadpan voice so as to avoid any hints of their own
subjectivity or of party prejudice. In time they evolved a very
distinct B.B.C. voice, speech and manner in their news broadcasts
that was a sort of modified Oxford lingo, and often they sounded
to me as if they were speaking with a heated stone lodged in their
mouths. They sounded like very proper, well-brought-up Englishmen who never lost their cool even when speaking of the most
horrendous events. Pity or sadness or a sense of tragedy had no
place in their delivery. I was not greatly surprised one evening
when I called on a friend just after he had given the news spiel
and found him in a dinner jacket. He explained that Reith would
never permit an announcer to face the microphone unless he was
suitably dressed in black tie and tux.

While I found the B.B.C. news announcers a little hard to
listen to, I remembered them with fondness years later when I
was subjected to the high jinks of the fast-talking, smooth, syrupy
American announcers, or the highly emotional commentators
such as Gabriel Heatter. I also recalled fondly the fine music
concerts and dramas, uninterrupted by commercials, and the
stimulating talks by persons of every kind who had something to
say. And as time went on, the B.B.C. news improved, in objectivity and in variety and depth. Millions of listeners of various
nationalities on the Continent turned to it for the facts and the
truth. Its shortwave news broadcasts in a score of languages were
the most listened to in Europe.

Two other aspects of broadcasting in Britain pleased me
greatly. No political party in Britain during an election, or at any
other time, could buy time on the radio to put over its propaganda. At election time each party was given an equal amount of
time—free. The abuses that later came to America, especially
with television, when the richest party bought the most time—
some would say, "bought the election"—were spared the British.
Secondly—and this was true elsewhere, as well, but I first experienced it in Britain—radio not only exposed the political windbags

and made them sound ridiculous, but it was unkind to most of the great orators who had been so successful in moving live audiences at large public meetings. Lloyd George and Ramsay MacDonald, the leaders of the Liberals and of Labor, respectively, were the two finest public speakers of the time, but their flowery, emotional oratory did not come over well on the tube. Baldwin, a rather ineffectual speaker at large gatherings (though sometimes superb in the narrow confines of the Commons) far surpassed them on the radio with his relaxed and simple manner. Only Winston Churchill, who rivaled the Liberal and Labor chiefs as a public orator, sounded just as good, or better, when he spoke to the people in their homes over the radio, but he had little opportunity for this in those days—his turn would come later.

Our public figures at home, it seems to me in retrospect, were slower than the British in learning how to use the radio. Calvin Coolidge and Herbert Hoover were terrible. They put you to sleep. The old-time politicians, with their overblown rhetoric, were even worse. Hardly any of them knew how to read a speech as if he were not reading, which was one of the secrets of communicating over the radio. All that would change with Franklin Roosevelt.

Outside of work, my life was rather miserable those summers in London. The blue laws, especially the Sunday blue laws, were a blight. They seemed calculated to make life as unpleasant as possible, particularly for those like me whose work, or lack of means, kept them in the gray, drab city over the weekend.

London on Sundays was a dead city. Almost all the restaurants and all the pubs were closed. To get a bite to eat one had to go to a Lyons tea shop, where the food was abominable. There was no public place where one could get even a beer to drink. The theaters shut down. Most of the buses were taken off the regular routes. Subway service was curtailed.

The well-off, of course, went to the country for the weekend and were able to continue the good life there. I had to work Saturdays and Sunday mornings at the office and could not get away to the country, even if invited. Trapped in the lifeless city I sent a desperate S.O.S. to Yvonne to come over, but she could not. Still desperate two summers later, in 1929, I begged Zora, whom I meantime had met in Vienna, to join me and she did. Together we survived the London weekends.

Fortunately, the museums stayed open on the Sabbath, and there were the parks. Sunday afternoons we prowled through them. The National Gallery was not the Louvre, but it was very good. The British Museum was unique in the world, being not only a great library but housing, among other things, the best sculpture of ancient Greece to be seen outside Greece, from where it had been carted away by Lord Elgin and others— "stolen," the Greeks said. But most of the world's great museums were full of stolen goods, the Louvre in Paris perhaps above all, and we citizens of great Western powers did not have too many qualms.

Hyde Park was jammed with trippers on Sundays, but at least it provided a little fresh air and green grass. One could always stop and listen briefly to the crackpots declaiming from atop their stepladders or soapboxes. If the press and radio were not very free, Hyde Park at least nurtured complete free speech. The freaks could say anything that crossed their empty minds and occasionally they were amusing.

When it rained, as it often did, even in August—though the late summer of 1929 was one of the driest on record—we could sit at home and catch up on our reading. That summer Zora and I read to each other in French most of Proust and Gide, improving perhaps just a little our foreign accents, Hungarian and American, respectively.

The perfidious blue laws were not suspended altogether even on the weekdays. The closing laws for pubs, bars and cafés were so complicated that I could never get them straight. During the day they would open and close at all kinds of hours. Usually when I arrived they would be shutting down. Evenings, after the theater or a concert, one would make a mad rush to a café to try to get in a drink and a snack before the midnight closing. But this usually was a losing proposition. The places were crowded and the service was slow. You were lucky to get one drink. The law stipulated that food had to be ordered with a beverage. The waiters would bring you a rubber-sandwich which had lain about the place for days and was not supposed to be eaten—could not possibly be eaten, though it cost you a dollar—but which satisfied the dictates of the law.

The English put up with all these ridiculous curtailments of their life with surprising stoicism. It seemed rather masochistic to me. Apparently the blue laws had been passed during the spartan days of the war, when they had made some sense. No one in Parliament or in the government had thought to change them after the war was over. An oversight, perhaps. As an American, I really had little right to complain. At home, with our idiotic Prohibition laws, it was far worse. The British, in this respect, had not been as barbarous as the Americans.

Occasionally there were pleasant interludes those summers which took me away from the routine of office work or from the drabness of London, or both. I loved the fortnight at Wimbledon that began toward the end of June. It was both a social and a sporting event. The stands were full of lords, ladies and one or two members of the royal family. On the fast grass courts you saw the best tennis in the world. Helen Wills, fully recovered from her appendicitis operation of the year before, had returned to Paris in 1927 to take the women's singles championship and then come on to Wimbledon to win her first of eight titles. No other woman could match her powerful strokes. Tilden and the other Americans, who had dominated world tennis for so long, began to fade, replaced by the French: Lacoste and Cochet in the singles, Borotra ("the bounding Basque") and Brugnon in the doubles.

Though I knew no more about golf than I had, in the beginning, about tennis, I was assigned to cover the big golf championships in 1929, when Walter Hagen took the British Open at Muirfield, Scotland, and Joyce Wethered of Britain beat Glenna Collett of America in the 36-hole final of the Women's British Open after being five down over the first thirteen holes at the famed St. Andrew's course by the sea. Joyce Wethered was the finest woman golfer of her time. Bobby Jones, who was to score the "grand slam" the following year, taking the British and American Open and Amateur championships, said she was the equal of any male golfer, including himself.

The erroneous idea of my Chicago editors that I had been a sports writer also led them to assign me to cover the Winter and Summer Olympics in 1928. The Winter Olympics were something new, reflecting the increasing interest in winter sports in Europe and at home. The summer games had been revived in Athens in 1896, after a lapse of some two thousand years, and had continued every four years except during the war, when the meeting scheduled for Berlin was called off because of hostilities. Chamonix, high in the French Alps, had hosted the first Winter Olympics in 1924 and now, in 1928, the second were taking place at St. Moritz in Switzerland. I found it a colorful, exciting spectacle: the ski jumping, the slalom and downhill races, the bobsled runs, the graceful figure skating, the hockey matches with their speed of action. The February setting in the picturesque valley below the towering snowy mountains had a beauty that you could find in no other gathering of sports.

The much vaunted Olympic spirit, which was supposed to bring the athletes of the world together in brotherly sportsmanship, was, however, somewhat lacking, and it would be no better during the summer games that year in Amsterdam. Nationalist rivalries were too strong. The young men and women were imbued with a fierce spirit not only to win for themselves but for their country. The judges were the most chauvinistic of all. In events that had to be judged, like figure skating and the form of ski jumpers, they favored either their compatriots or those from countries they liked. They cheated many a performer. The United States, which had done badly at Chamonix, came up at St. Moritz with a long-distance skater who beat out the favored Scandinavians and Finns in the 10,000-meter race. But his gold medal was taken away from him when the judges decided to call it "no race" because of the soggy conditions of the ice for the late skaters. As they said at home, "he was robbed." One young Norwegian lass captivated the fans that year, triumphing even over certain judges. This was the fifteen-year-old Sonja Henie in the women's figure skating. She had first competed at Chamonix at the age of eleven. Now she was supreme, a dazzling, lovely figure on the ice. She would go on to win two more Olympic titles and to fame and fortune.

The IX Olympic Games at Amsterdam, in the first fortnight of August, 1928, turned out to be the finest athletic spectacle I had ever seen and the most successful modern Olympiad yet held. More than four thousand young men and women from forty-six countries competed. For the first time since the war the Germans participated—ten years after the Armistice the bitter hatreds of the war had finally dissipated. The Russians were not invited—out of fear, apparently, by the International Olympic Committee that they might contaminate the innocent youth of the rest of the world with "godless" Bolshevism. In time, of course, this fear, too, would fade and after another war the Soviet Union would vie with the United States in dominating the games.

Olympic and world records fell in almost every event that

splendid summer in Amsterdam, the Americans setting most of them in track and field, and in swimming. But for the first time since the war, athletes from other countries successfully challenged the Americans in a number of races. Lord Burghley, of Great Britain, beat out the favored American in the 400-meter hurdles; a South African edged out an American in the 100-meter high hurdles, setting a new world record. Another Englishman, Lowe, won the 800-meter run, for an Olympic record. A Canadian won both dashes, which the Americans had been expected to take. And the great distance runner Paavo Nurmi, the "flying Finn," in the 10,000-meter run added a fourth victory to his three previous Olympic triumphs of 1920 and 1924.

In ancient Greece the Olympics were not open to women athletes—indeed, women were barred from witnessing them (the men performed naked)—with the solitary exception of the priestess of Demeter, goddess of all the fruits of this earth, who sat alone and apart on a white marble pedestal in the stadium. Bowing to the times, the Olympic fathers now introduced at Amsterdam a limited track and field program for women. It proved very popular. An unheralded pretty, blue-eyed, blond young woman from Chicago, Elizabeth Robinson, became the darling of the spectators when she flew down the cinder path, her golden locks flying, to win the 100-meter dash in world-record time. For a correspondent of a Chicago newspaper this was a break. The *Tribune* transferred my account of her victory from the sports pages to the front page and badgered me for more copy until I had practically written a biography of this attractive, unassuming young woman.

The International Committee had abandoned keeping an official point score of the games, perhaps to dampen national rivalries, though we American correspondents kept an unofficial tabulation, pleased no doubt that it showed the Americans far ahead of the others. General Douglas MacArthur, president of the American Olympic Committee, was too much the proud patriot not to keep one himself, even incorporating it in the grandiose report he presented later to no less a person than Calvin Coolidge, President of the United States. Counting first, second and third places in all events, he gave us a total of 131 points, with Finland far behind in second place with only 62 points and Germany third with 59. In the purple prose which he later would make familiar to his compatriots he reported to the President the names of each of the American winners and commented: "In achieving these victories America made seventeen new Olympic records, seven of which are world records. This represents the greatest number of Olympic and world records ever achieved at one time in any set of games, either Olympic or otherwise, by any nation, either American or foreign, in the history of athletics."

The large American team had come over to Amsterdam in the specially chartered S.S. *President Roosevelt,* on which the athletes lived during the games. The general kept a tight ship and most of the athletes resented the strict discipline he imposed. This was not the Army, after all. He would brook no breaking of the rules and personally saw to it that his curfew was observed, that no one took advantage of the lack of Prohibition laws in Holland to break training even with a beer, that "socializing" of boys and girls be monitored and limited, and that his young charges behaved at the games and in the streets of the Dutch city in that virtuous manner he expected of young Americans.

One day toward the end of the games, General MacArthur invited me to his quarters on the ship for a cocktail and some talk. It was the first time I had met this man, who was not yet nationally known but who was regarded in Washington, I believe, as the most brilliant officer in the Army, and who, indeed, in 1930, would become Chief of Staff and go on from there to his glorious (and sometimes inglorious) military career. No one could have predicted that in 1932 it would be he who with tear gas, bayonets, tanks and charging cavalry, the last commanded by a swashbuckling major named George S. Patton, Jr., and with his troubled and disapproving aide, Major Dwight D. Eisenhower, at his side, would drive the bonus-army veterans out of the nation's capital. Nor could I have foreseen the fame and glory that would come to him in the next war when he commanded our forces in the Pacific, nor the tarnish when President Truman had to sack him during the Korean War for insubordination. Or that in 1948 and 1952 he would entertain the idea of becoming a candidate for the Republican nomination for President, backed by the extreme right wing of the party.

On this day General MacArthur, puffing his pipe and offering me his tobacco for my own, was genial, eloquent—and arrogant. He was proud of all the American triumphs in the Olympics. "There is no substitute," he said, raising his well-modulated voice

378 | 20TH CENTURY JOURNEY

and tightening his jaw, "for victory"—a phrase that did not strike me as particularly original but which I recalled years later when he proclaimed it on a famous and more warlike occasion. His pride in the American athletes was genuine but it was tempered by his disappointment that they had resented the discipline he insisted on.

"We're becoming an undisciplined people," he observed, "forgetful of the old spartan virtues of hard work, dedication and respect for lawful authority that made us great. Our young men and women, splendid athletes that they are, reflect the country."

In some ways, he thought, the country was in bad shape. It had no army, for one thing. The prosperous nation was dangerously complacent about that. I wondered why he had brought the subject up—perhaps he knew of Colonel McCormick's obsession with it. I knew nothing about the Army, except that we had one of sorts. But he proceeded to enlighten me.

"Do you realize," he went on, warming to the subject, "that we have one of the smallest armies in the world—nineteenth or twentieth among the nations? Even those little countries we created after the war, Rumania, Czechoslovakia, Yugoslavia, Poland, have a bigger army than the United States of America. At home there are practically no armed forces at all. Most of our soldiers are overseas or down on the Mexican border or sitting at desks. In case of an emergency we could count on a combat force of only two divisions—about twenty-five thousand men out of an army of a hundred and twenty-five thousand."

"What about the National Guard?" I asked, just to show my interest.

"No damned good—I mean, until you give them six months' intensive training."

The U.S. Army was not only minuscule in size, he said, but its equipment "wasn't worth a damn." It had nothing but obsolete tanks, obsolete planes, obsolete artillery, and not even a single "mechanized" regiment.

"We have the worst-equipped army in the world," he said. "And the terrible thing is that our people don't give a damn. They're too busy making money. I'm truly concerned."

I said I was too. But I did not feel called upon to explain that my concerns were somewhat different from his and focused more on what might become of a country full of frenzied dollar-chasers. The future of the U.S. Army did not lay heavily on me. We had a little small talk and I finished my drink and left, rather impressed by the general. He seemed above the stripe of what I imagined our professional soldiers to be. He was forceful, articulate, thoughtful, even a bit philosophical, and well read. Only his arrogance bothered me.

It was an interesting and happy interlude for me, that fortnight of the Olympics in Amsterdam. Yvonne made it even happier by breaking away from Paris to join me. She never looked more lovely. She became delightfully excited by almost every race—on the track, at the swimming stadium, out at the rowing. She thought the women divers were the most graceful young women she had ever seen. She liked the racy talk of the sports writers from home, learned a great deal of Americanese from them and took their admiration for her in stride. While I was writing the evening dispatch she would sit at the telephone and check on various events I had been unable to cover personally. Evenings we dined and danced far into the night. It was one of the finest two weeks we ever had together away from Paris. I was still madly in love.

Two assignments in London kept up my new interest in aviation, which had been kindled by my covering the landing of Lindbergh in Paris. On June 18, 1928, Amelia Earhart, with two male companions as copilot and navigator, landed her pontooned plane at Burry Port in Wales, after a flight from Newfoundland, thus becoming the first woman to fly across the Atlantic. The *Tribune* hustled me down to Wales to cover the event in a tiny chartered Moth biplane which was so slow it could, and did, land on a vacant lot close to the center of town. Miss Earhart was a freckle-faced, pert, gracious young woman of thirty, and though, like Lindbergh, she had sold her story exclusive to *The New York Times*, she generously provided me with enough details of the flight to enable me to write a dispatch. In a way the flight was anticlimactic after Lindbergh's feat.[1] Half a dozen American

[1] Miss Earhart went on to become the best-known woman aviator of the next decade. While on a round-the-world flight she was lost over the Pacific between New Guinea and Howland Island in July, 1937. No trace of her was ever found. There was speculation that she had made a forced landing on a Japanese-fortified island and was executed, but it was never substantiated.

flyers, with their crews, had now flown the Atlantic in the last thirteen months. Each had stepped up public interest in the possibility of establishing regular commercial air service across the ocean. The problem was to build a plane powerful and large enough to accommodate several passengers and mail, and to increase its speed.

Progress in speed was stimulated in those days by the Schneider Cup races, which drew entrants from Britain, Italy, France and America. The race in September, 1929, which I went down to cover in the waters off Ryde, on the Isle of Wight, not only produced speeds far in excess of any previously achieved by aircraft but, unknown to us correspondents at the time, provided Britain with the prototype of a plane that would help it survive when the next war came.

One of the British entries, a Supermarine S6, flew the thirty-one-mile triangular course at a speed of 328 miles an hour. It was awesome to watch as it streaked by a few feet overhead, faster than any plane had ever flown before. All the aircraft in the Schneider races were pontoon planes, taking off and landing on water. Aeronautical designers did not then know how to land such high-speed machines on wheels on a runway. This would have to wait for the development of the flapped trailing edge on the wings, which would enable planes to slow down to a safe landing speed.

The first Schneider Cup race in 1913 at Monaco had been won with a speed of 45 miles an hour, and even after the war, despite all the development of fighter aircraft, the fastest plane at the 1920 race at Venice had made only 103 miles an hour. In nine years the speed had been tripled. In my dispatch I calculated that at a speed of 328 miles an hour a plane could fly from London to New York in ten hours and on to Chicago in three hours more.

The news caused some excitement in Chicago, where the *Tribune* gave my story a banner headline on page one. The newspaper had nagged the aviation industry for its lack of enterprise—Europe was far ahead of us in the development of commercial aviation. Our fastest new commercial aircraft had a top speed of only 150 miles an hour and regular service between our cities was sporadic. The flight from New York to Chicago took from six to eight hours, with luck. The prospect of a three-hour service aroused the imagination of Chicago. At that time most people took the train—an eighteen-hour journey. The prospect of a regular service across the Atlantic was even more exciting, but it would take another ten years before it became a reality.

During the races I saw a bit of the British aviators, who were all test pilots in the Royal Air Force. They were very close-mouthed but I did gather from them that they hoped the Super-marine S6 would be a model for a new British fighter plane as soon as a way could be found to land it on wheels. I did not then understand the significance of this. Only later would I learn that the plane that won the Cup races that September day of 1929 would become the Spitfire fighter and eleven years afterward, converted to a land plane but with the same speed, save the country in the Battle of Britain, driving off the attacking German bombers and fighters in one of the most crucial battles in history.

With this story my apprenticeship in London's Fleet Street over three long summers came to an end. Already the year before I had become a sort of roving foreign correspondent, the best job you could have in this field. I began to travel and to see the world.

BOOK SIX

ROVING CORRESPONDENT, 1928-1930

O ccasionally in those first years as a roving correspondent my assignments out of London and Paris took me to ancient countries that, as it happened, had reached turning points in their long and troubled history, and I could get back to the kind of reporting I liked best.

Again, ridiculously enough, covering sports opened the way. By a curious quirk of fate two of these assignments in 1928 came as a result of my having to report on Gene Tunney. He had won the heavyweight boxing championship of the world from the great Jack Dempsey in Philadelphia in 1926, successfully defended it against Dempsey a year later in Chicago in the famous battle of the "long count,"[1] knocked out Tom Heeney of New Zealand at Yankee Stadium in July of this year and then announced his retirement from the ring. Richer by $1,742,282, according to the sports pages, from his last three years of fighting, he had gone on to Yale to lecture, had come over to Europe in August to visit the home of his ancestors, Ireland, and planned to go on from there to Italy to marry what the newspapers described as "an heiress," Mary (Polly) J. Lauder of Greenwich, Connecticut. My Chicago editors asked me to go down to Southampton to meet him as he got off the *Mauretania* on August 21 and to accompany him for a while on his European travels.

The assignment started out as a lark. Tunney, surprisingly

---

[1] Knocked down, and apparently out, in the seventh round, Tunney got an extra four seconds to recover when Dempsey was slow in moving to a neutral corner. The champion came back to win on points. So exciting was the fight, even when reported blow by blow over the radio, that eight fans, listening to the broadcast, died of heart failure.

articulate and well read, was pleasant company, except when he lectured me at length on "marine painting" after we got off Shakespeare and some of the more modern writers we both loved, though toward the end of his travels I could see that he was rather looking forward to slipping away for a walking tour with his friend Thornton Wilder, whose novel *The Bridge of San Luis Rey* was a best seller that year, and who, he told me, would be his best man at the wedding in Rome.

The Tunney assignment, which began as a pleasant interlude, brought me at the end my first look at, initially, Ireland, free from the British at last after murderous centuries of oppression, killing, burning, and robbery, and then Italy, at a moment when Mussolini had finally wiped out his democratic opposition by means of a sensational and brutal murder and the promise of others, and was now ready to stamp his mindless Fascism on an old, attractive and civilized people who deserved better. In Rome I would also get my first glimpse of the Vatican—not only its art treasures and library, but the workings of its vast religious empire, so mysterious to a Yankee Presbyterian—and one day of the Pope talking earnestly in German to a small group of Austrians.

By the summer's end in 1928 when I arrived in Dublin, the Irish Free State had survived for six years—survived the Irish themselves, their old quarrels, their lust for killing one another. Even the fiery, American-born Eamon de Valera, the "President" of the self-constituted "Republic," who had opposed the establishment of the Free State because it had not been allowed to break away completely from Britain, had the year before finally taken his seat in the Dail, abandoning his opposition by violence for a more peaceful and democratic kind. I had not followed very closely the story of Ireland's winning its virtual independence after the war, though it had aroused the passions of millions of Irish-Americans at home. A few days in Dublin talking to politicians, editors, writers and some of the fanatics of the Irish Republican Army educated me rapidly.

The Free State, which had been granted Dominion status on the Canadian model, had scarcely been born at the beginning of 1922 before it was plunged into the bloodshed of a civil war. Michael Collins, who with Arthur Griffith had negotiated the treaty with Britain after De Valera pulled out of the secret talks, and who was now head of the Provisional Government, was killed in an ambush by members of the I.R.A. Led by Rory O'Connor and De Valera the I.R.A. had occupied the Four Courts building in Dublin and had blown it up, with all its records. O'Connor was arrested but De Valera escaped, only to be caught later and sentenced to a year in prison—a bitter pill for this fanatic Irish patriot to endure from his own countrymen. The hated British had always been his jailers before.

For nearly a year, as the Provisional Government and the Dail met daily, the first to try to run the country, the second to draw up a constitution for a regular parliament and government, their offices in Dublin resembled a fortress, heavily guarded against the insurgents by troops with machine guns. By the beginning of December, 1922, a constitution was finally hammered out and a regular government was established with William Cosgrave as President of the new Free State, but when the Dail met on December 8 Cosgrave opened it by announcing that one member had been shot dead and another wounded on their way to the meeting. The new government promptly decided to meet terror with terror. Next day four insurgent prisoners, including Rory O'Connor, were shot without trial. Martial law was proclaimed and more executions were carried out. In the countryside, burning and bombing of public buildings and private homes continued. Rail and road communications were paralyzed.

"Is there to be no living Irish nation?" Griffith had cried out. If the fighting continued there would be only dead Irishmen and, as Collins said just before his assassination, "our belief in ourselves as a nation will perish." Gradually their cries were heard and by May of 1923, when the number of executions had risen to seventy and ten thousand Irishmen crammed the Irish prisons, De Valera called a halt, declared hostilities at an end and ordered his followers to bury their arms. But it took him three years to cool off. In 1926, perhaps sobered by a year in prison, he broke away from the Sinn Fein, which he had led so long, on the issue of members of Parliament taking the oath of allegiance to the King of England, as required in the Constitution. De Valera, foreseeing that the only path to power for his Republicans lay in playing the parliamentary game, decided to take the oath to the King "only as an empty political formula," formed a new party, the Fianna Fail, and with it entered the Dail for the first time in 1927, the year before my visit. He would have to wait another five years before taking over the government. Then he would lose little time in abolishing the oath, breaking the last ties with the British Commonwealth and finally, after the Second World War, proclaiming a Republic—achieving at last the final goal for which he had fought all his life. But all that lay in the future.

Though he was only the leader of the parliamentary opposition, and that barely for a year, De Valera was easily the most interesting figure I met that fall in Dublin. Like most Americans, I knew something of his tempestuous career, for at home he was a great hero to the Irish-Americans and his exploits in behalf of freedom for Ireland had often been chronicled in our press. Nearly every evening after Tunney had returned from a day visiting this and that, or being hailed here and there, a group of Irish would gather in his hotel suite for drinks and talks that usually continued far into the night. One evening De Valera called to pay his respects to Tunney and, though he did not drink, he stayed for a chat. He was a little dismayed to find an American newspaperman present and I had to promise that I would not use anything he might say as the basis of an interview for the *Tribune*, or quote him directly in any way, though I told him that tens of thousands of Irish-Americans in Chicago as well as most of the rest of our readers would be intensely interested to learn what was in his mind now that he and his followers had entered the Dail. I think he was still hurt by the compromise he had had to make and the fear that many Irish in America, who had raised so much money for his cause, might have felt betrayed by his giving up on his fight for a Republic of Ireland. He certainly had no intention of explaining himself through me and my newspaper. He was then forty-five, tall, gaunt, ascetic, highly intelligent and articulate, with a warm voice, a bit of a brogue and that fine pronunciation of vowels and thickening of consonants that make the Irish speaking English so delightful to hear. As he spoke I kept thinking of what I had read and heard of his remarkable and dangerous life.

De Valera had been born in New York in 1882 of a Spanish father and an Irish mother. His birth in America saved him later from certain death. His father died shortly after he was born and at the age of two he was sent to Ireland, where he grew up in the home of his maternal grandmother in County Limerick. With the aid of a scholarship won for his prowess in mathematics, he attended Blackrock College near Dublin, took his degree at the

Royal University and taught mathematics in a local high school. He had a passion for mathematics, continued to study it, especially when he was in prison, and after he left that evening someone told me he was the only man in Ireland who understood the Einstein theorem of relativity. He had begun to study it in 1918, before it became generally known, while doing time in Lincoln Jail in England.

He had early become a fervent Irish patriot and revolutionary. By 1916, in the midst of the Great War, he was at thirty-three one of the leaders of the Irish Volunteers and of the Sinn Fein, and when a remnant of these—some two thousand men—staged the Easter rebellion in that year, proclaimed the Irish Republic and tried to take over Dublin, De Valera was one of the sixteen leaders, commanding a group of fifty armed men who blocked the road from Dublin to the sea. After four days of fighting, British troops put down the uprising and all the leaders, including De Valera, were court-martialed and sentenced to death. Fifteen were executed, but not De Valera. His sentence was commuted at the last moment to life imprisonment after the military tribunal learned that he had been born in New York and could claim American citizenship. The British at that time were sensitive to American public opinion. The fortunes of war had turned against them and more than ever they needed the support of the United States, already their chief arsenal. They were aware of the Irish-American vote and how it might delay, or even prevent, America coming into the war on their side.

So the life of De Valera was spared and he was sent to Dartmoor Prison in England to begin a life sentence. The following year, to play further on American sympathies as well as to ease the spirit of rebellion in Ireland, the British government gave a general amnesty to the Irish prisoners. De Valera returned to Dublin and, as the only surviving leader of the Easter uprising, was made head of the Sinn Fein. Even then, De Valera now told us, the Irish people felt in their bones that the Easter rebellion was the turning point on their road to independence. Failure though it was, and so costly in lives, especially of their leaders, out of its ashes rose what soon would become free Ireland. The date would be celebrated by the Irish as their Day of Independence, much like our Fourth of July. As in our own case, independence had subsequently to be won.

De Valera did not stay out of prison for long. In May of 1918 he was arrested again, charged with fomenting rebellion, and was carted off to Lincoln Jail in England, where he spent much of his time studying Einsteinian mathematics and probably more time planning to escape. This he did, in the following February. Object of a massive manhunt, he managed to evade capture in England and then in Ireland and finally got away on a ship to America disguised as a stoker. Now proclaimed the "President of the Irish Republic" he received a tumultuous welcome in New York, Boston and other cities, where he raised more than five million dollars for the cause. He returned clandestinely to Ireland in 1920 and immediately launched a new war against England, one of the bloodiest and cruelest ever fought in Ireland. The British sent in the Black and Tans, an irregular force of bloodthirsty desperadoes, who killed and burned from one end of southern Ireland to the other. The Irish, under De Valera and Collins, met terror with terror. No one's life or home was safe.

The terrorism of the Black and Tans aroused the Irish hatred of the British to a new pitch. Soon in England that terror was being denounced by public men of every sort, including the Archbishop of Canterbury. Arthur Henderson, a leading figure in the British Labor Party, returned from a visit to Ireland and told the Commons that what was happening there was "a disgrace to the human race," and Lord Asquith, a former Prime Minister, exclaimed: "Things are being done in Ireland which would disgrace the blackest annals of the lowest despotism in Europe." The British government was accused of deliberately conducting a policy of murder and terrorism. Under the pressure of public opinion it finally gave way. It agreed to negotiate with De Valera himself, a truce and then self-government. A treaty was made and the Irish Free State was created, though De Valera in the end would not accept it. Now, by 1928, he had. It was only a matter of time, I was told by both his friends and enemies, before he would become its head, and that evening in Dublin in his quiet but determined way he seemed quite confident of it.

From his manner and his talk it was obvious that his eminence and all the hero-worship he was subjected to had not spoiled him nor deflected him from leading a simple personal life. He lived, I was told, in a small house, where his wife, Jennie O'Flanagan, like him a former schoolteacher, whom he had married in 1910 when she was teaching him Gaelic at the Gaelic League, did the cooking and the housework. He shunned convivial parties so dear to most Irishmen, preferring to spend as much time as possible at home with his wife and children, reading a lot and listening to music, and occasionally doing a little horseback riding.

Hero as he was to so many Irish, who regarded him as the father of the revolution that had brought Ireland freedom from the British at last, this complex, fiery man had remained strikingly modest at heart. Would he remain so, I wondered, if and when the big prize, as head of government, was won? Or would he in the end become seduced by the footlights of high public office and succumb to the adulation and flattery that accompanied it, as Ramsay MacDonald, the British Labor Prime Minister, had. The trappings and power that surrounded prime ministers and presidents had turned the heads of so many.

His subsequent road, to skip ahead, disclosed that De Valera, like Gandhi, whom I would shortly get to know, would not succumb to these temptations. For most of the forty-one years from 1932 until he retired in 1973 he led Eire, as it became officially called, as either Prime Minister or President, one of the very few men of greatness in my time who remained unspoiled by fame, uncorrupted by power.[1]

"What do you want for Ireland that you haven't got?" I asked him that evening, during a pause in the conversation.

"A great deal!" he answered, his face lighting up. "More education, for one thing. We are still an uneducated people. We need more social services. The lack of them now is a disgrace. We have to do a great deal more for the workingmen, for the poor. Fighting the British for so long made us forget what a wretched condition these people are in. Above all"—he raised his voice; you could hear in it and see in his face the old fighter coming to life—"above all, we've got to break away completely from the British, their king, their parliament, their government, their empire. And we will!" And they did. De Valera and Gandhi were the only two revolutionaries I would know in the course of my work

[1] He died in Dublin at the age of 92 on August 29, 1975, mourned, revered and honored not only by the Irish but by the world. "All my life," he told a nun shortly before his death at the nursing home where he spent his last days, "I have done my best for Ireland. Now I am ready to go."

who ultimately won what they set out to get: absolute independence for their countries—in both cases from the British. Probably I should add Thomas Masaryk in Prague, who achieved his lifelong goal of national independence for the Czechs and Slovaks after the collapse of the Hapsburg Empire in 1918. But the independence, in its true sense, of Czechoslovakia was short-lived. Hitler smashed it in 1939. Revived in 1945, after the second war, Czechoslovakia became pretty much an appendage of the Soviet Union after the Communist coup in 1948.

What were the Irish doing with the new-won freedom in 1928? After centuries of British oppression they seemed to me to be simply happy to be running their own affairs—and in a democratic way. But political freedom, I saw, did not bring complete freedom for the Irish people. Freedom to divorce was not allowed; the Catholic Church saw to that. One of the worst things to me was the censorship the Irish imposed on themselves, and here, too, could be seen the hand of the Church. The books of their greatest novelist were banned. You could not buy a copy of Joyce's *Ulysses* in any Dublin bookstore. The works of many others, Irish, English, American, were not to be had. Forbidden!

On the whole, though, I was struck by the tolerance of the overwhelming Catholic majority for the small minority of Protestants. The bloody civil war in the South had never been a war of religion as in the North. The three million Catholics in the Free State did not hate the quarter of a million Protestants, as the latter hated the minority Catholics in Ulster. Church-ridden though the State might be, it accorded freedom of worship and political freedom to the Protestants. A Protestant, Douglas Hyde, the great Gaelic scholar, would be elected the first President of Ireland in 1938 after it had proclaimed itself a sovereign, democratic state. And later a Jew would be elected Lord Mayor of Dublin. Finally, in a referendum in 1972, the Irish would vote to strike out a provision of the Constitution which had given the Roman Catholic Church a privileged position in the Republic.

And what a joy it was that autumn to hear the English language spoken as only the Irish could speak it—with a lilt and a rhythm that made it sound like pure music! English, after all, was for them an acquired language, acquired from their conquerors. They not only spoke it well but wrote it beautifully. Was not

Yeats already the foremost poet in our language? Joyce the foremost novelist? Synge and O'Casey among the finest dramatists? Not to mention George Bernard Shaw, who had transplanted himself from Ireland to England, and at home Eugene O'Neill, of Irish forebears. They were enriching the language in all its splendor.

To arrive in Rome for the first time after a summer in dreary London was to come out of a dull and depressing gray drabness into the splendor of the sunshine that made radiant the Eternal City and brightened life again. Rome was not as beautiful or as well laid out as Paris but it had a nobility that no other capital I had seen possessed. The history of its long life—two millenniums—cropped out everywhere, and in my first days I spent most of the time gazing at the splendid ruins that brought one's mind back to the time when Rome was the center of the greatest empire ever built and Paris and London merely small colonial towns. I spent whole days roaming about the Forum, under the Capitoline Hill, where so much of ancient Roman life took place and from which the country and the empire were governed, crossing past the Arch of Constantine to the Colosseum, where I would sit on a stone seat high above the arena, munch a sandwich for lunch, and contemplate what scenes had transpired there, the great meetings, the circuses, the gladiators thrown to the lions, fifty thousand Romans packing the stands. Roaming the city one could see history moving forward through the centuries toward our own day—through ancient Roman, early Christian, medieval, Renaissance and baroque. One meandered through the narrow, winding, teeming streets, always to emerge on an old church, a splendid fountain, a baroque palace, a triumphal arch, a graceful piazza. I was so entranced one afternoon in stumbling on to the Piazza Navona, once the stadium of Domitian, that it has remained my favorite place in Rome ever since, a quiet haven of inexpressible charm and beauty where one can eat and drink leisurely and tarry on the terrace or on a bench and meditate.

Rome, of course, is a double capital—of Italy and of the Roman Catholic Church—and one ended up inevitably in St. Peter's Square to gaze upon the great church, the Michelangelo masterpieces in the Sistine Chapel and the art treasures in the Vatican museums. The Pope was still "a prisoner in the Vatican" then but I gathered that negotiations were already under way between him and Mussolini to make the Vatican a sovereign state, a solution of the Roman Question which was reached the next year, in 1929, when the Lateran Treaty was signed.

Learning of this reminded me that I had not come to Rome as a tourist but that I had work to do: to cover the wedding of Gene Tunney and to remain in Rome for a couple of months in replacement of our regular correspondent, David Darrah, the former editor of the Paris *Tribune,* who had hired me three years before and was responsible for me being on this Continent at this moment, and who had now gone off on a lengthy assignment in South America. After the former heavyweight champion's wedding I was to turn to more serious work: cover the daily news, get to the bottom of the Matteotti murder and its consequence for Fascism in Italy, and try to find out how the Vatican worked. I was successful in the first two, but not in the third. The secrets of the Holy See, its finances, its politics, its diplomacy, and the workings of its world-wide organization that held the Church together and furthered its interests and maintained its power, were too well guarded to be penetrated by a youthful, unsophisticated foreign correspondent from Chicago, and a Presbyterian Protestant from the Corn Belt to boot, though for the next twelve years, on and off, when assignments brought me back to Rome and the Vatican, I gave it a try.

One crisp autumn day at the beginning of October, 1928, in the charming Hotel de Russie, around the corner from the Piazza di Spagna, Gene Tunney was wed to Mary J. Lauder. It was a front-page event for the newspapers at home, more important to them than anything else that was happening in Europe, and some sent over their sports reporters and even their society editors to cover it. Tunney and his bride were a radiant and attractive couple but I recall the wedding chiefly because it gave me an opportunity to meet and talk with Thornton Wilder, the best man at the ceremony. His latest novel, *The Bridge of San Luis Rey,* as I have mentioned, was going very well and this obviously pleased him. Every day before the wedding I would find him sitting in the spacious lobby of the hotel reading a Tauchnitz paperback novel, unmoved by all the bustle of the reporters and photographers, or by the stratagems of the bridal couple to avoid them. He was reserved, but amiable enough, and when you sat down for a chat you were struck by his modesty.

Also by his keen interest in the novel, and particularly in the new American novelists. He spoke admiringly of Hemingway, who had burst into fame two years before with *The Sun Also Rises,* of Dos Passos, who was beginning to be noticed, of Fitzgerald, whose *Gatsby* he thought probably the best of all the postwar American novels. The early promise of Fitzgerald, he thought, had now been fulfilled. He disagreed with me about Gertrude Stein. She, too, would soon be recognized. He spoke glowingly of these and there was no hint of rivalry, let alone jealousy. He did not want to talk of his own work. Except for Miss Stein, no writer I knew did. Talking with Wilder was a pleasant experience. I never met him again but watched his development in the ensuing years, impressed by his staying power, which was greater than all the other American writers of his generation. He was still writing well and publishing when he died in 1975.

I remember one moment of comedy from the wedding: when the solemn, dignified Arnaldo Cortesi, the Rome correspondent of the staid *New York Times,* no less, emerged from the wedding feast, from which the press had been barred, disguised as a waiter. It was in the finest tradition of a tabloid stooping to anything to get a "scoop." Cortesi, with his old-world manners and values, and considering the decorum of the paper he worked for, had seemed the least likely among us to try it. Even for the more earthly *Chicago Tribune* I had not thought it worth going to such lengths. But the appearance of Cortesi, who had the bearing and the long, lean face of a Renaissance Italian aristocrat, slipping furtively out of the banquet hall attired in a waiter's white tie and tails, a napkin thrown over his shoulder, his white-gloved hands grasping a tray, was a sight to see. There was a great roar of laughter from a hundred reporters and photographers and then a burst of applause. Some of us speculated on the probable *Times* headline:

VETERAN TIMES ROME CORRESPONDENT
DISGUISED AS WAITER GETS EXCLUSIVE
STORY OF WEDDING OF FORMER HEAVYWEIGHT
CHAMPION WITH WELL-KNOWN AMERICAN HEIRESS

That would have given Adolph Ochs, with his lofty ideals for the *Times,* something to ponder over breakfast next morning.

My own coverage of the event was not very inspired. In truth I was getting tired of having to report on the goings on of American notables in Europe. In Paris and London and on the Riviera or at Deauville or Biarritz we had to spend too much time keeping track of their marriages and divorces and other games. In Rome that fall after the Tunneys were wed, I was glad to get back to more serious reporting. Something new in contemporary history was happening here: the rise of Fascism. I wanted to find out what it was all about.

Is there not almost inevitably, I began to wonder, a turning point in the affairs of a revolutionary government, whether of the Right or the Left, which has come to power in a land, though it has had to share some of that power with other groups, a moment early in its life when its fate hangs in the balance and it either goes under or survives by the skin of its teeth and takes advantage of its luck by destroying its enemies and making its power absolute?

It was easy to recall examples of the first, of governments that failed to hold on: several in France after the great revolution of 1789 until Napoleon took over and made himself emperor and dictator; some in Europe after the liberal uprisings of 1848; and more lately at the end of the Great War, of which the short-lived Kerensky government in Russia was one. The Bolshevik regime, which replaced Kerensky, was a recent example of the second. Though it constituted a minority among the parties that helped to overthrow the Czar, it had held on, smashed its opposition by trickery or force and established its Communist dictatorship.

In Rome I began to see that Mussolini had successfully passed through that trial in the years just previous and that he had turned what looked like almost certain defeat and ouster from office as Prime Minister into a victory that soon led to his dictatorship. The forces of Italian democracy, divided though they were, had almost succeeded in maintaining a free country and in sinking the Fascist leader and his movement. But, as later in Germany and for the same reasons—their irresolution and sheer stupidity—they had let their chance slip by. In Italy it had taken the murder of just one man to precipitate the crisis and then to turn the trick.

How was this possible? How had it happened? In the weeks

that followed—there was not much spot news or, mercifully, any more American weddings to cover—I spent most of my days and nights in search of the answers. This was my first experience with Fascism. One could see at once the awful cost to a civilized people of having their freedoms trampled upon. But how, I wondered, had these roughneck black-shirted Fascists, with their castor-oil squads and their bullyboys, of whom Mussolini was the foremost, got away with it? And in one of Europe's oldest and most sophisticated societies.

The turning point, it became increasingly clear, the more I delved into the story, had come with the murder of the Socialist deputy Giacomo Matteotti by Fascist thugs. Son of a wealthy landowner from the Po valley, Matteotti, like so many youths of his class, had early embraced Socialism, been a comrade, though not a friend, of Mussolini's in the early days of the Socialist Party before the war, eventually studied law and entered Parliament as a Socialist deputy in 1919. From the beginning of Fascism he had been its implacable enemy, denouncing in the Chamber its terror and corruption, even when it had come to power in 1922 after the so-called Fascist March on Rome.[1]

In a tumultuous session of the Chamber on the afternoon of May 30, 1924, with inkwells and other objects being hurled about like hand grenades and the deputies scuffling in the aisles, Matteotti had stood at the rostrum for two hours patiently expounding, when he could be heard, on how the recent elections had been rigged to give the Fascists a majority, how opposition candidates had been murdered or beaten, their meetings broken up, their newspapers suppressed, and how the ballot boxes had been stuffed by Blackshirt ruffians. All through the speech and at its end the Fascist deputies hurled insults at the speaker and threats against his life. Matteotti was not unmindful of them. Turning to a colleague as he took his seat he said: "Now you may write the eulogy for my funeral."

Eleven days later he was dead.

Mussolini himself had sat through Matteotti's speech silent but livid with rage. Back at his office he told his henchmen that something would "have to be done" about Matteotti. He could

[1] Most of the Fascist squads had arrived in the capital aboard trains and Mussolini himself had taken the overnight Pullman train from Milan to Rome.

not be allowed to make another such speech. The more rugged of his followers needed no further encouragement. On the afternoon of June 10, while Matteotti was walking from his home to catch a streetcar to the Chamber, he was seized by six men, overpowered after a fierce struggle, pushed bleeding into an automobile and stabbed to death. That evening, under cover of darkness, his body was thrown into a shallow grave in the woods of Quartarella, fourteen miles north of Rome.

The leader of the murder squad was typical of those who wormed their way up to the inner circles of Fascism. He was Amerigo Dumini, a St. Louis gangster, who had returned to the land of his ancestors after the war and become fixer and hatchet man for the Fascists. He openly boasted that he had carried out eleven "homicides." The others were Fascist scum, all with prison records for violent crimes. For them the elimination of Matteotti had been just another assignment. Before the night was over they were boasting of the deed and Mussolini was informed of what had taken place.

But for several days he feigned ignorance. To Matteotti's wife, who called on him two days later and begged that her husband be returned to her, "dead or alive," he assured her that there was nothing to worry about and that he was certain her husband would soon be back. To the Chamber the same day he said that the police were diligently searching for the "missing deputy" and that he hoped "that Deputy Matteotti will shortly be able to resume his seat in Parliament."

The assassins had left too many clues for the police to cover up the crime for very long. The blood-soaked automobile had been found the next day parked at the Ministry of the Interior. On June 14 detectives arrested Dumini as he was about to leave Rome. In his suitcase were found the bloodstained trousers of Matteotti. The newspapers were ordered to suppress news of the discoveries but word soon leaked out and there was a violent revulsion throughout the country. In Milan and other cities thousands of party members in public demonstrations hurled their party cards into the gutters. When Mussolini tried to mobilize his Fascist militia, most of its members refused to report for duty. On June 13 all the opposition deputies save the Communists walked out of the Chamber and proclaimed that they would not return until Matteotti's abductors had been caught and brought to trial and law and order restored. They appealed to the King to dismiss Mussolini and form a new government. They called themselves the new Aventine, recalling the hill to which once in Roman times the plebeians had withdrawn in protest against the usurpation of their rights by the upper classes. They met separately and protested and protested. But that was all.

The little King was of no help, nor was the Senate.

The diminutive King Victor Emmanuel III—he was barely five feet tall—had been largely responsible for inflicting Mussolini on the country in the first place. Frightened by the postwar chaos and fearing a takeover by the Socialists, it had been he who had called Mussolini to power on October 28, 1922. Unmindful of the fact that most of the disorder in Italy that fall was caused by the Fascists, who were mobilizing their militia, seizing key centers in many cities and taking over trains for the March on Rome, he had paid no attention to the assurance of his Army Chief of Staff, General Pietro Badoglio, that "five minutes of machine-gun fire will scatter that [Fascist] rabble." When the government declared a state of siege and directed the Army to put down the Fascist shock troops, the King refused to sign the proclamation. Instead he wired Mussolini in Milan to hurry to Rome and form a government.

Now in 1924, two years later, though disliking the rowdiness of the Fascists, he was pleased that they had restored "law and order" and had been content to share power with the traditional parties. Mussolini, despite his threats, had not yet made himself dictator. His Fascists held only four of fourteen Cabinet posts. Parliament functioned. There was constitutional government and freedom of speech and of the press, more or less, despite the Blackshirt terror. But the murder of Matteotti had provoked a sudden crisis. Later Mussolini would admit that it was the greatest crisis of his regime—until toward the end, when Fascism began to crumble under the strain of a losing war. For days the Duce was panic-stricken. The party was falling apart. There were angry demonstrations under the window of his office in the Chigi Palace. He knew that the opposition parties were pressing the King to throw him out and he feared the monarch might give in.

But this was to overestimate the courage of Victor Emmanuel. When the deputies of the Aventine called on him, produced evidence of Mussolini's complicity in the murder of Matteotti and demanded his dismissal, he turned a deaf ear. After all, he pointed out, the Senate, two weeks after the disappearance of the Socialist deputy, had given Mussolini an overwhelming vote of confidence, with Benedetto Croce, the revered philosopher and himself a senator, applauding the result. Furthermore, the King reminded the opposition deputies, in the Chamber itself Italy's three venerable former Prime Ministers, Orlando, Giolitti and Salandra, all of them Liberals, had declared their support for the shaky Mussolini. Even after August 16, when Matteotti's butchered remains were found by an alert police officer, and a new cry for Mussolini's ouster rose from one end of the country to another, the King would not budge. The opposition parties had been confident that this time he would, if only out of a sense of revulsion at a crime carried out by his own government. When the King turned them down they were at a loss as to what to do next. They never got another chance.

Mussolini, sensing their hesitation and irresolution, recovered from his panic. He struck. On January 3, 1925, he delivered a speech in the Chamber which, as I now read it more than three years later, seemed to me to pronounce the end of any semblance of democratic, constitutional government and the beginning of the totalitarian, one-party police state. Emboldened by the failure of the opposition to get him when he was down, he now proudly proclaimed his responsibility for all that had taken place. "If Fascism has become a criminal association," he said, "I am its leader." If force was necessary to ensure Italy's 'tranquillity" he would employ it. "Rest assured," he concluded, "that in the next forty-eight hours the situation will be clarified."

It was, though it took the next three years, the period just prior to my arrival, to complete the job fully. Opposition political parties and press were suppressed, as was freedom of speech and assembly. Special courts were set up to try political offenders and a secret police was established to ferret them out. As Mussolini would write in 1944, shortly before his own execution at the hands of partisans: "By my action of January 3, 1925, with the suppression of all parties, the bases were laid for the totalitarian state."

Well, at least he knew what he wanted, and given the shocking disarray of the forces of democracy, he knew how to get it.

"Law and order" were restored. "Social peace" prevailed. The trains began to run on time.

From abroad foreign dignitaries applauded. In England the Archbishop of Canterbury began to see the strutting Italian dictator as "the one giant figure in Europe" and even Winston Churchill, the Chancellor of the Exchequer, was taken in. Meeting Mussolini in Rome shortly before my arrival he hailed him as a great European leader and especially for his "struggle against the bestial appetites of Leninism." At home the banker Otto Kahn said of Mussolini: "The world owes him a debt of gratitude." And Thomas Edison thought him "the greatest genius of the modern age."

The esteemed *New York Times* did not lag far behind. It had been almost outraged at the charge that Mussolini might have had a hand in the murder of Matteotti. "There was not a breath of suspicion against Mussolini himself," it said. "Nobody questions Mussolini's integrity and honesty and his determination and ability."[1]

The assassins were let off. At a trial in 1926 in the remote village of Chieti, far removed from Rome, where passions might easily have caused trouble, two defendants were acquitted and Dumini and two others were found guilty of "manslaughter without premeditation" and sentenced to six years in prison. Two months later Mussolini pardoned them and they were released from prison. So far as the government was concerned the case was over. Murder had paid off. Mussolini had used it to make himself dictator.

On October 28, 1928, the anniversary of the "March on Rome," I went down to the Piazza Venezia to hear the Duce address the multitude. It was the first but by no means the last speech I would hear him make over the years. Some of the foreign correspondents in Rome thought he was the finest orator in Europe, but I was disappointed. The pitch of his voice was too high and the pace of his words too feverish. He screamed at his listeners. You could see at once, though, that he was a born actor. After an explosive phrase he would jut out his chin, throw back his head and wait for the roar of applause, which he obviously loved. Then as he swung back into his rolling, turgid periods he would flail his arms. The gestures seemed to be overdone and somewhat ridicu-

---

[1] Quoted by Laura Fermi in *Mussolini*, p. 241.

lous. But the crowd was obviously fired by them and by the torrent of screeching words. There was no doubt that he was an
artful manipulator of the masses. He not only swayed them with
his oratory but also, I knew, with his fiery journalistic writing.

He had developed his skills as a young Socialist leader before
the war. As the youthful editor of *Avanti,* the Socialist daily in
Milan, he soon proved to be the best journalistic writer in the
revolutionary movement and quickly built up the circulation and
prestige of the newspaper. He had broken with the party over the
question of Italian intervention in the war, which he favored, had
been expelled and had then gone off to the front as a common
soldier. Regarded as a renegade by the Socialists when the war
was over, he had founded the anti-Socialist Fascist movement in
Milan as an outlet for his immense energies, and somewhat to his
surprise had seen it mushroom in the chaos of the postwar world.
Intelligent and widely read in history, whose lessons he thought
he understood, he had known how to profit from the twentieth
century's confusion and despair.

But he was flawed, I thought. He strutted too much. He was
too bellicose. He was much too ambitious not only for himself but
for his country. Now that he was dictator he seemed to envisage
himself as a modern Caesar who would restore to Italy the glory
of Rome. He allowed himself to be carried too far away to realize
that Italy simply lacked the natural resources to become a great,
imperial power, which in our time depended upon industrial
strength, and that the Italian people, moreover, were too civilized, too down to earth, to be interested in his ambitions, which
they saw as false. Certain industrialists, bankers and landowners,
to be sure, were learning how to profit from the regime. They
were relieved to be free from the threat of socialism and strikes.
The always conservative and backward peasants apparently supported him. But the bulk of Italians, most of the middle class and
all of the workers (and almost all of the intellectuals), so far as I
could see, did not take Fascism very seriously. They were too
intelligent for that. They suffered it but seemed to be sure that it
would not last very long, that it was a passing phase. They had
passed through so many periods of aberration in their long and
colorful history. As an Italian historian, who had been ousted
from his university chair, put it to me one day, behind the façade
of Fascism there was only emptiness, and inside Mussolini's strutting figure there was only sawdust. George Seldes, a colleague of

mine on the *Tribune*, had seen that. He had called the Duce "a sawdust Caesar" and had been expelled from the country forthwith.

But few people abroad were as discerning as my professor friend, Seldes and the majority of the Italian people. As I have mentioned, most of the leaders in the Western democracies praised Mussolini to the skies. Even one so intelligent and cynical about the human race as George Bernard Shaw was taken in. He spoke out his admiration for the man. He was even going to write a play about him, he said. My own guess was that Mussolini, like all dictators, would eventually overreach himself. Power would corrupt and corrode him, as it did all tyrants. I would feel the same about Adolf Hitler in the early years of his dizzy successes. But for many years, in both cases, it looked as if I couldn't have been more wrong.

I did not, as I have said, get very far that year in my efforts to penetrate the workings of the Vatican. Naïvely, I tried, for instance, to find out something of its finances: what its revenues were, where they came from and how, and what its expenditures might be and how they were broken down. A stone wall guarded that kind of information. My newspaper was interested in this because that year Cardinal Mundelein's Chicago diocese had lent the Holy See $1.5 million in 5 percent sinking fund twenty-year bonds secured by Church property in the city. What was it to be used for, my editors wanted to know, and what did it mean to the Vatican? Was Rome in some financial trouble? I failed on this assignment, too. The finances of the Holy See, I was told, were its own business. So was the fact that it never published a budget or a balance sheet.

Like all the other foreign correspondents I had to depend on a paid tipster inside the Vatican for most of what little news I could get. This was Monsignor Orlando (as I shall call him), a fine Renaissance Italian whom you could not help but like even after you realized he was deceiving and swindling you at almost every turn. Sometimes when one of my colleagues beat me on a story from the Vatican and Chicago complained, I would query the good father, who I knew was on the payroll of every American correspondent in Rome, though he denied it.

"Ah, you see, my good friend," he would say, his eyes twinkling, "that was special piece of information—worth two thou-

sand lire itself. It not included in regular coverage. You see, eh."
I think he took me for a Protestant idiot.

He had to have more money, he said, and if I was interested
he could supply me with some "exclusives," too. "But it cost you a
little extra, eh, two thousand lire, maybe three, maybe five, if it
really big news. You tell me how much you can pay. Your newspaper, I believe, very rich. What is few thousand lire to big
American newspaper?" He would grin and grasp my arm. "After
all, my good friend, it not out of your pocket, is it? We understand?"

The good Monsignor Orlando never explained his pressing
need for money except to mention once or twice that he had a
poor mother with a large family in the north. But we all suspected. He was reputed to have a regular mistress and numerous
passing ones. He dined in the finest restaurants and undoubtedly
was a connoisseur of expensive wines and good food. Well, I concluded, you didn't meet many Renaissance men nowadays, even
in Italy. Occasionally I would curse him to his fat, fleshy face,
but I kept him on, as did the others. With him things evened up.
He betrayed us all, but in the most charming, old-world fashion,
and always with a straight, smiling, kindly face.

On my own I did get on to one important story that would
soon mark a turning point in the history of both the Vatican and
Fascist Italy. I learned that the Roman Question was about to be
solved. It was an old problem, going back to 1870, and it had
plagued both the Holy See and the Kingdom of Italy ever since.
By 1870, with the capture of Rome, Italian armies of the Risorgimento had completed the conquest of the old Papal States which
had begun in 1859. Rome was proclaimed the capital of reunited
Italy under the House of Savoy. The centuries-old temporal reign
of the popes came to an end. But Pius IX refused to acknowledge
it. He refused to recognize the new kingdom or its government.
He declared himself "a prisoner in the Vatican" and neither he
nor his successors had set foot outside its narrow confines since.
Cavour, the chief architect of the reunited country, had sought
before his death in 1861 to negotiate with the Vatican, offering it
financial compensation for its loss of territory and a guarantee of
the sovereignty of Vatican City, but the Pope had refused to talk
to him. For fifty-eight years the Roman Question had remained
unsolved.

With the arrival of Mussolini in power in 1922, the attitude of the Vatican began to change. The Church welcomed the advent of Fascism because it believed it might save Italy from anarchy and from being taken over by Socialists or Communists. But it had two doubts. The first was about the Duce himself, who in his Socialist years had thundered against the Church, preached atheism, proclaimed that "Christ is dead and his teachings moribund," and even in the first years of building up the Fascist movement had insisted on the party's taking a stand against the Church, calling for the confiscation of its ecclesiastical property. The second doubt was whether the Fascist regime would be stable enough to last and thus be worth negotiating with. As to the latter, the Vatican had a problem of its own. One of the main threats to Mussolini's continuing in office came from a political party which the Vatican itself had helped form after the war. This was the Catholic Popular Party, led by a brilliant Sicilian priest, Don Sturzo. By 1922 Don Sturzo had gathered a large following and his party had 107 deputies in the Chamber, which made it the second largest, after the Socialists, in the nation. And it had allied itself with the democratic opposition, including the Socialists, against Fascism.

This presented a dilemma to the Church. The new Popular Party, thanks largely to the magnetism of Don Sturzo, had won over a considerable part of the masses and thus constituted a political bulwark against the Socialists. But it was democratic and opposed to Fascism, which the Vatican was now leaning toward. Three months after becoming Prime Minister, Mussolini had made his first overtures to the Holy See. He had met secretly with Cardinal Pietro Gasparri, the veteran Papal Secretary of State, and made clear that he wanted a solution to the Roman Question which would be acceptable to the Pope. Not only the Socialists but the Catholic party, he observed, stood in the way of setting up a "stable" government that could negotiate a lasting agreement.

This difficulty, so far as it concerned the Popular Party, was quickly removed by the Vatican. In June, 1923, the Pope ordered Don Sturzo, as a priest, to resign his leadership of the party and cease political activity. This doomed the Catholic party, and it soon began to lose strength. Mussolini, encouraged by this move of the Vatican, had begun further talks with it that had stretched out ever since. In the meantime he took certain steps to make clear that, whatever he had said in the past, he now wished to restore the Church's position in Italy and to encourage the Catholic religion throughout the land.

The one-time atheist and archfoe of the Church hastily had his children baptized. Then he arranged for a religious wedding to his wife, whom he had married years before in a civil ceremony. Guardedly he began to speak well of the Church, which previously he had so vilified. More openly he urged Italians to pay more attention to religion. He ordered the crucifix, which the Risorgimento had banished from state schools and hospitals, restored. He allotted large sums for the repair of churches in northern Italy damaged by the war. The Vatican took appreciative notice. Leading prelates commenced to send out friendly signals. Certain cardinals made public statements lauding the Duce for ridding Italy of "the threat of Bolshevism."

In 1926, just after the banning of all the opposition democratic parties, including the Catholic Popular Party, negotiations between the Vatican and Mussolini were stepped up. Though they were conducted in the greatest secrecy, I learned that the parties, then working on the fifteenth draft, were nearing agreement. It was signed in Rome a couple of months after I left, on February 11, 1929.

Vatican City was recognized as an independent, sovereign state. Though with only 110 acres of territory, and therefore the smallest in the world, it was also one of the most powerful. The Italian government agreed to pay the Holy See $50 million as compensation for the loss of the Papal States. It recognized the Church as the official church in Italy and Roman Catholicism as the official religion. It agreed to make its laws conform to the wishes of the Church by making religious instruction obligatory in the public schools, religious marriages compulsory and divorce illegal. The Church thus was given back its old place and power in Italy and its political sovereignty in the world. In recompense the Vatican recognized the Kingdom of Italy and its Fascist government as the temporal power in the country and agreed to keep the Church out of politics.

For Mussolini it was the greatest success of his career. Not only in Italy but abroad he was hailed by Catholics and non-Catholics alike for his statesmanship. Catholics rejoiced that he had freed the Pope from his "imprisonment" and made the Holy

See a sovereign state, to which the nations of the world could now send their diplomats and receive the Pope's envoys in return. Pope Pius IX himself praised the Duce extravagantly, as a man sent by Divine Providence.

> We have also been favored. A man was needed like the one that Providence has placed in Our path; a man who did not share the preoccupations of the liberal school.

From that day on Fascism was greatly buttressed by the support of the Church. Now no enemies were left in Italy to oppose Mussolini's dictatorship. It was not the last time the Vatican would do a favor for a Fascist dictator. Shortly after Adolf Hitler established *his* dictatorship in Germany, at a time when Nazi excesses, particularly the persecution of the Jews, the harsh measures against both Protestants and Catholics, the crushing of the democratic parties, had caused world-wide revulsion, the Vatican signed a concordat with Nazi Germany. Coming when it did, the concordat gave the Hitler government much badly needed prestige, both among its own people and in the outside world.

I left Rome at the end of 1928 with mixed feelings. I loved the old city, its antiquities which recalled so much of history, its pink and yellow walls, however crumbling, its narrow streets and spacious piazzas, its very air and light, especially at sunset, the sound of its church bells that pealed the day long, and the lovely hills around. It had fastened its nobility and charm on me for good, and I would return from time to time to the end of my life.

But the takeover of such a beautiful and civilized country by Mussolini and his rowdies clouded the picture and depressed one. Democracy here was dead. The present and the immediate future, at least, belonged to Fascism. This was a bleak prospect for such a sunny people. Was Fascism the wave of the future, as some here and abroad thought, and as Anne Lindbergh would predict a decade later when the Nazi brand was riding high in Germany? I could not believe it—not in the long run. The Italians on the whole were more patient about it than I, with my raw, Yankee impulsiveness. They had a better sense of history than I had as yet developed. They said to you: "This too shall pass."

. .

One crisp late afternoon in early December, as the sun was setting over the dome-lined rooftops, I took my leave of the Eternal City. I had a vacation due. I wanted to see the hill towns, Assisi, Perugia and Siena, stop over for a few days in Florence and then go to Venice, which from all I had read and heard was one of the marvels of the world. After that I had a rendezvous with Yvonne in Grenoble for a little pre-Christmas celebration. The Alps, which surrounded the town, would be covered with snow by then. We thought it was a beautiful and romantic place to meet.

It was a trip that has haunted my memory ever since. To roam the hill towns and Florence and Venice for the first time in your life is an unforgettable experience. No matter how often you returned to them in later years to widen and deepen your acquaintance, they could never be quite the same. For once, the first time, the reality surpassed the imagination. They were different, in beauty above all and in art, from anything your mind or experience had prepared you for. Like Rome, but more pointedly because they were smaller, they brought back not only a great deal of history but vividly so many figures of the past who had appeared vaguely in your American education, but who had once lived and worked and loved and governed and written and painted and sculpted in towns and surroundings the like of which you could not possibly have envisaged as other than make-believe.

Now suddenly on the hilltop perch of Assisi you could imagine St. Francis striding this town, looking down in contemplation on the verdant valley below, finding the light of the Lord, preaching the Gospel and feeding the birds; and the pious genius Giotto, later painting in a labor of love his twenty-four frescoes of the life of the saint along the high walls of the upper basilica of the Church of San Francesco. Florence was almost too much to try to take in over a few days, the city of Dante and Beatrice, of Petrarch, Boccaccio and Savonarola, the Medicis, and the supreme artists Cimabue, Masaccio, Fra Angelico, Filippo Lippi, Botticelli, Raphael and, above all, Leonardo and Michelangelo. And finally in Venice, rising majestically from the sea, to look for the first time on what you had seen previously only in scattered illustrations: the Doges' Palace, the Grand Canal, the Rialto, the

Piazza San Marco and the basilica, the merchant of Venice, who so fascinated Shakespeare, and the works of the great Venetian painters, Bellini, Giorgione, Veronese, Tintoretto, Titian, the last the teacher of El Greco.

There was so much in that brief trip of exploration that became imprinted on my consciousness forever: the sight the first evening, as the train approached the station in the valley below, of the thousands of lights of Assisi sparkling far above on the hilltop, looking as if they were strung across the night sky. The translucent, amber sky of Florence as you walked along the quais of the Arno and crossed the Ponte Vecchio, the bridge lined with gold, silver and jewelry shops that had been in business since the sixteenth century. The wonder of the first days wandering through that city's two great art museums: the Uffizi, with its Botticelli room and Leonardo's *Annunciation* and so much else; and the Pitti Palace, crammed with Raphaels, among them the *Madonna of the Chair*, Andrea del Sartos, Titians, Tintorettos and Rubenses, and outside it the Boboli Gardens, lovely and restful even on a chilly, sunny winter day. In Florence, still, the Church of San Marco, a place to sit and contemplate and also to take in the great frescoes of Fra Angelico, some fifty of them adorning the walls of the cells and corridors. Ruskin called them "the most radiant consummation of the pure idea of Christianity in all art." Among them was the artist's masterpiece, *The Annunciation*.

I had seen copies of many of these Florentine paintings, even in Iowa, where as a youth I had subscribed to some juvenile educational service that mailed them to you. But to see them in the original and, in the case of the frescoes, in their natural habitat, and with colors that had withstood the aging of centuries, was an altogether new and exhilarating experience. Sometimes, especially in Florence, I kept running into paintings and sculptures that were entirely new to me. One day strolling along the far bank of the Arno I stopped in the Church of Santa Maria del Carmine to discover in the dimly lit Brancacci Chapel the frescoes of a Florentine painter of the early fifteenth century, Masaccio, of whom I had scarcely heard. An elderly English lady I had met in a bar had mentioned them. Masaccio was the first, she said, though earlier Giotto had tried, to break away from two-dimensional painting and liberate objects from flat surfaces. "For his time," she said, "the first years of the fifteenth century, he was 'sensational.' He is the father of Renaissance painting. Did you know," she asked, "that Leonardo and Michelangelo came often to the Church of Carmine to study him?" I didn't, and I thanked her for the information.

Though the chapel was poorly lit and the frescoes were dimmed by what must have been smoke caused by dust and candle wax, the Masaccio frescoes were a revelation nonetheless. In *The Expulsion of Adam and Eve, The Payment of Tribute* and another, *St. Peter Baptizing*, the familiar figures, which in all previous paintings look as though they were pasted to flat surfaces, step out from the background, itself now in perspective, breathe the light and the air, and move about like human beings. In earlier painting I had seen, the faces of men and women were masks. They looked alike. In Masaccio they take on personalities of their own. They are individuals of flesh and blood, full of passion, fear, doubt.

I had made an exciting discovery, at least for myself. I made another the next day when, crossing the street from the Cathedral, I came across the bas-reliefs of Ghiberti on the East Door of the Baptistery. Depicting ten scenes from the Old Testament, beginning with the temptation of Adam and Eve, they are as dynamic and harmonious as the greatest paintings. I had never seen sculpture so alive. Michelangelo, I read later, called this Ghiberti door the Gate of Paradise, and that is the title that has come down today. I had discovered it for myself, before I had read or heard of it, and I would come back from time to time to gaze at it for the rest of my life.

Almost drunk from the wonders of Florence I finally tore myself away and took a train to Venice. It, too, was more than I had dared to imagine, a Venus rising from the sea, utterly unlike any other place I had seen, or would ever see, in America, in Europe, in Asia. Implanted on my memory for good would be the first late afternoon when upon arrival at the railroad station I took a gondola that wound its way down the Grand Canal to the Danieli, past the marble palaces where the patricians had lived, or perhaps still lived, for they all seemed occupied though a bit run-down. The gondolier, in his sailor suit and straw hat, was all that I had read about, breaking into song one moment, pointing out a palace the next, resting his oar when we came to the Ponte di Rialto so that I could have a good look at its high and graceful arch (high enough, I would read somewhere, for an ancient armed galley to pass under).

And there was the first day on the Piazza San Marco, puttering through the Church of San Marco, with its Byzantine façade and above the central doorway the celebrated four bronze horses, which the Venetians had taken from Constantinople at the beginning of the thirteenth century only to see them carted away by Napoleon at the end of the eighteenth and finally returned (one of the few pieces of artistic booty the French did return) at the demise of the Napoleonic empire. An aging monk, who attached himself to me, imparted this information and took me through the basilica. I was looking for the fine Byzantine mosaics, but he tried to rush me past them. His strong point seemed to be not so much art but history. He insisted, at great length, that the bones of St. Mark lay buried under the high altar of the chancel, brought to Venice from Alexandria in the ninth century. Outside he pointed with pride to the towering Campanile, one hundred meters high, he said it was, adding that after standing for nine centuries it had, unfortunately, collapsed in 1902 and been rebuilt by Italian genius. "You cannot tell new one from old, I think. I have seen them both," he said. Finally he took me through the Doges' Palace, a lovely pink-and-white marble edifice, with spacious ornamental halls and rooms. "The symbol of Venetian power and glory," he exulted, as if he regretted that they were no more, and that the splendid palace by the water's edge, once the nerve center of the glittering Venetian empire, was now merely a center of attraction for gaping tourists like me.

Weary from the walking and the rubbernecking, I parted from the old monk, after donating to what he called his "charities," and made my way through a swarm of pigeons on the Piazza San Marco to the Café Florian for some sustenance. Some two hundred years old, it was still, I found, one of the best cafés in the world, and, like the city itself, unique. The food and wine were good, the coffee and ice creams excellent, and the conversation of the Italians, at least, seemed animated. It was a good place to gather to eat, drink and talk and I could see why it had remained so popular and had attracted, among others, so many poets from the north, Goethe, Byron, Wagner, George Sand and Musset, Ruskin and many others, all of whom sang its praises.

As in Rome and Florence I tramped for days through the

narrow streets and over the bridges of the canals (my monk had told me there were 400 bridges over 150 canals, and I missed very few). When I got tired I took a gondola to here or there. Except for the unpleasant chugging of the motorboats—fewer then than now—a golden silence hung over the city, broken only by the gondoliers bursting into song or shouting at you for a fare from their moorings near the Paglia bridge, or by the yelling of vendors pushing their large two-wheeled carts over the cobblestones and warning you *"Le Gambe! Gambe!"*—Look out for your legs!

There was also something voluptuous about the city. It may have been in its heyday a place of corruption, intrigue, cruelty and business skulduggery—the merchants and bankers of Venice were by all accounts a sharp lot; and no doubt it was full of cheats, spies, thieves, procurers, gamblers, even murderers, as the storybooks tell. But it must also have been a place of much pleasure, happiness, love-making and refinement, and it still was. I kept seeing an inscription on the sundials: *Horas non numero nisi serenas*—I count only the happy hours.

"I must tell you terrible thing," my monk had told me as we parted. "This beautiful city, this Venice unique, it is slowly sinking into sea."

I could not believe it. That a city of such grace and beauty, unlike any other in the world, should not be there to uplift man's spirits to the end of time was unthinkable. As I left it to return to France and to the down-to-earthness of earning my living, I felt happy, though, that I had seen it still standing proud above the eroding waters, and that I would not be around should it disappear forever beneath them.

The very thought of that fate had overwhelmed Byron, and I recalled his lines:

> *Oh Venice! Venice! when thy marble walls*
> *Are level with the waters, there shall be*
> *A cry of nations o'er thy sunken halls,*
> *A loud lament along the sweeping sea!*

There was nothing down-to-earth about the ensuing days Yvonne and I had in Grenoble. I had never seen her so vivacious, so full of a *joie de vivre*. Her hair and eyes seemed blacker, more luminous, than ever before. Everything about her was exciting and seemed as new to me as though we were meeting for the first time. A young man and woman could never have been more in love—and in more majestic surroundings, with the snows of the Alps above us as we walked and talked. It was an idyllic interlude.

Then, stupidly, I made a mistake. I couldn't let well enough alone. We decided on the way back to Paris to stop off a couple of days in Lyon, an ugly commercial city, but full of good restaurants we wanted to sample. I felt so deeply in love that I wanted to cement it forever. That was my mistake. In Lyon I again urged Yvonne to get a divorce and marry me. She would not hear of it. She saw no reason why we should not go on as we had—"forever," she said, "if we want to." At any rate, she would not abandon her family. And she teased me about being so bourgeois and so foolish. "Why spoil so great a love by marriage?" she said. "It shackles you. Now we are two free spirits. It is the only way to be in love."

I was not entirely convinced, but we dropped the subject, made up and feasted festively for two days—it was part of our Christmas celebration, after all—on the fine food and wine of the region.

It must have been in that ugly city of Lyon, or perhaps it was in Paris the next few days during the holiday season, when Yvonne was taken up with her family and Christmas was bleak for me, that my doubts about our future, which had depressed me occasionally before, began to grow. A resentment, too—that I could not be with her every hour of every day. From that time on, to tell the truth, and especially after I arrived in Vienna two months later, I began to become interested in other women. In that lovely baroque city by the Danube I would soon find one to whom I was drawn by a deep affection and with whom I would live, there and in the following summer in London. Vienna would prove fateful for me that way and eventually I would meet another there with whom I fell in love and married. By that time Yvonne would begin to change her mind, but it was too late. I could not change mine back.

There was a thread in my life with Yvonne which I later thought resembled a theme that Thomas Hardy had dwelt much upon in his novels: that one of the tragedies, or at least one of the sorrows, in existence was that a man and a woman rarely experience their love in the same way at the same time. There was a time-lag between them. What one felt at a given time would be felt by the other only later, by which time the feelings of the first had changed, and it was too late to fuse their lives.

Hardy had died early that year at the age of eighty-eight, a much venerated novelist and poet, and his ashes had been buried in Westminster Abbey. The pessimism about life in his novels, his belief that life was largely determined by blind chance and not by what a man and a woman tried to make of it, had outraged the prim late-Victorian critics in England (and in America), and after *Jude the Obscure*, in 1896, tired of the mindless criticism, Hardy had abandoned the novel and turned to poetry. I had read or reread his novels since coming over to Europe and they had deeply affected me, affirming some of my own skepticism about our life on this earth. Yet I could not deny that these last three and a half years in Europe had been the fullest, the happiest, of my life. I could not deny, to myself at least, that I was ambitious, seeking some achievement as a journalist and later, I hoped, as a writer. I knew it depended a good deal on chance, just as my getting the job at the last moment, which had enabled me to stay in Europe, had been a matter of sheer luck.

What a man achieved, what became of him, Hardy thought, depended on the throw of the dice, and the dice, he believed, were loaded against him. True, to a considerable extent, I conceded. But not entirely. Perhaps it was my youth. I believed that unless fate was inexorably against you, you could still, to quite a degree, shape your future.

Fate, to be sure, seemed against me so far as my future with Yvonne was concerned. Though I attended a gay reveillon in Paris that Christmas Eve, and another on New Year's Eve, I could not get up much holiday spirit. I must have been in an evil mood. How else explain the preposterous quarrel I provoked in the middle of a merry New Year's reveillon at Gillotte's bistro, after work that evening, with Camille, a lovely, athletic, dark-blond girl from California, who was on the news staff of the Paris *Tribune* and who had become one of my dearest friends. Perhaps I was drowning my misery in too much good champagne. Though I did not realize it I blurted out something that evidently deeply hurt her, and I have never forgotten how suddenly, livid with anger, she tossed the contents of her champagne glass in my face and stomped out, followed by the gentle Elliot Paul, who said he would bring her back and I could apologize for whatever I had said. They did not return. But one good thing came from that ugly, inexcusable (on my part) scene. A romance began that New Year's Eve between Camille and Elliot and in due time they were married.

Sobering up the next day and feeling contrite I tried to find Camille, but she did not come to work. Eventually I found her and apologized and we resumed a friendship that would endure for decades. Having sobered up, I looked back on 1928, and I had to admit that it had been a pretty good year, not only in personal happiness and fulfillment but in the way it had widened and deepened my experience as a foreign correspondent.

The assignments in Britain, Ireland and Italy, at a moment when these ancient countries had reached a certain turning point in their history, had provided a further education, and to them was added one assignment that brought considerable disillusionment and a realization that one of the dreams of man in the second decade of the 20th century was not coming true. After covering the Winter Olympics in St. Moritz, I had been instructed to proceed down to Geneva to report on a session of the League of Nations. It was my first opportunity to see at first hand how Woodrow Wilson's dream, rejected by his blind fellowcountrymen, was working out in practice.

Most people in Europe that year believed that the old Continent, devastated by war since the beginning of history and almost destroyed by the last one, had finally come to its senses. They felt they had at last entered upon a long period of peace and that whatever crises arose between the nations would be settled by the statesmen, who, having learned the lessons of the last bloody world conflict, would now compose their differences around the conference table of the League of Nations. Even for Winston Churchill the year of 1928 marked the end of the "world crisis."

Two years before, in 1926, Germany had been admitted to the League and given a permanent seat on its Council, alongside the victorious Allied powers, Britain, France, Italy and Japan. It was believed in Geneva that the League would keep Germany in check and encourage it to work decently with the other nations in the pursuit of peace. True, the League was not quite universal. Two great powers remained outside. The United States would have nothing to do with it. And Soviet Russia, though anxious to join, had not yet been invited. To the Europeans, who dominated Geneva, this did not seem to matter much. America to them was submerged in an empty-minded materialism and selfish isolationism. For the present at least it could not have made a very valuable member of the League. Nor could Russia, with its "godless Communism and its free love." Some day, it was thought, the Yankees would see the light and the Russians would abandon their godless ways and then both could join.

In the meantime the League of Nations, the Parliament of Mankind, as some hopefully called it, could press forward. Its chance had come: to keep the peace of the world, assure a little decency and justice for all peoples, and gradually do away with the burden of armaments, which would no longer be needed by any nation. Who could deny that the sights of Geneva were high, its goals noble, and that it was the answer to the finest aspirations of the human race?

Alas, it took only a few weeks in Geneva that midwinter to disillusion this young reporter. The eloquent statesmen of the nations of the world did not gather here to compose their differences but to gloss them over by hypocritical talk. It was not really their fault. The fault lay in the state of mind of nations, in their fanatical nationalism, in the zeal of the people of each nation to guard their country's sovereign rights. No nation, no people, were ready to delegate authority to a world body. They would not subordinate national to world interests. This was the stumbling block. The League never overcame it.

The hypocrisy of the statesmen, who paid lip service to the League's ideals, was a marvel to watch. Over the years till the bitter end I would come back from time to time to Geneva to watch the spectacle. It was fascinating, and it provided a correspondent with much good copy; but it was also sad and depressing.

Most of the "stars" of European statecraft and diplomacy, foreign ministers and slightly lesser fry, showed up for one meeting or another and I watched them at first hand playing their shabby parts. Ramsay MacDonald, the handsome and eloquent Scot, was the first Foreign Minister of a big power to come to Geneva and the only British Prime Minister, and in this smaller setting I had a better chance to observe him than I had in London. With disbelief and sorrow one watched the swift decline of this great man, the architect of the Labor Party's rise to power, Britain's first Labor Prime Minister, warm and charming in public, a moving speaker, a shrewd politician, a successful negotiator, but in the end through some flaw of character a victim of his own increasing, and finally overweening, vanity. Of obscure origin—he was born illegitimate—he had fought his way to the top, battled the citadels of privilege in Britain, only to succumb in his last years in office to the flattery of the rich and wellborn, finding his working-class friends, who had helped him attain his highest political goal, uncongenial. In the end he cast off most of his Labor friends to become head of a "national" government, which was overwhelmingly Tory.

By the time he came back to power in 1929, he had been much taken with Lady Londonderry, in whose company he was said to spend a great deal of his time. His wife had died years before and he had not remarried. Lady Londonderry was often at Geneva when he appeared at the head of the British delegation and they seemed inseparable. Nonetheless, the American correspondents were somewhat taken aback once when he insisted on bringing the lady to a stag luncheon we had organized for him. The morning of the gathering he had remarked casually that he wanted her to sit on his right side at the table. When someone got up nerve enough to tell him that it was a stag affair, that no women had been invited (this was decades before women's lib) and that perhaps Lady Londonderry would not wish to be the only woman present, he bristled and made it clear that we must take her or he would not come.

As time went on, MacDonald's woolliness in speech became more and more pronounced, so that you could not understand what he meant or where he stood. He seemed more moody and tired. His powers seemed to be waning—all but his vanity, which continued to flourish. In 1935 he stepped down as Prime Minister of the "national" government and was defeated for re-election that year in his old seat at Seaham. He died two years later, a rather pathetic figure, lonely, almost forgotten, except by his old Labor colleagues, who despised him. Later, with the healing of time, they would look back on him more fondly and more generously, realizing that with all his faults he was the greatest leader Labor ever had.

Other luminaries came and went, and some of them left their mark on your memory. Pillar of the League in those days, and a man who did more to try to make it work than any other, was Aristide Briand, a shaggy-faced Frenchman with a drooping mustache, long hair that fell over his ears, and a foul-smelling cigarette always dangling from his lips. But one remembered him most for his golden voice, which had the rich, deep tones of a cello, wonderfully modulated, and for the gestures that accompanied his glowing words, his hands being so delicate and artistically expressive that they reminded me of those of Paderewski at the piano. For the last seven years of his life—from 1925 to 1932—as French Foreign Minister in eleven successive governments, in four of which he was also Premier, he tried to breathe life into the League of Nations. He conciliated Germany, restored the entente with Great Britain, tried to give teeth to the League so that it could enforce the peace, joined with the United States, a nonmember, to "outlaw war," and promoted the idea—and ideal —of a United States of Europe. He was a man of reason, compromise and conciliation and for a time it looked as though with these qualities he might succeed. But they could not suffice to meet the harsher realities of rampant nationalism that hardened as the 1930's began. You could see the old man beginning to break, in spirit and body, as he commenced to realize that all his work had been in vain. But in 1928 he was still hopeful, even confident. I counted him the finest orator the League had ever heard and I did not yet realize that first time at Geneva that words, moving as they were and issuing in such a golden voice, were not enough.

Not far behind Briand in oratory and magic at the tribune was his colleague Senator Joseph Paul-Boncour. He was a handsome man, a *bon vivant*, a man of letters, a "first-nighter" at the theater, a skilled debater. He seemed to have all the attributes to propel him to the top in French politics and at the League. But he never quite made it and I never understood why. Perhaps it was the luck of life. He finally became Premier at the end of 1932, but lasted only six weeks, and never got another chance. But he was a fixture in Geneva. He moved the Assembly and the Council with his eloquent words.

Two years before, in 1926, Briand had shared the Nobel Peace Prize with Germany's Foreign Minister, Gustav Stresemann. Together they had worked out the Pact of Locarno, by which the Western powers guaranteed their mutual frontiers and promised never to go to war over them again. Briand liked his counterpart personally and for years at Geneva they got along better than anyone expected a Frenchman and a German could. Stresemann was not an attractive-looking man but almost everyone at Geneva, including us correspondents, liked him. His slit eyes, his bulging sausagelike neck, his cropped hair covering a bullet-shaped head, made him look like a pig. But he was a congenial man and laughed heartily over a sumptuous meal, beer, brandy and cigars. No one of us, not even Briand, however, suspected how devious he was. That was revealed much later when the German secret papers became available. These make it clear that during the time he was seemingly negotiating so sincerely with Briand to end the deadly, centuries-old enmity of France and Germany, and giving Germany's word that the western frontiers, violated in 1914, would henceforth be respected, and proclaiming Germany's loyalty to the League, he was telling his German confidants, including the Crown Prince, that Germany was joining the League and adhering to Locarno only because it was weak. As soon as it was strong, Germany would act differently. Five weeks before he signed the Locarno Pact and brought Germany for the first time into the League of Nations, Stresemann wrote the Crown Prince in confidence:

> Entry into the League does not mean that we are choosing the West and turning our backs on the East. We can only choose when we have behind us a military force . . . That is why German policy must at the start follow the policy which Metternich, I believe, adopted in Austria in 1809: be devious and balk at big decisions.

We correspondents did not detect Stresemann's deviousness, and neither did Briand right up to his death in 1932. By that time Stresemann, too, was dead; he died in 1929.

Another familiar figure in Geneva in those days was the British Foreign Minister, Sir Austen Chamberlain. He always struck me as a cold potato of an Englishman, an early-nineteenth-century character who seemed a little ill at ease in the more rambunctious twentieth century. Metternich and Talleyrand were his idols and he tried to emulate them. His elegant monocle seemed glued to one eye—I never saw him without it—and he gave off a glacial air even when he was warmly backing the League on one issue or another. Glacial but also capped with that tinge of British superiority which non-Britishers found so annoying. I often wondered what made him tick. He had long been a power in the Tory party. Twice, in 1922 and 1923, he had a chance to become Prime Minister, a goal his celebrated father, Joseph Chamberlain, just failed to achieve, and which still eluded his younger half brother Neville. But he would not take it. He was content now to be Foreign Minister. He seemed to enjoy basking in the limelight in Geneva. He had not been unsuccessful as Foreign Minister since 1924, though the job in that relatively peaceful time had not been very difficult. Still, around the League he seemed a relic of the past.

The future, perhaps even in England, belonged to younger men. The brightest light for me in the British delegation was a strikingly handsome, impeccably dressed young man, Anthony Eden, who two years before had become parliamentary private secretary to Sir Austen and invariably accompanied him to Geneva. Behind his old-school-tie Oxford manner was an attractive personality and, if he trusted you, a disarming frankness. Older British diplomats were a little suspicious of his idealism. He not only talked of peace but seemed to believe it was possible. Achieving peace was almost an obsession with him and this was due, I think, to his experience in the war. Unlike most of the other envoys at Geneva, who were too old to have personally known the hell of war, and who babbled emptily about peace without being willing to make any concession to help keep it, he had known what war was like—first hand, in the trenches. Two of his brothers, the eldest and the youngest, had been killed in the war and he himself had been gassed and wounded.

Gradually, as was perhaps inevitable as he climbed toward the foreign ministership, which he achieved for the first time seven years later, his idealism faded and he faced the realities of European foreign politics as cynically as any of his colleagues. He went along with the British surrender to Mussolini after Italy attacked Abyssinia, in what many of us thought was a betrayal of the League. He took a lead in setting up the hypocritical Non-intervention Committee which, as he well knew, allowed Hitler and Mussolini to intervene massively in the Spanish Civil War, while preventing Britain and France from sending arms in any quantity to the beleaguered Spanish Republic. He tricked France, I thought, from reacting to Hitler's invasion of the Rhineland, though it didn't take much to make the French, who had lost their senses, hold back. Finally though, to his credit, he reached a point where he could no longer stomach his own government's appeasement, under Neville Chamberlain, of the Fascist dictators, Hitler and Mussolini, and he resigned in protest as Foreign Minister in 1938. He would regain his post when the second war came.

Over the years I saw him occasionally in Geneva, London and once in Berlin when he came there to try to negotiate with Hitler. He was more considerate of the foreign correspondents than any other British officeholder, and once or twice told me more of his problems than he perhaps should have. But I began to see that, like all the rest, he was flawed. When finally after the second war he achieved his goal of becoming Prime Minister, he threw it away by joining France in sending troops to take over the Suez Canal. It was a foolish enterprise, inexplicable that it should be backed by such an experienced and intelligent man, and it finished his political career suddenly, and forever.

Eduard Beneš, the Foreign Minister of Czechoslovakia, was another fixture at the meetings of the League of Nations in those days. Son of a peasant, he was a stocky little man with a peasant's blunt face, tough, doggedly persistent, yet strangely pedantic and professorial. He had abandoned his early socialism to devote his life to building an independent, democratic Czechoslovak state out of part of the ruins of the old Hapsburg Empire. As a penniless youth he had worked his way through the University of Prague and then three graduate schools in Paris, picking up a knowledge of history and four foreign languages, which he spoke with a strong Czech accent. He had returned to Prague during the war and under Thomas Masaryk, the ultimate founder of the new nation, had worked in the underground and then fled to Paris, where during the rest of the war and at the Peace Conference he had nagged Allied statesmen with demands for a new Czechoslovak nation.

Now in 1928 he had become the leader of the smaller states that owed their existence to the Allies and that saw in the League of Nations the best guarantee of their future. Without eloquence or elegance, but persistently, he spoke for their interests and labored prodigiously to strengthen the League. Foreign politics was his life; he seemed to have no personal existence outside it. I saw him from time to time in the next years, especially in Prague, where in 1935 he became his country's second President, succeeding the retiring Masaryk. By then, with the advent of Hitler in Germany, his hopes for Czechoslovakia were fading, though he would not admit it in public. I had gone over to radio broadcasting in 1937 and urged him, when I put him on the air for us, to let America and the rest of the world know the desperate situation of Czechoslovakia, which Hitler was determined to destroy. But he could not bring himself to do it. "I am an optimist," he would say, as the prospects for Czech survival grew dimmer in the face of Nazi threats. He was not a false man, yet I was sure his optimism was false.

I remember running in to him in the hall of Broadcasting House in Prague on the evening of September 10, 1938, when the Sudeten crisis had reached its climax and Hitler was screaming that he would have the Czechs, one way or another, preferably by force. With the walls of this sturdy little nation crumbling, Beneš had spoken out on the radio calmly and reasonably. "Nothing but moral force, good will and mutual trust is needed," he said. "Let us be optimistic." He had spoken in German as well as in Czech, so that I had caught his words, and when I bumped in to him coming out of the studio I wanted to say: "Why do you speak like that? The British and the French are betraying you. And you are dealing with gangsters in Berlin." But his face and manner were so forlorn, quite in contrast to the words he had uttered on the radio, that I did not have the heart to say it. We exchanged a few meaningless words, and he went out into the night, a sad figure, stooped under the terrible burden, a remnant of the proud man I had seen so often at the tribune of the League. Only afterward, when Czechoslovakia had been doomed by the Munich Pact, sold down the river by Britain and France, did Beneš admit: "We have been basely betrayed." He resigned as President and fled to London for his life.

I visited him in London during the war, when he headed the Czechoslovak government in exile. He was full of plans for the rebirth of his nation when Allied victory came. He was more sensible about the minorities—there had been three and a half million Germans, a million Hungarians and half a million Ruthenians in the old Czechoslovakia, which they hated—than he had been. But he did not foresee—none of us did—the strength of the Communists or the determination of the Soviet Union to make them dominant in the new Czechoslovakia. He was betrayed by them, too, after he returned in 1945 to resume his presidency of the reborn country. When the Russian-backed Communist coup took place in 1948, Beneš realized that it was the end of a democratic Czechoslovakia. He stepped down as President. Broken in body and spirit he died the same year. He was sixty-four.

That first time in Geneva in 1928 I could not foresee such ends to men's dreams. As my experience deepened and as time went by I would see it happen several times—to good men and bad: to my friends Negrín and Del Vayo, Premier and Foreign Minister, respectively, of the Spanish Republic; to Blum, Daladier and Reynaud, the last leaders of the French Third Republic; to Mussolini, who dreamt of a new Roman Empire; to Hitler, who looked forward to ruling Europe for the German Master Race. Only to Gandhi, who befriended me in India, would it be left to realize his dream—of freedom and independence for his country—and to feel confident (though he was killed by an assassin's bullet soon after reaching his goal) that what he had fought for all his life would endure. It had happened to De Valera too, as I have mentioned.

The biggest story during that winter meeting of the League which first brought me to Geneva in 1928 was exploded by the Russians, who had not yet been invited to join the world body but who participated in the preliminary disarmament meetings as outsiders. On February 22 they tossed a bombshell into the dull, hypocritical meetings of the so-called League Committee on Security and Disarmament, which had purposefully been getting nowhere. The terrible Bolsheviks simply proposed that the way to disarm was to disarm—completely, within four years. During that period all the world's armies, navies, air forces and fortifications would be scrapped, along with their arms. After that an international control commission would police the world and keep the peace. It would be a very special body, outside the League, so as to take in Russia and the United States, and from which, the Soviets suggested, would be excluded all bankers, industrialists, gunmakers, generals, admirals and former ministers. In their stead would be representatives of legislative assemblies and trade unions. Peasants might be brought in later "when they had mastered the principles of international law."

The august delegates of the nations at Geneva, large and small, were horrified. Scrap all armies, navies, air forces? Unthinkable! The Bolsheviks must be fooling. Of course they were. They knew perfectly well that the rest of the world was not going to disarm. Secretly, with the help of the disarmed Germans, they were pushing their own rearmament feverishly. But the Soviet delegates enjoyed the discomfiture of the capitalist delegates, who, when they had recovered from their shock, popped up to say that the Soviet proposals were "interesting, but impractical and certainly premature."

The League and the subsequent disarmament conferences, of course, got nowhere. The Allied powers began to increase their arms. All they were interested in was keeping Germany disarmed, and when Hitler realized that, he pulled Germany out of the League in the very first year of his power and launched a massive, secret rearmament program of his own.

What feeble strength there was in the League began to waste away. Japan withdrew after the League condemned it for invading and occupying Manchuria, though the world body had not gone beyond words; it had taken no action. Italy resigned when the League feebly and ineffectively opposed its conquest of Abyssinia. Three of the five big powers in the League were now out of it. Russia was finally admitted, but not for long. In 1939, five years after it joined, it earned the dubious distinction of being the only member of the League of Nations ever to be expelled. Japan had not been thrown out after it invaded Manchuria, nor Italy after its aggression against Abyssinia. Nor had the League condemned Hitler for marching into the demilitarized Rhineland in 1936 and into Czechoslovakia in the spring of 1939 or for launching the Second World War by attacking Poland on September 1, 1939. But when the Soviet Union attacked gallant little Finland on November 30, 1939, the League threw it out a fortnight later, the only time in its frustrated history that it ever took such a drastic step against an aggressor or acted on anything so promptly.

It always seemed to me that the League of Nations suffered the most fatal blow of all when it failed to stop Mussolini from conquering Abyssinia in 1935. Never did the statesmen of the Big Powers, especially Britain and France, behave more disgracefully. They condemned Italy for its aggression in ringing words and then slunk from applying the sanctions demanded by the League Covenant, which would have brought Mussolini's very vulnerable country to its knees. It could not have survived oil sanctions, but these were never applied. If this was the shabbiest moment in Geneva's drab history, ironically its most moving moment came when Haile Selassie, the dark, black-bearded Emperor of Ethiopia, his country now overrun by the Italians, his soldiers dead or maimed from mustard gas, his cities in ruins from bombing, stepped to the tribune of the League Assembly on June 30, 1936, and in his halting but eloquent French appealed to the conscience of Geneva and of the world to undo the crime against his country.

The answer given to Haile Selassie was predictable. It was that the League could do nothing for the stricken country. Sanctions, mild though they had been, were abandoned.[1] Italy was begged to return to Geneva. From then on the League was condemned to death. Its main pillars, France and Britain, fell over themselves to regain the good graces of the sawdust Italian Caesar. In Berlin I noted that Hitler had taken due notice of the impotence of the League and the spinelessness of the two Western democracies. It was a good augury for the plans he was hatching.

But in 1928 we could not see that far ahead. Though I took a dim view of living in Geneva, the home of Calvin and Calvinism, which still flourished in all its drab narrowness, I enjoyed this first crack at covering the League of Nations. Though my Wilsonian illusions were quickly dampened, it was educational to watch the world statesmen floundering about in a sea of hypocrisy. I got some good stories; several of them were front-paged. And when my friend Wythe Williams of *The New York Times* had to leave Geneva suddenly for personal reasons, I covered for him, too. For the first and last time in my life some of my dispatches were front-paged in that august newspaper, though under Williams' name. I felt fairly satisfied with myself.

---

[1] Haile Selassie returned to his country in 1941 after the collapse of the Italian forces in Africa and resumed his rule, reigning for another thirty-three years until in 1974 he was deposed by a military coup. He died on August 27, 1975, at eighty-three.

February 23 was my twenty-fourth birthday. There was a good story that day about the League cracking down on Hungary for importing forbidden arms—it did crack down on the small, weak nations—and that evening with some friends I celebrated the anniversary at the Casino, whose gambling tables and bar were off limits to the Calvinistic Genevois. I guess I felt a little smug. At twenty-four, I told myself, I had reached the big time in journalism, hobnobbing with veteran and renowned correspondents and statesmen twice my age or more, and daily recording history for the "World's Greatest Newspaper." For an American youngster less than three years out of a prairie college, I was not, I thought, doing badly.

In the midst of these birthday self-congratulations there came a blow that quickly deflated me. Colonel McCormick cabled Henry Wales in Paris:

WALES. SHIRER'S STORIES FROM GENEVA HEAVY AS A BRIDE'S CAKE. PROCEED THERE IMMEDIATELY AND TAKE OVER.

And I had thought I was doing so well! The *Times*, if not the *Tribune*, had even cabled some encouraging words about one of my stories.

I returned to Paris in a dismal state. The terrible colonel's cable probably meant I would be fired, but he must have forgotten to follow up. I was allowed to remain in his lordly employ. My firing was postponed—for several years.

So from time to time I returned to Geneva to watch the depressing antics of the statesmen fiddling around while the world drifted toward another hideous war. By the late thirties it was easier than in 1928 to see why the League of Nations had failed. No nation would sacrifice its interests to those of the world. The spirit of nationalism was too strong for that. The League could stop the aggressor only if its members lived up to the Covenant and agreed to collective action. Each country shrank from that, though the power of the combined nations, even without the United States, would have been enough to halt any aggression had it been used. The absence of America did weaken this world body, but too often it was used as an excuse, particularly by France and Britain, to do nothing. Gradually we saw that the stupid human race was not yet ready for Wilson's idea and ideal and might never be, as long as nations insisted on following, exclusively, their selfish interests and believed there was something to be gained by war, or the threat of war.

In 1938, a year after going over to radio, I made my home and headquarters in Geneva, and though I was rarely there, because the coming war was being hatched elsewhere, I occasionally used to gaze upon the sprawling marble palace of the League, which looked over the waters of Lac Léman toward the snows of Mont Blanc. It was now a vast and stately tomb, in which lay buried so many decent hopes and aspirations that war-weary men had dared to entertain.

I saw it for next to the last time on July 5, 1940, when I returned to see my family after reporting the battle and the fall of France. The League was dead, the Secretariat silent and empty. The war had dealt the final blow. That evening, sitting on the shore of the lake, I felt a sadness, and that night I expressed it in my diary.

> This evening in the sunset the great white marble of the League building showed through the trees. It had a noble look, and the League had stood in the minds of many as a noble hope. But it has not tried to fulfill it. Tonight it was an empty shell, the building, the institution, the hope—dead.

The new year of 1929 had hardly started before I was on the move again. In mid-January Wales sent me down to the Riviera to cover the funeral of Grand Duke Nicholas, whose death, it seemed to us, heralded an end of an era and of the hopes of the Russian refugees of reviving a Romanov dynasty in Russia. After that, I was to remain on the Riviera and report on the empty lives of the rich and titled, American and European, who whiled away the winter there. The assignment did not attract me. It was sure to bore the daylights out of the likes of me. But there was not much news in Paris and Wales thought he was doing me a favor. "We've got to cover the bastards down there," he growled. "And besides, you can get some sun and some rest. It'll be the life of Riley for you, Willy." He did not see that I was too young and restless—and perhaps too ambitious—to be content with that.

It was rather touching to see all of the Romanovs who had escaped execution at the hands of the Bolsheviks and all the Russian aristocracy who had got out of the Soviet Union alive pay a last tribute to Grand Duke Nicholas. Their slim hopes of one day returning to Russia seemed further dimmed by his death, for he had been the ablest of the last Romanovs, the only one, they thought, capable of replacing the hapless Nicholas II. A grandson of Czar Nicholas I and a cousin of Nicholas II, who with his family had been slain by the Bolsheviks at Ekaterinburg just ten years before and only eight days before White troops arrived at the town to liberate him, the Grand Duke had commanded the Russian armies during the war and earned the respect of Hindenburg and Ludendorff as the best of the Russian generals. He had escaped from the Crimea on a British warship in 1919 and settled at Antibes, refusing to have anything to do with efforts to make him a pretender to the lost throne. That role had been assumed by another cousin of the Czar's, Grand Duke Cyril, whom we used to see occasionally in Paris and who had set himself up in a castle in Brittany and proclaimed that he was "Czar of all the Russias."

Hope, however faint, lingers on among émigrés, and this was especially true of the Russians. Thousands of them from all over Western Europe flocked to Nice, including two of the Czar's sisters, the Grand Duchesses Zenia and Olga, and many other notables, overflowing the little Russian Orthodox church. As I mingled among them I caught a feeling not only of their sense of loss at the passing of Grand Duke Nicholas but of their despair of the future. All through the first years of their exile they had believed that God would strike down the "godless" Bolshevik regime and that they would return to Mother Russia, their old privileges and property restored. Now nearly twelve years had passed since the revolution and the abdication, and the heirs of Lenin had clamped a tight Communist grip on the land, their government recognized as legitimate and sovereign by all the great powers save the United States.

"Thank God!" a bearded old general, whom I had met in Paris, exclaimed as we walked slowly out of the cemetery. "You Americans, at least, have the decency not to recognize those Red criminal usurpers in the Kremlin." I did not have the heart on such an occasion to answer that I, at least, disagreed with my own government, which was not yet wise and honest enough to acknowledge the fact that diplomatic recognition of a country does not imply approval of its regime. We recognized other dictatorships, especially of the Right.

I suppose in time the fading faith of the Russian émigrés turned to ashes, for many of them, the most prominent above all, lived to a ripe old age in their various places of exile. Grand Duchess Xenia had been given a house in England by the royal family and over the years when I was in London I would see in the royal calendar in *The Times* a line that she had taken part in some small ceremony at the side of the King and Queen. She was eighty-five when she died, in 1960. Her younger sister, Olga, lived in Copenhagen until after the second war, at first with her mother, the Dowager Empress Marie Fedorovna, who died in 1928 at eighty-one. After the war she moved to Canada, lived piously but unostentatiously, the last years in a small flat she shared with a Russian couple over a barbershop in a slum in Toronto. She, too, died in 1960 at seventy-eight. Both had lived long enough to know that the three-hundred-year-old Romanov dynasty, of which they were among the last remnants, would never be restored in Russia—nor would any other dynasty.

After all the exciting assignments of the previous year, staying on on the Riviera to cover "society" was a comedown. I didn't give a damn about "society." I couldn't care less what Yankee millionaire was having an affair with what countess, who was marrying or divorcing whom, what silly American woman was trying to trade a fortune for a title. The place seemed full of American women as mindless as birds. It was the era of the tango, and the plush night clubs were crowded with slick-haired Argentine gigolos catering to the desires of these hapless women, bitchy, aging, ugly divorcées—and some who were not divorced —who seemed to be trying to make up for sex-starved lives at home. All of this I found profoundly uninteresting and not worth writing about. Watching the idle rich convinced you that there was something wrong with the distribution of wealth in this world, and that maybe the socialists, who wanted to redistribute it and give a little more to those who toiled, were right. Obviously in this field I was a lousy journalist, refusing to acknowledge that what bored me titillated our readers in Chicagoland.

Frustrated, I found myself shutting myself up in my room most of the day and evening (when I should have been out gathering tidbits of gossip), rereading Proust and sinking into the wonderful novels of Balzac and Stendhal—the last an exciting discovery. Some evenings in desperation I would skip over to Monte Carlo and try my luck at the gaming tables. But this, too, bored me. I lacked the gambler's fever. Or I would prowl through the rain-spattered streets of Nice (the sun on the Riviera, at least that year, was the invention of the French Tourist Bureau—it rarely shone), restless and depressed, ending up sometimes in a café where the French newspapermen who got out the local daily gathered after work. I could now speak their language and occasionally there would be good talk, though on the whole they were a provincial lot.

Then one bitterly cold rainy day (for the warm temperatures of this winter resort area were also a figment of the commercial imagination of the promoters) I got a telephone call from Wales in Paris.

"Willy," he said, "I've got good news for you, since you claim to be so miserable down there. Get up to Vienna as fast as you can and take over the bureau there for a while."

It was dying, the vast and beautiful city that for centuries and up until so recently had been the gay and glittering capital of the Hapsburg Empire. It had a somewhat dilapidated appearance now that it had been reduced to being the center of what little was left of Austria, a small country along the Danube that could not possibly support the capital's two million inhabitants, or even itself. The stately public buildings and palaces, from which Austria-Hungary had been governed, were molting, the plaster and paint peeling off the classical or baroque façades. Some of the light-opera houses, concert halls and theaters in this city which had a passion for music and drama were dark, the once-splendid restaurants and cafés half empty, the smart shops bereft of customers, the dress of the people in the streets a little shabby. Before the employment offices there were long lines of men and women stomping their feet in the snow.

And yet much of the beauty and charm remained. You could not destroy these overnight or even in a generation. I fell in love with Vienna at first sight. It did not replace Paris in my heart. But it came very close. After the French, the Austrians and especially the Viennese were the most attractive people I had seen, the women particularly.

The old monarchy had put its stamp of imperial splendor on Vienna since the days when its troops had repulsed the Turks at the city's gates four hundred years before. But now Vienna itself was ruled by the Socialists, the only metropolis in the world that was. No matter. The Socialists were as aware and as proud of the splendor and charm of the capital as any archduke. Only they were seeing to it that the workers got a chance to enjoy it as well as the rich and the titled. They had a stake in its future. In fact, they denied that Vienna was dying—it was merely adapting to the new times and circumstances.

Maybe so. It was difficult to see how a city of two millions, which once catered to the needs of an empire of fifty-two millions and received its sustenance from it, could live on as the capital of what was now a country of less than seven millions. A capital that contained almost a third of a nation's population, it seemed to me, was bound to wither away. But the fickle, fun-loving Viennese were not worrying about that. The Socialist municipality was busy giving the common people some of the good things of life that the rigid, reactionary monarchy had long denied them: good public schools, kindergartens, children's nurseries, clinics, hospitals, swimming pools, skating rinks and, above all, modern housing. The Karl Marxhof, one of the immense new apartment complexes, stretched out for nearly a mile, and several others were almost as large. The slums had been torn down. For the first time a worker had a decent place to live in. And good public schools, and free medical and hospital care. At a time when social security was unknown at home, Vienna provided the best in the world. I was impressed, and I showed it in my dispatches. Accurate and objective though they were, Colonel McCormick did not like them. He reminded me sharply that socialism was the work of the devil and all socialists lazy bums. It was incredible how childish, stupid, ignorant the rich barons of Chicago were. And hypocritical—for I remembered from my youth the ghastly slums out by the stockyards.

The old city, when I arrived, lay under a thick mantle of snow, and the next few weeks would turn out to be the coldest and snowiest in Central Europe since records were kept. The snow only made Vienna seem more lovely to me. I bought some snow boots and, as always in a new place, began prowling through the streets to get a feel of the city.

One started with the Ringstrasse, the finest boulevard in Europe except for the Champs Élysées. Some 200 feet wide, and lined with trees, with separate channels for motorcars, streetcars, pedestrians and horseback riders, it was built on the old fortifications and enclosed the inner city on three sides. Walk its two-mile length and you saw most of the landmarks of the town: the stately Early Renaissance Opera House, the first love of the Viennese; the sprawling Hofburg, the imperial palace of the Hapsburgs, which housed the National Library, one of the great ones of the world; the imposing museums of natural history and art, the latter possessing one of Europe's finest collections of paintings, many of them, no doubt, like those in the Louvre, booty from foreign conquests. Farther up the Ring one passed the Palace of Justice, still burned out from the workers' riots of two years before, and the Parliament—both in Greek classical style, which seemed rather foreign to the Viennese temperament but no more so than the same kind of architecture in Washington. Farther on, the Rathaus, the city hall, a beehive of Socialist officials who ran the town, a sprawling modern Gothic edifice which would have been more suited to the Rhineland. In its vast cellars were pleasant beer halls and restaurants. Behind it the complex of the university, one of the prides of these people, who told you it was Europe's oldest, dating back to the fourteenth century, and which had been and still was the intellectual center of *Mittel-Europa*. Opposite the Rathaus, on the other side of the Ring, was the Burg Theater, the largest theater I had ever seen—it covered a whole city block and was also one of the prides of the city. Here eventually, after I had learned the language, I would see most of the Austro-German classical repertoire.

Behind the Opera was Vienna's most famous hotel, Sacher's. In the small, intimate, magenta-walled salons of its fine restaurant the nobility and aristocracy—all the archdukes and archduchesses, princes and princesses, counts and countesses—had wined and dined before the war, and I doubt if the likes of me would have found a table there in those days. But after the fall of the Hapsburgs it became a little more democratic, though the titled folk still came. Indeed, Frau Sacher, the formidable proprietor, a heavyset, dynamic and rather imperious woman, had fed them for free during the days of hunger after the war. She still strode about when I was there, superintending the service, greeting old friends, a long pencil-like cigar in her mouth or hand. Sometimes she would stop and discreetly point out for me the notables at adjacent tables.

I saw them all, a thousand or more, one evening at the annual military ball at the Hofburg. The *Fasching* pre-Lenten festivities had begun and a fading countess I had met invited me to take her there. It was a curious gathering, amusing and yet a little sad. All that were left of those who had fluttered about the court in the old days were there—the old soldiers in their antique prewar bemedaled dress uniforms, the women attired in finery they must have worn when presented to the Emperor. The odor of mothballs hung over the gathering. For a few hours that evening in the great chandeliered halls these remnants of a bygone day forgot the bleak present—with all those red Socialists now running the town!—and faded back to the past with all of its frivolous trappings, dancing the night through to the waltzes of Johann Strauss. My countess was in raptures, and I was highly amused, though I felt I was betraying a little my humble origins and present sympathies (with those terrible reds) in such company. The dancing and the champagne were fine, but the conversation was terrible.

From the Opera, the Kärntnerstrasse wound down to the Graben and the Cathedral of St. Stephen, an imposing fourteenth-century Gothic structure, the center of religious life in this Catholic country. The narrow street was lined with smart shops that appeared empty except for two, Gerstner's and Demel's, the renowned pastry shops, which were bitter rivals, vying with each other to serve an astonishing assortment of cakes, cookies, candies, tortes and other confections for those with a sweet tooth. Both shops were crowded with women. At the cathedral the Kärntnerstrasse became the Rotenturmstrasse and led one down to the Danube Canal. In my ignorance I had expected to come upon the broad Danube River itself. But the storybooks and the lyrics of the waltzes to the contrary, the great river does not flow past the city, as it once did. A new bed had been dug for it two or three miles away, beyond the Prater. Leopoldstadt, across the canal from the inner city, was full of office buildings and Jews—it was the center of a rich Jewish life. How could one know in that snowy winter of 1929 that that Jewish life would not go on there for long—for only nine more years, to be exact, until Hitler, an

Austrian himself and a long-time resident of Vienna, where he lived like a bum before the war, came.

Later, when spring arrived, I used to go out to the Prater, a magnificent park of two thousand acres of woods and fields where you could stroll to your heart's content and then, if you felt like it, take in a vast amusement center which boasted, among other things, the largest Ferris wheel in the world. From its top, if you were not giddy from the height, you got a panoramic view of Vienna. On one edge of the Prater I finally reached the Danube. It was a disappointment. It was not blue, as in the songs, but brown (had it ever been blue, as Johann Strauss sang in his waltzes?). But on a spring or summer day, when you gazed down on it from the hills of the Wienerwald, the color of the river changed, and from there it looked like a ribbon of silver trailing off between the green vineyards of the hillsides toward the Hungarian plain and thence, in your mind, a thousand miles down through the Balkans to the Black Sea.

Vienna was an old city and, like Paris, Rome and London, had a history that stretched back to the Roman times, when it was known as Vindobona, a thriving town at the crossroads of Central Europe. Marcus Aurelius, who composed some of his meditations along the Danube while directing his armies, is believed to have died there, in 180. The Nibelungen was composed up the Danube at Passau, and Attila and Kriemhild were wed, according to the saga, at Vindobona. Twice—in 1529 and in 1683—the repulse of the Turks before the city's walls had preserved Austria and all of Central Europe for Christendom. Over some seven centuries under the Hapsburgs, Vienna had served as the capital of an expanding empire that finally stretched to the Adriatic in the south, to the northern borders of Bohemia, and to the east to the Carpathians. Despite the ups and downs of the greedy, autocratic Hapsburgs, the empire, as one century followed another, must have seemed to its inhabitants to be a very permanent thing, one of the great powers of Europe, and Vienna the most beautiful and civilized capital on earth. Life softened and was enriched during the nineteenth century, and the pursuit of pleasure, of wine, women, singing and waltzing became ingrained in the lives of the inhabitants.

Even those born thirty years before, around the turn of the century, as I had been, must have taken for granted that the charming, dreaming, happy-go-lucky life of the great city would go on forever. As the bells rang in the twentieth century the good citizens had recalled that Emperor Franz Josef had been sitting on the throne for fifty-two years and seemed destined, despite his limitations, to go on sitting on it for a good many years to come.[1] His last mistress, Frau Kathi Schratt, a retired actress, to whom he was utterly devoted, was still living when I arrived in 1929 and soon my newspaper would be after me to go to see her about writing her memoirs. Such continuity! But the war had come in 1914, and the old Emperor had stupidly helped to start it by his idiotic demands on little Servia after Archduke Ferdinand, the heir, and his wife had been assassinated by revolutionists from that country at Sarajevo. Revolution had followed, a rude awakening, and the seven-centuries-old dynasty had toppled. Now Austria, reduced to the small space of its language frontiers, was a republic. And yet the old ways of life lingered.

Music and baroque, I realized after I had begun to get the feel of things, were the keys to the character of the city and of the Viennese. Most of the great composers of the late-eighteenth and nineteenth centuries did their finest work there. Some were native, like Haydn, Mozart, Schubert, Johann Strauss, Bruckner and Mahler. Others, like Beethoven and Brahms, were drawn there from Germany. With such towering composers working and creating in its midst, Vienna became the music capital of the world. And the Viennese reacted; they in turn developed a deep love for music. In no other city that I have lived in—Paris, London, Berlin, New York—have I seen so many so passionate about music. But more than that, they not only were auditors but players and singers, not only many of them professionals but many more amateurs. There were half a dozen good professional quartets playing in Vienna when I arrived but there were also hundreds of amateur ones. It was in listening to both that I first got my own passion for chamber music. After all, most of the great quartets were written by Haydn, Mozart, Beethoven and Schubert. Ever since my Vienna days I could never hear enough of them.

Vienna appreciated the works of this galaxy of creative

[1] He did, for sixteen more years, until his death in 1916 at eighty-six, after reigning since 1848.

geniuses, but not always the composers themselves. One could not forget that Mozart died poverty-stricken and that he was buried in an unmarked grave in the pauper's field at St. Marxer Cemetery after a so-called "third-class funeral." (In Austria even the funerals, like the railroad coaches, were divided into three classes.) And after composing so much sublime music, and in every conceivable form: symphonies, quartets, sonatas, concertos, masses, operas! Dead at thirty-five, when most creative artists are just approaching their prime.

Schubert, too, had lived in poverty despite the tremendous outpouring of his genius—six hundred songs, among which are some of the loveliest I've ever heard, symphonies, masses, quartets and piano pieces. I remember the flood of emotion I felt at first hearing, in Vienna, Schubert's quartet *Death and the Maiden* and the *Trout* quintet. Aside from five or six quartets of Beethoven's they are the most glorious chamber music ever written. Schubert died even younger than Mozart—he was only thirty-one. He got a better burial, two or three graves away from that of Beethoven, whose genius he had worshiped and at whose funeral he had served as a pallbearer the year before. I heard more Hadyn, Mozart, Beethoven and Schubert in a few months in Vienna than I had heard in all my previous life.

In this respect I soon felt attuned to the Viennese, sharing their passion for music. It was an important part of their lives, and it became one of mine. Music was in their blood and left its mark on their character.

Baroque, too. You could not understand the Viennese unless you realized what baroque was, and how it, too, had become a part of them and their style of life. The contours and forms of baroque appealed to the senses. Baroque was a call to the pleasures, fantasies and dreams of life, a reaction against the pure spiritualness of the Gothic and the severity of Protestant architecture in the north. It was warm, sensuous and full of movement. In Vienna, at least, it led to a special vision of life. Through the harmony and fantasy of form it managed somehow to bring heaven and earth together, to abolish the boundary between life and the dream, between the real and the unreal, and to reconcile the antagonisms of pain and joy, death and life, nature and man, faith and knowledge. It was a dynamic thing, full of human passion, for it recognized man's longings and the deep creative urges as well as the frailties. Above all, in Vienna, it was a call to dream. All the Austrian writers of the nineteenth century dwell on the theme. For Hermann Bahr, one of the most popular of Viennese writers, life around the turn of the century was essentially baroque. To him and his fellow-countrymen, he said, it meant that

> life is postponed until after death. It begins there; here all is unreal: the serious business is on the other side. Here we only dream, since life itself is a dream. But never forget you are but dreaming.

And so in Vienna, until the bubble burst, these giddy men and beautiful, elegant, flirtatious, frivolous, fickle women dreamed on, passing the pleasant days and nights waltzing and wining, in light talk in the congenial coffeehouses, in listening to music and viewing the make-believe of theater and opera and operetta, in flirting and making love. An empire had to be governed, to be sure, an army and navy manned, communications maintained, business transacted and labor done; but as little as possible of the mind and the energies was devoted to such things. The real life of the Viennese began with the fun and the pleasures and the dreams.

It was passing now under the stark realities of postwar life but a surprising amount seemed to remain. It was summed up in the word *"Gemütlichkeit,"* a word that has no equivalent in any other language. It meant many things that you soon noticed in the Viennese character: gaiety, frivolity, easygoingness, carelessness and, I think, laziness. My countess had tried to explain it one day.

"Our secret," she said, laughing, "is that we have learned how to combine a minimum of work with a maximum of pleasure."

It wasn't exactly the kind of life I, with my grim, Protestant, Midwest background, was seeking. Brought up on the Presbyterian work ethic, I thought the Viennese life was a bit frivolous and unreal. But it was pleasant mingling with these people who lived it. It must have had a mellowing and civilizing effect on a raw American youth. It provided a further education.

. .

In truth I had a lot of work to do, and in these felicitous surroundings, or in spite of them, I swung into it with relish. I had to cover not only Austria, but all the other countries of the Danube, which had sprung up or been augmented or deflated at the fall of the Hapsburg Empire: Czechoslovakia, Hungary, Yugoslavia, Rumania and Bulgaria. Like every other nation in Europe, where the Great War had brought immense changes, they were trying to cope with the problems of a new era. With the exception of Czechoslovakia, which under the great Thomas Masaryk, its seventy-nine-year-old founder and thrice re-elected President, was making democracy work for the first time there, they were not doing very well. The rest were living under dictatorships or semidictatorships whose rulers might seem comic, and were, but who were as oppressive, stupid and cruel as any former Austrian tyrant. I would spend a good deal of time in those countries trying to see men in prison, or just out of it, and listening to their accounts of the stifling of freedom and decency, of the brutality of torture of those who dared to dissent. In this respect, there had been little change down through the ages. Central Europe at this time provided one of my first lessons: that though a people may win freedom for their country, they do not automatically win it for themselves as individuals. Everywhere I found repression, fraud and chicanery, with ordinary common people the victims, as they always had been no matter what the regime.

But there was a lot of fluffy stuff to write up, too, some of it as foolish as a Viennese comic opera, and this was what our readers in Chicago liked best, I suspected. Something out of romantic Vienna and the Blue Danube, or from picturesque Budapest, or from Bucharest, with its ridiculous Hohenzollern-Sigmaringen monarchy, whose throne the once king and now playboy Prince Carol was plotting to regain with the help of his red-headed Jewish mistress, the fiery Magda Lupescu. In Vienna itself there was always "colorful copy" in Maria Jeritza, the beautiful, temperamental star of the Opera, who was frequently being brought to court—once by a maid she hadn't paid for ten years: "She was no good," she would plead; another time by a starving composer who sued her for payment of an opera she had commissioned him to write: "It stunk," she argued.

In Vienna, too, there were stories from the learned doctors—

quacks, they seemed to me—who were stirring Europe with their claims of discoveries of how to retain eternal youth by the transplant of monkey glands or the injection of the hormones of some other beast into one's body. We often made the front page with such flummery—such is the craze of some, especially in America, to remain young, as if aging beyond thirty or so was life's curse. More legitimate and much more interesting to me were the feuds of Freud with his former disciples Jung, Stekel and Adler. Psychoanalysis was bursting into the world at that time and Freud was its prophet. No doubt he was a genius and he had an immense impact on the twentieth century, but he could brook no criticism from the men he had trained and who, defying him, began to break away and to question some of his theories and methods. It was a delight to get into the fray, even for one so ignorant as I. Adler was especially helpful to me in getting his side of the argument in print. He was never a man to shun publicity. Freud did, but got publicity by the very act of shunning it. He declined all requests for an interview. The only chance I got to see him was when he read a paper at some congress of psychoanalysts. He was an imposing figure at seventy-three, rather fatherly, self-confident, and with an intensity in his face, and especially in his eyes, that was striking and denoted, I thought, immense powers of mental concentration. He chain-smoked large cigars, and it may have been this habit that later caused cancer of the throat. Seeing him and hearing and reading so much controversial talk of him in Vienna encouraged me to begin to read him—we had not been much concerned with Freud out in Iowa —and to try to comprehend some of the light he had shed on the mind and the unconscious and dreams and the sexual drive and the guilt feelings and the Oedipus complexes of the nervous, neurotic human beings of our time.

One wintry afternoon at a boring diplomatic tea party, which a correspondent attended in the line of duty and in the faint hope of picking up the trail of a story, I met Zora. We fled from it together, and I walked her home to her apartment in a street named, I know not why, Taubstummengasse—Deaf and Dumb Street; my German was progressing from zero far enough to translate it. She was a Hungarian, though her English was almost flawless, and she had dark-blue eyes that expressed a sort of merriment at one moment and a sadness at another, and that were set unusually far apart over high cheekbones. She had silky dark-brown hair and her voice was deep and resonant. Someone had introduced us early in the party and we hit it off immediately. After having met so many beautiful but dumb countesses, I was immediately struck by her lively mind and her sense of humor.

"Thank God, you're not another one of these Viennese countesses," I said, as we clinked our glasses. She smiled.

"You look as bored here as I am," she said after a second drink. "Let's get out of here."

At her apartment we had another drink. And then we went around the corner for dinner at a simple but pleasant little restaurant. And we talked and talked as if we had known each other for a long time.

"You probably won't come to see me again," she said as we drank our coffee.

"Why not? I'd certainly like to."

"I didn't have the heart to tell you, after what you said about all those boring countesses you had met here. But . . ." She hesitated and her eyes were teasing.

"But what?"

"I'm one of them. By marriage, I mean. Does that disturb you?"

"As a matter of fact, no," I said. "Let's say you're an exception."

She had married old Count "X" during the war, she said, and regretted it ever since. They were now separated—he was off puttering around in his icy *Schloss* in the country and she had returned to Vienna and taken an apartment. She had been trying for years to get a divorce, but in Catholic Austria it was difficult, even with the "godless" Socialists in the Rathaus.

I remembered that it was my Austrian assistant's night off, and I suggested she come with me to the office and help translate the news agency file and early-morning newspapers. My German was not yet quite up to it. At the office she proved to be more helpful than my assistant, translating rapidly, spotting stories of interest and providing amusing background to some of the dispatches.

"Maybe you will take me on as your second assistant," she

said jokingly when we stopped at a coffeehouse on the way home. It had started to snow again by the time we headed back to "Deaf and Dumb Street," and we romped down the Ring, shaking off the snowflakes and laughing. The city looked beautiful in the snow, and so did Zora. We finally reached her home and I never left it, until I had to leave in May to cover the tennis in Paris and then go on for another dreaded summer in London.

"Why don't you join me in London?" I asked her, as we drove to the Westbahnhof, where I was to catch the Orient Express for Paris.

"Maybe I will," she said. A deep affection had grown, a lively interest in each other. I could not bear to think that we would not come together again.

Over the years in Vienna—for I would soon return for a longer stay—many friendships were made, some of them for life.

John Gunther arrived the next year as a correspondent for the Chicago *Daily News,* and though our newspapers were rivals, which raised certain professional problems, we became close friends and so remained until his death more than forty years later. A native of Chicago, like Sheean and me, he, too, had come over on a cattle boat three or four years before me and finally landed a job on the *News.* John was a big, rangy man, bursting with energy and an enormous curiosity about life and people. Journalism, at which he was very good, was only a stepping-stone, he confided to me. He wanted to be a novelist, and already he had published three novels, one of which, *The Red Pavilion,* had done well in England if not so well at home. What better preparation for a novelist than newspaper work, he would exclaim, and cite Dreiser, Sinclair Lewis and Hemingway as examples. Later I would have a similar ambition but, like Gunther, after a few novels that did not cause any splash at all in the world, would scrap it for another kind of writing. We were young enough to be confident that we were on our way to somewhere that would bring some kind of achievement and recognition, first in journalism and then in writing books, and we never tired of talking, of the problems and hurdles and of everything else under the sun while walking through the Wienerwald or sitting at a table in a café or going off together on a jaunt to Budapest, Belgrade and Bucharest in search of a story and more experience.

The dialogue continued, as time went by, all over Europe—long after we had left Vienna we were continually running in to each other in the most unlikely places, as once in Danzig on the eve of the second war—and it lasted as lively as ever through the post-war years when we lived within a stone's throw of each other in New York. The dialogue and the friendship.

Fodor became another friend. He had been the mentor of Dorothy Thompson when she came to Vienna after the first war on her first newspaper job and later he became the mentor of Gunther. "He educated Dorothy and me practically from the cradle," John would say. He helped in my education, too. I have never known a man, and especially a journalist, who gave so much of himself and his knowledge to others. Fodor was a short, round, bubbling Hungarian. Even his closest friends never called him by anything but his last name, for he detested the sound of his given name, Marcel. Educated as an engineer, he had gone to England to work before the war, been interned there when the war broke out, and had used his time in camp to add English to the half-dozen languages he already knew. He had drifted into journalism in the chaos of the first years of peace and had become the Vienna correspondent of the *Manchester Guardian* and later, through Dorothy Thompson's intercession, also of the New York *Evening Post*.

Fodor loved Vienna, its people, its cafés, its restaurants, the food and the wine, and, above all, good talk. He would sit up all night with you jabbering about everything, but especially about what was going on in Vienna, Budapest, Prague and all the other capitals of Central Europe. His knowledge was encyclopedic, but he wore it well and he displayed it in a courtly manner, though he could become as passionate about a cause—man's freedom, for instance—as the rest of us. I can still hear his voice rising and his accent becoming a little heavier: "But, Bill, don't you see? That so-and-so [he was too courtly to use strong Anglo-Saxon words] in Budapest [or Belgrade or Bucharest] is a crook. You see! We must start there. Now, you see, there's a plot. He . . ." Sometimes I teased Fodor that he saw plots and counterplots being hatched like chickens in a henhouse and that maybe there were simply historical currents at work; and indeed he called his first book *Plot and Counterplot in Central Europe*. Martha Fodor, his wife, was a dark-haired, dark-eyed Slovak, beautiful and enigmatic, who as our pleasant evenings together wore on to the small hours of the night would say: "Enough! I think I have heard enough of politics. Now listen to me!" And she would grab her guitar and start to sing gypsy songs in a low, sultry voice, her dark eyes full of passion and then sadness. It was a good note on which to end a long evening. The Fodors, like the Gunthers, became an intimate part of my life.

Whit Burnett and Martha Foley, too, when they later came to Vienna as correspondents for the New York *Sun* syndicate. Even more than Gunther and I, they already had literary ambitions, and though they were conscientious journalists, their heart was in a more lasting kind of writing. Whit was writing short stories and they were very good but very Hemingway. Already, though, he was beginning to discover where his best talent lay. This was in editing. Soon the Burnetts were at work in the *Journalistenzimmer,* a room provided by the State Telegraph and Telephone office for the newspapermen and whose rickety Mimeograph machine they used to get out the first issue of *Story.* Whit had a genius for discovering young writers who had never been published before, and *Story* contained the very first published stories of such writers as William Saroyan, Truman Capote, Norman Mailer, Mary O'Hara, Carson McCullers, Joseph Heller and J. D. Salinger. No other magazine in the thirties (the Burnetts later published it in Majorca and then New York) introduced so many good young writers.

Robert Best of the United Press presided at the Café Louvre, where the correspondents hung out. A big, genial, somewhat portly fellow, who never lost his native Carolina accent whether he was speaking English or German, he was well liked by the other correspondents, for whom he was never too busy to do a good turn. In all the time he was in Vienna, from 1923 on, he virtually lived at the Louvre. It would not have occurred to anyone to telephone or meet him any place else at any time of day or night. He had an apartment somewhere, in which he lived with an aging countess, but no one ever saw it or her. Bob was the best of companions, like most American Southerners a born storyteller, and indeed in his manners and mind and speech he seemed still to be implanted in his Carolina mountains. But this would change. He never went home to renew his roots, and gradually he began to put down new ones in the worst weedy patches of Central

Europe. This would transform him into a pitiful remnant of what he was when I first knew him as he sat at his *Stammtisch* at the Louvre and exchanged news, gossip and good talk with the rest of us. Yet none of us could faintly imagine what would become of him in the end—it will be told in due course.

Among the frequent American visitors to Vienna was William C. Bullitt, who remained there the winter and spring of 1932 working on a book, he said. He was a handsome, polished, warm and friendly, rather debonair man of forty from an old Philadelphia family. Gunther and I saw a good deal of him for he not only shared our passion for European history and current politics but he brought to us a good deal of information about what was going on at home. He was sure that Franklin Roosevelt, governor of New York, was going to get the Democratic nomination that summer and that he would easily defeat Hoover for the Presidency in the fall elections. He had been working informally for the governor, he said, sending back reports on the situation in Europe, and when spring came that year he was restless to get back to America to work for the nomination.

Besides being a congenial companion, Bullitt was also something of a hero to Gunther and me. As a twenty-eight-year-old member of the American delegation to the Peace Conference in Paris after the war, he had been sent by President Wilson to Moscow early in 1919 to negotiate a preliminary peace agreement with the new Bolshevik government and to report back to the Allied statesmen on whether Lenin's revolutionary government was stable enough to survive and, if so, whether it could be dealt with by the Western capitalist powers. John and I had only a vague recollection of Bullitt's role, but in many talks at lunch or dinner, or hiking through the Wienerwald, he filled in the details —he was a superb raconteur.

He had set out for Russia with the blessings of Wilson and with instructions from Colonel Edward M. House, Wilson's aide and confidant, and from the British Prime Minister, Lloyd George, taking with him the ebullient Lincoln Steffens, one of the great muckraking American journalists of the era, who made no bones of his sympathies for the Russian Revolution. In Moscow Bullitt saw Lenin and spent weeks in secret negotiations with Tchicherin and Litvinov, the Soviet Commissar and the Assistant Commissar for Foreign Affairs.

According to Bullitt—and Steffens confirmed it in his memoirs—he brought back from Moscow all that House and Lloyd George had asked for, and more: agreement to an armistice on all fronts, abandonment of claims to Russian territory in Poland and the Baltic, and the assumption by the Soviet Union of the debts of Czarist Russia in return for the diplomatic recognition of the U.S.S.R. by the big Allied powers, the lifting of their "hunger" blockade, loans in the form of food for the starving country and withdrawal of Allied forces. Young Bullitt returned to Paris in high spirits, confident that he had scored a diplomatic coup and that his information, after so much misinformation that the Bolshevik regime was crumbling, would be of the utmost value to the Big Four statesmen, who were drawing up the terms of peace and redrawing the map of Europe.

To his surprise and then growing indignation Wilson and his colleagues were not in the least interested. The answers Bullitt had brought back from Moscow did not seem as important to them as they did to him and—he was sure—to history. At that moment Allied armies (including American) were attacking the Bolsheviks from Archangel and Vladivostok and were supporting and supplying White armies elsewhere. What Wilson, Lloyd George and Clemenceau wanted in Russia was the destruction of Communism and the revival of the capitalist state. They could not face being told by a confident young junior American diplomat that the Lenin regime, despite its difficulties, had too strong a hold on Russia to be replaced and ought to be dealt with while its weaknesses could still be exploited for concessions.

Wilson, who had sent Bullitt to Russia, refused to see him in Paris. Lloyd George returned hastily to London to tell the Commons that he had never heard of the "Bullitt mission." The conservative young Philadelphian was branded "a Bolshevik," though neither then nor thereafter did he have any sympathy for Communism—indeed, he hated it. And his standing was not helped when Lincoln Steffens on returning to Paris from Russia made his famous statement: "I have seen the future, and it works."

It was from this double cross, as he saw it, by the President of the United States, whom he had idolized, that Bullitt's hatred toward Wilson sprang. Disillusioned not only by the failure of the Allies to deal with the Soviet Union, but also by the terms of the peace treaty, Bullitt resigned his post and returned home. There he denounced the treaty and Wilson before the Senate Foreign Relations Committee, giving effective ammunition to Senator Henry Cabot Lodge and the other Senate diehards who were determined not only to reject the treaty but to destroy Wilson, which they did.

It was obvious from his talks with us that Bullitt's feelings of resentment against Wilson had festered all these years. But I did not comprehend their extent until years later. I knew that he was seeing a lot of Freud that year but I did not connect this with the book he said he was writing. I thought probably he was in analysis with the Master himself. It was thirty-five years later, in 1967, that I made the connection, upon publication of *Wilson—A Psychological Study* by Sigmund Freud and William C. Bullitt. In it all of Bullitt's feelings of resentment and hostility to Wilson, pent up all these years, seemed to spill out. Perhaps it was only human, in view of the President's repudiation of him at Paris in 1919.

But why had the great Freud lent himself to such a book? He had written not only the Introduction but whole chapters of the work. Strangely, Freud's bias turned out to be as strong as Bullitt's, though the Viennese psychoanalyst had never met Wilson or, it was obvious, known very much about him except what his young American friend fed him. But as he "confessed" (his word) in his Introduction,

> the figure of the American President, as it rose above the horizon of Europeans, was from the beginning unsympathetic to me, and this aversion increased in the course of years the more I learned about him and the more severely we suffered from the consequences of his intrusion into our destiny.

The book showed, to me at least, the pitfalls for even a Freud trying to psychoanalyze historical figures—he had done it with Moses, Leonardo and others. We all knew that Wilson, like almost everyone else, had his neuroses; he was the victim of a strong-minded father whom he alternately revered and hated, and ultimately he had turned on his closest friends and associates, such as Hibben at Princeton and Colonel House at Paris, conjuring them up as his deadly enemies and cursing them for their alleged betrayals, which were without basis, except in his nerve-racked mind. But the Wilson presented by Freud and Bullitt is to me too ridiculous to be good history or biography. At least one psychoanalyst, who was working closely with Freud in Vienna during my time there, took an even stronger view of the book. This was Erik H. Erikson, a neighbor of mine in the Berkshires and a teacher at Harvard, who wrote a devastating review of it in the *New York Review of Books.*

I can only believe that Bill Bullitt, whom I much liked as a person though disagreeing with him more and more as the years went by, fell too easily into bitterness and resentment against those he believed had crossed him, or double-crossed him. Wilson was not the only one. Later as the first American Ambassador to the Soviet Union, after President Roosevelt resumed diplomatic relations in 1933 with a country which for fourteen years we had refused to recognize, Bullitt seemed to me to harbor a festering hatred of a regime and its system not so much because of the horrors of Stalin's terror, though they appalled him, but because he felt the Soviets were not living up to the agreement he had helped the President negotiate with them as a condition for recognition, and also because it seemed to him that the Bolsheviks did not sufficiently appreciate what he had tried to do for them in 1919, when they were alone, friendless, starving and besieged. His hatred of the Soviet Union and of Communism became a phobia and ill served his friend Roosevelt or his country when he became Ambassador to France in the years just before the war, and a close adviser of F.D.R.'s on European affairs. That judgment is based not only on a reading of all of his secret dispatches to the President and the State Department from Paris, but on the opinions expressed to me by the French Premiers at the time, Édouard Daladier and Paul Reynaud, who liked him immensely but who felt that his phobias about Communism and the Soviet Union, which grew to immense proportions during his ambassadorship in Paris, sometimes marred the cool and objective judgments a good diplomat ought to make regardless of his personal feelings.[1]

[1] For example, I found one Top Secret cable to President Roosevelt from Bullitt in Paris on May 17, 1940, vividly describing a Communist revolt in the French Army, then being driven rapidly back by the Germans on Paris, which never took place.

In cooperation with the Germans and on orders of the Soviet Government one regiment of Chasseurs, which was composed of Communists from

Bullitt had been married to Louise Bryant, an intriguing and romantic figure in that fabled and colorful generation just ahead of us, that Gunther and I admired and somewhat envied. It had come of age mostly out of the Ivy League colleges shortly before the war and had centered around Provincetown, Greenwich Village, Paris, Moscow, and the ambulance drivers and correspondents in the war. It had included Edna St. Vincent Millay, Mabel Dodge, Eugene O'Neill, John Reed, Dos Passos, Scott Fitzgerald, Hemingway, Sinclair Lewis, Lewis Gannett, E. E. Cummings, Edmund Wilson and Walter Lippmann, among others. John and I had been much taken with their bohemian lives and loves and their journalistic, literary and, in O'Neill's case, playwriting achievements.

Louise Bryant was typical of the group. She had been married to a dentist in Portland, Oregon, when John Reed, on a visit home, had snatched her away and taken her to live with him in Greenwich Village. O'Neill, a friend of Reed, had fallen in love with her for a while, as had others, but she finally married Reed and set off for Russia with him to cover the Bolshevik Revolution. Out of that had come in 1919 Reed's classic eyewitness account, *Ten Days That Shook the World*, a book that, despite its passion-

---

the Paris industrial suburbs, revolted three days ago, seized the vital town of Compiègne on the German path to Paris and are still in possession of the town. They number 18,000 and I'm informed that they will be attacked by the Air Force and tanks this evening.

That was an unusually big regiment! No regiment in the French Army, or in any other army, contained 18,000 men.

Bullitt concluded his cable to Roosevelt: "Please for the sake of the future, nail every Communist or Communist sympathizer in our Army, Navy, and Air Force."

This horrendous tale, along with a second in the same cable saying that since "all the heavy French tanks were manned by Communist workmen from the Renault works," they refused to advance when ordered and instead sabotaged their tanks, was invented either by Bullitt or by an informant whom the Ambassador ought to have known better than to believe. I came into Compiègne a few days later as an American correspondent with the advancing German armies and talked to the local inhabitants, none of whom mentioned this "red" revolt in Compiègne or any place else. I also went through the voluminous testimony of the commanders of the four French armored divisions as well as that of the two over-all commanders of tanks, most of whom were as anti-Communist as Bullitt, if not more so. There was not a word from any of them of a Communist revolt or of Communist tankmen refusing to advance or sabotaging their machines. On the contrary, they maintained that the French tank crews without exception fought magnificently before they were wiped out.

ate sympathies with the Bolsheviks, who were portrayed in the American press as devils incarnate, had become a best seller, and had immensely impressed me when I got to it as a freshman in college. Louise, too, had achieved fame for a series on the revolution that she wrote for Hearst's New York *American.* Then, the next year, in 1920, Reed had suddenly died and been buried in the Kremlin wall, which later became the shrine of the heroes of the revolution.

Bullitt, a friend of both Reed and his wife, whom he had seen much of in Moscow on his mission in 1919, had married Louise Bryant in 1923 and they had spent a good deal of time in a home they had in Paris, where I had first caught a glimpse of her. She was not beautiful but terribly attractive in a provocative way, with her reddish hair, slim figure, enigmatic eyes, and a restlessness for men and adventure. "When that girl touches me," O'Neill had once confided to a friend about her, "it's like a flame," and other men apparently had felt it, too. With the unbohemian Bullitt she had appeared to settle down. But not for long. The old restlessness returned and with it a great deal of drinking and cutting up. This was too much for the fashionable young Philadelphian and in 1930 Bullitt had divorced her on the grounds of "personal indignities." They had had a child, a daughter, to whom Bullitt was utterly devoted. Also, it was obvious from his talk, when it turned to the old days, that he still cherished the memory of Louise Bryant. Her spell, as it had on O'Neill and on so many others, lingered on.

One early-spring Sunday, with the snow still high on the ground, Bullitt, Gunther and I went for a walk in the Wienerwald, stopping to lunch at a rustic restaurant in a clearing in the woods. Bullitt was in high spirits and insisted on ordering champagne and we had a fine meal and much sparkling wine and talk. He was anxious to return to America, he said, and start working for the nomination of Governor Roosevelt, about whom he spoke at great length and with burning admiration. Only Roosevelt, he contended, could rescue the country from the Depression, which was far worse, he added, than Gunther and I, preoccupied with the problems of Europe, realized. Very few at home, he said, knew what a potentially great man Roosevelt was. Bullitt was indignant at a column recently published by his friend Walter Lippmann describing Roosevelt as too much of a playboy to be

President. He grew quite emotional and I could see that the passion of his hatreds (for Wilson, the Communists) was equaled by the passion of his loves.

John and I left the table for a few moments to call our offices in Vienna to see if any news was breaking this Sabbath afternoon. There was little of interest, we were told, except a news agency report from Moscow that Louise Bryant had died. John and I debated how to break the news to Bullitt and decided to tell it straight. He paled, lapsed into silence and finally asked us to call his home and tell his chauffeur to drive out to fetch us as soon as possible. The lunch, begun in such high spirits, ended on this melancholy note.

The report, as happened so often in Vienna, proved to be false. Louise Bryant did not die until four years later, in 1936, in Paris. It was a sad ending for so glamorous a woman. According to the newspaper accounts, she had been drinking heavily and had fallen down the stairs of a decrepit little Left Bank hotel in which she had been living her last grubby years, and suffered a cerebral hemorrhage. She died a few days later at the American Hospital. She was forty-one.

There were a number of rather strange American "characters" in Vienna in those days who had come to the city for one reason or another, fallen in love with it and the Viennese, and remained. Some had come, in the first place, to be psychoanalyzed by Freud or one of his associates, a process that often continued unending over the years without, I thought, spectacular results, one way or another. Of all these "characters" we found one the most interesting and compatible. This was Dr. Darwin Lyon, who claimed some kind of descent from the great Charles Darwin, author of the *Origin of Species*. I always suspected that the doctor's father had simply given him the Christian name out of admiration for the great British scientist. "Doc" Lyon, as we called him, was a gangly, effervescent, fast-talking American in his middle forties, I suppose. Perhaps his somewhat emaciated face made him seem older, or it might have been because I was only twenty-five, and a twenty-year age difference made men seem older than they were.

"Doc" was what the French call a *fantoche*, delightful and a little crazy, though in one respect not so crazy as we thought. He had come to Vienna as a doctor with the American Red Cross at the war's end to organize medical care and food supplies for the starving Austrians. He had fallen in love with the city and its inhabitants, who long remembered him gratefully for his services in their time of need and accorded him a special status which he enjoyed and would have had no place else. He continued to do a little medical work, for which, I believe, he was not licensed, and some research at the medical school of the university. At the time I knew him he was absorbed principally in working on rockets. He was in touch with Dr. Robert H. Goddard, a physicist at small Clark University in Worcester, Massachusetts, who long had been regarded at home, I believe, as a crazy visionary about rockets but who, in 1926, I had read somewhere, had actually fired the world's first liquid-fueled rocket and who now, in the 1970's, is recognized as the father of rocketry.

"Doc" Lyon tinkered away at his rockets in an old workshop he had set up, and on many an evening he would drop by for a drink and dinner and regale Gunther and me about the future of rockets. Very soon, he claimed, men would be sending rockets to the moon. I suppose that is why Gunther and I thought "Doc" was a little daffy. He would talk on and on about the feasibility of boosting liquid-propelled rockets into the stratosphere from whence they could be guided to the planets. It all seemed too fantastic to take seriously and John and I would tease the poor man about being crazy and proffer him another drink, which he never turned down. Sometimes "Doc" would lure us to his cluttered workshop, where he had fashioned a conical object about fifteen feet high which he said was a rocket that he was going to take down to the Italian Alps and that, with luck, might penetrate the stratosphere. One spring he set out with his contraption in an old truck and promised to send us a wire if the thing worked. Sure enough, in a few days we got a long telegram from him saying that his rocket had taken off from an Alpine peak and "disappeared into outer space." If true, John and I had a "scoop" for our respective Chicago papers, but we were very skeptical and cabled such guarded accounts that they were tossed into the wastebasket by our editors. Later, Doc's mistress, a curious Viennese woman with whom he was feuding before they left for the mountains and for whom the rocket experiment apparently was the last straw, for they broke up shortly afterward, told John and me that the rocket had sizzled and come down from a few hundred feet in the air, but "Doc" said she was crazy and that the experiment had been a wonderful success. Unfortunately, he said, he had no instruments to monitor the rocket after it got out of sight and he had no idea where it had landed—perhaps in China, he thought. Perhaps so. But I doubt it. At any rate, looking back on Dr. Darwin Lyon nearly half a century later I no longer see him as crazy as we then regarded him. He was a minor pioneer in a field that would later dazzle us, with rockets landing men on the moon and guided, in some instances, by men on earth to planets far beyond the moon. It was Gunther and I who were crazy not to have believed.

Both of us incidentally became "crazy" in quite another way. This was over a beautiful and temperamental young actress at the Reinhardt theater named Luise Rainer. She was to us, at least, the most exciting ingenue on the Vienna stage. Dark, with large dark eyes that could be sad or blazing and with a personality to match, she rather intimidated me just by her presence, and maybe she saw John and me occasionally mostly to perfect her English. She was working on the language because she had her heart set on Broadway and Hollywood, and very shortly she would make the move and in *The Good Earth* win an Oscar and become one of the finest movie actresses of the thirties.

It is odd, as I look back, how many friends were made in Vienna whom I would continue to see, here or there, in Europe or America, for the rest of my life or theirs: Luise Rainer, Bill Bullitt, the Fodors, the Gunthers, the Whit Burnetts, Virgilia Peterson, who was tall, willowy, beautiful, sensitive, vivacious and a good writer. "Gilly" had come first to Vienna to write a novel but also, I think, to be near to Poland, where Prince Paul Sapieha lived, and whom she soon married. She seemed the winter in Vienna that I saw her to have some doubts about settling down to a life in the Polish countryside, but these she soon overcame. Much later, at home, we would see a good deal of each other and to our surprise, since we had been old friends so long, fall in love. I was with her the day before Christmas Eve one snowy winter in the Litchfield hills of Connecticut—the day before her untimely death in a blizzard as Christmas dawned.

And all through one winter in Vienna (1932–1933) there were Dorothy and Red—Dorothy Thompson and her then husband, Sinclair Lewis. Lewis was then at the height of his fame. Two years before, he had won the Nobel Prize, the first American author ever to be given the coveted award. Three novels, *Main Street* in 1920, *Babbitt* in 1922 and *Arrowsmith* in 1925, had won him acclaim at home and abroad, and if those that followed were not nearly as good, *Mantrap, Elmer Gantry, The Man Who Knew Coolidge, Dodsworth* and *Ann Vickers*, the last published while he was in Vienna in January, 1933, they added something to the public figure—at least he kept on writing as well as he could— and brought him a considerable fortune.

Dorothy Thompson had a reputation of her own, not as the colorful wife of a famous novelist, but as one of the best American foreign correspondents in Europe. Except for my *Tribune* colleague in Berlin, Sigrid Schultz, Dorothy was the only woman who had made the grade and I counted her among the top American correspondents, the equal of her good friends Edgar and Paul Scott Mowrer, H. R. Knickerbocker, John Gunther and Vincent Sheean, and better known at the time than any of them. Not until they started writing books, Sheean with his *Personal History* in 1935 and Gunther with *Inside Europe* the following year, would their names rival Dorothy's. She was never a good book writer; she wrote her books too hurriedly. But as a journalist she was superb.

Dorothy was also an extremely attractive woman. I never thought her beautiful, as so many did—the large features of her face, her strong chin and her rather bulky frame did not quite allow for that—but she was engaging-looking and her vivacious-ness, her vitality, her warmth and passion, her enormous appetite for life, her intelligence, and her powerful and original person-ality made her one of the most interesting women I have known. She did talk too much. It was difficult for her not to dominate a conversation and often turn it into a monologue. Though her diaries and letters would later show that she often questioned herself sharply in private, I was not aware of this at the time. She almost never did it in my presence. Outwardly she bubbled with confidence—about herself at the time and about her future. In the course of many decades after Vienna we would often argue passionately until we ended shouting at each other—most often about the Germans and Germany, with both of which she had a love-hate relationship that I did not share. But the violent exchanges did not destroy our affection. And for periods we agreed on a truce: we would refrain from discussing the Germans. There was always plenty else to talk about.

Dorothy and Red arrived in Vienna at the end of the summer of 1932 and rented a large apartment in the Wohllebengasse and a spacious villa on the Semmering, two hours by train south of Vienna in the mountains. At first they seemed quite happy, especially Dorothy, who was soon holding forth, as was her wont, in her salon crammed with admiring journalists, diplomats, statesmen and what was left of the German, Austrian and Hungarian aristocracy, discussing everything under the sun—art and love, but above all politics. This had been a problem for the Lewises ever since they were married four years before in London. Dorothy was at home in Europe among Europeans; Lewis was not. Much of the conversation at Dorothy's gatherings was in German, in which she was extremely fluent but which Red scarcely understood. He felt shut out of the talk, and his inevitable reaction, which was mercurial, was to stomp out and leave not only the party and the dwelling but the city. He was always taking off in a huff for other parts. Except for the American correspondents, Red could not stand Dorothy's friends. Nor, even when he understood it, their talk. Politics did not interest him and he developed a phobia for her obsession about "The Situation."

"If she would just stop talking about 'The Situation,' for Christ's sake!" he would say as I followed him to a bar, after he had made a hasty exit from one of Dorothy's talkfests. "If she'd just call it off for five minutes! But she can't. I've got to listen day and night to her prattle about the *goddamn Situation.*"

Someone—probably Gunther, who knew Dorothy and Red much better than I—had told me that they had come to Vienna this time to make a last heroic effort to save their marriage, or as Sheean put it, "to recapture the vanishing dream." But it soon became obvious to their friends that the effort, however heroic, was failing. When he was not off to Italy for a week or two, Lewis was mostly on the Semmering, while Dorothy remained in Vienna, happy with her friends. She had always loved Central Europe and its capitals, Berlin, Vienna and Budapest, having what Sheean called an "extreme susceptibility to the Danubian pretension." Most of her journalistic life had been spent in these parts. They were more attractive to her than any other section of

Europe. Here were most of her old friends. She spoke the language, knew the people, the history, the land, the politics. Red couldn't have cared less—for the region, the people or her German-speaking friends there. His heart was always in America, but if he was in Europe, as he had often been since *Main Street* had brought him a modest fortune, he preferred France or Italy but, most of all, England, where he could speak the language.

All through the winter in Vienna and on the Semmering he grew more irritable and drank more heavily, spending most of his time in the villa in the mountains, away from Dorothy. Already in their New York apartment, someone remembered, they had reached a point where they needed not only separate bedrooms but separate living rooms.

"Sometimes I think you don't see me at all," Dorothy would write him from Vienna after he had taken off for Italy following a quarrel, "but somebody you have made up, a piece of fiction, like Ann Vickers." It was his excessive drinking that bothered her most, and she would confide to his biographer of their life at this time that when he came to her room, late at night and drunk, he smelled of rotting weeds.

The prospect, as the winter passed, of a breakup of the marriage depressed Dorothy, I think, more than it did Red, who never could have been happy very long in any marriage or in any other relationship with women. Dorothy's first marriage to Josef Bard, a handsome, romantic Hungarian writer, had been a bitter and disillusioning experience and at one point it had almost driven her to suicide. She had loved him passionately and exclusively, while he had taken a more European view toward a wife, straying away from time to time with other women, and this had broken her heart. She had hoped for better luck with Sinclair Lewis.

But she had not really loved him. "What moved me," she would write of her marriage to Lewis, "was a compelling sense of his need."

Yet neither I nor any other woman who had come into his life before or was to come afterward could fulfill whatever that need might be. . . . He was an elementary force in himself, driving and driven . . . In the end all women left him, driven away perhaps by the impossibility of penetrating the curtain that screened him from any real intimacy; or he left them, forever disappointed.

Perhaps, as Sheean, who knew him much better than I did, concluded, it was Lewis' feeling of sexual inadequacy that made it impossible for him to have a lasting relationship with a woman. It apparently tortured him and may have been the main reason why he always seemed at war with himself, why he took refuge from his failures with women in drink. I myself, for whom Lewis had been a literary hero since *Main Street,* was struck by the feeling of insecurity which lay beneath his bombast during the many talks we had that winter. He seemed depressed sometimes by his physical appearance, which he feared was repulsive to women, and he would dwell on it in jest, which scarcely hid how sensitive he was to it, pointing to his acned face, the scars from which, as he said, made it resemble a pockmarked battlefield. Yet I had seen him charm a roomful of women with his wit, his takeoffs in the vernacular on dozens of characters from a dozen lands—he was a superb mimic—and by the warmth of his feeling for them.

One thing happened to Dorothy at an extravagant party the Lewises threw on the Semmering over the Christmas holiday that year that even Red did not notice or probably ever learn about. I did not attend the gathering and I learned this about Dorothy only thirty years later.

One day Jimmy Sheean called me up in New York, where he was turning Dorothy Thompson's papers into a memorable book, *Dorothy and Red.* His voice crackled with an excitement unusual for him.

"Listen!" he said. "You won't believe what I just found in Dorothy's diary. And I thought I knew her—after all these years. But I never knew this."

"Knew what?" I asked.

"Remember that Christmas party Dorothy and Red threw on the Semmering—the one you and I, fortunately, missed? Well, Dorothy fell madly in love with Christa Winsloe—you know, Baroness Hatvany. It's all in her diary—pages of it. And it wasn't the first time, she says."

"I can't believe it," I said. "Dorothy was, despite all the years in Europe, such an all-American girl."

"Listen to this," Jimmy said, and proceeded to read from the diary. Later he published the entry *in toto* in *Dorothy and Red.*

I remembered Christa Winsloe as a beautiful, witty, rather charming and sensitive German woman, an artist who sculpted mostly animals, and who had achieved a name as a writer suddenly with a novel, *Mädchen in Uniform,* that in the late twenties had become a best seller on both sides of the Atlantic and was turned into a moving film. It was the story of a young schoolgirl, Manuela, who fell in love with a woman teacher and, unable to adjust to the inevitable rejection, had plunged to her death down a staircase in the school. Dorothy had met Christa Winsloe in Berlin in the twenties and had been more attracted to her husband, Baron "Laci" Hatvany, a debonair Hungarian who shared her passion for politics. Still, she had found the dark and sophisticated Christa interesting and had been so moved by the novel that she had wanted to translate it. Suddenly, after six years, during which Dorothy had not seen the Hatvanys, they appeared for the Christmas party on the Semmering. Dorothy fell in love with her at first sight this time.

> So it has happened to me again, after all these years [she wrote in her diary on December 28, remembering that it had happened the first time in America when she was twenty with a woman of thirty-seven and again briefly in Berlin with a "sapphic love"].
> . . . To love a woman is somehow ridiculous. *Mir auch passt es nicht. Ich bin doch heterosexual.* [It doesn't suit me. I *am* heterosexual.] . . . Well, then, how account for this which has happened again. The soft, quite natural kiss on my throat, the quite unconscious (seemingly) even open kiss on my breast, as she stood below me on the stairs . . . I love this woman. . . .

There is much more about her new-found love for this woman in the diary—they would spend much time together in the ensuing months when Lewis' absences became more frequent and Dorothy felt the need for love. Christa Winsloe followed Dorothy to America and for a short time they seemed inseparable, in New York and on Dorothy's Vermont farm. When they were separated they wrote endearing letters to each other, Christa once declaring "nothing on earth can come between us—not a man." But a man did come between them in the form of Ezio

Pinza, the great basso of the Metropolitan Opera, whom Christa pursued across the American continent during a tour of his, though not very successfully. In 1935 she returned to Europe and settled in the south of France, and for a time during the war Dorothy sent her an allowance of fifty dollars a month and discounted rumors that her friend was living with a Swiss woman named Simone Gentet. Dorothy lost track of her when the Germans occupied southern France in 1942, and was crushed when she heard immediately after the war rumors that both women had been shot in 1944 as alleged German spies by the French maquis. Dorothy could not believe it and asked Henri Bonnet, the French Ambassador in Washington, to check. He got the French police to investigate and reported to Dorothy:

> Miss Christa Winsloe died on June 10, 1944. . . . She was not captured by the maquis but murdered by a man named Lambert, who killed her, falsely pretending that he was fulfilling orders from an underground movement. In fact, Lambert was nothing but an ordinary criminal . . .

I do not know how Dorothy took the news of this sad end. By this time she was married to Maxim Kopf and embarking on the only happy marriage of her life.

I had some good talks with Lewis that winter on the Semmering. I took the precaution of staying at the Sudbahn hotel, near his villa. He was drinking heavily, especially after New Year's, starting with a tumbler of brandy at breakfast, and a weekend could be rather long if you accepted his invitation to stay at the villa. Dorothy was never present and we could talk of things that interested him and me, though of course I shared Dorothy's passion for politics. But I was also interested in writing and writers, and that was what he mostly talked about. I had begun to wonder why so many good American writers petered out in the prime of life, at the very time most European authors were just getting into their stride. Later Thomas Mann, who greatly admired Lewis, and Fitzgerald and Hemingway even more, would suggest to me that this decline in power might be due to the early success that came to so many writers in America, and with it, sudden money and sudden fame and adulation. These things, he thought, if they came too soon, when a writer was not old or mature enough to cope with them, strangled him. They not only strangled him as a writer but, in some cases, strangled his life, as happened just after the second war to Ross Lockridge and Tom Heggen, who could not endure the immense acclaim that came with their very first novels and, in their helplessness, killed themselves. Their first novels had been their last.

I found Lewis very much preoccupied with this phenomenon, as well he might be, for he sensed—though he hated to admit—that his own novels had fallen off after *Arrowsmith* in 1925, seven years before. Red and I had one day gone to a lunch in Vienna given by some Austrian authors for two of their best, Franz Werfel and Stefan Zweig, and one of them—I can't remember which, though I believe it was Zweig—had touched on the subject of American writers fading so early and at the end turned to Lewis for a response. But he had remained silent—perhaps he had not followed the speeches, which were in German.

He couldn't understand, he said, in our Semmering talks why so many American writers ran out of steam when they had so many good years ahead. He mentioned Dreiser and Sherwood Anderson, whom he did not like personally, but whose works he had praised in his Nobel Prize speech.

"And what," he would say, "has happened to Fitzgerald since *Gatsby* [1925] or even to Hemingway since *A Farewell to Arms* [1929]. Frankly, I don't know. They're so young compared to some of us oldsters."

He himself was far from through, he said. In fact, he said, he was projecting what he thought would be his greatest novel, a work that would be nothing less than a history of America. Perhaps he was thinking of his labor novel, on which he had been working, on and off, for years, and which, he had told me, would encompass three generations of American workers.[1] Actually, as I learned later, he was working out the skeleton of a lesser novel, *Work of Art*, that dealt with hotels, which had always fascinated him, and which, when it came out two years later, struck me as

---

[1] According to Dorothy Thompson in an article in the *Atlantic Monthly* in 1960, Lewis finally threw the manuscript of the labor novel away "with the dictum that few labor leaders were really concerned with helping the rank and file; rather, they were concerned with feathering their own nests and grabbing power. I went with him to an AFL convention in Canada, and he railed at its leaders all the way back."

one of the least of his novels and which Sheean thought so bad as to be "unsuited for publication." It was scarcely a work of art.

And in truth it was all downhill for Lewis from now on, as it had been, gradually, for five or six years, though he would turn out nine more novels, the last, *World So Wide,* shortly before he died. All downhill for his marriage with Dorothy, too. The winter in Austria had not saved it, as they had hoped. Probably nothing could have saved it. Almost any marriage between a great writer and a great journalist, I concluded, was doomed. Their egos, their compulsive drives, were too great to fit into a compatible union, though Dorothy would never concede this. She opposed a divorce to the bitter end.

Though I was never an intimate, I saw Lewis occasionally when I was home on leave during the second war, and immediately afterward. He was a lonely man. The marriage had finally broken up in 1937, I believe, when Red stomped out of their house in Bronxville for the last time, claiming that Dorothy's career had ruined everything and that she had eroded his creative powers. But the formal parting did not come until 1942, five years later, when at Lewis' urging she finally agreed to a divorce.

Three years before this, in 1939, when he was fifty-four, he had taken up with a pretty, young stage-struck woman of eighteen, Marcella Powers, and since then they had been constantly together. I saw them mostly at the Gunthers'. At last, it seemed, he had found an attractive woman who was too young and inexperienced to be unduly critical or to question his freedom. She obviously admired the great writer, and he was very happy with her. Together they toured in his play *Angela Is Twenty-Two* and he did everything he could to further her career on the stage. But this union, too, was doomed. She, at least, realized that the difference in age was too great to bridge and in the end, to his sorrow, she married a younger man.

Sinclair Lewis' last years were a bleak despair. He moved from one big house to another, bought and sold them, first in America and finally in Italy, searching for something—some resting place?—he could not find. He had abandoned most of his friends, or they had abandoned him. More lonely than ever before, he finally took on as a secretary-companion a young clerk from the Thomas Cook & Son travel agency in Florence by the name of Alexander Manson. They had met over a bottle of brandy in the bar of a hotel in Assisi, and the young man had introduced himself as a major, recently of the British Army. According to Dorothy the young man's background was "obscure," his nationality "undistinguished," and Bernard Berenson, after meeting him in Florence, where Lewis had rented a gaudy villa not far away, concluded that he was "a minor Central European adventurer." True or false, this young travel-agency clerk was Lewis' constant companion for the last wretched year of his life, sharing the Florentine villa and all the traveling, for the great writer was constantly on the move—up and down Italy, across to France and back again, through Switzerland, by motorcar along all the highways and byways of southern Europe. Constantly on the move, and constantly drinking. After his first heart attack a succession of Italian doctors, anxious to help a man they regarded as one of the world's greatest writers, warned him that unless he stopped drinking he would die. But he could not stop, and probably by this time it was too late.

On the last day of 1950, in Rome by now, he was stricken. He was taken by Manson to an obscure hospital on the outskirts of Rome, where the doctors diagnosed his condition as acute delirium tremens. He never fully regained consciousness and would not have been able to recognize any friends had they come to his bedside, though none did. No one in Rome outside of Manson (who later claimed to be his heir) knew where he was. Utterly alone this great American novelist died on the morning of January 10, 1951, of paralysis of the heart, less than a month short of his sixty-sixth birthday.

Today it has become rather commonplace for so-called literary critics and probably a good number of readers of books to write off Sinclair Lewis as a novelist. And indeed his brilliant biographer Mark Schorer concluded that Lewis was "one of the worst writers in modern American literature" though he added that "without his writings we cannot imagine modern American literature." Many of us were swayed, I think, by that brilliant generation of American novelists that came after Lewis, especially Fitzgerald, Hemingway, Dos Passos and Faulkner, who burst on the American literary scene between the wars and greatly enriched it. Compared to them Lewis lacked style and a sense of the poetry of words in prose. Yet his impact on modern

American life and manners, on our American character, was greater than all of the other four writers together.

Main Street and *Babbitt* shook up the country as no other books had before or have since. The very title *Main Street* became lodged in our consciousness as the essence of all the drab small towns in America, and so did many of Lewis' characters. "Babbitt" became a word to denote the small-town booster Rotarian, against which my own generation in the smug Midwest towns had revolted. In Elmer Gantry we recognized all the phoney evangelists and preachers who afflicted the land. And when one thinks of the novels in America in the years just prior to the appearance of Sinclair Lewis, with their bloodless gentility, which even the works of Howells suffered from, one can see that it was Lewis who, more than any other writer of our time, liberated American writing and finally aroused America to see what it really was. He cleansed the country of its sentimental nonsense, its false optimism, its provincialism, smugness, conformity, ignorance and bigotry—or at least he tried to.

It is true, as many have said, that for all his exposure of the American way of life, its emptiness, its tawdriness, Lewis lacked the tragic sense of life. But surely he awakened us to its often frightening reality. Many of his characters nowadays strike the young, I am told, as superficial, often mere caricatures, figures on the surface that Lewis could not get underneath. Dorothy, not without her prejudices, thought he had never "really penetrated the human soul."

For me Lewis will live as perhaps our greatest writer, not, to be sure, a Tolstoy or a Dostoevsky, a Balzac or a Proust, or even a Dickens, to whom many have compared him. But no other writer in America captured and recorded as he did the nature of American life, its foibles, its frustrations, its aspirations, its generosity, its hocus-pocus, its speech and its wonderful absurdities. Sinclair Lewis never wrote the novel he talked to me about that winter on the Semmering, one which he hoped would be his greatest and nothing less than a history of America. Apparently shortly before his death he became reconciled to the realization that it could never be done—at least by him. "America is too big for the Great American Novel," he told an American reporter. "America is impossible to grasp." Perhaps so. But he grasped it better than anyone else.

. .

Back home in America after her years in Europe Dorothy Thompson became, with her newspaper column syndicated by the New York *Herald Tribune,* her radio program, her public speeches and magazine articles, one of the foremost ladies in the land, second only perhaps to Eleanor Roosevelt. Her fame added to her self-confidence but never spoiled her and we continued to see each other, usually in New York, occasionally at her farm in Vermont, where I stayed with Jimmy Sheean in the guesthouse. Our lifelong discussions and arguments (especially, predictably, about the Germans) continued.

I did not see so much of her after Maxim Kopf, her third husband, died in 1958—a blow from which she never fully recovered. She moved about a good deal after that, living at Dartmouth for a time and then in Washington and only occasionally in New York. After Maxim's death she had sold her beloved Twin Farms in Vermont, which had been the geographical center of her personal life for thirty years, and sublet her apartment in New York. From time to time she wrote she had been ill.

One day shortly before Christmas in 1960 she came to see me in New York for what proved to be the last time. When I answered her ring and opened the door I scarcely recognized her. This big, robust, dynamic woman had shrunk into a wispy, withered, stooped, tiny, gray-haired woman. The voice that had been so forceful spoke in whispers. She was unsure on her feet and I took her arm and helped her up the stairs to the living room. Once there she revived and seemed to be happy to be with old friends from the days in Europe. The Sheeans and the Gunthers, probably her closest surviving friends, were there. We had some drinks and much good talk. She was off to Lisbon, she said, to spend Christmas with Bernadette, her daughter-in-law, recently separated from her son, Michael Lewis, and their two young children. They were the only grandchildren she had, and she loved them. She died in Lisbon five weeks later. She was sixty-seven.

Friends and acquaintances from London sometimes dropped by in Vienna, happy to be away from the chill and the fog. Most of them were young Labor Party M.P.'s who wanted to look into the Socialist government of Vienna and study what it had done for the workers and the poor. Nye Bevan and Jennie Lee were among them, as was Russell Strauss, Labor backbenchers at the time, but later to become Cabinet ministers in subsequent Labor governments. Our friendships lasted for life.

The biggest stir was caused by the arrival from London one spring of H. G. Wells and Baroness Moura Budberg. If Sinclair Lewis was to me at that time the foremost of American writers, Wells was the greatest writer in England—a judgment I would ultimately abandon. But he had no small talk, at least with us American journalists who met him at the Gunthers', nor did he seem interested in talking about writing and writers. He was obsessed with his plans to save the world, and they seemed rather unrealistic to me.

Moura Budberg seemed more interesting, probably because what I had heard of her life was so romantic. She had the distinction—at least for me—of being at this period (the early thirties) the lover of two of the most famous writers in the world, and at one and the same time, Wells in England and Maxim Gorki in Russia. Before that, during the Bolshevik Revolution, she had had an affair with the flamboyant Bruce Lockhart, the acting British Consul-General and actually a British agent, and was arrested and imprisoned on the suspicion of having been involved in an alleged plot by Lockhart to overthrow Lenin's regime. Later, in his book, *Memoirs of a British Agent,* Lockhart would write of her: "Where she loved, there was her world, and her philosophy of life had made her mistress of all the consequences."

Wells and the baroness were old friends, having met back in 1914 in Petrograd, when she served as his interpreter and guide. They met again in 1920 when Wells arrived in Moscow to see his old friend Gorki and to have a meeting with Lenin, and again the young Russian woman acted as his guide and interpreter. She had been born Marie Zakrevskaia, daughter of a wealthy Russian landowner and senator, and at her father's urging had learned English, French, Italian and German. Before the first war she had married a Count von Beckendorff, who was shot during the revolution. She rarely mentioned the Baltic baron whom she next married except to say that she had divorced him because of his addiction to gambling. But she retained his name, Budberg, to the end of her life, though at one juncture H. G. wanted to make her Mrs. Wells.[1]

When she came to Vienna Moura Budberg had just turned forty, and was very attractive in a Slavic way, with high cheekbones, a wide face and expressive eyes. She was remarkably erudite in the literature of not only her native Russia but of England, France, Italy and Germany and for a time lived mainly from her translations and her work as a literary agent. Like so many others I met in Vienna, she and I saw each other at rare but memorable intervals in the years that followed, usually in London or in New York.

Once in New York shortly after the end of the second war, Moura kept me up all one night with her vivid account of the death of Gorki, in 1936. Gorki, I think, had been her greatest love. In 1922 she had followed him from Moscow to Italy, where he had returned for reasons of health, having lived there as an exile from the Czarist government after the 1905 uprising until shortly before the 1914 war. When Gorki went back to Russia in 1928, first tentatively because he had not liked the repressions of the Soviet government, especially the harsh treatment of independent-minded writers, Moura did not go with him. She thought, she said, it might be embarrassing to him as he, now regarded as the greatest living Russian writer, tried to adjust to the absolutism of Stalin's murderous regime—he who had fought so long against the absolutism of the Czar.

But she was with him at his dacha near Moscow when he died. Though she had refused to publish anything about it, she now told me she was convinced that Gorki had been poisoned at

---

[1] This was in 1934. George Bernard Shaw, reporting to a friend that Wells "has fallen to the charm of Moura," said that H. G. had complained to him: "She will stay with me, eat with me, sleep with me. But she will not marry me." Shaw was pleased. "Moura," he wrote, "looking back at his past adventures, refuses to give her independence and her title away. And no wonder!"

Actually, they maintained separate homes when she finally settled in London. She was adamant against marriage. "I'm not going to marry," Moura told a friend. "He only *thinks* I am. I'm not such a fool." This may have been because of her close relationship to Gorki, who was still living and whom she saw on visits to Russia.

At any rate Wells quickly became reconciled. "We live in open sin," he wrote a friend. "But for two grandparents with lives of their own there is neither marrying nor giving in marriage."—Norma and Jeanne MacKenzie: *H. G. Wells—A Biography,* p. 388.

the behest of Stalin. The great proletarian writer had kept protesting to the dictator about the treatment of Russian writers, and finally Stalin apparently had had enough. No one else nagged him about such things—if one wanted to live. The blow of Gorki's death, the loss of a lifelong friend and lover, was bad enough. But now, that night, with Gorki's body barely cold, she had to think of getting away alive. Stalin would certainly have her killed because she knew too much. Once again, as during the Bolshevik Revolution nineteen years before, she went into hiding and eventually succeeded in escaping abroad. So far as I know, she never made public this version of the last days of Gorki and how he died.

Three or four years before her death I saw a good deal of her one summer in London and at Luise Rainer's place in the country. She was then sorting through piles of material from cardboard boxes that littered the living and dining rooms of her house in Cromwell Road. She had finally given in to the pleas of her friends to write her memoirs and had begun to sift through her voluminous papers. The work seemed sometimes to bore her and exhaust her and she would telephone and urge me to come over for tea and vodka. She was then a year or two short of eighty, and as alive and alert as when I had first seen her at forty. Sprawled all around us were the records of as full a life, I believe, as was lived by any woman of the time. Moura Budberg died in Italy in 1974 at eighty-two, shortly before these lines were written.

One fine spring day in 1929—much that I have just recounted took place in Vienna in subsequent years—I took leave of the beautiful city and of Zora and caught the Orient Express for Paris to cover the tennis there and then go on to London for Wimbledon and a third and last summer's work in the grimy city.

I wondered what Yvonne would be like after so long a separation and how I would feel about her now that I had, to some extent, broken away. She met me at the Gare de l'Est, and she was as lovely as ever and as exciting, as if nothing had happened between us, and I fell in love with her all over again. She spent nearly every afternoon with me at the new tennis stadium. Mornings we walked along the boulevards, full of the fragrance of the chestnut tree blossoms, ending up to lunch on the terrace of a restaurant on the Place de l'Alma, where you could look across the Seine toward the Invalides and the Eiffel Tower. It was a lovely spring and a good time to be together. And a bad time to have to wrench myself away to go to London.

London turned out to be somewhat brighter for me that summer. I made some friends. That spring the Labor Party had been returned to office and with it a number of Labor M.P.'s of about my age, with whom I soon became acquainted. Two of the brightest and most attractive were a fiery young Welshman and an equally fiery and even younger and very pretty Scottish girl, Nye Bevan and Jennie Lee. Both had had fathers and grandfathers who had been coal miners. Both had grown up in poverty and had got into politics early in order to try to do something to alleviate it and to make life in Britain a little fairer. Both had struggled for an education. And each of them spoke with the strong accents and lilt of their respective native lands, Wales and Scotland, and spoke passionately and eloquently. They were such an engaging couple that I suppose it was inevitable they would marry, which they did five years later, in 1934.

Jennie actually had been elected from North Lanark in a by-election in February that year, upsetting the Tory candidate and turning a 2,000-vote majority which his predecessor had enjoyed into a thumping 6,000 majority for herself and the Independent Labor Party. She was only twenty-four, the youngest M.P. in the House of Commons, and one of the very few women.

Aneurin Bevan had gone to work in the coal pits of Wales at fourteen and remained in them for seven years, gradually working his way up in the local and district Miners' Union. After the war he won a two-year scholarship to the Central Labor College in London, but apparently got little out of it, and when he returned home was unable to find work in the depressed mines or at anything else. He never forgot the three dismal years of unemployment but he did not waste his time in self-pity. He began to educate himself, reading voraciously in history, economics and literature—poetry was a lifelong love—working in the union and serving on a County Council, where his eloquence and sharpness in debate began to attract attention. In the 1929 spring elections he won the House seat from Ebbw Vale with a majority of 13,000 over the combined vote of the Liberal and Unionist candidates. His political career had begun at the age of thirty-one and it would go far: to the highest councils of the Labor Party, to several Cabinet posts in Labor governments after the second war, and almost to the prime ministership, though this eluded him in the end. Had he lived a little longer he would, I think, have made that, too.

Bevan struck me as an audacious young man when I first met him—he was not impressed with authority, in his own party or in Parliament or elsewhere—and I was not surprised at his debut in the Commons. In his maiden speech he took on Churchill, with whom he would duel on the floor for the rest of his life, and in the ensuing weeks he added Neville Chamberlain, eventually to become Prime Minister, and Lloyd George, a fellow Welshman and the wartime Prime Minister, as the targets of his vehement attacks. No freshman member had ever dared to make such a bold beginning. Overnight he became a sensation, and something of a darling of the parliamentary correspondents, for whom he was a breath of fresh air in the dusty halls of Westminster.

Nye Bevan remained a lively, provocative friend. With no one else save possibly Dorothy Thompson did I have so many heated arguments—they went on from year to year whenever we met—and also so many illuminating talks: about politics, capitalism, socialism, communism, history, philosophy, poetry, novels, and even food and wine. We did raise our voices sometimes in the heat of our passion, and once in London during the second war, when Nye had asked me to invite John Steinbeck, whom he wished to meet, there was so much shouting that John, a peaceful, amiable and rather apolitical man, feared we would come to blows. John did not know on that first occasion that he was hearing the natural expression of old, affectionate friends, who, whatever their differences, agreed essentially on raising hell with the world as it was—a world too smug, too greedy, too unfair.

I had a deep affection and admiration for Jennie Lee, too, and we argued a little less. Perhaps I went overboard in the Foreword she asked me to write for her second book, *This Great Journey*, but not by much. I hailed her then as "one of the remarkable young women of our time—our own country has had no one quite like her," and spoke of her "dark, laughing, Scottish beauty and great charm." Jennie, too, would rise in the Labor Party, though not quite as high as her husband, and eventually she, too, would attain Cabinet rank. Success never spoiled her.

A simple little French restaurant on a corner in Soho, where

I often took refuge from English food, was a pleasant gathering place for a number of people from the stage, the universities, Parliament, the press and the trade unions. It was here that A. J. Cook, the aggressive, fire-eating head of the Miners' Union, had introduced me to Bevan. I had met Cook earlier and had written a somewhat sympathetic portrait sketch of him in the Paris *Trib*. Since he was considered a left-wing radical by the Establishment this had not endeared me either to many readers, who wrote in in protest, or to my employers. Cook had led the great miners' strikes after the war and was one of the most uncompromising of the union leaders in the bitter General Strike in 1926. Now in 1929, as we talked on many an evening at the little restaurant, he seemed a little spent.

"Don't you see why?" Nye Bevan put it to me. "He has burned himself out in a flame of protest against the unjust conditions posed on his people."

I think Cook, who had also been a leader in the Independent Labor Party, which was left of the official Labor Party, had also come to the conclusion that nothing could be expected from the new Labor government.

"Ramsay MacDonald [the Labor Prime Minister]," he would say, "is at heart a Tory. He has forgotten where he came from. Don't expect him to do anything about the workin' class."

The recession was worsening that summer. Unemployment was approaching two million and the Labor government was under pressure from the Tories and the business and banking establishments to reduce, instead of increase, the pitiful unemployment dole. Cook had no illusions that MacDonald would hold out long against them. He was still, like young Bevan, in whom he took much pride, a revolutionist but he had abandoned whatever hope he had once had that there would eventually be a truly socialist society in Britain. He was only forty-five, but he seemed reconciled to his lifelong hopes being dashed. This made him more mellow. Like Nye, he enjoyed good food and wine. And above all, good talk.

Paul Robeson sometimes came by for a meal on his night off or before his performance at the Drury Lane in *Show Boat*. He had made an enormous splash in London by his singing of "Ol' Man River" in the popular musical. But he had taken his acclaim modestly and seemed to prefer the company one found in the simple restaurant to the more dazzling kind that surrounded the stars of the stage. He was then thirty-one, tall, handsome, amiable, and he had a magnificent baritone voice. I do not recall that he was very political at that time or even very bitter at the treatment of his fellow-Negroes at home. He was happy though, he said, to be living and working in London, where he found much less racial prejudice than in America. And it may be that his talks with many of the young Labor Party people and with union leaders like Cook began to open his mind to politics. Later, after he had gone home, he grew increasingly bitter at the oppression of his people and I think it was this feeling that propelled him toward a sympathy with Communism and Soviet Russia. He thought they offered hope to blacks.

I always admired him for sticking to these new beliefs, naïve as I believed them to be, sticking to them despite all the indignities inflicted on him by super-patriot Americans and their government. I did not see him for many years, and I do not know if he finally became disillusioned with Communism or with the Soviet Union. We were fellow-passengers on the *Queen Mary* from New York to Europe late in the summer just before the second war came. He had put his children in school in Russia and told me how wonderful it had been for them to grow up in a society where there was no racial prejudice. He was on his way to Moscow to see them.

Constantine Oumansky, the Soviet Ambassador in Washington, was on the boat, and Robeson and his wife spent a great deal of time with him. Oumansky was an intelligent, cynical man and he seemed to exercise quite a bit of influence over Robeson, which I tried mildly to counteract. Oumansky, certainly with tongue in cheek, had gone down to Third Class one day to lecture to some American students on "Soviet democracy," of all things, and he had taken my kidding good-naturedly. He knew well enough there was no democracy in the Soviet Union. But Robeson disagreed. He was sure there was. And he was sure Stalin's Russia would line up in the coming war on the side of the democracies, Britain and France. Perhaps Oumansky already knew better, though he pretended to believe, and he said, that there would be an alliance of the Soviet Union with the West against Nazi aggression—unless Paris and London tried to maneuver Russia into a war against Germany alone.

That was the trouble, I admitted. That indeed was what Prime Minister Chamberlain and Premier Daladier had been trying to do since Munich, when they had sold Czechoslovakia down the river to Hitler, and no doubt Stalin knew it. Oumansky, too. But it was not succeeding. By that summer (1939) Britain and France, having foolishly sacrificed the Czechs, with their splendidly armed army and formidable fortifications, had got themselves irretrievably committed to coming to the aid of Poland, which had a poorly armed army and no fortifications, should the Germans attack. Oumansky, I think, saw that. What he did not know, judging by the long talks I had with him, was that Stalin was already secretly negotiating a deal with Hitler to keep Russia out of the war in return for which the U.S.S.R. would get a slice of Poland and the Baltic States, which had been taken from Russia in 1918.

Robeson's reaction to the Nazi-Soviet Pact, which was signed in Moscow a few days later, I never knew. Perhaps it disillusioned him, as it did so many other admirers of the Soviet Union. No matter. However naïve he may have been about these things, he remained for me a great artist, one of the finest singers and actors we have had, and a warm, sincere, decent, generous, courageous human being.

With such friends and acquaintances as these and a few more, such as Russell Strauss, a rich young man who was also elected a Labor M.P. that year and joined Bevan and Jennie Lee at the extreme left of the party (he, too, would attain Cabinet posts), and his wife, Patricia, a beautiful, blond young actress, life in London was greatly improved for me over previous years.

Zora made it even better. After some hesitation she came out from Vienna to live with me that summer. And though she was still a countess, she did not seek out the titled and the rich. We were openly "living in sin," after all—it was not so prevalent nor so widely accepted then as now—and she was happy among my more bohemian and working-class friends. I was relieved. I don't recall meeting anyone, or trying to, in London's upper crust. Later when the new war came and I had earned a modest name and the German bombs had produced a great leveling, this would change. Many great town houses (those that had not been destroyed) and country places were opened up to American correspondents—now become "war correspondents"—and Cabinet ministers, generals, admirals and air marshals, press lords, old aristocrats and famous hostesses such as Lady Colefax and Lady Cunard pressed invitations on us. On the theory—or excuse—that a good journalist must learn all sides of life I did not exactly shun some of these offerings, though I never sought them, and sometimes, no doubt, I got from them useful information or tips and even a little fun. But in London, my heart was always elsewhere, among the friends I had made among mostly the Labor people in my young days in Fleet Street.

Some of one's American colleagues became friends from the start, men like Negley Farson, the gusty roving correspondent of the Chicago *Daily News,* and a good writer of books, and Webb Miller, the shy, modest, intelligent head of the United Press for all of Europe. Webb was one of the great correspondents and our paths often crossed elsewhere, on the Continent and in Asia. A good deal older and more experienced than I, and the most generous of men, he helped me over various hurdles on several difficult assignments. He was a great deflator of pompous asses. He had had no illusions about Hitler keeping the peace, and he had gone home once for a speaking tour—being inordinately shy he hated public speaking—in order to try to warn American newspaper editors and others as to what was coming in Europe. He used to smile at that experience.

"No one paid the slightest attention," he would say. "Everyone—newspaper editors, senators and congressmen, people around Roosevelt and in the State Department—told *me* what the situation in Europe was. They knew, they said, as Senator Borah proclaimed, there would be no war."

When it came, in September, 1939, it profoundly depressed Miller. He was afraid that Hitler could not be stopped, and when the Nazi armies overran Denmark and Norway in the following April, he was in despair. He knew, as did we all, what the next step would be. Two days before it came that late spring, when we knew that Hitler was about to hurl his armies against the West, through Holland and Belgium, toward France, Webb Miller was found dead on a railroad track at Clapham Junction, near London. The news shocked me.

That night in Berlin, after I had heard it from the U.P. office, I wrote in my diary: "I wonder what killed him? Tired? Sleepy? I know it wasn't suicide." But later I wondered. No one will probably ever know for sure. Webb had been overworking in blacked-out London. He could have been tired or sleepy or both. The compartments of trains were also blacked-out and it was difficult to tell when you arrived at your station in the suburbs and easy to step out in the darkness. The Nazi press in Berlin behaved with its usual lack of taste and truth. It said that Webb Miller had been murdered by the British Secret Service.

Another American correspondent I got to know in London met death in a different and even sadder way. He was the victim not of the war but of incomprehension and callousness in his home office. This was nothing new to a foreign correspondent. We were constantly at the mercy of nincompoop editors who hadn't the faintest idea of what the world beyond the American shore was like—or the problems their correspondents had working in it. Somehow this was too much for this sensitive man. He headed the London bureau of the New York *Herald Tribune*, one of our best daily newspapers (despite its staunch Republicanism) and certainly, at that time, the best written. He had been, I believe, a Rhodes Scholar at Oxford and was probably a little more learned than most of us. Having lived long in England he had assimilated to some degree English ways: a slight Oxford accent, tweedy clothes and an addiction to pipe-smoking (I had taken up the pipe in high-school days, and it was never held against me). He was, I always thought, a very intelligent newspaperman.

Apparently back in New York it was felt among some of the editors that the *Herald Tribune* needed a bureau head in London who was a little less British and a lot more red-blooded American. They picked a police reporter from the New York beat to take over in London, recalling my friend and assigning him to a job in the newsroom at home. It broke his heart. Somewhere in the mid-Atlantic on the ship taking him back to his native land he jumped overboard.

There was one person in London that summer I very much wanted to meet. One evening Zora and I went to the London Pavilion to see Noel Coward's latest musical, *This Year of Grace*. For weeks the London newspapers had been raving about a beautiful and vivacious young dancer named Tilly Losch, who, they said, had "made" the show—some said she had "saved" it. Zora had seen her in Vienna when she was the prima ballerina at the State

Opera. At the show she struck me as being one of the finest dancers I had ever seen, and of astounding beauty.

"If you think she's so wonderful, why don't you go backstage and introduce yourself," Zora suggested in her bemused way. But I was much too timid. Somehow, though, I was sure I would meet Miss Losch some day, and I did, eleven years later in New York. We became devoted friends for the rest of our lives.

By the end of that last summer in London, Zora and I, despite a great deal of happiness together, had come to a friendly parting of the ways. We had decided we could not make it together—for one thing, I could never get Yvonne out of my head. During our last weeks Zora went out a good deal with friends in the Hungarian colony, and there she met a diplomat in the Hungarian Legation whom she liked and married soon afterward. We kept in touch until the war and occasionally I visited them in Budapest. She seemed fairly happy. She was killed, I was told after the war by a mutual Hungarian friend, in the upheavals that followed the arrival of the Red Army in Hungary and the establishment of a Communist regime. Most of her life, I reflected, Zora had lived through war and revolution and turmoil, the fate of those who lived on the Danube in that long, troubled time. There had been the first World War, lost, and the several revolutions in Budapest that had followed, and then the second war, also lost, and the Communist revolution at its end. In between the wars, much chaos and hunger and repression. Born and raised in the glitter of the Hapsburg Empire, she had seen that old order collapse, and then one shaky world after another fall apart. Perhaps by the time the Russians arrived in 1944 she had had enough.

I was glad to get out of London at the end of the summer and return to my first loves, Paris and Yvonne. Moreover, a plan was beginning to take shape. I had now been in Europe four years and it had become home to me. Yet there was another home, where most of my roots would always be. I wanted to see what it was like now. I cabled Colonel McCormick for a month's home leave. After the thrill of a month back in Paris, it seemed like an attractive adventure to recross the Atlantic. Yvonne came to the boat train to see me off and on November 9, 1929, I boarded an American liner at Cherbourg for New York.

• •

America had abruptly changed.

The gaudy, goofy 1920's, the dazzling "Coolidge-Hoover Prosperity," the wild chasing of the dollar, the mania to get rich quick on the stock market, all the frenzy for the tinsel of life, all the swollen confidence of Americans that the immediate future was bright and paved with gold, had come to a precipitate end a few days before my boat docked in New York. The mighty stock market had crashed, wiping out the savings of millions and the fortunes of many. The Depression, which would become the worst in our history, had begun.

The front pages of the New York newspapers, which I glanced at while waiting for baggage inspection by irritable customs officers at the dock, were studded with lurid accounts of brokers, bankers and other gamblers with other people's money as well as their own jumping out of windows or otherwise ending what they must have thought were their broken lives, though it was only their bank accounts that were broke, only money that was lost. As I drove from the dock to my hotel I saw a sight in the streets that I had never seen in my prosperous native land before. Men and women, shabbily dressed, but with good, strong American faces that had a bewildered look, were standing on the curb selling apples. Crudely scrawled signs propped against their tray of fruit gave the price: "5 CENTS."

As I made my way west to Chicago and across the Mississippi to Cedar Rapids, Iowa, I scarcely recognized the proud country and the proud people I had left only four years before. The good citizens, recently so cocky, seemed stunned. They couldn't grasp what had hit them. Nor could I. Preoccupied in Europe, I had not faintly comprehended what had happened so suddenly at home. Even what had happened to my mother when she told me that more than half of her modest widow's savings, which my younger brother, a financial expert in New York, had conservatively, as he thought, invested for her in "gilt-edged" stocks—U.S. Steel, General Electric and the like—had gone down the drain in Wall Street. (For the rest of his life he never forgave himself.) I tried to catch up on what had happened, starting in New York for the first few days and feverishly continuing my education in Chicago and Iowa. But everyone was in a state of shock. Incoherent. The bankers, the brokers, the businessmen, above all. It would take years for me, as for everybody else, to sort out what really had taken place. And why.

On September 3, 1929, the Great Bull Market had soared to new highs on the New York Stock Exchange. A fortnight later, on September 19, less than two months before my return, the market, after a slight setback, had reached even higher levels. Then it had begun to slip again to what the brokers called "first-class bargain levels." U.S. Steel was down from 261¾ to 204, Radio from 114¾ to 82½. General Electric had fallen more than 50 points. "A good time to buy," said the pundits. But no one jumped in to buy, not even the wiseacres of Wall Street, and this was noticed in the press and picked up by the public. It was strange and depressing news. For nearly a decade the Great Bull Market had been going up and up, and by 1927, prices of stocks had begun to soar into the wild blue yonder. There seemed to be no limits.

That was the trouble. But very few realized it and those who did were branded as positively unpatriotic if not downright un-American. "Be Bullish on America!" one brokerage firm exhorted in a newspaper advertisement. "Never Sell the United States Short!" exhorted another. The previous November (1928) Herbert Hoover, "the great engineer," had been elected President by a landslide and the news of his election had set off a spree of buying on the Stock Exchange that sent up prices to new levels. All through November new highs were registered and new records for shares changing hands. The New York Stock Exchange had begun to go, as someone said, "crazy." The frenzied trading on November 20 led *The New York Times* to comment that "for cyclonic violence yesterday's stock market has never been exceeded in the history of Wall Street." Wall Street was gripped not only by frenzy, then, but by "cyclonic violence."

This paranoiac state of affairs among the grown-up citizens who handled most of the nation's money would continue for nearly a year. "The market," one financial expert, one of the few who had not lost his senses, exclaimed, "is discounting not only the future but the hereafter!" Few noticed that as the volume of sales and the prices skyrocketed there was a tremendous increase of trading on margins and that they were becoming thinner, as little as 10 percent on the purchase of a stock. "Buy now, pay later" was the slogan and it was ballyhooed not only for the purchase of stocks but for buying more durable goods on the installment plan. Credit began to pile up astronomically. By summer, 1929, brokers' loans to those who bought stocks on margin approached six billion dollars, twice that of 1927, and by October reached nearly seven billions. They were carrying 300 million shares of stock on margin.

Everyone—from the President of the United States down to Cabinet members, business tycoons, big bankers and even professors—joined in the ballyhoo. When the somnolent Calvin Coolidge left the White House in March, 1929, he was moved to observe that business was "absolutely sound" and that stocks were "cheap at current prices." The unsuspecting public did not know that he had been warned several times in his last two years in office by the Federal Reserve Board that speculation in Wall Street was getting out of hand. Probably most people would not have paid attention if they had known. The fever of speculation to get rich quick had spread over the whole land. It not only dominated people's minds and conversation and the news they read or heard but the whole culture of the Jeffersonian Republic. Whatever other values were deemed of worth in our society, the one most deemed now in the closing frenzied years of the 1920's was making money—a lot of it, fast. This could only be done by "investing" in the stock market—gambling, that is.

All the best minds in business and finance, even in academia, strongly recommended it. John J. Raskob, a director of General Motors, an associate of the Du Ponts and Chairman of the Democratic National Committee, wrote a widely read piece in the *Ladies' Home Journal* entitled "Everybody Ought to be Rich." Who should know better than he, who had made himself rich, and now wanted to share the secret. It was easy, he explained: Save fifteen dollars a month, invest it in "good, solid common stocks," leave your dividends in to accumulate, and lo! in twenty years you will have eighty thousand dollars at a minimum and an income of at least four hundred dollars a month. "The way to wealth," he advised, "is to get into the profit end of wealth production in this country." Still, twenty years was a long time to wait. The more impatient ones, and they were legion, borrowed up to the hilt and bought on margin. Others, only slightly less patient, took advantage of a plan recommended by the inimitable Raskob and bought shares in an "investment trust." These concerns not only invested, say, a man's savings of one thousand dollars in market stocks but purchased another thousand dollars in his name on credit, all the stocks being posted as collateral. As stocks soared, the modest man could sell his two thousand dollars in shares for, say, three thousand dollars and not only repay the debt but make a handsome profit. Then he could start all over again. It was taken for granted that stock prices would soar—forever.

Investment trusts, like the market, boomed. Not only brokerage firms but the big banks leaped into this lucrative business. It seemed the perfect answer to the modest investors, men and women who had neither the time nor the facilities to "study the market." Instead of putting their money in specific stocks on the Exchange, they could do better, they were told, by placing it in the stock of an investment trust, whose managers, with a profound knowledge of the market and devoting their full time to it, would wisely invest it in various stocks on the board. For one thing, this meant that the small investor could spread his risk. But more important, his investment in stocks was being handled by experts. As the stocks on the market went up, so would the stocks of the investment companies. It was estimated that more than four million Americans channeled their investments through these companies. In 1928 there had been 186 investment trusts or companies. A year later there were 265. That year they sold three billions' worth of shares in themselves, or a third of all the capital issued that year. Just before the crash their total assets were in excess of eight billions. Most of this tidy sum would evaporate after the Wall Street debacle.

My brother, who was thinking of leaving his job as an economic statistician at Standard Statistics to go into teaching, was troubled by the complicity of so many university professors in the stock-market mania and subsequent crash. They had joined the bankers and brokers, he said, in the most idiotic forecasts of the golden future for those, of however modest means, who plunged into the market. They had outdone the slick financiers, he said, in praising the wisdom, the downright genius, of the dubious money handlers in Wall Street.

Many of the academicians had lent their names to mushrooming investment trusts as advisers or directors. Professor Edwin W. Kemmerer, the renowned monetary expert at Princeton, had become a director of American Founders Group, a conglomerate of investment companies, and Dr. Rufus Tucker, another academic wizard, had become its staff economist. But all their expertise had not prevented the Group's assets of a third of a billion dollars from evaporating after the crash, its highly touted stock falling from seventy-five dollars a share in October, 1929, to less than seventy-five cents. From the University of Michigan had come a Dr. David Friday to advise another Wall Street combine. His reputation as a forecaster was then immense. One Michigan trust stressed the brainpower at its disposal. It had three eminent academic advisers: Irving Fisher of Yale, Edmund E. Day of Michigan and Joseph S. Davis of Stanford. Professor Fisher was regarded as the most eminent economist of the time, the supreme American oracle, widely quoted in the press and on Wall Street on every occasion. Though my brother thought he was in other fields a brilliant economist, he also thought poor Fisher would be remembered most for his famous pronouncement just before the crash: "Stock prices," said the eminent man from Yale at that crucial moment, "have reached what looks like a permanently high plateau."

The record of the Ivy League, in fact, my brother thought, was especially bad. Harvard even had its Harvard Economic Society which pontificated regularly on the state of the market and the economy. Even after the Wall Street crash these Harvard economists were insisting that there would be no depression.

Two learned professors, my brother thought, had been particularly obnoxious. They had no patience with the grumblers who thought, as did the Federal Reserve, that speculation was getting out of hand. Both published books forecasting the rosiest future for the market. Both books came out in 1929, the year the market was wiped out. My brother used to read me a few choice quotes from their opuses. If the times had not been so sad I would have laughed.

There was, for instance, a Joseph Stagg Lawrence of Princeton, whose press published his book, *Wall Street and Washington*. Professor Lawrence couldn't forgive the Federal Reserve for trying to dampen speculation. He castigated the Fed's "bias, a bias founded upon a clash of interests and a moral and intellectual antipathy between the wealthy, cultured and conservative settlements on the seacoast and the poverty-stricken, illiterate and radical pioneer communities of the interior . . . Blatant bigotry and turbulent provincialism had joined to condemn an innocent community." The professor's heart bled for "innocent" Wall

Street. His mind boggled at the uncouth provincials from the "interior" who dared to question the genius of the money men. Wall Street, after all, he contended, was the focus "of the world's most intelligent and best-informed judgment of the values of the enterprises which serve men's needs." Up to the eve of the crash Professor Lawrence, from his Princeton Olympus, contended that "the consensus of judgment of the millions whose valuations function on that admirable market, the Stock Exchange, is that stocks are not at present over-valued . . . Where is that group of men with the all-embracing wisdom which will entitle them to veto the judgment of this intelligent multitude?"

Where indeed? There were not many with even a little wisdom. One of the few, my brother told me, had been banker Paul M. Warburg, who that spring had called upon the Federal Reserve to restrict the lending of money to banks for speculation on the market. Unless the mania for speculation was halted, he warned, there would be a disastrous bust. It would not only ruin the market, he added, it "would bring about a general depression."

Warburg was derided by those who said they knew best. He was accused of "sandbagging American prosperity." So was Roger Babson, the eccentric statistician and forecaster, who once had been bullish about the market and the economy but who in the fall of 1929 was falling prey to doubts—and expressing them. On September 5 he had told the Annual National Business Conference that "sooner or later a crash is coming, and it may be terrific." He went even further, to the consternation of his listeners and those on Wall Street who read his doleful forecast the next day. He predicted something worse than a stock-market crash. "Factories will shut down," he warned. "Men will be thrown out of work . . . and the result will be a serious business depression."

My brother thought that Babson's dire warning was taken more seriously in the country than was generally admitted. It made some stop and ponder. But Wall Street denounced him even more vehemently than it had Warburg. "'The Sage of Wellesley,'" said *Barron's*, should not be taken seriously. People should remember his "notorious inaccuracy" in the past.

Wall Street preferred the honeyed words of the professors. Besides Lawrence of Princeton and Fisher of Yale there was Professor Charles Amos Dice of Ohio State University, who also published a book that last year of wonderland, *New Levels in the Stock Market*. Professor Dice thought they were just about right and would continue to rise. The ignorant forgot, he maintained, that there was taking place "a mighty revolution in industry, in trade and in finance" and that the stock market was but "registering the tremendous changes that were in progress." Professor Dice's prose, my brother said, could become awfully purple whenever the good man thought of the dazzling future in America. He was especially worshipful of the big plungers, men largely from the automobile industry, who in 1928 had thrown tens of millions on the market and shot up the prices of shares. Professor Dice was lyrical about their "vision for the future and boundless hope and optimism. . . ."

> Led by these mighty knights of the automobile industry, the steel industry, the radio industry . . . and finally joined, in despair, by many professional traders who, after much sack-cloth and ashes, had caught the vision of progress, the Coolidge market had gone forward like the phalanxes of Cyrus, parasang upon parasang and again parasang upon parasang. . . .

Parasang upon parasang? We had to look up the word in the dictionary. It turned out to be a Persian measurement of length—about three miles. The good professor, my brother thought, knew his Persian history better than he knew Wall Street.

The break on Wall Street, my brother told me in recounting what had happened, came on Thursday, October 24. The great crash followed on Tuesday, October 29—"Black Tuesday," it was called, though a good many gave the Thursday the same coloration. It had been black enough.

The market had opened steadily and then suddenly it had broken. Hundreds of thousands of shares of the best companies were dumped on the floor for sale. Prices fell off, and then plunged. By eleven o'clock there was a stampede to sell at any price. The ticker fell behind. No one knew at any moment what the prices were, and they feared the worst. Panic ensued. The traders were gripped by a terrible fright. They threw hundreds of millions in stocks on the market. Down and down went the prices: U.S. Steel from 205½ to 193½, General Electric from 315 to 283, Radio from 68¾ to 44½, and these were the blue chips. The life savings of many, the wealth of the few, were fast melting away.

Frightened by the debacle, New York's leading bankers met hastily at the offices of J. P. Morgan. Morgan himself was in Europe. Thomas W. Lamont, his senior partner, presided. They agreed to put up $40 million apiece for a pool of $240 million to, as they put it, "stabilize the market." Lamont explained the action to reporters in what Frederick Lewis Allen later described as one of the most remarkable understatements of all time. "There has been a little distress selling on the Stock Exchange," he said, and explained that this was due to "a technical condition of the market" rather than to any fundamental cause. He thought the situation would improve.

And indeed it did. Word that the country's leading bankers were supporting the market with their millions rallied the Exchange. Prices stopped tumbling. Some started to go up. America's great and wise bankers had saved the market and stopped the panic. Everyone was grateful and before the day was done the incurable optimism of the men of money began to surface again. Thirty-five brokers had the gall to issue a joint statement that, despite all that had happened, "the market was fundamentally sound," in fact "technically in better condition than it has been for months." Bankers and business tycoons offered similar statements of assurance. Even President Hoover chimed in (by request of the bankers, it was later learned) to assure the country that "the fundamental business of the country . . . is on a sound and prosperous basis."

On the following Friday and Saturday, though trading was brisk, the market held firm. Everyone believed that the panic was over and that prices would resume their upward trend. The belief lasted only over the weekend.

Monday, October 28, turned out to be another disastrous day. General Electric fell 47½ points, Westinghouse 34½, A.T.T. 34, U.S. Steel 17½. This was worse than Black Thursday. Again the bankers met at Morgan's. But this time they realized that not even their millions could stem the swirling downward tide. They were all overcommitted themselves and would have to join in the selling. The blind forces of the market, of fear and panic in the country, were stronger than the resources of the big banks. When it was learned that the bankers had thrown in the sponge, what followed the next day, Tuesday, October 29, was inevitable.

Later Harvard's economist John Kenneth Galbraith would look back on that day and conclude that it "was the most devastating day in the history of the New York Stock Market, and it may have been the most devastating day in the history of markets." There was a wave of wild selling as soon as the Exchange opened. Huge blocks of stocks were thrown on the floor to fetch what they could—in most cases almost nothing. One bright messenger boy, according to Allen, bid one dollar for a stock that had been listed at 11 the day before, and got it. The floor of the Exchange was in chaos. Members of its Governing Committee holding an emergency meeting in a room under the floor could hear, they said, the panic raging overhead. But there was nothing they could do. A record sixteen and a half million shares were traded for anything they could bring. The bottom had fallen out. The *Times* industrial averages tumbled a further 43 points. All the gains of the previous twelve gaudy months had been lost. An estimated $40 billion, a sum larger than the national debt, had been wiped out. Hundreds of thousands of citizens, too.

After a flurry of brief rallies the market hit rock bottom for the year on November 13, a couple of days before I arrived. The *Times* averages of fifty leading stocks, which had stood at 312 on September 3, closed at 164, down by almost half. Averages of twenty-five leading industrials dropped by even more, from 469 to 221. Such blue chips as American Can had fallen from 181⅛ to 86, Anaconda from 131½ to 70, General Motors from 72¾ to 36, Radio from 101 to 28. Other stocks had done no better.

The Great Bull Market, on which so many millions of Americans had pinned their hopes for miraculous riches, was dead. I think by the time I returned home from Europe in mid-November that year, this much was realized. You could never again get rich quickly on the stock market. That bubble had burst. But how much else was realized by the late autumn after the Wall Street crash? Not much else. Those you talked to in New York, Chicago and Cedar Rapids were still too dazed to make a judgment. It would take a year or two before Americans comprehended fully that the dizzy postwar era, with all of its illusions and all its foolishness, had ended and that hard times lay ahead. So many had come to take prosperity for granted, even though the vast majority of Americans had never shared in it. It had become a way of life for the lucky. When it suddenly ended they were bewildered and lost. Many were shattered.

> Prosperity [Allen would write later] is more than an economic condition; it is a state of mind. The Big Bull Market had been more than the climax of a business cycle; it had been the climax of a cycle in American mass thinking and mass emotion. There was hardly a man or woman in the country whose attitude toward life had not been affected by it in some degree and was not now affected by the sudden and brutal shattering of hope. . . . Americans were soon to find themselves living in an altered world . . .[1]

In the Depression that ensued they had time to reflect on why the bubble burst. The country had hastily erected a gigantic business and financial edifice on shifting sands. Credit had expanded recklessly, as had speculation and production. More goods were being produced than people had the money to buy. The combined purchasing power of the masses was not nearly enough to absorb them. Wages and salaries would have had to be raised and prices cut to achieve this, but they were not. Wages were kept low and prices high. Even Hoover would later see this—when it was too late. Looking back he thought "the debacle was largely contributed by a failure of industry to pass its improvement (through labor-saving devices) on to the consumer." New machinery and more skilled workers had increased the output of American labor by more than a third in the 1920's, and in such industries as automobiles by three times. But the manufacturers had kept the swollen profits, and after looking out for themselves with handsome salaries and bonuses, they had thrown much of the remainder into the feverish market. Between 1923 and 1928, for example, the index of speculative gains leaped from 100 to 410; that of wages rose only from 100 to 112. The chief problem of the American economy had become not production but consumption.

[1] Frederick Lewis Allen: *Only Yesterday*, pp. 306–307 (paperback edition). I am indebted to Allen and to Galbraith, *The Great Crash, 1929*, for recalling much of the above. But my brother's account held up very well.

Few Americans apparently realized this. Nor did most people, victims of the myths of "rugged individualism" and "competitive free enterprise" as they were, see that finance capitalism had largely replaced industrial capitalism in our country. As we have seen Raskob advising the multitude, the way to get rich was to "get into the profit end of wealth production," not of the production of goods. The rise of the holding companies during the decade was a good example. Company after company was pyramided into holding companies at the top, which controlled the empire though they were made of paper. Samuel Insull's three-billion-dollar enterprise in utilities was typical, and like most of the others it would collapse when the harsh realities of economic life confronted it.

Prosperity to be real and lasting had to be shared. But the mass of our people got only the crumbs. The fantastic rise of the stock market and its sudden crash in the fall of 1929 had not directly affected them. They were too poor. They had no money to invest or gamble. I simply could not believe what my brother told me about poverty in America. I had not realized that most of our people had not benefited from our renowned "Coolidge-Hoover Prosperity." The stark facts, which my brother proceeded to relate, and which I later checked when all the figures were in, were incredible. All through the giddy twenties we had had a sickening poverty in the midst of plenty—an old story to be sure and one that would be repeated even to the time of this writing, when, at the beginning of 1975, nearly half a century later, sixteen million Americans were dependent on food stamps to get enough to eat. All through my life the rich were getting richer and the poor poorer—another old story.

In 1929, after a decade of the greatest prosperity the country had ever had, I now learned some somber facts. The most surprising one was that in that golden year 60 percent of all American families lived below the poverty level. Their income, that is, was under $2,000 a year, the level then generally held—this was before the U.S. government itself established poverty levels—to be just enough to provide the basic necessities of life. Only a little over 2 percent of American families had incomes of more than $10,000 a year and they accounted for two-thirds of the country's total savings. Next was a cluster of 8 percent who received more than $5,000 a year. Nearly three-quarters of American families—

71 percent—got less than $2,500. Some 42 percent were below the $1,500 level, and more than 21 percent were below $1,000.

This was appalling. Perhaps, I thought, the country deserved what had hit it. But this was foolish. As things got worse and the Depression deepened, it would be the mass of the poor who would suffer the most. It was they who would go hungry, in their hovels, in their despair.

Back home in Cedar Rapids, Iowa, when I arrived that late autumn, no one was going hungry. The farmers said they were broke, as they had so often said in the years I was growing up here. And farm prices were down, compared to prices of everything else—an old story, too, in this rich farm belt. But at least the farmers grew enough to eat, and lived in solid homes. The Depression had not yet hit our towns. Businessmen said their affairs were not too bad. Not a single bank had failed, though one or two were in difficulties. Only a few persons had been wiped out by the Wall Street debacle though many, like my mother, had been hurt. There was none of the hysteria I had seen in New York the week before. Nobody was jumping out of windows. The grim years for the town, as for the country, lay ahead and no one could imagine that within three years the land would be nearly prostrate, with 85,000 business bankruptcies, 5,000 bank failures, 10,000,000 unemployed and so many beautiful farms in our own neighborhood, tilled by so many sober, hard-working owners for so long, snatched away from them by mortgage foreclosures, though sometimes not without armed resistance, for these decent folk, who had dutifully voted for Coolidge and Hoover and their prosperity, knew when they were being done in. Like so many other Americans they would be jolted out of their complacency, jarred loose from their clinging to the old myths of rugged individualism and its rewards, when hard times came.

Everything in Cedar Rapids seemed smaller than I remembered. Greene's Square, opposite the railroad station, where I had sat listening in awe to the hardened doughboys from the Rainbow Division when they got back from combat in France after the war; Washington High, beyond the square, where I had spent four years that by now had mostly slipped out of my mind; the First Presbyterian Church, across from the square, where my mother still held the family pew—it looked so squat and small after the cathedrals of France and England; the downtown section beyond the railroad tracks and its "skyscrapers"; the Cedar River below the dam, which had seemed so broad—as wide as I now knew the Rhine, the Danube and the Thames to be; the lawns that surrounded the old Victorian houses on First and Second avenues, which once had appeared so spacious; the campus of Coe College, where I had happily spent the last four years before I left the town; and finally our home out on Third Avenue, to which the family had moved from the old ancestral homestead while I was still in college.

They all seemed to have shrunk. At first this puzzled me. Was my memory so faulty? It had been only a little more than four years since I had gone away. Only later did I see that it was not the town that had changed but I. And one day, many years afterward, I found a passage in a book by André Maurois that expressed very well this phenomenon. It was in his *À la Recherche de Marcel Proust* (page 169) and he was writing of Proust's attempt to recapture the past in his great novel *À la Recherche du Temps Perdu* (Remembrance of Things Past).

> It is in vain [Maurois thought] that we return to the places we have loved: we will never see them again because they were situated not in space but in time, and the man who looks for them will be no more a child or an adolescent who embellished them with his imagination.

Still, it was good to be home—for a few days anyway. I was struck by how friendly the good people were, in contrast to the reserve of the English, the French, the Austrians, even the Italians, in whose midst I had spent the last four years. The local gentry, businessmen, bankers, lawyers, clergymen, whom I had scarcely known, greeted me warmly in the street. "Glad to see you, boy," they would say. "Been following you in the *Tribune*. You've been around, eh! Hope we can have a talk. How about . . ." There was no longer a morning newspaper in the town, and the *Chicago Tribune*, which arrived in time for breakfast, had acquired a considerable circulation. My by-line in it had been noticed. My mother recounted that people would stop her when she was shopping or dropping into the bank and say: "Interesting piece from Vienna [or London or Paris or Rome] Bill had in the *Tribune* this morning. My, your boy certainly gets around."

I think my mother was rather pleased at this. "It almost gives me a swelled head." She laughed. "But don't you get one, son. Pride goeth before a fall, you know."

Perhaps I was a little puffed up though by the welcome. There were pieces in the daily *Gazette,* the weekly labor *Tribune* and the *Coe College Cosmos* about my arrival. For the first time in my life I was interviewed—I who had done all the interviewing before. Some of the stories were a little embarrassing. They hailed me as "the hometown boy who had made good" and embroidered on what the reporters thought was the romantic life of the foreign correspondent I was supposed to be leading. "It's mostly just hard work," I had tried to tell them—to no avail. "He has covered Europe," wrote the editor of the labor weekly, "upon assignments with royalty, reported diplomatic assemblages and important conferences, mingled with statesmen whose names are known the world over . . ." but I forgave him for his purple prose. We had had a good two-hour talk. It was he, I remembered, who on my graduation from college four and a half years before had predicted in an editorial that this "green kid" would "go far" in the newspaper world. I kidded him about it now. "Well, goddamn it, I was right," he bellowed. "And the amazing thing is you're only— How the hell old are you?"

"Twenty-five," I murmured.

"Jesus! Only twenty-five!"

So I went about, I guess, in sort of a blaze of glory, lecturing to the students in journalism at the college on being a foreign correspondent and probably embroidering a little myself, visiting with old professors who exaggerated their pride in me and claimed they had always known how well I would do. And I had long talks with my mother about the state of the town and the country and her own problems of widowhood. She lived alone, but she was not lonely. Her active mind kept her occupied. Typically, she did not, as she never had, pry into my personal life, though she was impressed when letters from Yvonne began to arrive from Paris and I would show them to her. "My!" she would exclaim. "I can't read a word of it. What language is that?"

"French," I would say.

"And you can read it?! My, that's really something! I guess you've learned a lot since you left here." We had a fine time together. I had brought her a bottle of Benedictine, which I had smuggled in from Paris, and she, who had been so hurt by my drinking of poisonous, bootleg hootch in college, and had never touched strong liquor herself, loved the taste of the sweet French liqueur.

"My, this tastes good," she said when, rather reluctantly, she took her first sip.

"It's good for your health, too, Mother," I said. "But in moderation, remember!"

She chuckled, as though she was enjoying being just slightly wicked. It was still unlawful to drink alcoholic beverages in our fair land, but the law, I soon found, was being broken more and more, even by some of the town's most upright citizens.

I had a good time with Grant Wood one day in his studio in the loft of the barn behind the Turner mortuary where I had played as a boy when it belonged to the local meat-packer king, Robert Sinclair, and—how far back that went!—there were horses in the stalls below and carriages in the entrance. Grant had finally found himself. He had finished the portrait of his mother, which he was calling simply *Woman with Plants*. It struck me at first sight, as it has ever since, as the finest portrait an American painter had ever done. Grant was excited about a new work which stood half-finished on his easel and which, the next year when it was the sensation of the exhibition at the Chicago Art Institute, would bring him the national fame he deserved. Like writers, he did not want to talk much about it when he was in the midst of it, trying to cope with its problems. It would become shortly one of the most celebrated of his paintings: *American Gothic*. We talked about the Paris days, which he seemed glad to have behind him. There was so much around him right here in Iowa, he said, that aroused his imagination and that he wanted to paint. I left him again with the feeling that he was one of the most modest and warm-hearted men I knew. Did he have an inkling of his genius, which was just bursting forth? I don't know. He would never show it. But after seeing the portrait of his mother I was sure of it myself.

The blight of Prohibition still poisoned the country and it depressed me. I longed for a good glass of wine. Not that our uptight Protestant town was exactly dry. The best people served cocktails, which they drank throughout their meals. And because of our large Czech population, the beer, which they made, was pretty good. But the cocktails and highballs were raw, from too much crude alcohol, and almost everyone I saw drank too much of them. One night at the country club, where I had caddied as a boy, I was appalled by the number of leading citizens, women as well as men, who passed out.

Happy as I was to be home with my family and to see again the familiar places and faces of my youth, I soon began to feel restless to get away. This rural town, after all, was not for me.. You could not really go home again, as Thomas Wolfe would find. It was something that you had outgrown. It was rather startling to realize that I had become a stranger in my own land. I longed to get back to Europe, which now seemed home to me. And perhaps there was something brewing at the *Chicago Tribune* that might make it even more attractive. Before I left Paris, Wales had slyly hinted that the terrible Colonel McCormick had been impressed with my dispatches from Vienna. "Be sure and talk to the old man when you get home," he had advised.

In fact, the colonel had summoned me to his august presence. I explained to my mother what this meant, and took leave of her and of Cedar Rapids, as eager, I guess, to get away from the town as I had been that June morning more than four years before when I had set out for Chicago, New York and Europe, wondering what the future would bring to a youth of twenty-one. Now it no longer looked so hopeless. And perhaps the lord of the *Tribune* might have something new to offer, as Wales had hinted.

In Chicago I checked in at the office and soon received a message from McCormick to lunch with him and his editors. This proved to be something of an ordeal. As the editors plied me with questions about the state of Europe I kept feeling the steely eyes of the imperious colonel focused on me, sizing me up. This was of no help and I got the impression that some of the editors, mostly middle-aged or more, who were looking me over in person for the first time, felt I was a little young for my job. Perhaps—and the thought horrified me—they would suggest that I do a year or two on the home edition until I matured. As the luncheon and all the questions came to an end, McCormick jumped up briskly and said, "Come with me, Shirer."

We took the elevator up to his lair in the highest reaches of the Tribune Tower overlooking Lake Michigan and the sprawling city. He sat down behind his large desk and indicated a chair for me at one side. Almost instantly I got off to a bad start. In my nervousness I reached for a cigarette and lit it.

"Put that damn thing out!" he commanded. I felt sure this

was the end for me. I did as ordered. "Didn't anyone tell you?" he barked. "No one smokes here."

"I'm sorry," I said. The bottom seemed to be falling out for me—at the very outset. He glanced at some papers on his desk for what seemed an age, occasionally looking up as if he were enjoying my discomfiture, but saying nothing. Apparently he would have nothing more to say to me and I imagined myself slinking out and making my way down to chilly, windy Michigan Avenue, without a job, and four thousand miles from Paris.

After a while he suddenly sprang up and strode to a large map of Europe on the wall, beckoning me to follow him.

"You did a pretty good job there," he said, pointing to a spot on the map that I could not make out. He kept standing in my way as I tried to peer around him. "Some of your stuff was pretty good," he said. He kept his broad back to me—he was a large, tall man—but I could see his forefinger stabbing at some point on the map in the heart of Europe. Vienna? It began to look as if it were.

"I want you to go there," he said crisply. "I want you to take over the bureau." He finally stepped aside so I could see where he wanted me to go. I must say I was elated. Vienna was a place I really liked. And to have a bureau for the first time!

"I . . . uh . . . really appreciate it," I stammered. "I think there will be a lot of news there."

"That's why I'm sending you," he snapped. "You did pretty well there. But, one thing, Shirer. Don't fall for all those Socialists and Communists there. And don't let all the counts and countesses take you in. I know the place. I spent some time there in my youth."

"When your father was ambassador." I suddenly remembered it. "He's still remembered in Vienna," I said, though that was scarcely the naked truth. In fact, I had never heard his name mentioned.

"They liked us," McCormick said. "But we didn't fall for them, for all that Hapsburg stuff." The colonel, I knew well enough, did not like emperors and kings. He was a staunch republican.

So I had the Vienna post! I thanked him again as warmly as my muddled head permitted. He started back to his desk, and when I followed, he turned abruptly.

"How old are you, Shirer?" he snapped. I thought for a split second that I ought to add a few years but then had a second thought.

"I'll be twenty-six in February," I said truthfully.

"A little young," he said. "But give it a try." Then he turned on his best pontifical manner. "On the *Tribune,* Shirer, it doesn't make much difference. If you're good enough to make the paper, however young, you're good enough to take on any assignment." I was glad to hear this—from the top man himself. It was one reason why I liked working for his newspaper. It tossed you into the biggest stories—to sink or swim.

He held out his hand. "When are you going back?"

"I'm booked on the *George Washington* next week," I said.

"Well, don't waste any time. I want you there as soon as possible. Good luck." At that he turned away and the momentous interview was over. Well, not quite over. As I approached the door, or what I remembered as the door, it was no longer there. Only a great wood-paneled wall, and there was not a crack in it that I could see, though I could have sworn we had come through a door there a few moments before. I walked up and down the length of the panel. No door. I glanced over at the colonel, who was fiddling with some papers at his desk. It was a very large room and he seemed rather far away. I paced up and down again. There was positively no door. I glanced over at McCormick. He wore a slight smile. Again he seemed to be enjoying my discomfiture.

"Excuse me, sir," I called out. "I don't seem to remember where the door is." I think I saw his hand reach to the side of his desk and press a button.

"It's right behind you, Shirer," he said, burying his head in his papers.

As I turned, a piece of the panel was sliding open just in front of me. I hurried through it. As I looked back it was sliding shut again, and I thought I saw a chuckle on the colonel's face. A queer duck, I thought, as I made my way out in a pleasant daze to the icy blasts of Michigan Avenue and hailed a taxi for my hotel. "But he gave me Vienna!" I kept muttering. "Not bad for twenty-five."

One hot, sultry August day during the following summer in Vienna I received a curt cable from Colonel McCormick. I was just getting settled in my new post. It had been a pretty good year, so far. I had a lot of territory to cover—besides Austria, all the countries of the Danube from there to the Black Sea: Czechoslovakia, Hungary, Yugoslavia, Rumania and Bulgaria. And I was on my own, free to roam the vast region in search of material or to rush to wherever a good story broke.

A big one, as news went in those quieter days, had broken in June and put my dispatches on the front page in Chicago for several days. Prince Carol one day had flown secretly from London to Bucharest and regained the throne of Rumania which he had once before renounced. He had taken with him his mistress, the blowzy Magda Lupescu, the daughter of a poor junk dealer in the capital. The story in retrospect, and in light of all that has happened since in a warring world, seems of little importance. Carol himself—I had visited him and his lady, who dominated him, in England the summer before—was an empty-minded, weak-willed, pleasure-loving playboy from the old German House of Hohenzollern-Sigmaringen, and Rumania, though it had a solid peasantry, was a sort of comic-opera kingdom. But Carol's return seemed to be straight out of a child's fairy tale and it appealed to a Western world sinking into despair from the Depression. It was romantic, colorful, daring—the dash through the night in a rickety private plane of the Prince Charming and the reclaiming of the rickety throne from his own son, the boy king Michael. Day after day the *Tribune* front-paged my crazy dispatches from Bucharest.

I had had time, too, to call in Prague on eighty-year-old Thomas Masaryk, a delightful scholar and statesman, and the President-founder of Czechoslovakia, which, apart from Austria, was still the only truly democratic country in my territory. I had had time enough to become disillusioned by the dictatorship I saw King Alexander clamping on Yugoslavia, a country whose sturdy people, the Serbs, Croats and Slovenes, I came to love; to see feudal Hungary drifting toward Fascism, though to visit Budapest was always a delight; and Bulgaria, under King Boris (also from a German House, Saxe-Coburg-Gotha), whose chief pastime was sitting at the throttle of steam locomotives, pulling trains around the kingdom, a sleepy little country standing still, as if there were no passing of time there.

Actually these countries, which in whole or in part, except for Bulgaria, had formed part of the Hapsburg Empire, comprised one of the richest areas on earth, with sixty million people, who if they—or their leaders—had had the sense to see that their lands comprised a viable and natural economic unit, as they had under the Hapsburgs, might have lived prosperous lives. The soil was fertile, and underneath it lay almost all the minerals needed to provide raw material for manufacture. But the region was divided, quarrelsome, short-sighted, seized by a virulent and absurd nationalism, and it was slipping into poverty and anarchy. This gave a correspondent, however, something to write about, since in our topsy-turvy world bad news is always more interesting than good news and enables newspapers to build up circulation and thrive and provide their help with a living.

And Vienna again was a delight to live in and work in. Its charm held. Arriving in January when the cold weather and the big snows came, I had taken up skiing and ice-skating. The snowy mountains of the Semmering were but two hours away by train, and the city itself was dotted with fine outdoor skating rinks where bands played Strauss waltzes for you to skate to and there were restaurants serving decent food and fine coffee and beer.

The spring and summer in the city and in the woods of the Wienerwald had been lovely. The Gunthers were there, and the Fodors and Bob Best and other friends. And I had met a beautiful young Viennese girl, a budding drama critic and journalist. Zora had given up her apartment in Vienna and moved on to Budapest to marry her Hungarian. In Paris over the Christmas holidays I had been held up by an emergency operation for appendicitis, the attack occurring while I was on shipboard coming back and scaring me since I remembered vividly how my father had died from just such a sudden seizure. I had been rushed from Cherbourg to the American Hospital in Paris in time, and all had gone well. Convalescing, there had been time to see Yvonne again. She was as lovely and vivacious as ever and just as determined not to throw in her life permanently, or at least matrimonially, with mine. In Vienna, then, I felt free.

After the rash of summer stories and the dashing to one capital after another, August had begun quietly. The weather was hot and the air languid and the Gunthers, Fodors, my new young friend and I had spent a lot of time idling at the beaches at Voeslau and Baden by day and in the cafés and cabarets of Vienna at night, lazily enjoying life.

In the midst of this idyll, out of the blue, the colonel's cable had come. Just two words: "FLY INDIA."

It was a message, though I could not know it at that instant, that would transform my life. It would quickly lead to a widening and deepening of my understanding of the world and its turmoil, giving me my first actual experience of a revolution, dispelling much of the "mystery" of Asia and the Asians, and bringing me into a lasting friendship with the greatest revolutionary, after Lenin, of our age, and the greatest man, a frail little Hindu, half-clad in a loincloth, a saint and at the same time a shrewd politician and a charismatic leader of the masses, Mahatma Gandhi. What he wanted was simple enough: to free his people and his country from the British.

For the next two years I would watch him going about this task. There would be interludes when Gandhi and his aides would be clamped temporarily in jail and the momentum of the Indian revolution would slacken and I could take off for other places in Asia: to Kabul, in primitive, tribal Afghanistan, to see a new king set himself up after another bloody civil war; to Baghdad and Babylon, and to ancient Ur to the south of them on the day archeologists from the British Museum had dug down beneath the rubble to discover the remains of an old Sumerian civilization that had thrived there before the Biblical floods.

But these were interludes. For the best part of the next two years my principal concern would be the reporting of Gandhi's Indian revolution. All that I had previously covered in Europe somehow seemed trivial. But luckily, when tropical illness eventually forced my return to Europe, my work would throw me into the main currents of contemporary history which had begun to sweep the old Continent, and indeed to sweep the whole world, toward upheaval, the destruction of the West's colonial empires, the barbarism of Adolf Hitler and Nazi Germany, the inexplicable decline of the Western democracies, Britain and France, a terrible war the like of which the earth had never experienced and, finally, toward the development of the nuclear bomb, which could—and someday almost certainly will—blow our little planet to smithereens, bringing an end to life, with its splendors and its miseries.

What I saw of these things and what I understood of them will be set down in another volume.

INDEX

Abbott, Abbie S., 153–55
Abbott, Rev. Dr. Lyman, 87
Abd-el-Krim, 34, 228n
Abyssinia, 417, 421–22
Acosta, Bert, 324
Adams, Brooks, 173
Adams, Henry, 70, 95–97, 173, 201–202
Adams, John, 363
Adams, Samuel Hopkins, 177, 212
Addams, Jane, 77, 277
Adler, Alfred, 435
Aiello gang, 32
Akron, Ohio, 156
Alcock, Capt. John, 324
Alexander I (King of Yugoslavia), 490
Alger, Horatio, Jr., 108–109
Allen, Frederick Lewis, 39, 176–77, 479
Allen, Jay, 331–32, 336, 338, 345, 346–47
Altgeld, John Peter, 87, 88, 89
Amana, Iowa, 192, 197–201
Amana Society, 197–201
America and the Young Intellectual (Stearns), 219
America First, 179, 180, 353
American Expeditionary Force, 222, 316, 318, 352, 361
American Federation of Labor, 91, 190, 204
American Gothic (Wood), 276, 278, 486
American Hospital (Paris), 258, 260, 447, 491
American Legion, 224, 258, 277; in Paris, 316, 317–18, 319, 320
American Mercury, The, 17, 18
American Open (golf), 374

American Railway Union, 87, 90–91
American Revolution, 135–36, 358
American Tragedy, An (Dreiser), 44n
Amherst College, 164
Amsterdam, 261, 375–77
Anderson, Margaret, 30, 106, 229
Anderson, Maxwell, 46
Anderson, Sherwood, 22, 30, 44, 106, 108, 231, 239, 271, 295–96, 300, 456
Annunciation, The (Leonardo), 406
Ann Vickers (Lewis), 450, 452
Antheil, George, 241–44
Aquinas, Saint Thomas, 183
Aragon, Louis, 241, 308
Armour, Philip, 102n
Armstrong, Hamilton Fish, 267
Arrowsmith (Lewis), 450, 456
Art Institute (Chicago), 29, 30, 50, 187, 276, 486
Asquith, Lord, 387
Assisi, Italy, 405, 406, 458
Associated Press (A.P.), 176
Astor, Col. J. J., 369
Atlantic Monthly, 456n
Augustine, Saint, 182
Auric, Georges, 241
Austria, 202, 266, 322, 457; -Hungary, 145, 147. *See also* Vienna
Autobiography of Alice B. Toklas, The (Stein), 283, 293, 295–96, 300, 301

Babbitt (Lewis), 17, 275, 450, 459
Bach, Johann Sebastian, 244, 245
Badoglio, Gen. Pietro, 396
Bagehot, Walter, 358, 359
Bahr, Hermann, 434